A NEW VIEW OF ECONOMIC GROWTH

A NEW VIEW
OF
ECONOMIC GROWTH

Maurice FitzGerald Scott

CLARENDON PRESS   OXFORD
1989

Oxford University Press, Walton Street, Oxford OX2 6DP
Oxford New York Toronto
Delhi Bombay Calcutta Madras Karachi
Petaling Jaya Singapore Hong Kong Tokyo
Nairobi Dar es Salaam Cape Town
Melbourne Auckland
and associated companies in
Berlin Ibadan

Oxford is a trade mark of Oxford University Press

Published in the United States
by Oxford University Press, New York

British Library Cataloguing in Publication Data
Scott, M. Fg. (Maurice FitzGerald)
A new view of economic growth.
1. Economic growth
I. Title
339.5
ISBN 0-19-828674-0

Library of Congress Cataloging-in-Publication Data
Scott, Maurice FitzGerald.
A new view of economic growth / Maurice FitzGerald Scott.
p. cm
Bibliography: P.   Includes index.
1. Economic development. 2. Industrial productivity. I. Title.
HD82.S394 1989
338.9—dc19   88—25312
ISBN 0-19-828674-0

Typeset by Burns & Smith, Derby
Printed in Great Britain
by Biddles Ltd.
Guildford & King's Lynn

To Eleanor

PREFACE

Confronted by a book of some 600 pages on economic growth (albeit with a summary), readers may reasonably ask why it is so long, and whether the claim to novelty in the title is justified.

The book has four parts, of which the third, 'Construction', puts forward what I believe to be a new theory of economic growth. Orthodox growth theories explain both the level and growth of output by three main variables: employment, the capital stock, and technical progress. My theory does not attempt to explain the level of output, only its change over a given period, and in that respect is more historical. The capital stock is not of central interest, and there is no separate rate of technical progress. The growth of output is explained by two main variables: the growth of employment and the rate of investment.

There are several unorthodox growth theories which make technical progress endogenous, but mine differs from all those I am aware of in important respects. Many of them have retained some of the features of orthodox growth theory which I have discarded, such as a production function with capital and labour as its arguments, or vintages of capital equipment. One especially important difference from most other unorthodox theories is that I have sought to show that mine can be used empirically to answer the usual questions asked of any growth theory: why growth rates differ; why the shares of wages and profits are what they are, and have changed; why some alleged regularities (Verdoorn's, Kaldor's, and Fabricant's laws relating to productivity growth in different industries) exist; how taxation affects growth; what is the optimum rate of growth and whether there is a case for government intervention to secure it; and why growth slowed down in many countries after 1973. This application of the theory occupies Part IV of the book, 'Use', which is the longest part. Only orthodox theories, in my belief, have hitherto been used in substantial empirical studies to answer those questions.

Orthodox theories are therefore unchallenged in empirical application, and they also dominate the textbooks. Any new theory must, then, show its superiority to orthodox theories if it is to merit serious attention. Hence the lengthy Part IV, but hence also Parts I and II.

Part I, 'Materials', is needed in any case to preface Part III, 'Construction'. The materials for any growth model consist of concepts such as income and output, investment, maintenance and depreciation, as well as the historical record of these magnitudes. My aim in Part I is to show that existing interpretations of these concepts are mistaken or inappropriate.

Investment is better regarded as the cost, in terms of consumption forgone, of changing economic arrangements, than as physical increments to the capital stock—so many extra tons of steel, bits of meccano, sacks of corn, or cubes of jelly. That is the mental picture appropriate to orthodox production function theories. Orthodox vintage theories conjure up batteries of machines, each stamped with its date of manufacture and manned by its separate team of workers. Neither vision corresponds to the way in which I think of economic change and growth. Maintenance and depreciation have been confused both by national income accountants and by growth theorists, and their clear separation makes a crucial difference to one's conclusions about the effects of investment on growth. The different concepts have generally been defined in a circular way, and without giving proper recognition to the meaning of income.

Part I is therefore a necessary preface to Part II, the 'Demolition' of existing theories, as well as to the subsequent 'Construction'. Sceptical readers must judge for themselves whether orthodox theories can survive my attack on them. I have tried to concentrate on fundamentals, and to ignore what seem to me to be secondary issues (such as problems of aggregation, reswitching, etc.), which may be theoretically valid but have proved incapable so far of stopping the onward march of orthodoxy.

Each part of the book has thus seemed necessary to complement and justify the main novel proposal, which is Part III. The need to present them all together has meant that, until now, I have been unable to put that proposal to the test of others' opinions. Much of Chapter 1 and some of the arguments in Chapter 3 have, it is true, appeared in previous articles and lectures (Scott 1976, 1979, 1981 and 1984), but the more positive side has scarcely had an airing, since a long book seemed to be the only way I could communicate it.[1]

It will be clear that I have set myself an ambitious task in writing this book. It has occupied virtually all of my research time for more than ten years, and would not have been attempted had I not become somewhat obsessed by the subject. Nor would it have been published had I not heard, increasingly, 'time's wingèd chariot hurrying near'. It is unfinished business. My hope is that it will provoke others to take up a topic that has fallen out of fashion since the 1960s. The theory of growth was then left in the unsatisfactory state in which it still languishes.

I have tried to acknowledge my intellectual debts by references in the text. Here I will mention those whose help has been by conversation or letter, or in other practical ways, rather than through their published work.

---

[1] My Keynes Lecture to the British Academy in November 1986 did attempt to combine some of Part III with Chapter 3; see Scott (1986b).

However, my debt to Edward Denison is so great that I must record it here. Although I believe that his method of calculating the contribution of investment to growth is mistaken, I have learned an immense amount from his work, and have relied heavily on his estimates for the United States, Japan, and many European countries. Conversations and correspondence with Dennis Anderson, Max Corden, Walter Eltis, John Flemming, John Galbraith, David Henderson, Ian Little, John Martin, Sheila Pugh, James Riedel, Itasu Sakura, Dick Sargent, Frances Stewart, Geer Stuvel, Martin Wolf, and David Worswick have greatly helped me, as has their often much needed encouragement. At a crucial point, Kenneth Falconer provided mathematical help which was invaluable. Clive Payne's and Martin Range's computing assistance enabled me to run a great many regressions, and Monica Dowley prepared some of the tables. Robert Bacon and David Hendry gave me econometric advice. Charles Feinstein provided me with statistical series for the United Kingdom which were essential. My acknowledgements to all of these in no way implicates them in a controversial and imperfect book. Had it been a team effort, I am sure it could have been much improved; but somehow I doubt that this would have been possible.

My main practical debt is owed to Nuffield College, and to its founder, Lord Nuffield. They have allowed me the freedom and time to work out my own ideas over a long period. If the book is eventually judged to have made a contribution to the subject, I hope that this particular acknowledgement is remembered. Freedom of this kind is a rare commodity, and I hope that this example will encourage its greater provision.

Not long after I had embarked on the project, I was given a year's leave of absence by the College, which was spent partly at the Economic Growth Center, Yale University, partly at Ian and Dobs Little's house at La Garde Freinet, and partly in Oxford. That year took me over some difficult hurdles, and I am grateful to those who made it possible.

Finally, there is the considerable practical debt I owe to Trude Hickey, my secretary throughout the years in which this book was written, to Katie Draper and Elaine Herman, who undertook much of the typing of the concluding drafts, to Jonathan Mirrlees-Black, who helped with some of the charts, and to Sue Hughes, who edited the typescript for Oxford University Press.

March 1988   *Maurice FitzGerald Scott*
                                              Nuffield College, Oxford

READER'S GUIDE

While I rather naturally hope that readers will start at Chapter 1 and persevere to Chapter 16, I realize that not everyone will feel able to invest so much time in reading the book. Each chapter is preceded by an introduction which explains what it is about. The following summary also indicates each chapter's contents.

Those who need to be convinced that orthodox growth theories are severely flawed should read Chapters 1 and 3.

Those who want to get to the main novel and constructive theoretical ideas in the book should read Chapters 1, 2, 5, and 6. If time permits, they should continue with (at least) Chapter 9, and also Chapter 8.

But of what use is theory if it cannot be used to answer questions about the world? Readers can choose for themselves which chapters in Part IV to read for this purpose. Chapter 10, on why growth rates differ, is perhaps the most straightforward application. Chapter 16, on the slow-down in productivity growth after 1973, deals with the most recent period. Chapter 13, on Fabricant's laws, concludes, rather surprisingly, that labour productivity *tends* to grow at the same rate in all industries within a country and over a given time-period. These are the three chapters one might take first. Chapter 15, which concludes that there may be a large externality to investment, so that growth is appreciably sub-optimal, is perhaps the most doubtful and difficult, but possibly the most important.

CONTENTS

PART III   CONSTRUCTION

PART IV   USE

LIST OF MAIN ABBREVIATIONS
AND SYMBOLS

(Note: all symbols refer to the non-residential business sector unless otherwise stated.)

Symbol	*Meaning*
CSO	The Central Statistical Office of the UK Government.
GDP	The gross domestic product as conventionally defined.
GNP	The gross national product as conventionally defined.
NNP	GNP less capital consumption, as conventionally defined.
HMSO	Her Majesty's Stationery Office.
NIPA	National Income and Product Accounts of the United States, US Department of Commerce, Bureau of Economic Analysis.
NRB	The non-residential business sector. Broadly speaking, this excludes the output of public administration, defence, health, education, and dwellings from the GDP as conventionally defined (but see Statistical Appendix for more precise details).
OECD	Organization for Economic Co-operation and Development, Paris.
Y	Output, and income in a closed economy, at current prices, measured in practice by GDP at current factor cost; also value added (wages plus gross profits) in a particular industry or firm.
Q	Output, and income in a closed economy, at constant prices; Y deflated by P in a closed economy, but in an open economy exports and imports of goods and services are deflated by their own price index numbers in the conventional way. Gross investment, however, is deflated by P. Q can also refer to the output of a particular firm or

industry, in which case it can be measured in any suitable units whose price is P. Then $PQ = Y$.

C Generally, capitalists' take-out from their enterprises (gross profits less gross investment where there are no taxes or borrowing), but in Ch. 1 used to denote total consumption in the economy; at either current or constant prices, depending on the context, but generally the latter.

S Strictly speaking, investment (at current or constant prices, depending on the context) net of required maintenance; measured by gross investment as conventionally defined, but deflated by P when measured at constant prices.

P An index of prices (in principle, a Divisia index), in general of consumption. For NRB, measured by the conventionally defined price index of private and public consumption. In Chs. 9 and 13, also used to denote the price index of the output (value added) of a particular industry, *relative* to the general price index of consumption.

W Total wages, i.e. all payments (in cash or kind) to the factor labour. For NRB, measured by total income from employment, including social security contributions and income taxes and employers' contributions to pensions. The total income of self-employed persons is divided between wages and gross profits using the procedures described in Ch. 2 and the Statistical Appendix.

L A quality-adjusted index of employment.

H The same as L except that no adjustment is made to allow for changes in the efficiency of work resulting from changes in hours worked per year.

N Numbers employed, expressed as full-time equivalents.

w The price of labour, quality-adjusted. Hence $W = wL$.

λ The share of wages in output or value added. Hence $\lambda = W/Y$.

s The share of investment in output or value added. Hence $s = S/Y$.

t Time, measured in years.

g The exponential annual rate of growth of output at constant prices. Hence $g = (1/Q)(dQ/dt)$.

g_L The exponential annual rate of growth of quality-adjusted employment. Hence $g_L = (1/L)(dL/dt)$.

g_N The exponential annual rate of growth of numbers employed (full-time equivalents). Hence $g_N = (1/N)(dN/dt)$

g_w The exponential annual rate of growth of the price of labour. Hence $g_w = (1/w)(dw/dt)$

r The real rate of return on marginal investment to the owners of a firm. This is also (depending on the context) sometimes the owners' real rate of discount, and sometimes the average rate of return. Where taxation is considered, this is post-tax. Where borrowing is considered, it takes account of that.

σ The ratio of investment (measured at constant prices in consumption units) to output (measured in any suitable units). Hence $\sigma = S/Q$. If Q is also measured in consumption units (if, for example it refers to the output of the representative firm in the NRB), then $\sigma = s$; but in general, if P is the relevant price in consumption units of Q, then $s = S/PQ$, and $\sigma = Ps$.

q The exponential rate of growth of output capacity (at constant prices), resulting from investment, per unit ratio of investment. Hence, assuming that the ratio of output to capacity is unchanged (which is assumed unless the contrary is stated), $q = g/\sigma$. This is one investment 'characteristic'.

l The exponential rate of growth of quality-adjusted employment, resulting from investment, per unit ratio of investment. Hence $l = g_L/\sigma$. This is the other investment 'characteristic'.

EPC   The equal profits contour. Along this contour in q- and l-space, marginal investments yield the same rate of return. The EPC is a straight line.

μ The slope of the EPC, shown to depend on real wage rates (which determine λ for given output and

employment) and the rate of investment. Also used
to indicate the proportionate marginal product of
labour, as found, for example, from regressions of
the growth of output on employment growth and
the rate of investment. Firms are assumed to
behave so that the two meanings result in the same
value of μ.

IPC The investment programme contour. The
investments being undertaken by a firm at a given
time with a given rate of investment, σ, constitute
its investment programme. If their average
characteristics are q and l, thus defining the point
C in q- and l-space, then we know that the firm's
rate of growth of output and employment are
$g = \sigma q$ and $g_L = \sigma l$. Given μ, which depends on
real wage rates, the firm's owners will choose C to
be on the highest EPC they can attain. Keeping σ
fixed, but allowing μ (and so real wage rates) to
vary, C will trace out a contour which is the IPC.
The slope of the IPC at the chosen point, C, is
then μ. C may also be viewed as the centre of
gravity of a 'slice of cake' (i.e. the 'cake' of
investment opportunities), and C will vary as the
slope of the knife cutting off the slice varies, the
size of the slice (i.e. σ) being constant.

ϱ The 'radius' of the (average) IPC. The parameter
in the equation to the IPC, $f(q/\varrho, l/\varrho) = 0$, which
determines how far out from the origin the
(average) IPC lies.

V The value of the firm to its owners, equal to the
discounted value of all future sums taken out by
them.

D The rate of depreciation for a firm, expressed in
the same units as value added.

δ The ratio of depreciation to value added for a
firm. Hence $\delta = D/PQ$.

K The net capital stock of the firm. The integral of
its net investment, $S - D$, over its whole past
experience, when S and D are both expressed in
consumption units.

v The valuation ratio of the firm (Tobin's q). Hence

$v = V/K$. Also, the fraction of investment which gives rise to spurious inventory profits at rate $v\pi$.

q_m, l_m, ϱ_m Marginal values of q, l and ϱ. When there are 'physical' diminishing returns to the rate of investment, increasing that rate by a small amount results in the 'centre of gravity' of the marginal investments, i.e. their average characteristics, lying on an IPC that is closer to the origin than the average IPC of all the intra-marginal investments. The average characteristics of the marginal investment are then q_m and l_m, and the radius of the IPC on which they lie is ϱ_m.

ϱ_0 The radius of the outermost IPC, i.e. when a firm's investment tends to zero.

γ Coefficient which measures the rate at which ϱ_m shrinks as σ is increased, defined so as to be positive. Hence $\gamma = -\,d\ln\varrho_m/d\,\sigma$.

r_a The real rate of return on a firm's average investments, as distinct from r, the marginal return. $r_a > r$ when there are 'physical' diminishing returns to the rate of investment.

α The exponential rate of discount, *per annum*, of future benefits arising from 'impatience', or to allow for the risk of demise of a dynasty; 'pure' time preference.

β The elasticity of the marginal utility of consumption with respect to increases in consumption, defined so as to be positive.

m Marginal tax rate (per unit of income) for households. Also, the marginal rate of personal income tax paid on dividends received by the average household.

r_{sha} Marginal post-tax real rate of return received by shareholders, generally assumed to equal their average return. This may differ from r because the firm is controlled by a management that does not seek to maximize its value to shareholders.

π The prevalence of slumps, measured by the proportion of years in a period in which output is below its previous peak. Also, the exponential rate of inflation.

ν The income elasticity of demand for an industry's (or firm's) output (value added).

ϵ The price elasticity of demand for an industry's (or firm's) output (value added), defined so as to be positive.

η The ratio of marginal revenue to price. In simple monopolistic competition, and referring to output, $\eta = 1 - (1/\epsilon)$.

ϵ' The price elasticity of demand for an industry's (or firm's) output gross of material inputs.

ma The ratio of material inputs to output gross of them, i.e. to the sum of material inputs and value added.

i The rate of interest on bonds (real or nominal, depending on the context).

F The (net) rate of borrowing by a firm, expressed in the same units as S.

f The ratio of (net) borrowing to gross investment, so $f = F/S$.

f' The ratio of (net) borrowing to net investment, so $f' = F/(S - D)$.

u The fraction of profits, net of both interest payments and depreciation, reinvested by the firm.

an 'Animal spirits': the shadow premium added to marginal revenue by management which reflects its preference for output over profits. Hence, in effect, management behaves as if it were maximizing the present value of the firm to shareholders, but with the ratio of marginal revenue to the price of output given by $\eta + an$, instead of by η.

cu 'Catch-up': an indicator of the extent to which a country is 'behind' the leading country (the USA), and so of the extent to which investment opportunities should be better (ϱ greater) on this account. Measured by the ratio of output per quality-adjusted worker in non-residential business, excluding agriculture, in the country concerned to that in the USA in a base year, with the ratio extrapolated to other years using the ratio of Q/L

in the country to Q/L in the USA in the year in question, relative to the base year.

D_p Dummy variable set at 1 for post-Second World War periods and at 0 for other periods.

D_n Dummy variable set at 1 for interwar periods and at 0 for other periods.

D_{UK},   Dummy variables set at 1 for the relevant country
D_J,   and at 0 for other countries: UK = United
D_E Kingdom; J = Japan; E = any one of Belgium, France, Germany (Federal Republic), the Netherlands, Norway or Italy.

g_H The exponential annual rate of growth of H. Hence $g_H = (1/H) (dH/dt)$.

k_1 A variable which allows for the existence of imperfect markets for goods in the equation relating μ and λ (e.g. equation (6.2)). In the case of simple monopolistic competition, $k_1 = 1/\epsilon$. In a perfect market, $k_1 = 0$. 'Animal spirits' could be included in k_1, in which case, with simple monopolistic competition, $k_1 = (1/\epsilon) - an$, and so k_1 may be small even in imperfect markets.

k_2 A variable that allows for the existence of taxation of savings in the equation relating μ and λ (e.g. equation (6.2)). With zero taxation $k_2 = 1$, and with positive taxation $k_2 > 1$. k_2 can also include the effect of borrowing at an interest rate below shareholders' discount rate (both after tax) so that the firm's 'cost of capital' is reduced. Such borrowing would tend to offset taxation of savings, thus bringing k_2 nearer to 1.

g_p The exponential rate of growth of the price of output, in principle of the price of value added in the firm or industry but in practice usually the price of gross output. Indirect taxes are excluded.

T_w The tax rate (per unit) on wages (i.e. all incomes from employment) on a tax-inclusive basis.

T_c The tax rate (per unit) on take-out from enterprises on a tax-inclusive basis.

T_s The tax rate (per unit) on savings (or investment) on a tax-inclusive basis. While this is expressed as if it were a tax on investment expenditure, in reality it is a combination of taxes on profits and dividends with various allowances for interest payments, depreciation, and investment expenditures. In Chs. 14 and 15 the estimates also include the effects of the methods of financing chosen. While the estimates are of marginal tax rates, it is assumed for simplicity that average rates are the same.

S^* Tax-inclusive savings, as opposed to S, which measures the opportunity cost to society, in terms of consumption forgone. Hence $S = S^* (1 - T_s)$.

s^* The tax-inclusive savings ratio, S^*/PQ. Hence $s = s^* (1 - T_s)$.

p The pre-tax real rate of return on a marginal investment. Hence $T_s = (p - r)/p$.

τ The tax rate (per unit) on company profits, after deducting net interest paid. Depreciation allowances would normally be deducted, but these (as well as investment allowances and investment subsidies generally) are here allowed for in the initial cost of the investment (see A below). Consequently, all the additional profits (net of interest paid) resulting from a marginal investment pay tax at τ.

A The present value (per unit of a marginal investment) of tax allowances (e.g. depreciation allowances) and subsidies for that investment, whose net cost is thus $1 - A$.

c Under the imputation system of taxing company profits, cash dividends are accompanied by a tax credit equal to $c/(1 - c)$ times the dividends, c being the so-called 'rate of imputation'. For income tax purposes, the dividend receiver is deemed to have received an income, per unit cash dividend, of $1 + c/(1 - c) = 1/(1 - c)$ gross of income tax, and to have paid $c/(1 - c)$ of tax. If his marginal rate of tax is m, he ends up receiving $(1 - m)/(1 - c)$ net of tax.

θ The value of the dividend, before deduction of personal income tax, which can be paid at the sacrifice of a unit of retentions. Hence the sacrifice of one unit of retentions enables the shareholder to receive $\theta (1 - m)$ units net of tax.

f_b The fraction of the consumption cost, S, of investment that is financed by borrowing. To simplify matters, it is assumed that the marginal and average fractions are equal.

f_s The fraction of the consumption cost, S, of investment that is financed by the issue of new shares. To simplify matters, it is assumed that the marginal and average fractions are equal.

d The ratio of annual dividends (before deduction of personal income tax) to the market value of a company's ordinary shares.

r^* The real rate of return before deduction of personal income tax, on both shares and bonds (assumed to be the same).

r_s The real social rate of return on marginal investment.

q_{ms}, l_{ms}, ϱ_{ms} As for q_m, l_m, and ϱ_m, but referring to an IPC which measures the total changes in output and employment resulting from investment at the margin, rather than to the output and employment of the firm undertaking the investment as perceived by it.

γ_s As for γ, but referring to the rate of shrinkage of $\hat{\varrho}_{ms}$, rather than ϱ_m, as σ is increased. Hence $\gamma_s = (-d \ln\varrho_{ms})/d\sigma$.

r_{as} The real social rate of return on average investment.

r_{sh} The real rate of return received by shareholders after paying profit (i.e. corporation) tax but before paying personal income tax. The rate of return after paying personal income tax as well is r_{sha}. Average and marginal returns are assumed equal.

r_c A weighted average of the real rates of discount of shareholders (r_{sh}) and other creditors (i) before deducting personal income tax. The average 'cost of capital' to the firm. The weights are the proportions in which shareholders and other creditors finance gross investment.

$\bar{\varrho}_0$ The radius of the outermost IPC collectively considered, i.e. when all investment tends to zero.

$\bar{\sigma}$ The value of σ for all firms collectively considered.

po   The ratio of take-out to profits net of both tax and depreciation.

SUMMARY

This summary is intended merely as a quick guide to the contents of each chapter, and as an *aide-mémoire* for readers of them. Explanations, qualifications, evidence, and details are omitted, as are numerous other points of interest.

Chapter 1: Growth Concepts

1. Existing definitions of national income are circular, and therefore unsatisfactory. National income, as well as individual income, should be defined in Hicksian terms. The best available estimate is the sum of consumption and *gross* investment.

2. Maintenance expenditures, which must be deducted before arriving at national income, are those required to keep economic arrangements *physically* unchanged, or to make good income lost as a result of *physical* deterioration.

3. Investment is the cost, in terms of consumption forgone, of changing economic arrangements. It should be deflated by a price index of consumption so as to be consistent with the definition of income.

4. Depreciation, defined so as to distinguish it clearly from maintenance, results only from relative price changes which reduce the earnings of an asset. Within a closed economy, appreciation must be equal to, and must offset, depreciation. In a typical progressive economy, depreciation consists mainly in a transfer of income from capitalists to workers, whose human capital thereby appreciates.

5. For a closed economy, gross investment as conventionally defined is the best available measure of material (i.e. non-human) investment net of maintenance.

6. The most useful capital stock for the explanation of economic growth is cumulative gross investment. This prompts the question, How far must we go back? The answer is similar to that given by any historian. The starting point is arbitrary, and has to be left unexplained. All one can hope to explain is subsequent change, and so all one needs to measure is subsequent cumulative investment.

7. This measure of the capital stock cannot be used in the usual production function, but neither can either of the two measures generally used (see Chapter 3).

Chapter 2: Growth Facts

1. The 'stylized facts' of growth are that, abstracting from fluctuations in the ratio of output to capacity, the rates of growth of output and of employment, and the shares of 'wages', 'profits', and investment in total output, are all constant. The rate of return to investment is then also constant. When these conditions are all satisfied, the economy (or a particular industry or firm, if the conditions are satisfied for it) is said to be in a state of 'equilibrium growth', or 'steady growth'.

2. It greatly simplifies growth theory if one assumes that these 'stylized facts' hold, and that businessmen behave as if they expect them to hold indefinitely. This can be defended as being at least better than the more usual analysis of change in terms of comparative statics, or of convergence on a static equilibrium.

3. Furthermore, examination of the growth record of the non-residential business sector (to which attention is confined throughout the book) in the USA, Japan, and the UK since the late nineteenth century shows that one can divide it up into periods of roughly ten to thirty years, for many of which the 'stylized facts' are a reasonably good approximation to what happened, especially in the USA.

4. Growth of total employment should in principle be measured by weighting each worker in proportion to his or her marginal product. Such a measure of 'quality-adjusted' employment can behave very differently from a simple total of numbers employed. In particular, the UK's productivity record *vis-à-vis* the USA and Japan is markedly improved when this is done.

5. Although, in the long run, the growth of output probably does affect the growth of employment, it is the reverse direction of causation that seems the more important and on which the rest of the book is focused.

Chapter 3: Orthodox Growth Theories

1. The most widely used orthodox growth theories assume that there is a production function whose inputs are labour and capital, and which shifts through time as the result of exogenous technical progress. Vintage theories also assume exogenous technical progress.

2. In measuring the contribution of either labour or capital to the growth of output, it is assumed that they are homogeneous. New capital therefore reduplicates old capital. The growth of output is generally not fully explained, and the residual, which is generally large, is attributed to technical progress.

3. The main objection to this view is that technical progress is not independent of investment and that new capital seldom reduplicates old

capital. It is in practice not possible to distinguish between where it does merely reduplicate (so that one is moving along the production function) and where it does not (so that the function shifts). Nor is it interesting to do so. One wants to measure the *actual*, rather than some hypothetical, contribution of investment to growth.

4. In practice, the contribution of capital has been *assumed* to be equal to the change in the capital stock multiplied by the average rate of return (i.e. the ratio of profits to the capital stock). This is much too small, because the relevant change in the capital stock is best measured by gross investment (see Chapter 1) and not by either of the two measures generally taken: gross investment minus assumed scrapping, or gross investment minus depreciation. In competitive conditions, no output is lost when assets are scrapped, nor is depreciation a social cost. On neither count, therefore, should any subtraction be made from gross investment. It is this underestimate of the contribution of investment that has given rise to the residual, attributed to technical progress.

5. Vintage theories, which assume that technical progress is embodied in investment, do not escape criticism. Their essential assumption, which results in similar conclusions being reached as with the production function theories, is that technical progress proceeds at an exogenously determined rate. This assumption is shown to have implausible implications.

6. If, as suggested here, growth is explained by an equation relating it to investment and the growth of employment, can one integrate this equation to get something like the production function? The result will, in fact, differ in several important respects: the shift arising from technical progress disappears; *levels* are not explained, but only differences in level from an arbitrary base period; there are no diminishing returns to cumulative investment; and 'total factor productivity' must be abandoned, although the efficiency of investment can be measured.

7. Instead of diminishing returns to the capital *stock*, one should allow for diminishing returns to the *rate of investment*.

Chapter 4: Some Unorthodox Growth Theories

1. Unorthodox growth theories do not assume that technical progress is independent of investment and in that respect are preferable to orthodox theories.

2. While much can be learned from the theories briefly reviewed, they suffer from various defects: some provide no formal model; some incorporate the production function; some are complicated; most notably, none has formed the basis of substantial empirical work to rival that based on orthodox growth theory.

Chapter 5: Investment, Invention, and Scientific Discovery

1. Orthodox growth theories regard scientific discovery or invention as the ultimate determinants of the rate of growth of productivity. Investment is merely required to match the pace of scientific advance or invention.

2. However, Schmookler has provided empirical evidence for the conclusion that the rate of invention is determined by the rate of investment.

3. In fact, inventions are best regarded as a form of investment, and their volume depends, in like manner, on their expected profitability.

4. Investment opportunities are recreated by undertaking investment. There is no evidence that inventive opportunities in a particular field become exhausted for technical reasons, although they may do so for economic reasons.

5. Inventions may not be inevitable, but there is a high probability that prior circumstances will bring them about, as the existence of near-simultaneous discoveries by different people shows. Learning from prior experience is important not just in scientific or engineering matters, but in other fields such as business and social organization.

6. The pace of scientific advance can thus be neglected in constructing a theory of economy growth, at least at the beginning. Research and development can be merged with other forms of investment and not considered separately at this stage.

Chapter 6: A New Growth Model

1. The model in this chapter is based on various assumptions which are subsequently relaxed. It is assumed that the economy can be represented by a typical firm whose output (value added) is sold and whose labour is hired in perfect markets. The firm's investment is entirely self-financed, and is chosen so as to maximize the present value of the firm to its owners. The firm must decide on its rate of investment and on the rate at which its employment grows.

2. The firm is confronted by investment opportunities which are assumed to be constant in the following sense: for any given rate of investment (measured by the ratio of investment to output, s), and given the exponential rate of growth of employment g_L, it will be possible to achieve the same exponential rate of growth of output g.

3. The *characteristics* of the firm's investment programme are defined as $q = g/s$ and $l = g_L/s$. The constancy of investment opportunities can then be expressed as the assumption that there is a constant functional relation between q, l, and s, so that if any two of these are chosen the third is determined. This functional relation can be depicted on a diagram in which

q and l are the ordinate and abscissa respectively and contour lines (called investment programme contours, or IPCs), which slope up to the right and are concave to the origin, correspond to different values of s.

4. The assumption that the IPCs are constant may be contrasted with the stagnationist view that investment opportunities are gradually exhausted, and hence deteriorate as a consequence of undertaking investment, and with the orthodox view that investment opportunities are created by scientific advance or by inventive activity at a pace that is independent of investment. The view preferred here is that it is *undertaking investment which itself creates and reveals the further opportunities*, and this is probably the main innovation in the model. The assumption of *constancy* is merely a working hypothesis which has the merit that it is consistent with the 'stylized facts' of growth.

5. With diminishing returns to the rate of investment, the contour lines shrink inwards to the origin, as less g and g_L is achieved per unit of investment, and so q and l become smaller as s increases. For simplicity, it is assumed that q and l shrink equiproportionately. The distance out of the contours from the origin is measured by the parameter ϱ.

6. Changes in ϱ may be due, as in paragraph 5 above, to changes in s. However, ϱ may also change because factors outside the model cause investment opportunities to improve or worsen. This could be due, for example, to better communications leading to quicker learning, or it could be due to better selection being made from a given set of opportunities (due, in turn, to better management, or to better capital markets in a more realistic model in which borrowing occurs).

7. It can be shown that, at the point chosen by the firm, the slope of the IPC, dq/dl or μ, would equal the share of 'wages' in output, λ, if the firm were making a once-for-all investment in a static economy. This is equivalent to the ordinary assumption that the wage equals the value of the marginal product of labour.

8. For a steadily growing firm in a steadily growing economy, however, this becomes

$$\mu = \frac{\lambda}{1 - s}.$$

Hence the marginal product of labour exceeds the wage by an amount that depends on the rate of investment, s.

9. In equilibrium growth, the representative firm will choose to invest at the same one point on the same IPC indefinitely, so that g, g_L, s, and λ will all be constant, as required by the 'stylized facts' of growth. It is shown in Chapter 7 that the rate of return, r, will then also be constant. The determinants of s are discussed in Chapter 8, but, taking s here as exogenously determined, it can be shown how the firm will choose g and g_L when the rate of growth of wage rates, g_w, is exogenously given to it. For the

firm to be in equilibrium growth, it must start off from the right share of wages, λ. If actual λ differs from this, the firm will tend asymptotically towards the equilibrium values, but its rate of growth will not be constant until they are reached.

10. A very similar analysis can be used for a whole economy. In this case, however, it is the rate of growth of employment, g_L, which is assumed to be exogenously given along with s. Then g, g_w, r, and λ are determined. The adjustment of λ to its equilibrium value could, in principle, in this case be instantaneous, since it requires only an appropriate change in wage rates.

11. The model leads to a simple linear equation to explain growth in terms of the rate of investment, its efficiency, ϱ, and the rate of growth of employment:

$$g = a\varrho s + \mu g_L$$

12. It can be shown that, as long as equilibrium growth prevails, this equation is equivalent to another, which is closer to the orthodox growth accounting equation, viz.:

$$g = (1 - \mu) \frac{S}{K} + \mu g_L .$$

However, there are three important differences. (1) The rate of growth of the capital stock is measured by the ratio of *gross* investment, S, to the *net* capital stock, K, rather than the ratio of *net* investment to K. It is therefore much bigger. (2) The weights of capital and labour inputs are $1 - \mu$ and μ instead of $1 - \lambda$ and λ. (3) Finally, there is no term for technical progress. For once-for-all changes in an otherwise static economy, my equation would coincide with the orthodox one. Hence the mistake made by orthodoxy is to apply a comparative-statics analysis to a dynamic situation, and to throw the whole of the resulting error into a black box labelled 'technical progress'.

Chapter 7: The Rate of Return

1. Three different proofs are given of the following formula for the (private) rate of return to investment when there are constant returns to the rate of investment. (This is also the average rate of return whether there are constant or diminishing returns to the rate of investment.)

$$r = q - \lambda l.$$

As this formula in effect says that the *initial* quasi-rent earned is to be treated as a perpetuity, it is at first sight puzzling why it should hold in circumstances in which wage rates may be rising or falling and depreciation or appreciation occurring. The second proof, in particular, aims to solve this puzzle by showing how additional investment brings forward subsequent investments by the firm into periods in which wage rates are lower (if wage rates are rising) or higher (if falling).

2. A formula for the rate of return when there are diminishing returns to the rate of investment is given in the appendix to Chapter 7.

3. Formulae for the rate of depreciation as a share of output (which is also the rate of appreciation for workers),

$$\delta = \frac{\lambda g_w}{r - g},$$

for the net present value of the firm,

$$V = \frac{PQ\,(1 - \lambda - s)}{r - g}$$

(where PQ is the value of output), which is also equal to the net capital stock K (i.e. to cumulated investment net of depreciation), and for the valuation ratio

$$v = \frac{V}{K} = 1$$

are proved, assuming equilibrium growth, no taxation or subsidy, and constant returns to the rate of investment.

4. Using these formulae, average rates of return to investment and ratios of depreciation to output are calculated for the USA, Japan, the UK, and seven continental European countries for various periods. Both rates of return and depreciation ratios were much higher in the years following the Second World War than in the earlier years of the present century.

5. Comparisons are made for the post-Second World War years of the above rates of return and depreciation ratios in the USA and the UK with those derived from conventional estimates using the perpetual inventory method and (for the rate of return) the ratio of net profits to net capital stock. The conventional rates of return and depreciation ratios are appreciably lower, especially for the UK, and various explanations of this are given.

6. Rates of return received by shareholders before personal tax are only about a half of those earned by businesses. The explanation of this gap is attempted in Chapter 15.

Chapter 8: The Determinants of the Share of Investment in Output and the Complete Growth Model

1. The most widely accepted investment function is the modified acceleration principle (capital stock adjustment principle), but this is unsatisfactory for various reasons including, in particular, the fact that investment is explained by output, whereas in the (long-run) approach taken here output is explained by investment.

2. For the average firm in the USA and the UK, nearly all its gross investment is financed by its own gross saving. Borrowing is mostly offset by the acquisition of financial assets. Hence it seems reasonable, at least to start with, to regard investment as being determined by the supply of saving. The role of demand for output is important, but it depends crucially on the existence of imperfect markets, which are discussed in Chapters 9 and 15.

3. My preferred theory of saving is that, for managements that seek to maximize the value of the firm to its owners, savings and investment will be pushed to the point where the marginal return equals the owners' rate of discount.

4. In equilibrium growth, owners' rate of discount of consumption, r, is assumed to be given by the equation

$$r = \alpha + \beta (g - g_N)$$

where α and β are constants, g is the rate of growth of 'take-out' by shareholders from the firm, which is also the rate of growth of its output, and g_N is the rate of growth of the number of shareholders; α corresponds to the rate at which utility is discounted, or to 'impatience', while β is the elasticity of marginal utility with respect to increases in consumption. This is called the 'Ramsey approach'.

5. The Ramsey approach may be contrasted with the simple life-cycle hypothesis according to which individuals plan their life time patterns of consumption so that they are left with nothing when they die. This is a bizarre theory, since it ignores the powerful urge to perpetuate oneself. It is also at variance with the evidence on saving by old persons. Given the need for a simple theory, it seems preferable to take the Ramsey approach, which assumes that individuals regard their heirs as they would themselves.

6. The equation in paragraph 4 above closes the growth model, which consists of eight equations to determine the eight endogenous variables (for the whole economy): q, l, σ, s, λ, μ, r, and g. These have all been defined in this summary except for σ, which is equal to Ps, P being the price of output which can be set equal to 1 for the whole economy, so that $\sigma = s$. The relevance and importance of P appears in Chapter 9, where separate sectors of the economy are considered. For the whole economy, g_L, g_N, α, and β are exogenous constants, as also are the constants determining the shape of the IPC, ϱ, a, b, and c. For the individual representative firm, $g_w = g - g_L$ is exogenous, while g_L is endogenous.

7. A geometrical representation of the model is given, and used, by way of illustration, to show the effects on the endogenous variables of a fall in α, the rate of discount of utility.

8. An attempt is made to estimate α and β from data on average rates of return received by savers in the USA and the UK. $\alpha = 0.013$ and $\beta = 1.5$ are the best guesses.

9. While the Ramsey approach is over-simplified and unsatisfactory, a review of the literature does not reveal any more satisfactory quantitative study capable of explaining long-run investment and saving.

Chapter 9: Growth of the Firm and Industry

1. For equilibrium growth to occur in a particular industry, the price of its output must be constant relative to that of the whole economy.

2. The model described in Chapter 8 can be used to analyse the behaviour of a representative firm in a particular perfectly competitive industry, the demand for whose output is growing faster or slower than the output of the whole economy. There is now one more endogenous variable, which is the price of the firm's output, P, and one more equation, which determines the growth of demand at constant relative prices for the firm and industry's output.

3. A higher price now shifts out the effective IPC, and so results in a faster *rate of growth* of output. This is because the burden (measured by s) of achieving a given rate of growth of output is reduced by a rise in P. The given rate of growth of output requires a certain ratio, σ, of investment (measured in consumption units) to output (measured in 'physical' units), and this implies a smaller value of s the higher is P. A dynamic supply curve can then be constructed relating the *level* of P to the *rate of growth* of supply. Stability conditions require that this slopes upwards to the right, and this comes about because the required rate of return rises as the rate of growth rises. Alternatively, or as well, it could be the result of diminishing returns to the rate of investment.

4. There is a close correspondence between an improvement in investment opportunities owing to exogenous factors and a rise in the price of an industry's output. In fact, if the former resulted in a uniform outward shift of the IPC, it would eventually be completely offset by a fall in P, which would return the industry to the same equilibrium growth position as before, so that the whole benefit would accrue to consumers in the form of a lower price.

5. Where the firm is selling under conditions of simple monopolistic competition, the model's equations must be modified to allow for imperfectly elastic demand for output, and this can be done quite simply. In fact, it can be shown that the effect of a demand elasticity of ϵ (defined to be positive) is to shift the dynamic supply curve up in the uniform proportion $1/\{1 - (1/\epsilon)\}$. For a particular (small) industry, therefore, the rate of growth will be unaffected, but P will be raised in that proportion. Hence monopolization is similar to a worsening of investment opportunities (see paragraph 4 above).

6. For a whole economy, P cannot change as a result of monopolization.

In this case the effect is again like a worsening in investment opportunities (a fall in ϱ), and the rate of investment and rate of growth are reduced.

7. All of the above assumes that each firm produces a single product. Firms can, however, diversify, and in this way can avoid compulsion to grow at the same rate as demand for their products in the long run. A firm could even grow in an otherwise static economy by taking the investment opportunities that all others are neglecting; nor need this imply an ever falling rate of return on its investments. However, a faster rate of diversification and investment would probably imply a lower *level* of the marginal rate of return. Furthermore, faster growth in the rest of the economy will benefit a firm, increasing the rate of investment it can undertake at any given rate of return. This is the basis of the accelerator and locomotive effects.

8. Two other possibilities may be noted. A firm may incur 'capital' selling costs which shift the demand curve for its products to the right, and in that case a higher rate of investment can result in a faster rate of growth in demand. Secondly, since the rate of growth of a firm's supply depends on the price level of its output, the same may be true of the rate of growth of demand, because a lower or higher price will reduce or increase the rate of growth of supply by the firm's competitors.

9. So far, the firm has been assumed to be entirely self-financed. As one limiting possibility, suppose instead that it can borrow at a given rate of interest in a perfect capital market. This will then fix its rate of return, and if there are constant returns to the rate of investment, the dynamic supply curve must be downward-sloping. This is not consistent with stability in perfect product markets, but is in imperfect ones.

10. Another, perhaps more realistic, possibility is that firms can borrow at a rising cost. The marginal cost of borrowing will then be equated to the marginal return on investment, but the average cost of borrowing will be less. Borrowing will then tend to reduce the burden of investment for shareholders, and it will both lower the dynamic supply curve and make it slope upwards less steeply or downwards more steeply.

11. A large proportion of firms, even large ones, are controlled by owners (who may be other companies, as well as private individuals or families). However, managerially controlled firms are also important, and the question arises how far they pursue, and are constrained by market forces to pursue, the maximization of the value of the firm to its owners. The evidence suggests that many firms can and do pursue other objectives, such as size and growth, at least to some extent.

12. One rather simple way of modifying the model so as to allow for the pursuit of size and growth at the expense of the value of the firm to its owners is to assume that those who control the firm attach a premium, *an* (for 'animal spirits'), to each unit value of output, over and above its

marginal revenue. This enters into two equations of the model: that relating μ to λ (see Chapter 6, paragraph 8, above), where an must be added to the denominator on the right-hand side, thus tending to increase λ for given μ; and the equation for the marginal rate of return, where an will tend to reduce that return below the shareholders' discount rate. Animal spirits thus offset monopoly, since the latter tends to lower λ and to raise the required average rate of return.

Chapter 10: Why Growth Rates Differ, I

1. The linear equation used to explain why growth rates differ (see Chapter 6, paragraph 11, above) was

$$g = a\varrho s + \mu g_L.$$

Most empirical studies based on orthodox theory consist of growth *accounting*; they do not *test* the theory. To follow a comparable procedure here would have meant predetermining a and μ, inserting actual values of g, s, and g_L, and obtaining ϱ as a residual. Instead of that, the above equation, modified as below, was fitted to 26 observations for non-residential business in different periods and countries by ordinary least squares. The closeness of fit and agreement of the coefficients with theoretical expectations then provided a test of the theory.

2. A modified equation, obtained by integrating the above one, was also fitted to 177 annual observations, but it did not add anything significant, and so it is not reported in detail.

3. The 26 observations were weighted by the product of population, the length of period, and an index of statistical reliability so as to counter heteroscedasticity.

4. Before fitting the equation, the term containing ϱ was expanded to allow for various possibilities: diminishing returns to s, country and (long-) period dummies, and 'catch-up'.

5. The resulting values of the coefficients in the best equations were consistent with the theory, and the closeness of fit was reasonably good. There was only rather weak evidence for diminishing returns to s or for significant differences between countries. There was, however, strong evidence that ϱ increased markedly after the Second World War, and weaker evidence that it also increased after the First World War. 'Catch-up' was quite significant, but only after the Second World War.

6. A constant added to the equation to allow for separate 'technical progress' was negative and insignificantly different from zero. An equation of the form

$$g = a + bg_L$$

was also fitted, allowing for shifts in a from before to after the Second

World War, and for catch-up. This gave a worse fit than my best equation, yielded a coefficient b which was appreciably bigger than the theoretical value of 1 (assuming steady growth), and implied that technical progress, a, was negligible until after the Second World War, which is implausible.

7. Taking my preferred equation, the contribution of material investment, s, to growth on average exceeded that of quality-adjusted employment, g_L, but the relative contributions differed greatly between periods and countries. Investment was a much more important contributor to growth than orthodox growth accounting studies suggest. For example, for the USA for 1948–73, Denison has estimated that, including an allowance for economies of scale, investment accounted for less than a fifth of the growth of non-residential business output, whereas my estimates put its share at over half.

8. There are various explanations for the marked improvement in investment opportunities (increase in ϱ) after the Second World War. In my view, high capacity utilization, strong business confidence, an absence of severe fluctuations in demand and prices, improved communications, greater professionalism of management, better education, and more expenditure, which should be (but is not) classed as investment, were important.

9. The very slow rates of growth experienced before the Industrial Revolution may be explained by poor communications and low rates of investment by others, which reduced the supply of investment opportunities to any individual, while high rates of discount caused by insecurity meant that few opportunities were taken up. There were many anti-growth factors, with lack of freedom to pursue and improve one's own business, and lack of confidence that one could keep most of the gains, perhaps the most important of these. Growth is a rare plant in history, but there are reasons for hoping that it is robust.

Chapter 11: Why Growth Rates (and Factor Shares) Differ, II

1. Chapter 10 considers only the linear version of the IPC. By allowing for its curvature, owing to diminishing returns to labour, one can investigate the determinants of the shares of 'wages', λ, and profits $(1 - \lambda)$, in total income. In its simplest version, the model implies that μ, the slope of the IPC, equals $\lambda/(1 - s)$ (see Chapter 6, paragraph 8, above). In turn, μ depends on the labour intensity of investment (i.e. the characteristic $l = g_L/s$), and declines as l increases. *Ceteris paribus*, λ then depends on g_L and s.

2. This relationship is investigated using the same period data as in Chapter 10, together with estimates of λ. While the evidence is broadly consistent with the theory, it is clear that there are many other important

factors influencing λ which should be taken into account. These include market imperfections, 'animal spirits' (these two offsetting each other to some extent), taxation of savings, and the availability of cheap finance (again, these two offsetting each other to some extent), as well as factors discussed below.

3. It appears that λ in the USA was larger than the theory would predict in the earlier years of the period, whereas in Japan and the UK λ was smaller. Over time, these differences lessened, so that for all these countries λ converged towards predicted values (and rather above them in Japan). This behaviour could have been due to more plentiful supply of agricultural land in the USA than in Japan and the UK in the earlier years, coupled with the declining importance of food in total expenditure and its greater availability through trade in later years.

4. Another possible explanation is that labour markets were always more competitive in the USA than in Japan and the UK, where the growth of trade unions may have shifted bargaining power away from employers.

5. The relation between λ, g_L, and s just described provides a means of estimating the degree of curvature of the IPC, which can also be investigated more directly. The evidence suggests that curvature is slight, so that the linear approximation in Chapter 10 is a good one.

6. Examination of the residuals from fitting either a linear or a curved IPC to the data for the 26 periods shows that many of the biggest deviations from the regression line occur for the earlier periods, where the statistical quality of the data is suspect. Successive periods are often on opposite sides of the regression line, which could be due to the fact that fluctuations in the ratio of output to capacity have not been fully eliminated. The first decade of the present century was a low growth period in the USA, Japan, and the UK, but only the UK's experience in this regard seems to have been widely commented on in the literature.

Chapter 12: Verdoorn's and Kaldor's Laws

1. This chapter is concerned with comparisons of similar industries in different countries, while Chapter 13 considers comparisons of different industries in a given period in one country.

2. Labour productivity has grown at different rates in similar industries in different countries. Verdoorn's Law suggests that these differences should be explained by differences in the rates of growth of output, and are due to economies of scale.

3. However, a faster rate of growth (say) in a particular industry in country A than in country B could be due to several reasons: faster growth of employment as usually measured (i.e. without quality adjustment), faster growth of labour quality, a higher rate of investment, more efficient

investment which is not associated with economies of scale, and that which is associated with economies of scale. It would be quite common to find *all* of these factors at work simultaneously, yet it is only the last which is relevant to the economies-of-scale explanation. As it seems likely that much of the differences in labour productivity growth can be explained by labour quality growth and investment, without invoking economies of scale, the evidence for the latter from *this* type of comparison is weak. Nor is there evidence that the ratio of growth in output to growth in productivity is particularly stable; nor, finally, is the positive association between output and productivity growth always to be found.

4. Kaldor emphasized the importance of 'industry' (mainly manufacturing) in determining the growth rate of the whole economy. He showed that there was a close correlation between the rate of growth of GDP (or of GDP excluding manufacturing) and that of manufacturing output for twelve developed countries over the decade 1953/4–1963/4. He explained this as being due to the fact that the capital and labour required to expand manufacturing output had little opportunity cost (except in a mature economy, in which case only low growth would be possible). Growth in manufacturing output depended on demand, which could be export demand or demand by 'agriculture'. In so far as the latter was the case, the ultimate cause was land-saving innovation.

5. Kaldor's (earlier) explanation of the UK's slow rate of growth as being due to the fact that it was no longer possible to gain substantially by transferring labour from agriculture to the rest of the economy is confirmed in this book. However, his explanation of the correlation between the rates of growth of GDP and manufacturing output is open to several criticisms. For the world as a whole, or for the USA (for example), where foreign trade has been a small fraction of output, exports are zero or very small, and so cannot plausibly be regarded as the exogenous cause of the growth of manufacturing. Nor is it plausible to attribute the very different rates of growth of exports of manufactures achieved by different countries to *demand* factors, since they were all competing in the same world market. Why should innovations in services or manufacturing itself not be at least as important as in 'agriculture'? It is, in any case, unsatisfactory to treat innovation as exogenous, for reasons already discussed. It is implausible that capital and labour inputs into manufacturing in the countries considered by Kaldor had little opportunity cost.

6. My alternative explanation of the correlation is more *ad hoc*, which is also in keeping with the fact that the correlation virtually disappeared in 1970–83. In 1953–63 the pattern of final demand changed in a way favourable to manufacturing, whereas in 1970–83 it no longer did so. Ironically, it was in the later period, rather than the earlier one, that *net* exports of manufactures increased relatively faster.

Chapter 13: Fabricant's Laws

1. This chapter is concerned with comparisons of rates of growth in different industries over a given period in a given country.

2. In a study of fifty US manufacturing industries over some forty years, Fabricant noted various correlations, including the following. As in Verdoorn's law, labour productivity tended to grow faster where output grew faster. Also, with faster growth in output, wage costs per unit of output grew more slowly, as did value added per unit of (gross) output and price. In Fabricant's view, the causation could run in both directions, from rapidly growing productivity to declining costs and prices and so to rapidly growing output, or from the last, via economies of scale, to declining costs and rapidly growing productivity.

3. Similar patterns of relationship have been found in other countries and periods, and the challenge is to explain them, especially in view of the reasons that exist for expecting that slower, rather than faster, productivity growth should be associated with faster output growth, as pointed out by Kennedy (and cited in recent explanations of UK productivity growth). One cannot provide the same explanation as for Verdoorn's law in Chapter 12, since different industries may have different capital intensities, so that very different ratios of investment to output are quite compatible with similar rates of labour productivity growth.

4. Salter extended Fabricant's analysis by showing that both 'gross margin' costs and materials costs per unit of output were reduced, as well as wages costs, in industries in which output grew most rapidly. This led him to reject substitution of capital or materials for labour as the main explanation of faster labour productivity growth. Instead, he mainly emphasized different rates of technical change as being the cause of both different rates of productivity growth and, via their effects on prices, different rates of output growth. However, he also related economies of scale to technical change, and recognized that faster growth in demand could result in greater economies of scale which would thus reduce costs and increase productivity.

5. Kennedy provided the most careful and extended analysis of this phenomenon. He rejected several explanations of the association between labour productivity growth and output growth, including (as a *main* explanation) differences in the rate of exogenous technical progress. Arguing that the main direction of causation must be from output growth to productivity growth, and drawing on Arrow and Schmookler in particular, he suggested that faster output growth induced faster technical progress as well as economies of scale.

6. An explanation of Fabricant's laws in terms of my model can be

provided. Industries in equilibrium growth do not exemplify the laws. For these industries, although output may grow at different rates determined by different income elasticities of demand, etc., prices of output will not change relative to prices-in-general, nor will the shares of investment or wages in output change. This implies that wage rates must rise in each industry at the same rate as labour productivity. If, as is plausible, wage rates rise at approximately the same rate in all industries, then so must labour productivity in the equilibrium growth industries.

7. On the other hand, there are industries that are not in growth equilibrium because they have been subjected to shocks on either the demand or supply sides. The evidence, on the whole, favours supply shocks. A major invention, for example, could increase ϱ and this would temporarily increase the rate of investment and growth of both output and labour productivity. Equilibrium growth would be restored by a gradual fall in price which, as shown in Chapter 9, has very similar effects to a fall in ϱ. These out-of-equilibrium industries would thus obey Fabricant's laws, but their productivity growth rates would regress towards the mean.

8. The evidence reviewed in this chapter supports this explanation reasonably well. Most industries are in equilibrium, and do not obey Fabricant's laws, but a significant fraction are out of equilibrium, and they do.

9. An alternative explanation of Fabricant's laws in terms of the effects of economies of scale on ϱ is rejected, since it does not fit the behaviour of most industries. Yet another explanation, which assumes a relation between the growth of demand and the *level* of an industry's prices, requires further investigation.

Chapter 14: Taxation and Growth

1. The effects of taxation on growth depend on how the revenue is spent. Raising taxes can increase the rate of growth if the revenue is well spent, or reduce it if not. In what follows, the effects on growth via government expenditure are neglected.

2. Taxes may be subdivided into three kinds: on wages, on capitalists' take-out, and on savings. Many actual taxes are a mixture of these.

3. Increasing the tax on wages can generally be expected to reduce investment in human capital, and so reduce g_L and g. Further reductions in g will occur if workers are driven into the 'black' economy, or if there is real wage resistance leading to cost-push inflationary pressure.

4. Taxes on capitalists' take-out have no direct effects on growth since they leave the rate of return to material investment unaffected. The government, in effect, becomes a sleeping partner in every firm. However,

if tax rates are high enough to lead to tax avoidance or evasion, there could be adverse effects on growth.

5. A uniform tax on savings tends to reduce the rate of return and the rate of growth. Estimates of the effect of savings taxes on growth are given in Chapter 15 using the model in Appendix C.

6. Uneven rates of tax can be justified on various grounds. Where there is no such justification, uneven rates of taxation on consumption provide scope for once-for-all gains in output. By contrast, uneven rates of taxation on investment could reduce the long-term rate of growth.

7. OECD estimates of marginal effective tax rates on wages in twenty-one member countries in 1983 show that they varied from 40 to 73 per cent for the average production worker in manufacturing.

8. Marginal effective tax rates on saving in the USA and the UK in 1960, 1970, and 1980, based on King and Fullerton's study, but with different formulae (explained in Appendix C to the chapter), show that they varied widely depending on the asset, industry, and sector providing the savings. It seems doubtful that the differences in tax rates had an economic rationale.

9. There is evidence that tax discrimination greatly affected the forms taken by household savings, and resulted in pension funds and insurance companies holding an increasing proportion of equities, especially in the UK.

Chapter 15: The Optimum Rate of Investment and Growth

1. This chapter concludes that the marginal social return to investment is substantially greater than the marginal private return, so that, prima facie, both investment and growth are sub-optimal. The analysis throughout refers mainly to the UK and USA non-residential business sectors in the years following the Second World War up to 1973. All the estimates are very tentative — but are still interesting.

2. Some relevant formulae are set out. The *marginal social* return is below the average if there are 'physical' diminishing returns to the rate of investment collectively considered. The *a priori* arguments for diminishing returns can be countered by arguments against, based on economies of scale. Some weak empirical evidence for them is given in Chapter 10, and, in default of anything better, the resulting estimate of the extent of diminishing returns is used in the sequel. Whereas average social returns are put at about 16 (UK) or 17 (USA) per cent per annum, marginal social returns are then estimated to be 13 or 14 per cent per annum.

3. *Average private* pre-tax rates of return to investment approximately equal average social rates of return. However, *marginal private* (after tax) rates of return to the typical shareholder household are estimated to be only

6 (UK) or 5 (USA) per cent per annum. There is therefore, on these estimates, a very big gap of 7 or 9 per cent per annum between marginal social and private returns which needs to be explained.

4. Of this gap, marginal company and personal taxation taken together (judging by 1960 tax rates) accounted for little more than a third. This allows for cheap fixed-interest borrowing as, in effect, an offset to taxation.

5. Three other factors explain the rest of the gap: the learning externality, the demand externality, and 'animal spirits', each considered below.

6. The idea that investment creates and reveals further investment opportunities is discussed in Chapter 6. Many of these opportunities may accrue to firms other than the one undertaking the investment, thus resulting in an externality. The implication is that 'physical' returns to the rate of investment diminish more sharply for the individual firm than they would if all firms were to increase investment together. For this reason, marginal social returns exceed marginal private returns to investment, and in fact, virtually the whole of the gap between the two which is not explained by taxation may be due to this learning externality. This is because the demand externality and 'animal spirits' apparently offset each other in the period being considered (see paragraph 8 below).

7. Firms selling in imperfect markets receive lower marginal than average returns because of marginal selling costs (marginal revenue less than price) and/or marginal costs of diversification. This gives rise to 'market' diminishing returns to marginal investment, and could be avoided if all firms increased investment together, and if the ratio of output to capacity remained constant so that demand curves everywhere shifted faster to the right. This is similar to the 'locomotive' effect. There is then, again, an externality to investment, and marginal social returns exceed marginal private returns for this reason. The average extent of the difference depends on how elastic the average demand curve is. After reviewing evidence of price elasticities in foreign trade, I take a best guess of 6 for the average price elasticity of demand, and that implies, if true, that the demand externality accounts for rather more of the gap between marginal social and private returns than does taxation, but less than the learning externality.

8. This demand externality, however, appears to have been approximately offset by 'animal spirits', that is, by the tendency for firms to value increases in output by more than their value to shareholders. The evidence for this offsetting is that it is required to reconcile the estimates of μ in Chapters 10 and 11 with the estimates of λ, s, and tax rates on savings using the type of equation described in Chapter 6, paragraph 8, above. The estimated magnitude of 'animal spirits' depends on the value chosen for the average price elasticity of demand. The larger that is, the smaller is the coefficient of 'animal spirits'.

9. Optimum growth may be defined as the rate of growth that would occur if there were four changes to the existing situation: no marginal net taxation of savings; no learning externality; no market imperfections, so that there was no demand externality; and no 'animal spirits', so that managers maximized the value of their firms to their shareholders. In these circumstances, marginal social and private returns would be equal.

10. Appendix C to the chapter sets out a model that is used to estimate the effects of the above four changes on the rate of growth in the UK and the USA in the period considered. The optimum rate of growth is then estimated to go up from the actual 2.7 to 4.6 per cent per annum for the UK, and from 3.4 to 5.5 per cent per annum for the USA. In each country it would require a very big increase in the share of material investment in output to achieve this, and also a big increase in the share of profits in output. Workers' current sacrifice of wages would, however, result in a much faster growth in their real wage rates, so that, taking both the immediate sacrifice and future gains together, their real worth would greatly increase.

11. Achieving such an optimum might not be desirable and is in any case probably impracticable. A more realistic possibility is the abolition of taxation on savings: and, according to the model, this would raise the rate of growth by roughly $\frac{1}{2}$ per cent per annum, which would be a substantial gain, and much more than estimates made by others have suggested.

12. The existence of the learning externality has long been known, and a variety of measures (e.g. subsidization of research, patent laws, governmental assistance to 'high technology' industries) have been taken, which, however, may move one only a little nearer to a goal that cannot be reached.

13. There may, happily, be a causal link between the demand externality and 'animal spirits', so that their offsetting of each other is not just an accident.

14. In principle, the existence of externalities to investment calls for a subsidy to it, and my estimates suggest that a large one, of the order of 50 per cent, is needed. However, there are arguments against paying such a large subsidy, including the important one, stressed repeatedly in the chapter, that my estimates are very uncertain.

15. Instead of subsidizing investment, governments could run budget surpluses which, despite arguments to the contrary, would almost certainly increase total savings rates.

16. Appendices D and E consider other views about optimum growth. The Golden Rule of Accumulation has been derived from orthodox growth theory. According to my theory, following the rule would result in wildly excessive investment which would swallow up the whole of output. Neither the view that saving is sub-optimal because of 'impatience' nor the

'Isolation Paradox' provides persuasive arguments for governmental promotion of investment.

Chapter 16: The Slow-down in Productivity Growth after 1973

1. This chapter concludes that the large swings from inflation to deflation that occurred after 1973 explain most of the slow-down in productivity growth. An analysis of the mechanism that brought this about is given.

2. There is a brief summary of events. Productivity growth slowed down in many countries in 1973, although in some the trouble started in the late 1960s. This coincidence suggests that common factors, linked to the upsurge in inflation and growing unemployment, were at work.

3. In turn, the upsurge in inflation is attributable mainly to cost-push by wage-earners following the prosperity and full employment of the postwar years, together with the tax squeeze owing to rising government expenditure. Student and labour unrest, followed by expansionary policies, a commodity price boom, and then the first oil shock, provided the detonator and primer, and ensured that the explosion was accentuated by its simultaneous occurrence in so many countries.

4. There was a precarious recovery in the late 1970s, but after the second oil shock governments took tougher deflationary action, and real interest rates rose sharply. Unemployment climbed to levels not experienced since the 1930s, and output stagnated or fell. By 1985, the end of the period considered in the chapter, recovery had not proceeded very far.

5. Why did all this slow down *productivity* growth? There have been many attempts to answer this question, but the leading one for the USA, by Denison, comes to no firm positive conclusion, although it rules out many explanations that have been suggested. Only about half of the decline of 2.7 per cent per annum in productivity growth from 2.4 per cent per annum in 1948–73 to − 0.3 per cent per annum in 1973–82 is quantitatively explained.

6. If the equations fitted in Chapters 10 and 11 are used to account for growth in the non-residential business sectors of the USA, Japan, and the UK (excluding oil and gas for the UK), the residual, ϱ, which measures the efficiency of investment, shows a very sharp drop in 1973–85 compared with earlier postwar years. However, this result follows when g, g_L, and s are measured in the standard way. There are reasons for adjusting all three in the period being considered.

7. g_L may have grown more slowly because labour shifted from higher- to lower-paid jobs, and this is not properly allowed for. While the data on employment by industry do not bear this out, there does seem to have been a shift towards small-sized establishments or firms (especially in Japan), where wage rates are lower, which contrasts with a shift in the opposite direction before 1973. This shift may have been partly due to recession. The

evidence in the USA is not firm, but there are several reasons for thinking that the quality of the labour force deteriorated after 1973.

8. The correct measure of g to use is not the growth rate of output, but that of output at a constant rate of capacity utilization. There is evidence that utilization fell after 1973 (although the measurement of utilization, discussed at some length, is very difficult), and so g should be adjusted upwards to allow for this. However, g_L should then also be adjusted upwards, and the net effect of the adjustments on productivity growth is small. There is also a small adjustment to s required because of lower utilization.

9. Important explanations for the apparent fall in ϱ are mistaken and wasted investment, arising from the wide swings in demand and relative prices falsifying expectations, and from abnormal required maintenance. The last is a novel explanation, and is linked to 'animal spirits'. When profits are squeezed, as in the 1970s and early 1980s, managers feel compelled to attend more to profit maximization. They may then scrap capacity whose quasi-rent in marginal revenue terms is zero, although positive if valued at current prices. The resultant loss of output implies an increase in required maintenance, so that true net investment falls in relation to measured s. In good times, this adverse effect of market imperfections is offset by 'animal spirits', so that scrapping has zero social cost. In bad times, however, the cost could be substantial.

10. Taking into account the above, and some other, factors, it seems likely that three-quarters or more of the fall in $g - g_L$ in the three countries was reversible, in the sense that a reversion to the smoother and less depressed macroeconomic conditions ruling before 1973 would restore most of productivity growth thus measured.

11. However, productivity growth is usually measured by reference to g_N, the growth of employment *without* allowing for quality changes. In the USA and Japan, but not in the UK, $g_L - g_N$ may have fallen by about 1 per cent per annum for reasons that could persist, and could therefore continue to lower productivity growth measured by $g - g_N$.

12. Although a restoration of macroeconomic performance to pre-1973 norms would probably restore most of productivity growth, that may not be easy to achieve. The principle requirements are that wage-earners' expectations and the expectations of those benefiting from public services should become sufficiently modest, and that businessmen's 'animal spirits' should recover.

PART I

MATERIALS

Change is not made without inconvenience, even from worse to better.

Richard Hooker,
quoted by Samuel Johnson in the Preface to the
English Dictionary.

1

GROWTH CONCEPTS

1.1 Introduction

What is a theory of economic growth about? Presumably, about the growth of real output or income, but what are they? I do not know any standard theoretical exposition of growth theory which provides a carefully discussed answer to this question. It seems to be generally assumed that the literature on the measurement and definition of national income provides us with concepts that are sufficiently well defined. We can then launch straight off into our analysis with meanings of income, output, investment, depreciation, maintenance, capital, wealth, labour, and land which everyone knows and which are adequate.

Unfortunately, that is not the case. As shown in Chapter 3, the two ways in which capital is generally measured are both inconsistent with the capital stock employed in orthodox growth theories. Nor is this a small matter, since, if one corrects the error, one thereby destroys the empirical evidence for the belief that technical progress is a very important factor in economic growth which is independent of investment. This demolishes the foundation of orthodox growth theory. Moreover, in most expositions of theory, depreciation and maintenance are not properly distinguished from each other; nor, for that matter, are capital and wealth, or even capital and land. There is no consensus as to how widely investment should be defined, although this makes a big difference to one's theory of growth. When it comes to empirical work, some writers use national income (which excludes depreciation of capital) and others gross national product (which includes it); some net investment, and some gross. In short, one has to admit that economists' use of concepts has been sloppy, and that this has resulted in some serious errors. Faulty materials have been used to construct faulty models of economic growth.

No excuse is needed, then, for what follows. I have tried to define the concepts needed in a consistent and logical way, with later concepts defined in terms of earlier ones. Systems of national accounts often fail to do this, providing circular definitions, as is shown below. I have also tried to state the ideal concepts, even though one must content oneself with approximations to these in practice. Here, again, one must criticize systems of national accounts which often list the approximations without clarifying the ideals. Without the latter, one cannot judge, or even understand, the former. So far as possible, I have retained well established concepts and approximations. The book is an attempt to explain economic growth as it has been commonly measured and understood, and I have departed from existing concepts only when this has been both practicable and highly desirable.

To guard against misunderstanding, it must be emphasized that definitions are only definitions, and carry no implications for economic decisions or policy. Defining income in one way, for example, does not imply that consumption should never exceed it. Investment does not have to match depreciation, and maintenance can quite rationally be neglected in some circumstances. The definitions are chosen, not because they have straightforward implications of this kind, but because they form a logically coherent set of concepts with which it is useful and interesting to analyse economic growth. It is with reference to that purpose that they must be judged.

1.2 Consumption

No attempt is made in this book to provide a discussion of the meaning of consumption, or of how it should be measured. This is a very big gap, and I am well aware that the accusation of sloppiness which has just been hurled at my fellow-economists can, at this point, fairly be returned. One's views about economic growth might be markedly different if one were to adopt a definition that departed in some radical, but perfectly reasonable and defensible, ways from the usual one. Nevertheless, it is the latter definition that will be used here. That is to say, I shall assume that consumption is to be measured by private and public expenditures at constant prices as conventionally defined. My defence of sticking to the conventional definition is that it would be too big a task to revise it. That needs doing, but I cannot attempt it here.[1]

[1] The question of how consumption is best defined and measured has been long discussed. Fisher regarded consumption as consisting of psychic experiences, and the money cost of acquiring these as the best available measure of them. He wanted to deduct 'labour pain' to arrive at a measure of the net flow of enjoyment (Fisher 1906, 1930; see also ch.1 in Parker, Harcourt and Whittington 1986). Pigou started by restricting his inquiries 'to that part of social welfare that can be brought directly or indirectly into relation with the measuring-rod of money'. However, this was narrowed further when he took as a guide (following Marshall) the practice of the British tax commissioners, which excluded 'the services which a person renders to himself and those which he renders gratuitously to members of his family or friends; the benefits which he derives from using his own personal goods, or public property such as toll-free bridges'. Pigou, however, reserved 'full liberty, with proper warning, to use the term [i.e. the national dividend, or income] in a wider sense on all occasions when the discussion of any problem would be impeded or injured by a pedantic adherence to the standard use' (Pigou 1932, 11, 34). Kuznets, besides discussing similar questions to those discussed by Pigou asked whether governmental services should be valued by their costs (as is the current convention) or by the amounts paid through taxation for them, favouring the latter (Kuznets, with Epstein and Jenks 1941, 31-4). More recently, Nordhaus and Tobin (1972) made estimates of the level and rate of growth of 'measurable economic welfare' for the USA over the period 1929-64, in

Throughout this book, the unit of account is a representative bundle of consumption goods and services (public and private). All prices are, in principle, expressed in terms of that. Since we are all accustomed to thinking in terms of *money* prices, however, it avoids confusion if one assumes that the money price of the bundle is constant, and that assumption is accordingly made throughout. This still allows *relative* prices to vary: it is only the price index of consumption that is held constant. Readers will be reminded from time to time in what follows that in this sense the discussion refers to *real* consumption and related magnitudes.[2]

1.3 Income

(a) Hicks's definition of individual income

The purpose of income calculations in practical affairs is to give people an indication of the amount which they can consume without impoverishing themselves. Following out this idea, it would seem that we ought to define a man's income as the maximum value which he can consume during a week, and still expect to be as well off at the end of the week as he was at the beginning. Thus, when a person saves, he plans to be better off in the future; when he lives beyond his income, he plans to be worse off. Remembering that the practical purpose of income is to serve as a guide for prudent conduct, I think it is fairly clear that this is what the central meaning must be. (Hicks 1946, 172)

This, is in fact, the central meaning of income which has been used in this book, but it needs further qualification and explanation. What follows is basically a summary of the points made by Hicks. The phrase 'expect to be as well off at the end of the week as he was at the beginning' is 'systematically ambiguous' (to use Ryle's term).

What I *want* to mean by this phrase is that, if the man were to consume all his income in the week, and if his expectations were to remain unchanged during it, then he could expect to be able to maintain the same real rate of

---

which they adjusted conventional estimates for a variety of items such as changes in the environment, urbanization, 'regrettable necessities' (such as military expenditures), and changes in leisure time. Only the effect of the last of these was substantial, and whether and how it should be allowed for is controversial, different methods leading to substantially different growth rates, although not much affecting different countries' *rankings* by growth rates. See Beckerman (1980), who provides estimates for several OECD countries in the postwar period, as well as estimates allowing for changes in income distribution, whereby the consumption of a poor man is given more weight per unit of money cost than that of a rich man.

[2] The relevant price index is that of private and public consumption as conventionally measured in the national accounts. There is no discussion in this book of two important problems, on each of which much has been written. One of these is the question of how best to measure *real* consumption. (For a recent survey, see Sen 1979, and also see the controversy between Sen and Usher (Sen 1980 and Usher 1980a) and Usher's book (Usher 1980b)). The other is inflation accounting (see Whittington 1983, and also Scottt 1986).

consumption in all future weeks. Please note that this basic definition says nothing about the man's *wealth*. However, if real wealth is defined as the present discounted value of all future expected real consumption, then, in the circumstances just described, the man's wealth would be the same real amount at the beginnning as at the end of the week, so long as his real rate of discount was constant and unchanged. Hence, 'as well off' in these circumstances would also mean 'with unchanged real wealth'. If the man did not consume all of his income, then in these circumstances his real wealth would increase, and a change in real wealth would show that he had consumed less, or more, than his income. However, there are two other reasons why the man's real wealth might change, which should be ignored in calculating whether he has consumed all his income or not. The phrase 'as well off' must abstract from these reasons: viz., changes in rates of discount, and changes in expectations. These can be illustrated by means of an arithmetical example.

Suppose that the man expects that he will receive a constant real stream of payments of £1 per week stretching indefinitely into the future. Consequently, the present value of this stream of payments, discounted back to one week before the first payment at a constant real rate of discount, which I assume is 0.1 per cent per week, is

$$\pounds \frac{1}{(1+0.001)} + \frac{1}{(1+0.001)^2} + \frac{1}{(1+0.001)^3} + \frac{1}{(1+0.001)^4} + \ldots = \pounds 1000.$$

One week later, assuming that neither his expectations nor the discount rate have changed, and that he has consumed the first £1, he will be confronted by exactly the same prospect as before, which will accordingly have the same present value of £1,000. Clearly, the man's income is £1 per week.

Suppose, now, that the real rate of discount were 0.1 per cent for the first week, but that it was expected to become 0.2 per cent for every subsequent week. The present value of the stream of payments a week before the first payment would now be

$$\pounds \frac{1}{1.001} + \frac{1}{(1.001)\,(1.002)} + \frac{1}{(1.001)\,(1.002)^2} + \ldots = \pounds 500.50.$$

The present value one week later, however, would be exactly £500, if the man consumed £1 in the first week and if his expectations were unchanged and the (constant) rate of discount was 0.2 per cent per week. Hence, the man's wealth would have declined by £0.5 over the first week despite the fact that he consumed only £1 then, and that he could still expect to be able to consume the same £1 in real terms for ever more. The change in his wealth would have been entirely due to the (expected) change in discount rates, and *this* change must not be counted in reckoning his income, which clearly is £1 per week according to the basic definition, both in the first week and in succeeding weeks.[3]

Finally, suppose the real rate of discount is constant at 0.1 per cent per week, and that the man's expected real stream of receipts is £1 per week so that his wealth is £1,000 as before. Now let one week pass, in which the man consumes £1 as before; but then his expectations change. He now expects to receive £2 per week in real terms for ever more. His wealth is now £2,000 and his income is £2 per week. What was it in the previous week? The best answer surely is that, looking at the past week from the point of view of the present, the best estimate of his income is, to a close approximation, £2. This (or rather, something slightly less than this) is what he could have consumed in that week, and he still could have expected (*now*) to be able to consume the same amount, in real terms, in all future weeks. It is slightly less than £2 because he actually consumed only £1, and so he must have saved nearly £1, and this must have contributed towards his present expectation of exactly £2 per week for ever more. So, had he instead consumed a little less than £2, say £ $(2-x)$, and saved nothing, his expectation now would be of receipts at £ $(2-x)$ for ever more. It is quite clear that the increase in his wealth, from £1,000 to £2,000 arising from the change in expectations, must not be reckoned in as part of his income.

There are some who will find the above definition of income profoundly unsatisfactory, since it implies that one never knows one's income, whether past, present, or future. Income always depends upon expectations about an uncertain future, and one's estimates of it will perpetually change as expectations change, and this is true of one's estimate of past income as well as of present or future income. Surely, it will be urged, there must be a better definition than that! Hicks himself rejected the concept in *Value and Capital,* along with the other concepts which, I believe, form the essential basis for economic growth theory. In that part of the book dealing with 'The foundations of dynamic economics', he wrote:

Nothing has been said in the foregoing about any of a series of concepts which have usually been regarded in the past as fundamental for dynamic theory. Nothing has been said about Income, about Saving, about Depreciation, or about Investment (with a capital I). These are the terms in which one has been used to think; how do they fit here?

My decision to abstain from using these concepts in the last five chapters was, of course, quite deliberate. In spite of their familiarity, I do not believe that they are suitable tools for any analysis which aims at logical precision. There is far too much

---

[3] In case this is not clear, I remind readers that the man has consumed £1 in the first week, and, at the end of it, expects to be able to consume at the same real rate of £1 per week for the indefinite future. That is the basic definition of an income of £1 per week. The basic definition says nothing about the man's *wealth*.

equivocation in their meaning, equivocation which cannot be removed by the most painstaking effort. At bottom, they are not logical categories at all; they are rough approximations, used by the business man to steer himself through the bewildering changes of situation which confront him. For this purpose, strict logical categories are not what is needed; something rougher is actually better. But if we try to work with terms of this sort in the investigations we are here concerned with, we are putting upon them a weight of refinement they cannot bear. (Hicks 1946, 171)

Hicks rejected these concepts, partly because he found the concept of income 'complex' and 'unattractive', but also for other reasons. He regarded the comparison of prospects at two different dates (e.g. of wealth at the beginning of successive weeks) as nonsense—'The choice between them could never be actual at all' (p.177). Since he wished to base his economic analysis on objective choices, this was a material objection. Furthermore, since each person's income depends on his expectations, and since these may well be inconsistent with others' expectations, 'the aggregate of their incomes has little meaning. It has no more to its credit than its obedience to the laws of arithmetic' (p.178). Hicks did not deny that social income, investment, and depreciation were important. On the contrary, he wrote:

I hope that this chapter will have made it clear how it is possible for individual income calculations to have an important influence on individual economic conduct; for calculations of social income to play such an important part in social statistics, and in welfare economics; and yet, at the same time for the concept of income to be one which the positive theoretical economist only employs in his arguments at his peril. For him, income is a very dangerous term, and it can be avoided; as we shall see, a whole general theory of economic dynamics can be worked out without using it. (Hicks 1946, 180)

My defence of Hicks's concept of income against his own attack is, quite simply, that *some* concept of income is needed if we are to study economic growth, and that this is the best concept I know. It is undoubtedly complex and impossible to measure precisely. But these objections are no more serious than those that can be made to virtually every concept used in economics. What is 'a commodity'? What is 'a price'? Can 'production' be altogether distinguished from 'consumption'? If we let the philosophers loose on our concepts, they would have a field day. I do not believe that the difference in logic and precision between, say, general equilibrium theory and macroeconomic theory is a difference in kind. Both can be made to look like mathematics (at the sacrifice of realism), and both can be made to look like reality (at the sacrifice of precision).

(b) Some other definitions of individual income

Let me now defend the concept against some possible rivals. The strongest is probably Simons's (1938) concept of 'gain', which is also Lindahl's (1933) concept of 'income as earnings', and Hicks's 'income *ex post*'. It is consumption plus actual increase in wealth. According to Hicks, this concept has the great advantage of objectivity, so long as it is applied to income from property (material as opposed to human). One can then measure both consumption and wealth by reference to market values. In practice, there are important forms of non-human wealth which are infrequently sold, and about whose market value there is, then, a good deal of uncertainty (e.g. land, buildings and many companies regarded as going concerns); so even for this definition of income one cannot claim very much on grounds of objectivity. 'Gain' can fluctuate enormously from period to period as expectations and discount rates change. As both Lindahl and Simons point out, 'gain' has not the dimensions of a flow of value per unit of time. A change in expectations can lead to an instantaneous change in value, which implies an infinitely large flow per unit of time when the change takes place. It seems to me that this concept of 'gain' is far removed from the usual concept of income or output. No one has seriously suggested, to my knowledge, that the national income is much higher because the stock market is booming in a particular year, and lower (even negative!) in another one when 'billions are knocked off security values', yet that would be the implication of adopting 'gain'. It is clearly a concept that is quite unsuitable for a study of economic growth.

Another possibility is Fisher's concept of 'real income', by which he meant real consumption. While he is undoubtedly correct in describing this as 'the alpha and omega of economics' (Fisher 1930, in Parker and Harcourt 1969, 39), it is not what is generally meant by income, and to use it in that sense leads to confusion. It is better to call consumption 'consumption', and to reserve the term 'income' for the wider entity, consumption plus saving (see below).

Mention should also be made of Friedman's concept of 'permanent income'. In his discussion of the pure theory of consumer behaviour, Friedman remarks that 'income is generally defined as the amount a consumer unit could consume (or believes that it could), while maintaining its wealth intact', and he refers at this point to Hick's *Value and Capital* (Friedman 1957, 10). This definition coincides with the one adopted here, provided the price index of consumption remains constant and rates of discount are also constant, which Friedman at this point in his analysis assumes. In his subsequent statement of the 'permanent income hypothesis', however, Friedman abandons this concept of income in favour of one that is made to depend on consumer behaviour in regard to saving and consumption. He divides actual receipts and actual consumption each into two components, called transitory and permanent. He postulates a theoretical relationship between permanent income and permanent consumption, and remarks:

We are going to treat consumer units *as if* they regarded their income and their consumption as the sum of two such components, and *as if* the relation between the permanent components is the one suggested by our theoretical analysis. The precise line to be drawn between permanent and transitory components is best left to be determined by the data themselves to be whatever seems to correspond to consumer behaviour. (Friedman 1957, 23)

While this procedure may be appropriate for Friedman's purpose, it does not provide us with a concept of income which seems directly usable for growth theory. It is unsatisfactory to make the amount of income in a particular year depend on how much people choose to save out of it in that year—rather as if the size of a cake depends on how one chooses to slice it. Nevertheless, Friedman's permanent income and income as defined here are closely related magnitudes.

(c) National [4] or social income

It is the growth of the real income of a nation, or of some other large group of persons, that is the concern of studies of economic growth. Can the concept of individual income just described be applied to a nation? I think it can, although it is not the usual approach to defining national income, perhaps because it has been thought to be impractical. If fact, as we shall see, it makes the practical problem of estimating national income simpler in several ways than the conventional approach. Instead of having to estimate gross national product (GNP) at factor cost less capital consumption, which is the conventional definition of net national product (NNP) or national income, one can rest content with GNP. The difficult problem of estimating capital consumption is avoided. Many studies have done just that, but their authors have been open to the accusation that NNP is the more meaningful concept, and have had to defend GNP as an approximation they have been compelled to adopt through lack of estimates of capital consumption. While any practical measurement involves approximation, I hope in what follows to convince readers that not subtracting capital consumption improves, rather than worsens, the resulting figures. National income, in short, is best approximated by GNP, not NNP.

---

[4] I have used the term 'national income' in what follows, as that is the traditional usage. In the empirical work in subsequent chapters, however, it is *domestic* income or product that is used, as that refers to the geographical boundaries within which employment and investment explaining its growth occur. Domestic income equals national income *less net* property income from abroad. It thus includes property income earned within the country by non-resident companies, and excludes property income earned abroad by resident companies. The distinction between the two is not important in this chapter, for most of which a nation is treated as if it were a closed economy.

The usual approach to defining national income may be sketched as follows.[5] 'The national income is a measure of the money value of goods and services becoming available to the nation from economic activity' (Maurice 1968, 1). '. . . it can be measured not only as the sum of incomes but also by summing expenditures on these goods and services. National expenditure can be broadly divided between consumption and adding to wealth (or investment). . . . Adding to wealth is taken to mean the net increase in the stock of capital assets' (Maurice 1968, 3).

This approach may be expressed by the following identity:

$$Y \equiv C + S \qquad\qquad (1.1)$$

where Y is national income, C is consumption, and S is net savings or investment.

As already noted, I follow the same conventions in regard to C. I also arrive at an identity similar to (1.1) for national income. Any disagreement, therefore, affects the definition of S.

The conventional approach to equation (1.1) *starts* from there. No justification is provided for the equation itself in terms of concepts of income such as those discussed in the preceding pages. This is unsatisfactory, and may partly explain why an unsatisfactory definition of S has been widely adopted. It is not clear how one can define S satisfactorily except by reference to some previously defined concept of income. The conventional approach seeks to define S by reference to some idea of 'maintaining capital intact'; but, as is shown below, that is best done by reference to income, and, indeed, I believe that the conventional approach in the end does just that. The definition in (1.1) is then circular, since S is defined in terms of Y, while Y is defined in terms of S. All this will become clear in the sequel when we discuss the meanings of maintenance, investment, and depreciation.

Let us now revert to the Hicksian definition of individual income and consider how it can be applied to a nation which, for the present, is assumed to be a closed economy. National income is then the maximum value of the rate of total consumption which can be expected to be maintained for the indefinite future. If the whole national income were to be consumed for a long period, the economy's resources would then be devoted to producing consumption goods and services, leaving nothing for investment. I shall also assume that employment would be constant, as would the population, so that there would not be any form of human investment either. In fact, there would be a static economy. This could take an extreme form in which

[5] I have taken the official description of the UK national accounts (Maurice 1968) as representative, but it would have made no material difference had I used the United Nation's description (United Nations 1968), or many other descriptions.

nothing at all changed. I will call this a *completely static economy*, which is useful as a point of reference. One could also have an economy in which neither the rate of total consumption nor total employment changed, but in which *some* changes in the composition of consumption or employment might occur. This more realistic possibility is called a *static economy* without qualification. We begin with the simpler case of a completely static economy.

In such an economy the population has a constant age, sex, and skill composition, sons and daughters stepping into their fathers' and mothers' shoes. Likewise, the domestic animal population is constant, as also are forests and the area of cultivated land. Man-made assets are all physically maintained and, if they deteriorate through usage or time, are replaced by similar things. Some expenditures are, of course, necessary to maintain herds, forests, fields, buildings and works, vehicles, and machinery, but this is all to be regarded as a cost of producing output, and not as part of that output. The whole of output, net of such costs, can then be consumed, and that rate of consumption can be maintained indefinitely.

There is one important qualification which must now be made, and which will not be repeated. There will always be forces outside the economic system that impinge upon it, for good or ill. I am thinking here not only of such natural forces as changes in the weather, earthquakes, diseases, and the like, but also of social forces, of which wars are the most obvious. A theory of economic growth cannot encompass everything that affects the level of income. In what follows, therefore, it must be understood that we abstract from all such factors, labelled 'exogenous', and include the effects of only those factors that it is usual to include: demographic ones and investment in human and material capital. Technical progress, as normally understood, is included, and is discussed later.

If we could observe a completely static economy, and measure its consumption, we would *ipso facto* measure its income, which would thus be C. However, we need to be able to do more than that. We need a definition of national income which can be applied to a growing eonomy at any time t. The only way I can see of using the same, Hicksian, definition of income is to define it as the rate of consumption which that economy could have achieved at t, and for the indefinite future, if it had been given a long period of notice before t that, after t, it was to become static. We must imagine that, up to time t, the same cumulative amount of investment is to take place as has actually occurred. However, its *form* will differ, since all production after t is to be devoted to consumption. Consequently, capital goods industries will be run down and converted to consumption goods production. Since this conversion process takes time, one needs a long period of notice to bring it about. Similarly, the same employment level is to be achieved at t as is actually achieved, but its allocation between industries, and its skills, will be different, and this also requires time to bring about.

If we follow this path, we then need some way of estimating what the rate of consumption would be at t if, given long notice, the economy were to become static at t. If that rate of consumption is Y, and if the actual rate of consumption in the growing economy at t is C, then we could define the difference between the two, $Y - C$, as S, savings or investment. However, to understand what S then is requires further discussion of maintenance and investment.

Before turning to that, let me try to reassure those who feel that the definition of national income just given must be quite impractical, and ask them to persevere a little further before they dismiss it for that reason. It should, at least, be evident that it does provide a natural starting point for the analysis of economic growth. Income is the consumption that could be enjoyed, for the foreseeable future, if growth came to an end. Growth occurs when that potential consumption level is increased.

1.4 Required maintenance

In the static economy just envisaged, some expenditure must be undertaken to maintain assets in a constant physical condition. Some of these expenditures are fairly minor—oiling and greasing, painting and cleaning, for example. Others are substantial—reroofing a house, replacing a blast furnace. Most are irregular so far as individual assests are concerned, but that does not matter. In a completely static economy there would be a balanced age structure of assets as well as human beings; and so, in total, maintenance expenditures would be at a constant rate, and could maintain *groups* of asset (e.g. a forest or a herd or a fleet of taxis) physically unchanged even though *individual* assets could age and decay. Each group of assets could then contribute an unchanged amount to the total output of consumption goods and services, and that total would be constant. The total maintenance expenditure then being undertaken may be called *required maintenance*, since it is the amount required to keep output constant.

Let us now move from a completely static economy to a static economy in which *some* changes occur to groups of assets, although total consumption and employment are still constant. This allows for the realistic possibility that, for example, there is some mining, extraction of oil, and other exploitation of non-renewable resources.[6] Some assets are then not being maintained, so that other assets must be improved if total output is to be kept constant. Required maintenance will be undertaken if the loss of output resulting from the failure to maintain some assets is made good by the increase of output resulting from improving other assets.

[6] One might still approximate a completely static economy if the proven reserves of each type of mineral, say, were a small fraction of all reserves, and if one could reasonably expect new discoveries to prove enough reserves to replace those used up for the foreseeable future.

This is a perfectly general statement which enables us to define required maintenance for a growing economy. In such an economy, assets will generally be maintained for part of their useful lives, and probably for much the greater part. However, maintenance may be neglected as the asset nears the end of its useful life, and this will result in a fall in its output. Meanwhile, other assets will be improved, leading to an increase in their output. On balance, output must rise in a growing economy. However, we can divide the cost of improving those assets that are improved into two parts. One part results in an increase in output just sufficient to counterbalance the fall in output owing to the neglect of maintenance on assets that are deteriorating. That part must be regarded as part of required maintenance expenditure. The rest of the cost of improving assets is investment.

There is more to be said about maintenance, but we must first clarify the meaning of investment, to which we now turn.

1.5 Investment

Expenditures undertaken to improve assets (whether human or not), over and above required maintenance, constitute *investment*. Such improvements result, essentially, from rearrangements of things or of systems of work. Even learning can be regarded as rearrangement of the brain and nervous system. A great deal of investment, as Ian Little has remarked, consists in moving earth and stones from one place to another. The construction of buildings, fields, dams, roads, bridges, harbours, railways, airports, and such like accounts for most non-human investment and is largely covered by the description. But even machinery and vehicles are only rearrangements of metal and other materials. All this may sound trite and obvious, but this concept of investment is, in fact, very different from the conventional one of adding to stocks (or 'the stock') of capital goods.

For example, moving workers from the countryside to the town, where they can earn and produce more, is investment. It is a rearrangement of workers which costs something. It is only by straining the concept of a 'capital good' that one can regard this as an increase in the stock of some capital good; yet this has been an important source of economic growth. Similarly, improvement of the fertility of the soil through clearing, draining, ploughing, weeding, and adding fertilizer is investment. This too can be regarded as an increase in the stock of capital goods only by straining the concept; yet this too has been an important source of economic growth. Part of the cost of making rearrangements consists in obtaining new information about markets, processes, and sources of supply, and in drawing up plans. Part of it consists in informing buyers and sellers of new products that are available, or of new requirements. Persuading other people, whether customers, suppliers, managers, or workers, to change their arrangements can be a slow and costly process. All these costs form part of investment, but it is difficult to describe them as additions to stocks of capital goods.

By defining investment in this way as the *cost of change,* it is at once clear that all growth must result from investment, together with demographic change, which it seems most convenient to keep as a separate factor.[7] Without investment, and without demographic change, there is no change in total output in a static economy and no change at all in a completely static one, and so there can be no growth. There is no room then left for some third, quite separate, factor called 'technical progress', since it is already included in the effects of investment. This profoundly alters one's view of the causes of economic growth, as later chapters show.

The definition proposed here is a return to the old idea of investment as a sacrifice of consumption for future gain. It explicitly answers the question, Sacrifice as compared with what? Investment expenditures are all those undertaken to change, and hopefully to improve, economic arrangements *in excess* of required maintenance. Hence the sacrifice is in relation to the consumption that could be achieved in a static economy, given a long period of notice as already described. Investment expenditures are all those that would be unnecessary in a static economy.

There are many kinds of investment which need to be distinguished for different purposes. In this book I shall distinguish between only two kinds: investment in human capital, and the rest. For convenience, let us refer to the former as *human investment* and to the latter as *material investment.* Human investment includes education, training, and health expenditures in excess of required maintenance, as well as the cost of moving workers from job to job, including the loss of output arising from frictional unemployment and the cost of labour exchanges, job advertising, and selection (all in excess of maintenance). Material investment includes conventional expenditure on fixed capital and increases in stocks and work in progress, together with some items that are not conventionally included and are not well described as 'material': research and development, market research, advertising, and planning. All payments to Schumpeter's entrepreneurs should be included, since that is part of the cost of change, and entrepreneurs would be irrelevant in a static society (Schumpeter's 'circular flow': see Section 4.2 below). Once again, it is only the excess of these expenditures over required maintenance that must be included. In this book, the number of workers is treated as an exogenous factor, and, while

---

[7] An increase in the number of persons could be regarded as a form of human investment, other forms including education, training, movements of workers, etc. For a treatment along these lines see Kendrick, with Lethem and Rowley (1976).

an attempt is made to adjust the measure of labour input for quality improvements arising from other forms of human investment, the *cost* of such investment is neither estimated nor analysed. The main focus of the book is on material investment.

This does not mean that human investment is thought to be less important than material investment; nor, for that matter, that maintenance expenditure is less important. Both human investment and maintenance expenditure are very important, and many countries have suffered from a neglect of both, or from mistaken choices with regard to both. In Chapter 16 I have something to say about abnormal maintenance requirements in recent years in developed countries, and there are countless stories of wasteful neglect of maintenance in less developed countries, as well as an obvious need for human investment.

Suppose we can identify actual investment expenditures and add up their value, which is £S per annum. Let us also identify and add up actual consumption expenditures, which are at £C per annum. Then one estimate of income is the sum of C and S, as in equation (1.1). This estimate assumes that, on average, each pound's worth of resources used for investment could produce one pound's worth of consumption, given a long period of notice. While this assumption could be improved upon (e.g. by taking into account different rates of indirect taxes on investment and consumption), it is probably a reasonable first approximation.

Since, as already explained, I adopt conventional definitions of private and public consumption, S consists only of material investment. Conventional definitions include expenditures on education, health, personal travel, and housing in consumption, as well as other costs of child-rearing.[8] Most of human investment is thereby included, leaving only material investment to be included in S.

Estimating national income in the way just described implies drawing a borderline between maintenance expenditures and investment expenditures. In general, the former *restore* economic arrangements while the latter *improve* them, and that is the main criterion suggested here. It is also found in some descriptions of systems of national accounts.[9]

Expenditures such as oiling, greasing, repainting, pointing, and repairing all fit easily into normal concepts of maintenance. But the category is very wide indeed. It includes, for example, inflows into stocks of materials, work in progress, and finished goods, which make good the outflows from there.

---

[8] Strictly speaking, too much is included under these headings. If one regards educational expenditure, for example, as human investment, then a large fraction of it is required merely to maintain existing levels of education. This would then be part of required maintenance, which should be deducted before arriving at national income (Scott 1980).

[9] See, for example, Maurice (1968, 361–2). See also United Nations (1968, paras. 6.61 and 6.115).

It includes the cost of ploughing, sowing, weeding, and harvesting, periodic costs that must be incurred if food output is to be maintained. These examples are enough to show that the *total* of maintenance expenditures is not a particularly meaningful or interesting quantity, any more than is, for example, total turnover. Hence income or output gross of maintenance expenditures is not meaningful or even interesting. It certainly is *not* comparable to conventional GNP.

It is important to note how the *ageing* of assests is dealt with in the system proposed here. If an asset remains physically unchanged, then required maintenance is being met even though the asset is becoming older. An individual cow, for example, would *not* be maintained according to this criterion, even if its milk supply were unchanged. The cow *is* physically changing as it grows older, and it will eventually stop producing milk. Maintenance then requires that it be replaced by a younger cow. A herd of cows of constant age composition can be maintained, but not an individual cow. On the other hand, an individual building or a machine can be maintenanced, for all practical purposes indefinitely. It may become less valuable, because of obsolescence, but that (on my defintion) has nothing to do with maintenance, only with depreciation, which is discussed later.

Other critieria for distinguishing between maintenance and investment have been suggested, but are unsatisfactory. The United Nations, for example, identifies gross fixed investment with the purchase of new durable producer goods, and defines durable goods as those having an expected lifetime of use of more than one year.[10] However, the choice of one year is essentially arbitrary. It is not the only period of account, since quarterly national income estimates are common, and yet *they* do not redefine ploughing or sowing as 'durable' because their use extends beyond one quarter. Furthermore, painting and decorating and repairing buildings can last for several years, yet these expenditures (which are very large) are not classified as part of gross investment. The arbitrariness in this method of distinguishing between maintenance and gross investment has been pointed out by, among others, Samuelson and Hayek.[11]

Another criterion that might be used is single-use versus multiple-use. The purchase of new multiple-use producer goods is then gross fixed

[10] See United Nations (1968, paras. 6.115 and 6.116). However, the UN *also* uses the criterion of improvements (see paras. 6.61 and 6.115).

[11] 'The accountant arbitrarily uses one year or some other criterion to determine which way any item is treated. The result of a change in such an arbitrary decision is an arbitrary change in the level of GNP as we double-count more or less in the total. However, and this is one of the most important arguments for NNP, the net magnitude remains invariant under changes in accounting conventions' (Samuelson in Lutz and Hague 1961, 34, fn. 1).

Hayek remarks that 'the concepts of gross saving and gross investment ought to disappear from economic analysis with the sharp division between fixed and circulating capital' (Hayek 1941a, 337, fn. 2).

investment. This criterion is suggested by Stuvel, who immediately qualifies it by excluding 'all non-tangible assets, such as good will, and all those multiple-use assets the expenditure on which is either small or recurrent in character, e.g. hand tools, motor tyres, office desk equipment and normal repair and maintenance' (Stuvel 1986, 19). This qualification is justified only on grounds of expediency. Readers are thus left with no *principle* on which to distinguish between gross investment and maintenance, since the latter clearly includes very large expenditures on multiple-use producer goods (e.g. most maintenance and repair of buildings and works). In reality, the criterion of improvement versus restoration is surely the one that is being used together with a practical criterion of lumpiness versus smallness and smoothness of the flow of expenditure. We return to that practical criterion later.

The distinction between restoration and improvement is sufficient to classify nearly all expenditures as either maintenance or investment. However, it is not quite sufficient for all. In a changing economy, some maintenance will inevitably be neglected, and the output lost thereby has to be compensated by improvements elsewhere if output is to be maintained. Some part of required maintenance will then consist of the cost of improvements. Since the whole of required maintenance, no more and no less, must be deducted as a current cost of producing output, if we are to estimate national income correctly, the cost of improvements to be included in required maintenance needs to be estimated. Alternatively, one cannot include the cost of all improvements made in investment, S, and so there is a problem of estimating the cost of those that are to be treated as maintenance. In ordinary circumstances, I would expect that their cost would be small, for reasons that are best discussed after the meaning of depreciation has been considered (see pp. 31–33 below).

Although the cost of improvements to be included in required maintenance is probably small, this judgement (and the definition of required maintenance on which it depends) requires a prior definition of national income. Without that prior definition, the usual procedure, as already noted, is to define consumption and gross investment each on its own. But to define gross investment requires defining the borderline between it and maintenance, and we have seen that attempts to do so by reference to durability of goods, or single-use versus multiple-use goods, fail. The only satisfactory borderline that I know of is the one sketched out above, and that requires a prior definition of income. In its absence, I believe that the usual procedures are trapped into a circular series of definitions. One cannot satisfactorily define income as the sum of consumption and investment, investment as expenditures that are net of maintenance, and maintenance as expenditures necessary to keep income constant.

Investment has been defined in this section as the cost, in terms of consumption forgone, of improving economic arrangements. Income is the sum of consumption and investment so defined. An important corollary of this definition is that both income and investment at constant prices are to be measured in terms of purchasing power over consumption. In practice, therefore, only one price index is required to deflate C, S, and Y, namely, the index required for C. This solves a number of problems that have beset national income statisticians for many years, besides being much simpler and easier than the conventional method of attempting (with poor success) to devise suitable index numbers for expenditure on capital goods.

Since, in an open economy, investment abroad is one form of national investment, it should be deflated by a price index of consumption, and this deals with the vexed problem of correcting real national income for changes in the terms of trade. (For further discussion, see Scott 1979.) The idea of deflating savings or investment by a price index of consumption has been mentioned or proposed by several writers,[12] but does not yet seem to have been accepted by the 'national income establishment', despite the fact that it would make life easier for them.

1.6 Depreciation and appreciation

Conventionally, no clear distinction is drawn between depreciation and maintenance. There is a simple explanation for this, which is discussed later. The term used in systems of national accounts is *capital consumption*, which is the deduction to be made from gross product or gross fixed investment to cover the 'using up' of capital arising from *both* foreseen obsolescence *and* normal wear and tear (see Maurice 1968, 16, and United Nations 1968, para. 7.19). The former is due essentially to relative price changes and the latter to physical changes. There really are two concepts which have been run together, and the failure to distinguish them has led to confusion and error. They must therefore be separated, but as a result readers may find that the definition of depreciation put forward here is a departure from existing concepts. Its use certainly makes a big difference to the way one analyses the process of economic growth and its effects on the distribution of income between wages and profits. Nevertheless, as is shown below, there is a close relation between my definition and 'ideal' or 'economic' depreciation as defined by other writers, and accounting definitions can be regarded as approximations to these.

The distinction between depreciation and maintenance rests on that

---

[12] Denision (fn. 13, p. 227) and Kuznets (p. 276) in Conference on Research in Income and Wealth (1957); Hicks (1965, 303); Little (1950, 228); Usher (1976, 324–9 and 1980a, ch. 5, the latter of which provides the most thorough and extensive discussion of the alternatives.

between changes in prices and quantities. As defined here, depreciation is due entirely to changes in relative prices, and so corresponds to what is often called obsolescence, whereas the need for maintenance arises because of physical changes. The fact that, in a closed economy, national capital will be maintained if all *physical* changes of economic significance are restored or offset was pointed out long ago by Pigou, but may have been lost to sight because his view seemed to have been successfully challenged by Hayek. While Hayek's criticism contained a valid point, it is unfortunate that the essential truth underlying Pigou's definition has not been recognized.[13]

In order to get to grips with depreciation, we must consider individuals or groups of individuals as opposed to a whole closed economy, since, for the latter, there is no depreciation on my definition. I will first give an intuitive explanation for this, which may satisfy some readers and enable them to skip the more lengthy one which, I hope, will convince others.

The intuitive explanation is as follows. Depreciation is defined as loss of wealth arising from, and only from, relative price changes. Changes in physical quantities do not directly enter into its calculation. For example, real wages rise and so an employer suffers thereby a loss of profits and wealth, ignoring any consequential changes in employment. But within a closed economy any relative price change that harms one group must benefit others by exactly the same amount. In the example, the workers gain what the employer loses. So, within a closed economy, appreciation must be equal and opposite to depreciation, and the total of both for all individuals in the economy has to be zero. Those readers in a hurry may now turn to p. 30.

As this is an important point which is not generally recognized, some readers may wish to consider it at greater length. Let us then consider, as an example, a firm that is owned by a group of persons, and employs another group. I shall refer to the owners as 'the firm' and to the employees as 'workers'. Some simplifying assumptions are made in order to bring out the main points clearly, but the argument is more generally valid.

The firm is first set up at time T_0, when it starts selling a representative bundle of consumption goods and services whose quantity and value[14] remain unchanged until T_1, which is some years later, when the firm ceases to operate. The firm is therefore fully maintained (i.e. there are no physical changes) from T_0 to T_1. The number of workers employed by the firm is

[13] Pigou made several attempts to define the meaning of maintaining capital intact. His last was Pigou (1941), which was criticized by Hayek (1941b), both drawing a comment from Hicks (1942). All three are conveniently reprinted in Parker and Harcourt (1969). See also Scott (1984) for a review of the controversy in the light of similar views to those put forward here.

[14] Here, as elsewhere, it is assumed that the money price of a representative bundle of consumption goods and services is constant.

also constant from T_0 to T_1, and then becomes zero. The firm operates in a progressive economy in which real wage rates are rising. I do not need to explain *why* they are rising, as I am not at this point trying to explain how the economy behaves. That is the subject of later chapters. Here I am concerned only with definitions. However, in case some reader is worried, let me say that real wage rates could be rising because there is investment elsewhere in the economy and employers are competing for a limited total supply of labour. The firm buys no material, fuel, or other current inputs. *Value added* by a firm in general equals gross output (i.e. sales, assuming no change in stocks) less material, etc., inputs (i.e. purchases, assuming no change in stocks). In this example, the firm buys no materials, and value added is constant as long as the firm is operating, and equals gross output. It is distributed partly to workers as wages and partly to the firm as gross profits. The owners own all the capital of the firm, and so there are no interest payments, and I also assume there are no taxes. After their initial investment in setting up the firm, its owners make no further investment in it. They take out all their gross profits from it, which they either spend on consumption or else invest elsewhere. At T_1, when operations cease, the firm's assets are worth precisely nothing.

The course of the firm's value added, gross profits, and wages is shown in Figure 1.1. Value added is constant throughout the firm's life at $P_0T_0 = W_1T_1$. Initially, wages are W_0T_0, and so gross profits are P_0W_0. However,

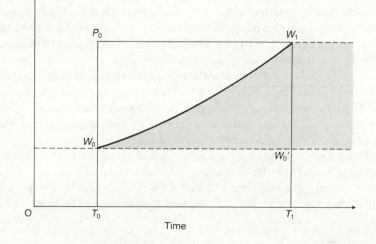

Fig. 1.1 ·Depreciation and transfer of income

as time passes and wage rates rise, wages absorb more and more of value added, until at T_1 they absorb it all. Gross profits are accordingly squeezed to zero at T_1, at which point the firm shuts down.

How should one measure the firm's income? Or the workers' income? Or the whole economy's income as affected by this component of it?

Let us take the firm first, as that is likely to be the most familiar case. After its owners made their initial investment, they could expect to increase their income as a result,[15] but not by the whole initial gross profit, P_0W_0. Let us assume that they correctly foresaw what was going to happen. Their income from this investment is then the maximum extra amount they can consume, because of the investment, and expect to continue to consume indefinitely. If they wanted to add this amount to their consumption, no more and no less, then they would have to invest some part of their initial gross profit, say an amount £D per year, and consume only the rest. In succeeding years, assuming they judged the amounts correctly, they would keep to the same rate of extra consumption, but this would be financed to a greater and greater extent from the income of their accumulated depreciation fund. Eventually, at T_1, it would *all* be financed in that way, and would continue so indefinitely.

If we can assume that the real rate of return earned on the depreciation fund is constant, say at an exponential rate of r per annum, then it is comparatively simple to work out the firm's income and hence to work out D at each moment in time. One simply needs to calculate the present discounted value of the firm's expected gross profits, which we may call A_0 at T_0, and the firm's income is rA_0 at T_0. Depreciation at T_0 is then gross profits less rA_0. In later years a similar calculation can be performed, so that, for example, at time T somewhere between T_0 and T_1, A_T is the present value of the remaining gross profits, rA_T is the income derived from them, and depreciation is actual gross profits less rA_T. This, of course, means that the income derived from the firm is declining, and eventually will vanish at T_1. However, the firm's owners will preserve their initial income if they invest the amounts of depreciation as calculated above, and in that case they will end up at T_1 with an income of precisely rA_0. Furthermore, in the interim from T_0 to T_1 they will have increased their consumption (as compared with the situation before the initial investment) by the same constant amount, rA_0, as a result of their initial investment.

A formal proof of the above is given in the appendix to this chapter, but an informal one may be given here. Anyone investing A_0 in a fund that yields r per annum can take out and consume a constant stream rA_0 per annum while leaving a constant amount A_0 invested in the fund. If nothing

---

[15] I ignore, in this example, the effect that undertaking this investment has on other investments undertaken by the firm. This could be an important omission, and is discussed further in Chapter 7.

were taken out, the fund would grow at the rate r. Consuming rA_0 stops this growth, no more and no less. If there were a perfect capital market confronting the owners of the firm in which the rate of interest was constant and equal to r, they could sell their prospective gross profits at T_0 for A_0. This is implied by the present value calculation. They could then exchange the firm for an income of rA_0, and that is, in effect, what they are enabled to do by investing depreciation allowances in a fund earning r.

The above example illustrates three different definitions of depreciation which have been used.[16] In the example, all three coincide. For a particular asset, the rate of depreciation at a given time may be:

1. the excess of net current receipts over income from the asset (or, equivalently, the excess of gross over net profits);
2. the amount that must be put aside for investment in a depreciation fund so as to accumulate the original value of the asset at the end of its economic life when its own value is zero; or
3. the rate of decline in the present value of the asset.

That these three definitions coincide in the example may be shown as follows. (1) Net current receipts equals gross profits for the firm's owners, and, as has been shown, income plus depreciation equals gross profits. (2) The firm has a present value of A_0 initially, if one uses r as one's discount rate, and that is also the value of the depreciation fund at T_1 when the firm itself is worthless. (3) If the owners of the firm consumed all their income, and if their only income were from the firm and the accumulated depreciation fund, then, since their income would be constant and equal to rA_0, their total assets would always have a present value of A_0. Hence the decline in the present value of the firm must be exactly offset by a rise in that of the depreciation fund. Since the latter equals payments into the fund, (3) is proved.

It is not difficult, all the same, to construct examples in which the three definitions no longer coincide; and in fact they will not if r varies through time or if expectations change—just those circumstances, in fact, that lead the Hicksian concept of income to diverge from Simons's concept (see p. 9).[17] I do not pursue the point further here, but merely remark that I regard (1) as the fundamental definition of depreciation since it is expressed directly in terms of income.

Conventional methods of accounting do not use any of the above definitions as such. Instead, the original *cost* of an asset is generally written off during its estimated economic life by a variety of formulae, such as

[16] For discussion of the first see Scott (1986a). For the second, see Hotelling (1925) and Wright (1964). For the third see Robinson (1959) in Robinson (1960, 209-21).

[17] Changes in the money price of consumption (e.g. inflation) can also cause differences, depending on how values are measured in (2) and (3).

straight line, declining balance, etc. However, if the original cost approximately equals the original present value, and if there is no inflation, then the accountant's method could approximate to (3), and so also to (1) and (2) as long as discount rates are approximately constant and expectations approximately fulfilled. While the approximations may be poor for particular assets in particular periods, they should be better for large groups of assets over long periods, when fluctuations in discount rates average out, as do bouts of over-optimism and over-pessimism. Corrections for inflation, however, would be essential.

So far, I do not claim to have stated anything novel in this example. Indeed, my hope is that readers will feel reassured that I am merely restating familiar points about economic depreciation. However, as we now turn to consider the income of workers, and then that of the whole economy, novel points will emerge.

Some further simplifying assumptions are now made for the workers. In calculating their income and wealth, they are treated as if they were immortal. This is the counterpart of our assumption for the firm, that it is fully maintained. For greater realism, one can imagine the workers consisting of a group of persons of constant age, sex and skill composition. Changes in these would complicate the argument without affecting its validity. The wages paid to workers at T_0 by the firm are the same as those they were receiving in their immediately preceding employment. Likewise, the wages paid to them at T_1 by the firm are the same as those they receive in their immediately following employment elsewhere in the economy. We need accounts for workers and firms which can be added together to give a consistent set of accounts for the whole economy (assumed to be closed). Consistency implies that like firms and workers are treated alike, both at a given moment in time and at succeeding moments in time. It is assumed that these workers pass from firm to firm, each of which is similar (although not identical) to the firm we are considering.

Let us now consider national income at T_0 just before the firm starts up, confining attention to those parts of it that feature in our story. If the economy were to become completely static just before T_0, and just before the firm's investment is undertaken (assumed to take a negligibly short period of time), the only contribution to income[18] that concerns us is that of the workers, W_0T_0. That, in fact, will absorb the whole value added of the firm or firms in which they are working, if their position is similar to that of 'our' firm at the end of *its* life (at T_1). So what we may regard as 'relevant' national income is W_0T_0.

Next, let our firm undertake its investment and start production. Relevant output in the rest of the economy falls by W_0T_0 as our firm's

---

[18] 'Contribution to income' is used here as equivalent to marginal product, and it is assumed that the sum of relevant contributions equals relevant national income and output. Perfect markets are assumed at this point, but that assumption is relaxed in Chapter 9.

workers leave their jobs there and join the firm. Our firm's output is $P_0 T_0$. Consequently, relevant output in the economy rises by $P_0 W_0$, the initial gross profits of the firm. The economy could now become completely static with output higher by that amount. Hence relevant national income has increased by $P_0 W_0$, the initial gross profits of the firm.

From T_0 to T_1 relevant national income does not change. Of course, actual national income will change, but those changes are not our concern, as they will be accounted for elsewhere, and we are confining attention to this firm.

Immediately after T_1 it is also the case that relevant national income does not change. True, our firm's output drops by $W_1 T_1$, but the firm's workers go elsewhere and are paid just as much, and that is not counted as part of the *additional* output produced by the firms they join. Their wages when they joined our firm, $W_0 T_0$, were not counted as part of the additional output resulting from our firm's investment at T_0. Consistency requires that $W_1 T_1$ should not count either as additional output resulting from other firm's investment. All that counts are those firms' initial gross profits.

Consistent accounting thus requires that national income rises by our firm's initial *gross* profits, $P_0 W_0$, when it undertakes its investment, and that this increment in national income *remains for the indefinite future*. This conclusion may surprise some readers, who may be inclined to regard it as the peculiar result of some peculiar assumptions. I will discuss the relaxation of the assumptions presently, but first I must follow through the argument a bit further. Those who are surprised that the initial gross profits are a perpetual gain to national income should reflect on its definition. If income is increased by £X, then that increment is indeed a perpetuity, and it will be eliminated only by subsequent disinvestment, or if some exogenous factor should produce an unexpected loss.

Workers' wealth at T_0 can be regarded as consisting of three parts, ignoring any material wealth they may own, and considering only their wages. There is, first the present value of their wages at T_0, assuming those wages to remain unchanged for the indefinite future. This would be their wealth were the economy to become completely static at T_0. Second, and in addition, there is the present value of the extra wages they are paid during the lifetime of our firm, from T_0 to T_1, together with the perpetuity $W_1 W_0'$. This is the present value, at T_0, of the shaded area (which extends indefinitely to the right) in Figure 1.1. Third, there is the present value, at T_0, of all the still further additional wages they can expect to receive in a progressive economy after T_1. The first and third of these parts must be accounted for elsewhere, when the accounts of the other firms, and of the workers working for them, are drawn up. Our concern here is only with the second part.

Let us assume that the discount rate used to calculate present value is the same for workers as for our firm, r. Let the present value of the second part of workers' wealth, just described, be A_{W0} at T_0. Then as for the firm, workers' income at T_0 is rA_{W0}. Ignoring any saving or dissaving by workers, and still confining attention to the flow of wages represented by the shaded area in Figure 1.1, it is clear that the present value of this flow will increase as time passes, and will reach a maximum at T_1, when it becomes the present value of the perpetuity W_1W_0'. So worker's income 'from the firm' rises from rA_{W0} at T_0 to W_1W_0' at T_1.

If we now consider the relevant *combined* income of the firm and its workers, we can see that it is constant, and equal to the initial gross profits of the firm P_0W_0. Likewise, their relevant combined wealth is constant, and equal to that of the perpetuity equal to these gross profits. The wealth of the firm is the present value of the area $P_0W_1W_0$ in Figure 1.1, whereas the relevant wealth of the workers is the present value of the shaded area, and together these make up the rectangular area whose height is P_0W_0 and which stretches indefinitely into the future. As time passes from T_0, the income of the firm declines, but that is matched and exactly offset by the increase in income of the workers. The decline in the firm's income gives rise to *depreciation* in the firms's accounts, but the increase in worker's income must (since total wealth is unchanged) give rise to an *appreciation* in their accounts which exactly offsets it. The sum of depreciation and appreciation must then be zero. This is consistent with our previous finding that, immediately after the initial investment takes place at T_0, relevant national income rises by initial gross profits indefinitely. Throughout our story, from T_0 onwards, the sum of the firm's income and the worker's relevant income is constant, and equal to P_0W_0, the relevant national income. However, more and more of that income, and eventually all of it, accrues to workers.

The essential feature of the above example is that there is only *one* physical change in the story, namely, that due to the initial investment which results in the initial rise in output of P_0W_0. Thereafter, changes in relevant individual incomes are due solely to relative price changes, which in this example take the form only of increases in wage rates. It is only because of these that the firm's income declines and that of the workers rises. It is self-evident that, if quantities do not change, as they do not in this example from T_0 to T_1, relevant national income does not change, but only its distribution between profits and wages. Hence, in so far as depreciation and appreciation result *purely* from such relative price changes, one equals and offsets the other.

Some readers may object that, when the firm ceases to produce at T_1, that is another physical change which must be taken into account. However, in the example given, that physical change has no *economic* significance. At T_1, the firm is producing nothing *additional* to what the workers will continue to produce when the firm has closed down. The closure of the firm is a physical change, but it has no more economic relevance than any other physical change that has no effect on national income. National accountants can ignore it, just as they ignore the effects of wind and weather on ruined castles and deserted villages.

Some readers may also object to the way in which attention is confined in the preceding argument to income arising from the firm directly, that is, to the rectangle formed by extending $W_1P_0W_0W_0'$ to the right indefinitely. If we consider the *firm's* present value and income at T_0, it is correct to confine attention to the area $W_1P_0W_0$, but is it correct for *workers* to confine attention to the rest of the rectangle (i.e. the shaded area)? At T_0, in a progressive economy, workers (whom we are treating as if they were immortal) will expect to receive further increases in wage rates after T_1. Their wealth at T_0 should include the present value of these further increases. Consequently, their incomes will be greater than is assumed in the preceding argument, and it will no longer be the case that the sum of their incomes and the firm's income will equal P_0W_0. Instead, it will be greater.

While this is an understandable objection,[19] it can be refuted as follows. There are two ways in which one might construct one's accounts for the economy at T_0. In the first, one could confine attention to the current situation, and assume that the economy is transformed into a completely static one there and then. In that case, P_0W_0 is the additional income resulting from the firm's investment, and it all accrues as gross profits, with no attention being paid to increases in wage rates above W_0. There is then, however, neither depreciation nor appreciation, since in a completely static economy no prices change, and the existing distribution of income remains unchanged. The sum of wages and profits (gross) equals national income.

The second way accords better with normal practice so far as profits are concerned. One attempts to predict the actual course of events after T_0. The firm's income is then its gross profits minus depreciation calculated in the way already described, that is, first working out the present value of the area $W_1P_0W_0$, and then multiplying that by r. In working out this present value, however, it should be noted that the calculation assumes either that the firm's owners consume all the gross profits as they accrue, or else that any profits reinvested earn r until they are consumed. If £1 is shifted from consumption at time T to consumption at time $T + \tau$, then it will grow to £ $e^{r\tau}$ if investment earns an exponential rate of return of r. The value of consumption discounted to any date you please will then be unaffected by transferring consumption through time, so long as the discount rate is also r. Thus the value of £ $e^{r\tau}$, consumed at $T + \tau$, discounted back to T, is £ $(e^{r\tau}e^{-r\tau})$, i.e. £1.

---

[19] In fact, I mistakenly took the same view as the imaginary objector in Scott (1976, 348, fn. 1 and 352), which led to mistaken conclusions about externalities to investment. In this book I argue that there are, indeed, large externalities, but for different reasons (see Ch. 15).

Now the higher wages accruing beyond T_1, if they are then to be paid out of higher output, can accrue (according to the views expounded in later chapters) only as the result of further investment. (Remember that I am abstracting from exogenous factors such as changes in the weather, earthquakes, etc.) Investment made up to T_0 is sufficient to pay wages up to the level W_1, but not beyond. If, then, we take account of the actual course of events beyond T_0, we must include in that course of events the cuts in consumption made before T_1 to pay for the investment necessary to achieve higher output after T_1. So long as that investment earns r, which is also the rate of discount, the effect on present value at T_0 of allowing for both the initial cut in consumption and the subsequent higher wages (and profits) is precisely nil, just as in the previous paragraph.

The *social* rate of return here is, in fact, the ratio of initial gross profit, $P_0 W_0$, to the cost of the investment by the firm. Since $P_0 W_0$ is the extra, perpetual, income accruing as a result of the investment, this seems a reasonable measure of the social rate of return. However, it will undoubtedly surprise some readers that it can also be the private rate of return. That is not obvious when profits dwindle away, as in Figure 1.1. Nevertheless, it is perfectly possible for the social and private rates of return to be the same. This is proved for the steady growth case in Chapter 7, which also derives formulae for the rate of depreciation for firms, and of appreciation for workers, in the steady growth case. That case is a better approximation to reality than the one-shot investment we have considered here.

I conclude, therefore, in regard to the objection that higher wages beyond T_1 must be brought into account at T_0, that it makes no difference to national income as to whether they are or not. It could, admittedly, affect the distribution of income between wage-earners and profit-receivers. That depends on how far investment is financed by reducing wages, and wage-earners' consumption, and on how far it is financed by reducing profit-receivers' consumption. One could construct cases in which the distribution was also unaffected.

The point just made has a wider application. In our example only one physical change is considered; but it makes no difference to one's estimate of national income at a given time, nor to the general proposition that depreciation and appreciation cancel each other out, how many physical changes occur. The firm, and other firms, can be undertaking investments more or less continuously, and, indeed, in the steady growth case considered in Chapter 7, it is assumed that they do.

Let us now relax some of the other assumptions in the example. The prices of the firm's outputs could be rising or falling in relation to our numeraire without that affecting the essential argument. A rise, for example, would prolong the life of the firm, and so reduce its rate of depreciation. However, the purchasers of its output would lose an equivalent amount, and would suffer faster depreciation (or slower appreciation) on that account. Taken over the whole economy, depreciation and appreciation would still sum to zero. A similar point applies to wage-earners. Some of these could have special skills whose value is reduced by investment elsewhere in the economy. Their wages might then fall, and they would suffer depreciation, just as did the handloom weavers in the Industrial Revolution. However, their loss would be someone else's gain.

The firm in our example purchased no material inputs, but, again, it makes no essential difference if we allow for these. If their prices rise or fall in relation to the numeraire, that will result in faster or slower depreciation for the firm, with opposite effects for the producers of the materials.

The existence of interest payments, taxes, and other transfers also makes no essential difference. One can either consider 'trading profits' before deduction of these amounts, as conventional national accounts do, to which the argument directly applies, or else treat, say, interest as a payment to a factor of production on a level with other factor payments.

The much more difficult assumptions to relax are those relating to discount rates, rates of return, and expectations. In fact, if the three different definitions of depreciation listed on p. 23 are to remain equivalent, one has to assume that there is a common, constant, real rate of return which is also the rate of discount, and that expectations are fulfilled and are also the same for all individuals, as in the example. I rather doubt that any simple way of accounting for depreciation can be devised unless these assumptions are made. The main comforting consideration is that, for defining *national* income, saving, and investment, it is unnecessary to estimate depreciation and appreciation in a closed economy, and even in an open economy, so long as its terms of trade with the rest of the world do not change. For large countries, at all events, national income can be closely approximated without estimating depreciation. This is because, for such countries, the ratio of trade to national income is relatively small, and also because imports and exports are probably more diversified and so there is less likely to be a persistent trend one way or the other in the terms of trade.

In practice, 'income' of both countries and individuals is most easily, and so most frequently, calculated ignoring depreciation and appreciation. As accountants tend to be conservative, they are more likely to attempt some estimate of depreciation, but even that is often ignored. For firms this gives gross profits, and for workers wages, and these are at least one measure of their respective contributions[20] to national income in a closed economy. Likewise, an open economy's gross domestic product at factor cost is one measure of its contribution to world national income.

Hicks's views on the unreliability of income as an economic concept (see

---

[20] See fn. 18.

pp. 7–8), as well as Hayek's (1941b) on the difficulty attached to the idea of maintaining capital intact, both stemmed in large part from the difficulties encountered in estimating incomes when discount rates and expectations vary, as they undoubtedly do. Fortunately, most of these difficulties disappear when we consider national income, since depreciation cancels out appreciation, and we can sum individual contributions to national income, which are much easier to measure. It is no wonder that practical systems of national accounts have largely confined themselves to GNP, GDP, and the corresponding magnitudes for property-owners and workers: gross profits and wages.

1.7   The confusion between gross investment, maintenance, and depreciation

One does not need to distinguish between maintenance and depreciation in order to estimate the income of a firm. It seems likely that it is this fact which explains their confusion in economic theory and national income accounting. The confusion would not matter were we interested only in individual firms; however, we are also interested in the income of a nation, and of a whole closed economy, and for them the distinction is important, and so too is the confusion.

A firm's rate of gross profits measured at constant prices[21] will be constant at a given moment in time if its employment is constant and if it is undertaking required maintenance. If, however, relative prices are changing, the firm's actual gross profits measured at current prices will, in general, be changing. If they are falling (as in our preceding example), then the firm is suffering depreciation. The firm's income (or net profits) then equals its gross profits *less* depreciation (or *plus* appreciation if price changes are favourable). These are the definitions put forward here.

It is clear that the firm's actual gross profits could be falling for either or both of two reasons: because of physical changes, or because of relative price changes. From the point of view of the businessman, this distinction is immaterial. Whether his assets are physically deteriorating or are becoming obsolete as relative prices change adversely really makes no difference. In either event, there is some expenditure he needs to undertake in order to offset these changes, and it is only after subtracting the cost of this expenditure that he can regard the remainder of his gross profit as Hicksian income or net profit, which could all be consumed indefinitely. Indeed, for the individual businessman the distinction between depreciation and maintenance has been made on different lines. 'Maintenance' has consisted of all those expenditures that are sufficiently small, frequent,

---

[21]   The prices are those ruling at the given moment in time.

and regular that one can, without too much distortion, estimate one's income by subtracting the actual expenditures instead of by setting up a fund and subtracting contributions to it. It is much simpler to do the former than the latter. 'Depreciation' has been concerned with expenditures that are too large and irregular to be treated in this way, and where a fund has had to be set up if estimates of income are not to be badly distorted. 'Depreciation' then consists of contributions to the fund, and gross investment consists of those expenditures that are not subtracted from revenues in estimating income. The distinctions between depreciation, maintenance, and gross investment have thus rested on simple practical grounds of convenience and approximation, and this is why criteria such as the length of the accounting period and the lumpiness of the expenditure have been used which seem quite arbitrary from a conceptual point of view.

So much for the practical businessman, but what of the practical social accountant? As we have seen, there are two important distinctions to be drawn: between gross investment and maintenance expenditures, and between depreciation and maintenance. I have suggested that the first distinction should rest on whether the expenditures improve or merely restore, but it must be admitted that this is not a precise distinction. To achieve precision, one could set up a fund for each and every asset, so that gross investment would then consist of all expenditures that changed assets (or, more generally, changed economic arrangements) without distinguishing improvements from restorations. Required maintenance would then be the sum of contributions to these funds. Unfortunately, this theoretically satisfactory solution is quite impractical, since it would enormously increase gross investment and the deduction for required maintenance. Ploughing and sowing change assets, as do painting and repairing, oiling and greasing, and a vast amount of other expenditure besides. In practice, therefore, one must fall back on the same criteria as the businessman: one avoids setting up funds and includes as many actual maintenance expenditures as possible with other current costs of production. The larger the group of assets in the aggregate, and the longer the period of account, the more closely will such actual expenditures approximate to notional contributions to the notional funds. It is at the closeness of this approximation that one must aim in deciding how to treat this or that item.

The important practical question is how closely expeditures that are classified as maintenance by national income accountants approximate to required maintenance, and whether they are smaller or greater than it in total. Conventional maintenance expenditures probably do physically maintain most assets until near the end of their economic lives,[22] at which

---

[22] As evidence for this one may cite Barna's view that most assets' economic lives are determined by obsolescence, rather than by physical wear and tear: 'it is obsolescence, rather than wear and tear, which is the cause of mortality—homicide to make room for a new

point maintenance tends to be neglected. This is true, for example, of a house standing on land which has much increased in value. When it becomes clear that it will pay to pull the house down and build flats, say, on the land, then it becomes pointless to continue to maintain the house. However, in all such cases the neglect of maintenance causes very little loss of income. True, the house may rent for as much as (or even more than) before; but nearly all that rent is attributable to the land, and virtually none to the building, so that when the building deteriorates and is finally destroyed, little or nothing is lost. This is similar to the shut-down of the firm in our previous example. Expenditures on some assests, such as replacements for a fleet of taxis, are in practice included in gross invest-ment, because they are lumpy, instead of in maintenance as they should be. In so far as that occurs, recorded maintenance expenditures fall short of required maintenance. However, this shortfall is made good, or more than good, by the inclusion in maintenance (or other current costs) of a great many expenditures that should be classified as gross investment: research and development expenditures, some managerial costs, some advertising expenditures, some costs of financial intermediaries, and so on. On the other side of the account, certain kinds of physical deterioration are ignored altogether, although they need to be offset by improvements elsewhere for maintenance to reach required levels. Examples are the depletion of minerals, the depletion of fishing stocks, and pollution of various kinds. Finally, it should be noted that many expenditures that are classified as maintenance in fact improve the assets concerned. Replacement is often made with an improved part, and, strictly, the cost of the replacement should then be split between maintenance and gross investment.

My own guess is that expenditures that are classified as current costs on balance probably overstate required maintenance for most developed countries in the Western world. It would be a major research project (well worth undertaking) to verify this, but, if it is correct, it follows that conventionally measured gross domestic investment probably understates true net domestic investment for these countries. It also follows that con-ventionally estimated depreciation, which is called 'capital consumption' in published systems of national accounts, should not be deducted from conventional gross domestic investment to give net domestic investment;

favourite, rather than natural death' (Barna, in Lutz and Hague 1961, 85). Kuznets took the view that maintenance and repair covers physical deterioration, while 'capital consumption' is due largely to obsolescence, which corresponds closely to the view taken here (see Kuznets with Jenks 1961, 396). See also Kuznets in Conference on Research in Income and Wealth (1951, 65): 'we know that the physical life of equipment is far longer than is assumed in depreciation charges; that maintenance cannot be long postponed without impairing operation; and that the rise in operating expenses within the ordinarily assumed lifetime of capital goods is relatively moderate. Consequently, the life period used in depreciation charges is cut short largely by considerations of obsolescence and the latter must account for a substantial part of depreciation charges.'

nor should it be deducted from GNP or GDP to give the net totals. If anything, GNP and GDP probably understate the true net totals.

In the rest of the book I proceed as if there is no discrepancy between conventional maintenance and required maintenance, or between conventional gross domestic investment and true net domestic investment, and I measure net domestic product by conventional gross domestic product. While this is a break from the received doctrine, in empirical work my procedure has frequently been followed, albeit with a guilty conscience which I hope I have shown to be inappropriate. Furthermore, the idea that depreciation, when it is due to obsolescence, is not a social cost is one that has been expressed by some well-known writers on national accounts.[23]

1.8 Capital and wealth

As defined here, capital is an input or cause, wealth an output or result. The simplest definition of capital is accumulated investment: the sum at constant prices, for as far back as we care to go, of past investment, not compounded by any rate of discount but simply added up. Capital is therefore backward-looking, and measures the total sacrifice of consumption made to bring the economy to its present state. Wealth is, by contrast, forward-looking, and measures the value of what has been achieved. It is the present discounted value of all future consumption. Let us consider each of these concepts in turn.[24]

In measuring capital, I want to find the total sacrifice of consumption made in the past. This requires an index of consumer goods prices, not

[23] 'In what sense does, therefore, obsolescence justify a deduction from captial, from the standpoint of society, however much it may be justified by business firms as a protection against loss in relative competitive position vis-à-vis newcomers who can reap the differential advantage of their newness? There is something absurd in a procedure that reduces the value of a capital good that is physically and otherwise unimpaired solely because there has been technical progress' (Kuznets, in Conference on Research in Income and Wealth 1951, 66. See also Kuznets 1974, 156).

'Technolgical progress frequently does destroy the earning power, and thus the money value, of already existing captial goods, and this type of obsolescence should and does enter into the depreciation allowances of businessmen. But technological progress causes no real loss to the economy as a whole. . . . Wherever appreciable technological advance does occur, therefore, reliance on the business concept of preserving the money value of capital intact as a measure of the decline in capital goods in the economy as a whole will result in an estimate of capital consumption that is too large' (Ruggles and Ruggles 1956, 114).

'Obsolescence, for instance, can be looked upon as the result of a transfer of wealth from owners of old types of machines to owners of new types of machines, labour, or consumers. The loss to the firm is genuine but the loss to the economy is counterbalanced by gains elsewhere' (Usher 1980a, 105). For a contrary view see Solow (1963, 61–2), whose argument that there is a social equivalent cost to obsolescence rests, however, on a model of growth in which there is exogenous technical progress—a model rejected here (see Chapter 3).

[24] Hicks, in Lutz and Hague (1961), is, so far as I know, the first to have distinguished between backward- and forward-looking concepts of capital. For a recent discussion of different concepts of capital, see Usher (1980c).

capital goods prices, to make investment in different periods commensurable, as already noted, and it is certainly simpler than conventional practice, which requires the estimation of capital goods prices.

It must also be noted that it is conventionally defined *gross* investment that is summed to give the capital stock, and *not* gross investment minus either scrapping or depreciation (capital consumption). This is because, for the reasons given earlier, gross investment is the best approximation to true net investment for a closed economy. Investment is net of maintenance, of course, but since depreciation and appreciation cancel each other out, there is no further subtraction. Both material and human investment should be included.

An implication of summing gross investment which may seem, at first sight, paradoxical is that an investment made, say, 100 years ago, and long ago written off in the books of the firm concerned, and possibly scrapped as well, will still feature in the capital stock. This is certainly not what would happen with conventional concepts, whether of the net or the gross capital stock. No investment remains in the conventional stock beyond its estimated economic life. With my concept, by contrast, investments once made remain in the stock for ever. How can this procedure have any useful meaning?

Let us first note that there is another concept of capital, to which we return later, which is close to the conventional concept of the net capital stock. This has its uses, and is the most relevant concept so far as capitalists are concerned. However, we are presently looking at matters from the point of view of the whole of a closed economy, and for this purpose there are reasons for preferring the capital stock defined above, rather than the conventional net capital stock. What are these reasons? There are four.

First, if we want to know the total sacrifice of consumption that has been made in bringing the economy to its present state, the sacrifice in each case being by reference to the alternative of stopping further change and resting content with the level of income achieved up to that point, then all past investment is relevant. It is quite irrelevant whether the actual configuration of matter directly resulting from the investment still survives or not. This is not, on reflection, so very strange. The cost of constructing a machine, after all, is the cost of making a rearrangement of iron ore, carbon, manganese, and whatever other materials are necessary. Included in the cost will be the moulds required for castings, even though these moulds may have been discarded. The cost of constructing a house is likewise that of rearranging bricks, cement, timber, etc., and it will include the cost of putting up scaffolding and shuttering, which must then be taken down. Capital is the cost of 'constructing' an economy, and not all the costs that have been incurred will leave tangible evidence of their existence.[25]

[25] Nor will all the costs themselves be tangible when incurred. Systems of national accounts generally exclude, for example, investment expenditures which are not embodied in tangible

Second, if we want to explain why the present level of output has increased from some previous level, then all the investment incurred between the two dates is relevant. Each bit of investment has helped to raise the level of output a bit, and we must sum up those bits and relate them to the sum of the investments. Again, it does not matter whether tangible evidence of those investments remains or not.

Third, if we want to explain shifts in the distribution of income between wages and profits, investments made at each stage in the process are relevant. The difference in distribution between two given periods must be explained, partly, by all investments made between them, regardless of whether they have physically survived or not.

Finally, if we want to relate capital to wealth, for the whole of a closed economy, the definition given here is the relevant one. This brings us to a consideration of wealth.

As already stated, wealth is the present value of future consumption; but to apply this definition we need to know what rate of discount to use and how the future is to be defined. In a real economy, there will be a wide range of possible rates of discount that might be used. Each individual or firm may have a different rate—indeed, not even a uniform rate, but rates that vary through time. If we want a relatively simple set of concepts applicable to the whole economy, we must content ourselves with something more manageable than the real jungle of discount rates. Just as we shall make use of a fiction that is the representative firm, so shall we employ a representative, or average, discount rate.

So far as the definition of future consumption is concerned, there appear to be two obvious candidates. One is an estimate of what future consumption will actually be. The other is the constant level of consumption that could have been achieved from the present time, t, onwards had notice been given a long time ago that no further changes would occur after t. If demographic factors are expected to make the labour force grow after t, then the present value of the former prospect will, generally speaking, exceed that of the latter. But if there is no demographic change expected, then under certain reasonable assumptions, with a reasonably chosen average discount rate, the two will be equal. The reason for this is that the present value of all investment on average will equal its cost (since that is how we choose the discount rate). Furthermore, with no demographic change, and on the view taken here (see later chapters), future growth of consumption must all be due to future investment. It then makes no difference whether, in the future, the economy invests or not so far as the present value of consumption is concerned. Investing means giving up consumption at some date for more consumption at a later date, but with the same present value. It does not increase present value. Consequently, in

assets such as research and development expenditures (see, for example, United Nations 1968, paras, 6.63, 6.102), but I can see no justification for that.

these circumstances both measures of wealth equal Y_t/r, where Y_t is income at t, and r is the appropriate average rate of discount (assumed constant).[26]

It is also the case that, if there has been no demographic change in the past, and if the average yield of investment in the past had been the same r, then total capital equals total wealth. The explanation for this is similar. With no demographic change, all present value has been due to past investment. (This is not strictly true—there must have been some initial income earned by the labour force before there was any investment; however, I assume that this would have been negligibly small in relation to current income levels). And since investments on average (given our discount rate) produced present value equal to their cost, if we total the costs, we reach the same total present value. All this is demonstrated for the case of a steadily growing economy in Chapter 7.

If there is demographic change, this must be allowed for. It is both a partial explanation of present income levels, and so of wealth measured by Y_t/r, and a partial explanation of increases in future consumption levels, and so of wealth measured by reference to that. One could construct a measure of capital which would include demographic change; however, that is not further considered here (see Kendrick 1976 for an attempt).

Let us now consider capital and wealth for an individual firm or family, each assumed to be immortal. Capital for the whole economy is the accumulated sum of past net investment (which approximately equals gross investment as conventionally defined). The same definition applies for the firm or family, but in their cases we must bring in depreciation or appreciation in order to calculate net investment. The latter equals gross investment minus depreciation, or plus appreciation. Capital then ceases to be backward-looking, since depreciation and appreciation are inevitably forward-looking. If expectations change, as they surely will, there should, in principle, be a recalculation of all past estimates of depreciation and net investment, and so of capital. One consistent set of expectations is strictly required to calculate them all.[27]

[26] I assume that at any given time t there is a unique constant discount rate which makes the present value, at t, of all future additions to consumption equal to the present value, at t, of the consumption sacrificed to obtain them. This equality of present value of consumption sacrificed to that of consumption gained need not hold for individual investments. All that is necessary is that is should hold for all investments taken together. That is the way in which the *average* discount rate is constructed. If there were no future investments, so that income was all consumed and a static economy obtained (there being no demographic change by assumption), then the whole of income at t, Y_t, would be consumed, and that rate of consumption would last for ever. Its present value, discounted at r (the same average discount rate), would then be

$$\int_t^\infty Y_t \exp\{-r(\tau - t)\}\, d\tau = \frac{Y_t}{r}.$$

[27] This definition of the net capital stock is the same as the conventional one so long as the original cost of each asset equals its present value when new, the rate of discount is constant and equals the yield on the depreciation fund, there is no inflation, expectations are fulfilled, and the amounts written off each year equal the decline in the present value of each asset. If expectations change, the values of assets must be revised.

If the average rate of return is constant, and equals the discount rate, and if there is no demographic change, then individual capital equals individual wealth, just as for a whole closed economy. Individual holdings then sum to the same total as for the whole closed economy, and the distribution of wealth corresponds to the distribution of past net saving. However, it does *not* correspond to the distribution of past contributions to (gross) investment. In a progressive economy, firms will have undertaken much more of total past investment than their share of wealth, since the process of depreciation and appreciation will have transferred much of the income from investment into the hands of workers. The growth model described in Chapter 6 and later chapters permits a further analysis of this process.

1.9   Land

What has happened to land in all this? We seem to have been able to get along quite nicely without mentioning it. Has it been forgotten? Or has it really been there all the time?

Surprising as it may seem at first, it *has* been there all the time. There are only two types of actor in our drama, human beings and everything else, and the latter must include land. In fact, it *is* land. Human investment is the cost of improving human beings, and material investment is the cost of improving land, i.e. everything else. I do not deny, of course, that there are important differences between things. There is land and land, just as there are people and people. All I am claiming is that it is a reasonable simplification to lump all things together, just as one often lumps all people together, and that much confusion can be avoided by *not* drawing a line between 'capital instruments' and 'land', as is conventionally done. Fields, for example, are the outcome of a great deal of investment. What part of them is 'land' and what 'capital instrument'? The question is unanswerable and uninteresting.

I agree with Scitovsky's note on land, which 'aims not at dealing with the factor of production, *land*, but at explaining why we are not dealing with it', and which concludes: 'From every point of view, therefore, land may be regarded as a capital good and the rent of land as similar in every respect to the gross earnings of a produced factor' (Scitovsky 1952, 227–8).

1.10   Capital in an aggregate production function

Some readers will object that the concept of capital proposed here is quite unsuitable as an argument in the aggregate production function $Q = f(K, L)$, and that conventionally defined capital (whether the gross stock or the net stock) is much better for that purpose. Capital, it will be argued, for this purpose should be the aggregate of capital goods, combined with weights proportionate to each good's marginal product. This is similar to the concept used to measure employment, each worker being weighted in proportion to his or her marginal product (see Chapter 2). Capital is then related to the productive power of capital goods, just as labour is related to the productive power of workers. A capital stock which includes capital goods that have been scrapped long ago cannot be used for this purpose.

While I agree with the last sentence, I do not agreee with the general argument. Neither the conventionally defined gross capital stock nor the net capital stock is at all suitable for use in the above production function. It is doubtful whether that function has a useful part to play in growth theory or empirical work, and it is not used in this book. The reasons for these conclusions are given in Chapter 3, where a critique of neoclassical growth theory is provided.

Appendix

In this appendix it is shown that, if the present value of a variable stream of gross profits lasting from T_0 to T_1 is A_0 at T_0, and if depreciation funds can be invested to earn a constant exponential rate of return of r per annum, then the income for the owners of the stream of profits at T_0 is rA_0.

Let the rate of gross profits at any time T between T_0 and T_1 be G_T. Then their present value is, by definition,

$$A_0 = \int_{T_0}^{T_1} G_T e^{-r(T-T_0)} dT = e^{rT_0} \int_{T_0}^{T_1} G_T e^{-rT} dT.$$

If *all* of gross profits were invested in the depreciation fund, they would accumulate at the rate r, and, at T_1, would amount to

$$A_1 = \int_{T_0}^{T_1} G_T e^{r(T_1-T)} dT = e^{rT_1} \int_{T_0}^{T_1} G_T e^{-rT} dT.$$

$$= A_0 e^{r(T_1 - T_0)}.$$

Now A_1 can be regarded as consisting of two parts, namely, the accumulated actual depreciation fund at T_1 and the amount that would accumulate at T_1 if income were also to be invested in it. Income is the maximum constant amount which can be consumed, and the rest of gross profit is depreciation, and so if both were invested from T_0 to T_1 one must accumulate A_1 by T_1. If income were rA_0, then its accumulated value at T_1 would be

$$C_1 = \int_{T_0}^{T_1} rA_0 e^{r(T_1-T)} dT$$

$$= rA_0 e^{rT_1} \frac{e^{-rT_1} - e^{-rT_0}}{-r}$$

$$= A_1 - A_0.$$

If follows that, if rA_0 is consumed, then the value of the fund at T_1 would be not A_1, but $A_1 - C_1$, which equals A_0. Now, since the fund is *ex hypothesi* invested so as to earn r per annum, it follows that rA_0 is the income from it at T_1. Hence the owners have been able to consume rA_0 from T_0 to T_1 and, at T_1, still have the prospect of consuming rA_0 for the indefinite future. Hence rA_0 is also their income at T_0.

2

GROWTH FACTS

2.1 Introduction

Theory needs facts, just as facts need theory. My concern in this chapter is to describe the main variables employed in subsequent chapters, to justify the simplifications made, and to set out the record, in terms of these variables, for the three countries with which we shall mainly be concerned: the USA, Japan, and the UK. My main aim is to present a theory of economic growth capable of explaining the behaviour of four principal summary statistics for these countries, and also for seven continental European countries for which suitable data are available for some postwar years. The four statistics are: the rate of growth of output, g, the rate of growth of quality-adjusted employment, g_L, the average ratio of investment to output, s, and the average ratio of 'wages' to output, λ. Later chapters consider industry data as well as national data, but the latter are the main concern. When I started work on this book, it was clear that a break in growth had occurred in many countries in 1973. I therefore used the available data up to 1973 for all my analysis, leaving post-1973 experience for later consideration (thus allowing more of it to accumulate). Until Chapter 16, therefore, which discusses the years 1973–85, almost all the analysis stops at 1973.

Chapter 1 discussed the concepts that should be used for growth theory, but how those concepts can be best approximated in practice is an art, and a very important one. This book could not have been written had not others devoted enormous time, effort, and skill to the compilation of the statistics I have used. I myself have devoted a large fraction of the time involved in writing the book to computations and research to obtain the figures I needed. Much more time could usefully have been spent on this task, and I have to admit that the estimates provided here are open to criticism. Interested readers will want to consult the Statistical Appendix at the end of the book before judging how far they are acceptable, and even so I have been compelled to omit most of the details of the calculations for lack of space. In this chapter, description has been kept to the minimum that seems to me necessary for a proper understanding of later chapters.

2.2 The main variables

In the rest of this book a great many different variables appear (see list at front of book), and are explained when they do. In this chapter attention is confined to the most important: g, g_L, s, and λ, the ratio of labour income (which we refer to as 'wages' for short) to output. These are the four variables with which most of our analysis is concerned. A fifth worth mentioning in this chapter is g_N, the growth rate of numbers employed, measured as full-time equivalents. All these are further explained below and in more detail in the Statistical Appendix, which also describes the sources used.

Exponential growth rates per annum are used throughout, in preference to the more usual percentage or proportionate growth rates, for mathematical convenience. Those unfamiliar with them should note that $100g$ is a close approximation to the percentage rate of growth (and g to the proportionate rate of growth), so long as g is small. More precisely, if the percentage rate of growth were $100x$, then

$$g = \ln(1 + x).$$

Mathematical convenience arises from the fact that exponential growth rates lend themselves easily to manipulation and, for example, can be added or subtracted without error in situations in which, if percentage or proportionate growth rates are used, an approximation is involved. Thus, the exponential growth rate of labour productivity is precisely $g - g_L$, no matter whether g or g_L is large or small.

Unless otherwise mentioned, I refer to the *non-residential business sector* rather than the whole economy.[1] As most growth theory, including that of this book, is framed in terms of profit-maximizing enterprises or individuals, it seems best to exclude governments and non-profit organizations. A further reason for doing so is that the growth rate of output of, for example, civil servants, armed forces, police, and education and health services is often poorly measured. Housing is excluded because its output is also often poorly measured as a result of rent controls. The services provided by other consumer durables are excluded from official estimates of national output, and it seemed best to exclude housing as well. However, the bulk of the gross domestic product is included: agriculture, forestry and fishing, mining,[2] manufacturing, construction, public utilities (gas,

---

[1] Thus following Denison's lead in Denison (1974), Denison and Chung (1976), and Denison (1979, 1985).

[2] Exceptionally, output of petroleum and natural gas extraction in the UK is excluded from 1970 onwards. (Output was negligible before then.) This was done because the way in which

electricity, and water), transport, distribution, and financial and other services (but excluding domestic servants and government, education, and health).

Output, *Y*, is measured gross of depreciation for the reasons given in Chapter 1. The preferred measure is *gross domestic product at factor cost*, this being, in my view, the best available approximation to true income in the sector.[3] *Domestic* rather than *national* product is used, since I do not want to discuss the determinants of net property income from abroad.

Output at constant prices is *Q*. In measuring the *growth of output at constant prices*, *g*, conventional estimates were adjusted by replacing gross investment deflated by its own price index numbers by gross investment deflated by the implicit price of index of consumption, for the reasons given in Chapter 1. It seemed most appropriate for this price index to include government expenditure on goods and services as well as private consumers' expenditure, since the consumption sacrificed or gained as a result of investment could be public as well as private. This departure from convention usually made little difference to measured rates of growth, except for Japan after the Second World War, when investment goods prices rose much more slowly than consumption goods prices. As a result, the Japanese growth rate in this period was reduced by the procedure followed here.

In principle, I should have liked to have measured growth using a Divisia index in which the price weights used were changed continuously. In practice, some of the available series (e.g. for the UK following the Second World War) approximated to that in that price weights were changed every few years. For other series, however, the changes in price weights were more infrequent, and it is unfortunately true that this could appreciably affect measured rates of growth. There can be substantial differences between growth rates measured at a particular year's prices and those measured at prices from a much earlier or later year, when relative prices may differ appreciably. However, the time available for the study left me no choice in the matter. It is one to which future research could profitably be devoted.

In measuring *labour input* I have followed Denison. Different types of labour are added together to form a single index of labour input. In principle, one would like to weight each type by its relative marginal product. The best approximation available is the wage, and even this is not available in the detail required, combined with matching employment data.

such output is measured in the official statistics is conceptually incorrect in that no allowance is made for depletion (i.e. required maintenance), and it seemed more interesting to study the behaviour of the rest of the economy, excluding this important and very rapidly growing element whose inclusion would have disturbed comparisons with earlier years and other countries.

[3] Unless there are changes in the sector's terms of trade, or abnormal required maintenance. Both are further discussed and estimates given in Ch. 16.

I have therefore, perforce, fallen back on approximations to this ideal which may be summarized as follows.

Where statistics of full-time and part-time workers are available, separately, the latter have been converted into equivalent full-time workers on the basis of estimates of the number of hours worked by each. This yields an index of *full time equivalent workers*, N, which is the crudest measure of labour input used.

Annual hours worked by full-time workers have varied greatly, and have generally tended to fall since the nineteenth century, as hours worked per week have shortened and holidays have lengthened. Absences owing to sickness and strikes have also varied. So far as possible, all these variations have been allowed for.

Workers' pay varies with both age and sex, with young workers and females earning typically much less than average males. Where statistics of workers grouped by age and sex are available, the effect of changes in the proportions of the different groups on labour input has been estimated, using average earnings for each group as weights.

Better educated workers generally earn more than less educated ones. Probably only part of this differential is due to the education itself, the rest being due to other factors such as parental upbringing and inherited qualities. That part which, it is assumed, is due to education can be related to the amount of education received by the work-force. As amounts of education have risen, this has tended to increase labour inputs by amounts that have been estimated.

Average earnings in agriculture and among the self-employed tend, generally, to be well below those ruling in the rest of the economy. Transferring workers from these sectors to the rest should therefore raise an index of labour input by amounts that have been estimated.[4] Exceptionally for the UK, no allowance has been made for this factor, since it is thought to have been very small over the periods considered.[5] Nor have the effects of shifts of labour between other industries been allowed for.[6]

[4] It could be objected that transferring labour from low-paid work in agriculture to higher-paid work in the towns may do little to increase the welfare of the workers concerned, because the cost of living is higher in the towns, or there are other net disadvantages. While this may be so, the relevant question here is whether *measured* output is increased by the transfer, and this should be so as long as relative measured marginal products correspond to relative measured wage rates.

[5] The effect of the shift out of agriculture in the UK was greatest in the earliest period considered, 1856–73, and this is to some extent allowed for in a 'nationality' quality effect estimated by Matthews *et al.* (1982, 101–2, 113 (Table 4.7)) and included in my estimates. This allowed for the fall in the proportion of Irish workers in the total UK work-force, agricultural workers being the biggest element of the Irish work-force. Some rough calculations suggested that, within Britain, the shift from agriculture to the rest of non-residential business improved labour quality by less than 0.2 per cent p.a. over 1856–73, by less than 0.1 per cent p.a. in 1873–1913, and by still less thereafter.

[6] For a good discussion of these effects, with some estimates for the UK, see Matthews *et al.* (1982, 260–6). For peacetime periods, their estimates suggest small positive effects of the order

There is a fair amount of evidence of various kinds that the efficiency of work increases as the number of hours worked shortens, and it seems reasonable to suppose that the gain in efficiency per hour diminishes as hours worked shorten. Denison has assumed, somewhat arbitrarily, a particular relationship between efficiency per hour and hours worked, and I have assumed the same one. A test of this relationship is provided in Chapter 10, although it cannot claim to any great reliability. The effect of making this adjustment for efficiency is that the big fall in hours worked, which occurred in both the USA and the UK before 1914, does not result in any substantial difference between our crudest measure of labour input N and the quality-adjusted index, which takes account of changes in full-time workers' hours of work, L. The fall in hours is more or less completely offset by the increased efficiency of average hours worked. Subsequent falls in hours, however, exert greater effects in reducing L in relation to N.

The index of labour input, L, used here makes allowance for all the factors mentioned. Because of the particular uncertainty attached to the last factor, the efficiency of average hours worked, an index that omits it but includes all the rest, H, is also constructed. We thus have three measures of labour input, N, H, and L, with three corresponding growth rates, g_N, g_H, and g_L. It is of some interest to see how they have varied both in relation to each other and to the growth of output, and this is examined later. It makes a big difference to the ranking of countries by rates of growth of labour productivity which of these measures of labour input is used.

The investment ratio, s, is the ratio of investment gross of depreciation to output as already defined. Depreciation is included for the reasons given in Chapter 1. In principle, required maintenance is excluded both from investment and output, and I have taken conventional estimates of gross

of 0.1 or 0.2 per cent p.a. They find a larger effect (about 0.5 per cent p.a.) across the Second World War, 1937–51. In principle, these estimates are *net* of age, sex, and educational effects, which are allowed for already in their other estimates, but educational effects had to be proxied by occupational ones. Furthermore, much of the improvement in quality, especially across the Second World War, was due to two shifts which are irrelevant to the analysis in this book, viz.: shifts into the relatively highly paid public and professional services, and shifts out of low-paid domestic service. These groups of workers are excluded from non-residential business. My own estimates of other inter-industry quality shifts for the USA, Japan, and the UK for the years after the Second World War yielded only small changes (see Ch. 16 for further discussion). Dennis Anderson has pointed out to me that there may have been shifts from lower to higher paid jobs *within* firms, industries, educational groups, etc., which are ignored here, and which lead to a substantial understatement of the true rate of growth of quality-adjusted employment. He prefers to approximate the latter by the growth of the real wage bill. However, in my opinion that overstates g_L, since it assumes that there is no increase in the average real price of quality-adjusted labour, which seems very implausible, given the information available on wages for particular occupations (e.g. builder's labourers, domestic servants, school teachers, etc.), where substantial real increases have occurred. Nevertheless, this is another field in which further research is needed. A really good index of the price of quality-adjusted labour would have many uses.

fixed investment plus investment in stocks (net of stock appreciation) as the best approximation available. As was pointed out in Chapter 1, conventional estimates are too big inasmuch as they fail to deduct some maintenance expenditures (e.g. for vehicles, mineral depletion, soil erosion, and pollution). On the other hand, they are too small inasmuch as they fail to include some kinds of investment expenditures (e.g. R&D, and parts of expenditure on advertising, financing, and management). For lack of time, I am compelled to make do with the available estimates, but this is another field in which more research is required. In Chapter 16 there is further discussion of abnormal required maintenance in the years after 1973. The investment ratio is measured at current prices, but, given the deflation procedures followed here, there would be little difference were it measured at constant prices.[7]

The share of wages, λ, is the ratio of income from employment plus the labour component of income from self-employment to output at current prices. Income from employment is as conventionally defined, and so includes employers' and employees' insurance and pension contributions, direct taxes, and payments in kind. In addition, the income of the self-employed has been divided into two parts, representing 'wages' and 'profits'. Broadly speaking, average earnings in similar employment multiplied by the numbers in self-employment gives 'wages'. However, Denison has used a somewhat more complicated method to perform the allocation for the USA since 1929 and for Japan in 1952–71, which I have followed. Total 'profits' then include the profits part of self-employed incomes plus all other, non-employment, incomes. Interest and the rent of land are included in 'profits', as are direct taxes on profits, interest, and rent.

2.3 Period data

My empirical analysis was conducted at two levels: using annual data, and using averages for selected periods. The latter turned out to be more fruitful, and most attention is paid to it in the rest of the book. A basic simplifying hypothesis is that steady growth, conforming to a modified version of Kaldor's stylized facts of growth, prevails. This is explained and justified later. Growth within each period approximately conforms to the hypothesis, but the approximation is poor, and the hypothesis less fruitful, if one combines periods between which there appears to have been a sharp

---

[7] In a closed economy, there would be no difference at all had investment been deflated by a price index of consumpion at factor cost (instead of at market prices—which was most readily available). For an open economy, differences can arise because of different ways of deflating exports and imports. For some further discussion and estimates of terms of trade effects, see Ch. 16.

break in behaviour. The two world wars and the depression of the 1930s are examples of breaks, and another occurred around 1973. While I attempt to explain why economies grew differently in one period compared with another, the unit of observation is, in effect, the period average. This involves a certain arbitrariness in the selection of periods, and I hope that others, armed with more powerful econometric batteries than my own old-fashioned cannon, will advance matters further. However, history is complicated and untidy, and I believe that it is not just better econometric techniques that are needed here.

The basic annual data consists of index numbers (1913 = 100) for Q, L, N, and H for the following countries and periods:

USA	1889–1985
Japan	1885–1940, 1952–1984
UK	1856–1985

These three countries were studied because relevant estimates stretching back over a long period were available in the English language. In addition, some period data were available for certain continental European countries as described below. While estimates for Japan for the years 1941–51 are not available, the later years are linked to the earlier ones although the links are weak. For each of the above three countries and years, s is also available. However, annual estimates of λ are available only for the USA from 1929 and for Japan from 1952. Rather unreliable averages of λ for earlier periods for these countries were estimated. For the UK, annual estimates for all the years are available.

From this annual data, period averages for g, g_L, g_N, and g_H were constructed as follows. Since the theory of growth is concerned essentially with the medium to long run, we need to abstract from cyclical fluctuations in the ratio of output to capacity. This can be done, to some extent, by fitting exponential trends to annual data, and this probably suffices where the periods being considered are twenty years or more. For shorter periods, and especially when fluctuations are large, more careful allowance for changes in the ratio of output to capacity is desirable. This subject is discussed at some length in Chapter 16 with particular reference to the years since 1973. For earlier years a rather rough and ready procedure was resorted to. The exponential trends were fitted to annual observations *excluding* those years judged to be substantially affected by excess capacity. Where output was appreciably less than its previous peak level, this was deemed to be the case. It was decided to exclude years affected by wars as well, since normal economic behaviour was disrupted then.[8] Periods stretching *across* wars were included.[9]

---

[8] For the slump and war years excluded, see the Statistical Appendix.

[9] To measure the trend rate of growth of output in the UK over the period 1913–24, I simply took the average exponential growth rate between the first and last years. Output in every year

The value of the investment ratio, s, is the unweighted mean of annual observations for all the years of the period except the last. (If the last year had been included, it would have appeared twice in successive periods.) In principle, it would have been preferable to measure s as the average ratio of investment to *normal capacity* output, rather than, as here, to actual output.[10]

The value of the share of wages, λ, is the unweighted mean of annual observations for all the years of the period excluding the last, and also excluding all slump years as defined above and excluding all war years. The wages share is cyclical, and we really need a cyclically adjusted share, assuming that it is this that governs investment and pricing behaviour (as seems reasonable). The procedure adopted gives a crude approximation to this. War years are excluded because it is thought that labour's share might then have been abnormal.

The periods chosen for the USA, Japan, and the UK can be seen from Table 10.1, which also shows data for seven continental European countries for 1955–62[11] based on Denison (Denison with Poullier 1967).

2.4   The 'stylized facts' of growth

A great deal of (perhaps most?) economic theory, and even empirical analysis, treats the economy as if it were in static equilibrium. Comparisons of different periods then become exercises in comparative statics. A step away from this type of analysis towards a more dynamic theory is to treat the economy as if it were converging on a static equilibrium. This is, for example, the assumption made by the capital stock adjustment principle. The speed of adjustment depends, usually, on the size of the gap between the actual stock and the (static) equilibrium stock.

In practice, it is obvious that modern economies are not in static equilibrium. It makes little sense to assume that they are converging on it, either. Yet the complexity of a fully dynamic analysis is such that one can sympathize with those seeking refuge in the above simplifications. I have chosen a different one, which I believe is closer to reality. I assume that an economy can be represented by a typical enterprise, and that this enterprise behaves as if it were in steady growth. Unless that rate of growth happens to

from 1914 to 1924 was less than in 1913. The procedure here followed that of Matthews *et al.* (1982), who took both 1913 and 1924 as benchmark years. There was a big fall in labour input across the First World War, as hours worked fell sharply, and so the fall in output may not have been due to a fall in the ratio of output to capacity.

[10] Generally speaking, there would be little difference. For further discussion and estimates for the years after 1973, see Ch. 16.

[11] Denison gave estimates for the years 1950–5 as well, but for several countries these were considerably affected by postwar recovery, and it was thought best to take the shorter period for all. It would also have been difficult to construct estimates for non-residential business for the earlier years. Denison's figures refer to the whole nation.

be zero, the enterprise is not, and never expects to be, in static equilibrium. It is undertaking investment all the time, and so it is changing its economic arrangements all the time. There are always investment opportunities confronting it, from which it keeps selecting (in some sense to be determined) the best. It is placed in an environment in which real wage rates[12] (typically, but not necessarily) are rising at a constant rate. The outcome of its choices is steady growth.

The simplification, which makes the whole analysis feasible and (I believe) useful, is precisely this: that steady growth *is* the outcome. It is this that enables one to analyse the enterprise's behaviour in a simple way, and to show how changes in various parameters influence g, g_L, s, and λ. The analysis is essentially one of comparing steady growth states, in each of which these four variables are constant. This is only one step away from comparative statics, but I believe it is in a better direction than that taken by theories of convergence on static equilibria. The simplification involves omitting the interaction between the cyclical behaviour of the economy and its trend behaviour. That is, admittedly, a heavy price to pay. In Chapter 16 some amends are made. It is clear that the slower trend growth of the years after 1973 cannot be satisfactorily explained without reference to the greater instability that then occurred. Nevertheless, for most of the book cyclical behaviour is ignored. It joins the list of items for further research.

An important justification for my approach is that economies can be described, to a reasonably close approximation and abstracting from cyclical fluctuation, as being in steady growth states for quite long periods of time. What follows is an attempt to demonstrate this. First, however, some historical background to the idea, together with a definition of steady-state growth, is needed.

In 1958, Kaldor suggested six 'stylized facts' as a starting point for the construction of theoretical models of growth.[13] For what I believe to be good reasons, I shall slightly change his list, and restate the 'stylized facts' as follows. Over quite substantial periods of time, say ten to thirty years, the four magnitudes, g, g_L, s, and λ, for the *non-residential business sector* of the economy, are all constant. In fact, of course, none of these *is* constant, since all are subject to cyclical fluctuations. However, growth theory generally seeks to abstract from these and to concentrate on trends within periods. Hence the assertion is that, apart from cyclical fluctuations, g, g_L, s, and λ are constant.

---

[12] 'Real wage rates' here refers to the price of (in principle) homogeneous labour, *not* earnings per man, since 'men' are heterogeneous. Hence the growth rate of real wage rates is the growth rate of labour income less that of quality-adjusted employment, g_L, not numbers employed, g_N.

[13] See Kaldor's 'Capital Accumulation and Economic Growth' in Lutz and Hague (1961, 178–9).

In a lecture given in 1969, Solow cursorily reviewed some of the available data referring to Kaldor's 'stylized facts'. The fulfilment of the leading four of them meant that the economy concerned was in a *steady state*, and

My general conclusion is that the steady state is not a bad place for the theory of growth to start, but may be a dangerous place for it to end. (Solow 1970, 7)

However, a more careful and critical review of the data (principally for the UK) by Hacche in 1979 came to a more negative conclusion:

The evidence reported in this chapter . . . suggests that . . . the steady state is not a particularly good place for the theory to start, either. (Hacche 1979, 298)

My own conclusion agrees with Kaldor and Solow, rather than Hacche. It refers, however, to the reformulated 'stylized facts' just given, and in particular to the non-residential business sector of the economy. It also refers to substantial periods of time, but *not* to periods of any length you please.[14] My interpretation of the 'stylized facts' is that they are a valuable way of summarizing certain key facts about long-term aggregate economic behaviour. In macroeconomics we habitually aggregate or average in order to make the welter of economic data tractable. So long as the central tendency is sufficiently strong, this procedure is justified. I think the facts of growth in the USA and the UK and in some other countries especially since the Second World War, are close enough to the 'stylized facts' to make them the starting point for theory in the way Kaldor intended. That is, one should ask of any theory that it should be capable of explaining those facts. In addition, the simplest versions of a theory can take these facts as the norm. Let us now consider what empirical evidence there is which bears on these assertions.

It might seem at first sight that, in order to test whether the trend rate of growth of output (for example) was constant over some period, one could proceed as follows. One would measure the closeness of fit of the equation

$$Q = a^* e^{bt}$$

to the observations for the period, Q being output at constant prices, t being time in years, and a^* and b being constants. Taking the natural logarithm of each side, this equation may be rewritten

$$\ln Q = a + bt \tag{2.1}$$

so that one would simply measure the goodness of fit, as shown by $\bar{R}^2$, of this linear equation.

Unfortunately, this simple approach is quite unsatisfactory, for reasons that become clear if Figure 2.1 is considered.

---

[14] By way of contrast, Hacche did not consider the stylized facts as approximations to behaviour within periods, but rather as referring to the whole of the period for which data are available.

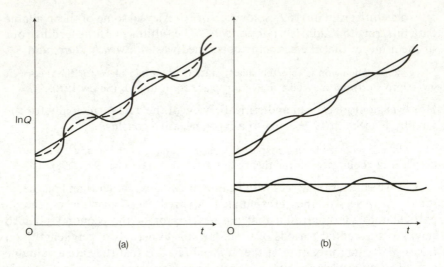

Fig. 2.1 Testing for steady growth

In Figure 2.1(a), two possible paths of output are compared, both of which consist of regular cycles about a linear logarithmic trend, similar to equation (2.1). Both paths could then be regarded as equally consistent with the 'stylized fact' of a constant rate of growth of capacity output, but the path with the greater amplitude of cyclical fluctuation would fit the linear trend much worse (would have a much lower $\bar{R}^2$). In Figure 2.1(b), another two possible paths of output are compared, both of which, again, consist of regular cycles about linear logarithmic trends. In this case, the amplitudes of the cyclical fluctuations are the same, but one path has a steeply rising trend and the other a horizontal trend. Again, both paths could be regarded as equally consistent with the 'stylized fact' of a constant rate of growth of capacity output, but the path with the horizontal trend would have a much lower $\bar{R}^2$ (indeed, zero) than the path with the steeply rising trend.

We need a test that is not open to the above objections. One such, which is adopted here, is to compare the goodness of fit of (2.1) with the goodness of fit of the same equation with the addition of one higher power of t on the right-hand side, [15] viz.

$$\ln Q = a + bt + ct^2 \tag{2.2}$$

We want to know whether the addition of this extra term, ct^2, improves the fit significantly. The extra term allows for the possibility of an accelerating or decelerating trend rate of growth. In the four cases illustrated in Figure 2.1, this term would not be significant, and so we would reach the correct

[15] Why only *one* higher power? We are abstracting from cyclical fluctuations, and the addition of further terms, which could significantly improve the fit, would bring them in.

conclusion that all four cases were equally consistent with a constant rate of growth of capacity output.

The same test can be used to determine whether the rate of growth of labour input, L, has been constant; and essentially the same test can be used to test whether the trend rates of growth of the investment ratio, s, and the share of wages, λ, have been zero. In the latter two cases we test to see whether the term bt in (2.1) is significant, with s or λ on the left-hand side instead of $\ln Q$.

In performing these tests I use two different, but closely related, measures. First, I see whether the coefficient of t^2 (for $\ln Q$ and $\ln L$), or of t (for s and λ), is significantly different from zero at the 0.05 and 0.01 levels of significance. The results of this measure are presented in Table 2.1.

Table 2.1   Significance of higher power of t in equations fitted to annual data for periods

	Dependent variable			
	$\ln Q$	$\ln L$	s	λ
Not significant at 0.05 level	12	13	14	5
Significant at 0.05, but not at 0.01 level	3	3	3	2
Significant at 0.01 level	4	3	2	5
Total no. of periods considered	19	19	19	12

Note
The equations for $\ln Q$ and $\ln L$ were similar to (2.2), while those for s and λ were similar to (2.1). They were fitted to the 19 periods for the UK, the USA, and Japan given the Table SA I, except for λ, for which data for only 12 periods were available (i.e. excluding years before 1929 for the USA, and before 1952 for Japan). The first and second columns in the table show the number of periods for which the coefficient of t^2 was not significantly different from 0 at the levels of the significance indicated. The third and fourth show the number of periods for which the coefficient of t was not significantly different from 0 at the levels of significance indicated. Lack of significance in the first two columns roughly speaking shows that constant exponential growth is a not significantly worse explanation than accelerating or decelerating exponential growth, while in the third and fourth columns it shows that zero growth is not significantly worse explanation than some growth, or decline. In short, lack of significance supports the 'stylized facts'.

Second, I measure the reduction in the average error with which equation (2.2) explains $\ln Q$ or $\ln L$ as compared with equation (2.1). This is simply the difference between the standard errors of the two equations. Likewise, for s and λ, I give the difference between the standard error of equation (2.1) (with s or λ on the left-hand side instead of $\ln Q$) and the standard deviations of s and λ. The results of this measure are given in Table 2.2. The meaning of the figures in these tables is explained in the notes accompanying them.

Table 2.2   Increases in the standard errors of equations fitted to annual data for periods explaining variables shown resulting from dropping higher powers of t from the equation

	$\ln Q$	$\ln L$	s	λ
Increases less than 0.001	4	8	13	4
Increases greater than 0.001 and less than 0.005	7	7	4	4
Increases greater than 0.005 and less than 0.01	4	2	1	2
Increases greater than 0.01	4	2	1	2
Total no. of periods considered	19	19	19	12

Note
The periods were as in Table 2.1. The first two columns result from a comparison of an equation like (2.2) with one like (2.1). For example, for the USA for 1948–73, the standard error of estimate of (2.2) was 0.03510 (so that, roughly speaking, the average discrepancy between the level of Q predicted by the equation for each year and the actual level was 3.51% of the level), while the standard error of estimate of (2.1) (i.e. having dropped t^2 from (2.2)) was 0.03615. The increase in the standard error was then 0.00105, so that this period was one of the seven for which the increase was greater than 0.001 and less than 0.005 shown in the first column of the table. For the second two columns, equations like (2.1) were fitted to s or λ, and their standard errors of estimate were compared with the standard deviations of s or λ, the latter being a measure of the average deviation of s or λ from a constant value equal to their respective means. Little increase in the standard error as a result of dropping t^2 (in the first two columns) or t (in the second two) supports the 'stylized facts'.

From Table 2.1 it can be seen that, in about two-thirds of the periods considered,[16] a constant exponential trend of output or employment was not significantly worse, at the 0.05 per cent level, than an accelerating or decelerating trend. Likewise, in more than two-thirds of the periods a zero trend in s was not significantly worse than a constant upward or downward exponential trend. For these three variables *individually considered*, the 'stylized facts' were rather a good description of the actuality. For the share of wages, λ, however, this was much less the case. The data here are dominated by observations for the UK—eight out of the twelve periods. For the USA and Japan there were only two periods each. In the case of the UK there was an appreciable upward trend in λ for most of the years considered, and especially in the periods 1873–1901, 1913–24, and 1937–51, two of which included wars. For the USA, annual data were available only from 1929 onwards, and the period of slump and war, 1929–48, was significantly better fitted by a falling linear trend than by a horizontal line. In the period 1948–73, however, there was no significant gain to be made as compared with a horizontal line. In Japan, the initial postwar years 1952–61 showed a significant fall in λ, but from 1961 to 1973 this ceased to be significant.

[16] The periods considered end in 1973. This is a reflection of the way in which the empirical work was undertaken (see Section 16.1 below), but in any case the very disturbed conditions following that year would make any trends uncertain.

In Table 2.1, I used the 0.05 per cent level of significance as my cut-off. This is perhaps conventional, but none the less arbitrary. In Table 2.2 I focus attention on a different, but equally arbitrary, cut-off, namely, an increase in the standard error of 0.005, i.e. of approximately one-half of one per cent in the levels of Q or L, or of one-half of a percentage point in s or λ. If assuming that the 'stylized facts' are true results in errors of only this (or lesser) magnitude, I consider that the approximation is satisfactory. This test is somewhat less severe than the preceding one, since now over half of the periods satisfy it for Q, over three-quarters satisfy it for L and s, and two-thirds satisfy if for λ (when the variables are individually considered).

It is not sufficient to consider the variables individually, however. We really need to know whether the 'stylized facts' are a satisfactory approximation for all four of them simultaneously. Taking the stricter test of the 0.05 per cent level of significance in Table 2.1, there are only two periods that satisfy it for all four variables simultaneously: the UK 1901–13 and 1964–73. On the less strict test of 0.005 additional error in Table 2.2, four additional periods pass muster: the UK 1924–37 and 1951–64, the USA 1948–73, and Japan 1961–73. Thus six out of the twelve available periods fit the 'stylized facts' to an approximation which I at least consider reasonably good. Furthermore, of the remaining six periods, three are dominated by wars and slumps (UK 1913–24, 1937–51, and USA 1929–48), and it is unsurprising that the approximation is so much worse then.

For the remaining seven of the nineteen periods, we have no annual data for λ, and so we can only ask whether the 'stylized facts' hold for Q, L, and s simultaneously. Using the stricter 0.05 per cent probability test, three out of the seven periods pass (the USA 1889–1900 and 1913–29, and Japan 1887–99). Using the less strict 0.005 increase in standard error test, one more period passes (the USA 1900–13).

Looking at it for each of our countries in turn, it is clear that the 'stylized facts' are a good approximation for the whole eighty-odd years of US experience, when it is subdivided into the periods considered here, and provided we put aside the nineteen years from 1929 to 1948. This is true not only for our three major variables required to explain growth (Q, L, and s), but probably also for the share of wages λ. For the USA we can test annual data for λ only back to 1929, but we have rough period averages back to 1889, and these do not suggest any pronounced trend, such as exists for the UK.

For the UK, the 'stylized facts' for all four of our variables could be said to hold reasonably well for the interwar and post-Second World War years, as well as for the years just before the First World War, 1901–13. In these years there was, admittedly, some upward trend in λ (as also in s in 1951–64), but it was not so marked as to render the assumption of constancy very erroneous. For the nineteenth-century periods, however, the 'stylized facts' are not such a good approximation.

For Japan, the 'stylized facts' are really a reasonably good approximation only for the period 1961–73. Before the Second World War, the Japanese economy was subject to major cycles of investment and growth which I have not succeeded in eliminating through my choice of periods. In fact, the 'stylized facts' form better approximations to longer periods then. Thus the three variables Q, L, and s (λ is not available) pass both my tests for 1887–1911 and 1911–36, regarded as two periods instead of the four into which I split them above. In 1951–61 the Japanese economy was still adjusting to a large influx of labour from demobilization and repatriation which was probably responsible for the big fall in the share of wages, and the big rise in the share of investment, in that period.

To sum up, in my view this evidence is enough to make one take the 'stylized facts' seriously as approximate descriptions of growth experience over periods that vary from about ten to about thirty years. A theory of growth which, in order to simplify matters, assumed that countries' growth over such periods could be described by the 'stylized facts' would have a good basis in past experience.[17] It is *not* claimed, however, that the evidence supports the view that the 'stylized facts' are good descriptions of growth over much longer periods than these. The two world wars disrupted growth behaviour in the past, and, as we shall see in Chapter 10, there is evidence not only that g_L and s changed significantly between periods, thus causing changes in g, but also that significant changes in the relationship between these three variables occurred.

A visual impression of the extent to which the data fit the 'stylized facts', as well as the difference between periods, can be gained from Figures 2.2–2.4. Within each of the periods, which are marked off by vertical lines, the trends of Q and L are roughly constant, but change from one period to the next. By contrast with the strong trends in Q and L, λ and s change little. However, in the very disturbed 1930s and 1940s in the USA and in the two world wars in the UK, the trends are swamped by large fluctuations. The First World War boom in Japan, the earthquake of 1923 (which made s negative), and the war boom of the late 1930s are also apparent. Figure 2.4 shows the very remarkable squeeze of capitalist's take-out which has occurred for the UK. Here there has been a trend increase in λ, as well as a rise in s since the Second World War. In Japan, prewar annual estimates of λ are lacking, but a similar squeeze almost certainly occurred, in contrast to the USA. This is further discussed in Chapter 11.

2.5 Productivity growth and quality-adjusted employment

Output per man is the most commonly used measure of labour productivity. Where data permit, output per man-hour is also frequently used, and is

---

[17] About two-thirds of the weight in the weighted regressions in Chapter 10 is given to periods for which the 'stylized facts' are a reasonably good description.

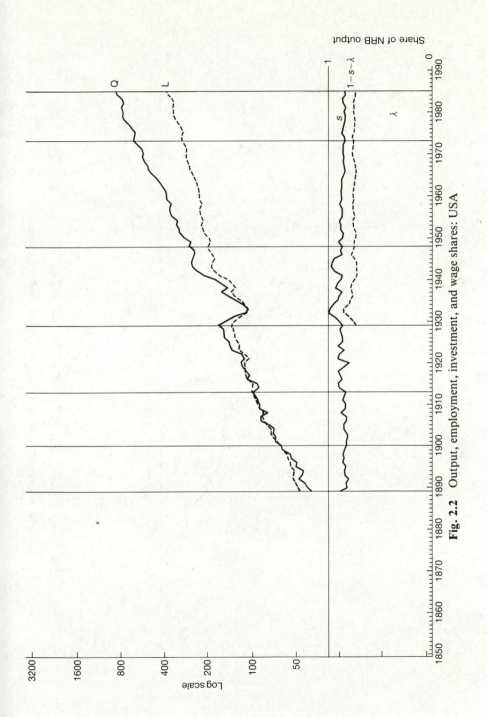

Fig. 2.2 Output, employment, investment, and wage shares: USA

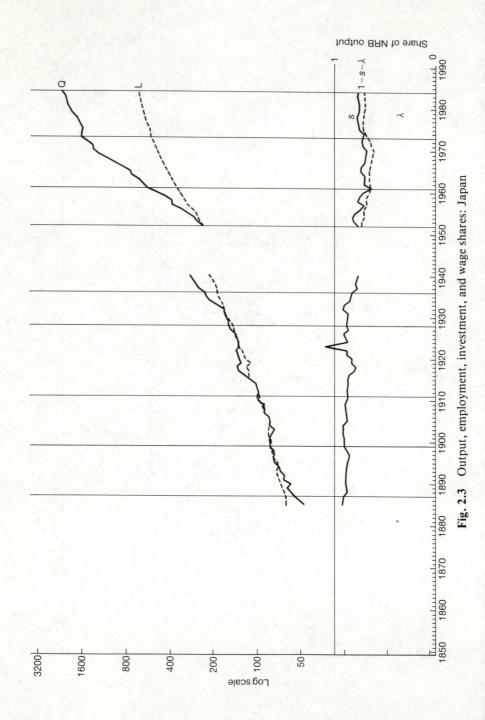

Fig. 2.3 Output, employment, investment, and wage shares: Japan

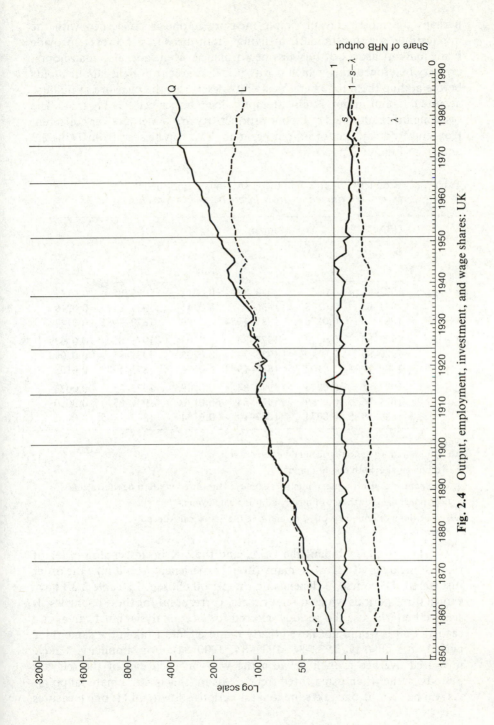

Fig. 2.4 Output, employment, investment, and wage shares: UK

perhaps the most relevant simple measure if one is concerned with the implications for the standard of living. Both measures, however, provide inadequate measures of business performance. Men, and also man-hours, are very heterogeneous, which is why it is desirable to weight labour inputs before adding them together. As already described, the measure of quality-adjusted labour input is an attempt, albeit imperfect, to do that. The resulting index numbers of labour productivity are sometimes very different from the crude indexes of output per man. This can be seen from Table 2.3 and from Figures 2.5–2.7.

Table 2.3 Productivity growth in the USA, Japan, and the UK
(Average exponential growth rate between years shown)

	USA		Japan		UK	
	Period	Growth rate	Period	Growth rate	Period	Growth rate
$g - g_N$	1973–85	0.0057	1973–84	0.0211	1973–85	0.0139
	1929–85	0.0178	1936–84	0.0341	1937–85	0.0219
	1889–1985	0.0176	1887–1984	0.0289	1873–1985	0.0147
$g - g_L$	1973–85	0.0022	1973–84	0.0103	1973–85	0.0162
	1929–85	0.0110	1936–84	0.0205	1937–85	0.0209
	1889–1985	0.0102	1887–1984	0.0136	1873–1985	0.0105
$g_L - g_N$	1973–85	0.0036	1973–84	0.0108	1973–85	−0.0023
	1929–85	0.0069	1936–84	0.0136	1937–85	0.0010
	1889–1985	0.0074	1887–1984	0.0154	1873–1985	0.0042

Notes

All figures are for the non-residential business sector.

g = exponential growth rate of output.

g_N = exponential growth rate of numbers employed measured in full-time equivalents.

g_L = exponential growth rate of quality-adjusted employment.

Derived from index numbers of Q, N, and L in the Statistical Appendix.

If asked to place Japan, the USA, and the UK in descending order of rates of productivity growth, many (in my experience) would take the order just stated. Of course, it depends on the period chosen. In Table 2.3 I have shown three periods which do not exactly correspond for these countries. It seemed better to use the periods selected for later analysis, but I can assure readers that it would not have greatly mattered had I taken the same three periods for all (say, 1973–84, 1937–84, 1900–84). For simplicity, I have measured average growth between the years at each end of the relevant periods, rather than using fitted trends. Again, this is not a material point. As will be seen, if one takes the longest periods shown, and if one measures

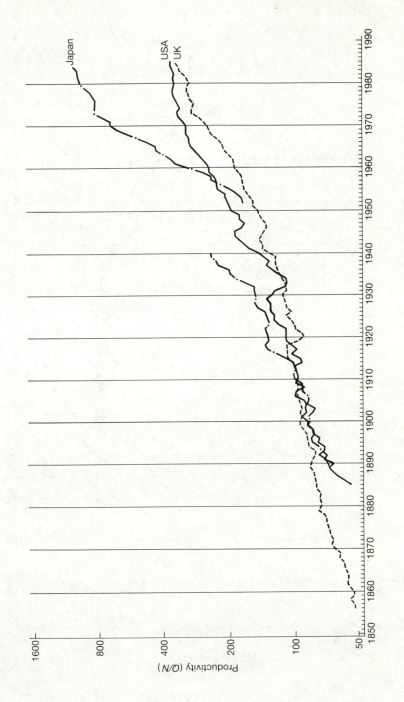

Fig. 2.5 Productivity: Q/N, USA, Japan, and UK (1913 = 100)

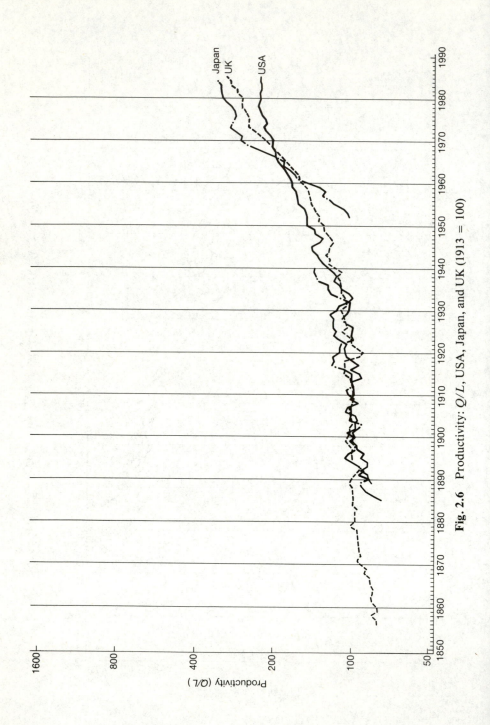

Fig. 2.6 Productivity: Q/L, USA, Japan, and UK (1913 = 100)

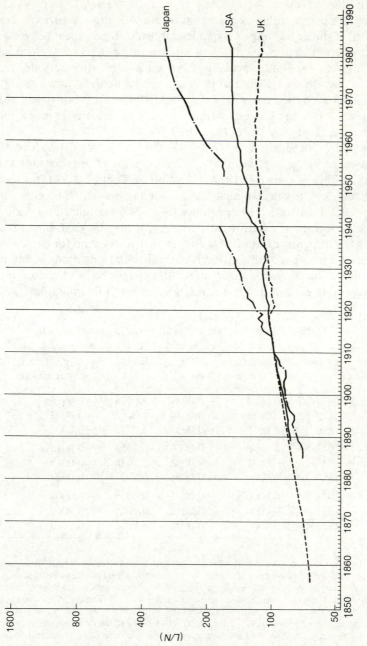

Fig. 2.7 *L/N*:USA, Japan, and UK (1913 = 100)

productivity by ouput per full-time equivalent worker (N), and its rate of growth by $g - g_N$, then Japan's rate of growth is easily the highest, and that of the USA comfortably exceeds that of the UK, thus confirming common opinion. If, however, one uses quality-adjusted employment (L) rather than full-time equivalent workers, and so measures the rate of productivity growth by $g - g_L$, and especially if one considers other periods, common opinion may be upset. Both in the most recent periods, and in the periods starting between the two world wars, the UK's rate of productivity growth is the highest. For the longest period, Japan's superiority is much reduced, and the UK is slightly better than the USA.

The clear implication is that the rate of quality improvement of employment (i.e. $g_L - g_N$) for the UK has been lower than that for Japan or the USA. This is shown in the last section of Table 2.3 and in Figure 2.7, and Table 2.4 provides an analysis of four factors which together account for $g_L - g_N$. Their relative importance depends on country and period, but, taking the longest period for each country, it may be seen that, for Japan, $g_L - g_N$ is a little more than 1 per cent per year faster than for the UK. About 0.8 per cent per year of this difference is due to the gain made in Japan from the reallocation of workers from agriculture to the rest of the economy, and virtually all the rest is due to the much greater fall in annual hours worked

Table 2.4   Analysis of difference between g_L and g_N
(Average exponential growth rates between years shown)

Country	Period	Reallocation of labour	Hours, etc.	Education	Age & sex composition	Total $g_L - g_N$
USA	1973–85	0.0004	– 0.0025	0.0074	– 0.0016	0.0036
	1929–85	0.0036	– 0.0020	0.0065	– 0.0013	0.0069
	1889–1985	0.0038	– 0.0009	0.0052	– 0.0007	0.0074
Japan	1973–84	0.0040	0.0000	0.0053	0.0015	0.0108
	1936–84	0.0071	0.0012	0.0038	0.0015	0.0136
	1887–1984	0.0080	0.0006	0.0061	0.0007	0.0154
UK	1973–85	0.0000	– 0.0071	0.0050	– 0.0002	– 0.0023
	1937–85	0.0000	– 0.0052	0.0055	0.0007	0.0010
	1873–1985	0.0000	– 0.0025	0.0052	0.0015	0.0042

Note
All the figures are based on index numbers in the Statistical Appendix, which also explains their meaning and gives sources. All refer to the non-residential business sector. Briefly, 'Reallocation of labour' refers mainly to the gain resulting from the transfer of labour from agriculture (and also self-employment in some periods) to other parts of the business sector; 'Hours etc.' refers to changes in full-time workers' annual hours worked, offset to some extent by assumed productivity effects; 'Education' refers to gains made when the composition of employment shifts towards workers with longer periods of schooling, etc.; and 'Age and sex composition' refers to the effects of changes in age and sex composition of employment. These four factors are all assumed to be multiplicative, so that their exponential growth rates can be added together to give the total difference between g_L and g_N.

in the UK than in Japan. The USA's gain from reallocation was substantial, but less than half of Japan's, and the fall in hours worked was not nearly so great as in the UK, although greater than in Japan (where annual hours are estimated to have risen[18]). The upshot is that $g_L - g_N$ was greatest in Japan and least in the UK, with the USA in between. It is these differences in labour quality growth that account for most of the long-term differences in the crude measure of labour productivity growth, $g - g_N$.

This is an important, and perhaps surprising, finding. It is, admittedly, uncertain, since the estimates of quality change are uncertain. Nevertheless, it encourages me to venture the bold hypothesis in later chapters (10 and 11) that fundamentally the same growth equation can be used to explain growth in these three countries—and I have added, for good measure, observations for seven other countries for which data are available after the Second World War. At a more mundane level, too, this is encouraging for a British writer. One is so used to evidence of Britain's poor growth performance that at least two cheers can be given for evidence showing that on one, important, measure of that performance it is close to average. Others, notably Kaldor (1966),[19] have made the main point about the much smaller scope for transferring labour from agriculture in Britain than elsewhere, owing to our early start. But the implication that business performance in this country stands comparison with that in the USA and even Japan is not widely recognized.

As a final point, it should be noted that, just as there are two ways of measuring labour productivity growth, so also there are two ways of measuring increases in the cost of labour. In the sequel, g_w stands for the rate of growth of wages per *quality-adjusted* unit of labour. It is more usual to find statistics of the rate of growth of average earnings per worker, without any quality adjustment. Sometimes, earnings per full-time worker, or full-time equivalent worker, are given, which is an improvement. Even so, the latter will diverge from the measure used here by $g_L - g_N$ which, as we have just seen, can be substantial. In my view, growth in the real cost of labour is much better measured by g_w than by growth in real earnings per worker, and the former is generally much below the latter.

2.6   The growth of employment

The preceding section has shown the importance of non-demographic factors, notably the transfer of labour from agriculture and self-employ-

[18] Reliable estimates of hours worked in Japan are available only for the years since the Second World War. I have *assumed* no change in hours worked before that. While this is a guess, it accords with the opinion expressed by Minami and Ono (1979, 210). See also the Statistical Appendix. As for the USA and the UK (see p.44), any reduction in very long hours of work (which may well have occurred) would have been more or less fully offset by efficiency gains without affecting $g_L - g_N$.

[19] Kaldor subsequently modified his views, however; see p.346.

ment to the rest of the economy and education, in determining the rate of growth of quality-adjusted employment, g_L. In the rest of this book I mostly neglect the factors determining g_L for the economy as a whole, and treat them as if they were exogenous. It is clear, however, that both the transfer of labour and investment in education are influenced by economic factors, and even demographic changes are too. The rate of growth of the economy undoubtedly affects g_L, just as g_L affects it, and I am here concerned with long-term effects and am abstracting from the short-term cyclical effect of output on employment. The assumption that g_L is exogenous can be justified only by lack of space and the need to tackle one thing at a time. By way of making some amends, we may now briefly consider some of the interrelations involved, before sweeping them back again under the carpet.

The relation between real wage rates and the supply of labour has been much studied, and a very useful survey of both theories and empirical studies is provided by Killingsworth (1983). While no firm conclusions can be drawn, it seems probable that the gross elasticity of supply (i.e. including both income and substitution effects) is absolutely small and quite possibly negative for males, although appreciably larger and positive for females. The results are derived from both cross-section and time-series studies, often of particular groups, among whom there may well be appreciable differences of behaviour. In both the USA and the UK there has been a large fall in manual hours worked per full-time worker over the last hundred years or so, accompanied by a very big increase in real wage rates, and this does support the idea of a negative elasticity, at least for males who have dominated the labour force. Admittedly, the real financial wealth of workers has also risen over this period, which could provide an alternative explanation for the fall in hours. However, wealth remains very unequally distributed, and the absolute increase in income owing to increased wealth has probably been small in comparison with the increase in real wages for most workers. Hence I do not give much weight to this alternative. Over the same period there has been a remarkable increase in female participation in the labour force, which confirms the idea of a positive elasticity there, although to some extent the changes probably resulted from different attitudes towards women's work arising, for example, from experience during the First and Second World Wars.

Since faster growth of output, with g_L constant, implies equally faster growth of real wage rates if the share of labour is to remain constant, the question then arises as to what effect this is likely to have on g_L. The answer may be, rather little, since the tendency for male hours worked to rise more slowly may be more or less counterbalanced by the tendency for female hours worked to rise faster. Admittedly, a growing proportion of women in the labour force should strengthen the latter in relation to the former, but the positive elasticity for women could itself become smaller as the fraction of women employed increases. Women may then become more like men.

Does faster growth of output affect the rate of investment in human capital? In so far as faster growth is accompanied by a higher rate of return to material investment, as one would normally expect, the rate of investment in human capital could be expected to fall. On the other hand, faster growth in real wage rates should increase the return to investment in human capital, which could offset that. The return would increase because the cost of the investment would be reduced relative to the benefits. The cost could take the form of teachers' wages, or earnings forgone by pupils, while the benefits could be some proportionate addition to the now higher earnings possible at a future date. Here again, the net effect might be rather small.

An effect that might not be small, however, is through expenditure by central and local governments on education. It seems likely that faster growth of output, and so of tax revenues, will induce or enable governments to increase their rates of investment in education, and this does seem to have happened during the period following the Second World War, with some tendency to reverse engines as growth has slowed down since 1973.

The only demographic factor I shall venture to discuss is migration.[20] Faster growth of output by country A in relation to country B, which is accompanied by faster growth in real wage rates, must tend to increase the relative attractiveness of country A in relation to country B. If migration is unrestricted, one may therefore expect that the net flow from B to A will tend to increase, thus raising g_L in A and lowering it in B. Again, the post-Second World War experience of many Western countries seems to bear this out. However, the importance of this effect depends very much on the tightness of controls over immigration, and this has tended to increase in some countries once immigrant populations have reached appreciable magnitudes.

To sum up this very inadequate discussion, it seems likely that faster growth of output will tend to result in a faster growth of the labour force. Hence, as between g and g_L, causation flows in both directions. I hazard the guess, all the same, that the effect of g on g_L is much smaller than the reverse effect in most Western countries. It may, then, be a reasonable first approximation to neglect the former, which is what is done here.

---

[20] This is in striking contrast to the classics, who paid considerable attention to the relation between births, deaths, and real wages. For an excellent discussion see Eltis (1984).

PART II

DEMOLITION

Ah Love! could thou and I with Fate conspire
To grasp this sorry Scheme of Things entire,
    Would not we shatter it to bits—and then
    Re-mould it nearer to the Heart's Desire!
    Omar Khayyam: done into English by Edward Fitzgerald

3

ORTHODOX GROWTH THEORIES

3.1 Introduction

The theories of economic growth that are labelled 'orthodox' here, and are briefly described in this chapter, are not accepted by all, or even nearly all, economists. Nevertheless, they are probably the ones that command most allegiance. They are the theories that have been developed by such well-known economists as Johansen, Meade, Phelps, Samuelson, Solow, Swan, Tobin, von Weizsäcker, and Yaari, building on earlier ideas coming from Domar, Harrod, Hicks, and Robinson. They have been applied in empirical studies to determine the magnitudes of different factors explaining economic growth, or in various analyses of productivity growth, by, for example, Abramovitz, Denison, Kendrick, Salter, and Solow. They have found their way into the textbooks on economic theory (see Section 3.2) and have formed the basis for innumerable doctoral theses. As one of the main practical inferences that have been drawn from their findings is that technical progress is a very important cause of productivity growth in the long run, while capital expenditure (which we shall hereafter call 'investment' for short) is relatively minor (and the *share* of investment in total national expenditure very unimportant in the long run), they may well have been partly responsible for the emphasis given to higher education, research and development expenditure, and 'technology-intensive' industries in many countries in the 1960s, which still lingers on here and there.

In describing and criticizing these theories, I shall be brief. My purpose is not to give a full exposition, or a survey of even the main work. Interested readers can find these elsewhere.[1] Rather, my aim is merely to remind readers of some of the main ideas underlying the theories, and to state objections to these. I try to avoid minor issues. Reality is very complex, and no useful theory can encompass it all. If a theory provides a good starting

---

[1] For a brief account which is still much fuller than that given here, see Solow (1970). For a longer exposition (which, however, makes no mention of vintage theory), see Meade (1968). Other good expositions including unorthodox theories are in Dixit (1976), Eltis (1973), Jones (1975), Hacche (1979), and Hamberg (1971). A historical survey with emphasis on the role of technical change is Heertje (1977). For a superb survey, placing the theory in the context of other theories, see Hahn and Matthews (1964), with further developments surveyed by Britto (1973). For readings, including some on other theories, see Hahn (1971), Sen (1970), and Stiglitz and Uzawa (1969).

point for the analysis of real problems, and if its main conclusions are at least approximately fulfilled in reality, it is a very good theory. It is because orthodox growth theory fails on both these counts that I want to demolish it. I do *not* wish to attack it because, for example, it makes use (in the most common versions) of aggregative concepts such as capital stock, labour force, or total output. Such concepts are doubtless imperfect, but they may nevertheless form a useful basis for theory. My criticisms are, I believe, more fundamental.

3.2 Which growth theory is orthodox?

In the sequel, what is generally known as neoclassical growth theory, and especially the one-sector growth model developed by Meade (1961), Solow (1956), Swan (1956), and others, is called 'orthodox'. One should not waste time on semantic issues, but it is of some importance to know what is 'orthodox'. Whatever it is must influence how succeeding generations of students of economics view the world about them, and must also shape, at least to some extent, those policies that aim to improve the rate of economic growth. Economic theory does not, and should not, exist in a vacuum. Out of all the theories born in the late 1950s and 1960s, when growth was at the centre of the profession's attention, why can one claim that it is the neoclassical theory that has triumphantly matured to orthodoxy?

One stringent test is the ability to survive in textbooks for students. Their writers are forced to select from the welter of theories available, and what they select is what most students learn. I have, accordingly, examined nine North American or British textbooks of macroeconomics,[2] two books of readings in macroeconomics,[3] and two particularly popular general economics textbooks,[4] all published at varying dates ranging from 1967 to 1984, and all devoting at least a chapter (or several readings) to growth. One conceptual apparatus of which all make use is the production function with total output dependent on inputs of capital and labour, with diminishing returns to each of these factors, and with technical progress shifting the function through time. This is the centrepiece of the neoclassical theory. Six of these books (and four out of the five most recently published) refer to 'growth accounting', which is based on this production function, and about the same number to the view that, in the long run, the rate of growth equals the rate of growth of the labour force plus the rate of technical progress, and is independent of the (constant) ratio of investment to output. Most

---

[2] Allen (1967), Brunhild and Burton (1974), Wonnacott (1974), Ott, Ott, and Yoo (1975), Zahn (1975), Dornbusch and Fischer (1978), Branson (1979), P. E. Kennedy (1979), Barro (1984).

[3] Mueller (1971), Surrey (1976).

[4] Samuelson (1973), Begg, Fischer, and Dornbusch (1984).

discuss whether technical progress is embodied or not, and some refer to vintage theories. The only other theories of growth that are discussed at any length in more than one book are the classical theories of Smith, Malthus, and Ricardo, the Harrod–Domar theories (these are discussed in all the earlier books, but more recently have begun to be ignored), and Kaldor's theories.

Vintage theories are discussed further below as a (rather complicated) modification of orthodox theory. They do not point to any fundamentally different conclusions. Classical theories, while of great interest in themselves, have been superseded by modern theories of growth and will not be further considered here.[5] The main interest of the Harrod–Domar theories lies in their position in the history of economic thought. They started from a dynamized version of the accounting identity between savings and investment, which opened up a discussion of stability. Our concern here is with long-term economic growth, and, since their theories did little to explain that, they are not further discussed. Kaldor's theories are briefly considered later. Here we may remark that they are discussed only in Allen (1967), Mueller (1971), and Samuelson (1973), and not in any of the later works.[6]

In addition to this textbook test, we can apply the test of empirical application. If a theory is successful, it will be used to explain historical growth and, possibly, to predict future growth. A theory that cannot be, or is not, used for either of these purposes is ultimately valueless, if we regard economics as having any pretensions to being a science. The main empirical application of orthodox theory to explain historical growth has been in growth accounting, which has not only been frequently done,[7] but has also led to some important conclusions which we examine further below. Orthodox growth theory has been less often used for prediction. Most econometric models are concerned with the short run, and for that purpose it is perhaps sufficient to rely, as they mostly have done, on simple projections of labour productivity. However, recently attention has been given to modelling supply more carefully; this has been done using aggregate production functions, and, in the case of the OECD's macroeconomic model, constant returns to scale and Harrod-neutral

---

[5] See Eltis (1984), for a lucid and fascinating analysis of these theories which includes Quesnay and Marx as well as Smith, Malthus, and Ricardo.

[6] Ott, Ott, and Yoo (1975) and Branson (1979) refer to Kaldor's theory of *saving*, but not to his theories of *growth*.

[7] The leading exponent is E. F. Denison (Denison, 1962, 1974, 1979, 1985; Denison with Poullier 1967; Denison and Chung 1976). Other important works are: the earlier studies of Fabricant (1954), Abramovitz (1956), and Solow (1957), all emphasizing the great importance of technical progress; the historical studies of France by Carré, Dubois, and Malinvaud (1976), of Japan by Ohkawa and Rosovsky (1973), and of the UK by Matthews, Feinstein, and Odling-Smee (1982); and see also the survey by Kennedy and Thirlwall (1972).

technical progress have been explicitly assumed (see Helliwell *et al.* 1986). By comparison with this, I know of no substantial body of empirical work on growth which is based on any other modern theory.

Many writers have questioned the assumptions underlying orthodox growth theory. Thus, three of the economists who perhaps did most to launch the theory initially—Meade, Solow, and Swan—all expressed their doubts about it. Nevertheless, no rival theory has yet appeared to take its place, and orthodoxy marches triumphantly on. I shall briefly outline its structure (which must be familiar to most readers) before criticizing it. While I think these criticisms should be fatal, I suspect their victim will survive until some better theory has appeared. The success of this chapter may, therefore, depend on that of later chapters.

3.3   A sketch of orthodox growth theory

The most important characteristic of orthodox theory which distinguishes it from other theories of economic growth, and in particular from the theory put forward in this volume, is the assumption that technical progress is independent of investment. Both production function and vintage theories share this assumption.

The process of economic growth is pictured as follows. At any given time, entrepreneurs are aware of a given technology. This has been described as a 'book of blueprints' (Robinson 1962, 116), and consists of knowledge of a whole set of techniques for producing output. In the light of their economic circumstances (prices, existing stocks of land, labour, and capital, market situation, etc.), entrepreneurs select the techniques they will use to produce outputs. As time passes, three main changes occur.

First, the labour force may change. In the simplest theories, labour is homogeneous, so changes in the labour force consist simply in an increase or decrease in numbers. It is perfectly possible, however, to allow for changes in the quality of the labour force, at least approximately, and still retain the highly convenient simplification of a single magnitude, L, to represent it. This can be done by the well-known device of weighting the quantities of different types of labour in proportion to their marginal products before adding them up (see Chapter 2). Each unit, appropriately weighted, has then the same (marginal) productive power, and so the total number of all weighted units is rendered homogeneous in at least that respect. By this means, the theory can include the effects on production of such things as changes in the age and sex composition of the labour force, or changes in the amount of education or training it has received. Denison is the leading exponent of this method.

Second, the quantities of different capital goods available may change as a result of two processes: on the one hand, new capital goods are produced;

on the other, old capital goods are consumed, or partly consumed. 'Capital goods' include stocks of finished and semi-finished goods and raw materials, as well as things like machines, vehicles, buildings, and construction work generally. They do *not*, however, include 'blueprints' or 'knowledge'. Just as it is highly convenient to combine different types of labour together so as to form a single number L, standing for the whole of the labour force, so it is convenient to form a single number K to stand for all capital goods taken together. It would seem that the best way to do this, in principle, would be to weight the quantity of each type of capital good in proportion to its marginal product, just as for labour. Surprisingly, and despite statements to the contrary, no one (so far as I know) has yet done this, even approximately. We return to this below, as the failure is an important criticism of empirical applications of orthodox growth theory, as well as a serious mistake in many expositions of the theory itself. As it is not, however, our immediate concern, we shall simply assume for the present that the weighting has been correctly done, in those cases where a total K is required.

The third main change to occur is in technology. More techniques become available, from which entrepreneurs select those which, in their circumstances, yield higher outputs for given inputs, or else lower inputs for given outputs, or some combination of these. The orthodox theory does not itself seek to explain why or how these new techniques become available: the process is exogenous to the economic system so far as the theory is concerned. There is a considerable literature on the subject, but the assumption of exogeneity has remained intact—not surprisingly, since changing it would profoundly alter the theory and its main conclusions, as we shall presently see. The implication is that technical progress cannot be appreciably speeded up, or slowed down, as the result of economic activity and, notably, as a result of increasing or reducing any kind of investment expenditure.

In principle, a fourth change is possible, namely, in the quantity of land available. This could be due to discoveries, or reclamation from the sea, or from the desert, or from clearing forests. While some theorists (notably Meade) keep land at least near the forefront of the exposition, others are inclined to forget about it, perhaps because changes in the quantity of land for the reasons mentioned are nowadays generally small, and (perhaps apart from discoveries) could in principle be treated as improvements to an already existing quantity of land, and so as an increase in capital. I shall continue to remind readers of the existence of land in what follows, although Chapter 1 explained how it could be assimilated to capital, so as to leave one with a two-factor theory of economic growth.

The simplest, and so most widely used, orthodox theory employs the following aggregate production function:

$$Q = f(K, L, A, t). \tag{3.1}$$

Here, Q is total real output or income, K is the total real capital stock, L is the total labour force employed, A is the total land used, and t is time. Q, K, L, and A must all be interpreted as some sort of index numbers which combine heterogeneous quantities by suitable weights in the manner just described. Increases in K, L, A, or t each increase Q. The increase that results purely from the passage of time, K, L, and A all being constant, is due to technical progress.

An apparent advantage of (3.1) is that it explains both the *level* of output at any given time and *changes* in that level from one time to another. I question this quite staggering claim below.

Let us now consider how the theory explains the 'stylized facts' of growth, or 'equilibrium growth' as we call it for short. In terms of that theory, these facts require that a constant rate of growth of real output or income, g, should be accompanied by:

1. a constant ratio of capital to output, K/Q, which implies that the growth rate of the capital stock, g_K, is the same as that of output, g;
2. a constant rate of return to investment, which I shall interpret here (as is usual) as a constant marginal product of capital, $\partial Q/\partial K$;
3. a constant rate of growth of the labour force, g_L, which, together with the assumption of a constant rate of growth of output, g, implies that the rate of growth of labour productivity, $g - g_L$, is constant;
4. constant shares of factor incomes, which, if we ignore land (as is frequently done), means that total output is divided in a constant ratio between labour and capital, and implies, given 3, that the rate of growth of wages rates, g_w, is equal to the rate of growth of labour productivity; i.e., $g_w = g - g_L$.

The last of these follows from the first and second, provided capital earns its marginal product (and land is ignored), for then the share of profits is $(K/Q)(\partial Q/\partial K)$, which is constant; condition 1 also implies that the ratio of investment to output is constant if, as the theory assumes, investment is dK/dt so that

$$g_K = \frac{1}{K}\frac{dK}{dt} = g = \frac{1}{Q}\frac{dQ}{dt}.$$

Then the share of investment in output is

$$\frac{1}{Q}\frac{dK}{dt} = \frac{K}{Q}\frac{1}{K}\frac{dK}{dt} = \frac{K}{Q}g,$$

which is constant.

Production function theory, for the most part, assumes that the function (3.1) is subject to constant returns to scale, so that if the quantities of capital and labour (ignoring land) were both to increase in the same proportion, say 1 per cent, then output would also increase in that proportion. This is in the absence of technical progress, and is based on the idea of reduplication (discussed further below). Since K and L are each homogeneous (and, in principle, infinitely divisible), 1 per cent more K plus 1 per cent more L yields 1 per cent more of every useful input that is already there, and should, one would think, produce 1 per cent more output. If there were economies of scale, rather more than 1 per cent extra output should result, but usually this is not assumed to be the case, since it does not fit in very easily with the assumption of perfect competition. To be consistent with that, the economies would all have to be external to the firm. This is, perhaps, unfortunate, but I do not regard it as a *major* objection to the theory. Some sort of allowance can be made for economies of scale, e.g. on Denison's lines (see p. 79 and fn. 9), as an afterthought.

Production function theory further assumes diminishing returns to the *stocks* of each factor. (This is an *additional* assumption, and does not necessarily follow from the constant-returns-to-scale assumption, as the simple function $Q = K + L$ quickly demonstrates.) This means that, for example, the higher is K/L, with given technology, the lower is $\partial Q/\partial K$, the marginal product of capital, and the higher is $\partial Q/\partial L$, the marginal product of labour.

In an economy with equilibrium growth in which labour productivity is rising, the labour force must be growing more slowly than the capital stock. The former grows at g_L and the latter (see condition 1 above) at g, and $g - g_L > 0$. It follows that the ratio of capital to labour, K/L, is rising. Yet, 2 above requires that the marginal product of capital, $\partial Q/\partial K$, should be constant, despite this rise in K/L. How is this explained by orthodox theory?

There are two possible explanations. First, technology can change in such a way that the *effective* quantity of labour grows faster than the *actual* quantity of labour. If, then, we measure the labour force in terms of efficiency units, E, instead of in natural units, we will find, says orthodox theory, that, after all, K/E does not rise, since E (in efficiency units) is growing as fast as output and the capital stock. This is known as 'Harrod-neutral technical progress'. According to Hahn and Matthews, no satisfactory explanation has been given as to why technical progress has been (at least approximately) of this kind, and it would seem to be something of a fluke.[8] It becomes even more of a fluke once one allows for land; for then the requirement is that land too, measured in efficiency units, must expand at the same rate of growth as output. It is also hard to see how one could ever test the proposition that technical progress was of this kind.

---

[8] However, C. Kennedy (1964) and others have attempted to provide an explanation, which is discussed on pp. 118–124 below.

The mere existence of equilibrium growth does not provide an independent test, since we are looking for an explanation of why $\partial Q/\partial K$ remains constant despite rising K/L (with L measured in natural units), and so we cannot adduce that fact as a demonstration that technical progress is Harrod-neutral. All this is rather unsatisfactory, and has caused at least one famous proponent of orthodox growth theory to reject this explanation as 'so special and peculiar that we shall pay no further attention to it' (Meade 1968, 98).

The second explanation, which Meade adopts, is that the production function is Cobb–Douglas, and so has an elasticity of substitution between factors of production equal to 1. It can then be written:

$$Q = Be^{mt} K^{\alpha}L^{1-\alpha} \tag{3.2}$$

where B is a constant depending on choice of units, and the term e^{mt} shows how (Hicks-neutral) technical progress expands output at the rate m when K and L are both constant. The exponents of K and L, which are α and $1 - \alpha$, sum to unity, which is in conformity with the assumption of constant returns to scale. Partially differentiating (3.2) with respect to K, we find that the marginal product of capital is

$$\frac{\partial Q}{\partial K} = \alpha Be^{mt}K^{\alpha - 1}L^{1-\alpha}$$

$$= \frac{\alpha Q}{K} \tag{3.3}$$

It is clear that, in equilibrium growth, since Q/K is constant, and since α is by assumption constant, $\partial Q/\partial K$ is also constant. This result would still hold if land were included.

It is worth noting that the Cobb–Douglas production function with technical progress as shown in (3.2) (which is Hicks-neutral) can be interpreted as showing Harrod-neutral technical progress. Thus, (3.2) can be rewritten

$$Q = BK^{\alpha}[L \exp \{mt/(1 - \alpha)\}]^{1-\alpha} \tag{3.2a}$$

so that labour, measured in efficiency units, grows at the exponential rate $g_L + m/(1 - \alpha)$, and $m/(1 - \alpha)$ is then the rate of Harrod-neutral technical progress. Orthodox growth theories imply (see below) that the equilibrium rate of growth equals the sum of the rate of growth of the labour force (in natural units) and of the rate of Harrod-neutral technical progress, which sum is simply the rate of growth of the labour force in efficiency units.

The Cobb–Douglas production function has the great virtue of simplicity. It still remains a rather special assumption, and one that some authors clearly regard as too restrictive. Nevertheless, because of its simplicity, it is undoubtedly the most widely used of any aggregate production function.

As has already been pointed out, constancy of distributive shares of profits and wages follows from conditions 1 and 2 of equilibrium growth, given that factors are paid their marginal products, so the combination of Cobb–Douglas and perfect competition is sufficient to satisfy the constant factor shares condition 4. It is worth noting, however, that the resulting theory of distribution is quite static, and that distribution (like growth in the long run; see below) is determined exogenously. No matter what happens to the ratio of investment to output, or to the rate of growth of population, or to anything else, the shares of profits and wages are unchanged so long as α is unchanged, since, for example, the share of profits is

$$\frac{K}{Q} \frac{\partial Q}{\partial K} = \alpha$$

(3.4)

(and that of wages is, naturally, $1 - \alpha$). Hence the theory has really nothing to say about what determines these shares.

An advantage of production functions that are not Cobb–Douglas is that they do permit the shares of income to depend on, for example, the ratio of capital stock to the labour force. They are still quite static—given this ratio (in efficiency units), and the other parameters of the function, the shares are determined, and do not depend upon *rates of change*. But at least the possibility of variation in response to some economic magnitudes is left open. However, to make use of these functions and still permit equilibrium growth requires swallowing the assumption of Harrod-neutral technical progress, as we have seen.

A striking conclusion of production function theories, which is a consequence of the assumptions that technical progress and labour force growth are exogenous to the system and that there are constant returns to scale, is that the equilibrium rate of growth of output is equal to the sum of the rate of growth of the labour force and the rate of Harrod-neutral technical progress. It is thus independent of the ratio of investment to output, and is exogenous to the system. We are thus left with the paradoxical conclusion that this theory of growth has nothing to say about what determines the equilibrium rate of growth.

The explanation for this result is that, although a higher ratio of investment to output increases the rate of growth initially, because it speeds up the proportionate rate of growth of the capital stock, this increases the ratio of capital to output. Hence a higher and higher investment ratio is needed merely to maintain the same proportionate rate of growth of the capital stock. With a constant investment ratio at the new higher level, the rate of growth of the capital stock must slow down until it tends to the same rate of growth as output. This is then the same as the rate of growth E of the labour force measured in efficiency units, since the rate of growth of output is a weighted average of the growth rates of the stock of capital and the stock of labour measured in efficiency units. Thus,

$$g = \frac{1}{Q} \frac{dQ}{dt} = \frac{1}{Q} \left(\frac{\partial Q}{\partial K} \frac{dK}{dt} + \frac{\partial Q}{\partial E} \frac{dE}{dt} \right)$$

$$= \frac{K}{Q} \frac{\partial Q}{\partial K} \frac{1}{K} \frac{dK}{dt} + \frac{E}{Q} \frac{\partial Q}{\partial E} \frac{1}{E} \frac{dE}{dt}$$

$$= P_K g_K + P_E g_E \tag{3.5}$$

where P_K and P_E are the output elasticities of capital and labour, and would equal their respective shares in income if each were paid its marginal product.

In equilibrium growth, we must have $g = g_K$, since K/Q is constant. Hence, in equilibrium growth,

$$g = \frac{P_E}{1 - P_K} g_E. \tag{3.6}$$

Now, with constant returns to scale, we must have

$$P_E = 1 - P_K \tag{3.7}$$

Therefore

$$g = g_E = g_L + g_T \tag{3.8}$$

In (3.8), g_E is measured in efficiency units, and so equals the sum of the labour force growth rate and the rate of Harrod-neutral technical progress, g_T.

If there are increasing returns to scale, and if the production function is Cobb–Douglas, it can be shown that it is still true that the equilibrium rate of growth is independent of the ratio of investment to output, but now it is greater than g_E by an amount that depends on the 'increasing returns multiplier'. If (again with increasing returns to scale) the production function is constant elasticity of substitution (CES), with an elasticity of substitution not equal to one, steady growth is not possible with a constant rate of Harrod-neutral technical progress (Eltis 1973, 254–62).

The result, (3.8), just established must not be interpreted to mean that capital contributes nothing to growth. The contributions of the different factors—capital, labour, and technical progress—are set out in the basic growth accounting equation which is very similar to (3.5), except that a separation is made between growth of the labour force in natural units, g_L, and the remaining growth in efficiency of labour which is due to technical progress. Thus we have

$$g = P_K g_K + P_L g_L + P_L g_T. \tag{3.9}$$

(Note that $P_L = P_E =$ output elasticity of labour.)

The assumption that factors are paid their marginal products is made, and so P_K and P_L are the shares of capital and labour in total output. It is then possible to estimate the residual, $P_L g_T$, by subtracting the known values of the contributions of capital, $P_K g_K$, and labour (in natural units),

$P_L g_L$, from the known growth rate of output. In equilibrium growth, when $g = g_K$ and all the other terms in the equation are constant, it is clear that the growth of capital *is* contributing to the growth of output. If g_L were to rise by Δg_L to a new higher level, the rate of growth of output would rise by the same amount if equilibrium growth were preserved; but that would require an increase in g_K, so that the rise in g would not *all* be due to the rise in g_L. The same is true of a rise in g_T.

Nevertheless, there are very many growth accounting studies which show that the contribution of capital to growth is smaller, and sometimes much smaller, than the contribution of technical progress. Some of the earlier studies (e.g. Solow 1957) exaggerated the contribution of technical progress by not allowing for quality improvement of the labour force, which should be included in g_L, and will be included if we weight different members of the labour force by their relative marginal products. Denison has made careful allowance for such quality improvements, and has assumed that a substantial part of growth is due to economies of scale so that the respective contributions of both capital and labour are larger on that account. He has also allowed for the effects of a number of other factors on growth, such as changes in the legal and human environment, changes in the weather, labour disputes, and changes in the intensity of demand—all of which, however, are rather minor over long periods. In his latest study of US growth, the contribution of his residual, 'advances of knowledge and n.e.c. [not elsewhere classified]', to growth was about twice as big as that of capital over the whole period surveyed, 1929–82.[9] Although Jorgenson and Griliches (1967) made estimates using the same basic methodology which appeared to show that there was virtually no residual at all for the US private domestic economy over the years 1945–65, these were subsequently (and in my opinion successfully) challenged by Denison, and Jorgenson and Griliches revised their estimates so as to show a much more substantial residual.[10]

In a recent study, Usher has pushed the argument for the importance of technical progress (as compared with investment), based on orthodox

[9] See Denison (1985, 107, Table 7-1). The figures all refer to contributions to the growth rate of national income in the non-residential business sector of the USA. For the period 1929–82, the contribution of capital is put at 0.38 percentage points per annum, and that of advances of knowledge and n.e.c. at 0.86 percentage points per annum. The contribution of economies of scale is additional to both of these and is put at 0.34 percentage points per annum. If it were allocated to capital and labour in proportion to their contributions as calculated assuming constant returns to scale, the contribution of capital would rise to 0.45 percentage points per annum. It must be said, however, that Denison's allowance for economies of scale is, at best, a well-informed guess. The relative importance of the residual is appreciably greater in the sub-period 1948–73, and far greater still in 1928–48. The residual is negative in 1973–82.

[10] Jorgenson and Griliches's original (1967) article with Denison's 'Examination' of it were reprinted in United States Department of Commerce (1972), along with Jorgenson and Griliches's 'Reply', Denison's 'Final Comments', and Jorgenson and Griliches's 'Final Reply'.

theory, to its logical (and, in my view, paradoxical) conclusion. In a chapter entitled 'No Technical Change, No Growth', he sets out to argue

that with one important qualification economic growth is entirely technological in origin, that without technical change there would be no economic growth at all, and that—as an accounting identity—the rate of economic growth is equal in the long run to the rate of (labour-embodied) technical change. I shall argue that these propositions are obvious, almost trivial, and that the source of confusion on this issue . . . is not ultimately empirical, or even economic, but linguistic. (Usher 1980a, 260–1)

By 'economic growth', Usher means growth of output or consumption *per head or per man-hour*.

Disregarding what seem to be relatively minor points in Usher's argument, the main points seem to be the following:

1. In equilibrium growth, the growth of output per worker equals g_T, the Harrod-neutral rate of technical progress.
2. If one explains the level of output in Canada (for example), and its growth, by means of a constant-returns-to-scale CES production function with labour, capital, and time as the only arguments, and if one sets it off in 1926 with the actual capital stock, and if one maintains the actual ratio of gross investment to output and the actual rate of growth of the labour force from then until 1974, but assumes zero technical progress, then 'only a few percentage points of the 549% increase in income per man-hour could be accounted for by investment' (Usher 1980a, 289).[11] The point here is that, in the absence of technical progress, diminishing returns reduce the marginal product of capital, and, as output grows more slowly, a given savings ratio provides a slower growth of capital stock.
3. Using the same assumptions and data as in point 2, when one asks the model to work out the rate of Harrod-neutral technical progress required to deliver the actual level of output achieved in 1974, one discovers that 'the rate of technical change is approximately equal to the rate of growth of output per head' (Usher 1980a, 289).

Usher's claim that the above points are 'obvious, almost trivial', is further evidence of the orthodoxy of production function theories of growth; but his references to a 'linguistic' source of confusion about the determinants of growth hits the mark. Chapter 1 demonstrated the need for new and better understanding of terms such as 'output', 'investment',

[11] In fact, the amount of growth in output per man-hour arising from investment, had there been no technical change, varies according to Usher from 104% to 3%, depending on the assumptions made about the elasticity of substitution between labour and capital, the initial share of labour in output, and the rate of depreciation (assumed to be 'by evaporation'); so the conclusion that 'only a few percentage points' could be accounted for by investment implicitly assumes something about these three parameters.

'depreciation', and 'maintenance'. Confusion over these concepts has undoubtedly led to a mistaken view of the determinants of economic growth, as I seek to demonstrate below. Before doing so, however, I must briefly review vintage theories of growth, whose main assumptions and conclusions are similar to those of the production function theories.

3.4 Vintage theories

Vintage theories are much more complicated than the simple production function theory outlined above and are accordingly much less used. They undoubtedly give additional insights into reality. Nevertheless, the fact remains that a great many of the most important conclusions of the two types of theories are the same, and they can therefore be considered, and criticized, together. This similarity results largely because both theories make the same assumptions of exogenous technical progress and perfect competition.

According to vintage theory, the assets created as a result of investment at any one time are superior to the assets created in earlier times, and inferior to those created later. Each vintage of assets gets better and better because of exogenous technical progress. In the absence of growth of the labour force (all vintage theories neglect land, so far as I am aware), growth of output occurs as labour is transferred from old to new assets, on which its marginal product is higher. Growth in the labour force is accommodated by transferring fewer workers to the new assets, while keeping more working with old assets.

Theories differ in accordance with their assumptions about the malleability of assets. At one extreme, all assets have fixed coefficients: so much labour must work with each machine to produce a fixed quantity of output, labour requirements falling in successive vintages. This is the 'clay-clay' assumption, since the coefficients are fixed initially and remain fixed for evermore. At the other extreme is 'putty-putty'. The coefficients are chosen freely, within the limits set by the given technology, when the machine is ordered. The choice will be determined by, for example, the level of real wages at that time. Subsequently, the coefficients can be varied in accordance with some production function (e.g. Cobb-Douglas). Thus, as real wages rise, the quantity of labour employed per machine will tend to fall as producers slide along their (predetermined) production functions. An intermediate possibility, perhaps thought to be the most realistic, is 'putty-clay', with coefficients freely chosen initially, but subsequently fixed.

An advantage of the 'putty-putty' assumption is that it is then possible to construct a model very similar to the production function model, and so much simpler than other vintage models. This has been done by assuming that the production functions are Cobb–Douglas (e.g. Solow 1963), which is, however, a rather restrictive assumption. If it is made, it is possible to weight each vintage of capital and add it to other vintages, and the total will behave like an aggregate Cobb–Douglas production function.

Vintage theory is not open to the objection, which can be made against production function theory, that income can grow even when investment (gross, in this case) is zero and the labour force is constant. Technical progress has to be embodied in capital goods, so that, without investment, it has no power to raise income. Vintage theory also seems quite realistic as a description of certain types of investment—that in vehicles and some kinds of machinery, for example. Here there do seem to be successive vintages, and there is a transfer of labour from old to new.

However, vintage theory does not well describe other important categories of investment, for example construction or investment in stocks and work in progress, or research and development. A road or a building can be improved, and this does not fit in with the usual clay–clay or putty–clay assumptions. Nor is it clear what labour is transferred to work with new rather than old roads or buildings or factories if improvements are being made to both; nor is the length of life of such assets something that one could set about measuring in any easily definable way. What has been the length of life of the Roman roads? Or of clearing the primeval forests? Or of draining, ditching, and working out boundaries on farm land? Vintage theory gets rid of the aggregate capital stock and replaces it by stocks of many capital goods of different vintages, and in some ways this is a step towards realism. But once one comes to consider a very large fraction of total investment, one realizes that it is not easily describable in vintage terms. It may be significant that one of the few attempts to test vintage theory directly (Gregory and James 1973) found no relation between labour productivity in factories and their date of establishment. With improvements proceeding more or less continuously to old and new alike, this is perhaps not so surprising, but it scarcely strengthens the case for vintage theory.

Vintage theories can explain the 'stylized facts' of growth, but they require the same sort of restrictive assumptions as the simpler production function theories. Just like them, vintage theories assume that technical progress is Harrod-neutral (Eltis 1973, 40), and in putty–clay models they also often take advantage of the simplifications that can be made by assuming that the *ex ante* production function is Cobb–Douglas (Hahn and Matthews 1964, 843). As with production function theory, the equilibrium growth rate equals the sum of the rate of growth of employment, g_L, and the rate of Harrod-neutral technical progress, g_T. A higher ratio of investment to output again speeds up the rate of growth temporarily, either by shifting more workers from old to new machines, thereby shortening their average life, or by increasing the average capital intensity of all machines. However, eventually the higher investment ratio is needed merely to keep the average life of machines as short as it has now become, or merely to keep new machines as capital-intensive as old ones. The increases in the rate of growth resulting from shortening average life, or from increasing average capital intensity, are then no longer possible, and growth resumes its previous rate.

Some have argued that it makes a big difference to one's view about the effect of investment on growth whether one thinks that technical progress has to be embodied in new machines (as in vintage theory) or not. However, the really crucial question is whether one thinks that the rate of technical progress depends on investment or not, as we shall see later. In vintage theory, each new vintage is superior to the older one by an amount that is assumed to be independent of the rate of investment. As Hahn and Matthews have put it,

The vintage approach does not as such involve necessarily any departure from the assumption that technical progress takes place at an externally given rate. The difference from the orthodox approach is merely that now the manna of technical progress falls only on the latest machines. This is not such a fundamental difference, so it is not surprising that vintage models can be made to yield results quite like orthodox ones. (Hahn and Matthews 1964, 837-8)[12]

So far as growth accounting is concerned, Denison has argued forcefully that his results, which are based on the disembodied technical progress model underlying equation (3.9), would normally be very little different if one were to assume, instead, that what he considered to be a reasonable proportion of technical progress had to be embodied in new investment. Very briefly, the reasons for this are that the average age of capital does not, he estimates, normally change very fast, and that, even when it does change, it does not affect the average quality of capital to the extent that simple vintage theories assume. Normally, large quality improvements will be made by only some part of new investments. These intra-marginal investments will take place every year, and fluctuations in the rate of investment will therefore affect investments for which the improvements are least marked. Simple vintage models, by contrast, assume that all investments in a given vintage carry the same amount of quality improvement.[13]

[12] Hahn and Matthews go on to point out that the vintage approach can be used with different assumptions about technical progress, as in Arrow's (1962b) and Kaldor and Mirrlees's (1962) models, which are discussed in Chapter 4.

[13] This is a very compressed summary of a complicated argument, and readers are urged to consult Denison (1964, 90–4; Denison with Poullier 1967, 144–50). Denison thought that some allowance should be made for embodiment in the immediate postwar years in the USA and some other countries, when especially high-yielding investment opportunities were available because of the lack of investment, and controls over it, during the war.

3.5   Criticisms of orthodox theories

The theories just outlined have been subjected to a barrage of criticism. In my opinion, some of this has been wide of the mark, and some that has hit the target has been as ineffective as if one were trying to stop a tank with a pea-shooter. Thus, all the criticism of capital aggregation, together with the reswitching problem, may be theoretically valid but unimportant.[14] Orthodox theories have survived, as we have seen, just as the use of other aggregates has survived, despite equally valid objections which have been made to them. Some bigger guns are needed, and readers must judge whether they are to be found in the following pages. Let me try to put the main objection in its simplest and starkest form. Those imbued with orthodoxy will not thereby be convinced, and I must plead with them to persist with the rest of the chapter and, indeed, with the rest of the book, since (to change the metaphor slightly while retaining its First World War flavour) I have to persuade them that there is a better hole to go to than the one they are in.

Figure 3.1, based on one given by Samuelson (1973, 601, Fig. 30-1), brings out the main point. The horizontal axis shows the real capital stock, K, which for the moment readers are invited to assume is measured in whatever they think is the best way. I shall later argue that it should be measured by cumulative gross investment in terms of consumption sacrificed. The vertical axis shows the rate of return, r, obtainable on marginal additions to the stock. Some will question the meaning of both K and r, but I am not concerned with these relatively minor points now. I assume, for simplicity, no change in quality-adjusted labour input throughout the analysis. As time passes, and growth proceeds, K increases from K_1 to K_2. With K_1 of capital, the marginal return is r_1. Then, says orthodox theory, in the absence of technical change, increasing capital to K_2 will shift equilibrium from P_1 to P'_2, and will bring down the rate of return to r_2. However, technical change will normally occur, shifting out the schedule of the marginal product of capital from $M_1P_1P'_2$ to M_2P_2. The rate of return could, then, either rise or fall. In the equilibrium growth case illustrated in Figure 3.1, the new equilibrium is at P_2 with the rate of return unchanged at r_1. This is the essential orthodox story.

My story is quite different. There is no downward-sloping marginal product of capital schedule. Instead, there is a schedule $r_1P_1P_2$, which is shown here as a horizontal line for simplicity, but which could in principle have other shapes, and could wander up or down. In what follows I stick to the simplest case. The line is then horizontal, because marginal returns

---

[14] It is significant that in hardly any of the macroeconomic textbooks listed on p. 70 is reswitching mentioned. It is mentioned in Samuelson (1973, 615), but that is in an appendix, and the section referring to it has a note saying 'This section may be skipped.' For an interesting discussion with some attempt to assess its likely importance, see Eltis (1973, ch. 5).

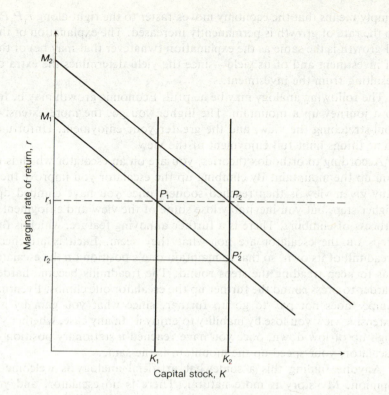

Fig. 3.1 Two ways of explaining steady growth

neither rise nor fall. Undertaking investment *means* changing economic arrangements, and when they are changed investors can see further opportunities for change of which they were unaware before, and which yield as much as their previous investments did.

The same facts are explained by both stories; that is, the economy moves from P_1 to P_2, with capital (and output) growing and the rate of return constant. However, the *implications* of the stories are different. According to the orthodox one, if the investment ratio is increased, the economy will move down the marginal productivity (MP) schedule and the rate of return will fall. Eventually, when the rate of return is again stabilized at a lower level such as r_2, the same rate of growth will be resumed. Ultimately, the rate of growth is determined by the speed at which the MP schedule shifts to the right, and that is not explained by the theory, but is exogenously determined. According to my story,[15] an increase in the investment ratio

---

[15] There is a qualification to the statement in the text required for diminishing returns to the *rate of investment* (not to the *capital stock*), which is explained later. It does not affect the essential argument, and so is neglected here.

simply means that the economy moves faster to the right along $r_1P_1P_2$, and so the rate of growth is permanently increased. The explanation of the rate of growth is the same as the explanation (whatever that may be) of the rate of investment and of its yield—since the yield determines the extra output resulting from the investment.

The following analogy may be helpful. Economic growth may be likened to a journey up a mountain. The higher you go, the more extensive and soul-stretching the view, and the greater your enjoyment. Unfortunately, some things limit full enjoyment of the view.

According to orthodox theories, you are on an escalator which is taking you up the mountain. By climbing up the escalator you improve the view. Any given view is then reached sooner, once you have climbed up to a higher step, but you inevitably lose some of the view and enjoyment in the process of climbing. There is a further annoying feature, which is that the steps on the escalator are not what they seem. Each is attached to a treadmill of its own, so that to maintain one's position on the escalator one has to keep treading the steps round. The treadmills become harder and harder to press round the further up the escalator one climbs. Eventually, it simply does not pay to go up further, since what you gain by a more extensive view you lose by inability to enjoy it. In any case, whether you are high up or low down, once you have reached a stationary position on the escalator, your speed up the mountain is the same.

Anyone finding this a somewhat artificial analogy is welcome to his opinion. My story is more natural. There is no escalator, and you are climbing up the mountain by your own exertions. While you climb, you cannot enjoy the view, so you stop every so often, but that, of course, slows your journey up. You are not sure of the best way up, and the speed you make depends not only on your exertions but also on your skill and luck in choosing the best way. You can see only a little way ahead, but, as you climb, more can be seen. There are others climbing, and you can benefit from their advice, especially if they are near you. Likewise, they benefit from yours. Different people climb up at different speeds, with those below perhaps climbing fastest if they ask those further up for advice and listen to it.

I have put more into this analogy than the main point which I set out to make. The main point is to establish whether there is or is not an escalator. The other points are ones to which we return later in the chapter and in later chapters.

3.6 The idea of reduplication

The simplest expositions of production function theories explicitly assume that 'capital' consists of homogeneous capital goods (e.g. 'corn', 'steel', 'tractors'). Implicit in this assumption is the view that actual investment in the real world can be regarded as the *reduplication* of existing assets. One is adding more to existing stocks of machines, vehicles, houses, factories, etc., and what one is adding is essentially the *same* as what is already there. For production function theories, this idea is quite fundamental. It is intimately related to the idea of exogenous technical progress, since any improvements in capital goods are attributed not to investment as such, but to this mysterious outside force.

The idea of reduplication is needed to justify three important characteristics of production functions.

First, most expositions of production function theory assume *constant returns to scale*, although some allow for increasing returns to scale. The assumption of constant returns to scale is plausible only if applied to equal proportionate changes in homogeneous inputs. Thus, it is plausible to suppose that, if twice as many men work with twice as many spades on twice the area of land, they will produce twice as much. But if we give twice as many men on twice the area of land some tractors instead of spades, no simple prediction about the change in output seems possible, even if we were told that the tractors cost twice what the spades cost.

Second, all production function theories assume that there are *diminishing returns to the capital stock*. Again, the implicit idea is that additions to the capital stock mean more of the same (more spades, not tractors instead of spades). If that were so, then indeed one could expect that the marginal product of extra spades would diminish as more were added to a given number of men working a given area. But if, when one invests more, one provides first better spades, and then tractors, and then better tractors, . . ., etc., then it is far from clear that more means worse. Does the existence of a past history of massive investment (i.e. a large capital stock) imply that investment *now* has a lower return than if there were a past history of meagre investment (i.e. a small capital stock)? Is the rate of return in Japan, say, lower than in the Sahara? Or was the rate of return in Japan in 1980 lower than it was in 1880? Or would the rate of return to *further* investment in the Sahara be lower if, before that further investment were made, a massive investment programme had been undertaken which succeeded in developing its water resources, covering it again with vegetation, changing its climate, and making the desert bloom? Put that way, diminishing returns to the capital stock cease to be so obvious.

Third, production function theories assume that technical progress shifts the function through time. This is bound up with the idea of reduplication because, in default of technical progress, reduplication is all that would occur. Hence the distinction between movements along the function and shifts of the function depends on whether reduplication is or is not occurring. In the theory put forward in later chapters, this distinction disappears. Since investment changes economic arrangements, it seldom is mere reduplication, and nothing crucial depends on whether or how far it is.

It should be clear from these three examples that the idea of investment underlying production function theories is quite different from the idea of investment as expenditure incurred in changing economic arrangements. It is only a very special kind of change, namely, the reduplication of existing capital goods, which is regarded as investment by production function theories. Since most investment is not of this kind, can one rescue the idea of reduplication in any way? The only way that I know of is the following artificial device which has been best explained by Denison.[16] Suppose the capital stock, defined in a way to be discussed below, is £K. Suppose net investment in some particular period is £ΔK. Then one *assumes* that the effect of this investment on output is *as if* each and every item in the capital stock had been increased in the proportion $\Delta K/K$. If the actual increase in output (abstracting from changes in the labour force) is greater than this (and the presumption is that it will be greater), then the difference is attributed not to investment but to technical progress, including the catching up of old-fashioned techniques with best-practice techniques (i.e. changes in the lag of application of techniques, as Denison calls it).

In this way, we can preserve constant returns to scale and diminishing returns to the capital stock. However, we have preserved these tautologically: there is no way of testing, empirically, whether they exist. They are simply assumptions, no more and no less. The question then to be answered is whether this is an illuminating and interesting way of describing reality, and whether the residual effect of 'technical progress' corresponds to anything interesting. I rather doubt it. There is no reason to suppose, for example, that technical progress, so defined, measures the effect of research and development expenditures. Indeed, I cannot think what it measures except (tautologically) the difference between an actual increase in output and a purely hypothetical increase, which is based on a set of definitions that I can see no reason for using.

So much for production function theories and reduplication. Vintage theories clearly do not assume reduplication from one vintage to the next,

[16] See, for example, the explanation of his basic method in Denison with Poullier (1967, 33–4). After first noting that he assumes constant returns to scale in this part of his calculations, and allows for increasing returns separately at a later stage, he asks, 'What fraction of the increase in real national income that would result from a 1 per cent increase in all factors of production is obtained from a 1 per cent increase in only one factor or group of factors?' He answers: 'Suppose, for example, that the factor is labour and that labour earns 80 per cent of the national income . . . A 1 per cent increase in the quantity of every type of labour in use will then be equivalent to an increase of 0.80 per cent in all types of input.' While Denison's illustration refers to labour, he applies the result to capital as well, and so he must be treating investment as if it were bringing about a uniform percentage increase in every type of capital.

and thus are more realistic than production function theories in this respect. However there is still an element of reduplication involved in each vintage. Thus, a higher rate of investment in a given year is assumed to add more 'machines' of that year's vintage than would investment at a lower rate. This, together with the fact that the improvement in 'machines' from one vintage to the next is exogenously given, means that there are still diminishing returns to the capital stock.

It might seem that, with vintage theory, there is no capital stock. However, there is just the same capital stock as production function theory has to put up with if it is to be applied: namely, some measure of cumulative investment along the lines discussed below. On a vintage view of the world, a larger capital stock in this sense at time t must imply a lower rate of return to investment at time t, at least if the capital stock has resulted from a process of more or less steady growth. The lower rate of return could be the result either of a shorter life of capital goods, or of more capital-intensive techniques being used for each vintage (or both) (see e.g. Eltis 1973, ch. 3).

3.7 No investment, no growth

Some may object that the preceding argument misinterprets production function theory. The assumptions of a homogeneous capital stock, or of investment as a uniform proportionate increase in every item in a heterogeneous capital stock, are *not* the only assumptions that can be or are made. On the contrary, it is possible to cover the case of a heterogeneous capital stock in which the different items are increased in different proportions by the usual device of weighting each increase by its marginal product. Jorgenson and Griliches (1967) are among the clearest expositers of this method. Since I shall use it in the sequel, so far as labour inputs are concerned, one may reasonably ask why it cannot be used for capital inputs as well. The answer is that it can, but that in practice, and so far as I am aware, it never has been, and certainly not by Jorgenson and Griliches. The result of using it is, inevitably, to eliminate the contribution of 'technical progress' to growth altogether.[17] Indeed, Usher's argument, just discussed,

---

[17] This is what Jorgenson and Griliches indeed claimed to have done (or nearly done—a small residual remained). However, as already noted, their demonstration was shown to be faulty by Denison (see p. 79), and their argument was not that given below. The objections that follow to the capital stock measures used by practitioners in this field apply to Jorgenson and Griliches's capital stock as well. Hence they reached the right conclusion for the wrong reasons.

In Section 6.9 below, I provide an equation, (6.10a), explaining growth which is similar in form to theirs, but with important modifications, which in my opinion protect it from objections that can be made to theirs. It is shown that the two would coincide in a static economy. Hence one could characterize their mistake as being the application of a static formula in a dynamic setting.

has to be stood on its head. His chapter should have been entitled 'No Investment, No Growth (Or Technical Progress)'.

Let us first consider how in practice changes in capital inputs are measured by those who have attempted to explain or account for economic growth. Two measures of the capital stock have been used, namely, the gross capital stock at replacement cost new, and the net capital stock. We take these in turn.

The gross capital stock at replacement cost new is generally calculated by the perpetual inventory method. An estimate is made of the average life, T, of each type of fixed capital asset, such as machinery. Gross fixed investment is estimated for T years back from the year, t, for which an estimate of the stock is required. Investment before that is deemed irrelevant, since none of the assets then created will have survived to year t. After converting these investment figures to year t prices (or to the prices of whatever base year is chosen for constant price estimates) by means of an appropriate index of machinery prices, the gross investments over T years are simply added together to give that component of the stock. This is added to other components, similarly calculated, for other types of asset with different lives. Finally, stocks of goods and work in progress are added to give the total capital stock. (For some mysterious reason, several authors omit this final step, as if such stocks had no marginal product.) Refinements are possible, in which assets of a given type are assumed to have lives that are not exactly the same, but are distributed around the mean—but we need not concern ourselves with this here.

This procedure could be justified in terms of the theory only if the marginal product of each asset were, throughout its life, directly proportionate to its original cost (brought to a common price level by index numbers of asset prices). This is unlikely to be the case. At the end of T years, the asset is going to be scrapped, not, in the majority of cases, because it has phyisically worn out,[18] but rather because the quasi-rent it earns has fallen to zero, or close to zero. In other words, its economic life is determined by economic factors (namely, competition from newer and better assets), and not by physical ones: by obsolescence rather than by decay (see Barna, in Lutz and Hague 1961, 85). That being so, the clear implication is that the asset's quasi-rent must fall over its lifetime, eventually becoming approximately zero. This is so despite the fact that the physical output, and other physical inputs, associated with the asset may all

---

[18] Of course, some assets are scrapped because of physical deterioration. This is true, for example, of cows and of some vehicles. I do not deny that such physical deterioration reduces output. In my terminology, it has to be offset by maintenance expenditure (which must include replacements of cows and taxis, for example) if output is to be maintained. However, for most assets I believe the most important explanation for scrapping is obsolescence, not physical decay. (See further below, and also the discussion of maintenance and depreciation in Chapter 1.)

remain approximately constant over the whole of its life. Because relative prices change (typically, real wages rise), the asset's quasi-rent will typically decline, and so will its marginal product.

Some may feel that, if the *physical* inputs and outputs remain unchanged, then the *relevant* marginal product, so far as the production function is concerned, has remained unchanged. They might argue that, measured at base-year prices, constancy of physical inputs and outputs implies constancy of marginal product. This would not be so, however, if a Divisia index were used, since then the price weights would change and, if the current value of the marginal product were zero, so would be its value at constant prices as measured by the Divisia index. For many countries, price weights are changed every few years, and so there is an approximation to a Divisia index. In any case, what *should* the marginal product be, given an ideal system of measurement? It seems to me self-evident that, if, to take the extreme case, and the simplest assumptions (perfect competition), an asset is scrapped whose quasi-rent is zero, the effect on output must be zero. The other factors of production associated with the asset must then be able to go elsewhere and produce as much as they were earning when they worked with the asset, and this must equal the whole of the output they then together produced. The economic contribution of the asset is then zero, and scrapping it does not reduce total[19] output. Yet it *does* reduce the gross capital stock, as conventionally measured. Hence it is patently inconsistent with the production function. The gross capital stock at replacement cost new cannot be the correct way to measure K if we want to use that function.

Let us now consider the other measure of K which is commonly used, namely, the net capital stock. This can also be estimated by the perpetual inventory method, but now each addition to the stock, after correcting for price changes to the base year, is written down over its lifetime by some depreciation formula (e.g. straight line, declining balance, double declining balance, etc.). The exact formula is not important for the argument that follows. The general effect is to reduce the value of any asset by an amount that increases with the age of the asset. An asset that is about to be scrapped should, in principle, have been reduced to zero value. At first blush, therefore, it would seem that this method should meet most of the objection made to the gross capital stock, since the depreciated values of different assets should be *roughly* proportionate to their marginal products, although the correspondence *would* only be rough, and would depend on the formula used and on the way in which the asset's quasi-rent changed over its life. Unfortunately, there remains a serious objection to this measure, which is

---

[19] It is *total* output that is not reduced. The output produced by the asset plus its associated factors does fall, but is replaced by new output produced by the associated factors. Should the latter become unemployed, the argument is not essentially affected. Instead of new output, we then have a fall in other inputs whose value is the same.

quite separate from the question of exact proportionality of depreciated value to marginal product for *existing* members of the stock. Instead, it relates to the method used to calculate net additions to the stock. With the net capital stock, the net addition to the stock equals gross investment minus depreciation.

At this point, it is necessary to ask readers to recall the discussion of depreciation and maintenance in Chapter 1, which is not repeated here. The main relevant conclusion was that, for all practical purposes, depreciation in a progressive economy should be regarded as essentially a transfer of income from capitalists to workers. The latter benefit from rising wage rates which result in appreciation which is omitted from conventional accounts. Were it included, it would offset depreciation on capital assets. It would then be clear that net investment for society as a whole is (approximately) equal to *gross* investment as conventionally measured, and not to gross investment minus depreciation. Hence, if the marginal products of existing members of the capital stock are, let us say, on average $\bar{r}$ times their net capital values, the marginal product of the *additions* to the stock are much more than $\bar{r}$ times *net* investment: instead, they are more like $\bar{r}$ times *gross* investment.

An analogy with the estimation of labour's marginal product may be helpful. Suppose we have a fixed quantity of land on which is employed a quantity of labour, OL_1, at a wage rate OW_1, which we assume equals its marginal product (Figure 3.2). Now let there be a small addition to the labour force L_1L_2, which causes the wage rate and marginal product to sink by W_1W_2 to OW_2. The contribution of the extra labour to output is correctly measured by the area $L_1P_1P_2L_2$, which, to a close approximation, is the new (or old) wage rate multiplied by the increase in employment. One would not think of deducting from this the fall in the wages earned by the existing labour force, $W_2Q_1P_1W_1$, which is merely a transfer of income from wage-earners to landowners. There is no net *social* cost involved in that (ignoring the question of weighting benefits received by different income-earners), since the landowners benefit as much as the wage-earners lose. My argument is that depreciation on capital assets is loosely analogous to the wage-earner's loss in Figure 3.2, and is offset by appreciation accruing to workers (like the extra rent accruing to landowners), leaving the net contribution of extra capital equal to something like $\bar{r}$ multiplied by gross investment.

The upshot of the argument so far is that neither of the two measures of the capital stock which have been used in practice correctly weights capital inputs by their marginal products. Both bias the estimate of the contribution of capital to growth downwards by a very large amount. In each case, the contribution to growth is proportionate to (say $\bar{r}$ times) the growth in the stock. With the gross capital stock, one measures the growth

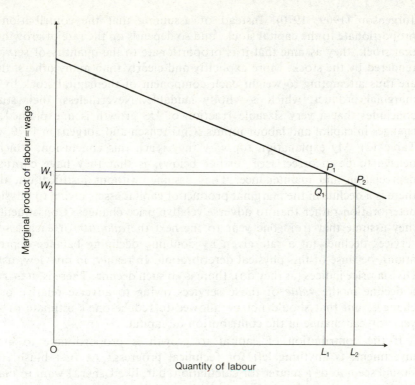

Fig. 3.2 Measuring the marginal contribution of labour to output

in the stock as gross investment minus scrapping, and scrapping is equal to the original cost of the scrapped asset brought up to some base-year price level. As we have seen, since in competitive conditions scrapped assets contribute nothing to output, this deduction is incorrect. With the net capital stock, one measures the growth in the stock as gross investment minus depreciation. Again, this deduction is incorrect since depreciation is essentially a transfer of incomes arising from relative price changes. The conclusion is the same in both cases: the contribution is proportionate to gross investment minus nothing.[20]

It may be useful to discuss a rather different way of estimating the contribution of capital to growth which has been set out by Christensen and

[20] This argument is essentially the same as in Scott (1976) and, more fully, Scott (1981). I have stated it here in a form that holds strictly only if there is perfect competition, or if firms behave in their scrapping decision *as if* there were perfect competition. In imperfect competition, assets may be scrapped while still capable of earning positive quasi-rents at current prices. Scrapping them does, indeed, reduce output and increase required maintenance. This 'abnormal required maintenance' was probably important after 1973, although not in previous postwar years. For further explanation and discussion, see Section 16.7 below.

Jorgenson (1969, 1970). Instead of assuming that the contribution is proportionate to the capital stock, and so depends on the rate of growth of that stock, they assume that it is proportionate to the quantity of services rendered by the stock. More explicitly and clearly than many others, they are thus attempting to weight each component of the capital stock by its marginal product, which is wholly laudable. Nevertheless, their study concludes that a very sizeable fraction of US growth is unexplained by changes in capital and labour inputs (Christensen and Jorgenson 1970, 47, Table 12). My explanation for why they reach this conclusion, which I believe to be incorrect (see further below), is that they have confused depreciation and maintenance. They assume, without justification, that there is a decline in the marginal product of capital assets owing to physical deterioration rather than to adverse relative price changes. Consequently, they assume that from one year to the next the *quantity* of each asset's services declines (at a rate given by doubling declining balance depreciation), because of this physical deterioration. In reality, in my view, using Divisia price indices (as they do), there is no such decline. There is, it is true, a decline in the *value* of those services owing to adverse relative price changes, but that should not be allowed to reduce one's estimate of the year-to-year change in the contribution of capital.

If the contribution of capital to growth is proportionate to gross investment, is anything left for technical progress? At first blush, this should seem to be a matter for calculation, but, like Usher, I want to make it a matter of definition, only not his! By defining investment as the cost of changing economic arrangements, I attribute to investment and labour force growth all the changes in output that occur, with two major exceptions. These are exogenous changes such as the weather, earthquakes, etc., and changes in capacity utilization, typically arising from the ups and downs of the trade cycle, but also possibly from fluctuations in labour effort, including that of management. Putting those aside, let us consider first the simplest case, in which there is no change in labour input. Unless there is a change in economic arrangements, we shall then have a static economy with no change in output at all. Technical progress cannot take place without a change in economic arrangements. The next step is to assert that changes in economic arrangements always cost something. Even if a few examples can be given which contradict this assertion, they are of such minor importance that they can be neglected. The conclusion is, then, that the whole change in output must be due to the change in economic arrangements, and hence to the investment that is the cost of making them. Of course, it may not be a simple matter to decide exactly what this cost is. One change leads to another, or, indeed, to several others, and so it is not easy, and may even not be possible, to trace the consequences of an investment forwards in time, or to trace the costs incurred to make some change backwards in time. All this means is that tracing cause and effect is very difficult in practice. I therefore represent complex reality by a much simpler model of it. In that model, the costs incurred to make each change are well defined, and it is incurring those costs (i.e. investing) that is deemed to have caused those changes.

Changes in labour input must now be taken into account, and here I follow essentially the same procedure as everyone else. I assume that employers ensure that changes in employment are pushed to the point at which their contribution to the net present values of the firms employing them is zero. I can then assume that the contribution of labour input growth to growth of output is measured by a simple function of the wage.[21] Subtracting this contribution from the actual increase in output leaves the contribution of gross investment.

The above procedure leaves nothing for a separate contribution by 'technical progress'. This does not mean that technical changes are not occurring. On the contrary, they are continuously occurring as every investment changes economic arrangements. What it *does* mean is that the attempt to separate the contribution of technical change is abandoned. Indeed, with my definition of investment, separation is strictly meaningless. Every investment changes something, and so is virtually bound to necessitate totally new knowledge in *some* degree. What is unclear is just how one can separate the additions to output arising from totally new knowledge from those arising from the application of already known techniques, and both, in turn, from those that would have occurred had the investment reduplicated existing assets. Furthermore, what is the point in trying to make this separation? If investment is inevitably a package, one of whose contents is an increase in knowledge, why try to calculate its contribution to growth as if this content were missing? Other writers have cast doubt on the attempt at separation (see in particular Kaldor 1957, 595-6), but some have cheerfully continued with models in which the separation is essential, and which have led to the paradoxical conclusions noted earlier.

To guard against misinterpretation, it must be emphasized that I am not *merely* asserting that all technical change has to be embodied. As has already been pointed out, standard vintage theories assume embodiment, and yet lead to much the same conclusions as production function theories. The reason they do is that the rate of improvement from one vintage to the next is exogenously given, and is independent of investment. That is not the assumption I wish to make, because it carries the following absurd implication. Imagine that, 100 years ago in a closed economy (or the whole

---

[21] In a static economy with perfect competition, wages equal marginal products, but in a growing economy, even maintaining the assumption of perfect competition, this is no longer true for the reasons given in Chapter 6.

world, say), all investment ceased, and also all population growth. For the next 100 years, capital assets were all maintained, so that each and every output remained constant. Arriving at the present after a century of stagnation, we start to invest again and what do we find? According to standard vintage theory, the machines available will be capable of producing jet aeroplanes, lasers, microcomputers, the whole array of modern drugs, and all the rest. Silently, without the need for any intervening investment, technical progress will have gone on, and the modern vintages actually available will miraculously be available in the hypothetical present too.

This is all wildly implausible.[22] It seems more plausible to liken economic progress to a journey with investment as the cost of travel. If the traveller pauses on the journey, he no longer incurs the cost, but neither does he progress, and when he starts off again, it is from where he stopped, not miles further on. One might try to preserve the standard vintage theories as an approximation to reality by maintaining that *some* investment is required to develop the new vintages, but that it is very small. The idea that R&D expenditures, plus costless inspirations, are the source of all productivity growth is, indeed, widely held, and must underlie production function theories as well as vintage theories. It is not, however, very plausible. It would imply that the rate of return to such expenditures was very high,[23] which makes one wonder why they are not increased.[24] It would also neglect the extent to which people learn from investments other than R&D expenditures. Acquisition of knowledge and learning from experience are undoubtedly of great importance in explaining economic growth, and are further discussed in subsequent chapters, as also is the externality to investment (excess of social over private return) which results therefrom. However, I doubt whether knowledge and experience can be acquired other

[22] Some, confronted by the argument just stated, react as follows. 'Well, yes, perhaps it is implausible. But vintage theory is still all right. After all, investment in developing countries in recent years *can* take advantage of the latest inventions available in developed countries. The former do not need to retrace the growth experiences of the latter.' I certainly do not deny that there can be learning and 'catching up' of this kind, and both feature prominently in later chapters. Nevertheless, a theory that is inapplicable to the world as a whole, or a closed economy, is unsatisfactory, to put it mildly.

[23] See Scott (1981, 214), where I estimated that, if Denison's residual growth rate of 1.41 per cent per annum in the US non-residential business sector from 1948 to 1973, which is attributed to 'advances of knowledge and n.e.c.' (Denison 1979, 92), had all been due to R&D expenditure during that period, its average rate of return would have had to be about 50 per cent per annum (and about 2300 per cent per annum if only basic R&D expenditure is included). It is noteworthy that Denison himself has credited R&D expenditures in the USA with explaining only '0.2 percentage points, or, at most, 0.3 points to the growth rate of measured output in nonresidential business during the post war period' (see Denison 1985, 28).

[24] A possible explanation is the failure of those undertaking R&D to capture most of its benefits. However, in that case why does not society subsidize R&D more generously, if the social benefits are so large?

than by changing economic arrangements and seeing what results; and if one cuts back the pace of change by cutting back investment, one must cut back the rate of acquisition of knowledge as well.

Suppose we grant that the contribution of capital to growth is proportionate to gross investment, without any deduction: is it possible to rescue production function theory? Let us assume that the rental of every capital asset equals $\bar{r}$ times its value in the net capital stock, K, so that gross profits are $P = \bar{r} K$. In any short interval, the capital stock increases because of gross investment, S, which is a *quantity* change and so is relevant to, and a cause of, increases in output. It also falls because of depreciation D, which is due to relative price changes, and so has no direct relevance as a cause of changes in output. Rather, it is a *consequence* of investment and rising real wage rates. The (quality-adjusted) labour force also increases by ΔL from its level L. Then, if Q is real output and w is the average wage, we might put

$$\Delta Q = \bar{r}S + w\Delta L. \tag{3.10}$$

This would give us a growth accounting equation which is in several respects similar to the orthodox one. It is *not* the equation that can be derived from the growth model proposed in Chapter 6, although it is similar in important respects.[25] Readers must wait until the model is developed in that chapter for further discussion of the relation between its equation and the orthodox growth accounting equation (see especially Section 6.9). Equation (3.10) serves at this stage to point up some very important differences.

First, there is no separate term for technical progress. If we can integrate the above equation to form a production function, that function is not shifting through time because of exogenous technical progress.

Second, integrating the term for capital does not give the net capital stock, but cumulative gross investment. To get the net capital stock we would have to integrate $(S - D)$, net investment, but that is not the relevant magnitude for explaining growth. It is then not possible to write the level of output as a function of K and L as in (3.1), with K as the net capital stock.

Third, however, if we substitute cumulative gross investment for K in (3.1), we encounter the following problem. How far must we go back? The perpetual inventory method places a limit on the period for which gross investment statistics are needed, which is the life of the longest-lived assets in the inventory.[26] If some other basis of asset valuation were used, such as insurance values or book values, we would not need to go back in time at

[25] In particular, it contains the same three principal variables, ΔQ, S, and ΔL, and contains no further variable representing technical progress.

[26] There are, however, some grounds for unease. 'Land' is usually left out, on the argument that it does not change appreciably in total. The age of some items in the stock (roads, hedges, cleared fields, drains, and even some buildings) can be much greater than the maxima assumed, and what 'age' means for some is unclear.

all. Cumulative gross investment, however, goes back in principle without any obvious limit. Admittedly, because of exponential growth, the amount of investment in earlier years becomes small, and could be neglected for that reason. However, this question suggests a more fundamental one which confronts every historian. Can one explain the present without going back an indefinite distance into the past? The production function appears to make the staggering claim that one can, but the strict necessity of substituting cumulative gross investment for the net capital stock suggests that the claim is false. Would it not be better to say that we can explain how the present has been reached from some point in the past, and that that point has to be chosen on grounds of practicality, such as the availability of data and of time and knowledge to provide the explanation? Should we not admit that we cannot really explain levels, but, at best, only changes from one level to another?

Fourth, if we make output a function of cumulative gross investment and employment, that function will not have the usual properties. In particular, and as already noted, there is no reason to suppose that the marginal return to investment will be smaller the larger is cumulative gross investment for given L. This in turn implies that equilibrium growth may well depend on the savings ratio, and that has important implications for tax policy and optimal growth, as we shall see in later chapters.

Fifth, a simple cumulation of gross investment is justifiable only if each unit of investment contributes equally to output. If there are diminishing returns to the rate of investment (discussed in later chapters), this is not the case.

Finally, we may note that, if both gross investment and the quality-adjusted labour force are regarded as inputs, and if there is no separate contribution from technical progress, 'total factor productivity' cannot be measured in the conventional way. However, economic efficiency can still be measured by the rate of return to investment, or by suitable application of an equation similar to (3.10) to changes in outputs and inputs, as is shown in later chapters.

3.8 Perfect competition, malleable capital, and the costs of adjustment

Production function theories generally assume the existence of perfect competition. In their simplest form they also assume malleable capital, as explained below. The effect of these assumptions is that costs of adjustment are ignored. It would be an exaggeration to say that growth theory without costs of adjustment is like Hamlet without the Prince of Denmark; perhaps it is more like Hamlet without the King of Denmark. Economic growth would certainly be a very different, and happier, experience if markets worked as smoothly and efficiently as they are assumed to do in perfect competition, and if capital were really malleable.

The firm in perfect competition is assumed to be able to buy as much as it wants of any factor, and to sell as much of any product, at going market prices. It can borrow unlimited amounts at going interest rates. But now there are difficulties, which have been pointed out by Richardson (1956, 1960) and Haavelmo (1960). How does such a firm plan its investments? The system is supposed to work by creating incentives, through changes in relative prices, for changes in supply to match changes in demand. But once an opportunity for earning an abnormal profit appears, what limits the rate at which firms can plan to take advantage of it? Conversely, once a subnormal profit appears, what limits the rate at which firms engaged in the relevant activity cease to do so? In reality, something has to limit the speed of adjustment, and adjustment cannot be costless.[27]

Perfectly malleable capital (and labour) are assumed in simpler expositions of static general equilibrium theory in which the economy's given stocks of capital and labour are allocated between different uses by means of price signals and in response to the wishes of consumers and owners of the factors of production. For standard two-good and two-factor models of international trade, for example, opening the economy to trade leads to a reallocation of the given stocks of capital and labour between the two industries in accordance with the dictates of comparative advantage. It is recognized that in reality there are costs of adjustment, and that a possibly lengthy transitional period may be required to reach the new equilibrium. All this, however, is neglected, the focus being on the initial and final positions.

The concept of capital underlying this type of analysis is of 'meccano sets' or 'jelly': its total quantity is important, but not its form. The idea of investment as the cost of change is very different. One cannot slide costlessly along a production possibility curve to a new equilibrium since all change is costly. One need never reach a static equilibrium, since each change reveals further desirable changes of which one was not previously aware. Costs of adjustment are not something to be separately allowed for, perhaps as an afterthought. They are regrettably necessary for economic growth to take place at all.

Economists who have introduced costs of adjustment into their models have often assumed that they increase the faster the adjustment is made, as seems plausible. (See, for example Nickell 1978, ch. 3.) In a similar way, it is plausible to assume that the faster changes generally are made, the costlier they become. Hence, while we have argued that there is no reason to suppose that there are diminishing returns to *cumulative gross investment*,

---

[27] If the investment opportunity is created by a continuously moving equilibrium there need be no problem, and this case has been analysed by Jorgenson's 'The Theory of Investment Behaviour' in Fettber (1967). If, however, the oppotunity is created by a discontinuous jump in prices or interest rates—or, indeed, in expectations—then the problem described in the text arises. See Nickell (1978, 12–13), who also discusses costs of adjustment at length in ch. 3.

it does seem likely that there are diminishing returns to the *rate of investment*. In the simplest orthodox theories, the marginal return to investment is the same as the marginal return to the capital stock, since investment simply is the marginal addition to the capital stock. As investment at any time is increasing the stock at only a small proportionate rate, large proportionate changes in the rate of investment should not make much difference to its rate of return, unless one allows for 'costs of adjustment'.

In the theory proposed in later chapters, the marginal return to any given rate of investment (measuring that rate by the ratio of investment to output) is independent of the amount of cumulative gross investment, and in that sense there are no diminishing returns to the stock of capital. However, the faster is the rate of investment, in general, the lower is the marginal rate of return. This is for at least two reasons. First, the knowledge of those undertaking investment at any given time is limited, and they will naturally try to select the best projects they are aware of first. So, more means worse. Their knowledge will come to widen as the investments are undertaken and more good projects come into view, but at any one time their horizon is limited. Second, most people resist change more fiercely the faster it becomes. Diminishing returns to the rate of investment are thus not an afterthought, but an integral part of the theory. However, as we shall see, they are likely to be much stronger for the individual firm than for all firms taken together. Indeed, they may well not exist for the latter.

3.9 Conclusion

Orthodox theories of economic growth make its main determinants non-economic. Usher's dictum, 'no technical change, no growth' (meaning no labour productivity growth), sums up one of the theories' most striking conclusions, which appears to be supported by many empirical studies. I have tried to show where the empirical studies have gone wrong, and why a better dictum is 'no investment, no growth'. If I am right, economics has more to say about the causes of growth, and that should please economists. The determinants of the volume and efficiency of investment are restored to the centre of attention, and both have long been the concern of economists. We can, with renewed confidence in their importance, study the behaviour of firms, project appraisal, the working of capital markets, the determinants of saving, systems of taxation, and their impact on savings and the volume and pattern of investment, all of which are very relevant to economic growth in the long run. We do not have to abdicate to scientists and engineers, or even to those economists who specialize in the study of technical change. I do not deny for a moment their interest and importance, but I do assert the importance of the economic aspects of economic growth.

4

SOME UNORTHODOX GROWTH THEORIES

4.1 Introduction

The main criticism of orthodox growth theories in the preceding chapter is that they assume that technical progress is independent of investment. The theories in this chapter have one thing in common: they do not make this assumption. In this respect they are much to be preferred. Nevertheless, they are all unsatisfactory in some other respects. In some cases (Schumpeter and Hirschman) there is no formal model, and while that has its advantages, it fails to satisfy a need that orthodox theory, in the absence of stronger competition, is then left to fulfil. In some cases the treatment of technical progress does not carry conviction, or does not lend itself to empirical investigations of growth. In fact, I am not aware of any substantial body of empirical work, comparable to that of Denison or Kendrick, which makes use of these theories. This may be because insufficient time has elapsed for them to gain acceptance, but it may also be because of weaknesses in the theories themselves.

One characteristic of them which I find a weakness, although others may regard it as a strength, is that they usually retain orthodox concepts, such as the capital stock and the production function, or vintages of capital goods, and graft on to these an extra relation between investment and technical progress. In my view, it is much better to jettison such concepts and start afresh with a more simple and direct analysis of growth. Perhaps it is their failure to do this which explains why these theories have not, so far, caught on.

In what follows, I describe and criticize the theories of individual authors. Once more, I am as brief as possible, and interested readers are urged to consult the original texts if they want a proper and fair exposition. What is given here is incomplete and one-sided; nor does it survey all the growth theories with endogenous technical progress which are available. Despite my criticisms, I have learned much from the theories reviewed, as the following pages show.

4.2 Schumpeter

Schumpeter's *The Theory of Economic Development*, originally published in German in 1911, with a second edition in 1926 which was translated into

English with minor revisions in 1934, has remained one of the great books on the subject. Unlike modern theory, no attempt is made to provide a formal model. Instead, the reader's attention is drawn to those aspects of the process which Schumpeter regards as important. This permits more flexibility than is possible in a model, since all sorts of interesting and illuminating points can be made—for example, about the motivation and character of entrepreneurs. Nevertheless, something is also lost. One cannot, for example, be sure how Schumpeter would have answered such questions as, How does an increase in the ratio of investment to output affect the rate of growth in the long run? How does it affect the distribution of income between wages and profits? Later writers, while often paying tribute to his ideas, have not constructed models that are closely related to them.

The book starts with a description and analysis of a static economy—the 'circular flow'. One of the main points made is that, in such an economy, producers and consumers learn by experience what they must do, and that this greatly economizes the need for rational decision-making or information-gathering. Price signals are not as important as the orthodox theory of a static economy would have us believe, and there is certainly no assumption of perfect markets or perfect competition.

If someone who has never seen or heard of such a state were to observe that a farmer produces corn to be consumed as bread in a distant city, he would be impelled to ask how the farmer knew that this consumer wanted bread and just so much. He would assuredly be astonished to learn that the farmer did not know at all where or by whom it would be consumed. Furthermore, he could observe that all the people through whose hands the corn must go on its way to the final consumer knew nothing of the latter, with the possible exception of the ultimate sellers of bread; and even they must in general produce or buy before they know that this particular consumer will acquire it. The farmer could easily answer the question put to him: long experience, in part inherited, has taught him how much to produce for his greatest advantage; experience has taught him to know the extent and intensity of the demand to be reckoned with. To this quantity he adheres, as well as he can, and only gradually alters it under the pressure of circumstances. (Schumpeter 1934, 5, 6)

The economy may change 'under the pressure of circumstances' (presumably because of such things as population growth, wars, the weather, etc.), but Schumpeter's interest does not lie there:

By 'development', therefore, we shall understand only such changes in economic life as are not forced upon it from without but arise by its own initiative, from within. Should it turn out that there are no such changes arising in the economic sphere itself, and that the phenomenon that we call economic development is in practice simply founded upon the fact that the data change and that the economy continuously adapts itself to them, then we should say that there is *no* economic development. (Schumpeter 1934, 63)

Hence one could interpret Schumpeter's view of the theory of economic development as being concerned with changes in the economy which are endogenous to the economic system: with endogenous technical progress, not exogenous.

Schumpeter emphasizes that he is concerned with *discontinuous* change. He explicitly excludes 'mere growth of the economy, as shown by the growth of population and wealth . . . . For it calls forth no qualitatively new phenomena, but only processes of adaptation of the same kind as the changes in the natural data' (p.63). 'Development in our sense is a distinct phenomenon, entirely foreign to what may be observed in the circular flow or in the tendency towards equilibrium. It is spontaneous and discontinuous change in the channels of the flow, disturbance of equilibrium, which forever alters and displaces the equilibrium state previously existing' (p. 64). He adds in a footnote that development in his sense 'is that kind of change arising from within the system *which so displaces its equilibrium point that the new one cannot be reached from the old one by infinitesimal steps.* Add successively as many mail coaches as you please, you will never get a railway thereby' (emphasis in the original).

My criticism of the idea of investment as a mere reduplication of existing assests (see Chapter 3) echoes this, although I would hold it to be true of virtually all investment, and would therefore disagree that there can be, to any important extent, 'mere growth of the economy' arising from the accumulation of wealth which is duplication of existing assets. The idea of discontinuity creates difficulties for any model of the economy. While recognizing that change is in reality discontinuous at the micro level, it seems possible to analyse growth at the macro level as if it were continuous, and this greatly simplifies the analysis. Furthermore, even at the individual firm level, change is probably more nearly continuous now than before 1914, when Schumpeter first wrote his book. Especially for large firms, new projects which change this or that part of the business are continually under review, and higher management's task to a great extent consists in initiating, considering, and activating such projects.

The main agents of economic change, according to Schumpeter, are producers, not consumers. Production means combining 'materials and forces within our reach' (p.65).

Development in our sense is then defined by the carrying out of new combinations.
    This concept covers the following five cases: (1) The introduction of a new good —that is, one with which consumers are not yet familiar—or of a new quality of a good. (2) The introduction of a new method of production, that is one not yet tested by experience in the branch of manufacture concerned, which need by no means be founded upon a discovery scientifically new, and can also exist in a new way of handling a commodity commercially. (3) The opening of a new market, that is a market into which the particular branch of manufacture of the country in question

has not previously entered, whether or not this market has existed before. (4) The conquest of a new source of supply of raw materials or half-manufactured goods, again irrespective of whether this source already exists or whether it has first to be created. (5) The carrying out of the new organisation of any industry, like the creation of a monopoly position (for example through trustification) or the breaking up of a monopoly position. (Schumpeter 1934, 66)

It can be seen that Schumpeter's idea of development covers nearly every kind of change in economic arrangements. Furthermore, he does not emphasize the accumulation of 'capital' at all. 'The carrying out of new combinations means, therefore, simply *the different employment of the economic system's existing supplies of productive means*—which might provide a second definition of development in our sense' (p.68; my emphasis). I regard this definition as of key importance, and take it as the basis for the concept of investment. Some readers may wonder why the point requires emphasis, since it seems obvious enough. Nevertheless, it leads to quite a different approach from that taken by most other growth theory, whether orthodox or unorthodox. There, growth is regarded as resulting from bigger *stocks* of labour, land, or capital, and technical progress is brought in most simply as a factor augmenting one or more of these stocks. The process of growth is thus to be analysed by considering, first, how the stocks have changed and, second, what effects this has on output, employment, prices, etc. If, however, one regards the process as one of introducing 'new combinations' of *existing* resources, the analysis can proceed directly to this second step: how have the new combinations changed output, employment, prices, etc.? This simpler and more direct approach is the one we attempt in later chapters.

Schumpeter emphasizes the role of the entrepreneur in development. By definition, he is the man who sees that the new combination is made. He is to be distinguished from the capitalist (who bears the risk) and from the inventor (who has the ideas), although it is possible for one man to be all three. He may be a manager, but need not be—a manager being, for Schumpeter, someone concerned with routine problems, whereas the entrepreneur is concerned with change. The difference between the two is stressed. 'Carrying out a new plan and acting according to a customary one are things as different as making a road and walking along it' (p. 85). Not only is the task different; it also requires a special kind of effort, since resistance to change exists both within oneself and in others.

Surmounting this opposition is always a special kind of task which does not exist in the customary course of life, a task which also requires a special kind of conduct. In matters economic this resistance manifests itself first of all in the groups threatened by the innovation, then in the difficulty in finding the necessary cooperation, finally in the difficulty in winning over consumers. (Schumpeter 1934, 87)

This idea of resistance to change is developed later, where I assume that the resistance increases the faster changes are made.

Schumpeter's sharp distinction between the entrepreneur and the capitalist, or owner or creditor, of the enterprise is not one that I have been able to follow. According to Schumpeter (1934, ch. IV), entrepreneurial profit is the reward for making successful new combinations. It is ephemeral, since competition from imitators will gradually eliminate it. The enterprise then becomes like any other part of the 'circular flow' and earns a normal profit for its owners, and creditors. This conception might be reasonable if new combinations were rare exceptions in what was otherwise a static economy, and is consistent with Schumpeter's view of them as occasional discontinuous changes. However, it is difficult to reconcile this view with the 'stylized facts' of growth. It seems to neglect depreciation as a *normal* phenomenon, and to reserve it as something afflicting only new combinations. They depreciate for a time, as entrepreneurial profit is competed away to zero, but thereafter seemingly enjoy constant normal returns to capital, and so depreciate no further. My conception is different. In a steadily progressive economy, depreciation is normal, since rising real wages tend to squeeze quasi-rents everywhere, on old and new combinations alike. An enterprise that wishes to pay out a constant real dividend must continually invest its depreciation funds, and this means that it must be continually changing. It must run hard merely to stay where it is. Consequently, although investment projects are indeed discontinuous, the need to undertake them to maintain the income of the owners of the enterprise is continuous. It is then difficult in a model of steady growth to separate off the temporary profits from each change made, and to attribute these to 'entrepreneurship', while attributing some sort of normal profit to the owners and creditors of the enterprise. Hence, while I certainly follow Schumpeter in assuming that imitation, and other new combinations, compete away profits made on old combinations, I do not follow him in distinguishing the functions of entrepreneurs and capitalists. In a more complicated model than mine one might want to draw such distinctions, but here I simply class all profit as a return on investment.

In a fascinating passage, Schumpeter distinguishes three motives for the entrepreneur:

'There is the dream and the will to found a private kingdom, usually, though not necessarily, also a dynasty . . . Then there is the will to conquer: the impulse to fight, to prove oneself superior to others, to succeed for the sake, not of the fruits of success, but of success itself. . . . Finally, there is the joy of creating, of getting things done, or simply of exercising one's energy and ingenuity. (Schumpeter 1934, 93)

As he points out, 'Only with the first groups of motives is private property as the result of entrepreneurial activity an essential factor in making it operative. With the other two it is not' (p. 94). True, profit is an objective measure of success which is needed to prove one's superiority for the second motive, but it need not be profit actually accruing to the entrepreneur himself. Hence a manager of an enterprise who holds no, or negligible, shares in it can still be subject to the second and third motives, and can strive to increase the firm's net present value. For the first motive to operate, he must either own a substantial part of the enterprise, or be rewarded a 'promoter's profit'. It is this last form of reward that Schumpeter regards as the purest case of entrepreneurial profit (p. 137-8).

Finally, we may note that Schumpeter's theory is concerned with enterprises, not with individual commodities, industries, or sectors of the economy. In this I follow him for the most part, although industries are considered in Chapters 12 and 13 below.

4.3 Hirschman

Hirschman's *The Strategy of Economic Development*, like Schumpeter's *Theory of Economic Development*, does not contain any fully worked out model, although, given its much later date of publication (1958), it is not surprising to find that some attempts at formalization are made. It shares the virtue of Schumpeter's book in being highly original and stimulating, and has the advantage of conciseness and readability. Although it is primarily addressed to the problems of the less developed countries, much of it applies, in my view, to those of the developed countries as well.

The book starts with a review of the factors which, at one time or another, have been regarded as prerequisites of economic development. Fashions have changed. In earlier times the provision of good natural resources was stressed. Then emphasis was given to savings and reproducible capital. Then attention shifted to human factors: entrepreneurship and managerial abilities and other skills. More fundamental value systems such as the Protestant Ethic, and psychological drives such as the drive to achieve success, were also put forward. All these alleged prerequisites, however, could be shown by experience to be either unnecessary (as when countries with poor natural resources developed rapidly) or else more or less universally present and therefore incapable of explaining differences between countries. It also became clear that the supply of many 'prerequisites' responded to development itself. Thus, investment led to profits, which financed more investment, and entrepreneurship and managerial abilities expanded through the performance of their own functions. Development could then be regarded as a virtuous circle. Hirschman concludes that 'development depends not so much on finding optimal combinations for given resources and factors of production as on calling forth and enlisting for development purposes resources and abilities that are hidden, scattered, or badly utilized' (Hirschman 1958, 5). He thus sets out to look for the 'inducement mechanisms' that will do this. 'If backwardness is due to insufficient number and speed of developmental tasks, then the fundamental problem of development consists in generating and energizing human action in a certain direction' (p. 25); 'development is held back primarily by the difficulties of channeling *existing* or potentially existing savings into available productive investment opportunities i.e. by a shortage of the ability to make and carry out development decisions' (p. 36). Hirschman calls this a shortage of the 'ability to invest'.

Hirschman next discusses 'the complementarity effect of investment', by which he means not merely that investment increases income and then also increases savings, but that in addition it induces further investment decisions; it makes them easier to take, because, for example, a new market is created for the output of the B industry when the output of the A industry is expanded, and, likewise, the new output from A may lowers costs of production in C. Hence investment in A has made it easier to decide to invest more in B and C. Hirschman makes use of the illuminating analogy of a jigsaw puzzle (pp. 81–2). One is trying to complete the puzzle as quickly as possible. It is easier to fit in a particular piece the more of its neighbours are already in place, while the hardest pieces to join on are those with only one neighbour in place. Development, however, unlike a puzzle, does not come to an obvious end. In a real puzzle, the task of fitting on new pieces become progressively easier as the stock of unfitted pieces diminishes, so that one has fewer and fewer possibilities to search among. To preserve the analogy, we must therefore imagine that the loose pieces are being added to as fast as they are being diminished by fitting them on to the existing picture. That picture then becomes like history, stretching back for a very long time and growing indefinitely.

This view of development is contrasted with the 'balanced growth' doctrine, of which Hirschman strongly disapproves.

'It is argued that a new venture—say, a shoe factory—which gets underway by itself in an underdeveloped country is likely to turn into a failure: the workers, employees, and owners of the shoe factory will obviously not buy all of its output, while the other citizens of the country are caught in an 'underdevelopment equilibrium' where they are just able jointly to afford their own meager output. Therefore, it is argued, to make development possible it is necessary to start, *at one and the same time*, a large number of new industries which will be each others' clients through the purchases of their workers, employers, and owners. For this reason, the theory has now also been annexed to the 'theory of the big push'.[1] (Hirschman 1958, 51)

---

[1] Rosenstein-Rodan (1957).

Balanced growth is attacked because 'The theory fails as a theory of *development*. Development presumably means the process of *change* of one type of economy, *into* some other more advanced type' (pp. 51–2).

The adherents of balanced growth, according to Hirschman, are escapist and also pessimistic. They give up the existing economy as a hopeless case, and wishfully think that a beautiful new economy, complete in itself, can be constructed all at once inside it. 'As Singer writes: "The advantages of multiple development may make interesting reading for economists, but they are gloomy news indeed for the underdeveloped countries. The initial resources for simultaneous developments on many fronts are generally lacking" ' (p. 53).

Balanced growth leads naturally to a desire for centralized investment decision-taking. This is to ensure that the externalities resulting from individual investments are internalized so that, to return to a previous example, the benefits of investment in A for B and C are fully taken into account when investment in A is considered. However, as Hirschman points out, there will not, in general, just be external *benefits*. There will also be external *costs*. Because of these costs, it is by no means clear that centralization of investment decisions will speed development. On the contrary, the success of capitalism may have owed as much to the ruthlessness with which such costs could be, and were, ignored. Centralization would have permitted the groups that lost out to mobilize resistance to change, which might have slowed down the pace of development substantially. Hirschman instances the guild system as an example of this.

In contrast to balanced growth, Hirschman envisages development as a chain of disequilibria:

Therefore, the sequence that 'leads away from equilibrium' is precisely an ideal pattern of development from our point of view: for each move in the sequence is induced by a previous disequilibrium and in turn creates a new disequilibrium that requires a further move. This is achieved by the fact that the expansion of industry A leads to economies external to A but appropriable by B, while the consequent expansion of B brings with it economies external to B but subsequently internal to A (or C for that matter), and so on. At each step, an industry takes advantage of external economies created by previous expansion, and at the same time creates new external economies to be exploited by other operators. (Hirschman 1958, 66–7)

There are many other fascinating insights provided in Hirschman's book. He has interesting things to say on the relationship between social overhead capital and 'directly productive activities', making the point that inducements to invest must, and do, operate on governments as well as on private businesses. His analysis of forward and backward linkages is well known, and exemplifies the ideas described above, as well as showing how economies of scale come into the picture.

Some of his ideas on linkages are further developed in an article that appeared some twenty years later (Hirschman 1977), where he gave many interesting examples of 'how one thing leads to another'. The linkages were not just of the direct input–output kind, but were also indirect. For example, an export industry could pay for imports which would open the way to subsequent import substitution (consumption linkages); or a mineral industry, perhaps foreign-owned, could offer an easy source of tax revenue for the government, and this revenue could then be used to develop other industries (fiscal linkages). Another classification introduced in this article, cutting across the others, is of inside and outside linkages. With inside linkages, the new activities would be undertaken by those operating the old ones, and would generally have to be technically similar to the old ones, leading to little further change. Outside linkages, requiring very different technologies, may also require different operators, and this may lead to a more continuing development.

The idea that one thing leads to another is at the centre of our later theory, although in a more abstract and general way than in Hirschman's writings. One pays a penalty for formalism, but it has its own reward.

4.4 Kaldor

Writing in 1964, Hahn and Matthews remarked, 'Kaldor's views have undergone a number of changes, and there is reason to believe that they have not yet attained their steady state' (Hahn and Matthews 1964, 797). I shall discuss here the model in Kaldor (1957), and, further below, the model devised by Kaldor and Mirrlees (1962). In addition to his contributions to the theory of growth, Kaldor made contributions of an empirical nature which have attracted much attention, as well as influencing economic policy. Some of these are discussed in Chapter 12 below.

In devising his 1957 model, Kaldor emphasized that

[it] eschews any distinction between changes in techniques (and in productivity) which are induced by changes in the supply of capital relative to labour and those induced by technical invention or innovation—i.e., the introduction of new knowledge. The use of more capital per worker ... inevitably entails the introduction of superior techniques which require 'inventiveness' of some kind, though these need not necessarily represent the application of basically new principles or ideas. On the other hand, most, though not all, technical innovations which are capable of raising the productivity of labour require the use of more capital per man ... A society where technical change and adaptation proceed slowly, where producers are reluctant to abandon traditional methods and adopt new techniques, is necessarily one where the rate of capital accumulation is small. The converse of this proposition is also true; the rate at which a society can absorb and exploit new techniques is limited by its ability to accumulate capital.

It follows that any sharp or clear-cut distinction between the movement *along* a 'production function' with a given state of knowledge, and a *shift* in the 'production function' caused by a change in the state of knowledge, is arbitrary and artificial. (Kaldor 1957, 595–6)

In order to give effect to these ideas (with which I very much agree), Kaldor postulated a 'technical progress function' of the kind illustrated by the line TT' in Figure 4.1. This assumes that the rate of growth of labour productivity, $g - g_L$, is faster the faster is the rate of growth of capital per worker, $g_K - g_L$. There are diminishing returns to the latter, so that TT' is concave viewed from below. However, the *position* of TT' does not depend on the ratio of investment to output.

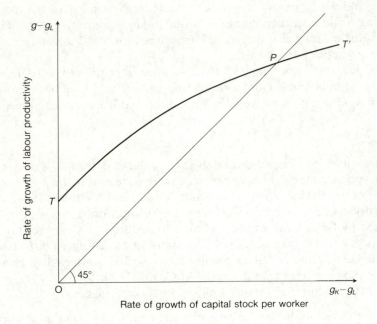

Fig. 4.1   Kaldor's technical progress function

In steady growth, as is usual, the capital–output ratio is constant, so that the rate of growth of capital must equal the rate of growth of output. So with $g = g_K$, we must be at P in the diagram in steady growth. Hence we reach the same paradoxical conclusion with this model as with orthodox models, namely, that the steady-state rate of growth of productivity does not depend on the ratio of investment to output: it depends only on technical progress.

The same conclusion, and more besides, can be seen from the linearized version of the model used by Kaldor. Writing the technical progress function in the neighbourhood of P as if it were a straight line that is the tangent at P, we have, with m and α constants,

$$g - g_L = m + \alpha(g_K - g_L)$$
$$\therefore \quad g = m + \alpha g_K + (1 - \alpha)g_L \tag{4.1}$$

Putting $g = g_K$ in steady growth, we get

$$g = \frac{m}{1 - \alpha} + g_L. \tag{4.2}$$

Equation (4.2) shows that the steady-state of growth is the sum of a constant and the rate of growth of the labour force. The constant can be interpreted as the rate of Harrod-neutral technical progress. Furthermore, equation (4.1) is precisely of the same form as (3.9) if we assume constant returns to scale for the latter (so that the coefficients of g_K and g_L sum to unity). In other words, we would arrive at precisely the same equation as (4.1) if we started from a Cobb–Douglas production function with Hicks-neutral technical progress at rate m (or Harrod-neutral at rate $m/(1 - \alpha)$). All this has been pointed out by Green (1960), Black (1962), and Eltis (1973, 154).

The remarks quoted earlier, however, do not suggest that it was Kaldor's intention that his model should turn out to be Cobb–Douglas, or that he thought that the rate of productivity growth in the long run should be independent of the ratio of investment to output. Hence the proposed technical progress function cannot be regarded as a satisfactory way of giving effect to the relationships that Kaldor had in mind.

Kaldor's model contained other interesting features distinguishing it from orthodox growth models; but I shall not comment on them here, as my principal concern in this chapter is in the different suggestions that have been made to incorporate technical progress into growth models. Accordingly, we turn now to his later model with Mirrlees.

4.5 Kaldor and Mirrlees

In his 1957 model, Kaldor used the concept of the total capital stock, despite the problems of measuring it which he recognized. In his 1962 article with Mirrlees, he discarded this concept, and used a (clay–clay) vintage model which required only the concept of gross investment. However, as with all vintage models, the result was an appreciable increase in complexity.

So far as the role of technical progress is concerned, the main innovation was a new technical progress function. This had the same shape as that illustrated in Figure 4.1, but with different magnitudes measured along each axis. Along the vertical axis, the dependent variable was now the proportionate rate of growth of labour productivity on the latest vintage of 'machines'. Along the horizontal axis, the independent variable was the proportionate rate of growth of gross investment per worker becoming available to man the latest vintage of machines per unit period. The technical progress function assumed that the greater was the latter, the greater would be the former, with diminishing returns once again.

Perhaps the chief difficulty with this set of ideas is that it is very complex and also difficult to relate to practical experience. It partakes of the usual conceptual difficulties of any vintage theory: if investment expenditure in a given period is spent so as to modify the nature of the work done by all, or even most, workers, some more and some less, what precisely is meant by 'the number of workers available to operate new equipment per unit period'? What precisely is meant by 'new machines'?

Apart from that, it is not at all clear why the *proportionate rate of increase* of gross investment should be the factor that determines the rate of growth of labour productivity on new 'machines'. Thus, consider the following example. Economy A achieves a certain stock of 'machines', manned by a certain labour force and producing a certain level of output, by a normal process of investment and growth. It then marks time for some years during which all 'machines' are physically maintained in an unchanged condition (with replacements to ensure this where necessary) and the labour force does not grow. The industries producing 'machines' simply remain idle, and output of 'machines' accordingly falls, but other output remains unchanged. Meanwhile, economy B, in complete isolation from A, starts off on exactly the same growth path and so reaches exactly A's position with the identical stock of 'machines' of each vintage, manned by the same labour force and so producing the same output. Just at the moment when B arrives at this point, A suddenly resumes investment at the same rate as B. One might think that A and B would then continue along parallel growth paths, but, according to Kaldor and Mirrlees's technical progress function, A's rate of growth of productivity on new 'machines' must be far higher than B's, at least initially, because the *rate of growth* of A's investment is infinite (from zero to some finite magnitude), whereas B's is whatever it normally is. It is difficult to understand the reason for this, and the authors do not really justify their technical progress function.

4.6 Arrow

In a famous and much quoted article (Arrow 1962b), Arrow devised a growth model to explore 'The Economic Implications of Learning by Doing'. After expressing his dissatisfaction with orthodox growth theory on the grounds that it leaves unexplained such a large part of the growth in productivity, which he agrees is due to a growth of knowledge, Arrow proposes 'an endogenous theory of the changes in knowledge which

underlie intertemporal and international shifts in production functions'
(1962b, 155). He offers two generalizations about learning gleaned from the
work of psychologists. First, 'Learning is the product of experience.
Learning can only take place through the attempt to solve a problem and
therefore only takes place during activity'. Second, 'learning associated
with repetition of essentially the same problem is subject to sharply
diminishing returns' (p. 155).

In the light of these generalizations, he sets out a clay–clay vintage model
of growth in which the quantity of labour required to man machines of
successive vintages (each machine having the same fixed output capacity)
declines. Unlike orthodox vintage models, however, Arrow does not assume
that this fall in labour requirements per unit of capacity output depends
only on time. Instead, he makes it depend on the amount of cumulative
gross investment, G, which has occurred from the beginning of time. He
takes this, rather than cumulative output, as an index of experience because
'Each new machine produced and put into use is capable of changing the
environment in which production takes place, so that learning is taking
place with continually new stimuli' (p. 157). Total output would be less
satisfactory as an index of experience, since it would, for example, continue
to grow in a static society in which nothing changed, so that learning could
hardly be supposed to occur.

Arrow assumes, then, that labour productivity per machine of vintage G
is given by

$$a = bG^{\mu} \tag{4.3}$$

where b and μ are constants, and μ would normally be assumed to be
positive but less than 1. It then turns out that the steady rate of growth of
the model, with full employment and a labour force growing at rate g_L, is

$$g = \frac{g_L}{1 - \mu}. \tag{4.4}$$

This yields the conclusion that an economy with a static labour force could
not grow in the long run, a conclusion that is hardly what someone believing
in endogenous technical progress would wish to accept. The reason why it
follows from Arrow's assumptions is as follows. In steady growth, both
gross investment and cumulative gross investment, G, grow at the same rate
as output, g. Labour productivity, from (4.3), must grow as fast as a, which
is as fast as G^{μ}. Since μ is positive and less than 1, it follows that labour
productivity must grow more slowly than G, and so more slowly than g. So
long as g_L is positive, it is possible for g to be the sum of the rate of growth
of productivity, say g_a, and the rate of growth of the labour force, g_L, with
$g_a < g$ and all these magnitudes constant. But if $g_L = 0$, we must have
$g = g_a$. It is then impossible to have $g_a < g$ as well, as is required by (4.3) in
steady growth.

Arrow's model is an interesting one, and the idea that investment itself leads to the growth of knowledge, and so makes further profitable investment possible, is one that I regard as fundamental. However, in view of the unacceptable conclusion just described, as well as the implication from (4.4) that the steady rate of growth does not depend at all on the ratio of investment to output, it does not seem useful to proceed with the model itself.

4.7 Eltis

Eltis has suggested a technical progress function which avoids the objections raised against those of Kaldor, Kaldor and Mirrlees, and Arrow. This function was originally put forward in 1963, and its applications in growth theory subsequently developed in Eltis's book *Growth and Distribution* (Eltis 1973). The function is

$$a = A + B\frac{S}{Y} \tag{4.5}$$

where a is the rate of Harrod-neutral technical progress, S/Y is the share of investment in output (net or gross depending on the further use made of the function; see below), and A and B are constants. This function permits technical progress to be partly exogenous and partly endogenous. Orthodox growth theories are reached by setting $B = O$, so that growth is wholly exogenous. Elitis justifies this function by reference to two phenomena: research and development expenditure (R&D) and learning by doing (Eltis 1973, Ch. 6), which I now consider in turn. My examination is necessarily too brief to include more than a very few of the interesting and stimulating ideas that Eltis puts forward.

Eltis hypothesizes that a typical manufacturer of capital goods (machines) will undertake R&D, which will enable purchasers of his goods to reduce their unit costs in the proportion a. The machine-maker will be able to charge more for his machines the greater is a. By increasing his annual rate of R&D, the machine-maker can increase a, although there are diminishing returns to this process. The rate of cost reduction that is achieved for the whole economy by these means then depends on (1) the size of a for individual machine-makers and (2) how many machines each sells in a year. Eltis argues that the more machines a maker of them can sell in a year, the more R&D in a year will it pay him to undertake, and so the bigger will be a for his machines.[2] Because of this, the average rate of technical progress will depend on the share of investment; i.e., B will be positive in (4.5) above. A may be positive or negative depending on whether, for

---

[2] See the discussion of Schmookler (1966) in Chapter 5 for evidence on this point.

example, doubling S/Y doubles a (when $A = O$), more than doubles it ($A < O$), or less than doubles it ($A > O$). According to Eltis, each of these is possible.

Eltis then considers whether steady growth is possible if all, or a substantial part, of technical progress is due to the above process. He argues that it will be possible if the labour force is constant, but not if it is growing. In the latter (more likely) case, the process should lead to accelerating growth in productivity, which Eltis considers is a possibility for which there is some evidence.

I shall argue in what follows that, if the process described above is a reality, one or other of three possibilities must be true:

1. the position must have been reached where there are very sharply diminishing returns to R&D;
2. the process only applies to a small fraction of total investment expenditure, and cannot be made to apply elsewhere (which comes to much the same as the first possibility);
3. there is a very high social return to further R&D.

In the event of 1 or 2 being true, we are to all intents and purposes back in the world of exogenous technical progress, since the rate of technical progress cannot be increased appreciably by increasing S/Y and, under 2, it cannot be reduced much either by reducing S/Y. Under 1, a fall in R&D could reduce the rate of technical progress, but it is unlikely to occur since it would mean abandoning very profitable intra-marginal R&D.

In order to see why 1, 2, or 3 must be true, consider an economy with a constant labour force which is growing at the expotential rate a, equal to the rate of Harrod-neutral technical progress. Let us first assume that the whole of this is due to the above process, and that expenditure on R&D is R_0 and output Y_0 per annum at time $t = 0$. Altogether, then, expenditure at the rate R_0 is causing unit costs to fall at the rate a, so that on *average* each pound spent on R&D per annum is causing unit costs to fall at the rate a/R_0.

Now consider a marginal increase in expenditure on R&D by £1 per year at $t = 0$, which is allowed to grow at the exponential rate a, so that the share of R&D in total output remains constant at a slightly higher level. This will, let us suppose, increase a by δa. Suppose the social rate of discount to be applied to investment is r. Then, at any future time t years from now, total output will be bigger, having grown at $a + \delta a$ instead of at a. So the benefit from this will be at the annual rate:

$$Y_0 \exp\{(a + \delta a)\,t\} - Y_0 \exp\{(a)\,t\}$$

The extra cost being incurred is simply e^{at} per year, i.e. £1 having grown to this amount by then. Discounting these benefits and costs at r, and summing over all future years, we get the present value of this marginal investment in R&D as

$$V = \int_0^\infty \left[Y_0 \exp\{(a + \delta a - r)\, t\} - Y_0 \exp\{(a - r)\, t\} - \exp\{(a - r)\, t\} \right] \mathrm{d}t$$

$$= Y_0 \left(\frac{1}{r - a - \delta a} - \frac{1}{r - a} \right) - \frac{1}{r - a}$$

For the marginal investment in R&D to be socially just worth while, we should have $V = O$. In that case, with a little manipulation, we get the result

$$\delta a = \frac{r - a}{Y_0 + 1} \longrightarrow \frac{r - a}{Y_0}$$

in the limit as the marginal investment shrinks towards 0. The marginal pound added to R&D increases a by δa, while the average pound, as we have already seen, increases a by a/R_0. Hence the ratio of marginal to average effects is

$$R_0\, \frac{\delta a}{a} \approx \frac{R_0}{Y_0}\, \frac{(r - a)}{a}.$$

Now R_0/Y_0 is the ratio of expenditure on R&D to national output, which is only a few per cent in most economies, given the usual definitions of R&D. Also, we may, as a rough guess, put the social rate of discount, r, at twice the rate of growth of output per head, a, which makes $(r - a)/a = 1$. (This would be consistent, for example, with an elasticity of the marginal utility of consumption with respect to consumption of 2 and a zero rate of pure time preference; see Chapter 8). Other values are possible, but I take this as being plausible, and to simplify illustraton of the point. It then follows that the marginal effect of increasing R&D on a is only a few per cent of the average effect, which implies that we have reached a point of very sharply diminishing returns, i.e. conclusion 1 above. Conclusion 2 would follow if we were to assume that R&D accounted for only a small fraction of a in all, say a fraction p. Then the average effect would be pa/R_0 and the ratio of marginal to average would be R_0/pY_0, which could be close to 1 if p were only a few per cent and so approximately equal to R_0/Y_0. Finally, conclusion 3 would follow if we had V substantially positive, which would permit the ratio of marginal to average effects to be substantially greater than with conclusion 1 and/or the investments covered to be a substantial fraction of the whole, but would imply that the social return to increasing R&D was very high.

If the above argument is correct, it is only if one believes in this last state of affairs, conclusion 3, that R&D, with effects of the kind posited by Eltis, can be an important explanation for the technical progress function he has suggested. I am sceptical of this possibility, and believe that 1 or 2 is more likely to be the case, so that, as already pointed out, we are to all intents and purposes back in the world of exogenous technical progress. If there is a great deal of socially profitable R&D waiting to be done, why have we not already discovered this?

We turn now to the second explanation advanced by Eltis for his technical progress function, which is learning by doing along the lines suggested by Arrow, but with an important difference. Whereas Arrow assumed that a q-times increase in cumulative gross investment would increase labour productivity q^μ times, with μ normally less than 1, Eltis assumes that it is the 'complete replacement of the capital stock by another with the same capital–output ratio' (Eltis 1973, 149) which increases labour productivity in a fixed proportion, namely, in the ratio e^R to 1, where $R >$ 0. He then argues that this complete replacement of the capital stock will take T years, and that T will be inversely proportional to the ratio of investment to output: roughly speaking, doubling that ratio will halve the time required for replacement. Hence labour productivity will increase in the proportion $e^{R/T}$ to 1 in one year, or at an exponential rate of R/T. If T is inversely proportional to S/Y, the investment ratio, then labour productivity must grow at an exponential ratio, that is directly proportionate to S/Y. This leads at once to the relation $a = BS/Y$ where B is a constant. We can then reach the technical progress function (4.5) if we allow for some exogenous technical progress, A, as well as technical progress arising from learning by doing.

This is an ingenious idea, but I am not clear as to exactly what is meant by 'complete replacement of the capital stock'. The forests cleared centuries ago still remain cleared, farm boundaries and ditches remain much as they were, old road alignments are preserved, and many buildings are over a hundred years old. Have we yet completely replaced our capital stock? In any case, why should complete replacement, if it can be defined, increase labour productivity in fixed proportion?

Let us, however, brush all these difficulties aside and consider the use to which Eltis puts his technical progress function. After all, the basic ideas underlying it seem plausible enough: that a faster rate of investment involves, *inter alia*, more R&D, which can be expected to speed up productivity growth, and that it also involves moving faster up any ladder of progress, with each new higher level of productivity, reached after learning more about new methods of production and new products, making possible the next advance.

Orthodox growth theory, as we saw in Chapter 3, makes the steady-state rate of growth equal to the sum of Harrod-neutral technical progress, a, and the rate of growth of the labour force in natural units, g_L, so

$$g = a + g_L.$$

Eltis makes use of the considerable intellectual capital invested in orthodox theory by retaining this relationship, as well as all the others we discussed in Chapter 3, but adding to them the equation (4.5). Hence his analysis of steady growth with endogenous technical progress consists of taking the Cobb–Douglas production function, or the CES production function, or one or other vintage models, and grafting on equation (4.5). This does considerably alter some of the orthodox conclusions. In particular, the steady-state rate of growth now depends on S/Y, and this variable also influences other magnitudes in ways that interested readers will find in Chapter 7 of Eltis's book.

This procedure, however, so far as production function theories are concerned, remains open to the various objections raised in Chapter 3 to the way in which the capital stock is measured, and in which changes in the stock are assumed to affect growth. So far as vintage theory is concerned, there remain the objections of complexity and lack of realism in various respects also mentioned in Chapter 3. In short, although past intellectual capital is utilized, the question arises as to whether it would not be better demolished and a fresh construction begun, starting with the same ideas of endogenous technical progress. Naturally I wish to persuade readers so, and the model in later chapters is constructed in that way. However, it does retain Eltis's concern with the ratio of investment to output as an important determinant of the long-run rate of growth of labour productivity.

4.8 Kennedy and some others

In 1964, Kennedy defended and developed the idea of 'induced bias in innovation' (a similar idea had been put forward by C. von Weizsäcker in an unpublished paper in 1962–3), which he traced back to Hicks (1932). This is the idea that a fall in the price of capital, relative to labour, will induce inventions of a labour-saving type. It had been examined, and discarded, by Salter (1960), who preferred to explain the historical rise in the ratio of capital to labour in terms of substitution between the two along known production functions. Salter's grounds for this rejection were that

The entrepreneur is interested in reducing costs in total, not particular costs such as labour costs or capital costs. When labour costs rise any advance that reduces total cost is welcome, and whether this is achieved by saving labour or capital is irrelevant. There is no reason to assume that attention should be concentrated on labour-saving techniques, unless, because of some inherent characteristic of technology, labour-saving knowledge is easier to acquire than capital-saving knowledge. (Salter 1960, 43–4)

It is interesting that Hahn and Matthews, writing after publication of Kennedy's article and with full knowledge of it, seem to have accepted Salter's view (Hahn and Matthews 1964, 831). It is also significant that Samuelson at first rejected Kennedy's argument, although, in the exchange between them, there is no doubt in my mind that Kennedy was victorious (Samuelson 1965, Kennedy 1966, Samuelson 1966). An admission of the Kennedy thesis is damaging to orthodox growth theory, since it vitiates the distinction between movements along a known production function involving substitution of capital for labour, and shifts of that function arising from 'technical progress'. As Kennedy pointed out in his original article, in his theory

it has not been found necessary to pose the question of how far a fall in labour requirements has been brought about by labour-saving innovation rather than substitution of capital for labour as a result of the cheapening of capital goods. Since this question is in principle unanswerable, there is some advantage in not having to ask it. (Kennedy 1966, 546)

Kennedy was not so much trying to produce a theory of growth, as defending the idea that innovation was responsive to relative factor prices, and showing how this response could explain constant shares between profits and wages in a steadily growing economy. He pointed out that earlier writers on growth (notably Robinson 1956, 170) had assumed that it was obvious that innovation would respond in this way. However, this view clearly could no longer be regarded as obvious since so much theory had been erected on assumptions that contradicted it. Since that still seems to be the case, and since the model in later chapters certainly assumes that investment and innovation (between which I do not distinguish) *do* respond to relative factor prices, it is worth while recalling Kennedy's argument, which is remarkably simple and clear.

The essential points are as follows. At any one time, entrepreneurs are faced by certain possibilities of reducing their capital and/or labour requirements per unit of output. (Both factors are for simplicity assumed to be measured in homogenous physical units.) These *possibilities* are assumed to be *technically* given; that is, they are quite independent of the relative prices of capital and labour. However, there is a constraint on the entrepreneur's ability to take advantage of them. If he opts for more capital-saving innovations, he has to forgo some labour-saving ones, for example. Kennedy did not explain this constraint, and I return to this weakness in his argument below. As it is at precisely this point that orthodoxy parts company with reality, it seems worth pointing out that the constraint must arise because the search for and exploitation of innovations is costly. In short, they require investment. Orthodox theory, by contrast, assumes that inovations are provided by 'costless inspiration', or that, at least, their flow cannot be increased by further investment. Were this really so, one would naturally accept with both hands whatever innovations the gods might choose to provide. But if the gods insist on being paid, and will sell more to those prepared to pay more, then the old economic problem has to be faced. There is then a constraint, and a solution that maximizes some objective function. In general, the lower is the price of capital relatively to that of labour, the more attractive become the labour-saving innovations relatively to the capital-saving ones, and entrepreneurs can be assumed to choose accordingly.

Kennedy proceeds from this to demonstrate that, under certain assumptions, steady growth will take place with constant shares of profits and wages, and technical progress will be entirely labour-saving. This then becomes an explanation for the existence of Harrod-neutral technical progress, although not one that has gained universal acceptance.

Kennedy's demonstration makes use of Figure 4.2. The axes measure the proportionate rate of fall in labour requirements (p) and capital requirements (q) per unit of output. We could equally call these the proportionate rates of labour augmentation (p) and capital augmentation (q) arising from technical progress. If the share of labour in total costs (or income) is λ, and that of capital is $(1 - \lambda)$, then Kennedy assumes that firms would like to maximize

$$r = \lambda p + (1 - \lambda)\, q$$

where r is the total fall in costs per unit of output. The choice between p and q is constrained to lie along the 'innovation possibility function' shown by

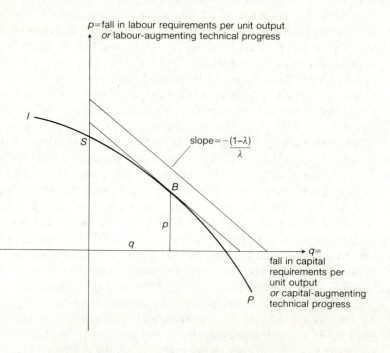

Fig. 4.2 Kennedy's innovation possibility function

the curved line *IP*. More p implies less q. So far as the firm is concerned, given λ, there is a trade-off such that a unit less of p loses λ units of cost reduction (r), while a unit more of q gains it $(1 - \lambda)$ units of cost reduction. Hence one unit of q is equivalent for the firm to $(1 - \lambda)/\lambda$ units of p. The family of straight lines of slope $- \{(1 - \lambda)/\lambda\}$ then gives, in effect, the firm's indifference map for p and q given by the point at which the *IP* curve touches the highest indifferent line, such as point B (for 'best') in Figure 4.2.

Clearly, the mix of labour- or capital-augmenting technical progress, on this analysis, depends on λ. The higher is λ, the more will the choice move towards labour augmentation and away from capital augmentation.

For there to be steady growth, capital measured in *natural* units must grow as fast as output, and also as fast as labour measured in *efficiency* units (see Chapter 3 above). Furthermore, output grows as fast as the weighted average of capital and labour in *efficiency* units. This implies that capital must grow at the same rate in natural units as in efficiency units, i.e. that there can be no capital augmentation in steady growth. Hence, for steady growth, we must be at S in the diagram. But why should firms choose to go there?

Suppose they are not there, but are, instead, at B. Then there is some capital augmentation going on. Assuming a constant saving ratio, however, capital in natural units must eventually grow as fast as output, which means that in efficiency units it must grow faster than output.[3] Since output growth is a weighted average of capital and labour growth rates in efficiency units, the rate of growth of capital must then be faster than that of labour in efficiency units. Then, so long as the elasticity of substitution between labour and capital, σ, is less than 1, the share of labour, λ, must rise. As I show above, a rise in λ moves B towards S. This process will continue until the steady-growth equilibrium at S is reached. At that point λ is constant, and so no further movement occurs, and we have purely labour augmenting technical progress.

There are several objections to Kennedy's analysis, if we regard it as the basis for a model of economic growth (see also Nordhaus 1973):

1. No attempt is made to explain the *position* of the innovation possibility function; that is, it is assumed that, for a given amount of labour-saving, there is a fixed amount of capital-saving that is possible. However, if the constraint that is operative is the investment cost of discovering and exploiting the innovations, it would seem only reasonable to allow for the fact that greater investment expenditure would permit more of both kinds of innovation simultaneously. In other words, more investment

---

[3] I say 'eventually' because we could have started from a position in which the given saving ratio made capital grow more slowly than output.

would shift the possibility frontier outwards.

2. Perfect competition is assumed. Not only is this limiting, but also it might be regarded as inconsistent with the idea that technical progress is endogenous (see Meade 1968, ch. 9).

3. The choice between different innovations is made entirely with reference to the immediate savings in current unit costs. Since we are considering what is essentially an investment decision, this myopic behaviour needs to be explained. It is not clear that it is the correct, wealth-maximizing, way to make the choice.

4. An aggregate production function with constant returns to scale in K and L is used to explain the level of output of consumption goods. This is open to the same objections as were given in Chapter 3 above.

Kennedy's idea of the innovation possibility function has been extended to a two-sector model by McCain (1972) and to an n-sector model by Kennedy himself (Kennedy 1973). It has been incorporated into otherwise orthodox growth models by Drandakis and Phelps (1966), and by Samuelson (1965, 1966). However, all of these extensions and applications remain subject to the above objections.

An interesting application of the idea which meets objection 1 is that of Conlisk (1969). He divides the economy into two sectors: one of these produces consumption goods, and the other he has christened the 'productivity sector'. Capital and labour are allocated between these sectors in accordance with savings decisions. The 'productivity sector' produces capital goods and also improves the efficiency of labour, and the choice between these is made essentially in the Kennedy way; in other words, the 'output' of these two 'goods' is constrained by a production possibility frontier similar to Kennedy's innovation possibility frontier. Firms choose their favoured combination of the 'goods' by reference to current factor prices. However, the *position* of the frontier is now no longer exogenously given, but is determined by firms' allocation of capital and labour to the 'productivity sector'. This is clearly an important step forward, but objections 3 and 4 above still apply to Conlisk's model. (He makes no assumption about perfect competition, so objection 2 may not apply; on the other hand, it is not clear how prices or wages are determined in his model.)

Nordhaus (1969) devised an interesting model which is similar to that of Conlisk in that technical progress is 'produced' at a cost. Nordhaus assumes that inventions can be costlessly imitated, but that inventors have a monopoly which lasts for a limited period (set by patent laws, or by their ability to keep the invention secret, or simply by slowness in imitation), during which they can obtain the benefits resulting from it. Objections 2 and 4 apply to Nordhaus's model, and, unlike Conlisk's, it does not explain the choices made between capital- or labour-saving technologies. A Cobb–Douglas production function is assumed for the whole economy, other than the 'invention-producing' sector, which ensures constant income shares with steady growth, but is open to objections already mentioned. Nevertheless, the role of *imitation* as a cause of productivity growth, which is a central feature of Nordhaus's model, is something I attempt to allow for in later chapters.

Ahmad (1966) both put forward his own theory of induced innovation and used it to criticize Kennedy's theory. Ahmad's theory assumed that businessmen could choose between different possible innovations, all costing the same time and effort, from a set called the 'innovation possibility curve'. These innovations enabled a given output level to be produced with less labour and/or less capital than in the existing situation, and the amounts of labour and/or capital saved would be chosen in the light of current relative factor prices. What was chosen was a production function, and there was in addition the possibility of substitution between labour and capital along this function. Ahmad's criticism of Kennedy was that the latter's theory constrained the shape of the innovation possibility curves in such a way that changes in factor shares could not take place, because changes in relative prices had to be offset by changes in relative quantities (rather like a Cobb–Douglas production function). My objection to Ahmad's theory is that it would require one to make some distinctions which it would be empirically difficult to make. Expenditure on 'innovation' would have to be distinguished from expenditure on 'capital'. Changes in quantities of labour and capital arising from movements along a given production function would have to be distinguished from those arising from shifts of that function. Ahmad did not discuss the problems involved in defining and measuring capital input.

Atkinson and Stiglitz (1969) criticized both orthodox views of technical change and the attempts to develop the Kennedy model mentioned above for their lack of an historical perspective. They pointed out that technical progress was likely to occur only in those techniques that were in current use, while techniques not being currently used would be passed by. There might be some spillovers, but one should not assume that the *whole* production possibility frontier would shift outwards. They also pointed out that investment decisions should allow for this. Thus, for example, a firm might opt for a more capital-intensive technique than current factor prices would justify because it could foresee that real wages were going to rise, and so it would be better placed in the future. It would be able to make improvements in capital-intensive techniques that would be suitable to the higher real wages of the future, and these improvements could not be made until it had built up some experience of such techniques.

I do not pursue the Kennedy model, and its developments, any further, for the reasons given. However, his idea (and that of Ahmad) of a set of innovation (and so investment) possibilities between which businessmen choose is central to the model described later, although I there recast it so as to get rid of the need to define or measure the *capital stock*. I have assumed, with Ahmad, Conlisk, and Nordhaus, that inventions are costly, and have allowed as best I can for imitation. I have also tried to incorporate Atkinson and Stiglitz's idea that, so to speak, you always start from where you are, so that the actual historical path you take is an important determinant of the nature of future progress. Finally, I agree with many of the points made by Streissler (1980), who has criticized neoclassical theories of growth, and has argued that economic growth and technical progress are due to investment, with emphasis on learning from investment.

4.9 Evolutionary theories: Nelson and Winter

The analogy between economic progress and biological evolution through natural selection has often been observed (see Hirshleifer 1977 for a survey). In the growth model put forward in Part III below, some of this analogy is preserved, in contrast to orthodox growth models. There are similar incremental changes, which can be regarded as improved adaptations to the environment. There is competition between firms as there is between species and within species. The environment for any particular firm is continually changing because of the changes made by other firms, and this changes the adaptations required. Every adaptation has to start from the existing situation, and creates a new situation from which new adaptations can be made. In orthodox production function theory, by contrast, the firm is free to choose the best 'blue-print' for all its employed factors at each moment in time. In Meade's exposition (Meade 1968, chs. II, XV), which is characteristically frank and ruthlessly clear, the firm sacks or sells all its factors of production at the end of each day, and hires or buys whatever it needs afresh, to suit the newest set of blue-prints, at the start of the next day. It is this potentially complete reorganization of production which preserves equilibrium continuously despite changing technology, and enables the theory to explain *levels* as well as *changes* (except that the changes in technology are not explained). It is as if a living organism could survive despite a complete mutation of all its genes, the mutations being selected to adapt best to the environment at all times.

In real life, as in my model of growth, only a small number of changes can be made in a small amount of time. Adaptation proceeds incrementally and endlessly, and is never perfect, if only because it itself changes the environment. Vintage growth models come much closer to this since only the latest additions to the capital stock, instead of the whole of it, are adapted to the current environment. But even this is a poor representation of life and of economic growth as well. In life, the mutations are not new species, or new members of existing species, which can be considered separately from the old species, or old members: they are small changes in existing species. It is only after a long period of evolution that they add up to something that can be characterized as a new species. Likewise, in my model the small changes resulting from investment are made to existing enterprises. In vintage models, however, the new vintages are something quite separate from the old ones, with their separate attached labour forces, material inputs and outputs. It is as if investment always consisted in adding entirely new (but small) factories on green-field sites, whereas most investment is not of this kind, but consists of modifications of existing factories, fields, roads, harbours, etc. It is this fact that has made vintage theory so difficult to apply empirically — the separate vintages are not really separately identifiable.

It is the nature of the mutations themselves, however, that constitutes perhaps the main difference between evolution of species and economic growth. In the former, the mutations are small *random* changes, and selection weeds out the unsuccessful. Success is measured by immediate survival, i.e. by adaptation to the *current* environment. Economic growth is more purposive. The changes are made with an eye to the future, and are not random. This means that economic change can be much more rapid, and that there is less waste. However, the contrast is not complete. On the one hand, natural selection will favour species that happen to have (by chance) taken a path that is most successful in the long run—leading to human beings rather than to dinosaurs, for example. On the other, businessmen can at best foresee the future as in a glass darkly. Their chosen adaptations are for the most part to the current situation, which they must survive if they are to take advantage of the longer term.

Another difference between biological evolution and economic growth is that competition (between species or between firms) typically results in no net gain to those involved in the former, but does typically result in net gain to the latter. Thus, Dawkins (1986) has pointed out the analogy between competition between predator and prey and arms races. Improvements on one side merely neutralize improvements on the other. The cheetah can run ever more swiftly, and so can the gazelle, so that slower members of both species are eliminated; but the numbers of each may be little affected, nor, so far as one can tell, is their enjoyment of life. Like the Red Queen in *Alice through the Looking-Glass*, one must run faster to stay where one is. It is different in economic competition. Firms of ever increasing efficiency may, it is true, become no more profitable, but their members, as consumers, benefit from the greater efficiency. There is still something of a 'Red Queen effect', for example in competitive advertising, but it no longer dominates.

There are other differences, and competitive selection is not the same as optimization, as Matthews (1984) has pointed out. *Both* are important ingredients in economic growth. Competitive selection is needed, partly as a spur, and partly because decisions are inevitably based on incomplete information, and involve guesswork and hunch. Selection eliminates mistakes. Optimization is needed to reduce waste and speed beneficial learning and imitation, as well as being a primary motive of invention. To some extent, competitive selection can be modelled *as if* it were conscious optimization (cf. Friedman 1953), and that is largely how it is treated in Part III, although one must admit that real differences exist.

Two writers who have chosen the opposite alternative, which is a very different approach to any of those considered thus far, are Nelson and Winter (1974, 1982). They share common ground in criticizing orthodox growth theories along lines similar to those already mentioned, and in drawing inspiration from Schumpeter. However, their 'evolutionary theory' jettisons the ideas of profit maximization and equilibrium, and substitutes a trial-and-error process in which firms are selected for faster or slower growth depending, to a large extent, on their luck in turning up successful innovations.

In an example of the kind of model they favour, firms are envisaged as operating according to certain 'rules' which determine their labour and capital requirements per unit of output, the way in which prices are fixed, and, as a result of their collective actions and a supply function for labour, the level of real wages. They reinvest all their profits after paying out a fixed rate of dividend, so more profitable firms grow faster than less profitable ones. They do not change existing techniques as long as the rate of profit is above some particular level, but engage in a search for other techniques if it falls below that. Inferior techniques that may be discovered are rejected, and superior ones adopted (without waiting to see if better ones still could be found by longer search). Competition for labour drives up real wages and squeezes out firms that are unsuccessful in finding better techniques. The model can be provided with parameters that make it simulate the aggregate behaviour of the US economy quite closely.

Several advantages are claimed for this type of theory, the main one being that it enables the theorist to make use of the empirical literature on the process of innovation, and its rate of diffusion through imitation. It also enables one to analyse the competitive struggle, and to assume, realistically, that some firms are more efficient than others. Likewise, the factors governing the rate of growth of particular firms, including those that limit its ability to obtain finance for investment, can be studied.

Nelson and Winter are critical of the way in which orthodox theory, with its macro approach based on aggregation, maximization, and equilibrium, hides the diversity and change which, they assert, are the central phenomena in economic growth. They admit that the problem is to reconcile diversity and change with analytic tractability and logical coherence, but believe that their approach enables this to be done. However, it does so, to judge by their example, only by resorting to computer simulation. Without that, it is hard to see how one could work out the implications of different pricing 'rules', or dividend 'rules', or search 'rules', etc., on the outcome for aggregate economic growth.

Perhaps it is, all the same, the only way forward. The complexity of the real world may be such that the attempt to portray it by a model simple enough to have analytical solutions, or diagrammatic solutions, is foredoomed to failure. Nevertheless, in later chapters such an attempt is made. In principle, allowance is made for diversity between firms, although in practice the issue is really fudged by assuming a 'representative firm'. That firm is in *growth* equilibrium and is maximizing its net present value,[4] neither of which assumptions would appeal to Nelson and Winter. However, the equilibrium is of a special kind. It does not mean that the firm, looked at from some timeless perspective, has done the best it can. The firm has reached its present situation as a result of an historical, incremental, process of change. At each step, the firm has made those changes that have appeared best to it, given the information then at its disposal. But likewise, each step has changed this information, so that each further step is taken in the light of new information. The firm never reaches a position where it can rest on its laurels, satisfied that no further changes are needed. Equilibrium simply means that the outcome of this process has been steady growth, rather than accelerating or decelerating growth.

One hopes that these assumptions mimic the outcome of selection through trial and error, but they may not do so very well. I have considerable sympathy with evolutionary theories, but believe that the hypothesis of profit maximization, in a different setting from those tried so far, may yet enable us to understand something more about economic growth, without having to reach for the computer.

---

[4] However, at a later stage allowance is made for managerially controlled firms which push growth beyond the point that would maximize net present value, and some evidence for this is given.

PART III

CONSTRUCTION

Yet all experience is an arch wherethro'
Gleams that untravell'd world, whose margin fades
For ever and for ever when I move.

Tennyson: *Ulysses*

5

INVESTMENT, INVENTION, AND SCIENTIFIC DISCOVERY

5.1 Introduction

What is the relation between investment, invention, and scientific discovery? We need to discuss this question because of the powerful orthodox view that investment is merely the exploitation of inventions, which, in turn, are merely the exploitation of scientific discoveries. According to this view, it is the pace of scientific advance that ultimately determines the rate of growth of productivity. Investment is required to match the pace of scientific advance. If it is more than sufficient for that purpose, the rate of return will fall, and if it is less, the rate of return will rise. The production possibility frontier, or the production function, shifts outward at a rate determined ultimately by the pace of scientific advance. An alternative view is that it is the pace of invention that is the determining factor, with the pace of scientific advance more in the background. But is either view borne out by what we know about the relations between investment, invention, and scientific discovery?

The main conclusion of this chapter is that scientific discovery and invention are best regarded as forms of investment, and that, at least to begin with, a theory of growth can be constructed without distinguishing between them. Furthermore, there is no evidence that investment opportunities become exhausted. Fresh ones are created by undertaking existing opportunities, since one learns from the changes made thereby. Consequently, instead of scientific discovery and invention being the creators of investment opportunities, investment itself creates them. To understand economic growth, therefore, we need, in the first place, to examine the rate, quality, and determinants of investment. It is a mistake to treat scientific advance and invention as processes that are independent of investment. This conclusion is the starting point for the construction of my model of economic growth.

5.2 Schmookler's *Invention and Economic Growth*

Let us first consider Schmookler's great book on *Invention and Economic Growth*, which is directly relevant. Schmookler defines an invention in the way relevant to the patent system 'as a prescription for a producible product or operable process so new as not to have been 'obvious to one skilled in the art' at the time the idea was put forward' (Schmookler 1966, 6). Sub-inventions are defined as 'obvious' changes in products or processes. 'Thus the average house designed by an architect, though differing in detail from all others, would be a "routine innovation", that is, a species of subinvention' (p. 6).

Schmookler examines, and lists in his book, 934 *important* inventions made in all countries in four industries between the years 1800 and 1957: 235 in agriculture, 284 in petroleum refining, 185 in paper-making, and 230 in railroading. An invention is judged economically important if it is thought, for example, to have made possible a sizeable percentage increase in output per unit of composite input, weighted by the relevant output's share in national output. It is judged technologically important if, with subsequent improvements of its essential idea, it led to one or more economically important inventions. The four industries are chosen as representing both old (agriculture and paper) and new industries, some relying considerably on science (petroleum and paper) and some not so much, some having large irms (petroleum and railroading) and some small, and all being important and having patent statistics which could be compiled relatively easily (see later). Schmookler instructed his research workers 'to record any suggestion in the literature that a particular scientific discovery (or any other event) led to the making of an important invention'. While for most of the inventions no initiating stimulus could be identified,

for a significant minority of cases, the stimulus is identified, and for *almost all of these* that stimulus *is a technical problem or opportunity conceived by the inventor largely in economic terms*, that is, in terms of costs and revenues. . . . In those few instances where the literature identifies a stimulus which is not an economically significant problem per se, that stimulus is an accident. . . . In contrast to the many accounts identifying economic problems as the immediate stimulus, *in no single instance is a scientific discovery specified as the factor initiating an important invention in any of these four industries.* (Schmookler 1966, 66–7; emphasis in the original)

Schmookler does not deny that, in some 'science-based' industries (he mentions the electrical, electronics, nuclear, chemical, and drug and pharmaceutical industries) invention and research is heavily dependent on scientific knowledge, and that in these industries there were many instances of important inventions being directly induced by scientific discoveries. However, he argues that, even in these industries, 'economically evaluated technical problems and opportunities arising in the normal conduct of business are dominant' (p. 68). Furthermore, even where an invention is directly stimulated by a scientific discovery, most of its social and economic significance derives from a host of other inventions which improve and adapt the basic one, and these depend on the economic value perceived to result from them. In general, Schmookler regards scientific knowledge as 'far more a permissive than an active factor in the inventive process' (p. 70). There are many more inventions that *could* be made on the basis of existing knowledge than *are* made, and those that are made are made because of their perceived economic value.

Just as important inventions were not, in the industries studied (and are probably not in most cases), directly stimulated by scientific discoveries, neither were they directly stimulated by other inventions. Again, however, Schmookler admits that there must be exceptions to this rule, although he believes them to be uncommon.

As a test of the hypothesis that inventions beget inventions, Schmookler compares the numbers of important inventions in his four industries with the numbers of patents in those same industries (Schmookler 1966, ch. IV). His patents refer to *capital goods used by the industry* to which they are allocated, since reasonably comprehensive statistics could be prepared for these, but not for other patents (e.g. for materials or consumer goods) (p. 20). He takes the number of patents as an index of inventive activity. He is well aware of the objections that can be made to this use of patent statistics, but he argues convincingly both that nothing better is available and that they are better than nothing. The main result of his analysis is a negative one: neither the long swings nor the shorter cycles show any clear relationship between the two series which could be regarded as showing that important inventions determine subsequent inventive activity.

Schmookler next considers the idea, put forward by Wolf (1912), and then by Kuznets (1930) and Salter (1960), of technological exhaustion in a field. As Kuznets puts it,

The stimulus for technical changes in other processes of industry is thus present from the moment the first major invention is introduced. . . .

While the stimulus for further inventions appears early, the number of operations to be improved is limited and gradually becomes exhausted. (Kuznets 1930, 31-3; quoted by Schmookler 1966, 87)

This view would imply, if it were true, that scientific discoveries and/or important inventions not only initiate an industry (or 'field'), but also limit its development. Once the initiating discovery or invention has been exhausted, further development comes to a halt, just as an oil well ultimately runs dry, or, at least, as it ceases to be economical to attempt to pump more oil out of it. In both cases, the exhaustion of opportunities is determined outside the economic system. It is a view that Schmookler clearly thinks is mistaken. There may often be rapid growth followed by decline, but the reason for the decline is essentially economic and not technological. Schmookler believes that it is the decline in the *value* of productivity advance, rather than increases in its *cost*, that is generally the decisive factor. As one example of this point he instances the horseshoe, which, since it was introduced in the second century before Christ, should, according to the theory, be a 'field' in which the technical possibilities for further improvement were exhausted long ago. Yet, as he shows, the annual number of US patents for horseshoes successfully applied for rose continually until the close of the nineteenth century, and then declined. 'Once the steam traction engine and, later, the internal combustion engine began to displace the horse, inventive interest in the field began to decline—because of a decline not in the technical possibilities of the field but in its economic payoff' (p. 93). Schmookler reinforces this example by another, showing that the numbers of patents for railroad track followed the same broad sweep of rise and subsequent decline as did the number of patents for all other railroad fields. Clearly, some third set of determinants, and not the technology in railroad track or in other railroad fields, must be invoked to explain this. His conclusion is reinforced still further by appeal to statistics of the numbers of patents in other fields, not closely related technically, which have yet followed similar cycles. Again, some determinants other than technology itself are required to explain why the cycles should coincide.

In fact, Schmookler's explanation of inventive activity is the expected profitability of inventions (pp. 112–15). This depends on the value of the expected sales of the relevant goods (he is considering capital goods inventions), less their costs of production and less the cost of making and developing the invention. Despite what others have said (see below), Schmookler does *not*, so far as I can see, assume that the cost of making and developing an invention is much the same for any good. All he claims is that the number of inventions will tend to vary with the expected value of sales of goods incorporating that invention. There is an omitted explanatory variable in his regressions, of which he is well aware; namely, the cost of making and developing the relevant inventions. Despite that, the regressions do provide evidence in favour of his hypothesis that expected profitability is an important determinant of inventive activity, and further evidence in favour of that is provided by other studies, notably those of Griliches (1957) and Mansfield (referred to below).

It is interesting that Schmookler discovered this explanation by chance, while searching for a relationship such as orthodox theory might suppose between inventive activity and subsequent productivity advance, and which he failed to find (Schmookler 1966, 104). This is itself an example of the way in which scientific discoveries are made.

Schmookler provides two kinds of evidence for his explanation, relating to time series and cross-sections, respectively. The main time-series evidence is for the relation between investment in railroading and numbers of patents of capital goods used in railroading. He considers both the very long swings over more than a century ending in about 1950, and deviations of seven- or nine-year moving averages from seventeen-year moving averages in the series. He also disaggregates the patents and investment statistics, and derives various lagged correlations. His conclusion, which is supported by the less adequate corresponding statistics for petroleum refining and building, is that both the longer and the shorter swings in number of patents are similar to those in investment, and that, for the most part, the patents lag behind investment at turning points, thus suggesting that investment is the cause rather than the effect (Schmookler 1966, ch. VI).

The cross-section evidence relates to about twenty industries and consists of the relations between investment in these industries and patents successfully applied for capital goods used by them (Schmookler 1966, ch. VII). If the logarithm of investment in an earlier year is regressed on the logarithm of the number of patents, the resulting r^2 is above 0.9 and the coefficient is not significantly different from 1.[1] Schmookler introduces employment as an explanatory variable in the regressions to test whether size rather than investment is the explanation for the correlations, but the resulting coefficients are not significant. He also rules out the hypothesis that *recent* past invention might explain both current invention and current investment, thus leading to the correlation observed between the latter two. Since the industries differ in amounts of investment by very large amounts (factors of 60 or 100), he considers it incredible that differences in recent past invention *could* result in such differences. 'No amount of technical progress could make barrel-making a major industry, and even with no technological progress whatever, the railroad industry would have had to replace a great deal of plant and equipment in 1947' (p. 147).

Schmookler provides further data and correlations, all of considerable interest, but I cannot summarize all of that here. Readers are urged to consult the original work. I must, however, consider a criticism of it, and in doing so will reveal more of his views.

5.3 Criticism of Schmookler

Rosenberg (1974) interpreted Schmookler as arguing that *only* demand mattered, and that the supply of inventions was, in effect, infinitely elastic. He recognized that Schmookler had allowed for great differences in the rate

---

[1] The two fitted equations are:

$$\log P_{1940\text{-}2} = 1.174 + 0.927 \log I_{1939}; \ r^2 = 0.918$$
$$\quad\quad\quad (0.080)\quad (0.070)$$

$$\log P_{1948\text{-}50} = 0.598 + 0.940 \log I_{1947}; \ r^2 = 0.905$$
$$\quad\quad\quad (0.116)\quad (0.070)$$

where P is the number of capital goods patents averaged over the years shown and I is investment in plant and equipment in $m. Standard errors are in brackets, and there were 21 and 22 cross-section observations respectively in different industries (Schmookler 1966, 144).

of development of science and technology in different fields, which differences had profoundly influenced the rates of growth of different industries. Thus, the rapid modern growth of the electrical, electronic, chemical, and pharmaceutical industries owed much, according to Schmookler, to scientific developments in those fields. However, this did not weaken the dominance of sales of capital goods in determining capital goods inventive activity (measured by the numbers of patents). If industry A spent twice as much on capital goods as industry B, then it would induce about twice as much inventive activity in producing capital goods for A as for B. Those capital goods might be increasingly electronically controlled, if the science and technology of electronics were advancing particularly fast. But that would be true for both A's and B's capital goods. Hence, while different rates of advance of science and technology would influence *which* fields would be drawn on to supply the new capital goods for *any* industry, about twice as much inventive activity would be devoted to A as to B if sales of capital goods were twice as big.

Rosenberg, however, wanted to give more importance than he thought Schmookler did to supply-side influences. He argued:

(1) that science and technology progress, in some measure, along lines determined by internal logic, degree of complexity, or at least in response to forces independent of economic need; (2) that this sequence in turn imposes significant constraints or presents unique opportunities which materially shape the direction and the timing of the inventive process; and (3) that, as a result, the costs of invention differ in different industries. (Rosenberg 1974, 95)

He thus attacked Schmookler's view that 'a million dollars spent on one kind of good is likely to induce about as much invention as the same sum spent on any other good' (p. 96), and also that 'From a broader point of view, demand induces the inventions that satisfy it' (p. 97). He contrasted the progress made in the techniques of navigation in the sixteenth and seventeenth centuries with those made in medicine. For both, there was a demand, but the former could draw on existing knowledge in mathematics and astronomy, whereas medicine had to await the development of the science of bacteriology in the second half of the nineteenth century, despite the interest, money, and talent devoted to it earlier on. Rosenberg argues that 'inventions are rarely equally possible in all commodity classes. The state of the various sciences simply makes some inventions easier (i.e. cheaper) and others harder (i.e. more costly)' (p. 98). He provides examples to prove his point. Schmookler had argued that 'society has now, and probably has had for a long time, a highly flexible, multipurpose knowledge base amenable to development at virtually all points' (Schmookler 1966, p. 173). Rosenberg, while agreeing with this up to a point, remarks that

it is easy to exaggerate the extent to which separate sub-realms of knowledge offer genuine options in the satisfaction of given categories of human wants, in the sense of presenting methods which are *substitutes* for each other. Such substitution is frequently non-existent and usually highly imperfect. (Rosenberg 1974, 100).

Furthermore, different branches of knowledge may be complementary, not substitutive. The new high-yielding varieties of rice, for example, require fertilizers and good techniques of water management. Although economic motives are more important in the development of technology than science, different developments may be more or less difficult to make. Thus, the substitution of coal for wood, which was becoming increasingly scarce in Britain in the second half of the sixteenth century, proceeded at very different rates in different uses, because of the different degrees of difficulty in overcoming technical problems. One of the last uses was also one of the most important, namely, metallurgy, so that demand influences cannot be held responsible for the delay of about two hundred years involved. 'Indeed, it may be confidently asserted that the solution came *last* in precisely that industry where the economic payoff was greatest: the iron industry' (Rosenberg 1974, 102). Even if demand determined the allocation of inventive *effort*, the payoff to the effort would depend on supply-side forces such as the state of scientific knowledge and of technological skills. 'These supply-side forces determine whether the output is of the kind associated with the medieval alchemist or the modern scientific metallurgist' (p. 103).

Rosenberg concludes by suggesting that we can learn much by a study of *un*successful inventions, to supplement the more usual study of successful ones. The supply curves of different kinds of inventions gradually shift downwards as knowledge advances. They are not always infinitely elastic, as Schmookler (according to Rosenberg) argues: 'The timing of inventions therefore needs to be understood in terms of such shifting supply curves which gradually reduce the cost of achieving certain classes of inventions' (p. 107).

Rosenberg's view may be characterized as 'supply-and-demand', his interpretation of Schmookler's as 'just demand'. It seems impossible to deny that inventions may be more or less costly in some sense in different fields, and that their costs vary depending, *inter alia*, on scientific discoveries and other inventions. All the same, I do not believe that Schmookler intended to deny that, even if some of his statements give that impression. He also states, quite clearly, that 'the relative efficiency of different technological means changes over time partly because of the rate and character of scientific and engineering progress' (p. 172), and that the faster rate of growth of some industries than others may be due to faster scientific and technological progress in fields relevant to them. Furthermore, he explicitly recognizes differences in the costs of invention in his more formal explanation (pp. 112–15). Indeed, it would hardly make sense to assume that all inventions cost the same and are in perfectly elastic supply. Mankind would then be in possession of Aladdin's lamp, since why should a desired invention not consist of anything one can imagine? Why should not the economic problem be solved once and for all? Schmookler certainly never assumed or argued that. He did, however, try to explain the empirical relationships summarized above—a problem that Rosenberg does not directly address.

Empirical studies of the importance of technological opportunity (i.e. the cost of invention) versus economic opportunity (i.e. the factors stressed by Schmookler) are surveyed by Kamien and Schwartz. They conclude that both are important.[2]

5.4 Conclusions

Schmookler's work, and that of others referred to below, points to five conclusions which are important for the growth theory developed in succeeding chapters.

1. The first conclusion is that invention is a particular form of investment. For some purposes (e.g. if one is writing a history of technology, or if one is analysing growth in a particular industry or field), it is essential to distinguish it from other forms; but for other purposes, and for the theory of growth put forward in this book, it is more important to emphasize the similarities to than the differences from other investments. Schmookler argued that the *prospective profitability* of an invention was the main determinant, in most cases, of its birth and survival. My understanding of Rosenberg is that he does not disagree with that, but rather seeks to emphasize the importance of what he sees as a missing element in Schmookler's account, namely, the existing state of relevant scientific knowledge which affects the costs of invention and so its prospective profitability. Mansfield's empirical work has shown both that the distribution of R&D expenditures among industries and the allocation of funds within a firm as between different research projects can be explained, to a large extent, by prospective profitability (Mansfield 1968; see especially chs. 2 and 3). To be sure, Mansfield points out that 'non-economic' factors must also have been important determinants of the allocation of funds. He mentions, for example, that company scientists have their own scientific and professional goals, which are not always consistent with the strictly commercial objectives of the firm; that intra-firm politics are important; that some kinds and sources of estimates are given more weight than others by decision-makers; that those who argue

---

[2] 'In fact, of course technological opportunity and economic opportunity are complementary influences on the course of invention. . . . Economic opportunity accelerates the exploitation of technological opportunity, and in the long run there is a feedback leading to new technological opportunities' (Kamien and Schwartz 1982, 64).

more effectively and persuasively for their proposals have a better chance of gaining approval; and that those projects promising 'success' sooner are often preferred to more adventurous projects whose higher expected returns will be longer delayed. However, very similar points apply to the allocation of funds to *any* investment projects, so that these points do not require us to distinguish R&D expenditures from other sorts of investment. A great deal of inventing is still done by self-employed inventors, rather than by hired technologists employed, for example, in research laboratories or firms.[3] Such inventors are in many ways like other small self-employed businessmen. Their motivation is complex, but expectations of profitability, and even perhaps dreams of riches, are probably as important for such inventors as for the businessman.

2.   The second conclusion is that, as with any investment project, prospective costs are an important determinant of prospective profitability, and can be such as to rule out some or enhance the attractiveness of others. This seems to be Rosenberg's main point, and I do not believe that Schmookler would disagree.

3.   My third conclusion is that investment opportunities are recreated by undertaking investment, and that their average quality does not change very much, at least so far as large sectors of the economy, or the whole economy, are concerned. Some of the evidence for this has been mentioned, notably that produced by Schmookler to show that inventive opportunities in different fields do not appear to become exhausted but decline, when they do, because demand for the relevant product declines.[4] Orthodox theory's reasons for believing that investment opportunities are *reduced* by undertaking investment is precisely that the flow of invention is exogenously determined. If the flow, on the contrary, depends on the rate of investment, which is suggested by Schmookler's evidence, and if, indeed, invention is just one *form* of investment, then there is no need to suppose that orthodoxy is right. It may be true that, if invention were brought to a halt, the marginal return on investment would fall: but that is not peculiar to invention. If investment in construction, or transport, or food supply, or

[3] See Schmookler (1966, Appendix B), who points out that a sample inquiry he undertook (also published in the *Review of Economics and Statistics*, August 1957) revealed that 'About 40 per cent of the inventions [in the USA] were *not* made by technologists or by hired inventors. Full-time inventors probably accounted for considerably less than half the inventions made. And non-college graduates were probably responsible for more inventions than were college graduates' (p. 260). However, both he and others have pointed out the *increasing* importance of inventions resulting from the R&D expenditures of firms, and especially large firms. Jewkes, Sawers, and Stillerman (1969) also stress the importance of independent inventors.

[4] I return to this point in Ch. 9, where it is shown that there is very close parallel between an exogenous fall in investment opportunities in a particular industry (such as would occur if, indeed, the scope for invention became exhausted), and a decline in the prices of the industry's products relative to goods in general (such as would occur if demand for those products were to fall). In both cases the scope for investment, and so also invention, is reduced.

many other things were brought to a halt, we would presently be forced to resign ourselves to a static economy. Schmookler's analysis of the way in which increased output of a particular good can be aided by inventions in a great variety of ways is helpful here. Improvements can be made in the good itself, or in capital goods to make the good, or in materials to make it, or in the organization of work to make it. And different industries and disciplines, different fields of science and engineering, can be the sources of each of these improvements. One may add that improvements that are unprofitable at existing prices can become profitable at higher prices—and this very important point, which is obvious but nevertheless forgotten, is taken up in Chapters 9 and 13 below.

There is a rather beautiful dispensation of Providence at work here. If one defines a good very narrowly, then the scope for improvement can vary 'exogenously' from time to time in the way stressed by Rosenberg. But the *effect* of such variations on the actual amount of investment in improvement, and so on the actual rate of improvement, can be mitigated by relative price changes. Thus, if the scope for invention and so investment increases in a particular industry, this will drive down the (relative) prices of its products, thus reducing the scope for further invention and investment. The rate of improvement in the industry will then revert to normal. If one defines a good very widely, relative prices cannot change so easily (and not at all, for the output of the whole economy); but then, just because the aggregate one is considering is so large, the scope for aggregate improvement is less likely to fluctuate. Hence, taking relative price changes into account, the scope for improvements, i.e. investment opportunities, may remain rather constant, in both large and small sectors.

4. So much for exogenous invention. But what about the exogenous rate of growth of the stock of scientific knowledge, which could be orthodoxy's *primum mobile*? It is surely implausible to believe that scientific advance is motivated by expected profitability, and that the cost of acquiring scientific knowledge can be regarded as just another form of investment. Yet does not the pace of scientific advance in the long run control the rate of technical advance? Rosenberg's emphasis on the importance of the stock of scientific knowledge accords with orthodoxy here. However, and despite all this, my fourth conclusion is that it is the rate of investment that controls the rate of technical advance, and that one can safely neglect the rate of scientific advance in constructing a theory of economic growth. This conclusion must not be interpreted to mean that I believe scientific advance is unimportant for economic growth, although it is probably true that, especially in the more distant past (including the Industrial Revolution in Britain), many inventions have been based not on scientific knowledge but on more directly practical knowledge.[5] In the

---

[5] This is, indeed, Principle 4 of Gilfillan's Social Principles of Invention, which reads

modern world, scientific knowledge has become increasingly important, and I have little doubt that further investment in it, *as well* as in many other things, is needed for growth to continue.

My reasons for neglecting it are as follows. First, the cost of basic research is a very small fraction of total investment costs, perhaps typically less than one-fortieth of them.[6] It seems implausible that long-term growth can be explained, or has to be explained, by this small fraction of the total, since the rate of accumulation of scientific knowledge can be changed by spending more or less on it. Firms in industries that are 'science-based' commonly undertake basic research themselves, or else commission it in universities or research institutes, and public expenditure on universities and research institutes is undoubtedly influenced by expectations that the research they carry out will contribute to economic growth, even if curiosity and fame are the chief motives of scientists themselves.[7, 8] Second, the existing stock of scientific knowledge is large, and, as Schmookler has

'Invention need not be based on prior science. It often precedes and evokes the apposit science' (Gilfillan 1970, 6). Cf. also Derry and Williams: 'The great majority of technological developments were the result of empirical discoveries by practical men: indeed, it has been remarked already that until comparatively recently technology contributed more to science than science to technology' (Derry and Williams 1960, 608).

[6] Basic research expenditure in the USA from 1948 to 1969 averaged rather less than 2.5 per cent of the value of gross investment in non-residential business. Basic research expenditures are as defined by the National Science Foundation and given in Kendrick (Kendrick, with Lethem and Rowley 1976, 169). The year 1969 is the most recent there given. Gross investment in non-residential business, which excludes all R&D, is from the sources given in the Statistical Appendix. For other countries, the corresponding ratio would very probably be lower.

[7] Schmookler's views on this are worth quoting at length:

The well-known controversy among historians of science concerning the relative importance of 'economic' and 'non-economic' factors in the growth of science really revolves mainly around the question of whether new scientific knowledge is demanded primarily as a consumer good or as a capital good. That the public's support of scientific research has increased over the past several decades precisely when its own capacity to understand the results declined as science became more complicated suggests that it is the demand for knowledge as capital that predominates in modern times. This inference is reinforced by the fact that marked increases in state support of science in recent centuries are demonstrably attributable to an increased demand for new applications generally associated with real, feared, or planned changes in the relative power of national states.

Thus, independently of the motives of scientists themselves, and with due recognition of the fact that anticipated practical uses of scientific discoveries still unmade are often vague, it seems reasonable to suggest—without taking joy in the suggestion—that the demand for science (and, of course, engineering) is and for a long time has been derived largely from the demand for conventional economic goods. Without the expectation, increasingly confirmed by experience, of 'useful' applications, those branches of science and engineering that have grown the most in modern times and have contributed most dramatically to technological change—electricity, electronics, chemistry and nucleonics—would have grown far less than they have. If this view is approximately correct, then, even if we choose to regard the demand for new knowledge for its own sake as a non-economic phenomenon, the growth of modern science and engineering is still primarily a part of the economic process. (Schmookler 1966, 176–7)

[8] It must be admitted that the economic payoff to basic research is so uncertain and difficult to measure that the yield to increments in expenditure on it could be high or low, and no one the wiser. Since the total expenditure is small, it would be prudent for the world to err on the side of excess. Nelson has argued that the mere existence of basic research expenditure by profit-seeking enterprises suggests that the total is inadequate. The amount carried out by

pointed out, many more inventions drawing on that stock could be made than are made.[9] I know of no evidence for the orthodox view that there are diminishing returns to cumulative investment because the stock of scientific knowledge at any one time is limited.

Third, scientific knowledge is by no means the only type of knowledge that is needed to enable investment opportunities to be discerned and undertaken. Such opportunities consist, after all, of *any* of Schumpeter's changes (new goods, new methods of production, new markets, new sources of supply, and new organizations of industry), and for even the first two, to which scientific knowledge is most directly relevant, other sorts of knowledge are required as well. Businessmen need the knowledge of accountants, lawyers, salesmen, personnel managers, industrial relations experts, engineers, architects, surveyors, and many others (including even, on occasion, economists) in order to recognize, formulate, and carry through investments. No one, so far as I know, has suggested that theories of economic growth must explain how such knowledge is acquired and developed, or how the stocks of it grow (if, indeed, such a concept can be given any meaning). Why then must I be compelled to explain and account for the growth in *scientific* knowledge? That it is an important and fascinating subject in its own right I do not for a moment deny. I wish I could have spent more of the time devoted to this book reading more of the history of science and technology.[10] I have had to conclude, however, that a useful theory of economic growth can be constructed without delving as far as I would have liked into such history. It is simply the case that other aspects of economic growth, of greater importance, need attention!

5.   My fifth, and final, conclusion relates to the process of learning, which is fundamental to the theory that follows. Both the history of scientific ideas and the history of technology show how improvements and extensions of knowledge depend on those that have gone before. It is difficult to find a really novel idea, and 'there is no new thing under the sun'. One should not think of history as a succession of geniuses whose original ideas changed the world. It is no disrespect to famous men and women to point out how they have drawn on the earlier work of others, and how very many different fields of knowledge often contribute to a single

subsidized institutions, such as universities, should be expanded until private enterprises find it not worth their while to engage in any basic research at all (or, at any rate, very little—the argument does not allow for the heterogeneity of research, as Nelson points out). See Nelson (1959).

[9] It is, for an academic, both awesome and faintly depressing to view the rows of books in a large library and to wonder how many of them will ever be read again.

[10] The following are studies which I found especially interesting and useful: Derry and Williams (1960); Singer (1959); and Crombie (1963). As guides to the subject of technical change and invention from an economist's point of view: Mansfield (1969); and P. S. Johnson (1975). A valuable study and survey of competition through innovation, and of the economics of innovation, is Kamien and Schwartz (1982).

invention.[11] The opposite theory, that inventions are inevitable,[12] goes too far the other way, but simultaneous, or near-simultaneous discoveries or inventions surely do indicate the great importance of the accumulation of past knowledge as well as the circumstances of the time, which, while they do not make a discovery or invention inevitable, do increase the probability of its occurring to a high degree.[13] In view of all this, it seems reasonable to regard the progress of science and technology as being akin to a journey in which each step moves one further along in the direction one chooses to go, and which can be speeded up or slowed down. The point reached by any step depends upon all the previous steps taken, and each step makes the point achieved by the next one possible.

A similar process of learning takes place in the business world. Lord Nuffield learned how to make bicycles by first repairing them, and how to improve the design of motor cars by repairing them too. His wartime experience of mass assembly of mine sinkers led him to carry further the principle of buying in components from specialist producers, rather than making them within his own factory.

In particular, he learned of the efficient production which could be achieved by quite small suppliers when their products were carefully designed from the point of view of the final assembly and when they were supplied with the necessary jigs and other equipment. (Andrews and Brunner 1959, 87)

A piece of machinery compels admiration because of the complexity of its design, and the skill used to make the parts that fit so smoothly and closely together. Likewise, an efficient factory, or large business organization of any kind, is very complex, and the way in which its different parts complement and reinforce each other is astonishing. Just as accumulated knowledge and skill are necessary to produce the machine, so are they

[11] For a vivid expression of this point of view, see Gilfillan (1970, 24–7), where a description of the invention of the steam engine is given by six imaginary people (a physicist, a mechanical engineer, a metallurgist, a lubrication engineer, a steam engineer, and a sociologist), each of which stresses the aspects peculiar to his own discipline.

[12] See Ogburn and Thomas (1922), which provides a list of duplicate or equivalent inventions, and which was attacked by Schmookler on the grounds that inventions having the same name or general description were in fact different.

[13] Despite Schmookler (see preceding footnote), I do not see how else one can explain such famous examples as Leibnitz's and Newton's more or less simultaneous and independent invention of differential calculus, Darwin's and Wallace's approximately simultaneous development of the principle of natural selection (which was itself anticipated, according to Darwin's Historical Sketch of the idea, given in later editions of his *The Origin of Species*, by other writers), and the more or less simultaneous development of the carbon filament electric lamp by Swan and Edison. For a discussion of the evidence that scientific discoveries are 'inevitable', which I find persuasive (and Schmookler's counter-arguments unpersuasive), see Merton (1961), reprinted as ch. 16 in Merton (1973). See also chs. 14, 17, and 18 in the latter. Merton points out that the existence of simultaneous or near-simultaneous discoveries has been long known, and that the concern of scientists to claim priority of discovery, and their fear of being beaten to the post, is itself evidence of 'inevitability'.

needed for the business organization. Again, rather than looking for differences, I want to stress the similarities.

Learning is the product of experience, and essentially of *new* experience.[14] New experiences result when we change the world, and investment leads to such changes. Broadly conceived, therefore, investment results in learning of all kinds: scientific, engineering, commercial, and social. There seems to be no need, at least at the beginning of a new theory of growth, to distinguish between the different fields of learning or investment. By merging all together, we avoid the necessity of tracing interactions between commercial experience and technology, or between technology and scientific knowledge, or between scientific knowledge and commercial experience. Causation flows in both directions, and it would be a complicated, though fascinating, exercise to relate each to the other. We also avoid having to draw some difficult distinctions between original scientific discoveries, inventions, innovations, and imitations. Let us first try to outline the theory satisfactorily before we attempt to sketch in the details.

One distinction that will be mentioned here by way of conclusion, since it is important subsequently (especially in Chapter 15), is between a firm's learning from its own experience (as in the examples of Lord Nuffield's learning given above), and a firm's learning from other firms' experiences, including, in the latter, learning from R&D expenditures by other firms or by universities and research institutes. By viewing a closed economy as a whole, we can ignore this distinction. Investment by the whole economy then generates learning and new investment opportunities for the whole economy. However, as I shall argue subsequently, much of this learning is external to the individual firm. P. S. Johnson (1975, 99) quotes a study by Langrish *et al.* (1972) of 51 innovations that received the Queen's Award to Industry in the late 1960s in Britain. They identified 158 important ideas that led up to these innovations, of which 102 came from outside the firm. According to Johnson, this finding of the importance of the transfer mechanism for ideas is confirmed by other studies. Gilfillan's view, for which he quotes support, is that 'The inventions which revolutionize a device or industry are commonly made by men outsiders to it yet informed regarding it; the far greater and more valuable mass of perfecting inventions are made by insiders' (Gilfillan 1970, 11-12, 88-91). 'Inside' and 'outside' here refers to the occupation or industry. So far as invention within the *firm* is concerned, and according to Schmookler, there has been a tendency, at least in the USA, to shift from independent to 'management-directed captive inventor'. This tendency may be slowing down, and in any case independent inventors are still very important (Schmookler 1966, 268). As I

[14] See the discussion of Arrow's ideas on p. 113.

show in Chapter 15 below, the fact that much learning comes from outside the firm implies that the social return to investment is greater than the private return, perhaps substantially so.

6

A NEW GROWTH MODEL

6.1 Introduction

The aim of this chapter is to describe the basic growth model which is further developed in later chapters, and is used to explain and analyse growth in a number of countries, as well as in particular industries in some of them. Some fairly simple model is badly needed to replace the battered and faulty orthodox models described in Chapter 3, since, in its absence, those models will continue to be taught and used, faulty or no. The model I shall put forward is, I believe, proof against the criticisms that can be made of orthodox growth models. It employs the concepts of income and output, maintenance, depreciation, capital, and, above all, *investment* described in Chapter 1. It abandons exogenous technical progress and the aggregate production function, and the distinction between shifts of that function arising from technical change, and movements along the function. The capital stock is no longer central, but merely a magnitude which it is interesting to calculate for some purposes. It abandons, also, the attempt to explain the level of output in terms of the existing state of the world. Instead, it takes the level as a datum and explains how that changes. The level at time t can still be explained in terms of the level at some earlier time, t_0, and the changes made in between, but that leaves the level at t_0 as the datum. The model is then very different from orthodox growth models, although it is used to provide answers to much the same questions: Why do growth rates differ, between different times within one country, between different countries, or between different industries within one country? What determines the shares of profits and wages? How does taxation affect the rate of growth? What is the optimum rate of growth?

6.2 Limitations and assumptions

The model is limited in the following ways.

1. Attention is given to changes in the capacity to produce, and variations in the ratio of actual output to capacity are not explained. I am concerned with growth over rather long periods, and not with short-term fluctuations. It is highly desirable to relate long-term to short-term behaviour, since, as has often been said, the long term is only a succession of short terms. Nevertheless, I have avoided discussion of short-term

economic behaviour. That Pandora's Box has been kept firmly shut, since otherwise this book would never have been written.

2. Almost all attention is given to steady growth or *equilibrium growth*, as I shall call it. The 'stylized facts', described in Chapter 2, were shown to be a reasonable approximation to quite long periods of different countries' histories. Growth differed from period to period and between countries, but it seems reasonable to take each period as a unit of observation, exemplifying the 'stylized facts'. This greatly simplifies the problem. Although the model could be adapted to analyse non-steady growth (and there is some discussion of this in later chapters), it is best designed for equilibrium growth.

3. The analysis is in terms of the behaviour of firms, with the economy consisting of a large number of 'representative' firms. The behaviour of governments, and the services rendered by consumer durables, including housing, are ignored. Consequently, the 'whole economy' means the non-residential business sector of the economy, and data refer to that (or to industries within it) wherever possible. Nationalized undertakings are included.

4. The representative firm is analysed in terms of its equilibrium growth behaviour. It is therefore treated as if it were immortal, or at least expected by its owners and managers to be so. Births, deaths, and marriages of firms are not considered.

5. The output of a firm, and of the whole economy, is measured by value added, which is the sum of gross trading profits and income from employment. Firms' purchases of materials, and their gross sales, are in general ignored. Implicitly, purchases of materials are assumed to remain a constant proportion of output gross of such purchases. This is a severe limitation, although one commonly made. It enables one to construct a two-factor theory of growth, capital and labour being the factors (with land assimilated to capital, as explained in Chapter 1).

6. Although there is some discussion of labour force growth at various points, for the most part it is treated as a datum so far as the whole economy is concerned. The growth of employment by the individual firm is endogenous, however. As explained in Chapter 2, it is the *quality-adjusted* rate of employment growth with which I am mainly concerned. This assumes that the effects of education and training can be treated in the same way as the effects of changes in numbers employed or hours worked. While this greatly simplifies matters, and some empirical support for the assumption is provided in Chapter 10, it is unsatisfactory. The role of education and training undoubtedly needs more attention than it is given here.

7. As already mentioned in the preceding chapter, material investment is treated as a whole, and is not analysed into its different components such

as research and development expenditures, machinery, vehicles and other plant and equipment, building and construction, inventories, and parts of expenditure on marketing, management, and payment for the services of financial intermediaries and other professions engaged in the transfer of property.

8. As was mentioned in Chapter 1, some important factors influencing output and its rate of growth are treated as exogenous and ignored. This applies, for example, to the weather, earthquakes, diseases, wars, and revolutions. It also applies, less satisfactorily, to what has been labelled '*x*-efficiency'—the ability of some enterprises to produce substantially more than others, which cannot be explained by differences in manpower, education and training, or plant and equipment. While all of these are important in particular historical instances, and may exert strong, once-for-all, effects, they do not fit easily into a theory of growth.

Further limitations will become apparent as the model is described. Although in sum these limitations are severe, they are no more so than is customary in models of economic growth. It would be good if some of them could be removed, but that requires further research.

Besides these limitations, which apply throughout the book, there are the following preliminary simplifying assumptions which are all relaxed in later chapters.

1. Firms are selling and buying in perfect product and labour markets, with no influence over prices received or paid, and no selling or buying costs.
2. However, firms are entirely self-financed, there being no lending or borrowing.
3. There are no taxes or subsidies.
4. The managements of firms seek to maximize the net present value of each firm to its owners.

The numeraire throughout is a representative bundle of consumption, which is also assumed to be in the model the final output of the non-residential business sector.[1] When it comes to the actual data, however, I am not entirely consistent with this, and use the sum of private and public consumption as numeraire. In principle, one can ignore the rate of inflation of money prices, but for simplicity it is often convenient to assume that the money price of the numeraire is constant.

6.3 The growing firm in a growing economy

At a given time, a given firm will have a particular organization, productive

---

[1] Readers may want to be reminded that, although final output equals the sum of consumption and investment, since I measure investment in terms of consumption forgone, the whole of final output is measured in units of consumption.

assets, and labour force. It will be buying a stream of current inputs consisting of materials (including semi-manufactures and services) of various kinds, which it then transforms using its assets and labour force into a stream of current outputs, which are sold. The firm could, in principle, keep its organization unchanged, maintaining all its assets and also its labour force, so that retirements are balanced by recruitments. It could then transform a constant stream of inputs into a constant stream of outputs. Its value added, or output, at constant prices would then also be constant.

However, prices may, and in general will, be changing. In terms of the consumption numeraire (whose money price I shall assume is constant), wage rates will generally be rising in a progressive economy. Then, even if the firm's material inputs and outputs do not change in price (so that it is, in that respect, representative of the whole economy), and the money value of its output then remains constant, a larger and larger fraction of that output will accrue to labour, and gross profits will fall. This fall in profits will cause the firm's assets to depreciate in value.

To offset this depreciation, the firm needs to invest, and thereby to change its organization. Investment will (if wisely done) increase gross profits, and, as we saw in Chapter 1, depreciation could indeed be defined as the amount of investment required just to offset the forces making for a fall in profits, so that a firm investing exactly its depreciation will experience constant gross profits. Such a firm will then be able to let its owners take out for consumption a flow equal to gross profits minus depreciation, and that flow will enable them to buy a constant real amount of consumption. That amount is then the net profit, or income, of the owners of the firm.

Typically, the firm will be investing at a faster rate than this. The owners will then be taking out less, but their take-out will be growing, because, with a higher rate of investment, gross profit will be no longer constant but growing.

The net present value of the firm to its owners is the discounted value of the future stream of amounts they take out from it. They are never going to sell the firm, but will only pass it on to their heirs, whom they treat as they would themselves. In effect, therefore, the firm and its owners are both to be regarded as if they were immortal. The future stream of take-out stretches away to infinity, growing all the time. In equilibrium growth, the rate of growth is constant, g, but so long as the rate of discount of the owners, r, is greater than g, the net present value is finite, and I assume that is so.

To maximize the value of the firm to its owners, the management must push investment to the point where its marginal rate of return equals their rate of discount. As the rate of investment is increased, the rate of growth of the firm's output is also increased. In equilibrium growth, the shares of profits and wages are constant, and so the rate of growth of profits must also be increased. Again, in equilibrium growth the ratio of investment to output (and so also to profits) is constant. Hence the ratio of take-out to profits and output is also constant. Take-out therefore grows at the same rate as output, and a higher rate of investment implies a faster rate of growth of take-out.

I assume that, if the owners of the firm receive a faster-growing take-out, they will raise their rate of discount. This is because the marginal utility of consumption to them will be falling faster as their consumption grows faster, and their rate of discount must reflect this faster fall in marginal utility. A higher rate of investment is also likely to result in the firm undertaking marginal investment with a lower rate of return. Hence there will come a point, as the rate of investment is increased, at which its marginal return falls to equality with the (rising) rate of discount of the firm's owners. At that point the optimum equilibrium rate of growth, from the owners' point of view, will have been reached, and the net present value of the firm will be at its maximum.

This shows the way in which the decision about how much to invest can be taken. There is only one other decision which the firm in equilibrium growth in the model is called upon to make, and that relates to employment. In choosing its investments from the opportunities confronting it, the firm can select those that increase employment more or less. For a given investment expenditure, a bigger increase in employment must be accompanied by a bigger increase in output in order that the higher wage bill is covered. The *extent* to which increased output is required for a given increase in employment depends on the real wage. Investment can be employment- (and output-) increasing, but it can equally be employment-reducing, with output growing less, or perhaps even falling where a lot of labour is saved. In short, the firm has to decide on the labour intensity of its investment projects, and that decision has implications for the rate at which both employment and output increase, and depends on the current level of wages.

A firm that is in equilibrium growth is then continually changing its organization, at a cost that is its investment expenditure. It is continually confronted by investment opportunities from which it selects only some. It makes two decisions: how much to invest (i.e. the rate of investment), and which projects to invest in. These decisions are interdependent, and both are taken with the same objective in view, namely, maximization of the firm's value to its owners. Undertaking investments alters the investment opportunities, not just by removing some, but also by creating others. The firm is always selecting the best opportunities it is aware of, but undertaking investments makes it aware of new opportunities since it learns by experience and by investing. Some of its investment consists of the cost of searching for opportunities. This is the case for research and development expenditures, which must be widely interpreted to include market research, investigation of new sources of supply, hire of business consultants and efficiency experts, etc. But almost any investment expenditure, by changing the world, enables something new to be learned. There is therefore no reason why investment opportunities should become exhausted. At any one time, it is true, the firm will be aware of a limited number of opportunities, some better than others. Hence increasing the rate of investment can be expected to worsen its average quality: more means worse. But there is no reason to suppose that the set of opportunities gets worse (or better) on average as time passes. Of course, they may do so, and for a particular firm there are bound to be fluctuations in the average quality of opportunities with which it is confronted. However, for the whole economy, and also for the *representative firm* in it, these fluctuations will tend to cancel out, and it is reasonable to assume as a working hypothesis that the average quality is (in a sense yet to be defined) unchanged. That, indeed, is the simplest hypothesis to take if we want to explain the 'stylized facts' of growth.

6.4   The basic growth diagrams

The ideas in the previous section can be given more precision and illustrated in Figures 6.1–6.4. Readers are asked to spend some effort to understand these diagrams, since I resort to them frequently in later chapters.

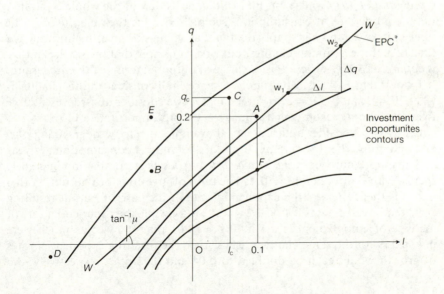

Fig. 6.1   Investment opportunity contour map

In all the diagrams I measure rates of change along the axes. These are exponential rates of change, and it may be helpful to think of them as proportionate changes achieved in some short interval of time. In the end, I treat time as continuous, as this simplifies the algebra. I discuss the difficult question of lags and gestation periods later on. For the present, it is assumed that investments result in instantaneous changes in a firm's organization. The vertical axis then refers to exponential rates of change of output[2] q, and the horizontal axis to exponential rates of change of employment, l. These rates of change are the result of investment undertaken by the firm. We thus confine attention to only two dimensions of change, output and employment.

The rates of change are measured *per unit of investment expenditure* that causes them; and the unit chosen, for a reason that will later become apparent, is the ratio of investment to the firm's output. Output refers to value added, but is measured in 'physical' terms. Thus, if both outputs and material inputs were physically homogeneous, it could be measured in tons, or by volume, or by number. With heterogeneous outputs and material inputs, it would have to be measured by value added at constant prices, output less material inputs, each at constant prices. The ratio of investment to output is S/Q, where S is the rate of investment measured in terms of its cost in terms of consumption forgone at constant prices, and Q is the rate of output, measured as above. We call this ratio $\sigma \equiv S/Q$.

It simplifies matters, and aids understanding, to consider the case of a *representative firm* whose output is the same as that of the whole economy, i.e. the numeraire of consumption (see p. 148). Q is then measured in the same units as S, and σ is simply the familiar savings or investment ratio. We shall take this case in this chapter, but first let us note that the savings ratio s is *defined* as S/PQ, where P is the price of output in terms of the numeraire. It follows that $\sigma \equiv Ps$. The simple case we shall consider in this chapter is where $P = 1$, and so $\sigma = s$. In later chapters we consider non-representative firms and industries in which P may vary, with important results.

Let us now consider an arithmetical example to clarify the meaning of q and l. Suppose the firm has an output of 100 units of consumption per year and invests 10 units per year with *characteristics* as at point A in Figure 6.1, that is, with $q = 0.2$ and $l = 0.1$. The ratio of investment to output, both σ and s, is then 0.1, and the exponential rate of increase of output resulting from that investment is $0.1 \times 0.2 = 0.02$ p.a., while the exponential rate of increase of employment is $0.1 \times 0.1 = 0.01$ p.a. If twice as much were invested, with the same characteristics, then the resulting exponential rates of growth would each be doubled to 0.04 and 0.02 p.a., respectively. An

---

[2] Strictly speaking, this is output at a constant ratio of output to capacity. Unless otherwise stated, capacity utilization is always assumed to be constant.

exponential rate of growth of 0.02 p.a. is close to (and slightly more than) 2 per cent per annum (see p. 41 above).

In general, therefore, if the ratio of investment to output with characteristics (q, l) is σ, then the resulting exponential rates of growth of output, g, and employment, g_L, are:

$$g \equiv \sigma q; \, g_L \equiv \sigma l. \tag{6.1}$$

These are definitions of q and l.

Let us now consider the characteristics of points $A, B, D, E,$ and F in Figure 6.1. Investment at A increases both output and employment. Investment at B increases output, rather less than at A per unit of investment, but saves some labour. Investment at D reduces output but saves a great deal of labour per unit of investment. It is not clear so far which of these investment characteristics is most profitable. Investment at F, however, which increases both output and employment, is clearly inferior to A since, for the same increase in employment per unit investment, output is increased less. It is also inferior to B, since employment is increased by more while output is increased by no more. E is the opposite case, being superior to both A and B.

In general, it can be seen that the better investment characteristics are those to the north-west ('North-west is best'). Investments in the south-east quadrant cannot be profitable, since they increase employment *and* reduce output. Investments in any of the other three quadrants could be profitable.

The firm wants to select the most profitable projects it can for any given amount of investment. As a first step in showing how this can be done, I define an *equal profits contour*, or EPC, along which the characteristics of all investment projects are equally profitable. It turns out that this is a straight line like the line WW in Figure 6.1. Before deriving the slope of this line for a growing firm in a growing economy, it is helpful to derive its slope for a static firm in a static economy, and I now proceed to do that.

Given my assumptions, a static firm in a static economy will find its profits unchanged if the value of the marginal product of any extra men employed is equal to the resulting extra wage bill. Consider, then, two investment projects with characteristics W_1 and W_2, each costing the same small amount of investment.

Let W_2's characteristics be Δq and Δl greater than those of W_1, where these differences may be large or small. We can imagine the small amount of investment as being undertaken at the rate $\delta\sigma$ and for a period of length δt.[3] Then, if this investment took place at W_1 with characteristics (q_1, l_1), the

---

[3] It might seem otiose to make both the incremental rate of investment, $\delta\sigma$, and the period for which it lasts, δt, vanishingly small. However, unless $\delta\sigma$ is small, we could encounter diminishing returns to the *rate* of investment (which are considered later on). In this particular case of a static firm in a static economy, it would not matter if δt were finite. With $\delta\sigma$

rate of growth of output and employment during δt would be

$$g_1 = \delta\sigma\, q_1; \; g_{L1} = \delta\sigma\, l_1.$$

At the end of δt, the levels of output and employment would be the opening levels, Q and L, increased by these rates of growth, that is,

$$Q\, e^{g_1\, \delta t} \text{ and } L\, e^{g_{L1}\, \delta t}.$$

To a first approximation, the increments in the levels of Q and L would then be

$$\delta Q_1 = Q\, g_1\, \delta t; \qquad \delta L_1 = L\, g_{L1}\, \delta t$$
$$= Q\, q_1\, \delta\sigma\, \delta t; \qquad = L\, l_1\, \delta\sigma\, \delta t.$$

Similar expressions can be derived for δQ_2 and δL_2 when the investment takes place with W_2's characteristics instead of W_1's. Then the difference in levels resulting from choosing W_2 instead of W_1 is

$$\delta Q = \delta Q_2 - \delta Q_1; \; \delta L = \delta L_2 - \delta L_1$$
$$= Q\, \Delta q\, \delta\sigma\, \delta t; \qquad = L\, \Delta l\, \delta\sigma\, \delta t.$$

Now if W_2 and W_1 are to be equally profitable, the value of the higher level of output, which is $P\delta Q$, must be exactly offset by the cost of the higher level of employment, which is $w\delta L$, where w is the wage rate ruling in the static economy. Hence

$$P\, \delta Q = w\, \delta L.$$

Therefore

$$PQ\, \Delta q\, \delta\sigma\, \delta t = wL\, \Delta l\, \delta\sigma\, \delta t.$$

$$\therefore \quad \frac{\Delta q}{\Delta l} = \frac{wL}{PQ} = \lambda$$

where λ is the share of wages in output (i.e. in value added).

Now $\Delta q/\Delta l$ is the slope of the line joint W_1 and W_2, which we shall call μ, and we have just shown that this must equal the share of wages in value added. Consequently, for a static economy, the equal-profit contours, EPC, are straight lines (since Δq and Δl can be large or small) with the slope λ. This result has been stated as if it were only a first approximation. However, it is the limiting case as $\delta\sigma$ and δt approach 0. Marginal investment at any point on WW is equally profitable.

This proof has to be modified for a growing firm in a growing economy, but the modification required is remarkably simple so long as we confine attention to equilibrium growth. I now assume that the firm is growing steadily at rate g, with employment growing at rate g_L, and with a constant ratio of investment to output σ, a constant price of output P in terms of the numeraire, and hence a constant share of investment in value added, $s = \sigma/P$. Also, since the rate of growth of wage rates $g_w = g - g_L$, the rate

---

vanishingly small, so too would be the changes in output and employment. However, when we come to a growing economy, wage rates are changing, and then δt must also be vanishingly small to obtain the result we need.

of growth of labour productivity, there is a constant share of wages λ. As before, the firm alters its investment programme for a short interval δt by choosing a more labour-intensive form of investment in respect of $\delta \sigma$ of investment, which is invested at W_2 instead of W_1 during δt. At the end of δt, output is then δQ higher, and employment δL higher, than it would otherwise have been. The firm then relapses back into equilibrium growth as before. In order that investment at W_2 shall have been equally profitable to investing at W_1, it must be the case that the firm's present value is unchanged as a result of making this alteration in its investment programme. In the static economy case, the higher level of output was just offset by the higher wage bill; in the growing economy case, a bigger gain in output than that is needed. For steady growth to be resumed, the firm must continue with the same *share* of investment, s, as before. Hence if output is higher, investment must be higher so as to maintain the same share. In fact the firm's present value will be unchanged if the owners' take-out, or consumption, is unchanged and grows at the same rate as before. Take-out equals output less wages and less investment. That is unchanged if

$$P\delta Q - w\,\delta L - \delta S = 0.$$

Now $\delta S = s\,P\delta Q$, since then the share of investment is unchanged, and so the unchanged take-out grows at the same rate as before.[4] It follows that

$$P\,\delta Q\,(1 - s) = w\,\delta L,$$

and if we now make the same substitutions as in the static case, we end up with

$$\mu = \frac{\Delta q}{\Delta l} = \frac{\lambda}{1 - s}. \tag{6.2}$$

The EPC are therefore straight lines with slope $\lambda/(1 - s)$. This is consistent with the static case when $s = 0$. It is interesting, and perhaps surprising, that the formula is independent of the rate of growth of wage rates, g_w. Our formula for the rate of return is also independent of g_w, and the reason for this is explained in Chapter 7.

It is worth noting that the slope of the EPC, μ, must be less than 1, whether in a stationary economy or in steady growth. In both cases, unless this is so, wages plus gross investment will exceed value added, and so take-out will be negative. A perpetual negative take-out can hardly be the objective of any firm, which would prefer instead to close down. This conclusion no longer holds, however, if there are imperfect markets and taxation of savings,[5] and it refers to the slopes of the EPC as perceived by the firm and so ignores externalities (see p. 376 below).

---

[4] Readers may regard this as an assumption at present. A defence of it is provided later.

[5] See p. 291 below for an equation for μ which allows for both of these, from which it can be easily deduced that $\mu > 1$ is consistent with positive take-out on *average*. However, it would then be the case that *marginal* investment *reduced* take-out, which would be plausible only if 'animal spirits' (see p. 277) were strong.

Consider now an EPC that passes through the origin of Figure 6.1. It is clear that the rate of return from investment at the origin must be 0, since nothing changes as a result of the investment, and so this is also the rate of return for all investments whose characteristics are on that EPC. EPCs that pass through points that are higher and higher up the q-axis will yield higher and higher positive returns to investments having their characteristics. If, then, we were to specify a minimum, cut-off, rate of return which the firm must earn on its investments, and if we were to instruct it to invest as much as it liked provided it could earn at least that rate, the firm's task would be as follows. Let us suppose that investments along WW all earn the minimum rate. The firm must undertake all available projects with characteristics lying on or to the north-west of WW.

We thus need to know what projects are available to the firm in that area and how much it would cost to undertake them. It seems reasonable to suppose that good projects are more scarce than less good ones. If we take bad projects, such as those at the origin yielding zero return, there is surely no limit to their number. A firm that is instructed to spend money in such a way as to leave output and employment unchanged should be able to devise an infinity of ways of doing this. As we move from these to the north, or west, or both, projects will be scarcer the further we move. Eventually, there may be no projects at all that increase output and/or save labour by very large amounts per unit of investment.

For any actual firm, the availability of projects at any one time will be patchy. There might be one with A's characteristics, one with B's, perhaps another small one with E's, but several like, or as good as, F's. Let us, however, consider a *representative* firm, which is thus a weighted average of the whole economy. For such a firm the availability of projects may be considered to be continuous in characteristics space. Let us measure this availability on an axis rising vertically out of the page in Figure 6.1. We measure availability in units of σ per unit area of the diagram. Thus, if we take a small area δa centred on A, and if the density of projects with characteristics as at A is h_A, then the share of investment which the firm can spend with characteristics as at A (or, strictly, within the range defined by the area δa) is $\delta \sigma = h_A \, \delta a$.

The magnitude h is analogous to height in an ordinary contour map, and from what has been said thus far, we can see that height will increase as we approach the origin (where it will be infinite) and will diminish, eventually going to 0, as we move away from the origin to the north or west. There is, so to speak, a cake of investment opportunities, most of them worthless or meagre, but some good and a few very good. Far enough to the north and west there is just the plate on which the cake sits, with no opportunities at all.

The shape of the cake is shown in Figure 6.1 by the contours joining points of equal height, *h*. The contours increase in height as we move from the north and west towards the origin. They cross the *l*-axis to the left of the origin and go off to the north and east. This is because projects which (per unit of investment) do not increase output must save labour, and the more they increase output the more labour they require (given their frequency). Finally, the contours are concave to the origin because of diminishing returns to labour. For a given frequency of projects, and a given amount of investment, adding further doses of labour increases output by successively smaller amounts.

Our representative firm, under instruction to pursue all the opportunities as good as or better than *WW*, will, in effect, position a large knife over *WW* and cut away the cake to the north-west of it. The volume of the cake will be the integral of $\delta\sigma$ (equal to sum of the volumes of little pillars of height *h* and base δa), and this will give σ, the ratio of investment to output for the firm.

We can also say what the effect of undertaking this investment will be on the output and employment of the firm. Each little pillar will contribute $\delta\sigma\, q$ and $\delta\sigma\, l$ to the exponential growth of output and employment, where *(q, l)* are the relevant characteristics of the pillar. If these contributions are summed across all the pillars, we will get mean characteristics q_c and l_c which will be those of the centre of gravity of the portion of the cake that has been cut off. Then if *C* in Figure 6.1 were the centre of gravity with characteristics (q_c, l_c), we would have

$$g = \sigma\, q_c = \Sigma(\delta\sigma\, q); \; g_L = \sigma\, l_c = \Sigma(\delta\sigma\, l).$$

The diagram needs to be further developed before we can use it as the basis of our model of growth. However, before proceeding any further, we can now relate it to the 'stylized facts' of growth. In equilibrium growth, the following magnitudes are all constant: g, g_L, s, λ, and the marginal rate of return which we call r. These magnitudes will all be constant for our representative firm, given our assumptions about its situation and behaviour, provided two more crucial assumptions are satisfied. The first is that the rate of growth of wage rates, g_w, must equal the rate of growth of labour productivity, which is $g - g_L$:

$$g_w = g - g_L. \tag{6.3}$$

The second assumption is that the cake of investment opportunities is continually remade, and has the same shape in the dimensions relevant to the diagram. Of course, in many other dimensions investment opportunities will differ. Output changes in a hundred different ways, as does employment and investment and the firm's organization. However, provided the same σ can be invested with the same mean q_c and l_c, then the same g and g_L will result. Furthermore, as our firm is representative of the whole economy, *P* remains unchanged and equal to 1, so that unchanged σ

implies unchanged s. Furthermore still, with wage rates growing at the same rate as labour productivity, so that $g_w = g - g_L$, the share of wages in output, λ, will be constant. With both s and λ constant, formula (6.2) for the slope of the EPC shows that μ must also be constant. Finally, therefore, if the cut-off rate of return, r, is constant, the firm will position the knife over the same line WW and, if the shape of the cake is the same, will cut off the same set of investment opportunities, which will then have the same q_c and l_c as before, and require the same σ as before.

The diagram has thus been constructed in such a way that the 'stylized facts' of growth are the result of the representative firm's behaviour when confronted by investment opportunities that remain constant in the sense already explained. Equilibrium growth can then be very simply depicted because the picture is essentially unchanged. Before developing the model further, we discuss what many readers will probably regard as its most crucial and novel part, and therefore the part that most needs explanation and defence if they are to accept it. That is the assumption that the set of investment opportunities is continually recreated and remains constant in the sense already explained.

6.5   The inexhaustible cake of investment opportunities

Let us begin by considering a whole closed economy, the world if you like, as if it were a single enterprise. We do this so as to exclude learning from outside, and to include all learning that there is. Later, we consider individual enterprises which learn a great deal from outside of themselves. Let us also pose the problem in terms of the model already described. At some given time, then, we can agree that our enterprise is confronted by a set of investment opportunities which is represented by the cake. The question is, What happens when some of these opportunities are taken? There are three possibilities which have been suggested at various times.

1. There is what might be called the stagnationist view, which received some support from Keynes,[6] and which may also have been the view of some classical economists and perhaps Marx. According to this view, investment opportunities are slowly exhausted, so that the returns to investment gradually fall. The slices taken out of the cake are then not replaced, and succeeding slices cut nearer and nearer to the origin, which could be reached, according to Keynes, within a generation. This view would make sense if we were omniscient, since then we would know the best

---

[6] 'On such assumptions [i.e. full employment and a 'not disproportionate' rate of investment] I should guess that a properly run community equipped with modern technical resources, of which the population is not increasing rapidly, ought to be able to bring down the marginal efficiency of capital in equilibrium approximately to zero within a single generation' (Keynes 1936, 220).

way forward, and we would choose the highest yielding investments first, and they would be succeeded by investments yielding less and less. In such a world there would be no invention or discovery. It is clear that we are not in that world, and that the view just described does not accord with experience or the 'stylized facts'.

2. There is the orthodox view, according to which investment opportunities are being created at an exogenous rate by 'technical progress'. If the slices match this rate, each slice will be the same as the previous one, since fresh cake will be made just as fast as it is being eaten away. The 'stylized facts' of growth can then be explained. If the slices are too big, the cake's growth cannot keep up with them and returns to investment will fall; if the slices are too small, returns to investment will rise. This view has been criticized in earlier chapters. It fails to explain why the cake grows. If growth is attributed to the advance of science, why do we not double the rather small amounts invested in that way and reap the enormous returns? Is it plausible to suppose that a failure to invest for a hundred years would be followed by a long period when returns to investment would be very high? The view has been defended on *a priori* grounds, and the only empirical evidence in support of it that I know of is the importance of the unexplained residual in many growth accounting studies. However, these studies have all measured the contribution of investment incorrectly, as pointed out in Chapter 3. There is no residual to be explained.[7]

3. There is the view taken here, that investment recreates investment opportunities. That the opportunities recreated should leave the same cake as was there before is a working hypothesis which has the merit that it is consistent with the 'stylized facts' of growth. That is an empirical justification, and further empirical justification is provided in later chapters where the model is used to explain a variety of phenomena. Perhaps that is all that needs to be said. However, some *a priori* reasons can also be advanced in defence. Investment leads to change and change is essential to learning. The more and the faster the change, the more and the faster the learning. As we saw in Chapter 5, invention is a form of investment. There is no evidence that technical 'exhaustion' sets in, and the rate of invention is maintained if the rate of investment is maintained. At first sight it may seem puzzling that good opportunities should be replaced by good and bad by bad, that being the implication that the cake is unchanged. On reflection, however, it seems reasonable. One way in which undertaking investment creates further investment opportunities is by imitation, and so undertaking a very productive investment leads to very productive imitation, while a bad investment sets a bad example. More generally, the scope for learning from

---

[7] See also p. 295 below for an econometric test of this assertion, and see Section 6.9 for a close comparison between the orthodox growth accounting equation and the one appropriate to my model, with no residual.

very productive investments should be greater, one might think, than the scope for learning from mistakes—although, like any generalization in economics, there will be exceptions. There is a temptation to think that investment opportunities that are *not* taken remain available, so that if good ones are not taken now they can be taken later, for example. But this temptation must be resisted. Investment opportunities do not remain in the cake unchanged until they are taken. In general, all are changed by the investments that *are* undertaken, so that what might have been good if done earlier could cease to be worth while—or could become even better.

So much for a whole, closed, economy. Let us now consider an individual firm's investment opportunities. To some extent it will learn from its own investments, and, in so far as that is the case, the preceding argument applies. To a great extent, however, firms learn from other firms' investments. There is then a flow of new ideas which is exogenous to the firm, and it might seem that the orthodox view 2 must apply.

I certainly do not wish to deny that there *is* an exogenous flow of new ideas and complementary investments which partly determine a firm's investment opportunities. But what is often forgotten is that, along with *this* flow, which is favourable inasmuch as it continually widens those opportunities, there is an opposite flow which is continually narrowing them. This adverse flow of competitive investments consists of the attempts being made by competitors of the firm to capture its markets and bid away its labour or materials. Both the favourable and the adverse flows result from the investments of other firms.

I believe that the net effect of these flows is favourable to a typical individual firm in the following sense. The faster is the rate of investment by other firms, the better will be the set of investment opportunities confronting the typical firm. In the model this will show up as an enlargement of the cake, so that it stands out further from the origin towards the north and west. This effect seems most obvious if one thinks of R&D investment by others (including investment in universities and research institutes). But one should not think of the effect as being confined to R&D investment: any investment by others may suggest investment opportunities to the typical firm, although some more than others. I am not here considering the effect of faster investment in permitting a faster growth of *demand*. That is an important effect, but it arises because of market imperfections, which we are assuming away at present. The role of demand is discussed later (see Chapters 9 and 15). The effects being discussed here are due to learning, complementarity, and competition.

Although faster investment elsewhere increases and improves the set of opportunities for the typical firm, I do not think that it makes them *grow*, or grow faster. For a given rate of investment elsewhere (i.e. given s), the set for the typical firm is given. The alternative view would be that higher s

elsewhere makes the set grow faster for the typical firm. The investment opportunities would accumulate faster, so that if our firm were to maintain its former rate of investment it would find its marginal rate of return continually increasing. I do not find that plausible, essentially because of competition from other firms. If the individual firm does not take up the better opportunities becoming available when *s* elsewhere rises, then others will. The simplest plausible assumption is, then, that the set increases as *s* elsewhere increases, but for given *s* elsewhere the set of investment opportunities remains essentially unchanged.

I do not mean by this that they are unchanged in a *physical* sense. Because of changes elsewhere in the economy, the firm's investment opportunities will be continually different in common sense terms. New inventions, new products, new capital goods, new markets, and new people will all alter the actual things that the firm must do to exploit its opportunities. The only sense in which I assume that the firm's investment opportunities are unchanged is in *economic* terms. Specifically, it is the map of investment opportunities in Figure 6.1 that is constant: the relations between incremental output, incremental employment, and investment. That it *is* unchanged is, of course, at best an approximation, and one that I expect to hold best for the typical or average firm.

Two qualifications must be made to the assumption of a constant set of investment opportunities. First, it does seem possible for parts of the world economy to lag behind other parts, and to benefit, as a result, from 'catch-up'. This phenomenon has been investigated by others, and some relevant empirical evidence is discussed later (Chapter 10). What may happen in such cases is that both the favourable stream of new inventions, etc., and the adverse stream of competitive pressures are shut off from a particular country for various reasons. Subsequently, the country is opened up to such influences. Investors in that country can then reap the benefits of access to the new inventions, etc. Since competition will not have forced up wage rates, investment opportunities will on balance be enhanced, although the lack of investment in the past will limit this enhancement.[8] As investment proceeds, and the country catches up, wage rates will be bid up and eventually the set of opportunities will become normal. This process of catching up can be envisaged for a country, or even possibly for a region within a large country, but hardly for an individual *firm*. The latter must compete in the same market as other firms for labour, and so is unlikely ever to be in a situation in which wage rates are much out of line with those paid by its competitors.

---

[8] In developing countries, the lack of investment in infrastructure, and the low level of education of the work-force, are often cited as factors that limit the profitability of private investment. This provides a counter-example to the conventional assumption of diminishing returns to the capital stock.

The second qualification is that the assumption that the set of investment opportunities is constant in the sense described is only a working first assumption. No one can foretell the future, and it is entirely possible that the set will shrink or expand. It is also possible that, in the past, there have been periods in which the set has shrunk or expanded. I know of no law of nature which requires a constant set. What has happened to the set in the past is a matter for empirical investigation. Some have claimed to be able to detect long waves of invention which should show up as expansions and contractions in the set of opportunities. My own investigations, described in later chapters, suggest a movement in one direction only—happily, that of expansion. However that may be, I suggest that, for the individual firm, the best working assumption at any given time will be that the set will remain constant.

This section has merely sought to show that an inexhaustible, constant, set of investment opportunities is a reasonable working hypothesis. The utility of the hypothesis can be demonstrated only by using it to explain growth phenomena, as in later chapters. For the present, it is to be hoped that readers are at least ready to open their minds to the possibility that this is one example where you can both eat your cake and have it too.

6.6   The investment programme contour map

The model is not yet simple enough to use. The next stage in its development is provided by Figure 6.2, which is similar to Figure 6.1, but adds a new concept, the *investment programme contour* (IPC). Armed with this, it is relatively easy to see how equilibrium growth is determined.

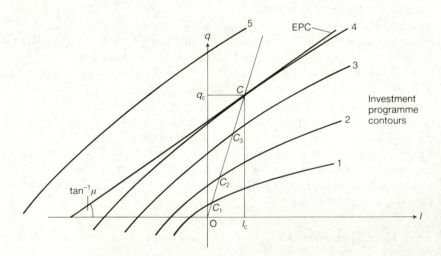

Fig. 6.2   Investment programme contour map

There is a map of IPCs, illustrated in Figure 6.2. To explain how they are derived, we perform a conceptual experiment which makes use of our first diagram, Figure 6.1. Point C in that diagram is the same as point C in Figure 6.2. In each, it shows the average characteristics of the firm's investment programme, that is, of all the projects the firm undertakes when it is investing at the rate σ, and given the slope of the EPC or knife, μ.

Now imagine that the firm keeps σ fixed, but varies μ. In Figure 6.1 the slope of WW, the EPC, will then change. The higher is μ, the more the knife is tilted round in an anti-clockwise direction, cutting off different slices of cake. Each of these different slices will have a different centre of gravity, and one can see intuitively that, as the knife tilts round anti-clockwise, the corresponding centre of gravity will also shift round anti-clockwise. *The IPC is the locus of the centre of gravity as μ varies for given σ.* For each value of σ there is a different IPC, and five are illustrated in Figure 6.2. For a given value of σ, a particular IPC shows the different possible average characteristics, q and l, for the firm's investment programme. The firm will select these characteristics so as to maximize its present value. It thus has to choose the best point (such as C in Figure 6.2) on the IPC, and its choice (for given σ) depends on the share of wages, λ. How this determines the best point is explained in the following review of the properties of the family of IPC.

There are two properties which can be shown to hold for any reasonably-shaped cake of investment opportunities.[9]

1. At any point such as C in Figure 6.2, the tangent to the IPC will have the same slope, μ, as the knife, WW, which is used to cut off that slice of which C is the centre of gravity in Figure 6.1. With IPCs shaped as in Figure 6.2 (see below), it follows that, if we are provided with a map of them, and if we are told the firm's rate of investment, σ, so that we know which is the relevant IPC, then the characteristics of the firm's investment programme, *(q, l)*, can be found once we know the share of wages, λ, and so long as we are dealing with a representative firm; for in that case we know that $P = 1$ and so $s = \sigma$. From our formula (6.2) we can then find μ. Then, so long as the tangents to any one IPC all have different slopes (as in Figure 6.2), there is only one point on the relevant IPC that has the required slope μ. The firm's rate of growth of output, $g = \sigma q$, and employment, $g_L = \sigma l$, are then determined once we know the map of IPC and σ and λ.
2. The IPCs are concave to the origin, as in Figure 6.2.

Besides these two properties, a third is self-evident.

---

[9] I do not prove properties 1 and 2 here, but have been provided with a proof by a mathematical friend, Dr K. J. Falconer, to whom I am duly grateful.

3. The greater is the rate of investment, σ, the closer will be the relevant IPC to the origin. In Figure 6.1, greater σ implies a larger slice of cake cut off. Hence the knife WW has to move in towards the origin, which implies that the centre of gravity of any slice (and the corresponding IPC) also moves in towards the origin.

We add a fourth property which can be regarded as a reasonable assumption.

4. The IPCs become parallel to the l-axis as $l \rightarrow \infty$, and tend to a slope of 45° as $l \rightarrow -\infty$.

If an IPC is parallel to the l-axis, further increases in the labour intensity of investment do not enable any further increases in output per unit of investment to be made. This is diminishing returns to labour once again. If an IPC has a slope of 45° with both q and l negative, this implies that, if investment is made still more labour-saving, the additional proportionate saving in labour is matched by an equal additional proportionate fall in output per unit of investment. In other words, the point has been reached at which the marginal product of labour has risen to equal its average product for further changes. Loosely speaking, therefore, this assumption makes the marginal product of labour vary between 0 and its average product as the labour intensity of investment is brought down from a very high to a very low figure.

Finally, we add a fifth property, which is little more than a simplifying assumption.

5. Along any ray from the origin, such as OC in Figure 6.2, the slopes of all IPCs are the same.

This property implies that, if σ is increased and if μ remains unchanged, then q and l will each shrink in the same proportion. I find it difficult to predict which of q and l is likely to shrink by more in such circumstances, and am therefore willing to take the simplest possibility. A weak defence of the assumption is as follows. It seems likely that, if σ is very large, the relevant IPC will be both close to the origin and sharply curved around it. This follows from property 3 and also from the fact that, if σ is very large, quite a small positive l implies rapid growth of employment, while quite a small negative l implies a very rapid fall of employment. One would expect the marginal product of additional labour to be low in the first case and high in the second, which would result in the sharp curvature. The result is that, no matter what μ we select within a wide range, with a high σ we end up with an investment programme in which both q and l are small. In the limiting case, as $\sigma \rightarrow \infty$, q and l both $\rightarrow 0$. Assumption 5 is consistent with this since, as σ is increased, no matter what is μ, we move in towards the origin as q and l shrink equiproportionately.

6.7   Equations for the investment programme contour map

The simplest curve having the properties of a typical IPC is the lower branch of a hyperbola. This is a second-degree curve, which is asymptotic to two straight lines. In our case, one straight line is parallel to the l-axis, and is the asymptote when $l \rightarrow \infty$, and the other straight line has a slope of 45°, and is the asymptote when $l \rightarrow -\infty$ and q also $\rightarrow -\infty$. If the first asymptote is $q = a$, while the second is $q - l = b$, then the equation to the hyperbola is

$$(q - a)(q - l - b) = c$$

where a, b, and c are positive constants. This must be restricted to $q < a$ and $q - l < b$ so that it refers to the lower branch of the hyperbola. It is illustrated in Figure 6.3.

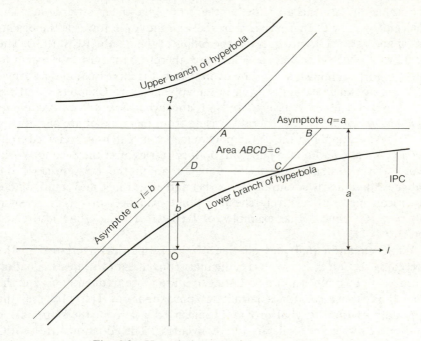

Fig. 6.3   Hyperbola $(q - a)(q - l - b) = c$

Property 5 makes the equation to the whole map of IPCs very simple. We merely need to divide q and l by a parameter ϱ, which we call the *radius* of the IPCs, and the resulting equation is[10]

[10] I owe the suggestion for the use of the parameter ϱ to Dr K. J. Falconer.

$$\left(\frac{q}{\varrho} - a\right)\left(\frac{q}{\varrho} - \frac{l}{\varrho} - b\right) = c. \tag{6.4}$$

The restriction now becomes $q/\varrho < a$ and $q/\varrho - l/\varrho < b$. ϱ is always positive, and is directly proportionate to the distance out along some given ray from the origin at which the IPC crosses it. Thus, in Figure 6.2, if the chosen ray is OC, and if we consider the IPCs numbered 1, 2, and 3, then ϱ for the first is directly proportionate to OC_1, for the second to OC_2, and for the third to OC_3. Doubling ϱ thus doubles the values of q and l along any ray.

The parameter ϱ conveniently measures two different effects. In the first place, it measures the effect of *diminishing returns to the rate of investment*. As the rate of investment σ, is increased, the knife WW (or EPC) in Figure 6.1 moves in towards the origin, and inferior, less profitable, investments are added to the firm's investment programme. The centre of gravity of that programme likewise moves in towards the origin, and q and l shrink. Consequently, the radius of the firm's IPC shrinks. The speed with which ϱ declines as σ increases therefore measures the extent to which returns diminish as the rate of investment is increased, and a formal treatment of this relation is given in the appendices to Chapters 7 and 15.

The second effect measured by ϱ is the *expansion or contraction of investment opportunities* generally arising from factors that are outside the model. An example of this is the phenomenon of 'catch-up' referred to in Section 6.5 above. For the same σ in both countries after the Second World War, ϱ was probably greater in Japan than in the USA because the Japanese had far lower output per worker and wage rates, and could imitate American methods relatively cheaply. Some evidence for this is given in Chapter 10 below. Other examples of factors affecting ϱ are also given later.

While equation (6.4) has all five of the properties mentioned in the preceding section, it is not always the most convenient or simplest equation to employ. Two other approximations to it are more frequently used in the sequel. First, we can use a parabolic approximation. This preserves the concavity of the IPC, but provides a linear equation for the slope of the tangent at any point, which is very convenient. The equations to the IPC and the tangent to it then are

$$\frac{q}{\varrho} = a + b\frac{l}{\varrho} - c\left(\frac{l}{\varrho}\right)^2 \tag{6.5}$$

$$\frac{\mathrm{d}q}{\mathrm{d}l} = \mu = b - 2c\frac{l}{\varrho} \tag{6.6}$$

where a, b, and c are all positive constants. This approximation is reasonable so long as q and l are neither very large nor very small (i.e. substantially negative—q or l can be close to or equal to 0).[11]

A second, and more drastic, approximation is a straight line, which (as usual) is highly convenient at times:

$$\frac{q}{\varrho} = a + b\,\frac{l}{\varrho} \qquad (6.7)$$

$$\frac{dq}{dl} = \mu = b. \qquad (6.8)$$

6.8 Explaining equilibrium growth: a trial run of the model

We have now reached the point at which I can show how the model can be used to analyse and explain equilibrium economic growth. This is only a trial run. All the simplifying assumptions listed in Section 6.2 are retained, and I do not explain how the rate of investment is determined. An additional simplifying assumption that I make is that there are no diminishing returns to the rate of investment. The cake of investment opportunities rises vertically from the plate and is as high as you please. Hence ϱ is independent of σ. These assumptions will be relaxed and deficiencies made good in later chapters, where we also explore the role of relative prices, which is of great importance when growth in particular industries or enterprises is our concern. Here, we confine attention to the representative firm and the whole (closed) economy, and so $P = 1$ throughout, and $\sigma = s$.

Furthermore, readers are asked to take on trust for the moment the equation for the rate of return, r, which is both the average and the marginal rate of return, given the assumption of no diminishing returns to the rate of investment. The equation is

$$r = P(q - \lambda l). \qquad (6.9)$$

The rate of return is thus the marginal profit per unit of investment, gross of depreciation. A proof of (6.9) is given in Chapter 7, but readers may recall the brief discussion of the rate of return on p. 28 above.

The model can refer to either the representative firm or the whole economy, the only difference being that for the firm the rate of growth of wage rates is exogenous and the rate of growth of employment, g_L, is endogenous, while for the whole economy it is the other way round.

Let us take the representative firm first. The relevant equations are then (6.1) (two definitions), (6.2), (6.3), (6.5), (6.6), and (6.9). These seven equations suffice to determine the seven endogenous variables: q, l, g, g_L, λ,

---

[11] For such extreme values one must employ the hyperbola, since the parabola reaches a maximum for q at a finite value of l, after which q declines. Likewise, when $q \to -\infty$, $dq/dl \to \infty$ instead of 1.

μ, and r. At this stage we are not explaining how σ is determined, and so it is exogenous, as are g_w and ϱ and the constants of the IPC, *a, b,* and *c.*

Turning to the whole economy, the position is just the same except that now g_L becomes exogenous (determined by demographic factors, education and training, etc., which are all unexplained within the model[12]), while g_w is endogenous. This means that the rate of growth of wage rates has to accommodate itself to the exogenously determined rate of growth of employment. Failure to do so would lead to either growing unemployment or labour shortages. We return to these possibilities in Chapter 16, but for the present shall assume that the labour market works efficiently so as to preserve full but not overfull employment over the average of the trade cycle.

The working of the model is illustrated by an arithmetical example in the appendix to this chapter and geometrically in Figure 6.4, which is similar to the earlier diagrams. There is only one IPC, since we are assuming no diminishing returns to investment. This simply traces the edge of the cake

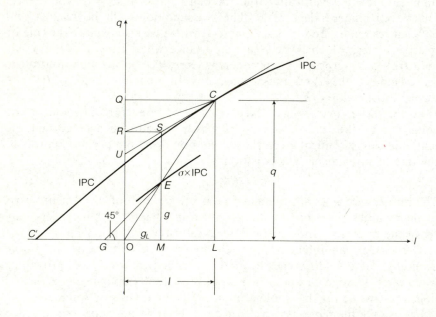

Fig. 6.4 Model diagram

[12] That part of g_L which is due to the transfer of labour from agriculture or self-employment to the rest of the economy is also treated as exogenous, although it seems likely that it would to some extent depend on, for example, s and g. This is one more area for further research.

on the plate, and is the curve $C'C$. We can then draw the additional curve shown as passing through E, which has the coordinates of $C'C$ multiplied by the rate of investment $s = \sigma$, which is a positive number less than 1. This curve is then a shrunken version of the IPC, and the point E, for example, has coordinates σ times the coordinates of C.

If we want to use the model to determine the representative firm's equilibrium rate of growth, we proceed as follows. Let the distance GO equal the (positive) rate of growth of wage rates in terms of the numeraire. Draw GE at $45°$ to the l-axis to cut the shrunken version of the IPC at E. Then E's coordinates provide the required rates of growth of output and employment, with $ME = g$ and $OM = g_L$. Projecting OE to cut the IPC at C provides the required characteristics of investment, with $LC = q$ and $OL = l$. That this is so follows from our construction, since $g = \sigma q$ and $g_L = \sigma l$, and since $g_w = GO = GM - OM = g - g_L$. Hence, if the firm invests at rate σ with characteristics (q, l) as at C, its rate of growth of labour productivity will match the given rate of growth of wage rates, and so λ will remain constant, which is a condition of equilibrium growth.

But will the firm *choose* to invest at C? As we saw earlier, given σ and λ, the firm's investment characteristics, and so its rates of growth of output and employment, are determined by the condition that the slope of the tangent at C must be $\mu = \lambda/(1 - s)$. For the firm to be in *equilibrium* growth at C, then, this condition must be satisfied. It follows that λ is determined, and it is, indeed, one of the endogenous variables. How can this be reconciled with our assumption that the firm is a price-taker?

The answer is that, unless λ equals the required value, the firm is not in equilibrium growth. In general, its rate of growth will not be constant, it will not be investing at C, and, even if σ is fixed exogenously, g, g_L, λ, and r will all vary. What ought to be demonstrated at this point is that, if the firm starts off from some value of λ other than the equilibrium value, it will gradually approach that value. However, I shall not provide any such demonstration. That is left to others better equipped than myself. All I shall provide is a non-rigorous argument to show why there is a tendency towards equilibrium.

My argument continues with the assumption that σ is fixed exogenously, and is constant. Let us denote equilibrium values by asterisks, and let us take the case where actual $\lambda > \lambda^*$, the equilibrium value. (The argument is quite symmetrical.) If the firm were to choose its investments *as if* it were in equilibrium growth, then (6.2) implies that we must have $\mu > \mu^*$. In that case, it must choose to invest at a point on the IPC to the left of the equilibrium point C, and, since $\mu < 1$, that implies that $q - l > q^* - l^*$. Multiplying this inequality through by σ gives $g - g_L > g^* - g_L^*$. Since, then, labour productivity is rising faster than in equilibrium, it must be rising faster than wage rates are increasing. Consequently, λ must be falling, and so moving towards the equilibrium λ^*. A weakness in this argument is the assumption that the firm behaves as if it were in equilibrium growth when it is not. Equation (6.2) holds in equilibrium growth, but not necessarily out of it. This would not matter if the firm were *close* to equilibrium, since then (6.2) is likely to give a good approximation to the firm's behaviour. However that may be, I cannot here provide a fully rigorous demonstration of the tendency towards equilibrium.[13]

Readers may (understandably) feel worried at this point. However, while I would like to satisfy them with a rigorous demonstration, I do not regard it as a high-priority requirement. This is because, when we come to the whole-economy case, there is another mechanism that can produce equilibrium growth, as we shall see. That case is the more important of the two.

We may now complete the representative firm case, proceeding on the assumption that actual λ equals its equilibrium value. All we have to show now is how the remaining important magnitudes (μ, λ, and r) appear in Figure 6.4.

The tangent to the IPC at C is USC, and so $\mu = UQ/QC$. We can now show that $\lambda = RQ/QC$. From (6.2) we have $\lambda = \mu(1 - s)$. Hence we need to show that $RQ/UQ = 1 - s$, i.e. that $UR/UQ = s$. But $UR/UQ = US/UC = OE/OC = s$, as required.

Finally, we can show that $OR = r$. This is because

$$OR = OQ - RQ = OQ - QC\lambda = q - \lambda l,$$

which is the formula for r in (6.9), remembering that we are dealing with the representative firm so that $P = 1$.

Let us now consider the whole-economy case, which can be speedily dealt with. Since g_L is now exogenous, we merely need to find where the vertical through M, with $OM = g_L$, cuts the shrunken version of the IPC at E. Everything else then proceeds as before, $GO = g_w$ being then endogenously determined.

This assumes, as before, that the endogenously determined λ equals the actual λ, since otherwise there could not be equilibrium growth. However, the mechanism by which equilibrium growth can be brought about is now quite different, and could in principle be as fast as you please, since it is simply a raising or lowering of wage rates. As before, let us take the case in which actual $\lambda > \lambda^*$, the equilibrium value. All that one need assume is that the effect of this is to lower the rate of growth of employment below its exogenously required rate of growth. There are at least two reasons why it should do so. First, as we saw in our discussion of the representative firm case, that firm is then likely to select a point on the IPC to the left of C, and

---

[13] In Chapter 8, where the model is completed by an equation that enables σ to be endogenous, the assumption that σ is fixed in the above argument must also be abandoned.

so, if σ is at its equilibrium rate, $\sigma l = g_L$ must be below it. Second, however, with $\lambda > \lambda^*$, and *a fortiori* with C to the left of C^*, we will have $r < r^*$. That is likely to make $\sigma < \sigma^*$, reinforcing the tendency for g_L to fall. Assuming, then, that we start off from a position of full employment (interpreted here as some sort of equilibrium in the labour market), unemployment will develop, and so, in an efficient labour market, wage rates will tend to fall. If wage rates were sufficiently flexible, the movement towards equilibrium growth could then be quite rapid. However, it must be admitted that, for all the well-known reasons, the economy need not be very stable, and so it could cycle around the equilibrium. The nature of these cycles is an important and fascinating subject, with an enormous literature, and we cannot venture into it here.

Having shown how equilibrium growth is determined in this preliminary version of the model, let us now consider a simple equation which may be used to explain economic growth. This is followed by a brief review of the three main exogenous determinants. We confine attention to the whole economy case.

6.9   A simple equation explaining growth

If the linear version of the model in equation (6.7) is multiplied through by $\varrho\sigma$, it becomes

$$g = a\varrho\sigma + bg_L$$
$$= a\varrho\sigma + \mu g_L \qquad (6.10)$$

using (6.8). This divides growth in any period into two parts: that arising from material investment, and that arising from growth of quality-adjusted employment. If the assumptions underlying this version of the model were fulfilled, these would be the rates of growth of output that would have occurred if, in the first case, investment, s, had been at the actual rate but employment growth, g_L, had been 0; and, in the second case, if s had been 0, while g_L had been at the actual rate.

To see this, consider Figure 6.4. Let us suppose that for a particular country and period, the actual growth rates of output and employment are given by E, and that investment at rate $s = OE/OC$ takes place with characteristics q, l, as at C. The simple linear version of the model, with no diminishing returns to the rate of investment, assumes that there is a unique IPC which must then be the straight line UC, cutting the q-axis at U (since μ is constant). It follows that, if $g_L = 0$, the characteristics of investment would have to be as at U, and at that point $OU = q - \mu l$. With s as before, the rate of growth of output must then be $sq - \mu sl = g - \mu g_L = a\varrho s$, from equation (6.10).

The case when $s = 0$ while g_L has its actual value is a little more tricky. If there is no investment, how can the increase in employment be absorbed? Surely some change in economic arrangements, and hence some investment, is needed? One way of solving this problem is to consider what happens as s approaches 0 while g_L remains fixed. It is clear from Figure 6.4 that point C must then move further and further to the right along the IPC, UC projected. Likewise, point L, vertically below C, will shift further and further to the right along the l-axis. However, point M must remain fixed, since $OM = g_L$. The ratio $OM/OL = s$ then shrinks towards zero. The point E moves down vertically towards M, and $ME = g$. The ray OE swings clockwise, becoming more nearly parallel to UC. In the limit, as $s \longrightarrow 0$, the angle MOE thus approaches the angle UCQ whose tangent is μ. Hence $g/g_L \longrightarrow \mu$, and so $g \longrightarrow \mu g_L$.

There will, of course, have to be changes made in economic arrangements to absorb the growing employment, and the above argument seems to make the incredible assumption that investment can become infinitely labour-intensive as it becomes infinitesimally small. This strains the linearity assumption beyond belief. However, there is an escape provided by maintenance expenditure. We noted in Chapter 1 that, even in a static economy, there would in practice be *some* changes, for example because of the extraction of minerals. *Total* investment can be zero, even if some kinds of investment are positive while others are negative, i.e. if maintenance is neglected. In an economy with a growing labour force, it would make sense to undertake the investment necessary to absorb this, while neglecting maintenance elsewhere, thus making total $s = 0$. This possibility means that one does not need to undertake infinitely labour-intensive investment projects. It also means that the linearity assumption may be better than one might think.

Equation (6.10) can be recast in a way that will be more familiar to those accustomed to the orthodox growth accounting equation. The latter (see equation (3.9) in Chapter 3 above) makes the rate of growth of output equal to the sum of three terms. The first two of these are the weighted growth rates of the capital stock and of employment, the weights generally being assumed to be equal to the shares of profits and wages in total output. The third term is the residual, which stands for technical progress. Equation (6.10) has only two terms and these can be rewritten as the weighted sum of the *relevant* rate of growth of the capital stock and of employment. There is no third term representing technical progress. In what follows, it is shown that the orthodox equation and equation (6.10) ought to coincide if one were dealing with a once-for-all change in an otherwise static economy. In this case there is no depreciation, which is why they coincide. In a growing economy, however, the orthodox equation treats depreciation incorrectly, and also gives incorrect weights to capital and labour, and this is why a residual appears in most growth accounting studies.

It was argued in Section 3.7 that, in competitive conditions (as assumed in this chapter), the increment in the capital stock that is relevant to explaining growth is gross investment, with no deductions. It is incorrect to deduct either scrapping (since scrapped assets have zero marginal product) or depreciation (since that is essentially a transfer of income from capitalists to workers, and not a fall in total income). That being so, the correct way to measure the rate of growth of the capital stock is to divide the rate of gross investment by the capital stock. While I call this 'the *relevant* rate of growth of the capital stock', it must be stressed that it is *the rate of growth of the capital stock that is relevant to explaining growth of output*, and *not* the rate of growth of either the net capital stock or wealth, the present value of future capitalists' take-out. To obtain them, one must indeed subtract depreciation from gross investment. However, one then obtains a rate of growth of capital that is *not* relevant to measuring the contribution of material investment to the growth of output, for reasons already discussed. (And the rate of growth of the so-called gross capital stock is no better.)

I shall measure the capital stock here by the discounted value of capitalists' future take-out, V. In Section 7.5 below it is shown that in steady growth, and making the same simplifying assumptions as here, this also equals the sum of all past investment net of depreciation, in other words, the net capital stock, K. Now capitalists' take-out, C, is a fraction $(1 - \lambda - s)$ of total output or value added. If the economy is growing steadily at g, and if the rate of discount of all capitalists, equal to the rate of return, is r, then take-out is also growing at g, and to obtain its discounted value we merely need to divide it by $(r - g)$. Hence[14]

$$V = \frac{C}{r - g} = \frac{(1 - \lambda - s)}{r - g} PQ.$$

The relevant rate of growth of the capital stock is S/V or, equivalently, S/K. It can then be shown that equation (6.10) can be rewritten as[15]

$$g = (1 - \mu)\frac{S}{K} + \mu g_L. \tag{6.10a}$$

---

[14] Since take-out, C, is growing at g, its amount t years from the present is Ce^{gt}. The present value of this is found by discounting it by capitalists' rate of discount r, that is, by multiplying it by e^{-rt}. Assuming that capitalists have an infinite time horizon (attaching as much importance to the future take-out that will accrue to their heirs as they would had it accrued to them), we can obtain the present value, V, by summing all future take-outs, after discounting. Hence

$$V = \int_0^\infty Ce^{(g - r)t}dt = \frac{C}{r - g}.$$

This assumes that $r > g$.

[15] This may be shown as follows:

$$(1 - \mu)\frac{S}{K} = \frac{(1 - \mu)s(r - g)}{1 - \lambda - s}.$$

Putting $r = q - \lambda l$ with $P = 1$, as in (6.9), this expression equals

It should be noted that the treatment of capital and labour (in 6.10a) is quite symmetrical (unlike the treatment in orthodox growth accounting). Both capital and labour are measured ignoring price changes, so that depreciation and appreciation are both ignored. Quantity changes, however, are included, as capital is net of required maintenance, and changes in employment equally allow for physical loss. Finally, each item of capital, like each item of labour, is in principle weighted in proportion to its marginal product.

There are three differences between (6.10a) and the orthodox growth accounting equation. First, the rate of growth of the capital stock is measured by S/K, i.e. with gross investment rather than net in the numerator. Second, the weights of capital and labour inputs are $(1 - \mu)$ and μ instead of $(1 - \lambda)$ and λ. Third, there is no term for technical progress.

Consider, now, a once-for-all change in an otherwise static economy. In such an economy there will be no depreciation, since real wage rates will not be changing. Consequently, the proportionate increment in the capital stock ought to be measured by S/K according to both the orthodox formulation and that proposed here. Furthermore, as was shown in Section 6.4, in a static economy $\mu = \lambda$ (since $s = 0$). Hence in a static economy the two formulations should coincide, and there should be no residual.

In a growing economy, however, they no longer do this. There will then, in general, be some depreciation, which in orthodox growth accounting is subtracted from S, and this greatly reduces the growth rate of capital as compared with my formulation. Although the latter gives rather less weight than orthodox growth accounting to capital growth, and more to employment growth (since $\mu > \lambda$ when $s > 0$), this is generally insufficient to offset the much greater contribution to growth resulting from material investment. Consequently, in my formulation there is no residual in a growing economy, any more than in a static one. It is the understatement of the contribution of capital in the orthodox procedure which results in the appearance of a residual. This conclusion is not just a theoretical one. It is borne out by the empirical data, as reported in Section 10.4 below.

There is one interesting situation in a growing economy in which, once again, the two formulations should agree on there being no residual. This arises when there is zero labour productivity growth, so that $g_L = g$. In that case there is no growth of real wage rates in steady growth, and hence no

$$\frac{(1 - \mu)\, s\, (q - \lambda l - g)}{1 - \lambda - s} = \frac{(1 - \mu)(g - \lambda g_L - sg)}{1 - \lambda - s}.$$

Now putting $\lambda = \mu(1 - s)$ from (6.2), the expression equals

$$\frac{(1 - \mu)\{g - \mu(1 - s)g_L - sg\}}{1 - \mu(1 - s) - s} = \frac{(1 - \mu)(1 - s)(g - \mu g_L)}{(1 - \mu)(1 - s)}.$$

$$= g - \mu g_L.$$

Consequently, when μg_L is added, we obtain g.

depreciation. Consequently, in both formulations the growth rate of the capital stock should equal S/K. Furthermore, we must have $S/K = g$, as is clear from (6.10a). It will still be the case that the orthodox formulation and my own give different weights to S/K and g_L, since with $s > 0$, $\mu > \lambda$. However, these different weights no longer matter, since they are being used to weight items that are equal to one another. This case is reminiscent of the constant returns to scale production function with no technical progress and with capital and labour both growing as fast as output.

Although (6.10a) and (6.10) are equivalent in the circumstances postulated, it seems preferable to use (6.10), and that is the equation that is used in the rest of this book. Were one to use (6.10a), one would need to estimate K, and this causes difficulties if an *independent* estimate is sought. One could, of course, simply define K in such a way that (6.10) and (6.10a) were identical, but then one might as well stick to (6.10). The choice between them matters only when they could give different results. Where that happens, I prefer (6.10), since I believe that the underlying model is more robust than that of (6.10a). The former requires that growth should be steady in the period under examination, which may be quite short (e.g. ten years). The latter, however, requires that growth should be steady *as well* during the whole period relevant to the measurement of K, which in principle is since investment began. Existing data on K are unreliable, since *(inter alia)* depreciation is based on estimates of asset lives which are unreliable and, in addition, price index numbers used to deflate investment expenditures are unreliable and theoretically incorrect. The inadequacy of available capital stock estimates is discussed at greater length in Chapter 7.

One further reason for preferring (6.10) to (6.10a) is that the former makes explicit the role of ϱ, the radius of the IPC, whereas in (6.10a) this is obscured. It is shown in Chapter 10 that an increase in ϱ is very important in explaining why growth was so much faster after the Second World War than before. In (6.10a) an increase in ϱ would show up as a factor tending to reduce V or K and so to increase S/K. This is in fact *not* likely to emerge from conventional calculations of K based on constant asset lives. Consequently, the use of (6.10a) may lead to erroneous conclusions.

We now turn to a brief review of the three determinants of growth in (6.10): g_L, σ or s, and ϱ.

6.10   Growth of quality-adjusted employment, g_L

The components of the growth of quality-adjusted employment have been analysed by Denison,[16] and I have nothing substantial to add beyond what

---

[16] See Denison (1962, 1974, 1979, 1985); also Denison with Poullier (1967) and Denison and Chung (1976).

is stated in Chapter 2. However, four points seem worth making here. First, much of g_L in the countries considered in this volume has been due to human investment, changes in hours worked, etc., rather than to demographic factors (see Tables 10.1 below and 2.4 above). Studies that confine attention to GDP per head of population, or even per worker, therefore omit much of importance. Second, studies that simply relate GDP growth to investment without regard to growth of the labour force at all, as some do, scarcely deserve to be taken seriously. g_L varies widely between different countries, and from one period to another, and has had very important effects on the rate of growth of output. Third, measurement of g_L is subject to considerable difficulty and uncertainty. In principle, one is trying to weight different workers by their relative marginal products; in practice, the detailed information required is not available, and so various assumptions have to be made (see Section 2.2 above). Finally, the contribution of g_L to output growth is appreciably bigger according to the model just described than according to orthodox growth models. Each 1 per cent addition to the growth rate of employment adds μ per cent, approximately, to the growth rate of output, whereas, according to orthodox theories making the same assumption of perfect markets, it should add only λ per cent. Since $\mu = \lambda/(1 - s)$, and since s can be as high as 0.32, the difference made can be appreciable.

6.11   Rate of investment, σ or s

Equation (6.10) shows that growth not due to g_L is due to σ. This also attributes more to that factor than do orthodox theories, which incorrectly subtract from gross investment either scrapping or depreciation, depending on the way in which the capital stock is measured. Having castigated studies of growth which omit employment growth, I must also castigate other studies which omit investment, confining attention to labour productivity growth. However, it is possible to learn something of interest from such studies, as Chapter 13 seeks to show. It is not possible, all the same, to provide a satisfactory quantitative explanation of growth if the rate of investment is omitted. On the other hand, the available data on investment are not satisfactory, and this reduces the reliability of any attempts to account for growth. The determinants of the rate of investment are discussed in later chapters beginning in Chapter 8.

6.12   The efficiency of investments, ϱ

Equation (6.10) shows that the extent to which a given rate of investment contributes to growth varies directly with ϱ, the radius of the IPC. ϱ depends on both the investment opportunities perceived and the way in which they are selected.

Selection occurs at two levels, and can go astray at each. First, there is selection by the individual firm from among the opportunities confronting it. Second, there is selection between firms. Ideally, one would like the whole economy to select as if it were a single giant firm (but taking prices as parameters). In practice, some firms may choose investments whose social rate of return is below that of investment opportunities that are being rejected by other firms. Capital markets do not work perfectly.

The knowledge, intelligence, originality, common sense, and effort of businessmen, inventors, and scientists are all highly relevant, as are the economic institutions that influence their perceptions and choices, including the degree of competition, taxes, and subsidies, the credit system, and product and factor markets generally. Learning from others' investments will be easier and quicker if communications and travel are easier and quicker. Decision-makers' motives are obviously important. Are they seeking to maximize present values, as we have assumed thus far, or are they pursuing other goals which may conflict with economic efficiency? How free and how decentralized are decisions to invest?

The analysis in this chapter has abstracted from diminishing returns to investment, but these are likely to be very important for the individual firm, and they could also be important for a whole economy. If returns to investment diminish because, as Schumpeter emphasized (see p. 104 above), there is resistance to change, which becomes fiercer as change speeds up, then investment is unlikely to be pushed very far, and only slow growth will be possible.[17]

It is clear that the isolation and measurement of g_L, s, and ϱ is only the beginning of an explanation of economic growth. Each, in turn, needs to be explained, and the inquiry could ramify into almost every department of knowledge. That is as it should be. One of the main criticisms to be levied against orthodox theories is the way in which they appear to eliminate so much from consideration, leaving an arid and unappealing field of inquiry.

6.13 Gestation lags and some other problems

I have treated investments as if they consist of well defined projects whose effects are instantaneous: when a cost δS is incurred, it results in an immediate change in the sustainable rate of output δQ coupled with a change in the level of employment δL. In reality, an investment project will typically require investment expenditures over a period of time that may be considerable (it took a hundred years to build some cathedrals!), also, its full impact on capacity to produce may require a considerable time to develop, as teething troubles will need to be overcome, the labour force has

[17] For further discussion of diminishing returns to the rate of investment, see the appendix to Chapter 7 and also Section 15.3 and p. 445.

to be trained in new methods, distributed stocks must be built up, and so on.

Another problem is that different projects merge into each other. A new factory may be built, and that could be regarded as a definite project; but the machinery originally installed in it will be changed from time to time, and the factory building itself may be extended or modified in various ways. If change is unceasing, what is a 'project'? Methods of project appraisal commonly assume that each 'project' has a 'life', and determinate benefits and costs; but if one thing leads to another, it is not clear that this assumption can be sustained.

One way of dealing with these problems is to look them squarely in the face, and then hurriedly pass on. Science abounds with models that abstract from the complexity of the real world, but nevertheless help one to understand it.

Another more intellectually satisfying approach to the first problem, which comes to much the same practical conclusion, is to recall the definitions of income and investment in Chapter 1. Income at time t is the maximum sustainable consumption rate at time t which an economy, *given sufficient notice*, can attain. The notice is required so as to convert investment activities into consumption-producing activities. If actual investment in the recent past includes expenditures whose full effects on output occur after t, then we must assume that income is measured at t so that it includes some, but not necessarily all, of those benefits. In principle, the same cumulative investment has to occur up to t as occurs in practice, but its *nature* is changed. Only investments whose effects on output and employment are fully realized by t must be allowed. There will then be no half-finished ships or buildings or roads at t. The economy will be fully geared to produce just consumption goods and services. Of course, *learning* from past investments cannot be completed, so in *that* respect the full effects of past investments will not be realized at t. But in other respects, investments will all be completed.

If output could be measured in that way, then investment would indeed affect it instantaneously. Investment in a half-finished ship, say, at t would affect output because, notionally, we would include in our measure of output the benefit from a substitute completed investment having the same cost. The practical question is how far existing measures of output depart from this theoretical ideal. There is some reason to hope that, at least in normal times, the *rate of growth* of output should not be greatly distorted, and that any bias in our measure of s and λ should be rather constant.

So far as the second problem—the separability of projects—is concerned, a theoretical answer can again be found. Although we arrived at the IPC map by a chain of reasoning which employed the concept of separable projects, we do not need to retain them at the end. All we require is that the equations should hold with respect to the relations between output, investment, employment, etc. It is convenient to think of investment as consisting of atoms of investment projects, each with its own characteristics, but in the end, all we need to know is how output and employment behave when the rate of investment is such-and-such.

6.14 Conclusion

The model of growth described in this chapter differs in important respects from orthodox growth models. Economic growth is explained in terms of the growth of the quality-adjusted labour force, the rate of investment, and the efficiency of investment. These in turn then need to be explained.

Stripped down to its essentials, the model is rather simple, and it can be illustrated by a simple diagram (Figure 6.4). A few more theoretical components are needed before we can set about testing its usefulness. In Chapter 7 three proofs of equation (6.9) for the rate of return are given. In Chapter 8 the determinants of the rate of investment are discussed and a rather simple theory is provided. In Chapter 9 attention is given to individual firms and industries, and the assumptions of perfect product markets, self-financing, and present value maximization are relaxed. This completes Part III.

The model assumes that in a particular sense investment opportunities of unchanged quality are always available. This is the assumption that most readers may want to question. In Chapters 3, 4, 5 and in this chapter reasons were given why investments should create new investment opportunities. The chapters in Part IV, where the model is used to explain past history, provide tests of this key assumption, and readers are invited to consider them before forming their own judgement.

Appendix: An Arithmetical Example

This appendix provides an arithmetical example of the model in Section 6.8. The numbers have been chosen for simplicity, but are also quite typical of the post-Second World War observations.[18]

Taking the model for the typical enterprise first, the exogenous variables are: $\sigma = 0.2$; $g_w = 0.02$; $\varrho = 1$; $a = 0.1085$; $b = 0.955$; $c = 0.4$. Throughout I set $P = 1$, and so $s = \sigma$.

The equations of the model are then:

$$\left. \begin{array}{l} g = 0.2q \\ g_L = 0.2l \end{array} \right\} \tag{6.1}$$

---

[18] Apart from ϱ. In Chapters 10 and 11 I arbitrarily set $\varrho = 1$ for the period before 1914, and its post-Second World War value for the USA, for example, is 2.622. Here, I set $\varrho = 1$ for simplicity. This only affects a in equation (6.5).

$$\mu = \frac{\lambda}{1 - 0.2} \tag{6.2}$$

$$0.02 = g - g_L \tag{6.3}$$

$$q = 0.1085 + 0.955l - 0.4l^2 \tag{6.5}$$

$$\mu = 0.955 - 0.8l \tag{6.6}$$

$$r = q - \lambda l \tag{6.9}$$

The solution for the seven endogenous variables is:

$$q = 0.2$$
$$l = 0.1$$
$$g = 0.04$$
$$g_L = 0.02$$
$$\lambda = 0.7$$
$$\mu = 0.875$$
$$r = 0.13$$

If we take, instead, the model for the whole economy, we merely replace g_w by $g_L = 0.02$ in the list of exogenous variables, which yields the same solution.

7

THE RATE OF RETURN

7.1 Introduction

In the first part of this chapter, three proofs of the formula for the rate of return are given. In order to keep them as simple as possible, and to bring out the essential points, all rest on the assumptions of perfect markets, no diminishing returns to rate of investment, no taxation, no borrowing, and no change in the general level of prices. The first two proofs, and to some extent also the third, as we shall see, maintain the assumption of steady equilbrium growth. The first proof is the most convenient one for subsequent relaxations of the other assumptions in the appendix to this chapter and in later chapters. The second and the third proofs, however, contrast more clearly with conventional formulae for rates of return. The second one assumes that there is a once-for-all marginal increase in the rate of investment, and the point at issue is why this results in a constant perpetual gain despite the fact that depreciation of all investments is occurring. This proof clarifies an important difference between the growth model put forward here and conventional growth models. The third proof makes use of a device that others have used, and one that apparently avoids the assumption of steady growth. A once-for-all investment in period 1 is followed by a once-for-all disinvestment in period 2, which restores the situation to where it would have been had the perturbation in period 1 not occurred. This proof thus appears to be more general, but it also shows up an important difference in regard to depreciation compared with orthodox formulae.

The second part of the chapter derives a formula for the rate of depreciation which approximates to the fundamental definition given in Chapter 1. This then enables us to examine the relations between net investment, the net capital stock, and the valuation ratio (or Tobin's q).

The final part of the chapter presents estimates of actual rates of return and depreciation, and demonstrates that the average rate of return on investment is much greater than the rate of return received by savers. Later, in Chapter 15, I attempt to explain this gap, which has important implications for tax policy and the question of whether actual growth rates are sub-optimal.

7.2   Proof no.1.   The steady growth case

Consider a firm whose current output (value added) is sold at a fixed price P, the quantity being Q so that the value is PQ. As is shown in Chapter 9, equilibrium growth requires that the firm's price, relative to prices in general, should not change. Since we are assuming that the general level of prices does not change, P does not change. As the firm is selling and buying in perfect markets, P is outside its control. The firm employs L workers who are paid a wage w, which is equally outside the firm's control. One would normally expect that w was rising, but it could be stationary or falling. In any case, it is changing at a constant exponential rate, g_w. The firm is investing at a rate S, and it keeps the ratio $S/PQ = s$ constant. The (fixed) characteristics of its investment programme are (q, l), so that the exponential rates of growth of its output, g, and employment, g_L, are

$$g = Psq; \qquad g_L = Psl.$$

These assumptions ensure that g and g_L are constant. In addition, for steady growth we require that the share of wages, $\lambda = wL/PQ$, is constant, and this implies that

$$g_w = g - g_L.$$

If the firm's rate of discount is r, then the present value of the firm is given by dividing the current value of the firm's take-out, which must be growing at g, by $r - g$. (For a proof of this, see Section 6.9 above.) Consequently the present value, V, is

$$V = \frac{PQ\,(1 - \lambda - s)}{r - g} = \frac{C}{r - g}\,.$$

It is worth noting that this formula for the present value of the firm in steady growth implies that there must be a positive take-out, C, if the firm is to have a positive value. This also implies that $1 - s - \lambda > 0$. Some have questioned why firms should pay dividends under a tax system that penalizes them more heavily than undistributed profits. Would shareholders not be better off if dividends were ploughed back? They could then reap the benefit in the form of more lightly taxed capital gains. Firms, and at least some of their shareholders, may, however, take a long-term view. If their behaviour then corresponds more closely to that of steady growth, they must permit shareholders to receive a net take-out (i.e. dividends in excess of investment) if the shares are to be worth anything to shareholders. In this context, Figures 2.3 and 2.4 are of some interest, since they show a great contraction in $1 - s - \lambda$ in the UK and Japan since the Second World

War (although taxation is not allowed for, nor is borrowing, so that $1 - s - \lambda$ does not equal the share of take-out for shareholders).

In order to obtain a formula for the marginal rate of return, which is also the firm's rate of discount if (as I assume) it is maximizing its present value, let us consider the following case. The firm increases its rate of investment by δs, (still with characteristics (q, l)) for a short interval of time, δt, and then relapses to its previous rate s, which it maintains indefinitely. During the time interval δt, the total amount of take-out sacrificed by the firm's owners is then $PQ \, \delta s \, \delta t$, and this must equal the increment to the present value of the firm resulting from the extra investment. The rate of discount that achieves this equality is then the firm's marginal rate of return r. I now work out the increment to the present value.

As a result of investing at a rate that is increased by δs, the rate of growth of output is raised by $\delta g = P \, \delta s \, q$, and the rate of growth of employment by $\delta g_L = P \, \delta s \, l$. Hence, at the end of the short interval of time δt, the level of output is δQ, and the level of employment δL, higher than it would have been without the extra investment, where (neglecting second-order terms)

$$\delta Q = PQ \, \delta s \, \delta t \, q; \qquad \delta L = PL \, \delta s \, \delta t \, l.$$

In order to revert to the previous rate of investment, s, a fraction s of this extra output must be invested. Consequently, at the end of δt, the rate of take-out is increased by δC where

$$\delta C = P \, \delta Q \, (1 - s) - w \, \delta L$$

$$= PQ \, \delta s \, \delta t \, P \, \{q \, (1 - s) - \lambda l \, \}.$$

The increment in present value is then $\delta C / (r - g)$. Setting this equal to the take-out sacrificed (i.e. $PQ \, \delta s \, \delta t$), and dividing through by $PQ \, \delta s \, \delta t$ gives

$$1 = \frac{P \, \{ \, q \, (1 - s) - \lambda l \, \}}{r - g},$$

from which, after multiplying through by $r - g$, we arrive at the formula (since $-g = -Psq$ cancels out from both sides)

$$r = P \, (q - \lambda l).$$

This proof can easily be adapted to a marginal investment made at any point along the equal-profits contour (EPC) through (q, l), which is a straight line whose slope is μ (see Section 6.4). Thus, for any arbitrarily selected point (q_a, l_a) on that contour such that $q_a - \mu l_a = q - \mu l$, the proof proceeds as above until we get

$$r - g = P \, \{q_a \, (1 - s) - \lambda l_a\}$$

$$= P \, \{q_a \, (1 - s) - \mu \, (1 - s) \, l_a\}$$

$$= P\{q\,(1\,-\,s)\,-\,\mu\,(1\,-\,s)\,l\}$$

$$= P\{q\,(1\,-\,s)\,-\,\lambda\,l\}$$

as before.

7.3   Proof no.2.   The perpetuity case

If the investment programme has characteristics (q, l), then q is by definition the proportionate increase in output resulting from a marginal unit increase in $\sigma = S/Q$. q is also the *absolute* increase in output resulting from a marginal unit increase in S. Likewise, l is by definition the proportionate increase in employment resulting from a marginal unit increase in σ, and $l\,(L/Q)$ is the *absolute* increase in employment resulting from a marginal unit increase in S. It follows that, if £1 more is invested with characteristics (q, l), the resulting increments in ouput, δQ, and employment, δL, are

$$\delta Q = q; \qquad \delta L = \frac{lL}{Q}.$$

The increment in gross profit is then

$$P\,\delta Q - w\,\delta L = Pq - l\,\frac{wL}{Q}$$
$$= r.$$

This is the initial increase in gross profit, but as time passes w may rise (as one would normally expect), or it could fall. It therefore is puzzling as to why the ratio of the *initial* gross profit to the cost of the extra investment should equal the rate of return. Surely it should do so only if the initial gross profit were to remain unchanged for ever, which seems to require that w should be constant? If, as in the normal case, w rises, the initial gross profit must be steadily eroded and eventually disappear. It then appears that the true rate of return would not be given by my formula, but would be less than that.

Now the erosion of profits by rising wage rates is precisely what causes depreciation in my model, and it certainly does occur. Despite that, it can be shown that, given my assumptions, the marginal rate of return is indeed the initial gross rate of profit, and this is so whether wage rates are rising, constant, or falling. This surprising result is explained at length in what follows. It contrasts very markedly with conventional views about the rate of return, which would subtract the rate of depreciation from the initial gross profit to get the net rate of return, equivalent to r. To anticipate, the reason why I get such a different result is that, unlike most conventional analysis, mine allows for the effect of extra investment now on investment in all future periods. The reverse direction of causation is generally allowed for inasmuch as depreciation that is due to obsolescence is allowed for. Thus, in my model, and in some conventional ones as well, future investment forces up the price of labour, and this erodes profits and results in depreciation, which is allowed for in estimating rates of return on current investment. However, it is also the case that current investment alters all future investment opportunities, and that is not usually allowed for in conventional theory, and certainly not in the way discussed below.[1]

It may be recalled that in Chapter 1 it was shown that, under the assumptions there stated, the initial gross rate of profit was indeed a perpetual addition to national income, and so could be regarded as providing a measure of the *social* rate of return from the investment causing it. Our concern now is with the *private* rate of return. Under the assumptions stated earlier, the proof given here will imply that the two rates of return coincide.

In the previous proof it was assumed that marginal investment resulted in increased output, which in turn resulted in increased investment, since the original ratio of investment to output was maintained. Hence, out of the extra $P\delta Q$ of output, a fraction s was saved and invested. Take-out therefore did not increase by the whole of the initial extra gross profit, because part of it was saved. The result was a smaller, but growing, increase in take-out. Now let us consider what happens when the *whole* of the initial gross profit is taken out. It is the previous absolute (and growing) *level* of investment that is restored after the interval δt. What I have to prove is that a constant absolute amount, equal to the initial gross profit, is added to all future profits. Since the latter were growing at a constant exponential rate g, the addition of a constant absolute amount to them does not leave the new total of gross profits growing at g. In fact, the rate of growth ceases to be constant, and this could lead to complications. In order to avoid these I adopt a different way of looking at the problem, which not only maintains simplicity but also clarifies an aspect of the model which might otherwise remain obscure.

The essential idea that I shall exploit is that there is a *sequence of investments* which the firm is going to undertake. If the firm undertakes a marginal extra investment now, that does not alter the sequence,[2] except

---

[1] If an allowance were made conventionally, it would be a negative one owing to the assumed diminishing marginal productivity of the capital stock, a concept that is rejected here. As is shown below, my allowance is positive in the normal case when wage rates are rising, and is negative only when wage rates are falling.

[2] However, the *sense* in which the sequence is unchanged requires careful interpretation. I am not asserting that it is unchanged in common–sense terms, only that the map of investment opportunities is unchanged in the sense discussed in Chapter 6.

that it brings it all forward in time. As has already been pointed out, each investment prepares the way for the next one. In my analogy of climbing up a hill, as we climb we see a little further up where we are about to climb. If, then, we speed up our climb, we shall see any given stretch of our future climb sooner, and we shall also climb any given stretch sooner. But the best path up the mountain itself does not change on present assumptions.

As was pointed out at the beginning of this section, if the characteristics of the investment programme are (q,l), each £1 of investment increases output by q, and employment by lL/Q. So long as the characteristics remain fixed (and I assume that they do), there is then a fixed linear relation between increased output and amount of investment. This relation is shown by the line PQ_1, PQ_2, PQ_3 in Figure 7.1. Along the horizontal axis is measured the cumulative sum of gross investment from a date that can be arbitrarily chosen so long as it predates the period we wish to consider (or it could start at the beginning of that period). I call this 'stock' G_t, so that, if T is the chosen starting date,

$$G_t \equiv \int_{\tau=T}^{t} S_\tau \, d\tau$$

As investment takes place, the increase in output per unit of investment will equal q, which is assumed to be held constant. Since P is also constant, the slope of the line PQ_1, PQ_2, PQ_3 is simply Pq.

Employment is not shown in Figure 7.1. In the normal case with growing wage rate and labour productivity, the ratio of employment to output gradually falls as investment takes places. However, so long as l remains fixed, as is assumed, the same output level is always accompanied by the same employment level. Since each £1 of investment always increases output by q and employment by lL/Q, if we start from some given L_T/Q_T and invest with characteristics (q, l), we must always reach the same employment level, say L_t, when we have made G_t of investment. The subscripts here refer to time, but they need not: one could simply put a serial number on investment, and the conclusions would hold.

The firm is in steady growth *without* the marginal investment. It follows that the ratio of the wage bill to the value of output must then be constant, and this is shown by the straight line w_1L_1, w_2L_2, w_3L_3 in Figure 7.1. So $w_1L_1/P_1Q_1 = \lambda$, and this also equals the corresponding ratios for 2 and 3. The slope of the wL line is then $P\lambda q$.

We can now see what happens when the firm undertakes a marginal investment. This takes place at time t_1, when cumulative investment is G_1. As only a small amount of extra investment is undertaken, I assume as a first approximation that it instantaneously increases the 'stock' to G_2. Hence, as shown in Figure 7.1, *with* the extra investment, both G_1 and G_2

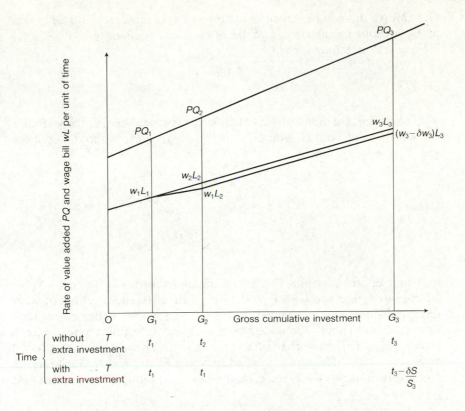

Fig. 7.1 Second proof of the rate of return formula

occur at t_1. Subsequently, the firm invests in each period at the same absolute rate as without the extra investment. Consequently, it arrives at G_3 *with* earlier than it did *without* by an amount of time that is worked out below.

We must now compare the *with* and *without* outputs and wage bills. The outputs are very simple. As each G is reached, the same output is reached. Hence at G_2 the value of output *with* is PQ_2, just as it was *without*. Likewise, at G_3 output is worth PQ_3.

As was pointed out above, employment is also the same *with* as *without*.

The only thing that is different (on my assumptions) is the wage rate. Since that is a function of time, dependent on investment and labour force growth in the rest of the economy, and since the times at which successive Gs are reached are earlier *with* than *without*, it follows that wage rates at a given G will be lower *with* than *without* so long as they are rising. How much lower?

Let the wage *without* minus the wage *with* when cumulative investment is

G_2 be δw (so this will be a positive quantity if wage rates are rising). Let time at G_2 *without* minus time *with* be δt (a positive quantity). If δS is the incremental investment, then

$$\delta t = \frac{\delta S}{S_1}$$

where S_1 is the rate of investment at G_1 in either case. Then, in the *with* case, the wage rate at both G_1 and G_2 is w_1, whereas in the *without* case it has grown to w_2 at G_2 where

$$w_2 = w_1 \, e^{\, g_w \delta t}$$

Hence

$$\delta w = w_2 - w_1$$

$$= w_1 \, g_w \, \frac{\delta S}{S_1}$$

to a first approximation. This is the initial wage rate difference. As we advance to higher and higher G, the wage rate difference declines (if wage rates are rising). This is because the time difference gets smaller and smaller, since it always equals δS divided by the current investment rate, which is growing at g. This more than offsets the fact that, with wage rates growing at g_w, this time difference is applied to a higher and higher wage rate. In fact, logarithmically differentiating the last expression with respect to time gives

$$\frac{d \ln (\delta w)}{dt} = \frac{d \ln (w)}{dt} - \frac{d \ln (S)}{dt}$$

$$= g_w - g$$

$$= -g_L$$

since with steady growth in the *without* case $g_w = g - g_L$.

Now the difference in the wage bill, *without* minus *with*, is simply $\delta w \, L$. Since, as I have just shown, δw is declining at the exponential rate g_L, and since L is growing at g_L, their product is constant. This demonstrates that the wage bill at any given G from G_2 onwards in the *without* case is a constant absolute amount higher than in the *with* case, as shown in Figure 7.1. The slopes of the wL lines are therefore the same in the two cases.

In order to compare profits in the two cases, we must compare like times. Initially, just when the incremental investment has been undertaken at time t_1 gross profit *with* is, as we have seen (p. 184), r per unit of incremental investment higher than it is *without*. Since absolute rates of investment thereafter are the same *with* as *without*, the absolute additions to rates of output are also the same in both cases. I have just demonstrated that the absolute additions to rates of wage bill are also the same in both cases (the slopes of the wL lines are the same): it follows that this initial r per unit of investment is preserved indefinitely. Since it is, then, a perpetuity, it is also the true marginal rate of return.

While the above demonstration has been in terms of a rising wage rate, it holds for a falling wage rate as well. The incremental investment then brings forward subsequent investments into a time when wage rates are *higher*, so that the new wage bill line is above, rather than below, the old one in Figure 7.1. This loss on subsequent investment offsets the appreciation that is due to falling wage rates on the incremental investment. Hence, as before, the total net effect is a perpetuity equal to r.

The proof is a logical deduction from the assumptions, but some may question their reality. The assumptions of perfect markets, no taxation, no borrowing, and no inflation are all relaxed subsequently. The assumption of steady equilibrium growth (in the *without* case) is not relaxed (despite the next proof). The assumptions of unchanged investment opportunities and of no diminishing returns to the rate of investment are the ones that some readers will not swallow easily. The former has already been discussed at length, and we may pause to consider the latter now.

If the set of opportunities that the firm is aware of at a given time consists of better and worse ones (as seems likely), the firm can be expected to select those that are best. Increasing the rate of investment should then result in a worse average set; the average rate of return will tend to fall as the rate of investment is stepped up; and the marginal rate of return will be below the average. All this seems plausible, although it must be remembered that powerful arguments in favour of increasing returns have been adduced as well. The importance and extent of diminishing returns is therefore an empirical matter which is investigated in Chapter 15. I conclude that there probably are quite strongly diminishing returns for the individual firm, although for all firms taken together the position is substantially different. Thus, if all firms together invest more, return may not diminish (or may diminish less than for the individual firm) because all benefit by learning more from each other. This is the basis for the learning externality discussed in Chapter 15.

If, as seems likely, there are diminishing returns for the individual firm, proof no. 2 no longer takes the simple form just described. Because of diminishing returns, the same absolute rate of investment is no longer consistent with an unchanged q and l, as I have assumed. Accordingly, I have worked out the formula for this case, using proof no. 1, in the appendix to this chapter. This has the advantage that, with the *share* of investment, rather than its absolute amount, held constant, q and l are also constant on my assumptions. Proof no. 1 therefore remains relatively simple.

7.4 Proof no. 3. The perturbation case

This proof is shorter and simpler than the first two. Some may regard it as more general as well, but, as we shall see, appearances are deceptive. It follows the idea put forward first (so far as I know) by Solow (1963), and repeated by King (1977, ch. 8). The firm has an investment, output, and input plan for future periods which it believes is optimal. This plan is made to undergo a small perturbation, so that in period 1 the firm invests one unit more and in period 2 it cuts back investment by whatever amount is necessary to restore the position in period 3 and all succeeding periods to the same as it would have been without the perturbation. Comparing the situations *with* and *without* the perturbation, there is a sacrifice of take-out of one unit in period 1. In period 2 there is an increase in take-out, for two reasons: first, there is the yield of the extra investment in period 1; second, there is the cut-back in investment. There are no other differences. The marginal rate of return is then that rate of discount that makes the *PV* of these differences, discounted back to period 1 (say), zero.

In conventional theory, the argument runs as follows. Let the yield per unit of extra investment, before deducting depreciation, be *MRR*. Let depreciation per unit of capital be at the rate of δ. Then in period 2, since the capital stock is $1 - \delta$ higher than it would otherwise be, we must cut back investment by $1 - \delta$ to restore it to its original position in period 3 and thereafter. Take-out in period 2 is then $MRR + 1 - \delta$ higher than it would otherwise have been. If r is the required rate of discount, the value of the extra take-out in period 2, discounted back to period 1, must equal the unit sacrificed in that period, or

$$1 = \frac{MRR + 1 - \delta}{1 + r}$$

Hence

$$r = MRR - \delta.$$

This argument needs to be modified in two important respects before it can be accepted. First, as conventionally presented, δ is essentially *physical* deterioration of the capital stock.[3] In the terminology of Chapter 1 it corresponds, then, to required maintenance, and *not* to depreciation. I certainly accept that the rate of return must be measured net of required maintenance, but would argue that gross profit, as conventionally

---

[3] This is explicit in King (1977, 230) and in Solow (1963, 29). Subsequently (see p. 61 *et seq.*) Solow also introduces the effect of obsolescence in the context of a vintage model with costless exogenous capital-augmenting technical progress. Objections to vintage models are given in Ch. 3 above.

measured, *is* approximately so measured. In any case, my disagreement with conventional theory is not about the subtraction of maintenance expenditures in calculating gross profit, but about subtracting allowances for depreciation arising from obsolescence (or relative price changes). Although King, for example, *starts* by making δ refer to physical deterioration, he subsequently uses data that are undoubtedly dominated by obsolescence. The confusion of the two must, as I have argued, be avoided. If one therefore adopts the conventions followed in this book of measuring profits net of maintenance, and if MRR is so measured, then δ must be eliminated, and this then leaves us with

$$r = MRR;$$

i.e., the marginal rate of return equals the initial profit gross of depreciation.[4]

This appears to be a much simpler, neater and more general proof than the preceding two. However, it rests on an assumption that I have not yet exposed,[5] and this is the second important modification to the argument. The crucial assumption is that, if the firm enters period 3 with the same capital stock *with* as *without* the peturbation, then it is in all other respects the same, so that the future course of events is unchanged. Under what conditions is this assumption likely to be fulfilled? It turns out that these conditions are just the same as those needed to justify the earlier formulae, namely, a constant map of IPCs and steady growth by the firm, at least as long as the formula is to hold.

The argument assumes that a unit less of investment in period 2 undoes the effect of a unit more of investment in period 1. Unless the characteristics of the investment in each period are the same, i.e. unless both Pq and Pl are the same, this will not be so. That q and l may differ is obvious if the map of IPC is changing through time, but even if it is constant, q and l could differ. Thus, if there are diminishing returns to the rate of investment, and if the rate of investment *without* is either increasing or decreasing from period 1 to period 2, then Pq and Pl will *not* be the same. For example, if the firm is increasing its rate of investment, a marginal investment in period 2 will be less productive than in period 1. In that case, the cut-back in investment in period 2 required to restore the *without* position in period 3 will be *more* than one unit. Consequently, r will be greater than the *MRR*.

---

[4] Readers may ask what has become of depreciation? Since we are here concerned with the *private*, and not the *social*, rate of return, the loss to capitalists that results when wages rise should, it seems, be allowed for. However, in the period analysis in the text, there is no such loss on the assets resulting from the peturbation. There is none in period 2, when *MRR* is earned, and in period 3 and later periods, when there would have been a loss had the investment remained, there is none because the original investment in period 1 has been offset by disinvestment in period 2.

[5] Again, this assumption is explicitly stated in King (1977, 229).

Nor is this all. Even if the rate of investment is the same in periods 1 and 2, that is not sufficient to ensure that the firm will choose investments in each period which have the same q and l as its marginal investments. For the same q and l to be optimal in both periods, not only must the map of IPC be the same, and not only must s be the same, but also λ must be the same. But the satisfaction of all these conditions amounts to specifying steady growth for periods 1 and 2. So the formula holds for period 1 as long as there is steady growth for periods 1 and 2. To make it hold for period 2 requires steady growth for periods 2 and 3. And so on.

One benefit we can gain from the above argument is the light it sheds on what may be called *supernormal (or subnormal) depreciation (or appreciation)*. I have argued that, under steady growth conditions, the marginal rate of return should make no allowance for depreciation, despite the fact that depreciation that is due to rising real wage rates may (and usually will) be occurring. *This* depreciation probably accounts for most, or indeed all, of total depreciation in a closed economy,[6] and so may be called *normal*. However, there will be industries and firms that are not in (approximately) steady growth, and they will be subject to *supernormal or subnormal* depreciation or appreciation. An example may help to clarify this.

Suppose that there is some important invention. This may be regarded as shifting out the IPC of the affected firms or industry, and so increasing the rate of return, volume of investment, and rate of growth of the industry. As time passes, competition and the rapid growth of output force down prices of output.

While the IPC are shifting outwards, Pq and Pl are tending to increase (assuming no change in P). While this is happening, the preceding argument shows that r will tend to be *less* than MRR. This is because the cut-back in investment in period 2 required to restore the *without* situation in period 3 and thereafter is *less* than one unit. If q and l increase in the proportion δ, which is to say if ϱ increases in the proportion δ, between periods 1 and 2, then the cut-back in investment in period 2 is $1 - \delta$, and the conventional result that $r = MRR - \delta$ holds. This case might be one in which the price of the relevant capital goods in terms of consumption was falling at rate δ per period, or in which their quality was improving at that rate.

The case when the price of output, P, is falling is different. The falling price means that MRR in successive periods declines, but it does not affect the result that each (short-period) $MRR = r$. It is still the case that, so long as q and l remain constant, the cut-back in investment needed to compensate for the initial unit of extra investment is one unit. However, this result does suggest that the long-period rate of return when P is falling

---

[6] In an open economy there will be, in addition, depreciation (or appreciation) arising from adverse (or beneficial) changes in the terms of trade.

is *below* the short-period one, and so below the initial gross profit per unit of investment. Out of steady growth, therefore, with P falling, one must subtract an allowance for depreciation from the initial gross profit; and one must add appreciation if P is rising. A similiar point applies if, out of steady growth, the share of wages is rising or falling, thus causing short-period rates of return to fall or rise.

In conclusion, let us revert to a point made earlier to explain the difference between the rate of return formula given here and conventional rate of return formulae. I pointed out in Section 7.3 that the formula allows for the effect of current investment on future investment, through shifting it forward in time into a period in which wages are lower (if wages are rising — higher if they are falling). This effect occurs for the *marginal* investment, which is the concern of this chapter. We have been considering the effect of investing and saving a little more, and so consuming a little less. In cost-benefit analysis this may well *not* be the relevant comparison. Instead, one is comparing a situation *with* a certain project and one *without* it. In the *without* situation, investment could be just as high as *with*, the difference being that it takes a different form. One is then selecting between alternative investment opportunities, rather than deciding how much to invest. In that case, the point about shifting forward investments does not apply, and it is certainly the case that, in comparing the alternatives, future relative price changes (including real wage changes) must be allowed for.

7.5 Depreciation, net investment, the net capital stock, and the valuation ratio, v

In this section formulae are derived for depreciation, net investment, and net capital stock for a steadily growing firm. Under certain conditions, which we investigate, the formulae are consistent with the fundamental definition of depreciation as being the amount of gross profit which, if it were invested, would leave the remainder of gross profit equal to the firm's income. Depreciation is due solely to relative price changes. Since steady growth is assumed, the formulae can serve, at best, only as approximations to reality in which growth is only approximately steady, but they may be useful none the less. One needs these concepts mainly as adjuncts in estimating income, and, as pointed out in Chapter 1, such estimates are inevitably rough and ready. The basic concepts discussed earlier can be used in more complicated situations than those of steady growth, but it would be out of place to discuss them here. They are best tailored to specific cases.

The basic formula is that for depreciation as a share of output (value added), which is

$$\delta = \frac{D}{PQ} = \frac{\lambda \, g_w}{r - g}$$

where D is the rate of depreciation, measured in the same units of value per period as the value of output, PQ, and the other symbols have their usual meanings. (But note that δ is no longer the ratio of depreciation to the capital stock, as in the preceding section, but is now (and henceforth) the ratio of depreciation to output.) This formula can be expressed in words as the present value of the future stream of increments in the wage bill per unit period that is due to rising real wage rates,[7] expressed as a share of output, and discounted at $r - g$ since the increments grow at g. Clearly, if real wage rates were constant, so that $g_w = 0$, depreciation would be 0. Also if real wage rates were falling, depreciation would become negative and so would become appreciation. I have chosen to define depreciation as a positive quantity, since that accords better with ordinary usage. However, it should be noted that depreciation for capitalists is (as pointed out in Chapter 1) matched by appreciation for workers. The formula thus also gives appreciation for workers, and this would have to be shown with a negative sign (i.e. negative depreciation) to be consistent.

There are several ways of deriving this formula, of which only one is given here. Let us call the net present value of the firm V. This is the present value of the future stream of take-out, C, which is growing at g, so that, as before,

$$V = \frac{C}{r - g}$$

and

$$C = PQ\,(1 - \lambda - s).$$

Now let us define depreciation as the amount that must be subtracted from gross investment, S, to give net investment which is equal to the rate of increase of the present value of the firm. This is one of the three definitions of depreciation discussed on p.23 above, and it is consistant with my fundamental definition, it may be remembered, only as long as rates of discount are constant and there are no windfalls, both of which assumptions are fulfilled in steady growth. Hence

$$\frac{\mathrm{d}V}{\mathrm{d}t} \equiv S - D.$$

Since $P, r, g, \lambda,$ and s are all constant in steady growth, and since

$$\frac{\mathrm{d}Q}{\mathrm{d}t} = gQ,$$

---

[7] Note that real wage rates are measured per *quality-adjusted* worker, and so will generally rise more slowly than real average earnings per worker, which grow $g_L - g_N$ faster. See Chapter 2.

it follows that, if we differentiate the above expression for V with respect to time,

$$S - D = \frac{g\,PQ\,(1 - \lambda - s)}{r - g}$$

$$\therefore \quad \frac{D}{PQ} = \frac{s\,(r - g) - g\,(1 - \lambda - s)}{r - g}$$

$$= \frac{s\,P\,(q - \lambda l) - g\,(1 - \lambda)}{r - g}$$

$$= \frac{\lambda\,(g - g_L)}{r - g}$$

$$= \frac{\lambda g_w}{r - g}\,.$$

The above proof uses our previous formula for $r = P\,(q - \lambda l)$, which applies only when there are no diminishing returns to the rate of investment. If there are diminishing returns, we can retain the formula provided we give it a special meaning: r must now be the *average* rate of return, since that is still given by the above formula, but then V has to be the present value of the firm using this average rate of return to discount the future stream of take-out. In practice, such average rates of return are frequently used.

Using the above formula, we can express the output (i.e. value added) of the firm as the sum of net profit, depreciation, and the wage bill, with net profit equal to rV. This can be shown as follows. Net profit equals

$$PQ - D - wL = PQ\left(1 - \frac{\lambda g_w}{r - g} - \lambda\right)$$

$$= PQ\left(1 - \lambda - s + s - \frac{\lambda g_w}{r - g}\right)$$

$$= PQ\left\{\frac{r\,(1 - \lambda - s)}{r - g} + \frac{(rs - g + \lambda g - \lambda g_w)}{r - g}\right\}$$

Now the second group of terms in braces on the right-hand side equals 0, since $rs = g - \lambda g_L$, and $\lambda g_w = \lambda g - \lambda g_L$. The first group of terms equals rV/PQ. Hence

$$PQ = rV + D + wL.$$

The circumstance under which rV is the true income of the firm are discussed later (p.197).

We can now introduce the net capital stock, K, which is defined as the accumulated sum of past net investment. Hence

$$K_t = \int_{-\infty}^{t} (S_\tau - D_\tau) \, d\tau$$

$$= \int_{-\infty}^{t} \frac{dV_\tau}{d\tau} \, d\tau$$

$$= V_t.$$

Hence, given our definition of depreciation, the net capital stock is the same as the net present value of the firm. This result is independent of steady growth, but the definition of depreciation accords with the fundamental definition only as long as rates of discount are constant and there are no windfalls. Changes in rates of discount and windfalls both can result in instantaneous changes in V, and one cannot include such changes in depreciation with the fundamental definition. Apart from any other considerations, the dimensions are wrong. Depreciation should be a *flow*, as it is the minimum flow of investment required if the real value of take-out is to be maintained. Depreciation defined, as above, in terms of changes in V is not a flow if there are discontinuous changes in rates of discount or in expectations. So if depreciation is defined in accordance with the fundamental definition, this will divorce K from V whenever such changes occur.

We have already seen that net profit is rV. If $K = V$, then the average rate of return equals net profit divided by net capital stock, a familiar relation;[8] i.e.,

$$r = \frac{PQ - D - wL}{K}.$$

Another familiar relation that may be mentioned is that the rate of growth equals the average rate of return multiplied by the share of (profit) income saved (Hicks 1965, 146, 258). Both income and savings are net of depreciation, so income is rV and savings are $S - D$. Hence.

$$r \frac{(S - D)}{rV} = \frac{1}{V} \frac{dV}{dt} = g.$$

This relation holds so long as the growth of income is due entirely to savings, and then it applies to the whole economy. Since depreciation for the whole economy is zero, net savings are S, and since $rs = g - \lambda g_L$, we have $rs = g$ if $g_L = 0$.

---

[8] And one that holds in a wide variety of circumstances besides steady growth: see Kay (1976).

We may now further investigate the circumstances under which the formula for depreciation is consistent with the fundamental definition of that concept given in Chapter 1. If a firm were to invest at the rate D with certain characteristics yet to be established, could that firm expect to take out a constant amount equal to its gross profit less D for the indefinite future? That is what is required by the fundamental definition of depreciation. The firm must be assumed to be investing D in the most profitable way open to it.

Let us assume that the firm was investing at (q,l) at rate s and growing at g, and that it is not subject to any diminishing returns to the rate of investment. If the firm is to invest instead a constant absolute amount D, and be left with a constant absolute take-out, then its gross profit must be a constant absolute amount. This can be achieved if its output is constant, and if its labour force shrinks at the same rate as the wage rate grows, so that the wage bill is constant. Let the characteristics of the firm's investment be (q_d, l_d). Then clearly we must have

$$q_d = 0; \quad Pl_d \delta = -g_w.$$

Let us assume, for the moment, that the firm's existing IPC, which passes through (q,l), is a straight line with slope μ. In that case, the point (q_d, l_d) must lie on this line, and so

$$q_d - \mu l_d = q - \mu l.$$

Substituting for q_d, l_d from above then gives

$$0 + \frac{\mu g_w}{P \delta} = q - \mu l$$

$$\therefore \quad \delta = \frac{\mu g_w}{P(q - \mu l)}$$

$$= \frac{\lambda g_w}{P(1 - s)(q - \mu l)}$$

$$= \frac{\lambda g_w}{r - g}$$

Hence we arrive at the same formula for depreciation as a share of output, δ, as before. Since the firm would be investing on its IPC, which is assumed to be a straight line, it would be earning the same rate of return, $r = P(q - \lambda l)$, as when it invested at (q,l) (see Section 7.2 for proof), and this would be the highest rate of return it could get.

However, all this assumes a straight-line IPC. More generally, we can expect the IPC to be concave to the origin. The firm could not then invest at the point (q_d, l_d) found above, but would have to make do with a lower return by investing at the point where the curved IPC cuts the horizontal axis. At this point, l_d would be arithmetically smaller, and this would mean that the amount of investment needed to make the labour force shrink at g_w would be greater. Consequently, the above formula for δ *under*states the true rate of depreciation, the degree of understatement depending on the curvature of the IPC. (The more curved, the greater the understatement).

There is, however, a consideration that tells in the opposite direction. In so far as there are diminishing returns to the rate of investment, the firm's IPC will move further out from the origin as it cuts back its rate of investment to D, and this could offset, or more than offset, the curvature loss just mentioned.

In conclusion, therefore, the formula for δ will give a close approximation to true depreciation so long as the degree of curvature of the IPC and the rate of diminishing returns to investment are both small, and, even if they are both appreciable, the approximation will be close so long as their opposite effects more or less cancel out.

The last point to be considered in this section is the valuation ratio, v,[9] which is defined (in the absence of taxation and of non-equity finance) as

$$v \equiv \frac{V}{K}$$

So long as there is steady growth and no diminishing returns to the rate of investment, since $V = K$, $v = 1$. However, in practice there are a great many factors that can make v diverge from 1. I consider the very important influence of taxation and its effect on v in Chapter 15; here I confine my attention to some other points.

Let us first consider what happens to v when there are diminishing returns to the rate of investment. I continue to assume that the firm maximizes its present value, using its *marginal* rate of return to discount future take-out, which I designate as r. The *average* rate of return on investment is r_a. It is then no longer the case that $V = K$, or $v = 1$. Since

$$V = \frac{C}{r - g}$$

while K, by the preceding argument, is what V *would* be if r_a rather than r were used to discount future consumption, so that

$$K = \frac{C}{r_a - g},$$

---

[9] The valuation ratio is often referred to as Tobin's q. However, as we need to reserve q for another use, we use v here instead.

it follows that[10]

$$v = \frac{V}{K} = \frac{r_a - g}{r - g} \geqq 1.$$

This result shows than the existence of values of $v > 1$ is perfectly compatible with long-run equilibrium.

Since available estimates of K are not made using my depreciation formula, but either rest on various accounting conventions or else use the perpetual inventory method and assume particular asset lives, it is clear that such estimates could result in measured values of K, and so of v, diverging from the theoretical value given above in either direction. We consider some possible reasons for divergence later in this chapter.

Observed values of V will reflect shareholders' (and other creditors') rates of discount. For a firm that seeks to maximize the value of the shares of the firm, the marginal return on investment should be set at a level that (taking into account taxation and the cost and availability of finance from non-equity sources) provides shareholders with their rate of discount. However, managerially controlled firms may pursue other objectives so that the marginal return on investment could be less or greater than the share value maximizing rate. This point is taken up further in Chapters 9 and 15.

Finally, one should mention the possibility of non-steady growth. If we define D as earlier from the relation $S - D \equiv dV/dt$, then there can be no divorce of V from K. However, as has been pointed out, if there are changes in discount rates or in expectations, this is unsatisfactory, since then D would not correspond, even approximately, to the fundamental definition. If, then, we stick to the fundamental definition of D, or to reasonably close approximations to it, changes in discount rates or in expectations will change the relation between V and K and so will alter v, either up or down. Let us, however, assume that neither discount rates nor expectations change, but allow that growth is unsteady in other respects. In that case, the fundamental definition is consistent with the relation $S - D = dV/dt$, so long as average and marginal rates of return coincide, and both equal the rate of discount. Then, even with unsteady growth in other respects, $V = K$ and $v = 1$. If, however, there are diminishing returns to the rate of investment so that the marginal rate of return is below the average rate, then it cannot be expected that average or marginal rates of return will remain constant as s changes; nor can one expect rates of discount to remain constant. In that case, in general $V \neq K$ and $v \neq 1$, and the relationships will change through time. Nothing very simple can then be said.

---

[10] See Kay (1976 456, eq (21)) for a similar result, but in a different context, the difference between r_a and r being due to accounting conventions (over-cautious depreciation allowances).

7.6 Some estimates of rates of return and depreciation

In this section I present estimates of the rates of return and of depreciation for my standard countries and periods made in accordance with the formulae described earlier. These are then compared with some more conventional estimates using the perpetual inventory method for the UK and the USA. There are often substantial differences, and I seek to explain these. I also consider estimates of the much lower rates of return received by savers. The large gap between the average return earned by businesses and that earned by savers is very relevant to the question of whether countries have achieved optimum rates of growth, which is examined in Chapter 15. Its proper consideration requires the intervening Chapters 9 and 14, which discuss the behaviour of individual firms and taxation.

The main estimates are displayed in Table 7.1. The first two columns show rates of return, and the second two, ratios of depreciation to output or value added. We take these in turn.

There are two different ways in which one can give effect to the formula for the rate of return. Either one can set $r = P(q - \lambda l)$, or, remembering that with perfect markets $\lambda = \mu (1 - s)$, one can set $r = P\{ q - \mu(1 - s)l\}$. The former has been used for column (2) of the table and the latter for column (1). They do not coincide because the estimate of μ for each country and period is derived from a regression equation in which μ is the estimated coefficient of the effect labour input growth on growth of output,[11] and this is not in fact precisely equal to $\lambda / (1 - s)$. We may therefore regard the estimates in column (2) as being estimates of the average *private* return to investment (before tax),[12] while those in column (1) are estimates of the average *social* return. The formula for the latter is, as is shown in Chapter 15, precisely that used for column (1). It can be seen from the table that the two sets of estimates do not differ much for years after the Second World War.[13] The largest differences occur where there is most uncertainty about the magnitude of λ, which is especially true for the Japanese prewar data, and that is a reason for preferring the estimates in column (1), which are independent of λ. In what follows I confine attention to those estimates.

The estimates are influenced by changes in the ratio of output to capacity. Although I have attempted to eliminate such changes by ignoring slump years and by using fitted trends (see p. 46 above), in practice they have not been altogther eliminated. A rising ratio may help to explain the high rates of return in the UK in 1964–73 and in Japan in 1928–36 and 1952–61, and a falling ratio the low rate of return in Japan in 1911–28. The low rates of

---

[11] See equation (11.3) below. μ was then $0.9034 - 2 \times 0.4193l/\varrho$; see equation (6.6) above.

[12] This is true even though markets are imperfect; see Chapter 15.

[13] Although *average* private and social returns were approximately equal, *marginal* private returns were probably well below *marginal* social returns, for reasons discussed in Chapter 15.

Table 7.1 Estimated average real rates of return on investment and shares of depreciation in value added in non-residential business, standard periods

Country	Period	Exponential rates of return per annum		Ratio depreciation to value-added	
		Formula (1)	Formula (2)	Formula (3)	Formula (4)
UK	1856–73	0.142	0.166	0.046	0.038
	1873–1901	0.084	0.098	0.030	0.057
	1901–13	0.034	0.044	−0.107	−0.082
	1913–24	0.037	0.020	0.039	0.109
	1924–37	0.096	0.109	0.032	0.062
	1937–51	0.141	0.149	0.062	0.089
	1951–64	0.127	0.128	0.139	0.153
	1964–73	0.186	0.186	0.180	0.188
USA	1889–1900	0.139	0.124	0.107	n.a.
	1900–13	0.074	0.062	−0.001	n.a.
	1913–29	0.127	0.126	0.087	n.a.
	1929–48	0.116	0.116	0.040	0.013
	1948–73	0.154	0.156	0.108	0.110
Japan	1887–1899	0.151	0.170	0.064	n.a.
	1899–1911	0.045	0.066	0.014	n.a.
	1911–1928	0.049	0.073	−0.021	n.a.
	1928–1936	0.236	0.272	0.063	n.a.
	1952–1961	0.258	0.252	0.198	0.155
	1961–1973	0.214	0.212	0.264	0.261
Belgium	1955–62	0.154	0.159	0.126	n.a.
Denmark	1955–62	0.155	0.156	0.154	n.a.
France	1955–62	0.210	0.213	0.146	n.a.
Germany	1955–62	0.217	0.220	0.181	n.a.
Netherlands	1955–62	0.125	0.127	0.180	n.a.
Norway	1955–62	0.116	0.116	0.250	n.a.
Italy	1955–62	0.194	0.204	0.130	n.a.

Notes

The formulae used were as follows (see text for explanation):

(1) $r = P\{q - \mu(1 - s)\,l\}$

(2) $r = P(q - \lambda l)$

(3) $\delta = \lambda(g - g_L)/(r - g)$

(4) $\delta = \lambda g_w/(r - g)$

Sources: data in the Statistical Appendix.

return in the UK, the USA, and Japan in the first decade of this century are notable, and are further discussed on pp. 333–4. Post-Second World War rates of return have generally been high, and some reasons for this are discussed in Section 10.7.

Turning to the estimates of depreciation in columns (3) and (4), we again have two variants of the formula given earlier. These would coincide in steady growth, since then the rate of growth of wages per unit of labour input, g_w , would equal the rate of growth of labour productivity, $g - g_L$. In practice they have not been exactly equal, and the share of wages in value added, λ, has changed slowly. In the UK the share has tended to rise so that, apart from the period 1856–73 when it fell, g_w has exceeded $g - g_L$, and depreciation in colunmn (4) (which uses g_w) has exceeded that in column (3) (which uses $g - g_L$). For the USA and Japan I have no annual estimates of λ for the earlier years from which the trend of g_w within periods can be estimated, and even the period estimates of λ are unreliable. Nor do I have annual estimates of λ for the continental European countries shown, but only averages for the whole period. Consequently, I confine attention to column (3) in the sequel.

Readers are reminded that these are estimates of depreciation as a share of value added, and *not* as a proportion of the capital stock, which is the way in which depreciation is expressed in neoclassical growth models. Since my fundamental definition of depreciation relates to income, the former seems the natural way to measure it. In order to convert the ratios in the table into proportions of the capital stock, we need to multiply by the ratio of GDP to the capital stock, a ratio I have not attempted to compute. Although this ratio has varied appreciably, its *proportionate* variation has not been anything like as large as that of the figures in column (3) (quite apart from the fact that some of these are even negative). Consequently, the remarks that follow about changes in the ratio D/PQ also apply to changes in the ratio D/K.

It is common practice to assume that D/K is constant, and to regard it as if it were physical decay of some kind or another. As was argued in Chapter 1, this is both misleading and theoretically unsatisfactory, and several writers have pointed out that depreciation is an economic and not a physical phenomenon, and may therefore be expected to vary with economic circumstances. On the definitions used here, depreciation of material investments is entirely due to rising real wage rates, so far as a closed economy is concerned. For the USA the ratio of external trade to GDP was probably small enough for us to neglect the effects of changes in the terms of trade on depreciation. For the UK, and Japan, and especially for some of the smaller continental European countries, such changes were more important, and it would have been better to have introduced them into the estimates. An improvement (or worsening) in the terms of trade benefits (or harms) the nation as a whole, and it would have been necessary to allocate this benefit (or harm) between material capital and labour. It is to be hoped that someone else will construct such estimates, which it would be very interesting to have. For the present, I proceed as if all the countries considered were closed economies or were not subject to changes in their terms of trade. That being so, the rate of depreciation varied considerably from period to period depending, in particular, on the rate of growth of real wage rates.

The most striking feature of the estimates is that depreciation rates were much higher after the Second World War than before it, this being the result of the much faster rates of growth of labour productivity. This is an important finding, since it suggests that conventional official estimates of depreciation at current costs in national income statistics are too low (and those of net capital stock too high) because they rest on rates of depreciation that ruled before the Second World War, whereas postwar rates were much higher.

The conventional estimates are based on the perpetual inventory method and make assumptions about the lives of different types of asset. For a more complete description of the procedures used readers are referred elsewhere,[14] but a very brief description is given on pp. 90–1 above. The method used to estimate depreciation and the capital stock did not allow for any increase in rates of depreciation following the Second World War. In the UK until very recently (see below) the assumed lives were the same, in many cases, as those used just after the war to determine depreciation allowances for tax purposes, and these in turn were largely based on prewar experience.[15] In the USA it was broadly the same. The lives used were 85 per cent of Bulletin F lives. Originally, these lives were fixed in 1931, but longer lives were then introduced in 1942, and it is 85 per cent of the latter lives that have been used (see Young 1975; see also King and Fullerton 1984, 205).

In the UK, the CSO, which is responsible for the official estimates of depreciation and capital stock, appeared to be satisfied in 1976 that its assumptions were still reasonable. It based this satisfaction on various studies which showed that the lives of capital assets were as long as the CSO assumed (Griffin 1976, especially Appendix 1). On the other hand, it was admitted that the resulting rates of depreciation were much lower than those used by companies in their own accounts. Thus, Griffin stated that 'The average period over which the depreciation is deducted is generally only about one half to one third of our estimate of average service lives' (Griffin 1976, 135). Subsequently, however, the official statisticians changed their minds. In the 1983 Blue Book, appreciable reductions were made in some

---

[14] For the UK, see Griffin (1976), who gives others references, of which should be mentioned the pioneering estimates by Redfern (1955). For the USA, see Musgrave (1976).

[15] The lives were set out in detail for machinery and plant in Board of Inland Revenue (1950). In fact, assumed lives were lengthened in the 1960s because Barna's fire insurance valuations implied that replacement cost was undervalued by the perpetual inventory method. See Barna (1975) and Dean (1964). See also King and Fullerton (1984, 46) and Smith (1987, 48).

asset lives. For example, industrial buildings' lives were reduced from 80 to 60 years. It was stated that 'Recent discussions with some larger under-takings in a variety of industries have indicated that the lives assumed hitherto for manufacturing plant and buildings have been unduly long' (CSO 1983, 114). Even so, a more recent official study seeking to reconcile differences in real rates of return, estimated from national and company accounts, states: 'Although no precise figures are available, the asset lives assumed in company accounts are thought to be, on average, around half those now assumed in national accounts' (HM Treasury 1984, 98). A still more recent study, which compared current cost valuations of vehicles, machinery, plant, and equipment (but excluding land and buildings) in company accounts with official estimates based on the perpetual inventory method, also concluded that, even after the adjustments to the latter in 1983, the asset lives assumed were too long. For the whole non-residential business sector (excluding agriculture), the current cost value of the *gross* capital stock was estimated to be about four-fifths of its value using the perpetual inventory method, and reasons were given why even this was an over-estimation (Smith 1987).[16]

It is undoubtedly convenient to derive rates of depreciation by the straight-line method by simply dividing the cost of the asset (suitably adjusted to current prices) by its estimated life. Nevertheless, it may not be possible to check the accuracy of this method as a measure of the true depreciation on my definition by making inquires about actual lengths of asset lives. As has often been pointed out, the meaning of an asset's life is ambiguous, since a piece of equipment or a building, for example, can be modified in various ways so as to prolong its period of use. Furthermore, machines can be kept on stand-by, with little use. In my desk drawer I still keep a slide-rule, which I occasionally use but would not really miss, and I even have an old hand-operated calculator. Are these pieces of equipment still 'alive'? Some items may be kept because their scrap value is negligible and they occasionally come in useful. If businessmen write off assets twice as fast as national accountants (without thereby gaining any tax advantage), one should perhaps conclude that the latter's rates of depreciation are too low, even if the former's are possibly too high. Nor is this conclusion refuted by the discovery that there are a great many old pieces of equipment and buildings which have not yet been scrapped or pulled down.

There does, then, seem to be some reason to suppose that rates of depreciation used in the official national income estimates in the UK are too low for the postwar period, and that this results in estimates of net capital stock that are too high. The same may also be true, although to a lesser

16 The sample used was biased in favour of larger companies, which have more capital per worker than smaller ones. However, the sample was grossed up using employment, and this therefore tended to overstate current cost capital.

extent, for the USA. I say 'to a lesser extent' for several reasons. There is a much bigger increase in the rate of depreciation in the UK than in the USA in Table 7.1 from the interwar to the postwar years. The lives assumed in the UK official statistics are typically much longer than those assumed in the USA. Finally, I have no evidence, comparable with that quoted above for the UK, that US companies use much shorter lives than do the official statisticians.

As we shall see presently, there is another important reason for mistrusting the postwar official estimates for depreciation and net capital stock at current cost. Before coming to that, however, let us compare the rates of return in Table 7.1 with some other estimates obtained in the conventional way by dividing net profit by the net capital stock. The estimates I shall refer to all subtract depreciation at current cost and also stock appreciation from gross trading profits to get net profit (before tax and before deduction of interest). The net capital stock is estimated by the perpetual inventory method in the way already described, and is net of depreciation but includes inventories and (in Table 7.3 but not Table 7.2) an estimate of land. We saw in an earlier section that in steady growth the average rate of return on investment, calculated as in Table 7.1, should coincide with the ratio of net profit to the net capital stock. However, in practice there are some wide divergences which need to be explained.

The estimates from Matthews *et al.* (1982) for the UK in Table 7.2 are for their benchmark years, which, on the whole, are years of high activity. They do not provide estimates for other years except in a chart, inspection of which suggests that the benchmark year figures are reasonably repre-sentative for the periods adjacent to them. The sector covered is similar to non-residential business, except that in Table 7.2 farming is excluded. This also implies that the exclusion of land from the net capital stock in that table should not be too serious, although it does bias the figures upwards. Comparison of them with the estimates in Table 7.1 shows that all the pre-Second World War figures in the latter are lower, and some much lower, whereas the reverse is true of the post-Second World War estimates.

Unfortunately, both sets of estimates must be regarded as very uncertain so far as the pre-Second World War estimates (and especially pre-First World War ones) are concerned. In Table 7.2 the estimates of capital stock are particularly uncertain,[17] while in Table 7.1 perhaps the major uncertainty relates to the rate of growth of the quality-adjusted labour force, g_L , and to the share of investment, s.[18]

---

[17] See Matthews *et al*, (1982), 616, Appendix N). The capital stock estimates before 1920 are graded D (margin of error ± more than 25%) and those after 1920 are graded C (± 15–25%).

[18] The formula for the rate of return in Table 7.1 may be written $r = \{ g - \mu (1 - s) g_L \}/s$.

Table 7.2 Average real rates of return in the UK 'trading' sector estimated by Matthews *et al*.

Year	Exponential rates p.a.
1856	0.175
1873	0.194
1913	0.167
1924	0.125
1937	0.159
1951	0.093
1953	0.105
1964	0.087
1973	0.046

Note
The rates of return given there for 1856–1937 have been multiplied by 15.9/14.2 to adjust for the change in the basis of the net capital stock estimates (see Matthews *et al*'s note to Table 6.13 and to Fig. 6.4, p. 185). The 'trading' sector is defined so as to include all gross property income (excluding stock appreciation) less the following: net income from abroad, non-trading rent (which includes the rent of dwellings), and farm rent and profit. Net profit equals this gross profit less depreciation at current prices in the same sector. Net capital stock equals the net domestic fixed capital stock excluding agriculture, dwellings, roads, and public and social capital, plus non-farm inventories, at current prices. Land is omitted. Average rate of return = net profit ÷ net capital stock. In the source, these are given as percentages, which have been divided by 100 to give the above figures. Ratios of net profits to net capital stock (if taken at mid-year) are estimates of exponential rates of return.
Source: Matthews *et al*. (1982, 186, Table 6.13).

In what follows, I shall focus attention on the more reliable post-Second World War estimates. The explanation of the differences for these may shed some light on those for the earlier years, which I must leave to others. The only point that will be made is that the comparison with Table 7.2 does at least show that the estimates in Table 7.1 are not *always* high by comparison with conventional estimates.

Turning, then, to Table 7.3, we see that, for the post-Second World War years up to 1973 in both the UK and the USA, conventional estimates give average rates of return for the non-financial corporate sector in column (2) which are substantially below those from Table 7.1 for the whole non-residential business sector, which are reproduced for ease of comparison in colunm (1). Why so?

The difference in coverage almost certainly increases the gap to be explained for the UK, and possibly also for the USA. In the UK, non-residential business includes public sector nationalized industries, which earn very low rates of return on a conventional basis and owned a large part of the capital stock. Unincorporated enterprises (excluding farming) may have earned much higher rates of return than the corporate sector, but they

Table 7.3   Average postwar real rates of return, UK and USA

Country	Period	Exponential rates p.a.			
		NRB	Non-financial cor-porate sector	Equities	Corporate bonds
		(1)	(2)	(3)	(4)
UK	1951–64	0.127	0.097	0.084	0.022
	1964–73	0.186	0.078	0.018	0.031
Avg.	1951–73	0.153	0.089	0.064	0.029
USA	1948–73	0.154	0.114	0.063	0.023

Notes

Col. (1) is the same as col. (1) of Table 7.1. The UK average for 1951–73 is derived in the same way as the figures for the sub-periods above, but is based on weighted averages of growth rates, etc., the weights being the lengths of the sub-periods.

Col. (2) is the ratio of net profits (before tax) to net capital stock for the non-financial corporate sector. Net profits = gross trading profits − depreciation at current replacement cost − stock appreciation. Net capital stock is at current replacement cost less accumulated depreciation and includes inventories and land. The UK series is based on estimates in Department of Trade and Industry, *British Business*, 21–27 Sept. 1984, p. 120, for years from 1960, linked to the estimates for 1955–73 given in Walker (1974), and to the estimates for 1951–70 given in Glyn and Sutcliffe (1972) and quoted in Burgess and Webb (1974, Table 4, col. 4). An adjustment was made to include land by multiplying the rates of return in the original sources by 0.884. This is very uncertain, and is based on information given in CSO *Economic Trends*, August 1984, p. 97. The USA series is from Feldstein and Summers (1977, 216). An adjustment was made to their original figures, which are stated to be net profits for the year divided by capital at the *end* of the year, to bring the capital stock to the middle of the year.

Col. (3) The yield is measured as the average dividend yield (before tax) plus the fitted trend rate of growth of real dividends over each period, the latter being the growth of nominal dividends per share deflated by an index of the price of the sum of public and private consumption derived from the national accounts. The same price index underlies the rates of return in col. (1). The UK series uses the FT Actuaries 500 Industrial Ordinary Share Index from April 1962, and the Actuaries Investment Index for earlier years. The data came from various issues of the CSO *Financial Statistics* and the *Bank of England Statistical Abstract*, no. 1, 1970, Table 30. The US series uses Standard and Poor's Composite (500 Stocks) index from US Department of Commerce, *Business Statistics*, 1977, pp. 106–7.

Col. (4) The yield is measured as the nominal yield to redemption of long-term (20-year in the UK) bonds, before tax, *less* the fitted trend rate of growth of the price of the sum of public and private consumption (as in col. (3)). The UK series is derived from the same sources as in col. (3), as is the US series, the latter being Domestic Corporate (Moody's) A-rating, this being the representative rating according to Furstenberg (1977, 356).

were outweighed by the low returns in the public sector.[19] I would guess that, if land were included, the conventional rate of return in farming would also have been lower than in the corporate sector. In the USA, some authorities believe that rates of return in unincorporated enterprises are

[19] See Matthews *et al.* (1982, 187, Table 6.14), whose estimates are, however, of gross rather than net rates of return.

much lower than in the corporate sector, but there is considerable uncertainty about this both because of the problem of valuing land and because of the problem of separating wage income from property income.[20]

There are two reasons associated with the measurement of depreciation and capital stock why the conventional rates of return in column (2) of Table 7.3 understate true average internal rates of return. The first of these has already been given: rates of depreciation assumed in the official estimates are almost certainly too low, especially in the UK. This results in an estimate of depreciation that is too small, which in itself exaggerates the rate of return, but also in an estimate of the capital stock that is too large, thereby understating the rate of return. Unless rates of return are very low, the second effect is the dominant one. For the UK, a simulation exercise was undertaken in which the conventional rate of return was calculated for the non-financial corporate sector assuming that asset lives were only half as long as the lives assumed in the official estimates. The result was to reduce the capital stock by about one-third during the years 1960–73 and to increase depreciation by rather more than a quarter. The increase in the average rate of return varied from 3.3 per cent p.a. in 1960 to 1.3 per cent p.a. in 1970 (HM Treasury 1984, 99).

The second reason why conventional rates of return are biased downwards in the postwar period is the very marked increase in price index numbers for capital goods which occurred from prewar to postwar years in the UK, and to a lesser extent in the USA. The prices of these goods rose in relation to the price index of private and public consumption by amounts shown in Table 7.4. The relevance of this is as follows. The rates of return estimated in Table 7.1 and in column (1) of Table 7.3 are true rates of return in that they compare consumption sacrificed in one period with extra consumption gained in later periods. In order that the conventional rates of return in column (2) of Table 7.3 should be comparable, both numerator and denominator of the fraction should be measured in terms of consumption. The numerator consists of profits gained at current prices, and the deduction for depreciation should measure the amount of gross profit that needs to be invested to enable a constant real amount of consumption to be maintained. Likewise, the denominator consists of the capital stock, and should measure the cumulative amount of consumption sacrificed in the past with depreciation measured as stated. It follows that, if the perpetual inventory method is to give effect to these requirements, the correct price index number to use to bring past investments to current prices is the price index of consumption. The same price index should be used for

[20] See, for example, the views expressed by Denison and Pechman and the caution by Feldstein, in Feldstein and Summers (1977, 228).

Table 7.4 Prices of capital goods relative to the price of private and public consumption
Index numbers, 1937 = 100

	1929	1937	1948	1960	1973
UK					
(1) Buildings & works (excl. dwellings)	93	100	125	113	125
(2) Plant and machinery	86	100	118	117	104
USA					
(3) Structures	89	100	115	115	125
(4) Producers' durable equipment	93	100	95	109	90

Notes
The price index of private and public consumption is the implicit deflator of the sum of consumers' expenditure and government expenditure on goods and services from the national accounts. The other price index numbers are the deflators of the relevant items of fixed capital expenditure. The sources used are those described in the Statistical Appendix.

both columns (1) and (2). In practice, as is shown in Table 7.4, the price index numbers actually used on the whole rose faster than the price index of consumption from the interwar period to postwar. This meant that both depreciation and the capital stock postwar were overstated, and both overstatements tended to result in an understatement of the rate of return in column (2) relative to that in column (1), with the extent of understatement being greater in the UK than in the USA. I have not attempted to quantify the understatement, but for the UK at least it could be significant, especially in the earlier postwar years.

It should be pointed out that neither of the two reasons just given for believing that conventional rates of return understate true rates of return in the postwar years apply, necessarily, to other periods. Before the war, and especially before the First World War, rates of depreciation were much lower than afterwards, and the national income statisticians' assumptions about these rates may, indeed, have been too high rather than too low. Similarly, it is not always the case that capital goods prices rise faster than the price of consumption, as is shown, for example, by the index numbers after 1948 in Table 7.4.[21] Consequently, these are not reasons for expecting conventional rates of return *always* to lie below the rates of return in Table 7.1—and, as Table 7.2 shows, they do not always do so in fact.

The two reasons both imply that the conventional capital stock estimates are too high, but the conventional depreciation estimates might be either too low or too high. In Table 7.5 the two types of estimates of depreciation for non-residential business are compared in columns (1) and (2). The

[21] For a further discussion of the unusually sharp rise in capital goods prices in the UK over the Second World War, see Matthews *et al.* (1982, Appendix H).

Table 7.5 Postwar ratios of depreciation to value added, UK and USA

Country	Period	Non-residential business		Non-financial corporate sector
		As in Table 7.1 (1)	Conventional (2)	conventional (3)
UK	1951–64	0.139	0.084	0.064[a]
	1964–73	0.180	0.102	0.070
	1951–73	0.156	0.091	0.067[b]
USA	1948–73	0.108	0.091	0.100

Notes
[a] 1955–64; [b] 1955–73

Col. (1) is the same as col. (3) of Table 7.1. Cols. (2) and (3) are the ratios of capital consumption, estimated by the perpetual inventory method, at current replacement cost, to the sum of gross trading profits (excluding stock appreciation) and income from employment. The data were obtained mainly from the official national accounts.

conventional ones all lie below those in Table 7.1, but the difference is much greater for the UK than the USA. Since the upward bias in the UK conventional estimates of depreciation is probably greater than in that for USA, given the price index numbers in Table 7.4, it follows that the downward bias arising from depreciation rates being too low in the conventional estimates must be *much* greater for the UK, as has already been remarked. Nevertheless, the differences in the UK are so large that it is difficult to believe that they could be explained by the two factors so far discussed. There must, surely, be some other factors at work as well.

Thus far we have considered only reasons why the conventional estimates of rates of return understate true rates of return. For the reason just given, it seems likely that, in the UK at least, the postwar rates of return and rates of depreciation in Table 7.1 are overstated. This could be due to the rate of growth of quality-adjusted labour input being understated. If g_L is too small, that tends both to increase $r = \{ g - \mu (1 - s)g_L\}/s$ and to increase $\delta = \lambda (g - g_L)/(r - g)$. The estimates of g_L are explained and discussed elsewhere. There is no particular reason to think that they are biased one way or the other, but, so far as it goes, the comparison with conventional estimates suggests that g_L may be understated.

Another possible explanation for the high UK rates of return postwar is that s is understated. Again, the estimates are discussed elsewhere, and there is no particular reason to think that they are biased. Furthermore, if estimated s were increased, that would acutally still further increase δ,[22] thus further widening the gap with conventional estimates of depreciation.

[22] Substituting for r in the expression for δ gives $\delta = \lambda (g - g_L)/(1 - s) (g - \mu g_L)$.

Moreover, if s is understated, it is virtually certain that conventional estimates of net profits, depreciation, and capital stock are also all understated. It is therefore unclear that understatement of s can be help to explain much of the observed divergences.

From 1951 to 1973 there was a 14 per cent improvement in the UK's terms of trade.[23] This would have reduced the amount of depreciation of material capital over this period, and so would help to explain the large gap between the estimates of depreciation in columns (1) and (2) of Table 7.5, since the ratio in column (1) for the UK should be reduced on this account. However, the extent of the reduction would be rather small.

The final factor that must be mentioned is that growth has not been steady. This complicates the estimation of rates of return, and means that rates of return to investment within a period need not equal the ratio of net profits to net capital stock, which is influenced by rates of return earned in past periods. Some of the difference between the two sets of estimates is probably due to this, but I have been unable to estimate how much.

I conclude, therefore, that average real rates of return on investment in the postwar period in the UK and the USA have very probably been higher than conventional estimates suggest, but that, at least in the UK, they were probably not as high as Table 7.1 suggests.

If that is accepted, columns (3) and (4) of Table 7.3 suggest that real rates of return received by savers (before deducting income tax) were well below those earned on investment. If we simply split the difference between the estimates in columns (1) and (2), for both countries the average rate of return on investment is 0.12 or 0.13, while the average return to equity is about half as much.[24] The real return on corporate bonds is much lower still.

There is considerable ambiguity about the rates of return received by savers. One way to measure that return is to imagine an investor buying £1 worth of shares, chosen so as to be representative of all shares, at the start of the chosen period, collecting and reinvesting all the dividends received in the period in similar shares, and selling out at the end of the period. The internal rate of return on this operation can then be reduced by the average rate of increase of consumer prices during the period to convert it into a real rate of return. It has been estimated that in the USA an operation of this kind, with the initial investment made at the beginning of 1948 and the sale occurring at the end of 1973, would have yielded an average (exponential)

---

[23] Calculated from implicit price index numbers for exports and imports of goods and services from the data in CSO, *Economic Trends Annual Supplement,* 1983., HMSO, London, 1983, pp. 7 and 12.

[24] I have combined the two sub-periods in the UK and taken the average for 1951–73, as seems preferable in view of the probable changes in the ratio of output to capacity over the sub-periods.

return of 0.087.[25] However, this method of estimating the rate of return does not provide a good comparison with the average rates of return considered above, since it includes the effects of changes in expectations and discount rates, whereas they do not. In a period in which expectations are improving and/or discount rates are falling, share prices will be rising, and this will increase the rate of return calculated by the method just described. The same actual performance of profits and dividends could yield a much lower rate of return if it disappointed expectations instead of exceeding them, or if it happened to be accompanied by rising rather than falling discount rates. Because of the volatility of expectations and discount rates, the rate of return thus calculated is sensitive to the dates chosen for purchase and sale.[26]

Instead of using the above method, the alternative preferred here is as follows. For a representative share, let the divided per share be C and the price of the share V. Assume that the shareholder expects the real value of the dividened to grow at an exponential rate g and that his real rate of discount is r. Then he will set

$$V = \frac{C}{r - g}.$$

Hence

$$r = \frac{C}{V} + g.$$

In words, the shareholder's real rate of discount, which also equals his expected rate of return, is the sum of the dividend yield and the expected growth rate of real dividends. Further details of the calculation are in the note to Table 7.3.

This formula ignores personal income tax (as did the previous one), but we can interpret r as the real rate of return that a company would have to earn on its investment, ignoring for the moment both profits taxation and fixed interest borrowing, in order that its shareholders should receive r before paying income tax. It is, in that sense, the *cost of capital* to the company. The individual shareholder's return after tax would then depend on his individual marginal income tax rate. If this were m, his return would be $(C/V) (1 - m) + g$.

The average cost of capital to the company is reduced below r in so far as it can borrow at a real interest rate below r, and column (4) of Table 7.3

[25] Calculated from Table 1A-1 in Sharpe (1981). The conversion to real yields was made using the consumer price index rather than the implicit deflator for private and public consumption. Had the latter been used, the rate of return would have been slightly lower.

[26] Using the same source as in the previous footnote, a sale at the end of 1974 instead of at the end of 1973 would have given a rate of return of 0.068, while one at the end of 1972 would have given one of 0.100.

suggests that that was the case in the period under review. The rates of return to corporate bondholders were less than 0.03. They are again before deduction of income tax, and are the nominal yields to redemption less the actual inflation rate.

In order to preserve comparability between columns (1) and columns (3) and (4) of Table 7.3, the inflation rate in all three is the same implicit price index of private and public consumption.

I postpone consideration of taxation to Chapters 14 and 15. For the present, we can regard it as one of the principal explanations of the gap between the average annual exponential real return earned on investment of, say, 0.12 or 0.13, and the real return received by the providers of capital, which before income tax was only about half as much for equity shareholders, and less still for bondholders. As is shown in Chapter 15, however, taxation is not by any means a *complete* explanation of the gap. The existence of such a large gap, and the explanations for it, have important implications for policy, which are discussed in that chapter.

Appendix: The rate of return with 'physical' diminishing returns to the rate of investment

Thus far, I have assumed a 'cliff' of investment opportunities, so that the rate of investment $\sigma = S/Q$, with characteristics (q, l), can be increased indefinitely without altering those characteristics. It might seem more plausible to suppose that, as σ increases, less good investment opportunities must be undertaken. So far as the whole economy is concerned, there is little confirmation of this in my empirical work, perhaps because of dynamic economies of various kinds (see Chapters 12 and 13). However, the evidence on this point is not firm, and in any case it seems likely that there are diminishing returns for the individual business even if not for the whole economy. Two reasons for such diminishing returns must be distinguished. First, there are those arising from the existence of market imperfections, which I call 'market diminishing returns'. The simplest example of these is where the firm that seeks to expand output at a faster rate has to lower its prices in order to sell more. Second, there are those arising from the existence of a given flow of new ideas and opportunities created by *other* firms' investments (but unrelated directly to demand for the first firm's output, since that is the first kind). If all firms were to increase their rate of investment together, *both* these source of diminishing returns would disappear—an important point to which we return in Chapter 15. However, *given* the rate of investment of other firms, a firm may find that a faster rate of investment forces it to select worse investments.

There are other reasons for diminishing returns to the rate of investment within a firm. Schumpeter, as we have seen (p. 104), drew attention to resistance to change which may be widespread, and not just confined to those likely to lose from it. Increasing the rate of investment increases the rate of change, and this is likely to meet increased resistance from customers and suppliers as well as from the work-force and even within the management team who are instigating it. Penrose has emphasized the importance of this team in limiting the rate of growth of a firm (often referred to as 'Penrose effects'):

Extensive planning requires the co-operation of many individuals who have confidence in each other. Individuals with experience within a given group cannot be hired from outside the group, and it takes time for them to achieve the requisite experience. It follows, therefore, that if a firm delberately or inadvertently expands its organization more rapidly than the individuals in the expanding organization can obtain the experience with each other and with the firm that is necessary for effective operation of the group, the efficiency of the firm will suffer . . . (Penrose 1959, 47)

The respect in which investments could be worse, which I class as 'physical', and consider here, is that the investment's characteristics q and l both diminish along any ray from the origin as the rate of investment is increased. If, for average investments, the characteristics are (q,l), then for marginal investments they will be smaller, say (q_m, l_m). To keep matters simple I further assume that both q and l shrink in the same proportion along any ray from the origin. This is brought about by a shrinkage of ϱ, the 'radius' of the IPC. The radius corresponding to marginal investment is then ϱ_m such that

$$\frac{\varrho_m}{\varrho} = \frac{q_m}{q} = \frac{l_m}{l} .$$

(7A.1)

It seems plausible to suppose that successive equal increments in the rate of investment result in smaller and smaller *absolute* reductions in ϱ_m. There must be an infinity of ways in which money can be invested for no result! Hence, ϱ_m can never shrink to 0, however great is investment. The simplest assumption consistent with these suppositions is that each equal *absolute* small increment in σ causes the same *proportionate* fall in ϱ_m, and the following equation gives effect to this:

$$\varrho_m = \varrho_0\, e^{-\gamma\sigma}$$

(7A.2)

Here ϱ_0 is the radius of the outermost contour when $\sigma = 0$, and, taking logarithms and then differentiating with respect to σ, we get

$$\frac{d\, \ln\varrho_m}{d\sigma} = -\gamma.$$

So γ measures the rate at which ϱ_m is proportionately reduced as σ is increased. [27]

In the proof that follows, we need to know the ratio of marginal to average ϱ, and this can be found from (7A.2). Average ϱ is the weighted average of ϱ_m, the weights being investment undertaken at each ϱ_m. Hence

$$\varrho = \frac{1}{\sigma} \int_{\sigma=0}^{\sigma=\sigma} \varrho_m\, d\sigma = \frac{\varrho_0}{\sigma}\, \frac{1 - e^{-\gamma\sigma}}{\gamma}$$

(7A.3)

[27] It will be noticed that I make ϱ_m depend on σ, not s, since it is, surely, the relation of S to Q that matters, and not that of S to PQ. Doubling or halving P should make no difference to the real investment opportunities, q and l, although it will, of course, enormously alter their profitability.

$$\therefore \quad \frac{\varrho_m}{\varrho} = \frac{e^{-\gamma\sigma}\gamma\sigma}{1-e^{-\gamma\sigma}} = \frac{\gamma\sigma.}{e^{\gamma\sigma}-1} \tag{7A.4}$$

I now employ a similar argument to proof no. 1 (section 7.2) to derive the formula for the marginal rate of return, r. A firm increases its rate of investment by $\delta\sigma = P\delta s$ for a short interval δt, so that the total additional take-out sacrificed is $PQ \, \delta s \, \delta t$. Since s is only marginally affected, there is no appreciable change in γ or μ, and so the slope of the marginal investment contour is unchanged and, given the assumption of equiproportionate shrinkage, the marginal investment takes place at (q_m, l_m) satisfying (7A.1). It follows that the extra growth rate achieved during the short interval is

$$\delta g = \delta\sigma \, q_m; \qquad \delta \, g_L = \delta\sigma \, l_m.$$

At the end of the short interval, the levels of output and employment will then be δQ and δL higher, where

$$\delta Q = Q \, \delta g \, \delta t; \qquad \delta L = L \, \delta g_L \, \delta t;$$

and the increase in take-out, C, will be

$$\delta C = P \, \delta Q \, (1 - s) - w \, \delta L.$$

$$= PQ \, \delta\sigma \, \delta t \, q_m \, (1 - s) - wL \, \delta\sigma \, \delta t \, l_m.$$

Remembering that $\delta\sigma = P\delta s$ and using (7A.1), we have

$$\delta C = PQ \, \delta s \, \delta t \, P\{q \, (1 - s) - \lambda l\} \, \frac{\varrho_m}{\varrho}.$$

This additional take-out grows at g, since, after the short interval, the previous rate of investment and rate of growth are resumed. Its present value is therefore $\delta C/(r - g)$, and this must equal the initial extra take-out sacrificed of $PQ \, \delta s \, \delta t$. Dividing through by that then gives

$$1 = \frac{P\{q(1-s) - \lambda l\}}{r - g} \, \frac{\varrho_m}{\varrho}.$$

Whence, remembering that $Pqs = g$, and writing $r_a = P(q - \lambda l)$ for the average rate of return, and using (7A.4), we obtain by rearrangement

$$r = r_a\left(\frac{\gamma\sigma}{e^{\gamma\sigma}-1}\right) + g\left(1 - \frac{\gamma\sigma}{e^{\gamma\sigma}-1}\right), \tag{7A.5}$$

which may also be written as

$$r - g = (r_a - g)\left(\frac{\gamma\sigma}{e^{\gamma\sigma}-1}\right). \tag{7A.6}$$

Note that when $\sigma \to 0$, $\{\gamma\sigma/(e^{\gamma\sigma} - 1)\} \to 1$, so that $r \to r_a$ (and $\varrho_m \to \varrho \to \varrho_0$). Also when $\sigma \to \infty$, $\{\gamma\sigma/(e^{\gamma\sigma} - 1)\} \to 0$, so that $r \to g$. Hence, for finite positive values of σ and γ, $r > g$ as long as $r_a > g$.

8

THE DETERMINANTS OF THE SHARE
OF INVESTMENT IN OUTPUT AND
THE COMPLETE GROWTH MODEL

8.1 Objections to the modified accelerator principle

There is no generally agreed theoretical framework for analysing and explaining long-run trends in capital accumulation. . . . Unfortunately, the theory of the investment function, especially in the long run, is not one of the strongest points in economic theory. . . . The most widely accepted investment function is the modified acceleration principle (capital-stock-adjustment principle). This asserts that there exists a certain capital–output ratio that is optimal for the firm, this ratio being determined by technology (including the pattern of consumer demand) and factor prices. Investment is such as to bring the capital stock, possibly with a lag, into this desired ratio to expected output. (Matthews *et al.* 1982, 326–7)

These quotations form a convenient starting point to the discussion. As they imply, most of the literature on the subject, and especially the empirical work, has been concerned with the short-term behaviour of investment over the trade cycle.[1] In these studies it may be natural, and perhaps satisfactory, to treat output as an exogenous variable which determines the desired capital stock and so investment. Nevertheless, such an approach is useless here. I have tried to explain the growth rate of output in terms of the rate of investment, *inter alia*, and it does not advance matters if I now try to explain investment in terms of the growth rate of output. Yet the modified or flexible accelerator does precisely that.[2] What is required is an additional equation (or equations) determining the *supply* of investible funds. This becomes clear when I set out the equations of my model more formally below. Taking the system as a whole, both the rate of investment and the rate of growth of output are endogenous.

Some other objections to the modified accelerator principle may be mentioned. First, in the theory underlying the empirical work, use is sometimes made of a production function to which I have theoretical objections which are given in Chapter 3. Second, much attention is paid to costs of adjustment, since the speed of adjustment of the actual to the

---

[1] For surveys, see Meyer and Kuh (1957); Eisner and Strotz (1963); Jorgenson (1971); Helliwell (1976); Nickell (1978).

[2] See the surveys just mentioned, and the empirical work of Jorgenson in particular.

desired capital stock depends on these (see, e.g., Nickell 1978, ch. 3), but, in principle, there is no distinction to be made between investment and costs of adjustment. Investment simply *is* the cost of change, and so should include all the costs of adjustment. However, I must agree that investment as conventionally measured does not always do so, and so some attention has to be given to the excluded costs. A related objection in principle is to the lag between investment and output. Again, if both were properly measured, there should be no lag, but in practice there often will be (see Section 6.13 above). Finally, the concept of a desired capital stock is fraught with difficulties.[3] Does it mean the stock that the owners of the existing stock would have, in some sense preferred? In what sense? Presumably, there must be some constraints to which they are subject. If *all* of the actual constraints are taken as they are, then why is not the actual stock the preferred stock? If the actual stock is equal to the preferred stock only in 'equilibrium', what does *that* mean? Does it mean that no one wants to change anything? If so, investment should be zero in equilibrium, and equilibrium is a state that no developed economy has reached for a good many years. It is not clear why a business should desire to hold a capital stock appropriate to a situation which it is most unlikely ever to reach.

The difference between the desired capital stock and the actual capital stock could be interpreted as referring to the difference between actual output and normal capacity output. The latter seems to me both meaningful and highly relevant to investment decisions. Its main relevance, however, is to the explanation of such decisions in the short run, over the trade cycle. It is likely to be much less important for the explanation of investment decisions in the long run, which is our concern here.

I conclude, therefore, that if the 'desired capital stock' has any useful meaning, it is in the context of short-run, cyclical, investment behaviour (which is, indeed, where it has been employed), and that to explain long-run investment behaviour we need a different conceptual apparatus. But although it is different, it still incorporates the central idea of the accelerator, which is that the rate of investment in a given firm depends on expectations about the rate of growth in the rest of the economy. The rate of growth of output is not, all the same, an exogenous variable determining investment. All this is explained later.

Instead of the modified accelerator principle, three other ways of modelling the supply of investible funds were attempted, which may be called the 'Ramsey approach', the 'eclectic approach', and the 'pure confidence approach'. In all of these, businessmen are envisaged as taking decisions not about stocks, but about flows. They are aware of a *flow* of possible investment projects. That is, in a given time interval they consider a

---

[3] Some of these are discussed in Nickell (1978, 31, 257).

certain number of such projects; in subsequent intervals, they consider further projects. Their problem is to decide how much to spend in the given time interval, and on which projects. I regard this as a decision about the *supply* of investible funds. Businessmen, financial intermediaries, and households are all taken together as if they were one group reaching a collective decision on how much to invest. This is, of course, a drastic simplification. The relations between these various groups are of great importance and interest, but I ignore them here (and return to them in Chapters 9 and 15).

Apart from simplicity, my procedure has one very important empirical justification. For most businesses most of the time, a very large fraction of their gross investment expenditure is financed by gross retained profits. Indeed, for many businesses, all of it is. Businesses do, it is true, usually borrow at short term, but they also acquire short-term financial assets, and their *net* borrowing is on average very small in relation to their expenditure on material investment (see pp. 266-7, 421-2, and Table 14A.1). There is, then, a very direct sense in which savers and investors are one and the same, at least so far as a large fraction of savings and investment are concerned.

In all approaches, as described in this chapter, imperfect competition, and so the role of demand and the accelerator principle, are kept very much in the background. This is done to simplify the exposition, and not because they are thought to be unimportant. In Chapter 9 and 15 they are discussed at some length. Here it must suffice to note that the expected rate of growth of demand undoubtedly influences investment decisions, but that this influence depends crucially upon the existence of imperfect markets.

8.2 The Ramsey approach

As I have interpreted it, the main idea underlying the Ramsey approach (Ramsey 1928) is that the marginal real rate of return on investment should be brought into equality with the real rate at which marginal consumption benefits are discounted. Alternatively, one can say that suppliers of funds attempt to maximize the present value of the future stream of consumption benefits resulting from their investments.

There are only two reasons considered here for discounting future benefits: first, because of diminishing marginal utility of consumption as consumption per head increases; second, simply because it is in the future (i.e. because of 'impatience' or 'lack of telescopic faculty'). Risk is not explicitly considered, but some average rate of discount for risk may be included in one or both of the factors just mentioned, and the second can, indeed, be considered as a measure of the estimated risk of the demise of the dynasty (see further below).

I consider only steady growth equilibrium, in which the rate of growth of output, g, is constant and the ratio of saving to income, s, is constant, as also is the share of wages, λ. It follows that the rate of growth of total consumption and of profits must both equal g, and I assume that this is also true of the rate of growth of consumption out of profits. The rate of growth of the (full-time equivalent) numbers in the labour force is g_N, and I assume that this is equal to the rate of growth of the number of savers who share in consumption out of profits. Some might prefer to take the rate of growth of population or some other number, but differences beween such numbers are usually small, and, as it is difficult to justify a choice of one or the other, I have chosen the most convenient, which is g_N. It follows that consumption per head of savers, in so far as their consumption is financed by income from their savings, is growing at $g - g_N$. As this is also the rate at which real wages per worker are increasing, total consumption per head may reasonably be assumed to be growing at this rate. If, now, the elasticity of the marginal utility of consumption with respect to increases in consumption is β, defined so as to be positive, then the rate at which the utility of consumption is falling through time is $\beta(g - g_N)$. If, for example, consumption per head were growing at 2 per cent a year, and if the elasticity, β, were 2, then the utility of consumption would be falling at (approximately) 4 per cent a year. To get our rate of discount, we have merely to add to this the rate of discount, for 'impatience' which is α. So, if α were 1 per cent a year, our rate of discount, r, would be (approximately) 5 per cent a year. In general, therefore, and measuring r, g, and g_N in exponential terms,

$$r = \alpha + \beta(g - g_N). \tag{8.1}$$

This formula, which is due to Champernowne,[4] makes simplifying assumptions additional to those of steady growth. Both α and β are assumed to be constant, and the underlying utility function is of a very simple form.

The utility function is additively separable, so that the total utility that is being maximized is simply the sum of the separate (discounted) utilities for each period. Furthermore, the utility of consumption in any period is independent of the amount of consumption in any other. Hicks has attacked this assumption as being especially implausible (Hicks 1965, 261). It requires that the marginal utility of consumption in a particular period be the same whether the levels of consumption in adjacent periods are well below or well above that of the period in question. Yet it seems more plausible to suppose that marginal utility would be higher if consumption in the adjacent periods were higher than if it were lower. While this may be so, it is not clear that it destroys the usefulness of the formula as a guide to

---

[4] See Robertson (1963, 240–3). Robertson states that Champernowne's article is 'regrettably unpublished'.

steady-growth behaviour, for then consumption in adjacent periods has to be in a particular relationship to consumption in the periods in question.[5] Hicks attacked the assumption of independence apparently because he was mistrustful of some other implications of the Ramsey approach. These were that $\alpha > 0$ and that $\beta > 1$. Unless $\alpha > 0$, the present value of a stream of future utilities which stretches to infinity, and which is always finite and positive, will not itself be finite. 'One cannot maximize something which is infinite. So that unless $\alpha > 0$, the whole construction breaks down' (Hicks 1965, 259). According to Hicks, Ramsey had not noticed this point, to which attention was drawn by Koopmans (1960). Hicks also objected to the implication that $\beta > 1$, which was required if $\alpha = 0$ (as Ramsey thought it should be) and if the optimum proportion of income saved in steady growth was to be less than 1, as it must surely be. According to Hicks, 'there is no intuitive reason why the marginal utility curves should be inelastic; it is odd that we should have to make them inelastic in order to make sense of the theory' (Hicks 1965, 259).[6]

For my own part, I cannot see that it is implausible to assume either that $\alpha > 0$ or that $\beta > 1$. Such evidence as I have, reviewed below, accords with both of these inequalities. 'Impatience' seems intuitively reasonable, as a description of behaviour, and also rational in a world in which destruction of oneself and one's heirs has always had to be reckoned with. $\beta > 1$ implies that there is a maximum level of happiness attainable through consumption expenditure, and that too seems highly plausible. I do not believe that a multi-millionaire is appreciably happier than a millionaire because he spends more on consumption.

It must be admitted that the assumption of *constancy* in both α and β is somewhat implausible. α would increase with insecurity, and β could well be small for poorer persons, and might therefore have risen as standards of living improved. There are also many other factors that must have influenced the supply of funds, which this simple formulation leaves out of account, and some of these are mentioned below. Nevertheless, the Ramsey approach has the strength of simplicity, and it seems worth pursuing on that account. It is an approach that has been much used in discussions of optimum growth, and I use it in that context in Chapter 15.

8.3 Savings and the rate of return: the Ramsey versus the life-cycle approach

The Ramsey approach to the supply of savings, just described, may be interpreted in different ways. If we regard it as a description of *individual*

---

[5] R. Solow (1970, 81) takes this view.

[6] Hick's definition of the elasticity of marginal utility is the reciprocal of that used here. Hence $\beta > 1$ implies a value of less than 1 on Hick's definition. It is unclear to me why this reciprocal definition has been used by several writers. My own is what I would take to be the usual one of the proportionate change in the marginal utility of consumption per unit proportionate change in the level of consumption that causes it.

behaviour, the coefficient α can be thought of either as reflecting the risk of extinction of one's dynasty,[7] or as reflecting one's preference for utilities that are enjoyed sooner rather than later. On either of these interpretations, the individual is as concerned for his descendants as for himself, and no particular attention is paid to his own certain prospect of death. The coefficient β implies that less weight is given to future marginal consumption expenditures if they are expected to grow, but the *same* weight is give to marginal *utilities*, no matter when they are enjoyed, and no matter whether they are enjoyed by oneself or by one's descendants. There is, then, a generally neutral treatment of one's own interests and those of one's descendants, although this is subject (possibly) to a preference for earlier rather than later enjoyment. All this is very much in contrast to the simple life-cycle approach to which we return below.

An alternative interpretation of the Ramsey approach is as a description of *aggregate* behaviour in a steadily growing economy. With population and consumption per head growing steadily, it might then be possible to reconcile the Ramsey approach with a wide variety of alternative explanations of savings behaviour. However, even on this view, there is at least one conclusion to which equation (8.1) points which would be regarded as very uncertain if one were to adopt the simple life-cycle approach. This is that, in certain circumstances (but not in others), there is a positive relation between the rate of savings and the rate of return. If the rate of return to the saver is increased by some factor (such as a cut in the tax rate on savings) which does not itself directly increase the rate of growth, g, and if the other terms in equation (8.1) (that is, α, β, and g_N) are constant, then g must increase, and in order for that to happen s must increase. There is then a positive relation between r and s. If, however, some factor increases both the rate of return and the rate of growth simultaneously, there could be a negative relation. As is shown later, an increase in g_L, for example, tends to increase both r and g and may well *reduce s*. That there is a necessarily positive relation in the first type of case is denied by the theory of saving considered below. Uncertainty about the relation has been increased both by this theory and by empirical studies, which have often pointed to its absence. However, as we shall see, those studies are open to criticism, and their failure to allow for negative relations of the kind just described must be numbered among their drawbacks.

Most work on the supply of savings that I know of has either developed from the consumption function, or has taken a life-cycle approach. A positive relation between the rate of return and the rate of saving has by no means been a universal finding of this work, and, indeed, its theoretical necessity has long been denied. Furthermore, recognition of individual death is essential to the life-cycle approach.

In the consumption function, the main interest has been the explanation

---

[7] See fn. 17 below.

of the level of consumption by the level of income, but many other factors have also been considered, including interest rates. Reviewing these studies, Boskin (1978) states that little attention was paid in the earlier studies to the apparently weak, and sometimes negative, relationship between savings and interest rates. He also remarks that 'little attention is paid to interest rates in consumption functions in the large-scale econometric macromodels in widespread use today' (Boskin 1978, 57). The earlier studies, however, used nominal before-tax interest rates rather than the more relevant real after-tax rates, which, as Feldstein (1970) pointed out, biased the estimated interest elasticity of savings towards zero. Boskin quotes two more recent studies (Wright 1969 and Taylor 1970) which did show a positive relationship between savings and interest rates, but concludes that 'there is very little empirical evidence from which to infer a positive relationship (substitution effect outweighing income effect) between saving and the real net rate of return to capital. Surprisingly little attention has been paid to this issue . . . and those studies which do attempt to deal with it can be improved substantially' (Boskin 1978, 58).

Boskin's own study, which used aggregate annual data for the USA in 1929–69, found a strong negative relation between real per capita private consumption and a measure of the real after-tax rate of return on capital for given levels of private disposable income, wealth, and unemployment (as an indicator of cyclical effects). There was therefore a positive relationship between savings and interest rates. However, this result was challenged by Howrey and Hymans (1978), who claimed that the significance of the interest rate effect was lost if a single year (1934) was omitted.

Doubt as to whether higher real interest rates promote savings has existed for a long time. It has been pointed out that, for those saving for retirement, the effect could go the other way, since the higher is the interest rate, the larger is the retirement annuity provided by a given rate of saving. This is presumably the income effect to which Boskin refers in the above quotation, and it is unclear *a priori* whether or not it is offset by the substitution effect. Feldstein has pointed out that, although a rise in interest rates lowers the price of future goods in terms of present goods, thus tending through the substitution effect to increase the demand for future goods, the amount of money spent on future goods (i.e. the amount currently being saved) may rise or fall depending on whether the price elasticity of demand for them is greater or less than 1. Hence even a tax reduction on saving compensated by a tax increase on consumption will not necessarily increase the current rate of saving.

The view that savings are primarily for retirement underlies the life-cycle approach to savings. Individuals are assumed to plan their levels of consumption over their lifetimes so as to maximize their total *individual* utility. This approach has been taken by several studies of savings behaviour and of the impact of taxation on savings (see Chapter 15). In its simplest version it does, however, suffer from a serious limitation. It fails to consider what Marshall called the chief motive of saving, namely, family affection.

That men labour and save chiefly for the sake of their families and not for themselves, is shown by the fact that they seldom spend, after they have retired from work, more than the income that comes in from their savings, preferring to leave their stored-up wealth intact for their families; while in this country alone twenty million a year are saved in the form of insurance policies and are available only after the death of those who save them. (Marshall 1920, 228)

Certainly, my own experience confirms Marshall's observation. Indeed, family affection is reinforced by another consideration. As people age, their desire to spend money often declines, probably because their ability to enjoy it declines, and also because their need to accumulate a stock of consumer durables declines. Then, so long as they remain in reasonable health, their expenditure dwindles away. It makes sense for them to pass on their wealth to younger descendants who will put it to greater use.

If the simple life-cycle model were true, individuals' wealth should decline after retirement, but there is little evidence of this. Personal holdings of wealth certainly increase with age up to retirement, as the life-cycle model predicts, but they go on increasing after retirement, which contradicts the model.[8]

[8] See Diamond Commission (1975, 115, Table 51). This table shows the proportion of total personal wealth owned by given age groups as a percentage of the proportion of the number of people in that age group. Men and women are separately distinguished, and figures are given for 1954, 1964–7, and 1972. A figure of 100 means that the average wealth of the age group is the same as that of the population of all ages. In general, the figures start below 100 at the 25–34 age group and rise to their highest levels (192 being the highest shown) for those over 84 years of age—i.e. well past retirement, and the highest age group shown. 'Wealth' here excludes accrued pension rights, which would admittedly alter the picture since they would decline after retirement. However, the same source estimates the total value of accrued rights in occupational pension schemes in 1972 at only about one-tenth of the balance sheet value of all other personal wealth in that year (see pp. 84 and 89). The value of accrued rights to *state* pensions is much larger (about three-quarters of other personal wealth, excluding pension rights), but since contributions to these are in the nature of a tax, I do not think they can be regarded as savings, nor the rights as wealth, which is comparable to other private savings and wealth. One suspects that the owners of most private wealth are not those who 'own' most accrued state pension rights.

Two further explanations of the increase in the average wealth of older persons were suggested in a later report (Diamond Commission 1977, 186). One of these was that wealthy people tend to live longer, so that 'in each successive age group the number of wealthy persons relative to the rest of the population will increase'. The other was that, since husbands tend to die before their wives and also tend to leave them a large part of their wealth, the higher age groups will include a higher proportion of widows who have gained in this way. This second explanation, however, contradicts the simple life-cycle model, and I rather doubt the power of the first explanation to overturn the conclusion that retired people do not run down their wealth, in contradiction to the life-cycle model. It is significant that Brittain (1978) found for the USA 'impressive evidence that substantial wealth accumulation continues beyond retirement' (p. 71).

Another feature of real life which contradicts the model is the extent to which wealthy individuals pass on their wealth to their children.[9] Some wealthy individuals also endow charitable foundations, and their wealth is then prevented from dissipation and may, indeed, often continue to grow.[10]

The urge to perpetuate oneself, whether through one's heirs or by some other means such as through the creation of institutions of various kinds, is perhaps the most fundamental urge governing our existence. Any model of savings behaviour that ignores it, as does the simple life-cycle model, is bizarre. If a simple assumption has to be made to produce a workable model, the assumption that saving is as if for an immortal family is much closer to reality. As has already been pointed out, it is this assumption that underlies the Ramsey approach of equation (8.1). It is quite consistent with *some* dissaving by the old as they spend their pensions. There is undoubtedly a life-cycle in an individual's earnings and expenditures, so that transfers between the generations occur. Such transfers will take place between the members of an immortal family whose individual members are born, grow old, and die. The family as a whole, however, may still save and so accumulate wealth in accordance with the Ramsey approach. Empirical evidence in its favour includes the fact that people continue to save beyond the age of retirement (fn. 8 above), that wealthy people have usually inherited more than average (fn. 9), and that high rates of return are significantly and positively related to high rates of investment (and so of saving) across countries (see later in the chapter). I do not claim that equation (8.1) is more than a rough approximation to aggregate behaviour and that, at best, it captures *some* important features of individuals' behaviour. Saving behaviour is very complex, and many factors are relevant to it, especially at the individual level.[11]

[9] See Diamond Commission (1975, 117–21), which cites studies by Harbury (1962), Harbury and MacMahon (1973), and Todd and Jones (1972). These studies provide evidence of 'a very strong correlation between the values of fathers' and sons' estates' in the estates left by top wealth-holders. This correlation held for estates left both in 1956-7 and in 1965, and comparison with a study for 1924–6 carried out by Wedgwood led Harbury to conclude that 'there was no very marked change in the relative importance of inheritance in the creation of the personal fortunes of the top wealth-leavers of the generations of the mid-twenties and the mid-fifties of this century. For either, the chance of leaving an estate valued at over £100,000, or even over £50,000 was outstandingly enhanced if one's father had been at least moderately well off.' See also Harbury and Hitchens (1979). Others who have used the empirical data available in the UK or the USA to demonstrate that inheritance is the major determinant of wealth inequality (which it could hardly be if the simple life-cycle theory were true) are Atkinson and Harrison (1978), Brittain (1978), and Oulton (1976).

[10] I write in a college founded by Lord Nuffield, a self-made multi-millionaire who died childless and made many other charitable gifts (especially for the advancement of medicine) during his lifetime. I write in a university in which the other colleges, and the university itself, have similarly benefited over the centuries from their endowments by wealthy men and women.

[11] Only about a half of those in any age group who die in the UK have the value of their estates recorded by the Inland Revenue, the rest presumably having small or negligible estates (see Oulton 1976, 97). That could be taken as evidence favouring the life-cycle theory for a

At the aggregate level, which is our concern here, a thorough investigation of the determinants of saving would need to take account of changes in the age composition of the population (as envisaged by the life-cycle theory) and of changes in investment in dwellings and in government and overseas savings and investment. All these important elements have been ignored here through lack of time. I have had to confine attention to the two main variables which distinguish different steady-growth periods: the rate of growth per head, and the rate of return.

8.4   The complete growth model using the Ramsey approach

Equation (8.1) completes my growth model, which can be expressed in terms of the following seven additional equations, all of which have appeared in earlier chapters.

$$r = P(q - \lambda l). \tag{8.2}$$

This equation for the rate of return was derived in Chapter 7.

$$\mu \equiv b - 2c\,\frac{l}{\varrho} = \frac{\lambda}{1 - \sigma/P} \equiv \frac{\lambda}{1 - s}. \tag{8.3}$$

This equation, which relates the slope of the investment programme contour, IPC, to the share of wages and the savings rate, was derived in Section 6.4.

$$\frac{q}{\varrho} = a + b\,\frac{l}{\varrho} - c\,\frac{l^2}{\varrho^2} \tag{8.4}$$

This is the equation of the IPC, explained in Section 6.7.

$$Psl \equiv \sigma l \equiv g_L; \qquad Psq \equiv \sigma q \equiv g. \tag{8.5}$$

These equations are really just definitions of l and q, and are explained in Section 6.4.

Equations (8.1)–(8.5) suffice to determine the eight endogenous variables: q, l, σ, s, λ, μ, r, and g. The rates of growth of the labour force, both quality-adjusted, g_L, and in numbers, g_N, are assumed to be exogenously given, as also are the various parameters of the model ϱ, α, β,

large proportion of *persons*, but *not* for a large proportion of *savings*, since most of these individuals were almost certainly poor and probably saved little even during their working lives. According to Harbury and Hitchens's estimates of a sample of large estates traced forwards from fathers to sons, about two-thirds of the sons in turn left estates worth less (after allowing for inflation) than those they would have inherited, on the assumption that they received equal shares of their fathers' estates, while only one-third left more (Harbury and Hitchens 1979, 54). This behaviour seems, at first sight, consistent with neither the life-cycle nor the Ramsey models. However, one must be cautious about drawing any inferences from this data, since both daughters and lifetime gifts were omitted, and the assumption of equal shares may have biased the results. Taxation, the sharply rising costs of maintaining and staffing large domestic properties, and agricultural depression between the wars may also have led to an unusually large amount of dissipation of wealth.

a, b, c. In this chapter, where we are considering a whole economy as if it were closed, we can set $P = 1$ and so forget it. Different values of P are needed only when we discuss different industries within an economy in Chapters 9 and 13. If $P = 1$, the difference between $S = S/PQ$ and $\sigma = S/Q$ disappears.

If we add the equation

$$g - g_L = g_W \tag{8.6}$$

to the above system, and if we now treat g_L as endogenous and g_w, the rate of growth of real wage rates, as exogenous, the model can be used to show the equilibrium growth of a firm or industry. If the firm is representative for the whole economy, then P again may be set equal to 1, but otherwise P becomes endogenous and so we require one further equation, which is provided by the demand conditions confronting the firm or industry. Discussion of this latter case is postponed to Chapter 9.

The model, as just presented, neglects various complications which are considered later,[12] notably, imperfect markets and selling and buying costs, 'physical' diminishing returns to the rate of investment, borrowing and lending, and taxation. Only steady growth equilibrium is considered.

By solving equations (8.1) – (8.5), expressing the endogenous variables in terms of the exogenous ones, and then partially differentiating with respect to the latter, one can determine the effects of small changes in them on the dependent variables. One is then comparing different steady-growth equilibria in order to see, for example, how a greater desire to save and invest (as shown by a fall in α) affects the share of investment, the rate of growth of output, the share and rate of growth of wages, and the rate of return.

No systematic attempt at this is made here.[13] In subsequent chapters the model is used in a variety of ways which amount to practical exercises of this kind, and one example of a geometrical analysis follows immediately. This illustrates a very important difference between its conclusions and those following from orthodox growth models, namely, that any factor which increases the share of investment in output, s, in the long run will also increase the rate of growth of output, g, in the long run. As was pointed out on p. 77 above, it is a striking conclusion of orthodox growth theories that g is independent of s in the long run. This difference has important implications for policy. Thus, for example, tax changes that increase the rate of saving yield much greater benefits if they increase the long-run rate of growth than if (as orthodoxy implies) they merely raise the level of output, leaving the long-run rate of growth unchanged. (See Chapter 15 for further discussion.)

[12] For a model that allows for the complications listed, see Appendix C to Chapter 15.
[13] A table showing the effects of small changes in exogenous variables in the model is given in Appendix C to Chapter 15.

8.5 Geometrical representation of the complete model with the Ramsey approach

Our usual IPC diagram, shown in Figure 8.1, may be used to tackle the problem posed above, namely, how does a greater desire to save affect the rate of growth and other endogenous variables in the long run? I have chosen to illustrate the equilibrium of a closed economy rather than a firm, but the latter requires basically the same diagram, as is pointed out below. The construction is as follows.

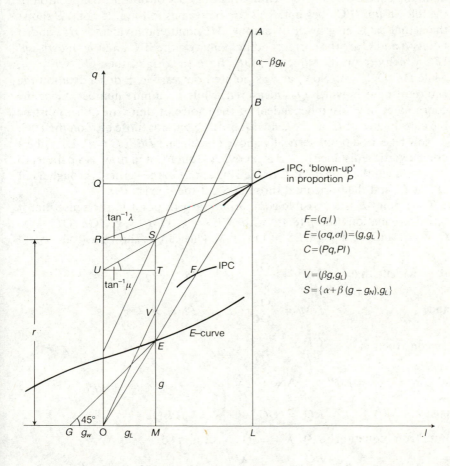

Fig. 8.1 Complete model diagram

We first need to draw the IPC curve 'blown up' in the proportion P, the price level. Since P in the case we are now considering is merely dependent on the choice of units, it may seem simplest to set it equal to 1, as already mentioned. However, in subsequent analysis we need to allow for different prices for different firms or industries, and so it is worth establishing the procedure here. If the IPC is given by (8.4), all we have to do is to draw the same IPC, but substituting $P\varrho$ for ϱ. This has the required effect of pushing out any point, such as F, in the proportion P on the ray OF from the origin. Hence, if the investment characteristics of F on the original IPC were (q, l), the coordinates of C are now (Pq, Pl), and $OC/OF = P$. The original coordinates (q, l), by construction, satisfy equation (8.4).

We may note in passing that, whereas the position of the IPC depends upon the choice of units to measure the quantity of output, the position of the 'blown-up' IPC does not. This can be seen as follows. If point E shows the actual rates of growth of output, ME, and employment, OM, and if points F and C are the corresponding points on the IPC and the 'blown-up' IPC which are on the same ray, OE, from the origin, then $OE/OF = \sigma$, while $OE/OC = s$. Now, as was pointed out earlier, σ depends upon the choice of units in which Q is measured, while s is a pure number. Since the coordinates of E are independent of the choice of units for Q, so must be the coordinates of C on the 'blown-up' IPC, but not those of F on the IPC.

Now let B be a point vertically above C such that $LB/LC = \beta$. Let A be a point a vertical distance $\alpha - \beta g_N$ above B. Join BO and draw AS parallel to it so as to cut the tangent at C to the IPC at S. Let the vertical through S cut OC at E, and the horizontal through S cut the q-axis at R.

Then point E is a possible equilibrium growth point in the sense that it satisfies equations (8.1)–(8.4), with $ME = g$, $OM = g_L$, $OE/OC = s$, $OR = r$, and the angle $CRS = \tan^{-1} \lambda$. This can be shown as follows.

It is evident that
$$ME = \frac{OE}{OC} LC = sPq = \sigma q = g$$

and
$$OM = \frac{OE}{OC} OL = sPl = \sigma l = g_L.$$

By construction,
$$\frac{UR}{UT} = \frac{TS}{UT} = \mu,$$

so $UR = \mu g_L = \mu sPl$.   Also, $\dfrac{UQ}{QC} = \mu$,   so $UQ = \mu Pl$.

Hence
$$RQ = UQ - UR = \mu Pl (1 - s).$$

But, from equation (8.3), $\lambda = \mu (1 - s)$, and so
$$\frac{RQ}{QC} = \frac{\lambda Pl}{Pl} = \lambda = \tan \text{ angle } CRS.$$

Also, $OR = OQ - RQ = P(q - \lambda l)$. Furthermore,
$$OR = VS + MV$$

$$= \alpha - \beta g_N + \frac{MV}{ME} ME$$

$$= \alpha - \beta g_N + \frac{LB}{LC} g$$

$$= \alpha + \beta(g - g_N)$$

$$= r.$$

Point E therefore gives g and g_L, corresponding to point C, satisfying equations (8.1)–(8.4). By choosing different points to start from on the IPC we can trace out the locus of all such points as E, and we may call this the E-curve. We can then find the equilibrium values corresponding to our whole economy case with equation (8.5) by finding where the E-curve cuts the vertical through the given value g_L. For example, if $OM = g_L$, then E would be the corresponding equilibrium point, and we could read off the equilibrium values of g, Pq, Pl, s, λ, and r as shown in Figure 8.1. Given $P = OC/OF$, we can also find q, l, and σ.

The diagram can be used to work out the effect of changes in the various parameters on the equilibrium values of the various variables. I will take only one example. An increase in the desire to save and invest is implied by a drop in α, the rate of discount of future utility. The line AS would then shift downwards, and would intersect CU to the right of the present S. As a result, the new E corresponding to C would be on OC to the right of and above E. Hence the effect of the increased desire to save and invest would be to shift the E-curve upwards. With g_L unchanged, g would be higher, the new equilibrium point being vertically above the old E. The new equilibrium C would then be to the left of old C, and it is clear that s would have increased, as Pq would have decreased. It is also clear that r would have fallen, since the tangent from the new C would cut the vertical through M below S. λ could fall or rise, although the former seems likely in most cases.

It must be pointed out that the direction of some of these effects depends on whether g_L is positive (as assumed above) or negative. In the example just given, a fall in α had the effect of shifting C leftwards, thus reducing l. If g_L is negative, however, a fall in α would shift C rightwards, thus algebraically increasing l. However, the E-curve would still shift upwards, increasing g and s and reducing r. Now, however, λ is bound to fall.

It is not difficult to adapt the diagram to analyse the equilibrium of a representative firm. The E-curve is constructed as above, but now equation (8.6) must be satisfied and g_L is endogenous. In order to ensure that $g - g_L$ equals the exogenously given g_W, we draw a line at 45° to the l-axis, starting from G on that axis, a distance g_W to the left of O (see Figure 8.1). The required equilibrium position is given by the intersection of this line and the E-curve.

8.6 Some empirical results with the Ramsey approach

In an earlier paper (Scott 1977) I attempted to estimate values for α and β from the behaviour of savers in the half-century or so before 1914 in the UK. The average yield on a safe long-term UK government bond ($2\frac{1}{2}$ per cent Consols) in that period was 3.04 per cent per annum, and was very stable. It seems likely that expectations about changes in average consumer prices were that they would be stable in the long run. Bowley's cost-of-living index fell from 112 in 1856 to 100 in 1913 (Bowley 1937, 121–2). Consequently, the 3.04 per cent yield on Consols may be taken as the real safe yield which a saver could expect to get in the long run before tax. Income tax was very low, and may be taken at 5 per cent (a shilling in the pound) on average, so the yield after tax was 2.89 per cent. In the source quoted, I used the rate of growth of net national income per head, deflated by the cost-of-living index, as a proxy for the rate of growth of real consumption per head, and put it at 1.64 per cent per annum. This estimate can be improved, and I now put the rate of growth at 1.06 per cent per annum, appreciably lower.[14] As in the earlier paper, one can then estimate maximum values for α and β, given that $\alpha > 0$ and $\beta > 1$, as follows:

$$\text{Maximum } \alpha = 2.89 - 1 \times 1.06 = 1.83 \text{ per cent p.a.}$$
$$\text{Maximum } \beta = 2.89/1.06 = 2.73$$

One can make estimates of maximum values of α and β on similar lines using data on real, post-tax, rates of return received by investors in equities in the UK and the USA in the years following the Second World War. It seems preferable to take equities rather than government bonds in this period since many tax-paying households, owning most of the relevant wealth, would (or at least *should*!) have avoided investment in bonds altogether. The relevant data are summarized in Table 8.1, which also lists the sources used. I have included in the table the data on rate of return and growth of consumption per head in the UK before 1914, already referred to. For the postwar data, the post-tax rate of return is the average dividend yield, after deducting tax, plus the growth rate of real dividends.[15] The saver is assumed to relate this real rate of return to the rate of growth of his consumption, which is in turn assumed to equal the rate of growth of real consumer expenditures per head for the whole population. This relation is as in equation (8.1).

---

[14] For the period 1870–1913 I have taken Feinstein's estimates of consumers' expenditure at 1900 prices from Feinstein (1976, Table 5). For 1856–1870 I have taken his estimates of GDP at factor cost (his Table 1) *less* his revised estimates of gross investment (see the Statistical Appendix), deflated by Bowley's cost-of-living index. Population is from Feinstein (1976, Table 55).

[15] If the dividend is C per share, which is expected to grow at g in real terms, and if the

Table 8.1 Estimates of α and β

Item	UK 1951–73	USA 1948–73	UK 1856–1913
(1) Average dividend yield, C/V	0.0437	0.0406	0.0299[a]
(2) Average rate of growth of real dividends, g	0.0249	0.0253	0
(3) Marginal tax rate for average household receiving dividends, m	0.561	0.431	0.05
(4) $r_{sha} = (C/V)(1 - m) + g$	0.0441	0.0484	0.0285
(5) Average rate of growth of consumption per head, g_{pc}	0.0224	0.0210	0.0105
(6) Maximum α (if $\beta = 1$)	0.0217	0.0274	0.0180
(7) Maximum β (if $\alpha = 0$)	2.0	2.3	2.7
(8) r_{sha} if $\alpha = 0.013$, $\beta = 1.5$	0.0466	0.0445	0.0288

Notes
[a] Not a dividend yield, but the average nominal yield on Consols: see text. Expressed here as an exponential yield.

Rows (1) and (2) for the first two columns were obtained as follows. The UK estimates are based on the Financial Times Actuaries 500 Index of industrial ordinary shares from April 1962 onwards as given in the CSO *Financial Statistics*, and in the *Bank of England Statistical Abstract*, no. 1, 1970. The latter source also gives the Actuaries Investment Index of industrial ordinary shares for the earlier years, which was linked on. The US estimates are based on Standard and Poor's Composite (500 stocks) index from US Dept. of Commerce *Business Statistics*, 1977. For both countries, dividends at current prices were deflated by the implicit price deflator of private consumption from official national accounts statistics so as to preserve comparability with the real rates of growth in row (5). The Consols yield in the third column of line 1 is the arithmetic average of annual averages from Mitchell and Deane (1962, 455), expressed as an exponential yield. Row (3) for the first two columns is the average marginal tax rate for households in 1960 given in King and Fullerton (1984, 83, 259). For col. 3, see Scott (1977, Table 2). Row (5) for the first two columns is derived from exponential trends fitted to data on real personal consumption per head given in CSO *Economic Trends Annual Supplement, 1983 edn.*, p. 45, and in the *National Income and Product Accounts of the USA, 1929–76*, Statistical Tables, p. 393. For col. 3, see fn. 14 in the text.

There are several doubtful estimates involved here. We have to assume that the typical saver's expectations about the growth of real dividends were correct, that his marginal tax rate was as assumed (see note to Table 8.1), and that his consumption did grow at the same rate as the average for the whole population. All of these assumptions could be questioned, and so the estimates of α and β that flow from them are correspondingly uncertain. If we simply fit equation (8.1) to the three sets of observations in Table 8.1 for the after-tax return received by the saver (r_{sha}) and his assumed rate of growth of consumption per head, we get $\alpha = 0.013$ and $\beta = 1.5$, and these

shareholder's marginal tax rate is m and real rate of discount r_{sha}, then the value of a share is $V = C(1 - m)/(r_{sha} - g)$, hence one obtains the formula for the rate of return in the text, viz.

$$r_{sha} = \frac{C}{V}(1 - m) + g.$$

See also p.212 above.

give estimates for r_{sha} as in row (8) of the table. This ignores differences in risk between equities and government bonds. It could be argued that the equity yields in the first two columns on Table 8.1 should be reduced to make them comparable with the bond yield in the third column. If this were done, it would reduce the estimate of β, and, in fact, I decided to leave the equity yield unadjusted. I rather doubt whether, in the years considered, there was a safer outlet for marginal house-hold savings than the purchase of a wide spread of equities. Full employment and rapid growth made them less risky than before the war, while investing in long-term bonds carried a severe downside risk, because of inflation. After expectations adjusted to inflation (which may not have been until after about 1958 in the UK), I question whether any competent financial household investor would have chosen to invest in long-or short-term bonds, except (as with cash) for liquidity reasons. Alternative estimates of α and β are discussed below, but in the end those just given seem to be the best available, and I employ them in the sequel. While the estimates must be treated with reserve, it is not easy to find any other comparable period of stability which would enable alternative estimates to be made on a similar basis.

Stern (1977) has provided a valuable review of attempts that have been made to estimate β. One method has been to derive it from demand studies for individual consumer goods. β has been shown by Frisch, on certain assumptions, to be a function of the income elasticity, the budget share, and the own (uncompensated) price elasticity for a particular good such that the utility derived from it by the consumer is additively separable from the utility derived from all other goods. Using this relation or similar ones, Stern quotes estimates of β nearly all ranging from about 1 to about 10 (with one estimate, however, as low as 0.4).

A second method used by Stern is closer to the one described above, and relates to savings behaviour. If a saver relies entirely on his income from savings, behaves as if he were immortal, and maximizes the present value of his future stream of consumption (with a utility function that has the simple form assumed above), then he will make the rate of return on his savings equal the rate of fall of the marginal utility of consumption, which leads to the familiar equation

$$r = \alpha + \beta g$$

with g now being the rate of growth of an individual saver's consumption. His capital will have to grow at g as well, and if the ratio of savings to income is s, then

$$g = rs.$$

It follows that[16]

$$s = \frac{1}{\beta}\left(1 - \frac{\alpha}{r}\right).$$

[16] This formula is also given by Hicks (1965, 258) and by Robertson (1963, 241).

Stern then states that 'The personal savings rate in the UK in the last decade or so has been around 10% (see Townsend 1976). Long-run (postwar) rates of return seem to be around 5% (see Merrett and Sykes 1973). Using these figures and $\alpha = 2\frac{1}{2}\%$ one has β approximately 5' (Stern 1977, 220).[17]

Stern also considers experiments that have been performed of choice under uncertainty, but concludes that they do not provide a satisfactory way of estimating β. Summing up, he states:

From estimates of demand systems for the allocation of expenditure to different goods we have formed a concentration of estimates of β around 2 with a range of roughly 0–10. The range for estimates of β from choice under uncertainty was negative to plus infinity. Our simple models of savings behaviour give estimates of the elasticity of the marginal utility of consumption around 4 or 5 with again a range from 0 to 10 or more. (Stern 1977, 221)

The estimates of α and β thus far considered are derived from personal choice behaviour. I turn now to see what can be learned from estimates of the rate of return and rate of investment based on my model and the 26 observations for different countries and periods. For this purpose, I have taken the very simple form of the model in Section 8.3 above and fitted equation (8.1) to the data. Several different versions of the equation were tried, some of which are given in Table 8.2, and the first of these is shown with the scatter diagram of the observations in Figure 8.2.

Inspection of the scatter diagram shows that there is, as expected, a strong positive relationship between the rate of return, r, and the rate of growth of output per head, $g - g_N$.[18] The first regression in Table 8.2, which is fitted to the 26 *weighted* observations, as explained in Section 10.2, gives a value for β of 2.2, which is quite close to that suggested by my

---

[17] I have replaced his symbols by mine. Stern bases his conjecture for α on the argument that it represents an allowance for the risk of 'demise of a dynasty', and that α is then, to a first-order approximation, the probability of this happening in a year given a 'Poisson process'. It should be pointed out that the personal savings rate is for *all* personal incomes, including those from work, and that, if savers expect that their incomes from work are going to change (and they did in fact grow in the UK postwar), the formula for s given above, and used by Stern, no longer holds. Robertson, based on Chapernowne, gives a formula for the case where income from work grows at g, which is

$$s = \frac{(1/\beta)\,(r - \alpha) - g}{r - g}$$

Using this formula with Stern's figures, and putting $g = 0.025$, gives β approximately equal to 1, not 5; and if α is put at an exponential rate of 0.013 as in my earlier estimate, β becomes about 1.3. The 5 per cent rate of return used by Stern is net of tax, and inflation-adjusted.

[18] The (real) rate of return could be measured either by $q - \lambda l$ or by $q - \mu(1 - s)l$, and I have chosen the latter, with values of μ taken for each period by inserting the appropriate values of l and ϱ in the equation $\mu = b - 2c\,l/\varrho$, and b and c coming from fitted equations described in Chapter 11, as also does ϱ. This alternative was preferred as some of the estimates of λ were thought to be unreliable. However, the first alternative, using λ, was also tried out, and, although the fit was slightly worse, the differences in the coefficients were small. In steady growth, $g - g_N$ would be the rate of growth of consumption per head as well as of output per head, but this was only approximately so for the actual periods.

Table 8.2 Regressions using the Ramsey approach

| Equation no. | No. of observations | Estimated values of coefficients | | | Coefficient of π | $\bar{R}^2$ | Standard error of estimate |
		α (constant)	β (coefficient of $(g - g_N)$)	Coefficient of $(g - g_N)^2$			
(1)	26	0.08308 (9.71)	2.1737 (8.96)			0.760	0.02537
(2)	26	0.03566 (2.42)	5.4954 (5.91)	−38.4827 (−3.65)		0.842	0.02062
(3)	26	0.03083 (1.00)	5.6810 (4.06)	−40.0955 (−2.87)	0.005719 (0.18)	0.835	0.02107
(4)	18	0.01405 (0.48)	6.3467 (4.82)	−46.0577 (−3.59)	0.03430 (1.22)	0.916	0.01381
(5)	16	−0.00608 (−0.25)	7.8118 (5.98)	−71.0268 (−3.88)	0.04220 (2.05)	0.918	0.01011

Note
The dependent variable throughout is the average real rate of return, and the equation fitted is (8.1) with the addition of terms in $(g - g_N)^2$ and π where indicated. All regressions are weighted. t-statistics are shown in brackets below the corresponding values of the coefficients. All regressions include a constant and $(g - g_N)$ on the right-hand side. Regression no. (3) includes, in addition, $(g - g_N)^2$, while regressions (3) and (4) include, in addition, π, which is an indicator of the prevalence of slumps. This is the proportion of years in each period in which output was below the level of the previous peak. Regression no. (4) excludes the observations for the UK 1856–73 and 1913–24; for the USA 1889–1900 and 1900–13; and Japan for all four periods before the Second World War. Regression no. (5) excludes the postwar observations for Japan as well.

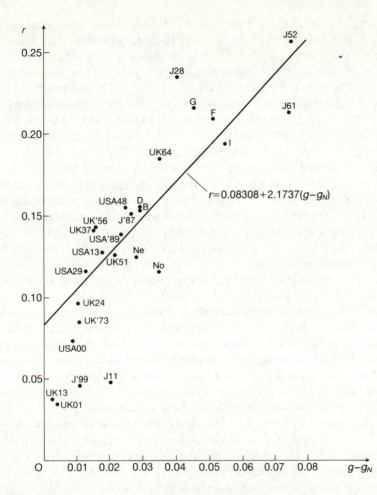

Fig. 8.2 Scatter diagram for the Ramsey Approach
For key to periods see e.g. Table 7.1. Each period's first year is shown above, and if this is in the nineteenth century it is shown with an apostrophe; thus, USA '89 = USA 1889–1900

method described above, and also accords with Stern's 'concentration of estimates' based on the allocation of expenditure to different goods.[19] However, the value of 0.083 for α (i.e. about 8 per cent p.a.) seems very high, and this is further discussed below.

Since the scatter diagram suggested a curvilinear relationship between r

[19] While it is smaller than Stern's four or five based on his model of savings behaviour, fn. 17 above gives reasons for thinking that a much lower estimate of β should have flowed from that model.

and $g - g_N$, equation (2) in Table 8.2 was fitted with an additional term in $(g - g_N)^2$. This is statistically significant, although its economic interpretation is unclear. The effect is to reduce α to 0.036, which is still rather high. We must now interpret β as the slope of the tangent to the curve, $dr/d(g - g_N)$. This now varies with $g - g_N$. The values for the more heavily weighted postwar observations are broadly acceptable (e.g., the USA, 1948–73 is 3.5, the UK 1951–64 is 3.8, the UK 1964–73 is 2.7, France is 1.5, Germany 1.9, and Italy 1.2) except for Japan, where the slopes are negative (-0.4 and -0.3 for 1952–61 and 1961–73, respectively).

Finally, it seemed worth trying out a variable measuring the prevalence of slumps, π, which is the proportion of years in each period in which output is below the previous peak. It thus gives an indication of average capacity utilization in each period, and the lower this was, the lower would have been the actual return in relation to my measure of it. One might therefore expect that, the greater was π, the greater would have been r, *ceteris paribus*. If one regards r as including some sort of risk premium, the same conclusion follows. Equation (3) in Table 8.2 shows that the coefficient of π has the expected sign, but is not statistically significant. Its significance increases, however, if we omit the eight observations that are, on statistical grounds, the most dubious, as in equation (4) and still more so in equation (5), where we omit, in addition, the post-Second World War observations for Japan (thus omitting *all* of the Japanese observations). However, I am reluctant to discard all the Japanese observations, and as the significance of π in equation (4) is not high, I have chosen to ignore it in the ensuing discussion.

If one compares my earlier method of estimating α and β with the results of the regressions in Table 8.2, one finds that the earlier method yields a much lower α, and also a lower β for some of the most important observations (such as the USA and the UK) but not for others (such as postwar Japan, or France, Germany, or Italy). There are at least three reasons that could help to explain the higher α in Table 8.2, and most of them would also explain a higher β.

1. Both company taxation and income taxation are complicated subjects, and there have been many special allowances for depreciation and investment grants, and special exemptions for particular forms of saving (e.g. through pension funds). The result has been a wide variety of marginal tax and subsidy rates for investment. The general effect has been to drive a wedge between the rate of return on investment and that received by the saver, and this would help to explain some of the difference in both α and β. Taxation is further discussed in Chapter 14.

2. The rates of return in the regressions are *average* ones, whereas in theory we need *marginal ones*, and the earlier estimates of α and β in Table 8.1 do in fact use marginal ones since the individual saver could regard the yield on ordinary shares or Consols as being independent of his own rate of

saving. I have given two reasons why the marginal return to investment might be below the average. First, there may be 'physical' diminishing returns to the rate of investment simply because the opportunities available become worse as the rate is stepped up. Second, there are 'market' diminishing returns, arising from selling costs, buying costs, and other so-called market imperfections, discussed at greater length in the next chapter. For both reasons, the marginal private return will be below the average social return which I have used, and so true α and β will both be smaller than the estimates in Table 8.2 imply.

3. My rates of return in the regressions may be exaggerated for other reasons as well, at least for the postwar periods, which carry most weight. Comparisons with conventional estimates of average rates of return in those years for the UK and the USA are given in Chapter 7, and these show that the conventional estimates are appreciably lower. While reasons are given in Chapter 7 for believing that the conventional estimates are too low, it is also possible that my estimates are too high, so that the truth lies somewhere in between.

There is a fourth reason which some might wish to include, which is the cost of financial intermediation. Like taxation, this could drive a wedge between the return on investment and that received by the saver. However, it seems unlikely that this explains any appreciable part of the difference between the earlier estimates of α and β and those in Table 8.2. In fact, I made no allowance for the transaction costs of buying or selling securities in the earlier estimates. One might, however, reasonably include some of the costs of financial intermediaries in social net material investment, and in that case all rates of return would be reduced somewhat.

Let me now summarize my conclusions on empirical estimates using the Ramsey approach to the determination of the supply of savings. It is clear that the regression equations in Table 8.2 leave out important factors: taxation, and the gap between average and marginal returns. They also rely on uncertain estimates of the rate of return and the rate of investment which are probably biased, the first upwards and the second downwards. The use of g_N as a measure of the rate of growth of the numbers sharing in the fruits of investment is open to question. The rates of return assume constant shares of profits and investment and project these and the rates of growth into the indefinite future, and no distinction is made between returns to equity or to those lending on fixed interest terms. The regression results are rather sensitive to the inclusion of the Japanese observations. For all these reasons, one cannot regard the estimates of α and β that emerge from the regressions as robust or closely comparable to my earlier estimates of α and β. At best, one can treat the regressions as 'empirical regularities' which reflect the combined results of a number of factors. As such, they must be viewed with suspicion, since the historical events underlying them may not be repeated in just that form.

8.7 Other approaches to the determinants of long-run savings and investment

Two other approaches were attempted, which may be called the 'eclectic approach' and the 'pure confidence approach'. In the eclectic approach it was assumed that the share of investment in output depended on the real rate of return, the share of labour income (or, by implication, the share of profits), and the prevalence of slumps (i.e. the variable π, already described on p.236). While regressions were obtained in which these variables had significant coefficients with the expected signs, the fit was less good than with the Ramsey approach, and the coefficients were also sensitive to the inclusion of Japan. In view of these less satisfactory results, and the stronger and simpler theory underlying the Ramsey approach, I discarded the eclectic approach and do not report the regressions here.

In the pure confidence approach it was assumed that the share of investment depended only on the prevalence of slumps, π, and the catch-up variable, $\ln cu$. The reason for including the latter was the supposition that business confidence would be stronger (and so investment higher) where investment consisted to a greater extent of imitation of well tried methods and was less of a venture into the unknown. In regressions with these variables, the coefficients were significant and had the expected signs, but, again, the fit was somewhat less good than with the Ramsey approach. The catch-up variable applies only to the postwar observations, and there it is perfectly correlated with ϱ, and hence may be acting as a proxy for the rate of return. I therefore decided to discard the pure confidence approach in favour of the Ramsey approach, and the results are not reported here. I believe that business confidence *is* undoubtedly an important determinant of investment and saving, and we return to consider it in Chapters 9, 15, and 16, where, as we shall see, it has an important part to play.

We consider later (Section 11.3) M. Olson's interesting thesis that differences in growth rates between countries can be partially explained by differences in the strengths of 'distributional coalitions', (Olson 1982). Olson suggested that such coalitions would be strongest in countries such as the UK, where the conditions for their formation had persisted for a long time, and that defeat and occupation by a foreign power in the Second World War would have weakened them in Japan and some continental European countries. Low growth in the UK, and high growth in the latter countries since the war, could thus be partially explained. However, the analysis in Section 11.3 concludes that differences in growth rates can be explained mainly by differences in rates of investment and rates of growth of the labour force. Olson's thesis does not appear to add anything to the explanation at that stage.[20]

Does it help in explaining differences in rates of investment? It does seem plausible that, where distributional coalitions are strong, resistance to change will be strong for all the reasons Olson gives (Olson 1982, 53–65 especially), and that this will tend to reduce the rate of investment and so the rate of growth. The Ramsey approach does not explain the rate of investment *directly*, but only indirectly, via the relation between the rate of return and the rate of growth of output per head. One might think that, where distributional coalitions are stronger, resistance to change might result in a lower rate of investment and growth of output per head for any given rate of return. Hence the observations for the UK should lie to the left of the regression line in Figure 8.2, while those for France, Germany, Italy, and Japan (postwar) should lie to the right of it. The results in the figure do not altogether bear this out, with about as many incorrect as correct. However, one must admit that this is not a very powerful test, since the fit in Figure 8.2 is not very good.

Matthews *et al.* (1982) believe that there was a downward shift of the supply schedule of finance (i.e. an increase in supply) in the UK after the Second World War as compared with before the First. Their evidence for this is that the rate of profit (net or gross of depreciation but before tax or interest deductions, at current or constant prices) fell while the rate of capital accumulation rose (p.350). Their measure of the rate of profit is the ratio of profits to capital stock, which, at best, measures the average rate of return achieved on the investment that constitutes the stock, and so is an average extending over a considerable period, varying with the lives of the relevant assets. It is also an *ex post* measure, whereas, strictly speaking, the supply of finance depends on expectations. (See Matthews *et al*, (1982, 345) for a discussion of these points.)

My own measure of the rate of return is also *ex post* and before deduction of tax or interest, but it is the average real rate of return on *investment*. It is therefore more relevant to decisions to save or invest, and is not subject to the uncertainties surrounding any measure of the capital stock. My estimates show an increase, rather than a fall, in the rate of return comparing 1951–64, and even more so 1964–73, with 1873–1901 or 1901–13 (but 1856–73 has a higher rate of return than 1951–64)—see Table 7.1 and Figure 8.2. There was certainly an increase in the rate of investment, as measured by s (Matthews *et al.* prefer to measure the proportionate rate of growth of the capital stock); but, if the rate of return did indeed rise, one cannot be sure that there was a shift to the right in the supply schedule. On the other hand, my measure of the rate of return overstates the average

---

[20] Although some weak evidence in its favour is provided by equation (10.2).

private return, and the degree of overstatement might well be greater after 1945 than before 1914, especially through neglecting taxation. It is also true that investment abroad was much more important before 1914 than after 1945, and the lack of competition for funds from that source may have increased the supply at home. Matthews *et al.* point out that depreciation and government saving both increased substantially, and they attach importance to the development of the joint stock company, the widening of the equity market, and the increase in the size and product range of firms as additional factors tending to increase the supply of funds. (See Matthews *et al.* 1982, ch. 12 for a discussion of these and other factors, and also ch. 5, pp. 139–51.)

For the USA and Japan, I have not found a discussion of the long-term factors determining the supply of investible funds which is comparable to that for the UK by Matthews *et al.*

For the USA, much more of the literature has been concerned with the explanation of personal savings and, in particular, with households' 'consumption functions'. Effort has been devoted to explaining the apparent long-term constancy in the ratio of household saving to disposable income, despite the large rise in that income, and two other, apparently contradictory findings: that the (short-term) marginal propensity to save exceeds the average, and that, in cross-section studies, richer people save higher proportions of income than poorer people. The permanent income hypothesis of Friedman, the life-cycle hypothesis of Modigliani and Brumberg, and the relative income hypothesis of Duesenberry all provide explanations of one kind or another. Much of the interest in these analyses, however, relates to short-term, cyclical, behaviour.

Longer-term trends have been measured and discussed by Kuznets (Kuznets with Jenks 1961). For the whole economy, he shows that the ratio of gross investment to gross national product in normal peacetime periods has varied very little (20.2 per cent in 1869–88, 20.9 per cent in 1909–28, and 21.3 per cent in 1946–55; p. 396). However, his estimates of capital consumption imply that the *net* investment ratio has fallen (13.0 per cent, 11.0 per cent, and 8.7 per cent over the same three periods). He therefore asks why, in view of the big increase in real income, there has been this fall. In his view, the answer is to be found not in a lack of investment opportunities, but rather in limitations on the supply of savings, and especially household savings, which have supplied the lion's share of total *net* savings. Kuznets has a long and interesting discussion of the long-term behaviour of household savings, in which he refers approvingly to Duesenberry's relative income hypothesis (p. 105).

Our interest lies, however, in total gross savings, and the figures quoted above show that capital consumption has been a large and growing proportion of this. Kuznets provides data and discussion on the main trends in the ratio of internal and external financing, both to total uses of funds (which includes investment in financial assets) and to total capital formation (which does not). Within the business sector as a whole, and in normal peacetime periods since 1900 (when the data first became available), these ratios are rather stable. Kuznets also has much of interest to say about the role of financial intermediaries, which has grown very greatly over the long term.

Perhaps because of the absence of clear trends in many of the key ratios in the USA, there is not a great deal that is directly relevant in these various studies to my own inquiry. The two most relevant points seem to be, first, that there is support for the assumption that, *ceteris paribus*, (gross) savings increase in the same proportion as income; and, second, that many of the hypotheses seeking to explain household savings behaviour imply that consumption lags behind income, so that the savings ratio will increase automatically if growth speeds up. This second point, however, which is echoed by Ohkawa and Rosovsky (see below), makes savings a passive consequence, rather than a cause, of growth. This contradicts both Kuznets's basic position, referred to above, and my own. While it seems plausible enough that *acceleration* in the growth rate will lead to higher savings as consumption habits lag behind, it is far less plausible to assume that households will fail to adjust to a steady rate of growth.

There is discussion of long-term fluctuations in the ratio of investment to output in Japan, including the great postwar increase, in Ohkawa and Rosovsky (1973). These writers clearly believe that the prospective rate of return is an important determinant (p. 149), but they nowhere provide estimates of even the *ex post* return. They measure it by the ratio of profits to capital stock (p. 151), but there is little discussion of this measure, which suffers, as we have seen, from deficiencies, ambiguities, and statistical uncertainties. Investment is apparently viewed as depending on the *growth rate* of the rate of return, rather than on its level, and estimates of this growth rate are provided (their Figure 6.3 and Table 6.4, pp. 150–1). The high post war rate of investment is then presumably due to the fact that the rate of return was *increasing*, rather than that the level was high. In fact, Ohkawa and Rosovsky seem to believe that in the long run there was no clear trend up or down in the rate of return. (This is stated as an *assumption* rather than an empirical fact: see p. 198). My own estimates, however, suggest that there was a very marked increase from at least the first thirty years of this century to the post-Second World War period. (The apparently high return in 1928–36 is problematic.) In the concluding discussion of the Ohkawa–Rosovsky model of long swings in the investment ratio, the exogenous factors appear to be demand and technological and organizational progress (see especially pp. 200–2). It seems unsatisfactory to treat the former as exogenous, and the latter cannot really be classed as an explanation.

Ohkawa and Rosovsky also briefly discuss the factors determining savings in Japan (pp. 167–72). They stress the importance of *personal* savings, which (at least since the Second World War) have consisted mainly of the savings of farmers and unincorporated enterprises. Corporations have financed much of their investment by borrowing from the personal sector. The personal savings rate may be increased (they say) by a high rate of growth of personal incomes (since there is a lag in the adjustment of consumption), by a backward social security system, by a lack of personal credit facilities, and by the need to pay for the education of children (p. 171). Apart from the fall in military expenditure by the government in the postwar period (p. 170), Ohkawa and Rosovsky seem to regard changes in the savings ratio as being mainly a response to changes in the rate of growth (p. 172).

This admittedly cursory survey of other attempts to explain saving and investment in the medium to long run has not revealed any satisfactory quantitative study. The Ramsey approach is by no means satisfactory either, but, all the same, it is the best I can offer for the time being. There is scope here for more research.

9
GROWTH OF THE FIRM AND INDUSTRY

9.1 Introduction

In this chapter we leave macroeconomics to delve a little deeper into the microeconomics of growth. Apart from its own interest, and its relevance to the empirical study of prices, output, and productivity in different industries in Chapter 13, the material in this chapter is needed for the macroeconomic Chapter 15 on optimum growth.

We start by considering the role of prices in determining rates of growth of supply in perfectly competitive industries. It is shown that the prices of a firm's products must be constant (relative to the general price level) in equilibrium growth. A dynamic supply curve is constructed which shows how the rate of growth of output depends on the level of prices ruling in the industry (relative to the general price level), and *not* on their rate of change. It is also shown that there is a close analogy between an exogenous improvement in investment opportunities, which might be due to a burst of inventions for example, and a rise in the industry's price level.

Firms selling in imperfect markets are considered next, at first with the simplest possible model, which assumes that each firm confronts a given downward-sloping demand curve for its products. A firm that produces only one product must then, in equilibrium, grow as fast as the demand for that product at constant prices, and its marginal rate of return and share of wages will both be lower than under perfectly competitive conditions. It is then as if there had been a worsening of investment opportunities in the industry, since the dynamic supply curve will be shifted upwards just as if that had occurred. Although these results are demonstrated only for the simplest case of monopolistic competition, there are other market structures that could lead to similar results.

A further step towards realism is to allow for the ability of the individual firm to escape from the above-mentioned constraint set by the rate of shift of the demand curve for its products. A firm that wants to grow steadily faster (or more slowly) than that can do so in either of three ways. First, it can do so by producing different products, or invading different markets, or, in short, by *diversification*. Second, it can invest more rapidly in various kinds of capital selling expenditures which shift the demand curve faster to the right. Third, there is the possibility that setting a lower level of prices for its products will also shift *its* demand curve faster to the right. This may occur because of a reduction in the rate of growth of competitors' supply.

Up to this point, the analysis has assumed that all firms are self-financing, and form the main outlet for their owners' savings. The supply of savings is a crucial determinant of the slope of the dynamic supply curve, and, under the circumstances postulated, upward-sloping supply curves would be the rule. The next step is to allow for borrowing by firms. Various possibilities are considered, including borrowing in a perfect capital market and borrowing by an owner-controlled firm in an imperfect capital market. The ability to borrow opens the possibility of a downward-sloping dynamic supply curve.

One must also consider the possibility of a divorce of ownership from control, and the important phenomenon of management-controlled firms. The chapter concludes with a discussion of such firms. How far are they able to pursue objectives other than those of the maximization of the present value of take-out, which I have assumed to govern firms' behaviour? Can I accommodate them within my model, and what modifications to it are then required?

I conclude, perhaps optimistically, that they can be accommodated, and that they do not require any essential change to be made in the *form* of the model's equations. However, the existence of borrowing, and the empirical evidence available, suggest that the supply of funds to firms will be much more elastic than if each were self-financed, and this makes downward-sloping supply curves more probable. The other main difference is that firms, on average, and because of 'animal spirits', are likely to be willing to sacrifice profitability for growth to some extent, and this offsets the opposing tendency arising from imperfect markets. It results, then, in more growth and a higher share of wages than would otherwise be the case. These macroeconomic implications are taken up in Chapter 15.

9.2 Equilibrium growth for a representative firm in a non-representative competitive industry

The analysis thus far has been in terms of a representative competitive firm and a whole economy whose output is the average bundle of consumer goods and services. (In so far as output consists of investment goods and services, the quantity of these is measured as if they were consumer goods and services.) Although the price, P, of output was retained in our formulae and in Figure 8.1, in fact one could set $P = 1$ without losing anything.

The next step is to consider a competitive firm in a *non*-representative industry, the price of whose output may, therefore, diverge from that of the average bundle of consumption. I still retain the assumption of perfect competition, but we can now gain some insight into the part played by prices in determining growth rates, and into the determination of relative prices under equilibrium growth conditions. As we discuss *only* those conditions, readers should be reminded of the warning already given: equilibrium growth at different rates in different industries is merely a first approximation—as is, for that matter, equilibrium growth for the whole economy. I adopt it because it greatly simplifies matters and because, as is shown later (Part IV), it does help to explain reality quite well.

For simplicity, I assume that the price of the average bundle of consumer goods does not change and I set it equal to 1 as the numeraire. Hence P, for a particular firm or industry, measures the price of the firm's output relative to that average bundle.

In equilibrium growth, P must remain constant. This is because both $\sigma \equiv S/Q$ and $s \equiv S/PQ$ have to be constant. I originally defined steady growth as being a state of affairs in which s, λ, g, and g_L were all constant, but this does not refer to constancy in σ. It might appear, then, that s can remain constant while P changes, because S and Q change in such a way as to offset the change in P. However, this possibility is ruled out by the following consideration. Let us suppose, for example, that P falls. Then, for constancy in s to be preserved, σ must fall. But since $g \equiv \sigma q$, $g_L \equiv \sigma l$, constancy in g and g_L then requires that q and l both increase, which implies a shift to the right along the IPC. That, in turn, implies a fall in μ, the slope of the IPC at the chosen point. Now since in equilibrium growth $\mu(1 - s) = \lambda$, with s constant a fall in μ requires a fall in λ, which is inconsistent with the requirements for steady growth. If the firm continued to invest at the same point on the IPC while P fell, it would need to keep σ unchanged to maintain growth unchanged, and s would then inevitably rise, which also would be inconsistent with steady-growth equilibrium.

This argument already indicates how relative prices influence the rate of growth. A fall in price increases the burden of maintaining the same rate of growth, while a rise in price alleviates it. A different way of expressing the same idea is to say that, if we keep the burden constant, that is if s is constant, then a lower price means that less growth will result, while a higher price means that growth will be faster. All this becomes clearer in the sequel.

For P to remain constant in equilibrium, the output of the industry of which the firm is a part must grow at a rate matching the rate at which the demand curve for that industry's products is shifting to the right. This requirement can be expressed most simply as

$$g = v\bar{g} \tag{9.1}$$

I assume that the firm is representative of the industry,[1] so that its rate of growth, g, is the same as that of the industry. v is the income elasticity of demand for the industry's products, and $\bar{g}$ is the exogenously given rate of growth of the whole economy.

---

[1] If it is not representative, P becomes exogenous, and the earlier analysis suffices.

I continue for the present to assume that the firm is entirely self-financed, and confine my attention to the Ramsey approach, and so equations (8.1)–(8.4) apply. The two identities (8.5) also apply except that g_L is no longer exogenously given: instead, the rate of growth of wage rates, g_w, is assumed to be exogenously given so that (8.6) applies. We then have, with (9.1), ten equations to determine the ten endogenous variables, q, l, σ, s, λ, μ, r, g, g_L, and P. The main difference from the previous analysis is that we have the additional equation (9.1) and the additional endogenous variable P.

One can illustrate the determination of equilibrium values by reference to Figure 9.1, which is the usual IPC diagram. Point E is first determined, since $OG = g_w$ (which is exogenous, and equals $g - g_L$) and $ME = g = v\bar{g}$ (also exogenous). On the vertical through E we then find S such that $MV/ME = \beta$ and $VS = \alpha - \beta g_N$. Then $MS = OR = r$. The IPC is given, and we find where it cuts the ray OE at F. Then $OE/OF = \sigma$, and the

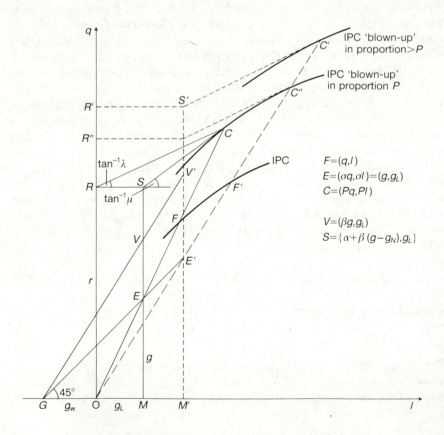

Fig. 9.1 Model diagram for non-representative industry

coordinates of F are l and q. We then draw SC through S parallel to the tangent to the IPC at F so as to cut the ray OE at C. Then, as before, $OC/OF = P$; the tangent of the angle $CRS = \lambda$; the coordinates of C are Pl and Pq; and $OE/OC = s$.

From this Figure one can derive two results which are important for subsequent analysis of the relation between supply and demand for the products of a particular industry. The first result is that a faster *rate of growth* of supply requires a rise in the *level* of the prices paid for the industry's products,[2] here represented by P. Again, readers are reminded that we refer throughout to equilibrium growth rates, such as at E in Figure 9.1, where the growth rate is ME. If this is to be raised to, say, $M'E'$, the new equilibrium point must satisfy the requirement that the rate of growth of labour productivity equals the exogenously determined rate of growth of wage rates g_w. Consequently, E' must lie on the projection of GE. It is then clear from the Figure that the ray OE' is to the right of OE. If there were no change in the price level, the new equilibrium position on the 'blown-up' IPC would be at C'', and the new rate of return would be OR''. This is higher than the previous rate of return OR, which implies that, for a firm producing under the assumed conditions, an increase in investment will result in both a faster rate of growth and a higher rate of return. One may ask, How, then, can point E have been a stable equilibrium position? The answer is that, in order for it to have been so, the *required* rate of return must increase faster than the achieved rate of return. How much the required rate of return increases when g increases depends on the parameter β (see equation 8.1)). In fact, the increase in the required rate of return is $\beta\Delta g$. The increase in the achieved rate of return when prices do not change depends on the shape of the IPC.[3] I shall assume that the equilibrium is stable, since otherwise the industry would not remain competitive, and consideration of imperfect markets comes later. It follows that the new required rate of return, OR', must be greater than the achieved rate of return when prices do not change, OR''. Hence prices must rise and push out the 'blown-up' IPC until the achieved rate of return equals OR'.

We can thus conclude that, in the postulated circumstances, an increase in the rate of growth of demand for the industry's products will result in a rise in their price level, P. It is also clear from Figure 9.1 that μ will be lower,[4] that the ratio of investment to output at constant prices, $\sigma = S/Q$,

---

[2] It must be noted that the demonstration of this result is based on the assumption that the industry can be regarded as being made up of representative firms, whose behaviour is analysed. To the extent that prices affect the rate at which new firms enter, or old ones leave, the industry, the supply curve is likely to be more elastic than the argument in the text suggests.

[3] If there were no curvature, the slope of the tangent at C'' would be the same as at C, and in that case the increase in the achieved rate of return must be less than in the required rate of return so long as $\beta \geq 1$. This is because the slope of the tangent at C is $\mu < 1$.

[4] μ falls as the ray OE swings clockwise, given the curvature of the IPC.

will be higher,[5] but that the share of investment at current prices could be higher or lower.[6] The share of wages, λ, equals $\mu (1 - s)$, and so falls if s increases (since μ certainly falls), and could still fall even if s falls.[7]

These conclusions, it must be remembered, hold under the special assumptions made here, which include perfect markets and complete self-financing. One might expect that small firms (for which perfect markets might be a reasonable approximation) would be likely to rely mainly on self-financing by the proprietors. However that may be, the conclusions can be very different when we allow for borrowing and imperfect markets, as is shown later in the chapter. A fall, rather than a rise, in the price level may then be required.

What is interesting about this result is that it is the *level* of price that matters, and not the *rate of change* of price.[8] Normal supply-and-demand analysis would suggest that, if the demand curve shifts faster to the right, then either prices will rise faster (if supply curves slope upwards: this includes the case where prices fall more slowly), or they will fall faster (if supply curves slope downwards: this includes the case where prices rise more slowly).[9] That is not the result obtained here. I hasten to add, however, that, since prices change from one equilibrium to another, there could be a long drawn-out period of transition when prices are rising or falling.

The second result that can be established with the aid of Figure 9.1 is a very important one. There is a close parallel, so far as the individual firm or industry is concerned, between an improvement (worsening) in the real investment opportunities confronting it and a rise (fall) in the prices of its products. If the improvement (worsening) in the real investment opportunities takes the simple form of a uniform outward (inward) shift of the IPC curve, that is, an increase (decrease) in ϱ, without any other change in its shape, then the parallel is exact so far as equilibrium growth is concerned. There are several ways of showing this. In Figure 9.1 such an improvement would shift F out along the ray OC. However, with the other exogenous variables unchanged, there is a uniquely determined equilibrium growth position at C. The 'blown-up' IPC has to pass through C, and investment has to have the 'characteristics' (see p. 152) at C, if equilibrium growth is to be restored. The only way this can happen is for the price of

---

[5] $\sigma = OE/OF$, and OE'/OF' must be greater as the slope of EE' is 45° while that of FF' must be less as $\mu < 1$.

[6] $s = \sigma/P$, so a sufficient rise in P could more than offset the rise in σ. Experiments with US 1948–73 parameters suggest that s falls when g is small and increasing, but rises eventually as g gets larger.

[7] The same experiments reported in fn. 6 suggest that λ falls over nearly the whole range of positive values for g.

[8] For a similar view to that expressed here, see Downie (1958, Ch. VI).

[9] The reconciliation of downward-sloping supply curves and perfect markets encounters some well-known problems.

output to fall in the same proportion as F has shifted out, so that price multiplied by OF equals OC once again. Initially, the improvement in investment opportunities with unchanged price would raise the rates of return and investment. The rate of growth of output would then increase, and this would drive down the price. The fall in price would tend to raise the share of wages, but this would be offset by the period of higher investment, and faster productivity growth. To reach the new equilibrium, the old value of λ would need to be restored, along with the old values of g, g_L, r, and μ. The improvement would thus lead to a fall in prices exactly offsetting it, so far as the industry was concerned, and the whole benefit would be passed on to consumers of the industry's products.

The equivalence of changes in P and changes in ϱ can also be seen from the equations of the system, (8.1)–(8.5). If ϱ, q, and l all change in the same proportion, they continue to satisfy (8.4). Likewise, g and g_L, and so g_w, will be unchanged with s unchanged if Pq and Pl are unchanged, and this requires that, for example, a doubling in q and l is offset by a halving of P. μ is unchanged if q/ϱ and l/ϱ are unchanged. λ is unchanged if μ and s are unchanged. Finally, r is unchanged if λ is unchanged and if Pq and Pl are unchanged.

Both of the conclusions just described are used in Figure 9.2 to show the relationship between the price level, the rate of growth of output, and investment opportunities in equilibrium. Rates of growth of an industry's output are measured along the horizontal axis, and the vertical line Dg shows the rate of growth of demand for that output which is assumed here to be independent of the *level* of prices charged, measured along the vertical axis. In equilibrium, as already stated, the level of prices is constant, and so the rate of growth of demand is given by the product of the income elasticity of demand, ν, and the rate of growth in the whole economy, $\bar{g}$. Subsequently I shall question the assumption that Dg is independent of P, but I maintain it for the present. It is the assumption usually made.

The curve Sg shows the rate of growth of supply. For the reasons discussed, this increases with the level of P,[10] and we normalize by setting $P = 1$ at the equilibrium point E where $Sg = Dg$. Points on either side of E are found by working through the system of equations already described. The parameters in the model are those defining the IPC (a, b, c, and ϱ), the supply of savings, (α, β, and g_N), and the rate of growth of wage rates (g_w). Given these, one can calculate P for given g, or vice-versa.

Changes in investment opportunities, ϱ, have the effect of shifting Sg down (if ϱ increases) or up (if ϱ falls). Figure 9.2 illustrates the effect of an 11 per cent increase in ϱ which results in a 10 per cent fall in P, so that $P\varrho$ is the same in the new equilibrium, E', as in the old one, E. Not only is $P\varrho$

---

[10] The earlier argument implies that the slope of Sg is flattened by a fall in β, but that stability requires some positive slope.

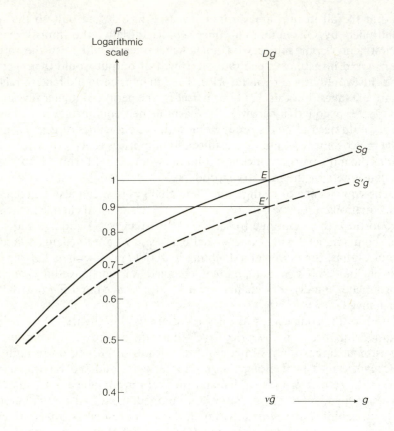

Fig. 9.2 Dynamic supply and demand

unchanged, but so are g, g_L, μ, λ, s, and r. This is the case discussed above with reference to Figure 9.1, in which point F shifts out along OC and price falls so as to preserve the old equilibrium at C and E.

Thus far, I have assumed that there are no diminishing returns to the rate of investment. We saw earlier (p. 213) that there were some factors that could lead to diminishing returns (e.g. 'Penrose effects'), but others that could counteract them (e.g. dynamic economies of scale). We return to the empirical question of the extent of diminishing returns later. It is not difficult to allow for them theoretically. A rise in the rate of investment at constant prices, σ, leads, then, to an inward shift of the IPC, and so to a fall in ϱ. Not surprisingly, this results in a more steeply rising curve in Figure 9.2. The required rate of return still rises with the rate of growth as before, and, as at each growth rate ϱ is lower because of diminishing returns, so must P be higher to offset the lower ϱ.

We may anticipate the discussion of borrowing by the firm at this point. It is obvious that access to a perfect capital market will peg the rate of return achieved by a firm to that ruling in the market. For a firm selling in a perfect market with no diminishing returns to investment, there could then be no stable equilibrium growth rate, since, as we have seen, the rate of return rises as the firm invests more and grows faster. Diminishing returns to the rate of investment could restore stability to such a firm by requiring a rise in prices to keep the rate of return constant when investment and the rate of growth are increased. Hence either diminishing returns to investment or a rising internal cost of finance could ensure stability in a competitive product market.

9.3 Imperfect competition: introduction

The analysis thus far has ignored the existence of imperfect markets and imperfect competition. The firms have taken prices as being outside their control, and have invested and produced accordingly. The role of demand in investment decisions has not been explicitly discussed because, for any firm, demand has not been a limiting factor. Everything that can be produced can be sold at given market prices, and whatever inputs are required can be bought at given market prices. These assumptions simplify the analysis, and so enable one to understand without being swamped by too much complexity at the beginning.

At the micro level of inter-firm competition, reality is much more complex and fascinating than my analysis can hope to reveal. My treatment of imperfect competition is elementary, and needs to be taken much further. Nevertheless, it is sufficient to show that imperfections affect not merely the level of output, as in orthodox static analysis, but also its rate of growth, and in a way that has not been generally recognized. In a nutshell, imperfections reduce the marginal private return on investment in relation to the marginal social return. There is then an externality to investment, and the rate of investment is, in general, too low, as also is the rate of growth. Besides this point, the form that competition takes can affect the rate of growth. Price competition is, in general, superior to other forms of competition.

9.4 Simple monopolistic competition

I start the analysis by the simplest departure from the assumption of perfect markets. The typical firm now confronts a downward-sloping demand curve for its products, whose position and slope it cannot influence. This demand curve shifts to the right at a rate depending on the rate of growth of the whole economy. Consequently, if the firm expands its output at the same rate, the prices of its products will not change. Any attempt, however, to expand output faster than this will drive prices down and must therefore tend to lower the firm's average and marginal rate of return. Likewise, slower expansion by the firm will cause the prices of its output to rise and so tend to increase both rates of return.

To keep the analysis simple, I assume that both price and income elasticities of demand for the firm's products are constant, the former being ϵ (defined so as to be positive), and the latter v. For the firm that is typical of the whole economy, $v = 1$.

I continue to assume that the supply of labour to the individual firm is perfectly elastic. This both simplifies the analysis and seems reasonably consistent with the observed tendency of wage rates to grow at about the same rate in all industries within a country, despite widely divergent growth rates in employment.

Let us first consider the equilibrium growth of the firm. The analysis is similar to that in Section 9.2 in that the price level for the firm's output is endogenous, and is determined at that level which ensures that its output grows at the same rate as demand. However, the formula for the firm's marginal rate of return and that relating the share of wages to the slope of the IPC are modified because of the less than perfectly elastic demand curve for output. They become[11]

$$r = P\{q(1 - \frac{1}{\epsilon}) - \lambda l\} \tag{9.2}$$

and

$$\mu \equiv b - 2c \frac{l}{\varrho} = \frac{\lambda}{1 - 1/\epsilon - s}. \tag{9.3}$$

It is clear from (9.2) that, for any given values of P, q, l, and λ, the marginal rate of return, r, is lower than in the case of perfect markets. Likewise, for given values of μ and s, it is clear from (9.3) that the share of wages, λ, is lower.

What difference do equations (9.2) and (9.3) make to the earlier analysis of supply and demand? Fortunately, the results are very simple. Consider a particular rate of growth of demand for the firm's products, g, which I assume depends on the rate of growth of the whole economy and the income elasticity of demand. Let us compare the equilibrium situations of the typical firm in a competitive industry with demand growing at g with that of a firm selling in imperfect markets with demand also growing at g. Let us suppose that, apart from the fact of imperfectly elastic demand in the second case, the firms are alike. They are thus both confronted by the same IPCs, and both are entirely self-financed, and their owners have the same α,

---

[11] See Appendix A at the end of this chapter for proof.

β, and g_N. It follows that both owners will require the same rate of return when output is growing at g, and, since output must grow at the same rate as demand so that price is constant in equilibrium, r must be the same for both firms. Both firms experience the same conditions in the labour market, so that g_w is the same for each. If readers will now turn back to Figure 9.1, they will see that for each firm the point E and the ray OE must be the same, and OE must therefore cut the same IPC at the same point F. Hence q and l must be the same, and so also must be σ, since $g = \sigma q$. Hence the 'real' rate of investment, S/Q, is the same for both firms.

We now come to the differences between the firms. These relate to P, λ, and s. For the competitive firm, P is lower and λ and s are both higher. In fact, it can easily be seen that, if we denote the competitive firm by subscript c, and the imperfectly competitive one by subscript m (for monopoly), then

$$1 - \frac{1}{\epsilon} = P_c/P_m = \lambda_m/\lambda_c = s_m/s_c . \tag{9.4}$$

Remembering that $\sigma = s/P$, substitution from (9.4) into (9.2) and (9.3) results in the same values of r and μ for the two firms.

It follows that the only modification needed to the supply curve Sg in Figure 9.2 to allow for imperfectly elastic demand is an upward shift in the proportion $1/\{1 - (1/\epsilon)\}$. The equilibrium price is raised in the same proportion, whatever the position of the demand curve. Although the rates of growth are the same under monopolistic as under competitive conditions, the higher price level with the former implies a lower level of output. This prompts the reflection that the effects on price and output are the same as if investment opportunities, as measured by ϱ, had deteriorated in the same proportion.

There are two further differences between perfect and imperfect markets in this simple case which are worth noticing. In perfect markets, and assuming no physical diminishing returns to the rate of investment, firms' average and marginal rates of return are the same, and equal to $P(q - \lambda l)$. This formula still gives the average rate of return in imperfect markets, although its value is higher,[12] and the marginal rate of return is below the average, as in (9.2).

The second difference relates to the conditions necessary for a stable growth equilibrium. For the competitive firm, as we saw earlier, there had to be either physical diminishing returns or a rising cost of internal finance. For the imperfectly competitive firm, stability can be secured without either

---

[12] From (9.4) we have, given that q and l are the same for the competitive and the monopolistic firm,

$$P_c(q - \lambda_c l) = P_m\{q(1 - \frac{1}{\epsilon}) - \lambda_m l\} < P_m (q - \lambda_m l),$$

so long as $q > 0$ and $1 < \epsilon < \infty$.

of these. This is because the firm's owners are now aware of the vertical demand curve, Dg, in Figure 9.2. They realize that a higher rate of growth than at E will drive down prices and reduce the marginal rate of return below their required rate. It might be thought that, since a lower rate of investment and rate of growth would raise prices indefinitely, it would pay them to cut back. However, that is not the case. Although prices rise, quantity falls, and the firm's present value is reduced. So long as the same conditions persist, the firm will therefore continue to invest at E, thus maximizing its present value, and with output growing at a rate matching the rate of growth of demand.

In the preceding section it was asserted that market imperfections affected not merely the level of output, as in orthodox static analysis, but also its rate of growth. Yet the case of simple monopolistic competition discussed above might be thought to contradict this. Only the level of output, and not its rate of growth, depends on ϵ. However, this conclusion holds only in a partial (growth) equilibrium analysis, and so applies to a small part of an economy—a firm, or a small industry. For a whole closed economy the burden of a given rate of real investment, $\sigma = S/Q$, cannot be altered by changing the price of output. In this case, as we have already seen, $\sigma = s$, since output is measured in the same units as investment, i.e. in terms of consumption. Consequently, if one compared two otherwise similar economies, one with perfect markets and the other with imperfect markets in which the typical price elasticity of demand was $1 < \epsilon < \infty$, then, if both happened to be growing at the same rate with the same real rate of investment, the marginal rate of return would be lower in the monopolistic economy. If α and β were the same in both economies, then both could not be in equilibrium growth. For example, if the competitive economy were in equilibrium, then the monopolistic economy would be growing too fast. Capitalists there would want to cut back the rate of investment and growth.[13]

---

[13] Assume that q, l, and σ are the same in both economies, that $P = 1$, and that there are no 'physical' diminishing returns to σ. Then g, μ, and $s = \sigma$ must also be the same in each economy. In the competitive one,

$$r_c = q - \mu (1 - s)l,$$

while in the monopolistic one

$$r_m = q \left(1 - \frac{1}{\epsilon}\right) - \mu \left(1 - \frac{1}{\epsilon} - s\right)l$$

if, in both, λ is set at its equilibrium value as in equation (9.3). Then

$$r_c - r_m = \frac{1}{\epsilon} (q - \mu l) > 0,$$

since $q - \mu l > 0$. If, now, $r_c = \alpha + \beta (g - g_N)$, then r_m must be less than this, its equilibrium value. For an estimate of the effect of a change in $\eta = \{1 - (1/\epsilon)\}$ on equilibrium g, see Appendix C to Chapter 15.

I consider various modifications of equations (9.2) and (9.3) in the sequel, where I discuss selling costs, both current and capital, and I also consider diversification by the firm. Later, I discuss borrowing and taxation. All these are important, but there is one fundamental difficulty which I do not satisfactorily deal with and which it is as well to recognize at the outset. I have considered only the simplest kind of monopolistic competition, and have not discussed oligopoly (which may be more widespread and is certainly important) or other market structures. I use equations similar to (9.2) and (9.3) in Chapter 15 to attempt to quantify the difference between private and social returns, and for that purpose need to estimate at least the order of magnitude of ϵ, the price elasticity of demand for the typical firm. The question then arises as to how one should interpret the available estimates, given that other market structures besides simple monopolistic competition are widespread. A few alternatives are mentioned below.[14]

One such alternative is that firms operating in an oligopolistic industry follow a price leader, who sets prices so as to maximize his own present value on the assumption that he will be followed, and after allowing for potential or actual competition by outside firms. The relevant value of ϵ would then seem to be higher than the elasticity of the total demand for the industry's products, since outside competition would provide more or less supply depending on the price set, thus reducing or increasing demand for the price leader's output over and above the effects on total demand by consumers. The importance of potential or outside competition has been stressed by several writers.

Another possibility, which is not very different, is that the firms within the industry reach a similar result by a process of trial and error or, alternatively, by collusion.

If the industry is monopolized by one firm, the situation is again similar, since it must still be on its guard against possible outside competitors.

Price leadership, collusion, or monopolization are all, perhaps, less likely if the products are highly differentiated, as there is then no obvious group of firms who stand to gain by such behaviour. Simple monopolistic competition may then be a reasonable approximation, and the relevant ϵ is that pertaining to the firm's own demand curve, which is in principle well defined (even if it is not empirically easy to estimate).

There are doubtless other possibilities which cannot be pursued further here. All I can do is to draw attention to the problem without, unfortunately, being able to resolve it.

Equations (9.2) and (9.3) assume that the only way in which the firm can increase the demand for its products is by lowering their prices. In reality, a

---

[14] See Hay and Morris (1979, chs. 4 and 5) for an excellent discussion with many references.

great many other ways are open to it, such as advertising, employing more or better salesmen, using more or more attractive selling outlets, better packaging, better after-sales service, or cheaper credit, or improving delivery to the customer. Different methods are appropriate to different products and different markets. All these methods cost money, and I refer to them in short as *selling costs*. All tend to shift the demand curve for the firm's products to the right, but one can in principle distinguish between those that have this effect only so long as a certain rate of expenditure is maintained, which we may call *current selling costs*, and those that produce a once-for-all shift, which we may call *capital selling costs*. Most of the examples just given are mainly current, but some advertising and some expenditure on increasing the number or attractiveness of selling outlets could be capital.

Data on selling costs are not generally available. Demand studies usually neglect them, and I have perforce done the same in Chapter 15, where an attempt is made to assess the degree of market imperfection of demand confronting the typical firm. I there refer to studies of demand in international trade, which have yielded a wide range of estimates of price elasticities of demand. As these elasticities refer not to output as measured by value added at constant prices, but rather to output gross of material inputs, an important modification of equations (9.2) and (9.3) is required. These can be rewritten more generally as

$$r = P\,(\eta q - \lambda l) \tag{9.5}$$

and

$$\mu = \frac{\lambda}{\eta - s} \tag{9.6}$$

where η is the ratio of marginal revenue to price. In (9.2) and (9.3), $\eta = 1 - (1/\epsilon)$, where ϵ is the price elasticity of demand for *value added* at constant prices. If, instead, one wants to make use of estimates of price elasticities referring to output gross of material inputs, which we may label ϵ', then it can be shown (see Appendix A at the end of this chapter) that

$$\eta = 1 - \frac{1}{\epsilon'\,(1 - ma)}$$

where *ma* is the ratio of material inputs to the sum of these inputs and value added. As *ma* can be of the order of 0.5, this makes an important difference.

The level and mix of selling expenditures that are *socially* optimal is a matter of considerable importance, and one that I can touch on only briefly here. Clearly, there are some expenditures which it is both privately and socially optimal for the firm to incur, including some advertising and some transportation costs. To leave the customer to search out the producer and take delivery of his goods at the point of production could be a very inefficient system of distribution. Likewise, to economize in selling staff and outlets by allowing customers to queue may be socially inefficient. On the other hand, there are well-known examples of advertising and other selling costs which serve mainly to counteract the impact of the similar expenditure of rivals without conferring a commensurate benefit on customers.

If demand were highly elastic with respect to price, the firm could be relied upon to incur only those costs of transport or selling that were socially optimal. It would incur them only if that gave it a cost advantage *vis-à-vis* other firms in satisfying its customers. In imperfect markets, however, the firm will incur costs with a view to their effects on prices, no longer outside its control. It may also seek to deter entry by investing in excess capacity or excess R&D, and in this way protect product prices from being undercut. This may give it an advantage over other firms, but at their expense rather than to the advantage of the customer—a zero-sum game. The social rate of return on some investments could then be zero or negative, although privately profitable. The moral seems to be that price information should be improved, freedom of entry preserved, and competition encouraged.[15]

9.5 Broadening the analysis of selling costs and imperfect markets

Thus far I have assumed that increases in the rate of growth of a firm's output which exceed the rate at which its demand curve shifts to the right can be obtained only by continually lowering the prices of its products or by continually increasing the ratio of selling costs to output. This implies that, if the firm is to achieve steady growth, it must be at the rate determined by the rate of shift of the demand curve for its products. To take a limiting case, in a static economy no firm, on these assumptions, could apparently achieve steady positive growth.

All this is unsatisfactory. It is unrealistic to assume that firms are confined to the production of a fixed set of products, and a firm that is hell-bent on growth will switch from those for which demand is growing slowly to those for which it is growing fast. Even within a given set of products, a firm can switch from slower to faster growing markets for those products. Even if there is a static economy, so that demand is not growing for any product and there are no faster growing markets to be found, the individual firm can still grow by taking over the investment opportunities of its supine competitors.[16] Finally, a firm can expand the value of its output by improving its quality or by introducing new products.

---

[15] For a recent discussion of different forms of competition and of competition policy, see the contributions by Mayer, Vickers, Hay, Sharpe, and Yarrow in Mayer *et al.* (1985).

[16] An individual firm can also grow by taking over, or merging with, existing firms. In what follows I ignore this, as it does not *directly* lead to any growth in the whole economy, which is our primary interest. It would also lead us too far afield.

These four possibilities are all covered by the term *diversification*, and are further discussed below. They provide the first route by which a firm that wants to grow can escape from the tyranny of the growth rate set in the rest of the economy. Two other escape routes will also be discussed. Investment may be used to shift the demand curve for the firm's existing products faster to the right. These are the capital selling costs already referred to. Finally, there is the possibility that the rate of growth of demand for the firm's existing products may depend upon the *level* of prices charged, rather than their rate of change.

9.6 Diversification

Consideration of a static economy brings out the issues most sharply. In such an economy, each firm is still confronted by investment opportunities. There are still improvements in economic arrangements which could be made, and which would cost something. What needs explanation is why no changes occur, and some discussion of this, in a historical context, is given in Section 10.8 below. Here let us assume for simplicity that firms' rates of discount, α, are so high that no changes seem worth while. Investment and saving are accordingly zero, and I also assume that there is zero growth in the labour force. So nothing changes.

Now suppose that one firm chooses to adopt a lower discount rate. Some of its previously rejected investment opportunities will now seem worth while, and when they have been undertaken the level of output in the whole economy will be a little higher and the firm a little bigger. If the firm has merely increased the output of the products it was already producing, their prices will be lower and/or the ratio of selling costs to output higher, and so further expansion of their output will appear less attractive. It might seem, then, that eventually the firm's growth, and so that of the economy, must grind to a halt. However, the firm's expansion will have changed the investment opportunities confronting other firms, and some of these might now have become sufficiently attractive for them to be undertaken, even at the high rate of discount used by those firms. Even if this is not the case, our original firm could decide to undertake some of the investments that other firms are rejecting. It may not be quite so well placed to do this, because it has not the special expertise or market position that the other firms have. Nevertheless, if its discount rate is appreciably lower, it may still be worth its while to take the investments over.

In principle, our original firm could undertake, more gradually and slowly, all the investments that would otherwise have been undertaken by other firms had they had lower discount rates and had the whole economy grown as a result. A similar growth process could occur (albeit much more slowly), with similar growth in incomes and outputs, the difference being that all, or most, of the investments would be undertaken by a single firm, which would thus enlarge its share of the output of the whole economy. However, since it would be a *growing* economy, there is no reason to expect that the prices of the firm's products would have to fall continually. With incomes growing as well as output, demand would grow with supply. The growing firm would not need to capture the markets of other firms, only the *increments* in demand which those other firms would be unable to supply because of their failure to invest. Admittedly, the growth of the economy would be much slower and less efficient if it occurred in this way, and the rate of return on the growing firm's investments might be low. This would be due to its lack of expertise, etc., as already mentioned. However, some limits to inefficiency would be set by the fact that other firms would be inclined to invest if the price of a particular product rose markedly because the growing firm was especially inefficient at supplying it.

One set of prices that would be continually bid up would be real wages. This would be the natural outcome of a static labour force and a growing demand for labour by our growing firm. This rise in real wages would squeeze the profits of static firms, and they would have to make provisions for depreciation in their accounts which would have been unnecessary had the economy remained static. This, in turn, might result in some defensive gross investment which matched the depreciation provisions, although such investment could be justified in present-value terms only if its rates of return exceeded the discount rate.

I do not wish to suggest that this example of growth in a previously static economy is particularly realistic. All I claim is that it does show how a particular firm can grow faster than the rate of shift of the demand for its products without its having to force down prices or increase the ratio of selling costs to output *indefinitely*. The essential requirement is that the firm should be prepared to accept a lower rate of return on its investment—a *lower* level, not a *continually lowering* level. One can generalize this by hypothesizing a relation between the rate of return and the rate of investment. A faster rate of investment requires a lower marginal rate of return. Hence for the individual firm that wants to diversify in imperfect markets, ϱ diminishes as σ increases. Further analysis of this case could then proceed along similar lines to that of our analysis of 'physical' diminishing returns for the competitive firm. (See the appendix to Chapter 7.)

An efficient firm will ensure that the marginal rate of return on investment in diversification is the same as the marginal rate of return on undiversified production, as set out in equation (9.5). The foregoing suggest a relatively simple way of incorporating 'market' diminishing returns into the model. Let us subdivide the firm into two parts, which we may call, not very accurately but briefly, the old and the new. The old part produces the existing products of the firm (albeit in ways that are being continually changed as investment takes place) and behaves according to the equations in Section 9.4. This part of the firm provides a substantial share of the markets it serves. If it is producing under conditions of steady growth, it must be increasing output only so fast as the demand for its products shifts rightwards, so that its prices are constant.

The new part of the firm, by contrast, is a newcomer to the markets it serves. I assume that it can expand sales as fast as it likes at prices determined by the market, which the firm takes as given. The new part of the firm is subject to diminishing returns to the rate of investment since it has to launch into products and markets in which it has less and less expertise. Its behaviour can therefore be described by the equations in Chapter 8, but with diminishing returns to the rate of investment, as in the appendix to Chapter 7.

The two parts of the firm are linked together by the requirement that the marginal return to investment in each part must be the same. That marginal return must also satisfy the utility-maximizing requirement that $r = \alpha + \beta (g - g_N)$, where g is now the rate of growth of the take-out from both parts of the firm put together.

Let us now consider the effect of changes in the rate of growth in the whole economy on investment and growth in our two-part firm. A low rate of growth in the whole economy, or a low income elasticity of demand for the firm's products, will reduce the rate of growth, the share of investment, and the rate of return in the old part of the firm. This will make the firm invest more in its new part, but will drive down the rate of return there as well because of diminishing returns as the firm invades markets that are less and less suited to it. We reach the conclusion, therefore, that a high rate of growth of demand for the firm's products will encourage it to invest more (the accelerator effect), but that the firm is not tied by iron bands to the rate of growth of demand. A firm with access to cheap capital, and so with a low rate of discount, will grow fast even if the rate of growth of demand is low —even, in the limiting case, in an otherwise static economy. Likewise, a firm endowed with high 'animal spirits', whose management values the power and prestige that comes from greater size, may sacrifice the value of its shareholders' capital to some extent in order to grow faster, thereby acting as a valuable locomotive for others. We return to this case later in this chapter; and further remarks on the accelerator and locomotive effects, and on the externality to investment which is implied by the existence of market diminishing returns, are to be found in Section 15.6 below.

In practice, there will often be a third part of the firm, which is engaged in producing and selling new products, or qualitatively improved products. For this part, demand is likely to be less than perfectly elastic, since the firm will have a temporary monopoly but the rate of growth of sales will depend chiefly on the firm's strategy. It may choose to expand output slowly while maintaining a high price so long as the monopoly persists; this will encourage substitute production by rivals. Alternatively, it may lower its price and expand its sales faster so as to acquire a dominant market position and discourage rivals.

The whole subject of competition in imperfect markets, through price-cutting, advertising, etc., innovation, or by other means, is both complex and fascinating, but cannot be pursued further here.[17]

9.7 Capital selling costs

Diversification requires the firm to produce new products, or to enter new markets, in order to grow. In this and the following section we consider ways in which demand for the firm's existing products in its existing markets can be increased so that a faster growth rate can be sustained.

It was earlier pointed out that there are some selling costs that are of a capital nature. An advertising campaign, or capital expenditure on new selling outlets, may cause a once-for-all shift to the right of the demand curve for the firm's products. This is, in fact, the only means that Solow (1971) assumed was open to the firm to procure a faster growth of demand in his analysis of the implications of different objectives that a firm might have. In fact, he assumed that the larger the fraction of its sales revenue which the firm devoted to investment in sales promotion, the faster would demand at constant prices grow. He also assumed that there were diminishing returns to this type of investment, so that successive equal increments in the fraction resulted in smaller and smaller increments in the rate of growth of demand. Promotion expenditure could be regarded as purchasing a stock of 'goodwill', and the level of demand at a given price depended on the size of this stock.

Capital selling costs are similar to the costs of diversification. A higher rate of investment by the firm, including these selling costs as a form of investment, enables the firm to grow faster, and there are probably diminishing returns to the rate of investment. As before, the marginal rate of return on this form of investment should be equalized with that on other forms. Consequently, equation (9.5) should still give us the firm's marginal rate of return.

9.8 The level of prices as a determinant of the rate of growth of demand

The orthodox theory of monopolistic competition provides the firm with a downward-sloping demand curve. At given prices, the rate of growth of

---

[17] For an original discussion of diversification, see Marris (1964, ch. 4). For a survey and analysis of 'Schumpeterian competition' through innovation, see Kamien and Schwartz (1982). See also Hay and Morris (1979, 289–99) for discussion and further references, and Mayer *et al.* (1985).

demand depends on the rate at which this demand curve shifts to the right. It is not generally held that this rate of shift of the demand curve itself depends on the level of prices set by the firm. However, there are some reasons for thinking that this could indeed be the case; as we shall see, some writers have taken that view, while others have denied it.

The earlier analysis showed that the rate of growth of *supply* from a firm, whether producing under competitive or monopolistic conditions, would depend on the *level* of prices it achieved. Now demand for one firm's products can be regarded as the difference between demand by consumers for it and its close substitutes *less* the supply of close substitutes by competitors. Even if total demand by consumers behaves in the orthodox way, net demand for a particular firm's products will grow more rapidly or more slowly, with the price level changed, if supply by its competitors grows more slowly or more rapidly. For this reason, the individual firm in monopolistic competition could find that the demand curve in Figure 9.2 was not vertical but negatively sloping. The rate of growth of demand for *its* products would depend on the level of prices it charged, because that level would influence the levels of prices charged by its competitors and so the rates of growth of their competing supplies.

A rather similar argument could be applied to oligopoly. Let us assume that a group of producers of a particular product either follow one of their number as price-leader or, by formal or informal means, act collusively in setting prices. The theory of the entry-preventing price has been put forward to explain how their prices will then be determined (see Sylos-Labini 1962; Modigliani 1958). They will attempt to set prices as near to the profit-maximizing point for a monopoly as is consistent with deterring entry. The implication is that a higher price level would lead to entry and so to a declining share of the market for the existing firms. Some have argued that it is more realistic to suppose not that entry is altogether prevented, but that the price is set so as to optimize the rate of entry so far as the existing firms (or the price-leader) are concerned (see Hay and Morris 1979, ch. 6, and the references there given).

Thus far we have distinguished total demand for a product, or group of similar products, from demand for the product produced by a particular firm. One might argue that such a distinction is invalid in a world of differentiated products. All products have substitutes, and every firm's products are unique in some respects. If the rate of growth of particular firms' supplies depends on the levels of prices they achieve, then it must follow that the rate of growth of demand for any particular product, and in general for any group of products, depends also on the level of prices at which they are sold.

This argument is very general. Both it and the preceding one are subject to the qualification that one cannot assume that different exponential growth rates will remain constant except as an approximation. This warning is similar to that given earlier. Differences in exponential growth rates result in changes which inevitably react back on the growth rates themselves.

Two final points may be made. First, if price levels do affect rates of growth of demand for any of the reasons given above, the same is likely to be true of current selling costs. Thus, for example, a higher ratio of selling costs by firm A is likely to force firms B, C, etc., to raise their ratios somewhat, and this, just like a price cut, will reduce their profitability and so their rates of growth, which in turn will increase the rate of growth of demand for A's products. Second, it is noteworthy that Solow was prepared to assume that (capital) selling costs could shift the firm's demand curve to the right at a greater or lesser speed, but was not prepared to assume that a price cut could do the same, except temporarily.[18]

The role of price levels as a determinant of rates of growth of demand is controversial. The main question is whether a relationship of the kind postulated is a useful approximation, and that is an essentially empirical matter requiring further research.

9.9 Borrowing and lending: introduction

Thus far I have assumed that the firm is entirely self-financed and, furthermore, that the firm's owners only invest in the firm. While this is a useful beginning, and also gives insights into the equilibrium for a whole closed economy (which cannot borrow from or lend to anyone else), it is inadequate. In this section I push the analysis a little further, but it remains far short of dealing with the complexities of real-life capital markets. In order to keep it simple, I confine attention to three possibilities. In the first, and simplest, I assume that the owners of the firm have access to a perfect capital market from which they can borrow, or to which they can lend, at a real rate of interest i. In principle, the determinants of that rate of interest can be analysed in the way already described for the whole of a closed economy. Now, however, I wish to consider the behaviour of a small part of that economy in these circumstances. This small part could be an individual firm or even a small country in the world capital market. In this alternative I

---

[18] 'This assumption has the peculiarity that spending a certain fraction of sales revenue on promotion generates a certain rate of growth of demand, while "spending" a certain fraction of sales revenue on price reduction generates merely a once-for-all increase in quantity demanded. . . . I suppose one could argue that the level of price affects the rate of shift of demand, by controlling the rate of penetration of new markets. Something like that does happen temporarily. But as a steady-state relation, it strikes me as absurd' Solow (1971, 321). While one must agree with the last sentence of this quotation interpreted strictly, it is unfortunately true that *anything* that leads to differential growth rates becomes ultimately absurd in a steady state. If one regards the steady state as merely a simplifying assumption which may yield reasonable approximations for periods that are long enough to be useful, it is no longer obviously absurd.

am really regarding the firm (or country) as one among many possible outlets for savers' funds. In the second alternative, by contrast, I retain my original assumption that the firm (or country) is the principal outlet, but now assume that the owners of the firm (investors in the country) can borrow at a rising cost of funds. The third alternative takes us nearest to theories of 'managerial capitalism' (Marris 1964). In this I assume, as in the first alternative, that the firm is only one among many outlets for savers' funds. However, I no longer assume that capital markets are perfect: instead, as in the second alternative, the firm can obtain funds only at a rising cost.

9.10 A perfect capital market

To maintain simplicity, no distinction is drawn between different types of creditor of the firm or different types of credit instrument. The undifferentiated creditors can earn a real rate of return i, assumed to be constant, on their money elsewhere, and so they require that the firm is operated so as to make at least the same return on its investments. If the firm is selling in a perfect market, there must be diminishing returns to the rate of investment, since otherwise there could be no stable equilibrium. The firm could increase its rate of return by investing at a faster rate, and there would be no limit to its rate of growth. In what follows, I shall ignore this possibility and consider only firms selling in imperfect markets. Such firms will have diminishing returns to investment in diversification and in capital selling costs, but the marginal rates of return there should be equal to the marginal rates of return in what we may call their main enterprises, which I assume is given by equation (9.5) (i.e. without diminishing returns, which are considered later).

What difference does the existence of borrowing in a perfect capital market make to the supply curve in Figure 9.2? The upward slope of that curve, it will be recalled, is due to the need to raise the price so as to increase the rate of return sufficiently to match the rise in the required rate of return. The latter is given by $r_r = \alpha + \beta (g - g_N)$, so that, when g increases, r_r increases by β times as much. Now, however, I am assuming that there is no increase in the required rate of return. All the finance the firm requires can be obtained at i. Since the rate of return achieved would increase if the price remained constant, the price must actually *fall* if the achieved rate of return is to remain equal to i. It then appears that the supply curve must be downward-sloping.

A downward-sloping supply curve is quite consistent with stability so long as the demand curve is vertical, as in Figure 9.2, and even if it has a negative slope (as Section 9.8 suggested it might), provided that the negative slope is steeper than that of the supply curve.

In our discussion of the competitive firm (Section 9.2), we saw that the existence of physical diminishing returns to the rate of investment would steepen the upward-sloping supply curve. The same is true of the firm selling in imperfect markets. Hence, if such a firm is subject to physical diminishing returns in its main enterprise, its supply curve will slope down less steeply; or it could be horizontal or upward-sloping, depending on how sharply returns diminish (i.e. depending on the size of γ).

9.11 An imperfect capital market

Let us now revert to the assumption that the firm's owners regard it as the principal outlet for their savings (which we reconsider later), but assume that they can borrow at a rising cost. The amount that they can borrow at a given marginal cost of funds depends on how much of their own savings they are prepared to invest. Lenders feel more secure the greater is the 'cover' for their interest payments, and in a steady state this 'cover' will depend on the proportion of the firm's total investment that is self-financed. If F is the rate at which the firm is borrowing and S is its rate of investment, then I assume that the marginal cost of funds rises with $f = F/S$. In fact, I assume a linear relation

$$i_m = i_0 + af. \tag{9.7}$$

It is intuitively obvious that the firm will equate the marginal rate of return on its investment to the owners, r, which is also their rate of discount, to the marginal cost of borrowing, i_m. Furthermore, the average cost of borrowing, i, will be midway between i_0 and i_m. Hence

$$i = i_0 + \frac{af}{2}.$$

Continuing with the assumption that the firm is selling in an imperfect market, but with no 'physical' diminishing returns to the rate of investment, the marginal rate of return on investment, r, to the firm's owners is increased by their ability to finance a fraction f of it at i, which is less than r (since $r = i_m$). In fact, as is shown in Appendix B to this chapter, r is now a weighted average of the previous rate of return given in (9.5) and i, with the latter being given a negative weight of f. Another way of expressing this is to say that the previous rate of return equals the 'cost of capital' to the firm, which is a weighted average of r (which the owners get) and i (which the creditors on average get), the weights being $(1 - f)$ and f, respectively. So

$$r = \frac{P(\eta q - \lambda l) - fi}{1 - f}. \tag{9.8}$$

Borrowing also affects the relation between μ and λ, by reducing the burden of saving on the firm's owners. As is shown in Appendix B,

$$\mu = \frac{\lambda}{\eta - s + sf\{1 - (i/r)\}} . \tag{9.9}$$

It can readily be seen that, if $f = 0$, these formulae are the same as (9.5) and (9.6), as they would be too if $i = r$. For given values of the other variables and parameters, borrowing clearly increases the rate of return, r. It also increases λ for given values of μ, η, and s.

The impact of borrowing on a firm's supply curve, as in Figure 9.2, is both to shift it downwards and to make it slope upwards less steeply or downwards more steeply. This can be seen as follows. First, consider a firm that is in equilibrium with $r > i_0$ but with a so large that borrowing is negligible. Contrast such a firm with another exactly similar one in which a is so small that $r \simeq i_0$. The second firm approximates to one borrowing in a perfect capital market. We saw in the preceding section that, while the first firm will have an upward-sloping supply curve, the second will have a downward-sloping one, so a decrease in a clearly reduces the upward, or increases the downward, slope. It is also clear that the second firm's supply curve must be lower at each value of g when the firm is borrowing. Borrowing must then raise the rate of return achieved for any given value of g and P. Hence, if the firm's achieved rate of return equals its required rate of return at some g and P without borrowing, it will do so at a lower P if it can borrow.

Lowering the cost of borrowing, through a fall in i_0 for example, will lower the firm's supply curve. This will not increase the firm's rate of growth in the circumstances postulated, since there is a vertical demand curve. The whole effect will show up as a fall in P. However, if we allow for the possibility of diversification, and so for 'physical' diminishing returns to the rate of investment, the rate of growth will increase. The cost of borrowing could be lowered for a number of different reasons, such as opening up a closed economy to capital imports from abroad, or less competition for funds by other borrowers, including the government. There could also be a reduction in the costs of financial intermediaries, whether because of greater efficiency or keener competition among them. The costs of borrowing may be high for small firms, since there are economies of scale in negotiating and monitoring loans. This may be especially important in developing countries, and may give rise to a virtuous circle whereby growth brings down the cost of borrowing, which encourages investment and so faster growth.[19]

All this only applies to the circumstances in which the firm actually borrows, so that $i_0 < r$. A firm could be in a situation in which its achieved rate of return was below i_0. Presumably there is some still lower rate of return, say i_l, at which the firm can lend. If r lies betwen these rates the firm neither borrows nor lends, and so the capital market is irrelevant to it. If r

[19] See Bottomley (1971, sec. 3) for an illuminating analysis.

sinks to i_l, presumably the firm will shut down, as its owners will prefer to lend their capital.

The above discussion limits firms to being either borrowers or lenders, or neither. In fact, many firms are both. All firms lend to *some* extent, whether by extending credit to customers or by holding liquid assets such as cash or bank deposits. Such loans earn a low or even zero direct financial return, but bring other benefits to the firm which could be regarded as part of their true return. One could seek to approximate this situation by regarding f in the preceding analysis as borrowing net of lending which will generally mean that f is quite small, and could even be negative.

Thus, for example, on average in the ten years ending in 1973, industrial and commercial companies in the UK apparently financed only some 5 per cent of their gross investment in fixed assets and in stocks and work in progress (before deducting stock appreciation) by *net* borrowing through financial assets, the rest being financed by their own gross saving.[20] Furthermore, issues of ordinary shares in the UK equalled about $3\frac{1}{2}$ per cent of gross investment, and that is finance provided by owners which is included in the above-mentioned figure of 5 per cent.

Because of intra-company investment flows across the boundary of the UK, and items unidentified in the accounts, one cannot be precise about the value of f for companies in the UK in this period, but it can be safely said that its average value was very small.[21]

One factor limiting recourse by firms to external borrowing is the risk of becoming highly geared. The larger the share of fixed interest charges in trading profits, the greater will tend to be the fluctuations in the residual accruing to owners. Not only may owners dislike this, but lenders also will feel less secure. This may result in a rising actual cost of borrowing, as in equation (9.7), but it is also possible that the *actual* cost may not rise and rationing of funds may be used instead. 'Rationing' loans by charging a higher interest rate may be imprudent, and both lenders and borrowers may prefer to be guided by conventional gearing ratios.[22]

[20] Apart from a small amount of capital transfers. See CSO (1974, Table 75).

[21] See also Singh and Whittington with Burley (1968, 43, 44). In a sample of over 400 quoted companies in the UK in four manufacturing industries, the average ratio of retained profits (after tax) to the increase in the book values of {fixed assets + current assets − current liabilities}, which they call 'internal finance of growth', was calculated for two periods, 1948–54 and 1954–60. Taking all four industries together, in about 40 per cent of the companies considered this ratio was exactly 100 per cent, and for about half the companies it was 100 per cent or more. The mean values were 84 and 77 per cent for the two periods. It should be noted that retained profits and assets are here measured net of depreciation allowances, whereas the figures cited in the text refer to the finance of investment gross of depreciation. Had depreciation been included in Singh and Whittington's mean ratios, they would have been substantially closer to 100 per cent.

[22] Modigliani and Miller (1958) argue that the average cost of capital to a firm is independent of its gearing ratio, but their argument rests on the assumption of a perfect capital

9.12 The firm's objectives and the managerially controlled firm

Thus far, I have assumed that firms pursue only one objective, which is the maximization of the present value of 'take-out'. Firms have been controlled by owners who use them as the principal outlet for their savings, apart from those firms operating in a perfect capital market where control could be by managers.

All this may be regarded as unrealistic. The divorce of ownership from control, the managerially controlled firm, and the pursuit by management of other objectives such as size, power, status, security, a quiet life, a large staff, and tax-free fringe benefits are, some would say, common features of contemporary capitalism.[23] Any study of growth that purports to be about the real world must be able to accommodate these phenomena. In this section, therefore, I address myself to the following questions: How important are managerially controlled firms? Is the maximization of the present value of the firm an important objective for such firms or, indeed, for owner-controlled firms? What discretion have firms to pursue other objectives, and how far are they constrained by market forces to maximize present values? What is the evidence that different forms of ownership result in different behaviour by firms? And, finally, what does it all add up to in terms of the model? Which equations need modification, and how?

Nyman and Silberston (1978), along with other writers, have challenged the view that the typical large modern corporation is run by managers with little proprietary interest in the firm. They criticize previous studies for taking too simple-minded a view of 'control' as depending on the proportion of the equity owned by one or a small number of individuals, for treating control by another company as not being ownership control, and for ignoring control by share-pyramiding and interlocking directorates. Their own main criterion for owner control is the power of an identifiable group of proprietary interests (which could be another company, a family, an individual, or small group of individuals especially with interlocking directorships) to change senior management. Their own classification of the top 250 companies in the UK in 1975/6, as ranked by either net assets or sales, suggested that over half were owner-controlled.[24]

Furthermore, they argued that the available evidence, though weak, suggested that this proportion was increasing rather than declining,

market and has generated considerable controversy, which is beyond the scope of the present work. See, however, p. 275 below for some further discussion.

[23] See, for example, Galbraith (1952, 1967); Baumol (1959); Williamson (1967, 1970); and Marris (1964).

[24] They estimated that 56% were owner-controlled, but thought this an underestimate for several reasons.

especially as a result of increasing control by financial institutions. They also stressed the wide variety of types of ownership control.

Another study that casts doubt on the idea that managerially controlled firms are the dominant type is that of Lawriwsky (1984). Of 226 Australian firms examined, only 79 were classified as managerially controlled, 71 were controlled by another company, and the remaining 76 were controlled by individual shareholders (mostly minority shareholders). Lawriwsky's study covered small- and medium-sized as well as large companies, which may partly explain why his proportion of managerially controlled firms is smaller than Nyman and Silberston's, which referred to the largest firms.

Even within managerially controlled firms, it is possible to reward management through stock options and other profit-related schemes, so that their incentive to maximize profits is strengthened. Such systems are apparently more common in the USA than in the UK and Australia (see Lawriwsky 1984, 80), and there have been several studies of their extent and of how top executives' earnings are affected by company performance. The results are disputed, and no attempt is made to summarize the debate here. Some writers view such schemes as providing an important part of top managers' remuneration and as being much influenced by profitability, but others take the view that they are unimportant, or are geared to sales rather than profitability.[25]

There is also the question of whether such incentives have a noticeable effect on firms' performance. Lawriwsky found that, for his sample of Australian firms, the use of bonuses was uncommon and that, where they were used, they represented only a small fraction of executives' salaries. He examined the relationship between director's shareholdings and firms' performances as measured by rates of return and growth of assets and found that it was positive but curvilinear. In other words, an increase in directors' (absolute) shareholdings tended to be accompanied by (and, he argued, to cause) an increase in the rate of return (or growth), but to a diminishing extent as shareholders got bigger. This relationship was quite strong for both managerially controlled and owner-controlled firms, but was weak for company-controlled ones.

These findings suggest two further points. First there is an implication that firms have some discretion about how profitable they will be. They are not *completely* constrained by market forces. Second, owner-controlled as well as managerially controlled firms may be operating below maximum profitability.

Let us take these points in reverse order. If we were considering the behaviour of firms that were each controlled and owned by one person, it would be difficult to distinguish between those that were trying to maximize

---

[25] For summaries of the debate with references, see Lawriwsky (1984, ch. 4) and Hay and Morris (1979, ch. 8).

the present value of take-out and those that were trying to maximize a more complex utility function, which included for example 'power' or 'achievement', or, more mundanely, the chairman's salary or expenses. If firm A experiences faster growth and a lower rate of return than firm B, is that because the owners of firm A give more weight to 'power' and less to financial wealth than those of B, or is it because they have lower values of α or β in our equation for their supply of funds? If chairman A drives a Rolls Royce and chairman B a Rover, we may want to include some of both their firms' expenditures on their cars as 'take-out', but this difference does not tell us anything clear about a difference in their objectives so far as maximizing its present value is concerned. It merely shows that their consumer preferences differ. It is therefore difficult to challenge the simple maximization model in these cases.

However, in many owner-controlled firms, the individual or group that controls it will not own all, or even a majority, of the shares. The owner/controller may take at least as much pride in the firm's size, rate of growth, the sophistication of its technology and equipment, or the contentment of its work-force as his opposite number in a managerially controlled firm. For the other shareholders, however, these may all be very secondary considerations, and maximization of present value may be their chief concern. Hence there may not really be a clear line to be drawn between owner-controlled and managerially controlled firms. In both, there may be a conflict of interest between those who control the firm and those who own some or most of it.

Let us now revert to the question of how much discretion managers have to pursue objectives other than present-value maximization. Firms are constrained by competition in their product markets, in their labour markets, and in capital markets. Some have apparently taken the view that these constraints are pretty tight. There is a process of natural selection at work which ensures that, regardless of their managers' objectives, only those firms that are most profitable survive. The most profitable firms also grow the fastest, and so come to supply most of demand, so that unprofitable firms can be safely neglected as being relatively unimportant.[26] While there is undoubtedly some truth in these propositions, the question still remains as to how ruthless the selection process is, how tight the constraints.

Some evidence in favour of the view that there is discretion is provided by the spread in rates of return earned by different firms even when averaged over periods as long as twelve years. Another indicator which points in the same direction is the valuation ratio, which is the ratio of the stock market

---

[26] '. . . . unless the behaviour of businessmen in some way or other approximated behaviour consistent with the maximization of returns, it seems unlikely that they would remain in business for long' (Friedman 1953, 22).

value of the firm to the net book value of the equity. These ratios also vary widely from firm to firm.[27] Unfortunately, neither rates of return nor valuation ratios can be regarded as wholly reliable indicators. Inflation leads to varying discrepancies between book values and replacement cost values of assets, depending on their lengths of life. Depreciation conventions also differ between firms, as do the methods used to value inventories. Stock market values can be very volatile.

To some extent, therefore, variations in rates of return and valuation ratios are due to measurement errors as well as to temporary economic factors. However, the view that managers have considerable discretion to pursue objectives other than present value maximization is strengthened if one can *explain* differences in profitability or valuation by differences in ownership or management. One piece of evidence of this kind has already been cited—differences in profitability explicable in terms of differences in directors' shareholdings. There are others.

Empirical work on the differences in performance between owner-controlled and managerially controlled firms has been surveyed by Hay and Morris (1979, ch. 8) and Lawriwsky (1984). Several studies showed little difference in rates of return and growth rates, but some are open to Nyman and Silberston's criticism that insufficient attention has been paid to the different ways in which proprietary interests can exercise control without necessarily owning a large proportion of the shares of a particular firm. Lawriwsky also points out that differences in performance can be due to differences in size and monopoly power as well as to differences in directors' shareholdings, and that allowance should be made for all of these

[27] See Singh and Whittington, with Burley (1968) for evidence regarding both rates of return and valuation ratios in the UK. Rates of return are measured as ratios of {trading profits + investment + other income net of depreciation + charges for *current* liabilities (e.g. bank interest) but including long-term interest and payments to minority interest in subsidiaries} to net assets, i.e. the book values of total fixed assets + current assets − current liabilities. Rates of return both pre-tax and post-tax are given, but in the latter case it is the net of tax return on equity assets (i.e. net assets less debentures, minority interest, and preference capital). These rates of return were averaged for two periods, each of six years, 1948–54 and 1954–60, as well as for both periods taken together. Taking the pre-tax return for 1948–60, the mean for 364 companies in the sample was 18.5% p.a. and the standard deviation, 7.0% p.a. The valuation ratio was the ratio of the stock market value of a firm's ordinary shares to the book value of the equity. The aim was to calculate the average of this ratio for 1954 and also for 1960, and the method used to average fluctuations in share prices was to take the mid-point of high and low values for each year (for details see the source, pp. 222–5). For 1954 the mean value of the valuation ratio for 402 companies was 0.94 and standard deviation, 0.48. For 1960, for 381 companies, the corresponding figures were 1.26 and 0.74. Another study which gives rates of return, based on ratios of profits to book values of net assets, is Lawriwsky (1984). These are for about 200 Australian quoted companies over the years 1965–6 to 1974–5 which are classified into three different types of control: by owners, by management, and by another company. For 145 small- and medium-sized firms the standard deviation of the return on net assets was between a third and a half of the mean return, but for 49 large firms the standard deviation was much lower, being between a fifth and a quarter of the mean return (Lawriwsky 1984, 264, 266).

in any attempt to estimate differences arising from control types. In his own study of Australian firms, Lawriwsky found that, among small- and medium-sized firms, managerially controlled firms earned higher rates of return, grew faster, and had higher valuation ratios and higher retention ratios than owner-controlled firms of comparable size. By contrast, these differences were generally reversed for large firms.[28] His explanation for this is that the smaller managerially controlled firms are under greater threat from take-over bids than are large managerially controlled firms, and that is why the former have such a good average performance. Owner-controlled firms, whether small or large, are difficult to take over. Thus, while there is an appreciable fall-off in performance in the larger as compared with the smaller managerially controlled firms, as they escape from the constraint of the 'market for corporate control', there is little difference in performance between larger and smaller owner-controlled firms.[29] As Lawriwsky points out, there is no doubt that firms want to survive, but profitability is not the only means to that end. Sheer size can help to ensure survival (although to a decreasing extent, it seems, in recent years), and so can concentrated ownership.[30]

I conclude, therefore, that, although managerially controlled firms may not be as dominant a form of organization as some have taken for granted, and although their top executives may sometimes be given profit-related incentives of various kinds, it is still true that they produce a large part of output and that in many such firms, at least in the UK and Australia and possibly in continental Europe as well, profit-related incentives are not important. Furthermore, as we have just seen, there is evidence that some of these firms (especially the large ones) have discretion to pursue other objectives than the maximization of present value. These other objectives may also be pursued by some owner-controlled firms in conflict with the interests of other shareholders, who may, in fact, collectively own a majority of the shares, although they are not sufficiently well organized to exercise control. The question then arises as to whether we need to modify the earlier models substantially to accommodate such firms.

[28] Except for the valuation ratio. Lawriwsky's comparisons referred only to rates of return, growth of assets, and retention ratios for firms of comparable sizes (1984, 202, 211). However, he also gives average valuation ratios on p. 171, which are referred to above. For large firms the averages differed very little as between managerially and owner-controlled firms.

[29] Another factor to which Lawriwsky draws attention is the extent to which different firms finance investment from external sources. Smaller managerially controlled firms that want to grow fast make greater use of the capital market as a source of funds than smaller owner-controlled firms, many of whom avoid it altogether so as to retain control. This exposes the managerially controlled firms to more external 'discipline'. For larger firms, access to the capital market is much easier since institutional investors, and others, prefer the greater liquidity and security provided by shares in larger firms. There is therefore less 'discipline' (Lawriwsky 1984, 162-4, 204).

[30] See Lawriwsky (1984, 222), who also cites Singh (1971) and Kuehn (1975).

Various 'managerial' and 'behavioural' theories of the firm have been put forward, for example by Marris (1964), Williamson (1967, 1970), and Cyert and March (1963). Marris hypothesized that managers would seek to maximize the growth rate (of assets) of their firms subject to constraints set by the capital market. Too much growth could be dangerous since it might depress the rate of return or reduce the ratio of dividends to earnings and so depress the firm's share price, thus exposing it to the threat of a take-over bid. We further discuss some aspects of Marris's theory of the supply of finance below. The behavioural theories are not considered here. As Hay and Morris point out, such theories face theoretical, empirical, and methodological difficulties, and 'the behavioural approach has not entered the main stream of economic study of the firm' (Hay and Morris 1979, 251). I am in no position to inaugurate that entry.

Solow compared Marris's and Williamson's theories with the orthodox theory that firms seek to maximize the present value of take-out. After drawing attention to certain difficulties, he concluded that:

growth-orientated and profit-orientated firms would respond in qualitatively similar ways to such stimuli as changes in factor prices, discount rate, and excise and profit taxes. On the evidence only of its behaviour in that kind of situation, an observer would find it hard to distinguish one kind of firm from another. But he might also find it unnecessary if his main object was to predict or to control the firm's behaviour. (Solow 1971, 341–2).

While Solow's conclusions are encouraging, one must still question whether the earlier model needs revision in some respects. This question can, in turn, be subdivided into two parts, referring to each of the two equations in the model which reflect management decisions. The first of these is the decision about how much to invest, which is governed by the equation $r = \alpha + \beta (g - g_N)$, using the Ramsey approach. The second is the decision about how labour-intensive any investment shall be, which is governed by equation (9.9) (or its earlier variants). We consider each in turn.

If the people who control the firm do not use it as the outlet for most of their savings, then the justification for the Ramsey approach disappears. This applies as much to firms that are controlled by another company as to firms that are management-controlled, assuming that, for the controlling company, its share of the controlled company is only a minor part of its total assets, as will usually be the case. This considerably reduces the applicability of the Ramsey approach. Despite this, the form of the equation governing the supply of funds to both management-controlled and company-controlled firms may be just the same as with the Ramsey approach. There are several reasons why this should be so, and some empirical support for them as well.

An equation (which is also an accounting identity, if the terms are suitably defined) that provides a useful starting point for the discussion is as follows:

or
$$\left. \begin{array}{l} g = u(r_a - if') + f'g \\ r_a = \dfrac{g(1 - f')}{u} + if' \end{array} \right\} \qquad (9.10)$$

where u is the fraction of profits net of both interest payments and depreciation which is ploughed back (undistributed); r_a is the *average* rate of return, and so equals $P(q - \lambda l)$; i is the *average* rate of interest paid on borrowings; and f' is the fraction of investment net of depreciation which is financed by new borrowing. Taxation is neglected. This equation is virtually the same as Marris's corresponding equations (see Marris 1964, 9, 206). It holds only in steady growth, and it is not difficult to see its logic.

The first version of the equation says that the rate of growth of the net assets of the firm, which is also the rate of growth of its output in steady growth, is composed of two parts. The first is financed by undistributed net profit belonging to equity shareholders. On each existing unit of net assets, the firm earns net profits of r_a, and pays out interest of if'. (Since f' is the ratio of borrowing to net investment, in steady growth it is also the ratio of accumulated debt to net assets.) Hence $r_a - if'$ are the net profits belonging to the shareholders, of which a fraction u is ploughed back. The rest of the growth of net assets is due to the growth of debt, and since in steady growth this must grow at the same rate as net assets, this provides $f'g$ per unit of net assets.

We have not allowed for new issues of ordinary shares so far, but, formally speaking, they can be regarded as a negative dividend. Ignoring taxation, one might think that it should make no difference to shareholders whether they subscribe to a rights issue of new shares or whether their dividend is reduced by the same amount. In practice, there are reasons for regarding these differently (including tax reasons), and we return to this matter below. For the present, we include new share issues in the first term, so that u could in principle be greater than 1.[31]

It is clear from the second form of (9.10) that, if f', u, and i are all constant, r_a must increase linearly with g. This conclusion can be expressed by saying that, if the firm cannot change its gearing or retention ratios, and if the interest rate on its borrowing is fixed, then the only way in which it can obtain more finance for faster growth is by earning a higher rate of return on its investments. In this simple case, therefore, the form of the equation governing the supply of funds is the same as $r = \alpha + \beta (g - g_N)$.

---

[31] However, u must be less than 1 in steady growth if shareholders are ever to receive any net benefit from the firm.

Furthermore, the coefficient of g in (9.10) could be very similar to β.[32] Equation (9.10) refers to the *average* rate of return, however, whereas r is the *marginal* rate of return.

In reality, firms can and do vary their gearing and retention ratios, and both ratios tend to be higher in faster growing firms (see Singh and Whittington 1968, 63–5), so we must allow for that. Let us consider, first, Marris's theory of the supply of finance. He argued that an increase in the gearing ratio, f', would generally benefit a firm since the interest rate on borrowing, i, would generally be below the average rate of return on investment, r_a. However, after some point, the risk of bankruptcy arising from a high gearing ratio would increase beyond an acceptable level. The firm would therefore push the ratio up to this maximum 'safe' level. Up to this point there would be no effect on the share price, and he also assumed that the interest rate would be unaffected (Marris 1964, 208).

Turning now to the retention ratio, Marris argued that, again beyond some point, an increase would tend to depress the share price for a variety of reasons. Given the information available to them, and given existing share prices, wealth-holders would hold existing shares in certain proportions in their portfolios, the shares representing claims to future expected streams of dividends. If a company wished to increase its proportion, by issuing new shares, or if it altered the expected stream by reducing present dividends in order to increase future dividends, then it must depress its share price in order to persuade wealth-holders to hold the extra shares, or to continue to hold the existing number with the altered dividend stream. Marris argued that the stock market would respond differently to an extra £1 of new issues and a £1 cut in the dividend (which we have merged in our u). By hypothesizing particular functional forms for the relation between the rate of discount applied by the market to a particular share, the rate of new share issues, and the 'true' retention ratio, Marris finally concluded that there would be an approximately linear relation between the average rate of return, r_a, the rate of growth, and the minimum safe valuation ratio (regarded here as a parameter) (Marris 1964, 220, eqn. 5.22). Once again, therefore, we end up with an approximately linear relation similar to the Ramsey approach.

Some of the steps in the above argument are open to attack. In two famous articles, Modigliani and Miller (1958, 1961) have shown that, under certain conditions, both the gearing ratio and the retention ratio should not affect the cost of capital to a firm, essentially because of arbitrage which can offset higher gearing or higher retention ratios by suitable sales or purchases of other fixed interest or equity securities. Thus, the mere fact

---

[32] If, for the sake of illustration, $f' = 0.1$ and $u = 0.6$, then the coefficient of g is 1.5, which is a reasonable estimate of β (see p. 231 above).

that a firm, in order to obtain more finance for investment, raises f' or u should not in itself require a rise in r_a. The supply of capital to a firm would then appear to be perfectly elastic at a cost depending on its risk class.

Modigliani and Miller's articles have provoked much controversy, which I will not attempt to summarize. Readers are referred to the invaluable survey by Hay and Morris (1979, ch. 10). They conclude that various types of market imperfection, the use of dividends as a signalling device,[33] shareholders' suspicion that managers are already retaining more profits than is in shareholders' interest, the threat of bankruptcy, and taxation are all possible reasons why Modigliani and Miller's conclusions may not hold. Although much empirical work has been attempted, it is not conclusive.

In view of this, it is desirable to retain as one possibility the perfectly elastic supply of funds case described in Section 9.10. However, it also seems desirable to allow for the possibility (and, in my own view, the probability) that firms are confronted by a rising cost of funds. This rising cost is at least one simple way of explaining a very widely observed phenomenon, namely, the tendency for faster growing firms to earn higher rates of return over quite long periods of time.[34] One must admit that this correlation between growth and rates of return could be interpreted as a disequilibrium phenomenon. A firm, for some extraneous reason, experiences a rise in its rate of return, and if it does not change its retention ratio or gearing ratio immediately in response, the rate of growth of its net assets must rise. Most of the studies referred to measure growth by the growth of net assets. Against this, however, it can be said that in some of the studies cited growth has been measured by index numbers of output or by value added,[35] and that some used averages extending over quite long periods of time. Hence, as a first approximation, I shall continue with a linear relation between the rate of return and the rate of growth of a firm. There are, however, two differences as compared with the Ramsey approach. First, the relation is between the *average* rate of return and the rate of growth, rather than between the *marginal* rate of return and the rate of growth. That may not make much odds if the marginal is close to the average return, but we discuss this further in Chapter 15. Second, the coefficient of the rate of growth (i.e. β in the Ramsey approach) is probably much smaller for most firms than the sort of magnitude one has in mind for β (i.e. perhaps around 2, and at any rate greater than 1). Precisely because firms have access to capital markets, and tend to increase the proportion of their investment that is externally financed as they invest more and grow rapidly, the supply of funds probably is much more elastic. As we have

[33] See further p. 413 below.

[34] See, e.g., Barna (1962), Weiss (1963), Parker (1964), George (1968), Kamerschen (1968), Singh and Whittington (1968), Radice (1971).

[35] Weiss (1963); Kamerschen (1968).

seen, even the possibility of an infinitely elastic supply (i.e zero β) seems worth considering, and a value for β of around 0.5 or even lower is suggested by some of the studies.[36]

We turn to the second of the two equations in the model which reflect managerial decisions, namely, equation (9.9) and its earlier variants, which governs the labour intensity of investment. Here there does not appear to be any body of previous theoretical or empirical work that is directly relevant. I therefore make only one point, which is taken up again in Chapter 15 where we consider some empirical data bearing on it.

As already remarked, several writers have taken the view that a managerially controlled firm may pursue the objective of size, or rate of growth, at the expense of profits, although the extent to which it will do so will depend on a variety of factors, such as the extent to which directors of the company own its shares, the existence of other profit-related incentives for management, the need or desire of the management to seek outside capital, and the threat of take-over bids, many of which factors will depend, in turn, on the size of the firm. Large firms may be freer to pursue non-profit objectives than small ones, and they account for a large part of total output. Nor are such non-profit objectives confined to managerially controlled firms, since owner-controlled firms can also pursue size and growth (etc.) at the expense of profitability to some extent. All this may result, then, in the observed share of wages, λ, being higher than would be the case if all firms were simple-mindedly seeking to maximize the present value of take-out as measured by the statistics on hand.

If, for example, managements employ staff in greater numbers or of higher qualifications than would be required on a strict calculation of profitability, this has an obvious effect in inflating λ. But the effect can be more subtle than that. A decision to go for a more labour-intensive form of investment implies choosing a faster rate of growth for a given volume of investment, and so a management that was prepared to sacrifice some profitability for faster growth would choose a bigger q and l than one maximizing the present value of take-out. It would be as if the firm valued every extra unit of output more highly than its marginal revenue. If, then, we rewrite equation (9.9) to allow for this, a simple way to do so is to add a shadow premium, say 'an' (for 'animal spirits'), to the term η, which is the

[36] Lawriwsky (1984, ch. 7) provides five equations in his complete model in which the rate of return on net assets is the dependent variable, and various independent variables as well as the growth rate of net assets explain it. His sample of over 200 firms is stratified both by size of firm and by type of control (owner, management, and company). The coefficients of the growth of net assets in these five equations range from 0.18 to 0.57, with the last being the most significant (t = 2.69 with 29 observations of large management-controlled firms). Marris (1964–5) gives five regression results in which the rate of return on net assets is the dependent variable and the growth of net assets is the only independent variable (as well as a constant). The coefficients on growth are all highly significant and range from 0.38 to 0.53.

marginal revenue of a unit of output net of selling costs. The equation then becomes

$$\mu = \frac{\lambda}{\eta + an - s + sf\{1 - (i/r)\}} \, . \tag{9.11}$$

Thus, for given μ, η, s, i, f, and r, the effect of this addition to the denominator is to require that λ should be greater. It offsets, to a greater or lesser extent, the opposite tendency, which results from market imperfections. In perfect markets with present value maximization, we would have $\eta = 1$ and $an = 0$. In imperfect markets with growth-oriented firms, we have $\eta < 1$ and $an > 0$, but if $\eta + an \approx 1$, the net result could be close to that of perfect markets. (See Baumol (1959, 77) for a similar suggestion.)

We may conclude the present chapter by discussing the supply of saving in the model of the whole economy in Chapter 15, since it is a natural extension of the idea underlying (9.11). Our concern is with the typical or representative firm. Such a firm is in reality an average of all firms, and all the problems of aggregation apply. I continue, as before, to neglect them, but want the typical firm to share some of the characteristics of managerially controlled firms in order that it shall be representative. In (9.11) the managerial element is introduced by allowing for a shadow premium on output. Consistent with that, the *same* shadow premium should influence the firm's decision on how much to invest. At one extreme, one could have an owner-controlled firm whose objective is the maximization of the present value of take-out; there would be no premium on output, and the marginal return on investment would equal the rate of discount of the firm's owners. If we now allow for some managerial control element, and some premium, the firm will (as Marris hypothesized) push for a faster rate of growth than its owners would consider optimal. The marginal rate of return on its investment will then fall below the owners' rate of discount, and the *extent* to which this happens *implies* a premium on output. The implicit premium can be found by comparing the actual marginal return with the owners' rate of discount, *the premium being whatever is required to bring the two into equality*.

To be more precise, let the actual marginal return be r and the shareholders' rate of discount be r_{sha}. Ignoring physical diminishing returns, but assuming imperfect product markets, we have

and

$$r = P(\eta q - \lambda l)$$

$$r_{sha} = \alpha + \beta (g - g_N)$$

where $(g - g_N)$ is now the typical shareholders' rate of growth of consumption per capita.

The implicit premium on output is then an, such that

$$r_{sha} = P\{(\eta + an) q - \lambda l\}. \tag{9.12}$$

So long as $an > 0$, we shall have $r_{sha} > r$. A *consistent* firm would, it seems to me, use the *same* premium on output, an, in (9.12) as in (9.11). The effect of this premium is to offset, to a greater or lesser degree, the anti-growth and anti-labour biases which would otherwise be the result of imperfect product markets. We return to this in Chapter 15, which provides estimates of η and an, and of the gap between r and r_{sha}. Chapter 15 also allows for taxation, and so refers to rates of return after tax.

Appendix A: Allowing for imperfect markets and material inputs

This appendix explains how equations (9.2) and (9.3) in the text are derived. Only the simplest form of market imperfection—a downward-sloping demand curve confronting the firm—is considered. No distinction is drawn between short- and long-run effects. Since steady growth is assumed throughout, this may not matter.

In working out the formulae for μ and r in Chapter 6 (p. 155) and Chapter 7 (p. 183), in each case we need to calculate the effect on take-out, C, of a small change δQ in output. Since perfect markets are assumed in both cases, the effect on take-out is simply $P\delta Q$. Where markets are imperfect, however, increasing output by δQ over and above what it would otherwise have been will drive down the price, and the increment to take-out will accordingly be less. We now define η such that the increment to take-out is $\eta P\delta Q$. Thus $\eta = 1$ if markets are perfect. If markets are imperfect, however, η equals the ratio of marginal revenue to price, which is then less than 1.

The formula for η is given below for two different cases. The implications for μ and r can be simply stated. The formulae are:

$$\mu = \frac{\lambda}{\eta - s} \tag{9A.1}$$

and

$$r = P(\eta q - \lambda l). \tag{9A.2}$$

Readers can check that this is so by reconsidering the original proofs of the formulae for μ and r, remembering simply to multiply $P\delta Q$ by η in the relevant places.

The output of the firm is Q, measured by value added at constant prices. If the demand function for this output has a constant price elasticity ϵ, defined so as to be positive, then, as is well-known,

$$\text{Marginal revenue} = \text{price} \left(1 - \frac{1}{\epsilon}\right).$$

In this case, therefore, μ and r are given by putting $\eta = \{1 - (1/\epsilon)\}$ in the above equations, and this is done in (9.2) and (9.3).

However, many empirical studies of price elasticities of demand refer to sales of goods, and not to output measured by value added. This is true, for example, of the attempts at estimating price elasticities of demand for exports and imports which are referred to in Section 15.6 below. For these, output must be measured gross of inputs of materials, and this makes an appreciable difference, as we shall see. We therefore need to consider what η becomes if we use ϵ', the price elasticity of demand for gross output, rather than ϵ.

Let the quantity of gross output be X and that of material inputs be M, with prices

P_X and P_M. Let us normalize by setting all prices to unity in the base period. Then, at base-period prices,

$$Q = X - M.$$

I assume throughout that materials are a fixed proportion, ma, of gross output, so

$$M = ma\ X.$$

What, then, is the effect on take-out of a small increase in output, after allowing for the reduction in price which results? In terms of value-added output it is

$$P\ \delta Q - Q\ \delta P = P_X\ \delta X - X\ \delta P_X - P_M\ ma\ \delta X.$$

Now by the same well-known result concerning the ratio of marginal revenue to price, we have

$$P_X\ \delta_X - X\ \delta P_X = P_X\ \delta X\ (1 - \frac{1}{\epsilon'}).$$

Also, because the ratio of material inputs to gross output is fixed,

$$\frac{\delta X}{X} = \frac{\delta Q}{Q}.$$

Hence

$$P\ \delta Q - Q\ \delta P = P\ \delta Q \left\{ \frac{P_X}{P} \frac{X}{Q} \left(1 - \frac{1}{\epsilon'} \right) - \frac{P_M}{P} \frac{X}{Q}\ ma \right\}.$$

The term in braces on the right-hand side is therefore η, and it may be simplified by cancelling out P_X, P_M, and P (all equal to unity), and replacing X/Q by $1/(1 - ma)$. Hence

$$\eta = \frac{1 - (1/\epsilon') - ma}{1 - ma} = 1 - \frac{1}{\epsilon'\ (1 - ma)}$$

which is the value used in (9.5) and (9.6). Since ma is often of the order of 0.5, it is important to incorporate it in the above formula if the elasticities being used refer to gross output (as they generally do), and not to use such elasticities with the previous formula for $\eta = 1 - 1/\epsilon$.

In the above argument, no reference is made to *selling costs*. One could define the price elasticity of demand with selling costs held constant when price changes. In practice, however, the demand studies already referred to do not hold selling costs constant. Information on selling costs is not generally available, and so the price elasticity emerging from such studies is one in which selling costs implicitly vary. One would expect that the observed price elasticity would be higher than if selling costs were held constant, since extra output would be sold by a combination of price cuts and increased selling costs. Unless the latter are taken into account, the observed price elasticities would tend to overstate η. This bias can be corrected by measuring ma as the ratio of material inputs to gross output excluding selling costs; the increase in ma then offsets the higher value of ϵ' in the equation for η. However, this does require an estimate of selling costs.

Appendix B: Borrowing at a rising marginal cost

In this appendix the derivation of equations (9.8), for r, and (9.9), for μ, are explained. Attention is confined to a firm selling in imperfect markets with no 'physical' diminishing returns to the rate of investment. In the absence of borrowing, r and μ would be given by equations (9.5) and (9.6). Our task is to show how these two equations are modified when the firm can borrow at a rising cost, as in equation (9.7), reproduced here for convenience:

$$i_m = i_0 + af$$

where i_m is the marginal cost of borrowing, i_0 is the initial cost when borrowing is negligible, and the marginal cost increases linearly with f, the ratio of the rate of borrowing to the rate of investment of the firm, a being a constant. As pointed out in the text, the average cost of borrowing i, is midway between i_0 and i_m:

$$i = i_0 + \frac{af}{2}.$$

The firm will then adjust f until i_m equals the rate of discount of the firm's owners, r. So

$$i_m = r.$$

With f fixed at this optimum level, we may now repeat the derivations for μ and r given in Chapters 6 and 7, as modified in Chapter 9 by the existence of imperfect markets for the firm's output.

We take the derivation of μ first. In this, we compare two points on the EPC, with investment characteristics differing by Δq and Δl, and imagine the firm to invest a small amount $Q\delta\sigma$ for a short interval of time δt at one point rather than the other. As before, output and employment are, as a result, different by

$$\delta Q = Q \, \Delta q \, \delta\sigma \, \delta t; \qquad \delta L = L \, \Delta l \, \delta\sigma \, \delta t.$$

For the two points to be equally profitable, take-out must be unchanged, but now we must allow for the effect of borrowing on take-out. Previously (p. 155) the change in take-out was

$$\delta C = P \, \delta Q(1 - s) - w \, \delta L = 0.$$

Two modifications to this must be made. First, we must allow for the fact that the ratio of marginal revenue to price is not unity but η. Second, a fraction f of s is borrowed, which increases take-out immediately, but subsequently reduces it because of the interest paid. These interest payments are most simply allowed for by subtracting their present value, discounting at r, from take-out. Hence

$$\delta C = P \, \delta Q\{\eta - s(1 - f)\} - w \, \delta L - P \, \delta Q \, sf \frac{i}{r}$$

$$= 0.$$

Since f is unaltered, the interest cost of the extra borrowing is i per unit, and, as this is a perpetuity, its present value is given by dividing by r. If we now substitute for δQ and δL, and divide through by $PQ \, \delta\sigma \, \delta t \, \Delta l$, we have

$$\frac{\Delta q}{\Delta l} \{\eta - s(1 - f)\} - \lambda - \frac{\Delta q}{\Delta l} \, sf \frac{i}{r} = 0.$$

Rearranging and putting $\mu = \Delta q/\Delta l$, then gives (9.9):

$$\mu = \frac{\lambda}{\eta - s + sf\{1 - (i/r)\}}.$$

Turning now to the formula for r as derived in Section 7.2, we imagine a firm to increase its rate of investment by $PQ\,\delta s$ for a short interval of time δt. At the end of this interval the levels of output and employment are higher than they would otherwise have been by

$$\delta Q = PQ\,\delta s\,\delta t\,q; \qquad \delta L = PL\,\delta s\,\delta t\,l.$$

As a result, take-out is increased by δC, and in Section 7.2 we had

$$\delta C = P\,\delta Q(1 - s) - w\,\delta L.$$

Again, two modifications to the above must be made. First, we need to substitute η for unity. Second, we must allow for borrowing and interest payments, each of which comes in twice. The first place they come in is with respect to the initial investment of $PQ\,\delta s\,\delta t$, of which a fraction f is borrowed. Since this does not change f, it leads to subsequent interest payments at the rate $i\,f\,PQ\,\delta s\,\delta t$, whose present value is obtained by dividing by the owners' rate of discount, r. The second place is with respect to the continuing, and growing, stream of additional investment which accompanies the higher, and growing, level of output δQ. Here, the extra borrowing is $P\,\delta Q\,sf$, and the present value of interest paid on this is i/r times as much, both these amounts growing at g.

As in Section 7.2, we set the initial sacrifice of $PQ\,\delta s\,\delta t\,(1 - f)$ equal to the present value of the extra take-out generated, the latter after deducting both of the sums of interest on borrowings mentioned above. Dividing through by $PQ\,\delta s\,\delta t$ gives

$$1 - f = \frac{P\,[q\{\eta - s(1 - f)\} - \lambda l - qsfi/r]}{r - g} - fi/r.$$

Multiplying through by $(r - g)$, and remembering that $Psq = g$, we get

$$(1 - f)(r - g) = P(\eta q - \lambda l) - g(1 - f) - gfi/r - (r - g)fi/r.$$

After cancelling out and dividing by $(1 - f)$, this gives (9.8):

$$r = \frac{P(\eta q - \lambda l) - fi}{1 - f},$$

which can be rewritten as the 'cost of capital' equals the marginal rate of return on investment:

$$(1 - f)r + fi = P(\eta q - \lambda l).$$

PART IV

USE

Experience has lately convinced all economists that no exercise in abstract economics, however closely deduced, is to be trusted unless it can be experimentally verified by tracing its expression in history.

George Bernard Shaw
Fabian Essays in Socialism 1889

10

WHY GROWTH RATES DIFFER, I

10.1 Introduction

The data described in Chapter 2 can now be analysed with the help of Chapter 6's model, which will also provide a test of the latter's usefulness. Attention in this chapter is confined to the linear version of the model, leaving the next chapter to deal with the curvature of the IPC. To anticipate, I conclude there that, while there is evidence of some curvature, it appears to be slight, so that the linear approximation is a good one.

The data consist of twenty-six observations relating to average exponential growth rates of output, g, employment (quality-adjusted), g_L, and rates of investment, s, in non-residential business in different countries and periods. Their derivation is explained in Chapter 2 and the Statistical Appendix, and, for the reasons given in Chapter 2, the periods stop at 1973. (Later years up to 1985 are considered in Chapter 16.) The basic equation fitted to these observations is (6.10), which is reproduced here for convenience (substituting s for σ, since $P = 1$):

$$g = a_Q s + \mu g_L. \tag{6.10}$$

The regressions thus enable one to determine a_Q and μ (Section 10.3). Their performance is compared with alternative explanations allowing for independent technical progress, which appear inferior (Section 10.4). A subdivision of g_L into three components is made and tested to see whether their aggregation is justified (Section 10.5). Section 10.6 provides a quantitative analysis of the proximate determinants of economic growth, based on the preferred fitted version of (6.10).

One striking conclusion of the analysis is that investment opportunities greatly improved after the Second World War. There is also some (weaker) evidence that they improved after the First World War. Thus, ϱ has greatly increased, and in Section 10.7 I consider various explanations for this, and suggest that high capacity utilization, strong business confidence, and an absence of severe fluctuations in demand and prices, as well as improved communications, greater professionalism of management, better education generally, and more expenditure of various kinds which should be classed as investment, were important.

A second conclusion is that there is not much evidence that $\cdot \varrho$ varies systematically between countries or that it depends greatly on the rate of investment. These are rather surprising findings, since it is generally thought that investment in the UK is less efficient than in Japan, for example. However, it is possible that one finding explains the other; ϱ for given s may really be greater in Japan, but this may not show up in the regressions because s is also greater, and there are indeed diminishing returns to the rate of investment (Section 10.3).

A third conclusion is that, following the Second World War, countries that lagged most behind the USA in output per quality-adjusted worker benefited through more productive investment (higher ϱ). Evidence of the benefits of 'catch-up' has also been found by others. It is interesting that I do not find any such evidence for periods before the Second World War, and this suggests that the flow of technology across international boundaries was weaker then. There is other evidence that inventions took longer to develop then, and were copied more slowly (Section 10.3 and 10.7).

I conclude (Section 10.8) by discussing various reasons why growth was so slow in the more distant past, before the Industrial Revolution. Poor communications, as well as other factors, reduced investment opportunities, while required rates of return were raised by insecurity. Lack of good government and freedom to pursue favourable openings must also have been important. Growth is a rare plant in history, but there are reasons for hoping that it is robust.

10.2 Some preliminary points about the regressions

The analysis reported here refers to the data for twenty-six periods already mentioned. In addition, annual data for Japan, the UK, and the USA were analysed, but the findings are not reported, as nothing additional of significance emerged from the analysis. The data were subject to auto-correlation of the residuals, a problem that did not seriously affect the period data.[1] Throughout, single equations fitted by ordinary least squares were used. I do not see why this should have led to any seriously biased estimates of the regression coefficients using the period data, although it could well have done so using annual data.

---

[1] The results obtained using US annual data agreed well with equation (10.3), but agreement was not good with much of the UK and Japanese data. I believe that this was mainly because I failed to eliminate cyclical influences satisfactorily. A comparison was also made of the goodness of fit of equation (10.3) to the pooled annual data with that of various other equations with explanatory variables such as employment and exponential trends which were allowed to vary between periods and/or countries. Equation (10.3) uses five explanatory variables, and comparisons were made with alternatives using four, six, nine and twelve explanatory variables. All gave worse fits than (10.3) except for the last; that used, for each of the three countries, employment and three time trends for pre-First World War, interwar, and post-Second World War periods.

In general, the econometric techniques used were of the simplest kind. This must be emphasized. I am conscious that my knowledge of econometrics is very limited, and that a more professional treatment of my data is needed. Inadequate expertise here (and in other places too) is the penalty of sole authorship. Despite that, I hope that readers will feel that I have managed to provide *some* empirical support for the theory. Perhaps I may add in defence that I know of hardly any other attempts to buttress growth theory with as much evidence as is provided in this and the following chapters. Most of the empirical work on growth consists of growth *accounting*, which is not a test of theory.

All the regressions reported here relate to (at most) twenty-six observations. This looks like a very small number, but it nevertheless covers a large part of historical experience for which data could be found. In that sense, the 'sample' is rather comprehensive. For the reasons given above, my analysis of 177 annual observations for the USA, Japan, and the UK, is not reported in detail. Since I give the data in the Statistical Appendix, others may like to try their hand at it. The mere fact that there are more separate observations does not, unfortunately, guarantee greater reliability of results, since the theory I am concerned with seeks to abstract from cyclical influences (and others, such as wars, strikes, and earthquakes) which affect annual observations much more than period trends.

The only sophistication introduced in the econometric analysis is the use of *weighted observations*, which deserves comment. It seems obvious that one should attach greater weight to an observation relating to growth for a period of twenty years than to one for a period of ten years. Likewise, one should attach more weight to an observation relating to the growth experience of a country with 100 million inhabitants than to that of a country with only 50 million inhabitants. Finally, more weight should be given to reliable data than to data that are statistically dubious. I have, in fact, allowed for all three.

The problem we are discussing is known to econometricians as *heteroscedasticity*. It is generally assumed, in fitting an equation to observations by ordinary least squares, that the variance of the error terms is constant. In other words, one assumes that there is no reason to suppose that, in fitting an equation to the observations, any particular subset of them will fit it better or worse than average. This is probably not the case, however, for the data considered here.

Thus, suppose that one regards the growth rate of a particular country over a period of n years as consisting of the mean of the n annual growth rates in each year of the period. Suppose also that the 'stylized facts' hold, so that the trend growth rate is constant. One's estimate of this trend must improve as the period is lengthened. The variance of the estimate of the trend will, in fact, vary inversely with n. This book's theory is not about growth rates in short periods, but over long periods. The longer the period, provided it is one in which the 'stylized facts' appear to hold, the more confident can one be that disturbances arising from cyclical factors will diminish in importance, and hence the more closely would one expect the theory to fit the data.

A similar argument applies to the size of a country. One would not expect the theory to hold at all well for a small region of a country, or for a small country. It requires, for its fulfilment, the averaging of many random influences on investment opportunities and behaviour. Hence the data for a large country should fit the theory better than the data for a small country, where all sorts of special influences could outweigh the broad tendencies with which we are concerned.

Finally, it is clear that, if the theory is correct, it should fit statistically reliable data better than unreliable data. The estimates of reliability of the data are somewhat arbitrary. I gave an index of 1 for all the post-Second World War data (except for Italy, where I gave an index of 0.5), and also for the UK over 1924-37, and the USA in 1929-48. For earlier periods for the UK I was guided by Feinstein's estimates of reliability, and for the USA and Japan I proceeded by analogy with the UK to some extent. The lowest weight given was one-third for the UK in 1913-24, and for Japan in 1887-1936. It should be emphasized that these estimates of reliability depend not just on the reliability of the basic sources used, but also on that of the modifications introduced here in order, for example, to obtain estimates for the non-residential business sector. Where I felt particularly uncertain about these modifications, I marked the index down.

The weights used to multiply the observations, before fitting the regression equations, were obtained by taking the square roots of the products of the three numbers mentioned, namely, the length of each period, the mean populations of each country in the relevant period, and the index of reliability. The result of doing this was to ensure that the regressions generally fitted US data 1929-73 very closely. If this procedure has indeed succeeded in reducing heteroscedasticity, it should have increased the reliability of the estimates of confidence intervals. The t-statistics, standard errors of estimates, and $\bar{R}^2$ are all, therefore, given based on the weighted residuals. For comparison, however, I have also given $\bar{R}^2$ based on unweighted residuals. Naturally, these are lower. Some of the more important equations were also fitted to unweighted observations, and the results are compared.

10.3 Fitting equation (6.10) to the data

Before equation (6.10) was fitted, the term $a\varrho s$ was expanded so as to allow for various possibilities. The parameter ϱ enables one to make allowance for possible parallel shifts of the IPC, which might be due to any or all of the following reasons.

1. As s increases, one would expect that the contour would shift inwards to the origin, since fewer and fewer productive investment projects would be included in the total programme.
2. The contours could shift through time for a number of reasons which are discussed later.
3. The contours could differ in different countries; for example, some might take the view that investment was especially productive in Japan (high ϱ) and especially unproductive in the UK (low ϱ).
4. Countries behind the leading country or countries could benefit by being able to imitate them, thus saving on research and development costs and also making fewer mistakes. The scope for catch-up is assumed to be measured by the ratio of output per quality-adjusted worker in the country and period in question to output per quality-adjusted worker in the USA in the same period, denoted by cu.[2] Output per worker is first compared with that of the USA in a base year, and the ratio is projected back and forward from then using Q/L for each country, as described above.[3] The base-period comparisons are based mainly on Denison (Denison with Poullier 1967; Denison and Chung 1976). However, I have adjusted Denison's figures where necessary so as approximate to non-residential business. I have also excluded agriculture, on the grounds that relative output per man there did not necessarily give a good guide to the scope for catch-up, being much influenced by the availability of land per head. Denison based his output comparisons on direct price or quantity comparisons so far as possible, rather than on values converted at ruling exchange rates. The quality of labour input was adjusted as described in Chapter 2. However, changes in the proportion of labour in agriculture were irrelevant once agriculture was excluded. There is some inconsistency in the projections back and forward inasmuch as agricultural output and employment and the transfer of labour from agriculture remain in the index of Q/L.

One can express the above four possibilities by putting ϱ as a linear function of the relevant variables, thus:

$$\varrho = \varrho\,(s, D_t, D_c, cu) = 1 + a_1 s + a_2 D_t + a_3 D_c + a_4 \ln cu.$$

The first term s, can be allowed for by adding a term in s^2 to the right hand

---

[2] An alternative, and possibly theoretically better, measure of the scope for catch-up is the ratio of real wages per quality-adjusted worker. This was not tried out.

[3] The US data reach back only to 1889, whereas the UK data start at 1856. For the years 1856–89 the average exponential rate of growth of US productivity was assumed to be the same as from 1889 to 1913.

side of (6.10), and one would expect the coefficient of this term to be negative.

The next two terms refer to time and country dummies. Terms $D_t s$ and $D_c s$ are added to the right-hand side of (6.10), where D_t has the value 0 for some time periods (e.g. before the Second World War) and 1 for others (e.g. after the Second World War), and where D_c has the value 0 for some countries (e.g. all except Japan) and 1 for others (e.g. Japan).

The last term, for catch-up, could be treated in two different ways. Since the USA was taken throughout as the leading country, cu is always 1 for the USA. The effect of catch-up is always 0 for the USA, and this is ensured if one makes ϱ linearly dependent on either the logarithm of cu or $(1 - cu)$. The first of these formulations in effect assumes that the same *proportionate* reduction in cu has the same beneficial effect in raising ϱ. The second formulation in effect assumes that the same *absolute* reduction in cu has the same beneficial effect in raising ϱ. I have no strong preference for either, and it turns out that the data are just about equally consistent with either. As the fit is marginally better for $\ln cu$ than for $(1 - cu)$, I have used the former. Hence the term $s \ln cu$ is added to the right-hand side of (6.10). Furthermore, in order to see whether the influence of catch-up varied with time, this variable was combined with time-dummies. One would expect the coefficients of the catch-up variables to be negative, since the smaller is cu, the more scope there is for catching up.

By allowing for variations in ϱ, one allows for *parallel* shifts in the investment programme contour. However, the shifts might not be parallel, and to test for this I tried out various other combinations of the variables mentioned with dummy variables. None proved satisfactory.

Statistically, the best equation found was as follows (D_p is a dummy variable set at 1 for post-Second World War periods and at 0 for all other periods):

$$g = 0.9119g_L + 0.06879s + 0.06756D_p s - 0.05401D_p s \ln cu. \qquad (10.1)$$
$$\quad (8.05) \qquad\quad (2.93) \qquad\quad (3.35) \qquad\qquad (-3.16)$$

$\bar{R}^2$ (weighted residuals) = 0.954; $\quad \bar{R}^2$ (unweighted residuals) = 0.870
s.e. (weighted residuals) = 0.00491; s.e. (unweighted residuals) = 0.00781

Here, as elsewhere, the figures in brackets beneath the coefficients are the relevant t-statistics. All are highly significant (at the 0.005 probability level on a one-tailed test). The equation was fitted to weighted observations, but values of $\bar{R}^2$ and the (normalized) standard errors are given derived from both the weighted and the unweighted residuals, the former being naturally more favourable to the equation. While it is thought that weighting is preferable, for the reasons given in Section 10.2, the magnitudes of the coefficients are not significantly different in a similar equation fitted to unweighted observations. The coefficients of $D_p s$ and $\ln cu$, however, then cease to be significantly different from 0 (their t-statistics being 1.05 and -1.34, respectively). This is what might be expected to result from heteroscedasticity, and it is thought that the t-statistics given above are more reliable.

An alternative equation that could have been used to test this linear form of the theory can be obtained by dividing through equation (10.1) by s, when one obtains an equation in terms of q and l, instead of g and g_L. One can test the effects of exactly the same variables on q as on g with this alternative equation, and, indeed, the resulting coefficients are very similar. However, as the fit of the equation is rather worse,[4] equation (10.1) was preferred.

Let us now consider the meaning and values of the coefficients, and then possible interpretations of the whole equation, which also requires consideration of other variables which were found not to be significant.

The coefficient of g_L is very much in line with the theory. It should equal μ, the slope of the investment programme contour. In the theory this slope should vary, since the contour is curved. Here we have only a linear approximation, in which most weight is given to post-Second World War observations. The weighted mean value for λ is 0.697 and that for s is 0.154. According to the theory (equation (6.2)), $\mu = \lambda/(1 - s)$. However, this assumes perfect markets and no taxation. It is shown in Chapters 9 and 14 that, allowing for these, one should put

$$\mu = \frac{\lambda}{1 - k_1 - k_2 s}$$

where with imperfect markets $k_1 > 0$, and with taxation of savings $k_2 > 1$. Were we to put $k_1 = 0$ and $k_2 = 1$, as with perfect markets and no taxation, the above weighted mean values would give $\mu = 0.824$. The value of $\mu = 0.9119$ in equation (10.1) is therefore consistent with the existence of some degree of imperfection and/or some taxation on savings. In Chapter 15 we return to this point, after some estimates of k_1 and k_2 have been made. It is interesting to note that the coefficient of g_L is appreciably greater than the mean value of λ, which might be one view of its 'proper' value. A steady-state orthodox theorist might expect the coefficient to equal 1, but would also require different accompanying variables on the right-hand side, so we return to that question later.

The coefficient of s depends on which periods we are considering. For pre-Second World War periods, the coefficient is 0.06879. For post-Second World War periods one must add to this the coefficient of $D_p s$, making 0.13635. The implication of this approximate doubling of the coefficient, in

---

[4] If the sum of the squared residuals (weighted) from the equation in q and l is multiplied by the square of the mean value of s, the result is 0.385, which is greater than the sum of the squared residuals (weighted) from equation (10.1), viz. 0.325. I am grateful to Professor D. Hendry for suggesting this test.

terms of the theory, is remarkable. It implies that ϱ doubled from periods before to those after the Second World War, which in turn implies that the contribution of investment to growth, per unit of investment, also doubled. This resulted in the increased rates of return shown in Table 7.1.[5]

The coefficient of s also depends on *catch-up*, the last term in equation (10.1). The lower was cu, the ratio of a given country's labour productivity to US productivity in the given period, the more negative was lncu, and so the more *postive* was $-0.05401s$ lncu, i.e. the higher was the growth rate and also the social rate of return. Thus, for example, the value of cu for Japan in 1961–73 was 0.4537, and s was 0.3175. Catch-up therefore added -0.05401×0.3175 ln$0.4537 = 0.01355$, or about 1.4 per cent per year to the Japanese growth rate, according to equation (10.1). It did this by adding $0.01355/0.3175 = 0.0427$ to q and so to the rate of return.

I have now explained the meaning of all the terms in equation (10.1). I must next point out a number of important qualifications, and also comment on variables that do *not* appear in it. The significance of the dog that did *not* bark in the night can be great.

The discussion in Chapter 6 as well as at the start of this section (the first of the four reasons why ϱ might vary) assumed that, as s is increased, less productive and less profitable investment projects have to be included in the investment programme. Were this true, it would imply that marginal rates of return would be lower than the average rates of return given in Table 7.1. This possibility was tested by adding a term s^2 to the right-hand side of equation (10.1), whose coefficient should have been negative. In fact, the coefficient was 0.03929 with a t-statistic of 0.31. It had therefore the wrong sign and was not significantly different from zero.

A possible explanation for this result is that s tends to be high in countries where the investment programme contours are shifted outwards for reasons exogenous to the discussion thus far. If, for example, the contours were shifted outwards in Japan, and inwards in the UK, because Japanese management was especially good while UK management was especially poor, or because Japanese labour was especially co-operative while UK labour was not, then this could explain why a higher s in Japan than in the UK led to a ϱ that was no different (apart from catch-up, which equation (10.1) allows for). The higher s in Japan, on the *same* map of contours, would have resulted in a lower ϱ there. But the map was not the same. The

---

[5] Setting $P = 1$, we have $r = q - \mu(1 - s)l$, and, if we divide (6.10) through by s we also have $q = a_\varrho + \mu l$. It follows that $r = a_\varrho + \mu g_L$. The changes in rates of return from before to after the Second World War in col. (1) of Table 7.1 were thus due to changes in both ϱ and g_L. However, for both the UK and the USA, g_L was lower than in previous peacetime periods, and so tended to offset the effects of the rise in ϱ. In the case of Japan g_L was higher, thus reinforcing the rise in ϱ, with the result that post-Second World War rates of return were extremely high.

contours were shifted outwards, and this was why s was higher in Japan and ϱ was no different.

In order to test this possibility, dummy variables D_{UK}, D_J, and D_E, having values of 1 for observations for the UK, Japan, and continental Europe, respectively, and otherwise 0, were each multiplied by s and added to the right-hand side of equation (10.1). We may first note that, when this was done, and *before* a term in s^2 was added, none of these country dummies was significantly different from zero. The coefficients and their t-statistics were as follows:

	coefficient	t-statistic
$D_{UK}s$	-0.02926	-0.92
$D_J s$	0.00601	0.22
$D_E s$	0.00488	0.18

The coefficients of $D_J s$ and $D_E s$ were clearly much too small to pay any attention to. That for the UK was negative (as some might expect) and quite substantial, even if not significant as judged by the t-statistic. There is thus a hint, if no more, of some factor which reduced investment opportunities (or else worsened the choice made from the opportunities available) in the UK.

When a term in s^2 was added to the equation along with the above terms with country dummies, some interesting, though inconclusive, results were obtained. The equation in full was as follows:

$$g = 0.6527g_L + 0.1483s + 0.04769D_p s - 0.07486D_p s \ln cu$$
$$\quad (3.31) \qquad (2.50) \qquad (1.85) \qquad (-2.01)$$

$$\quad - 0.04716D_{UK}s + 0.02488D_J s + 0.004434D_E s - 0.2269s^2 \qquad (10.2)$$
$$\quad (-1.32) \qquad (0.78) \qquad (0.16) \qquad (-1.07)$$

$\bar{R}^2$ (weighted residuals) $= 0.952$; $\quad \bar{R}^2$ (unweighted residuals) $= 0.828$
s.e. (weighted residuals) $= 0.00500$; s.e. (unweighted residuals) $= 0.00898$

None of the coefficients of the additional variables (i.e. the last four) is significant at the 0.05 probability level on a one-tailed test. Nevertheless, the signs of the coefficients for the UK and Japanese dummies, and for s^2, are as one would expect, and they are moderately significant. Hence the data give some weak support to the view that investment opportunities in the UK are more restricted than in the USA, that they are better in Japan than in the USA, and that there are diminishing returns in all countries to the rate of investment. (The continental European countries must be regarded as being about the same on average as the USA on this evidence.) This support is further weakened, however, by the fact that the coefficients of g_L and s are now much less satisfactory than in equation (10.1), the coefficient of g_L being too small and that of s and $D_p s$ rather too big.

In what follows, I generally neglect both country differences and diminishing returns to the rate of investment, as this makes for simplicity. Nevertheless there is quite a strong presumption on general grounds that diminishing returns exist, and so they must be recalled at various points in the analysis. It would also be rather surprising if there were *no* country differences. So, although equation (10.2) is neglected here, it is to be hoped that subsequent research will be able to advance further than this.

Although (10.1) is statistically the best linear equation found, it is worth considering equation (10.3), which is nearly as good, since it provides some (albeit weak) evidence that ϱ increased after the First World War, as well as again after the Second. This is quite important when we come to review explanations for these increases in ϱ in Section 10.7. When a dummy variable D_n, having the value 1 for periods that were deemed 'interwar'[6] and 0 otherwise, was multiplied by s and added to the right-hand side of (10.1), the following results were obtained:

$$g = 0.9034g_L + 0.05228s + 0.03329D_n s + 0.08480D_p s - 0.05428D_p s \ln cu. \quad (10.3)$$
$$(8.11) \qquad (2.01) \qquad (1.36) \qquad (3.61) \qquad (-3.23)$$

$\bar{R}^2$ (weighted residuals) $= 0.956$; $\bar{R}^2$ (unweighted residuals) $= 0.889$
s.e. (weighted residuals) $= 0.00482$; s.e. (unweighted residuals) $= 0.00786$

The term $D_n s$ is not significant at the 0.05 probability level on a two-tailed test, and an F-test at the 0.05 probability level shows that dropping this term does not significantly worsen the fit of the equation. Hence, if we stick to these tests of significance we should drop this term. On the other hand, at a lower level of significance, 0.2 on a two-tailed test, the term *is* significant. Also, analysis of the curvature of the investment programme contours in Chapter 11 supports the case for equation (10.3) rather than (10.1).

Taking the coefficients in (10.3) as they stand, we may note that they are very similar to (10.1) so far as g_L and $D_p s \ln cu$ are concerned. The coefficient of s is smaller and that of $D_p s$ bigger. Hence the main effect of introducing the interwar dummy is to suggest that the average rate of return (assuming $g_L = 0$[7] and with no catch-up) was about $5\frac{1}{4}$ per cent per year before the First World War (instead of about 7 per cent per year, as in (10.1)), and that this rate of return rose to about 9 per cent per year in the interwar period, before rising still further to about $18\frac{1}{2}$ per cent per year after the Second World War.

---

[6] For the UK, 1913–24 was classed as pre-First World War, and 1924–37 and 1937–51 as interwar. For the USA, 1913–29 and 1929–48 were both classed as interwar. For Japan, 1911–28 and 1928–36 were both classed as interwar.

[7] See fn. 5 above.

10.4   Alternative ways of explaining the data

I have now completed the exposition of the best linear equations conforming to the theory of growth that I could find. Their coefficients are reasonable in terms of that theory, and appear consistent with other relevant information. Equation (10.1) 'explains' 95 per cent of the weighted, and 87 per cent of the unweighted, variance in growth rates between different periods and different countries, and equation (10.3) rather more. A scatter diagram that illustrates equation (10.3)'s goodness of fit is discussed in Chapter 11, after we have considered nonlinear versions of the model (see Figure 11.2 and Section 11.3 (a)). Before proceeding any further, it seems worth while comparing this performance with that of some other possible ways of explaining the same data which might be commonly used.

One obvious modification that might be made to equation (10.1) is to add a constant term to represent 'technical progress' which is independent of the rate of investment or the growth of the labour force. This was tried, but the constant was negative, tiny (-0.00054), and insignificantly different from zero ($t = -0.12$).

Orthodox steady-state theories with constant returns to scale assume that the rate of growth is the sum of the rate of growth of the labour force and the rate of technical progress. It takes a long time to approximate the steady state closely, but if observations extend over many countries and periods, one might expect that the distribution of observations about it would be random. Hence one could fit an equation of the form

$$g = a + bg_L$$

in which b could be expected to equal 1. Even those who do not assume that the steady state is a good approximation often use an equation of this form. The trend of labour productivity is assumed to be exogenous, but one might want to allow for the possibility that it differed between countries, and also that it shifted from, say, the interwar to the post-Second World War period. It would also be reasonable to allow for the possibility of 'catch-up', so that the constant a would be larger for countries the further they lagged behind the USA. After experimenting with a number of different equations, the best that I could find had, in fact, only four variables (country dummies and interwar dummies proving to be insignificant as judged by F-tests at the 0.05 level of significance):

$$g = 0.001853 + 0.01361D_p - 0.02384D_p \ln cu + 1.2157g_L \qquad (10.4)$$
$$\quad (0.53) \qquad\quad (3.79) \qquad\qquad (-4.65) \qquad\qquad (8.48)$$

$\bar{R}^2$ (weighted residuals) $= 0.893$; $\bar{R}^2$ (unweighted residuals) $= 0.817$
s.e. (weighted residuals) $= 0.00748$; s.e. (unweighted residuals) $= 0.00925$

This equation is not such a good fit to the data as equation (10.1). Its weighted standard error, for example, is half as big again. Some of its coefficients are also theoretically unsatisfactory. The first coefficient implies that there was negligible technical progress until after the Second World War, which seems implausible. The coefficient of g_L is appreciably larger than the expected value of 1. (The excess is about 1.5 times its standard error.[8]) This comparison therefore tells in favour of my theory.[9]

10.5　Alternative ways of measuring labour input

In this section we consider two alternative ways of measuring labour input to the one adopted. For the first, labour input was measured by full-time equivalent numbers of persons employed (the crudest measure), N. The second alternative incorporated quality adjustments for age, sex, education, and (except for the UK) the transfer of labour away from agriculture and self-employment; in addition, it measured man-hours rather than men. This measure, H, differed from the preferred measure, L, only in excluding the effect of the somewhat controversial and arbitrary allowance for changes in the efficiency of an hour's work.

Table 10.1 gives estimates of g_N and g_L, and of the two adjustments made in proceeding from g_N to g_L, for my standard countries and periods. The first adjustment, $g_H - g_N$, shows all the quality adjustments made to g_N save one, namely, that for changes in the efficiency of an hour's work. That is shown in the third column of the table headed $g_L - g_H$. The final column, g_L, then equals the sum of the first three columns. All of the adjustments follow Denison, and are described in Chapter 2. The averages given at the foot of each column show that the quality adjustments on average rather more than doubled the rate of growth of full-time equivalent numbers to give the final measure of employment growth, g_L, that was used. There was appreciable variation in the relations between the entries in the columns, but g_N is positively correlated with g_L and 'explains' about 60 per cent of its variance.[10] The aim of the following tests is to see whether the adjustments made to g_N to get g_L can be justified on empirical as well as general theoretical grounds.

The first test was to substitute g_N and g_H for g_L in equation (10.1). The result in both cases was to worsen the fit, especially when g_N was used.[11] The coefficient of g_N was 1.18 and that of g_H was 0.81. In my opinion, neither of these is as plausible as the coefficient of 0.91 obtained for g_L.

---

[8] However, a coefficient larger than 1 could be attributed to increasing returns to scale (see p. 78). (I am grateful to J. R. Sargent for pointing this out.)

[9] One could interpret equation (10.4) as a reduced-form solution to the complete model, described in Chapter 8, in which s is endogenous and ϱ and g_L are exogenous.

[10] The equation $g_L = 0.0074 + 1.3685g_N$ was fitted to the 26 observations, with $r^2 = 0.617$.

[11] The sum of the weighted squared residuals, as compared with equation (10.1), was more than doubled in the equation with g_N, and it was increased by one-fifth in the equation with g_H.

Table 10.1 Three components of employment growth

Country	Period	Full-time equivalent numbers g_N (1)	Quality adjustments and hours $g_H - g_N$ (2)	Efficiency of an hour's work $g_L - g_H$ (3)	Total g_L (4)
UK	1856–73	0.0083	0.0023	0.0035	0.0142
	1873–1901	0.0100	0.0072	0.0008	0.0180
	1901–13	0.0114	0.0062	0.0017	0.0193
	1913–24	−0.0040	−0.0088	0.0093	−0.0035
	1924–37	0.0089	0.0078	−0.0010	0.0157
	1937–51	0.0034	0.0021	0.0022	0.0077
	1951–64	0.0045	0.0014	0.0009	0.0068
	1964–73	−0.0093	−0.0031	0.0005	−0.0120
USA	1889–1900	0.0184[a]	0.0045	0.0031	0.0260
	1900–13	0.0239	0.0045	0.0051	0.0334
	1913–29	0.0131	0.0020	0.0051	0.0201
	1929–48	0.0099	0.0052	0.0035	0.0186
	1948–73	0.0080	0.0071	0.0004	0.0155
Japan	1887–99	0.0054	0.0135	0.0000	0.0189
	1899–1911	0.0034	0.0112	0.0000	0.0147
	1911–28	0.0026	0.0227	0.0000	0.0253
	1928–36	0.0114	0.0190	0.0000	0.0303
	1952–61	0.0196	0.0303	−0.0014	0.0485
	1961–73	0.0131	0.0213	0.0003	0.0347
Belgium	1955–62	0.0045	0.0050	0.0031	0.0126
Denmark	1955–62	0.0101	0.0008	0.0041	0.0150
France	1955–62	−0.0023	0.0174	0.0009	0.0161
Germany	1955–62	0.0116	−0.0057	0.0091	0.0149
Netherlands	1955–62	0.0105	0.0029	0.0029	0.0163
Norway	1955–62	−0.0016	−0.0001	0.0041	0.0024
Italy	1955–62	0.0061	0.0231	0.0053	0.0344
Mean, weighted		0.0093	0.0083	0.0017	0.0193
Mean, unweighted		0.0077	0.0077	0.0024	0.0178

Note
See text for meaning of g_N, g_H, and g_L, and Section 10.2 for description of weights.
Source: Statistical Appendix.
[a] Owing to an error, this was taken as 0.0153 in all relevent regressions.

This test, so far as it went, therefore tended to confirm the choice of g_L, although it should be pointed out that the original choice of equation (10.1) resulted from a process of trial and error in which g_L was the variable employed. Had I started with g_N or g_H, I might have obtained better-fitting equations for them.

In the second test, three variables were substituted for g_L in equation (10.1). These were g_N, $g_H - g_N$, and $g_L - g_H$. Regarding g_L as the aggregate of these three, I wanted to see whether, in fact, this made much difference to the equation and whether all three were significant. Furthermore, if the coefficients of all three were the same, and equal to the aggregate coefficient 0.9119, the aggregation could be justified. The result of this test was to leave all the other coefficients in equation (10.1) not significantly different and to obtain the following coefficients (and t-statistics) for labour input:

	coefficient	t-statistic
g_N	0.771	3.60
$g_H - g_N$	1.078	5.02
$g_L - g_H$	1.443	2.27

All three coefficients are significant at the 0.025 per cent level (and the first two at the 0.005 per cent level) on a one-tailed test. They are not equal to each other or to 0.9119, but each differs from that figure by less than its standard error. Unsurprisingly, the coefficient of $g_L - g_H$, the effect of changing efficiency resulting from changes in hours worked, is the least satisfactory. Nevertheless, these results go some way to support the chosen aggregate labour input measure, g_L.

10.6   The proximate causes of growth

Equation (6.10), the simple linear version of the model, divides growth in any period into two parts: that due to material investment, and that due to growth of quality-adjusted employment. In turn, the contribution of investment in the equation depends on a_ϱ, and that of employment growth on μ. To undertake this analysis of growth rates, we then need estimates of a, ϱ, s, μ, and g_L, and these are provided by the regression equations reviewed already. It is worth emphasizing that this explanation of growth differs from the growth accounting explanations of, for example, Denison, in that the separate effects of investment and employment are derived from regression equations and not *a priori*. In ordinary growth accounting, the contribution of employment growth, for example, is *assumed* to be given by the product of the share of labour income and the growth rate of employment. There is no corresponding assumption here. Consequently, the residuals here are different from the ordinary growth accounting residuals. The expected value of the residual here is zero, while I suppose one must regard the expected value of the residual in conventional growth accounting as positive (since it represents exogenous technical progress). There seems to be no hypothesis that is being tested by conventional growth accounting—it *is* just accounting, and with no obvious means of checking the final balance! By contrast, the closeness of fit of the regression equations does test my simple linear model's explanation of growth.

In Table 10.2, equation (10.3) has been used to obtain values of the explanatory variables. All the terms involving s are shown under column (1), except for catch-up, which is shown separately under column (3). The

Table 10.2   The proximate causes of growth

Country	Period	Parts of rate of growth arising from:				
		Investment	Growth of labour force	Catch-up	Unexplained	Total
		(1)	(2)	(3)	(4)	(5)
UK	1856–73	0.0052	0.0128	0	0.0061	0.0241
	1873–1901	0.0055	0.0162	0	−0.0006	0.0212
	1901–13	0.0050	0.0174	0	−0.0063	0.0161
	1913–24	0.0028	−0.0032	0	−0.0008	−0.0013
	1924–37	0.0069	0.0142	0	−0.0017	0.0194
	1937–51	0.0077	0.0069	0	0.0041	0.0188
	1951–64	0.0232	0.0061	0.0076	−0.0105	0.0265
	1964–73	0.0266	−0.0108	0.0077	0.0038	0.0272
USA	1889–1900	0.0088	0.0235	0	0.0079	0.0402
	1900–13	0.0090	0.0302	0	−0.0059	0.0334
	1913–29	0.0116	0.0182	0	0.0019	0.0316
	1929–48	0.0075	0.0168	0	−0.0006	0.0237
	1948–73	0.0195	0.0140	0	0.0000	0.0335
Japan	1887–99	0.0069	0.0171	0	0.0088	0.0328
	1899–1911	0.0059	0.0132	0	−0.0037	0.0154
	1911–28	0.0119	0.0229	0	−0.0103	0.0244
	1928–36	0.0116	0.0274	0	0.0137	0.0528
	1952–61	0.0344	0.0438	0.0155	0.0023	0.0961
	1961–73	0.0435	0.0313	0.0136	0.0002	0.0887
Belgium	1955–62	0.0226	0.0114	0.0050	−0.0043	0.0347
Denmark	1955–62	0.0262	0.0135	0.0064	−0.0059	0.0403
France	1955–62	0.0251	0.0145	0.0055	0.0049	0.0500
Germany	1955–62	0.0305	0.0135	0.0073	0.0073	0.0587
Netherlands	1955–62	0.0312	0.0147	0.0089	−0.0152	0.0396
Norway	1955–62	0.0389	0.0021	0.0077	−0.0143	0.0344
Italy	1955–62	0.0265	0.0311	0.0080	−0.0042	0.0613
Mean, weighted		0.0177	0.0175	0.0028	0	0.0380
Mean, unweighted		0.0175	0.0161	0.0036	−0.0009	0.0363

Note
The weights used are described in Section 10.2.

Source: Based on the data in the Statistical Appendix and equation (10.3); see text.

residuals are in column (4). Mean values are given at the foot of each column. Looking first at these, it can be seen that the contribution of material investment averages a little more (especially if catch-up is included) than that of employment growth, but for particular periods and countries the relative contributions have varied greatly, and there is virtually no direct relationship between them.[12] Catch-up has been unimportant on average, but, if we exclude the years before the Second World War when it is estimated to have been negligible, and also the leading country, the USA, it has been quite important. I defer comment on the unexplained residuals until Chapter 11.

Table 10.2 is merely the beginning of an explanation of why growth rates differ. Further analysis of the growth of the labour force appears in Section 10.5 and Chapter 2. The marked increase in the contribution of investment, $a\varrho s$, following the Second World War was due both to higher s and to higher ϱ. The determinants of s are discussed in Chapter 8, and in the next section we review different explanations for the rise in ϱ.

10.7 Why were investment opportunities better after the Second World War?

Equation (10.3) implies that, apart from 'catch-up', investment opportunities, as measured by ϱ, increased by about 60 per cent[13] from the period before to that following the Second World War, and that they also increased substantially from before 1914 to the interwar period (although that increase is less certain). These are very remarkable changes. The acceleration of productivity growth following the Second World War has been remarked by others, and various explanations have been suggested, which we now review.

1. High levels of demand, together with expectations of rapid growth of demand, have been mentioned by some writers. For example, in Beckerman's view,

Economic growth is very much dependent on expectations concerning the future growth of demand. If entrepreneurs expect demand for their products to expand rapidly they will expand capacity more rapidly. In the course of doing so they will also generally achieve a faster rate of increase in productivity per unit of new capacity than if they were expanding capacity slowly. This may be partly the result of a deliberate and purposeful increase in entrepreneurial ingenuity and energy responding to the challenge to produce more in the face of the wider market opportunities. And it may be partly the automatic effect of economies of scale, both

---

[12] The correlation between col. (1) and col. (2) of Table 10.1 is $r = 0.12$.
[13] The coefficient of s, which is $a\varrho$, increased from $0.05228 + 0.03329 = 0.08557$ in the interwar period to $0.05228 + 0.08480 = 0.13708$ (ignoring 'catch-up') after the Second World War.

internal (to the firm) and external, or of the greater 'embodied' technical progress accompanying a higher rate of gross capital formation. But we do not yet have enough data for evaluating the likely relative importance of these possible alternative mechanisms by which confident expectations are transposed into a faster growth of productivity per unit of additional input of capital (and labour). In Henderson 1966, 65-6)

According to Beckerman, 'As well as fitting the facts remarkably well, this view of the growth process seems also to have been more or less accepted by a cross-section of expert opinion in different countries represented on an OECD working party' (in Henderson 1966, 67). The above quotation does not do full justice to the view, which emphasizes the importance of international competitiveness in engendering confident demand expectations. The emphasis is, moreover, on expectations of *growth* of demand rather than on the *level* of demand.

Another writer who has emphasized demand, including its level, has been Maddison:

In the post-war period, it has become clear that the buoyancy and stability of demand can also be a major factor determining productivity growth. There was a backlog of opportunity on the 'supply' side which enabled productivity in these economies (i.e. the OECD countries) to respond very favourably once the right climate of demand and expectations of future demand had been created. . . . The main instrument by which high demand created high productivity growth was by raising the rate of investment and the growth of the capital stock . . . There were other transmission mechanisms favouring growth in this virtuous circle situation, which were of lesser importance than accelerated investment but none the less significant in their contribution to growth. High demand flushed surplus labour out of low productivity occupations, both within countries and by promoting international migration; it improved efficiency and induced economies of scale. (Maddison 1982, 99-101)

Matthews *et al.* (1982, 533-5) also attribute some of the faster growth in total factor productivity in the UK, comparing 1951-73 with the years before the Second World War, to both faster growth in demand and a higher level of demand in relation to capacity. They point out that a higher level of demand can have both beneficial and harmful effects, and conclude that the net effects were probably beneficial in 1951-73. However, they are then faced with the difficulty that total factor productivity grew faster in the interwar years than before 1914, whereas the level of demand was undoubtedly lower. While one *could* believe that the beneficial effects of lower demand then preponderated, they do not assert that this was so.

It does seem very likely that high demand was partly responsible for the unusually high rates of investment after the Second World War; but neither this, nor the effects of demand on the rate of growth of the quality-adjusted labour force, are at issue here. The question we are discussing is whether high demand resulted in still further increases in output, over and above those arising from the extra supplies of capital and labour it may have induced. Beckerman and Maddison (and the OECD working party, apparently) and Matthews *et al.* seem to have believed that there was a bonus of this kind, although Maddison at any rate regarded it as less important than the effects via increasing supplies of capital and labour.

If the average utilization of capacity was higher after the Second World War than before it, as seems probable, that would have increased the average efficiency of investment as measured by ϱ. The same quantum of investment will increase output twice as much if the average utilization ratio of output to capacity is twice as great. The efficiency of investment appears to have fallen since 1973, and lower capacity utilization is probably part (although only a small part) of the explanation (see Chapter 16). Confident expectations of growth could also explain some of the greater efficiency of investment before 1973, and a weakening in confidence could explain the decline in efficiency thereafter. This is a novel point which requires fuller explanation, and that is best deferred to Chapter 16. It is related to the point made in Chapter 9 that 'animal spirits' can offset monopolistic tendencies. A weakening in 'animal spirits', with more attention being given to profit maximization in imperfect markets, can result in socially valuable assets being scrapped, thus causing a loss of output. A final point relates to the absence of severe *fluctuations* in output and prices during most of the postwar years up to 1973. This probably resulted in less wasted investment than occurred in either earlier or later years.

Nevertheless, while all these factors undoubtedly played an important part in explaining why ϱ was so high from 1948 to 1973, there were other factors. The investment programme contours did not shift *in*wards in the interwar years and, indeed, probably shifted outwards, as compared with the years before the First World War. The interwar years cannot be regarded as ones in which demand was high, or expectations of demand confident. It seems to me that we need to find some factor that acted over both periods, and this does not point to a high level of demand or to confident demand expectations.

2. Another possible explanation is 'catch-up'. Maddison remarks:

There is no evidence that the postwar acceleration was due to a faster pace of technical innovation. The frontier of technology lay predominantly in the US economy, whose pace of productivity growth did not increase. The acceleration of growth outside the USA is basically explicable in terms of a reduction in the technical lag. (Maddison 1982, 124)

However, according to my estimates, there are two things wrong with this view. First, there *was* an appreciable acceleration in the rate of labour productivity growth in the USA after the Second World War (and this is true whichever of the three ways described in Section 10.5 one measures labour input). Nor can this, according to the theory developed here, be fully explained by a higher rate of investment. Second, while catch-up does explain a part of the acceleration outside the USA, it by no means explains the whole. In short, there appears to have been a general acceleration in the rate of growth, in the USA as well as elsewhere, not attributable to growth of inputs or to catch-up. This is consistent with catch-up having been *part* of the explanation for the increase in ϱ outside the USA, as equations (10.1) and (10.3) imply.

3. A somewhat different version of the catching-up idea is that technical progress occurs in an irregular fashion. There is a bunching of major innovations which results in a subsequent period of rapid growth of productivity as they spread throughout the system, and spawn a host of minor innovations. As their influence dies away, so the rate of growth of productivity declines, until a new bunch of major innovations occurs. The timing of these major cycles may also be influenced by wars. Writers who have expounded variations on this theme have been Schumpeter, Rostow, Mensch, Freeman (and others), and perhaps also Hicks. It terms of the theory that I am putting forward, one could imagine that there is a cyclical behaviour in ϱ, which shifts outwards while the major innovations are taking effect, and then inwards as these effects die away. At first sight this cyclical behaviour does not seem to explain the present observations, since they consist simply of two outward shifts of ϱ: from before 1914 to the interwar years, and from then to after the Second World War. However, this neglects two periods of slow growth in productivity: from about 1900 to about 1914 in the UK, the USA, and Japan (the only three countries I have considered before 1914), and since 1973 in these three and a great many more countries. Is it possible to relate the apparent shifts in ϱ to major innovations? Or can the slow-downs in both of the periods just mentioned be explained in other ways?[14]

4. The liberalization and rapid growth of world trade since the Second World War have been mentioned by Maddison (1982, 111–15). He points out that there were several different ways in which productivity growth could have been affected. There are, first, the well-known gains from greater specialization in line with comparative advantage, which, however, are generally estimated to have been rather small. Maddison himself gives estimates which also allow for economies of scale and greater competition, and which are appreciably larger than Denison's estimates. Nevertheless, for the larger countries, even Maddison's estimates are small, and for the USA they are negligible (0.01 per cent p.a.), so that this can hardly be

---

[14] Some discussions of the causes of the slow-down in the UK in 1900–13 is given in Section 11.3(c). The slow-down after 1973 is the subject of Chapter 16.

regarded as a significant contribution towards explaining a shift in ϱ that was substantial for the USA as well as for other countries. This view is reinforced when one remembers that the interwar period was one when trade contracted severely as trade barriers were increased all round, and yet ϱ, if anything, shifted outwards compared with before 1914.

The post-Second World War expansion of trade, however, had two other effects which Maddison mentions. First, it strengthened business expectations, and was one of the causes of the rapid growth of demand and the high level of investment. Matthews *et al.* (1982, chs. 14, 15, and 17) pay considerable attention to the role of external factors in causing fluctuations in demand in the UK, and to the favourable world environment following the Second World War. Also, for Beckerman (in Henderson 1966) as well as Lamfalussy (1963), export-led growth was very much 'the name of the game'. All this, however, has already been considered in explanation 1 above, and confronts the same difficulty as there mentioned, namely, how to explain the fact that ϱ did not fall, and probably rose, in the interwar period as compared with before 1914. It is Maddison's second further effect that seems to me more important, namely, trade as a method (and also, perhaps, a symptom) of quicker, and wider, diffusion of knowledge of investment opportunities. This, however, brings me to the last explanation that I shall consider here.

5. The number and quality of the investment opportunities confronting investors, together with the skill with which they are chosen and the amount of investment expenditure, determine their average social yield. In terms of my theory, they also determine ϱ. If investors become aware of more and better opportunities, or if they select them more wisely, ϱ will increase. There has been a very considerable improvement and cheapening of communications over the last hundred years, and especially, with cheap and quick air travel, over the last forty. The very rapid growth of foreign trade and foreign investment since the war has helped to increase business contacts world-wide. Coupled with this, there is the managerial revolution, which has increased the professionalism of management, and there has been a big increase in the proportion of the labour force employed in managerial and professional occupations, as well as improvements in education more generally. In some countries (the USA for example) there has been an increase in the share of R&D expenditures in total output. All these factors have probably contributed to a greater awareness of developments in places that used to be considered remote, but are no longer. A higher proportion of the work-force is now on the look-out for investment opportunities, and the workers involved are probably more skilful at choosing them. The hypothesis is that it is these factors that have increased ϱ, and that they have acted both within countries and between countries. The USA and other countries have benefited from them, but countries lagging behind the USA

(provided certain other conditions are right, including the availability of a sufficiently educated work-force) have benefited especially, since there is more scope for them to learn and to catch-up. This is consistent with finding that the catch-up variable in equation (10.1) is not significant before the Second World War, but is significant thereafter.

It is interesting that Matthews has also noted that catch-up was apparently not operating significantly before the Second World War, but that it did operate afterwards. He conjectures:

Still within the conceptual framework of the catch-up model, one could postulate that after the Second World War the facilities for international transfer of technology suddenly increased, say because of the more rapid growth of world trade or because of the activities of multinational companies or because of the removal of obstacles to transfer, formerly created by xenophobic governments. (Matthews 1982, 12)

Here, the additional point is made that similar developments were at work *within* countries and between countries.

Another independent piece of evidence in favour of this hypothesis is that the time lag between inventions (defined as 'the first idea, sketch, or contrivance of a new product, process or system, which may or may not be patented') and the relevant subsequent innovations ('the first introduction of a new product, process, or system into the ordinary commercial or social activity of a country') has apparently shortened appreciably over the last century,[15] and the rate of diffusion of mature technologies has speeded up.[16]

To some extent, the increase in ϱ, owing to the above factors, was a statistical artefact. Using my preferred definition of investment, i.e. the cost of improving economic arrangements, management resources devoted to searching for and implementing investment projects are themselves a part of investment, as are research and development expenditures. Neither is

---

[15] An equation $G = ae^{bT}$, where G is the gap in years from invention to innovation and T is the date of the invention, was fitted to the data given on 62 inventions in Freeman, Clark, and Soete (1982, Table 3.1(a), (b) and (c)), the dates used being those of the authors. The resulting correlation was highly significant ($r^2 = 0.435$), with $b = -0.0305$. The inventions listed had dates ranging from 1874 to 1961. The result is biased since inventions made in recent years which had not yet resulted in innovations are inevitably excluded, and only those whose innovations have appeared in a fairly short time are thus included. The rate of fall of the 'gap' is thus exaggerated. (The value of b implies that the 'gap' falls to about a fifth of its value in 50 years.) But it is nevertheless probable that there has been a significant and substantial fall. The definitions of invention and innovation quoted are from Freeman *et al.* (1982, 201).

[16] See Ray (1984, 88): 'Vastly improved information and communication must have contributed to the fact that the decline of the open hearth method of steel-making was much faster than the decline of the Bessemer method, the previous dominant steel-making process . . . The study of float glass conveys the same message: it has replaced the earlier processes of making flat glass within a relatively shorter time; the previous technology stayed at its peak for a long time but its fall has been precipitous.'

included in the conventionally defined gross investment figures I have had to use. Hence it is probable that, if investment were measured as I should ideally like it to be measured, there would be a greater increase in its share, s, from before to after the Second World War than I have allowed for. A smaller increase in ϱ would then be needed to explain the observed increase in g, the growth rate. However, while this is a qualification that must be borne in mind, I very much doubt that it seriously changes the main picture. A very sizeable increase in ϱ does seem to have occurred over this period.

An interesting implication of the foregoing is that there may be two levels at which certain kinds of investment affect the rate of growth. Thus, for example, investment that improves communications may directly increase output (by reducing working hours spent on travel, say) and may in addition improve investment opportunities (i.e. increase ϱ) by speeding up the diffusion of innovations and increasing an awareness of improvements being made elsewhere. Some expenditures on education and on research and development may also be of this kind, as may investments which improve the competitiveness of the market system. Institutional changes that foster growth can be of many kinds, and may cost something to bring about. This leads us to the subject of the following section.

10.8   Why was economic growth so slow in the past?

The causes of the Industrial Revolution, or, more generally, of economic growth in the modern era, have been much studied. It is interesting to turn the question round and to ask why growth in earlier centuries was negligible by comparison with current norms. Were investment opportunities lacking? Or were they simply not taken? And, in either case, for what reasons?

Kuznets is one of those who has emphasized the accumulation of 'empirical and tested knowledge'.

That the accumulation of empirical and tested knowledge is at the base of the enormous growth of population and economic production during the recent two centuries is a truism . . . the rate at which additions are made to the stock of tested knowledge will affect the rate at which that knowledge will be applied in economic production, and the latter may spell important differences in the rate as well as structure of economic growth. And this difference, which we cannot measure in our present state of ignorance, between modern times and the earlier centuries in the rate of additions to scientific knowledge must account, in large part, for unusually rapid rates of economic growth in recent centuries. (Kuznets 1966, 60)

This view of the primacy of scientific knowledge was criticized in Chapter 5. Technical knowledge has not depended on prior scientific knowledge in many fields, even if it has in some. Growth of technical knowledge is the *result* of investment, and not a prior cause of it. Hence it is not enough to point to the undoubted fact that an enormous growth of knowledge has accompanied the growth of the world economy in the last two centuries. That does not explain why either of them occurred, or why they did not occur before.

Kuznets expressed very similar views again in 1980, and was criticized by W. Fischer and I. M. D. Little.[17] Fischer thought that much could be learned by studying the reasons why some countries have *not* succeeded in taking off into self-sustained economic growth. He pointed out that the Chinese and Islamic civilizations were for centuries technically superior to Europe and yet failed to take off, and that one great historian of Chinese science and technology, Needham, 'tends to look for the answer not in his own field of expertise, but in the socio-political institutions and behaviour' (Giersch 1981, 60).

Indeed, it is worth interposing a significant quotation here from Needham:

In other words, not to put too fine a point upon the matter, whoever would explain the failure of Chinese society to develop modern science had better begin by explaining the failure of Chinese society to develop mercantile and then industrial capitalism. Whatever the individual prepossessions of Western historians of science, all are necessitated to admit that from the fifteenth century AD onwards a complex of changes occurred; the Renaissance cannot be thought of without the Reformation, the Reformation cannot be thought of without the rise of modern science, and none of them can be thought of without the rise of capitalism, capitalist society, and the decline and disappearance of feudalism. We seem to be in the presence of a kind of organic whole, a packet of change, the analysis of which has hardly yet begun. . . . I would be prepared to say that, if parallel social and economic changes had been possible in Chinese society, then some form of modern science would have arisen there. (Needham 1963, 139)

Fischer briefly mentions various explanations which have been suggested for the failures, but most are at least incomplete. Thus, the decentralization of power and competition between many political and social groups favoured Europe over China—but then, 'the Islamic world was never centralized over a long period'. Nor was it religion, with Islam and Christianity being closer to each other than to other world religions. He also mentions economic needs, social institutions, and 'a particular European frame of mind called "rationality" ', but then prudently refrains from giving answers to 'these really big questions'. However, he does make some suggestions. Since growth inevitably involves changes which disrupt traditional ways of life, some way of resolving the resulting conflicts must be found, or change will be blocked (this is also stressed by Kuznets), and this points to the necessity of the rule of law and internal peace and good government.

---

[17] See the contributions by the three authors cited in Giersch (1981).

Good government in this sense allows people to pursue their own goals without fear of being penalized for becoming wealthy, it allows regions and social groups to develop differently, it allows "economic forces" to work themselves out, for example, to allocate the factors of production in an efficient manner. In Giersch 1981, 63)

Fischer concludes by stressing the need for a society to be flexible and open in its response to challenges, with the Italian city-states in late medieval Europe, the Netherlands in the sixteenth and seventeenth centuries, England in the eighteenth, and America in the nineteenth and early twentieth centuries as the leading examples.

At the end of his comments, Fischer has drifted away from his starting point of considering failures to grow to the more usual one of singling out successes. Ian Little, the other commentator on Kuznets, devotes most attention to slow growth and the reasons for it. He points out that, until the eighteenth century,

improvements and dissemination seem to have been almost incredibly slow. The breastplate harness of horses, which tended to throttle them, reduced their efficiency, as compared with a padded collar, from 15 manpower to 4 manpower. It took 3000 years or more for a rudimentary padded collar to evolve, and another 1000 years for it to develop and become general. It similarly took thousands of years for fore and aft rigging and a swinging boom to appear. Yet such improvements did not have to wait upon new materials, or concentrated power; nor did they require, by way of 'science', more than observation, wit, and ingenuity. Glancing through the 3000-odd pages of the Oxford History of Technology, one finds dozens of statements like—'the general form of war galley had not changed very greatly 1500 years later' (i.e. in AD 1500), or 'Thus by *c.* 1500 BC three basic glass-making techniques were in use. It was not for another 1500 years or so that a new process was developed (glass blowing).' (Giersch 1981, 66)

Little considers, but regards as unsatisfactory, an ecological explanation that modern growth is a response to population pressures on limited land. He suggests that low and inefficient investment may be the reasons, the inefficiency being investment in cathedrals, tombs, and armies.

Does historiography support the hypothesis of a rapid rise in, and redirection of, investment starting in the late Middle Ages? I do not know. Even if this investment theory were substantiated, one could ask further what determines investment, and its efficiency. This would bring us to capital markets, and beyond them to social, religious, and psychological theories.

At which point he abandons the quest.

Not being an historian, I have no commission to pronounce on these matters, but I am rasher than those whom I have quoted. Little's suggestion that low and inefficient investment explains low growth is the one I naturally start from. How can that, in turn, be explained? Let us first consider the investment opportunities available. If equation (10.3) is accepted, the average rate of return on investment when there is no growth of employment was only around 5 per cent per annum before 1914. Employment growth would have added one or two percentage points to this in the UK or Japan, and two or three in the USA, but, if we are thinking of the centuries before the Industrial Revolution, zero is a reasonable approximation for employment growth. Furthermore, communications were a good deal worse then, as Little's vivid examples show, so learning from others' investment was very slow; in addition, with a low rate of investment elsewhere, there was in any case less to learn. Average rates of return were thus possibly well below 5 per cent per annum. There could still have been, and certainly were, *some* investments earning far higher returns, but they were thin on the ground. Where returns were high because of gains at others' expense (e.g. through fraud), little or no growth would have resulted.

Nevertheless, with very little growth in prospect, rates of discount should also have been low, were it not for risk and uncertainty. There is evidence that rates of discount were, in fact, often high.[18] Fischer's good government, with some assurance that profits earned could mostly be kept, was lacking in most countries most of the time. Insecurity made it sensible to 'invest' in military strength, and the feudal system, with its curbs on the liberty of the individual, was perhaps an efficient response. Insecurity also meant that the best investments for the individual were often gold, jewellery, or land, which could be hidden or at least not easily destroyed. Individual acquisition of these did little or nothing to transform society. It merely reshuffled ownership, and did not represent investment by society as a whole: hence, a zero-sum game. The energies and interests of the most powerful, able, and best educated members of society were devoted not to investment, but to politics and war. Acquisition of wealth was indeed often a negative-sum game.

Another reason for the lack of investment was the class-ridden nature of many societies which was inimical to change of any kind. Those at the top had an interest in laws and conventions that kept each man in his station, while those at the bottom were too weak to upset the order. The Indian caste system is an example of this, and it is close to the theme of Olson (1982).[19]

Yet another reason was widespread illiteracy, which meant that

---

[18] Thus, for example, McCloskey and Nash (1984) cite evidence from the movement of grain prices from harvest to harvest, and of ratios of returns to costs for owning sheep or cattle, as well as other evidence, all tending to show that rates of discount were over 20 per cent p.a. in Europe in the Middle Ages, but fell to something under 10 or 12 per cent in the 16th century.

[19] See p. 334 for further discussion of this stimulating book.

accumulated knowledge, other than that which could be passed on by training on the job, was available to only a small fraction of society. Investment in education was in turn hindered by the view that it was unnecessary, unsuitable, and even dangerous for most people.

Finally, one may mention the power of organized religion, partly because it absorbed the energies of many of the best educated, partly because the building of tombs, temples, cathedrals, and churches absorbed a great deal of savings, and partly because it was sometimes inimical to scientific inquiry.

The list of anti-growth factors could be extended. Perhaps, however, the most crucial was lack of freedom—economic, social, and political. Hartwell (1983) has pointed out that economies have always contained a mixture of three main systems for making production, consumption, and distribution decisions: namely, traditional–collective, command centrally administered, and market–free enterprise. 'It was the gradual freeing of man's entrepreneurial talents from the bonds of custom and command that finally resulted in the remarkable economic growth of the industrial revolution'.

In terms of human history, sustained economic growth is rare, and this suggests that several conditions (Needham's packet), rather than merely one or two, have had to be met before it can occur. It is also the case, however, that its occurrence has at least in some respects made its survival more probable. Investment has improved communications, and increased education, which has weakened class systems and religion. Increased income has made it easier to save, and widespread increased wealth has given more people an interest in maintaining law and order. The free societies are the richest, and best able to defend themselves; nor do men who have tasted freedom abandon it without a struggle. One can also think of greater dangers that have resulted from increased wealth, and doom-mongering is always in fashion. Some less fashionable optimism is needed as a corrective.

11

WHY GROWTH RATES (AND FACTOR SHARES) DIFFER, II

11.1 Introduction

Chapter 10 was concerned with only the linear version of the model. In this chapter we move on to consider the theoretically more satisfactory curvilinear version in which the investment programme contour (IPC) is concave to the origin. I maintain the assumption that there are no diminishing returns to the rate of investment, and hence that there is only one IPC, since that is both simple and consistent with the data. However, by allowing for curvature of the IPC, one can investigate the determinants of the shares of labour and capital in total income.

Interest in theories that seek to explain the functional distribution of income reached a peak in the 1950s and 1960s, and I review some of the relevant literature below. That the theories were never very satisfactory is attested by two surveys of them:

The present state of distribution theory is most unsatisfactory. This statement would probably always command a wide measure of assent, irrespective of time or place; but to-day, in view of some recent contributions, it has perhaps more than ordinary pertinency. (Reder 1959, 180)

The theory of income distribution is in a highly unsatisfactory and controversial state. (Scitovsky 1964, 15)

The theory put forward here is also unsatisfactory; but I hope that readers will conclude that it is more satisfactory than its predecessors.

Curvature of the IPC results from diminishing returns to labour when more and more labour per unit of investment is added to already existing employment. Because of the curvature, one should observe that more labour-intensive investments are chosen when the share of labour, λ, is low than when it is high (see Chapter 6).

The most obvious way to test the theory is to see whether a second-degree curve, such as equation (6.5), gives a better fit than a straight line to the period data. Two versions of this direct approach were tried, and are reported in Section 11.3 (b) below. In one of these, all of the coefficients of the explanatory variables were left to be determined by the regression. As this left nine explanatory variables to be so determined, with only twenty-six observations, it is perhaps not surprising that few coefficients were significant. In the other version, ϱ was prespecified by making use of equation (10.3). (Equation (10.1) was also tried but proved less satisfactory.) The results were consistent with the preferred, indirect, approach described below, but did not really add anything to it. The second-degree term which determined the amount of curvature was not significantly different from 0. It was concluded that the degree of curvature was probably not very great, so that a second-degree curve did not emerge as clearly preferable to a linear equation for explaining growth.

As an alternative to this direct approach, use was made of the data on labour's share to estimate the degree of curvature indirectly. This was done by relating labour's share to the labour intensity of investment in the way described in Section 11.2 below and using equations (6.2) and (6.6). The resulting fit was not particularly good, but this was to be expected, as it was not possible to make allowance for a number of variables (such as the degree of imperfection of markets, 'animal spirits', taxation, and the cost and availability of fixed interest finance) which probably differed between countries and periods and which would have affected labour shares. Furthermore, it seems quite likely that the shape of the investment programme contours differed between countries and periods for other reasons (some of which are mentioned in Section 11.2), and this would help to explain the poor fit of the relationship observed. Despite these uncertainties, I believe the evidence is consistent with the view that labour's share *is* smaller when the labour intensity of investment is greater, *ceteris paribus*.

The relation between the two implies a certain, rather slight, degree of curvature of the investment programme contours. In Section 11.3 the implied second-degree curve is fitted to the data, and the resulting errors compared with those in the best linear equations. While the fit is worse, it is only very slightly so, and I conclude from this that all the data taken together (i.e. including those relating to labour's share) can be quite well explained in terms of the theory. I do not know of an alternative theory that would explain the data so well.

There is one further point to be made in this introduction. The theory of distribution shares, and of the relation between those shares and the labour intensity of investment, is also a theory of employment. It provides an explanation for changes in employment, *given* the rate of investment and *assuming* that the ratio of output to capacity is unchanged. Employment will grow faster for any given rate of investment the lower is labour's share of value added. Throughout, I treat each period as if it were one of equilibrium growth, and hence as if rates of investment and shares of labour were constant, resulting in constant rates of growth of employment and output. This is a simplification of reality which has been followed throughout the growth model and its application. It does violence to the facts, since (as was noted in Chapter 2), labour's share rose in the UK, and the rise was appreciable in some periods. There were also changes in some other countries (as well as some trends in shares of investment). I have not distinguished, so far as the explanation of employment trends is concerned, between periods in which there is a particular average share of labour with no trend, and one in which there is the same average share of labour with an upward trend. In the latter, the rate of growth of real wages will have been faster than the former, and, according to most theories of employment, this might have been expected to result in a slower growth of employment in the latter than in the former. Further investigation of this seems necessary, but it is left (like much else) to others.

11.2 Explaining the share of labour: the preferred approach

(a) The alternatives and the main results

Equations (6.2) and (6.6) are repeated here for convenience, with (6.2.) modified by including the variables k_1 and k_2 to allow for imperfect markets, 'animal spirits', borrowing, and taxation of savings (see pp. 278, 291, and 399):

$$\frac{\lambda}{1 - k_1 - k_2 s} = \frac{dq}{dl} = \mu = b - 2c\,\frac{l}{\varrho} \qquad \text{(6.2) and (6.6)}$$

The following variants were considered.

1. The dependent variable is $\lambda/(1 - s)$. I had no data on k_1 and k_2, and so took the limiting cases in which markets are perfect and firms maximize profits or, alternatively, 'animal spirits' offset the imperfections ($k_1 = 0$), and where net taxation is 0 and any fixed interest finance is available at an interest cost equal to the firm's own discount rate ($k_2 = 1$) (or, alternatively, cheap finance offsets taxation).
2. The dependent variable is λ. This gives

$$\lambda = b\,(1 - k_1) - bk_2 s - 2c\,(1 - k_1)\,\frac{l}{\varrho} + 2ck_2\,\frac{g_L}{\varrho}.$$

Whichever variant is chosen, there are two alternatives as regards ϱ:

(a) we could derive ϱ from equation (10.1) or (10.3), and insert these prespecified values into variant 1 or variant 2;
(b) we could let the regression equation itself determine ϱ.

The above gives four alternatives (and six if we consider both equations (10.1) and (10.3) in (a)), all of which were tried. I decided that the most satisfactory of these was (1a), using equation (10.3) to prespecify ϱ. The advantage of prespecifying ϱ (i.e. using alternative (a) rather than (b)) is that the resulting equation is consistent with the best equation explaining growth. Alternative (b) requires more explanatory variables, and this results in equations with ill-determined coefficients, especially when combined with alternative 2. Where significant values were obtained, their standard errors were such that there was no reason to reject the coefficients in the preferred alternative. Hence little more could be learned from following alternative (b).

Within alternative (a), equation (10.3) was preferred to (10.1) because it results in a better fit for the final curvilinear equation explaining growth (see Section 11.3 below).

Alternative 1 was preferred to 2 because one cannot place much confidence in the coefficients of 2, whose standard errors are again large. The same fundamental difficulty applies to alternative 2 as to (b). In each case, the resulting increase in the number of explanatory variables is large in relation to the number of observations, and it seems preferable to constrain the equation rather tightly, because we have good reason to suppose that we are omitting important explanatory variables (relating to taxes, subsidies, finance, and the structure of the economy), which mean that the coefficients are ill-determined. It seems better, then, to make maximum use of the information gained from equations (10.1) and (10.3), and to use the additional information provided by the labour share data to estimate only one more coefficient relating to curvature (i.e. c).

I first report and discuss the results of the preferred alternative. The results of the other alternatives are summarized briefly in Section 11.2 (e).

Figure 11.1 is a scatter diagram in which $\lambda/(1 - s)$ is plotted against l/ϱ, the values of ϱ being derived from equation (11.3). The line shown is

$$\frac{\lambda}{1 - s} = 0.8774 - 0.8386 \, \frac{l}{\varrho}. \tag{11.1}$$
$$(67.44) \quad (-5.73)$$

$\bar{R}^2$ (weighted residuals) $= 0.679$; $\quad \bar{R}^2$ (unweighted residuals) $= 0.700$
s.e. (weighted residuals) $= 0.0306$; s.e. (unweighted residuals) $= 0.0375$

which is fitted to all the points shown (weighted as before)[1] *excluding* all the Japanese observations, the US observations for 1889-1900 and 1900-13,

---

[1] While I believe that the weighted regression is more reliable, fitting an unweighted one leaves the coefficients little affected:

$$\frac{\lambda}{1 - s} = 0.8690 - 0.9608 \, \frac{l}{\varrho}.$$
$$(76.11) \quad (-7.24)$$

$\bar{R}^2 = 0.774$; s.e. $= 0.0325$

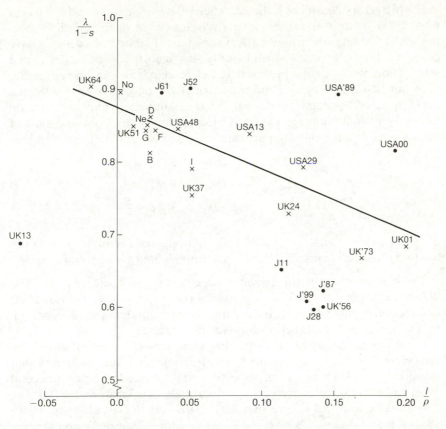

Fig. 11.1 Scatter diagram relating λ/(1 − s) to l/ϱ
Regression line shown is equation (11.1), fitted to observations indicated by crosses; observations indicated by dots are excluded. For key to periods see e.g. Table 10.1. Each period's first year is shown above, and if this is in the nineteenth century it is shown with an apostrophe; thus, USA '89 = USA 1889–1900

and the UK observations for 1856–73 and 1913–24. Explanations for these exclusions are attempted below, but inspection of the diagram shows that they are all outliers to the fitted line.

The equation 'explains' rather more than two-thirds of the variance of the sixteen observations to which it is fitted, and both cofficients are highly significant. The constant, 0.8774, should in theory be close to the coefficient of g_L in equation (10.3), which is 0.9034, and the difference between them is insignificant. The coefficient of l/ϱ has the expected sign, and its magnitude implies only slight curvature of the investment programme curve, as we shall see later. So far, then, the equation is really very satisfactory considering the fact that I have omitted k_1 and k_2, which must differ between countries and periods, as well as structural differences in their economies which could affect the share of labour. However, I have obtained this satisfactory result only by ignoring the outliers, and satisfaction can be maintained only if a defence of this can be mustered.

In the first place, one should note that if the outliers are included the coefficients of the equation do not change significantly and both remain highly significant, although the fit of the equation is then poor and most of the variance is unexplained. The equation fitted to *all* the observations is

$$\frac{\lambda}{1-s} = 0.8729 - 0.7611 \frac{l}{\varrho}. \tag{11.2}$$
$$(40.16) \quad (-3.38)$$

$\bar{R}^2$ (weighted residuals) = 0.294; $\bar{R}^2$ (unweighted residuals) = 0.113
s.e. (weighted residuals) = 0.0654;   s.e. (unweighted residuals) = 0.0978

The best estimate of the curvature coefficient, c, would thus be little affected whether one included or excluded the outliers. Nevertheless, one's *confidence* in the estimate, and in the theory underlying it, depends on finding a plausible explanation for excluding them.

It is clear from Figure 11.1 that the US observations are all above the regression line, implying a higher share of labour than the norm, and that this divergence from the norm lessened through time. By the post-Second World War period the divergence had virtually disappeared. The UK, by constrast, lies below the regression line (apart from the last observation for 1964–73), and, again, this divergence on the whole diminshed through time, being greatest in 1856–73 and becoming very small in 1951–64. An exception is 1913–24, however. The Japanese observations before the Second World War are especially unreliable, but they follow a somewhat similar path to that of the UK, lying below the line before the Second World War, and then going above the line in the postwar period. There is then a strong contrast between the USA on the one hand, and the UK and Japan on the other, in the earliest years, but this contrast diminishes as time passes.

A possible explanation for all of this is the availability of agricultural land or a substitute for such land through trade. In the latter half of the nineteenth century land was plentiful in the USA, but scarce in the UK and Japan, in relation to labour. Furthermore, food (and especially if one excludes the processing and distribution of food) represented a more important component of consumers' expenditure. As development proceeded, the economic important of land declined. In the USA a smaller and smaller fraction of the population worked on farms and a smaller and smaller fraction of consumers' expenditure was spent on food. In the UK and Japan, trade increasingly provided a cheap substitute for home-grown food. UK agriculture reached a peak around 1870, from which it began a long period of stagnation which lasted until the Second World War. Farm rents in 1938 were £35 million, compared with £62 million in 1872 (Feinstein 1976, Table 23). In 1951, T. W. Schultz wrote a famous article on 'The Declining Economic Importance of Agricultural Land' in which he contrasted the economics of Ricardo, where diminishing returns to labour in agriculture played a major role, with the *'Dynamic Economics'* of R. F. Harrod, who he quoted as saying 'I propose to discard the law of diminishing returns from the land as a primary determinant in a progressive economy . . . I discard it only because in our particular context it appears that its influence may be quantitatively unimportant' (Harrod 1948, 20). Schultz produced evidence from the USA, the UK, and France in support of two propositions he considered to be 'historically valid in representing the economic development that has characterized Western communities':

1. a declining proportion of the aggregate inputs of the community is required to produce (or to acquire) farm products; and
2. of the inputs employed to produce farm products, the proportion represented by land is not an increasing one, despite the recombination of inputs in farming to use less human effort relative to other inputs, including land. (Schultz 1951, 727)

In terms of the theory presented here, when farm land and farm produce were important, an economy with plenty of farm land in relation to labour was one with plenty of labour-intensive investment opportunities. On the investment programme map, the frequency of investment opportunities to the north-east was high. With the availability of free land in the USA, it needed labour, but not a great deal of saving, to expand farm output.[2] The investment programme contours thus sloped upwards more steeply in the USA than in the UK and Japan, where there was no good farmland in free supply, and where labour-intensive investment opportunities were therefore relatively less plentiful. The importance of these differences declined, however, as farm products declined in economic importance (Schultz's propostion 1), and so investment opportunities in the USA and in the UK and Japan became more alike.

This is one possible explanation for the outliers in Figure 11.1, but it may not be of sufficient quantitative importance to explain them fully, and it is in any case worth considering other possible explanations. One such relates to differences in social structures. Both the UK and Japan inherited social

---

[2] See also fn. 13 below with reference to the labour intensity of US agriculture in the latter half of the 19th century.

structures from a very long period in which the forces of a free economy were restricted and controlled in numerous ways. The USA, by contrast, and especially after the Civil War, was a land in which individual initiative was probably much less influenced either by actual controls of one sort or another, or by conventions that carried as much or more weight. Employers in the UK and Japan may have been able to keep down the share of wages by collective behaviour of a kind that was impossible in the USA. In terms of our theory, k_1 may have been substantial in the UK and Japan because of the monopsonistic behaviour of employers, so that for the same $\mu = \lambda / (1 - k_1 - k_2 s)$ and the same s, λ in those countries had to be much smaller than in the USA. The weakening of these monopsonistic influences and the strengthening of trade union powers, so reducing k_1, would have then shifted up the share of labour, λ, for given values of μ and s in the UK and Japan but not in the USA.[3] This does not, however, explain the apparent *down*ward shift in $\lambda/(1 - s)$ in the USA which is shown in Figure 11.1. Part of the explanation is the statistical point that the shares of labour in the USA in both 1889–1900 and 1900–13 were estimated from period average (rather than annual) data, and so no allowance could be made for slump years in which the share of labour was especially high. In other periods these slump years were removed before striking an average (see p. 47 above). As a further explanation, one might invoke increases in taxation on investment (or profit), which would have increased k_2. These increases also occurred, however, in the UK (and probably in Japan?), and so one would have to suppose that there they were outweighed by the forces acting in the opposite direction which were reducing k_1.

Differences in taxation and finance may also explain the post-Second World War observations for Japan, which lie appreciably above the regression line in Figure 11.1. Profits tax rates in Japan were relatively low and the gearing of large Japanese firms was relatively high, and banks provided finance at real interest levels which were well below the real rates of return being earned on investment. For Japan, therefore, k_2 may have been relatively low in the postwar period, thus inducing a high value of λ for given μ and s. Another possible explanation for the postwar Japanese observations is that 'animal spirits' were especially strong there. The managers of Japanese firms may have given more weight to growth and so relatively less to profit maximization than their Western counterparts, as some observers have alleged. The effect of this would have been to reduce k_1, and even to make it negative.

The importance of custom and inertia seems to be required, however, to explain the 1913–24 observation for the UK. This estimate is statistically

[3] As is shown below, whereas the weakening of employers', and the strengthening of labour's, bargaining power has been cited by some authors as an explanation of the rising share of labour in the UK and Japan, several writers have argued that unionization in the USA has had a negligible effect on labour's share there.

suspect. The share of labour, λ, is the average for the years 1913, 1920, 1922, and 1923. The war years and the slump year 1921 were excluded (and, as always, the final year of the period), but the years included, apart from 1913, were abnormal in several respects. The other relevant variables (g, g_L, and s) for this period are subject to appreciable measurement errors. Taking the estimates as they stand, the share of labour is much too low in terms of our theory, given the decline in employment per unit of investment. This could have been due, however, to stickiness in the wage share, since for the years either before or after this period, the same or similar wage share *was* roughly appropriate; i.e., the observations for 1901–13 and 1924–37 lie quite close to the regression line in Figure 11.1.

One last factor, peculiar to the UK, which must be mentioned is the nationalization programme undertaken after the Second World War. The nationalized industries invested heavily but were not very profitable. One would not expect to find private industries in steady growth in which the combined shares of wages and investment exceeded value added, leaving less than nothing to be taken out by the owners. This, however, was typically the situation in the nationalized industries after the war, and it must have tended to raise λ for given s for the whole non-residential business sector.

(b)   The results for the UK further discussed

Matthews *et al.* (1982, 194–7) discuss the fall in the share of profits and the rise in labour's share in the UK since about 1870. They do not provide a quantitative explanation of the kind attempted here; instead, they provide several qualitative explanations. The first is in terms of the neoclassical production function, and states that technical progress was biased in such a way that, given the actual growth experienced in labour and capital, the share of capital fell. Strictly speaking, an explanation in these terms could be made to fit any change in the share, and is not so much an explanation as a description of what must have happened if one believes in the neoclassical production function and if one makes some assumption about the elasticity of substitution between labour and capital. (Matthews *et al.* assume it is less than 1.) There is always, then, *some* bias in the rate of technical progress which can explain what happened. Since I reject the neoclassical production function on theoretical grounds, I do not believe that this provides a useful approach. Even were one to accept the production function, it would not seem to be very useful, unless it could be shown that the relationships involved were stable, or explicable in stable terms by some other changes that could be observed, and this is not attempted by the authors.[4].

[4] For a criticism of this type of analysis, which shows very clearly how any pair of observations of relative prices and relative quantities of labour and capital can be 'explained' by making appropriate assumptions about the bias of technical progress or the elasticity of substitution between labour and capital, see Johnson (1973, 194–5).

A counter-attack could be made on my own approach along similar lines. Is there not some combination of shifts in the position and slope of the investment programme curve (which, in this context, is the counterpart of the neoclassical production function) which can 'explain' any change or difference in the share of labour income? There is, but I am trying here to point to observed changes or differences in *other phenomena* (such as changes or differences in the importance of agricultural land, the power of employers versus employees, taxation and the cost of finance, etc.) which can account for such shifts. I am not simply labelling the shifts 'biased shifts in the investment programme curve', which would be the equivalent procedure. My equation does explain a sizeable part of the rise in labour's share for the UK from 1873–1901 to 1964–73. Given the actual changes in g, g_L, and s, and taking the estimates of ϱ based on equation (10.3), equation (11.1) explains a little less than half of the rise in λ between these periods.[5] This still leaves half to be explained, and for that we must turn to the other factors Matthews *et al.* discuss.

A second explanation provided by them is similar to that given above in terms of the weakening of employers' monopsonistic power in the labour market and the strengthening of trade unions. However, they do not think that this helps to explain the rising share of labour in 1870–90, or in the interwar period, presumably because neither of these was a period when trades unions became manifestly stronger. In both periods, Matthews *et al.* point out, there was increasing foreign competition which may have squeezed profits. They reject, however, a long-run decline in the degree of monopoly in *product* markets as an explanation for the fall in the share of profits over the whole period (1870–1973) as being implausible.

In contrast to the suggestions made here, Matthews *et al.* do not attach importance to the decline in agriculture as an explanation for the fall in the share of property income in GNP. In their very interesting discussion of this question, they point out that 'most of the falls in the shares in GNP of farm property income [6] and of total agricultural income occurred before 1913' (Matthews *et al.* 1982, 175). In fact, they give a table which shows that farm property income as a percentage of GNP fell from 10.1 in 1856 to 2.4 per cent in 1913, and then further to 1.1 per cent in 1973.[7] However, although this statistically accounted for well over half of the total fall in the share of property income between 1856 and 1973, they add:

[5] The equation explains two-thirds of the rise in $\lambda/(1 - s)$ between these periods, as can be seen from Figure 11.1, but only about half of the rise in λ.

[6] Farm property income includes rent on farm land and buildings plus profits of farmers, including the property component of the incomes of self-employed farmers. It thus includes everything that I have included in 'profits' as opposed to 'wages'.

[7] A small part of the decline from 1913 to 1973, viz. 0.2%, is attributable to the exclusion of Eire from the UK after 1920.

It would be wrong, however, to infer that the decline in agriculture's importance was a major force in diminishing property's share in GNP. Property's share in agricultural output in 1856 was in fact only fractionally higher than property's share in GNP (or the share of domestic property in GDP). The decline in the relative importance of agriculture, taken by itself, would therefore have done little more than alter the sector of the economy where property income was earned; it would have resulted in an increase in other property income's share in GNP nearly equal to the fall in farm property income's share. (Matthews *et al.* 1982, 176-7)

As a proposition about a hypothetical alternative in which agricultural output remained with the same share of GNP (or GDP) as in 1856, while other average output also maintained the same share (instead of gaining), this is impeccable. Had the shares of property income in total output in agriculture and non-agriculture remained as in 1856, the difference between this hypothetical alternative and one in which the share of agriculture fell as it did would have been very small so far as the share of property income in GNP is concerned. This structural change cannot statistically explain the actual fall in property income's share.

It is another matter, however, to conclude that the supply of cheap food from abroad, plus the low income elasticity of demand for food (which, as Matthews *et al.* point out, were the main reasons for the fall in the share of agriculture in GNP), were unimportant parts of the explanation for this fall in property income's share. The question of how the economy would have developed in the absence of these factors is much more difficult to answer, and cannot be answered merely by an appeal to the above sorts of statistics. With similar rates of investment and labour force growth, but with a higher income elasticity of demand for food, the demand for food would have grown faster, and, in the absence of imported food, the main source of supply would have had to be internal. Food prices, instead of falling in relation to average prices from 1856 to 1913,[8] would probably have risen substantially. Food production would probably also have risen appreciably more than it did. Farm rents would probably have risen dramatically. Real wages throughout the economy would have risen less, perhaps much less, and the share of 'profit' in total output might then have fallen much less than it did.

(c)   The results for the USA further discussed

There does not seem to be any American study, corresponding to that of Matthews *et al.,* that is very helpful in explaining the US data on income shares. Two studies that are frequently referred to in the literature are those by Johnson (1954) and Kravis (1959). Both of these relied on estimates by

---

[8] They fell by about 14% in relation to the GNP deflator from 1856 to 1913 (Matthews *et al.* 1982, 643).

King (1919) and Martin (1939) for pre-1939 data. These estimates, not to mince matters, appear to be very unreliable, as was pointed out, for example by Lebergott (1964). In my estimates I have not used King or Martin, but have preferred Budd's (1960) estimates, which are independent of these sources.

Both Johnson and Kravis found that there had been an increase in labour's share of national income (including an allowance for the labour income of the self-employed) from 1900–09 to the early post-Second World War period. Both pointed to the rise in the share of government employees as part of the explanation for this, but, even when they are excluded, a modest rise in the labour share remains. In my figures, which refer to non-residential business and are gross rather than net of depreciation, there is a rather larger rise in the labour share from 1900–13 to 1948–73. In looking for explanations for the rise in the share, when government employees are excluded, Johnson confined himself to factors *other* than shifts in demand and supply. He mentioned that the decline of agriculture, a relatively capital-intensive industry (including land in 'capital'), was part of the explanation, but he was not inclined to put much weight on an increase in the bargaining power of labour.[9] Kravis was also sceptical about the latter, and referred to Reder (1959), who in turn referred to Kerr (1957) and concluded that 'so far the available evidence is entirely compatible with the view that unionism has had but a negligible effect upon labour's share' (Reder 1959, p. 185). One may add that the studies discussed in Bronfenbrenner (1971) confirm that view.[10] There thus appears to be a contrast between the UK and the USA in this important respect, and it is certainly consistent with my own findings: whereas in the case of the UK one needs to explain why labour's share rose as much as it did, in the case of the USA the opposite is the case (see Figure 11.1).

Most of Kravis's attempt to explain the increase in labour's share is couched in terms of changes in the relative quantities and prices of labour and capital with implications drawn about the bias in technical progress (Kravis 1959, 935–45). Reasons have already been given for rejecting this approach.[11]

Three other American studies may be mentioned, but none is helpful here. Reder's study, already referred to, concluded, on the basis of Solow

[9] Because 'almost half the increase in the shares was achieved by the decade 1920–29' (Johnson 1954, 179). Johnson also pointed out that, to some extent, the rise in the share of labour was not matched by an equal rise in labour's real income because the cost of living was lower for farm workers than for other workers, and the numbers of farm workers declined as a share of total workers (p. 180).

[10] See his Chapter 4, Section 8, where Bronfenbrenner refers to studies by Denison (1954), Levinson (1954), Phillips (1960), and Simler (1961).

[11] See p. 319 above. It may be noted that Johnson (1973, pp 193–4) made similar criticisms of Kravis's explanation.

(1957), that an aggregate Cobb-Douglas production function explained the private non-farm share of labour income well, since its trend was more or less constant over the first half of the twentieth century, and since the actual share corresponded well with the value found for the output elasticity with respect to labour input (Reder 1959, 192-200). Kendrick and Sato (1963) provided data on the shares of labour and capital in the private sector of the economy from 1919 to 1960, and also on the associated changes in labour and capital input. However, they did not provide an explanation of the observed increase in labour's share over this period. Instead, they provided what were essentially accounting identities.[12] Finally, Haley (1968), referring to Budd's and Kravis's studies already cited, put his main emphasis on the decline in the importance of agriculture,[13] as well as the increase in the importance of the government sector.

One problem that confronts anyone attempting to explain the shares of labour and capital in the USA is that they apparently changed remarkably little as compared with, for example, the UK or Japan.[14] This means that there is little that any theory can bite on. As Reder suggests, a Cobb-Douglas production function performs quite well, but so do other theories, both neoclassical or otherwise.[15] In my opinion, one needs to contrast the US record with that of other countries if one is to learn anything useful, or provide a good test of any theory. Since none of the writers cited did that, and since, in addition, most of them used the neoclassical production function, I have not found them very helpful for my own inquiries.

[12] They also, however, suggested a constant elasticity of substitution production function for the US economy with an elasticity of substitution of about 0.6, which was deduced simply from the relative rates of growth of the quantities and prices of labour and capital—a procedure that involves assuming neutral technical progress.

[13] Rather surprisingly, Haley attributed both the *decline* in labour's share shown in Budd's estimates for the 60 years up to 1910 (these were not the estimates I have used, but those estimates of Budd which used King's estimates) and the *rise* shown in the subsequent half-century by Kravis to the decline in the importance of agriculture. He argued that agriculture was relatively labour-intensive in the first period and relatively capital-intensive in the second (and also much smaller by then in relation to the rest of the economy). The relative labour intensity of agriculture in the earlier period may help to explain the high labour share then which is apparent in Figure 11.1.

[14] Solow (1958) questioned what was meant by 'remarkably little' in statements of this kind, and suggested a comparison between the variability of the aggregate share and the variability of the shares in individual industries. By 'remarkably little' one might have meant that there was negative correlation between movements of the shares in individual industries, so that the variability of the aggregate share was damped. In the USA in the years he considered, the reverse, if anything, was true. By comparison with the UK or Japan, however, the US aggregate share *does* seem to have changed 'remarkably little'.

[15] Reder found that Kaldor's theory of distribution fitted the US data well, but that, because of the constancy of relative shares, the fit was about as good whether one assumed equal or unequal propensities to save out of wage and non-wage incomes. He also reported that, of five production functions fitted by Solow to the US data, there was no purely statistical reason to choose between four (including the Cobb-Douglas) (Reder 1959, 188-95).

(d)   The results for Japan further discussed

We turn now to studies of Japanese income shares, of which only five (in English) are considered. The most recent are two that form part of Ohkawa and Shinohara (1979). One of these, by Yamada and Hayami (Chapter 4), deals with shares in agriculture, and the other, by Minami and Ono (Chapter 11), deals with shares in non-agriculture. The pre-Second World War data are based on these two studies, which I have used to get as close an approximation as possible to the labour share in non-residential business for comparison with the post-Second World War data, which are derived principally from Dension and Chung (1976). The two remaining studies, whose data were not used, were by Ohkawa (1968) and Ohkawa and Rosovsky (1973). It must be stressed that all the pre-Second World War estimates are particularly uncertain, there being some sizeable differences between the sources just cited, some substantial differences between estimates of total incomes and total output (see Minami and Ono 1979, 216), and some strong assumptions made in arriving at many of the estimates. Even the post-Second World War data are very uncertain, since the importance of self-employed and family labour is so much greater in Japan than in the UK and the USA (and continental Europe), and the allocation between labour and capital is open to question (see fn. 19 below). Because of these great uncertainties, I have placed most reliance on regression equations which exclude the data on Japanese income shares. It is, nevertheless, of some interest to see how the best estimates available do fit the regression line, and this is shown in Figure 11.1.

All the sources agree on there having been an appreciable increase in the share of labour from the interwar years to the post-Second World War period. While a sizeable increase in $\lambda/(1 - s)$ over this period is predicted by my theory (since l/ϱ falls), the actual increase, according to the above estimates, is far bigger: s rose sharply, and this alone would have raised $\lambda/(1 - s)$ by more than equation (11.1) requires, given the fall l/ϱ. There should, therefore, according to the equation, have been a fall rather than a rise in λ. Another way of putting this is that, whereas the postwar levels of λ were somewhat higher than predicted by the equation (explained, I have suggested, by low taxation, high gearing, and cheap finance), the prewar levels of λ were far below the predicted levels—from 11 to 14 percentage points of total income too low. It is this that requires explanation.

Minami and Ono believe that

labor was in unlimited supply for the nonagricultural sector until the end of the 1950s or the beginning of the 1960s. Although the interwar period was one of substantial flux, until this turning point, the nonagricultural sector could employ unskilled workers at the almost constant real wage level prevailing in the agricultural sector. (Minami and Ono 1979, 210)

They add later:

Labor's share of income is higher in the early postwar period than at the end of the prewar period. This can be attributed to the destruction of capital equipment during the war, which resulted in the marked reduction after the war not only of output per worker but also of real wages. However, the reduction of wages was smaller than that of output per worker, because workers could not be employed at wages below the subsistence wage for any length of time.

During the growth of the late 1950s, wage increases lagged behind productivity increases, causing labour's share to decline from 75% in 1955 to 70% in 1960.[16] However, the decline stopped around 1960 and has remained at about 70% through 1968, the last year for which data are available. The stability of income shares is attributable to the low level of surplus labour in the countryside, requiring entrepreneurs in the nonagricultural sector to increase wages steeply, to draw additional workers from the agricultural sector. (Minami and Ono 1979, 212)

This explanation takes us back to that given above (pp. 316–17) for the contrast between the USA on the one hand and the UK and Japan on the other in the late nineteenth century, the one with plenty of agricultural land per worker and the others with comparatively little. I argued that the possession of little agricultural land per worker was a factor tending to lower the share of labour as it implied (in terms of my theory) a relative scarcity of labour-intensive investment projects. For Japan, like the UK, the situation was relieved by foreign trade, which enabled the country to obtain a growing proportion of her food supplies from abroad. However, Japan's dependence on her domestic agriculture was much greater after 1900 than was that of the UK: her land–man ratio was much lower, the proportion of her work-force engaged in agriculture was much higher, and the rate of growth of her population was also much faster. Minami and Ono's unlimited supply of labour from agriculture to the non-agricultural sector at an approximately constant real wage was the result of all this, and, as they point out, the situation persisted until after the Second World War.

It is still somewhat puzzling that the share of labour was so high in the 1950s since there was 'surplus' labour then. Minami and Ono's explanation is in terms of a minimum real wage set by subsistence, but this might have been expected to lead to heavy unemployment if it was much in excess of the amounts businesses deemed it worth paying.

Perhaps one can account for what happened as follows. In the early 1950s, over two-thirds of workers (excluding government workers) were employed in the unincorporated sector; even if one excludes agriculture, half of the workers were in the unincorporated sector.[17] The bulk of these

---

[16] These shares refer to *net* income in non-agriculture, including government employees but excluding housing. The decline in the share of labour in non-residential business was even greater, according to the estimates I have used: namely, from 69% in 1955 to 62% in 1960, the average for 1961–73 being 61%.

[17] See Ohkawa and Rosovsky (1973, 254). Financial sectors as well as agriculture are excluded in the second statement.

workers were proprietors and family workers.[18] The estimated share of labour in the unincorporated sector is based partially on the assumption that these workers earned the same wages as hired workers.[19] For unincorporated enterprises with no hired workers, and there were probably many like this, the actual marginal products of the proprietors or family workers could have been lower than the wages of hired workers. In the absence of unemployment benefits, it was necessary to support family members by a subsistence 'wage' even if the work done in return contributed less than this to the revenues of the enterprise. It could make sense even to hire workers in this situation, since their skills might be superior to those of available family members. Hence, while the wage rate (and so marginal product) for hired labour could not fall below subsistence, the *marginal products* of proprietors and family members could. If one were able to value all labour at its (lower) marginal product, it is then likely that the share of labour in the 1950s would have been appreciably lower than the estimates we have used. Further evidence in support of this is the fact that Minami and Ono's estimates show a big rise in the share of labour in unincorporated enterprises (always excluding agriculture) from the interwar to the postwar period, whereas there is little rise shown for the corporate sector: the former goes up from 53 to 71 per cent comparing 1920–36 with 1953–9, while the latter goes up from 73 to only 75 per cent. The explanation for the rise seems therefore to lie in the unincorporated sector, and it may be more statistical than real.[20]

Apart from Minami and Ono's explanation of the rise in the share of labour since the last war, the only other explanation I can discover in the sources mentioned is Ohkawa's reference to postwar institutional changes:

[18]   See Ohkawa and Rosovsky (1973, 262) for figures for 1958.

[19]   See fn. 20. The Denison–Chung estimates which I have used for non-residential business from 1952 to 1971 are based on an average of two methods similar to the two described in the next footnote, which deals with Minami and Ono's estimates. However, Denison and Chung estimated the labour share in the unincorporated sector for 1970, and assumed that the share was the same in all earlier years. This could explain why the estimated share in the 1950s was high despite the 'surplus' labour available *then*—but not in 1970. See Denison and Chung (1976, 172–4).

[20]   Some doubt, however, attaches to this comparison. Minami and Ono state that they have included all employees in the corporate sector, thus exaggerating its wage share, and land and house rents are excluded prewar but possibly not postwar. For the prewar period they estimated the labour income of unincorporated enterprises by assuming that the workers in it earned 'the average wage in the non-corporate sector'. For the postwar period, as well as estimates on that basis, they also estimated the labour share by assuming that the ratio of non-labour income to captial in the sector was the same as in the corporate sector. It is not clear to me which basis was in fact used in their final table of estimates for postwar, or whether some average was taken (Minami and Ono 1979, 206–7, 217). It is also somewhat disconcerting to find that in Ohkawa's (1968) estimates the behaviour of labour's share in the corporate and unincorporated non-agricultural sectors is precisely the opposite of that according to Minami and Ono. According to Ohkawa, it was labour's share in the coporate sector that rose sharply from the interwar years to the period 1953–62, while labour's share in the unincorporated sector *fell*! (p. 183).

the dissolution of the Zaibatsu, which liquidated monopoly elements, may have had a downward effect on the share of income from assets, and the nation-wide development of trade unions may have affected labour's relative share through the strengthening of labour's bargaining power. (Ohkawa 1968, 180)

(e) Other approaches

In Section 11.2(a) four alternative ways of explaining the share of labour are listed. The preferred alternative, 1(a), has been described at length. By comparison, the other three were all unsatisfactory and are summarized here only briefly.

Alternative 1(b) kept $\lambda/(1 - s)$ as the dependent variable, but did not prespecify ϱ. When an equation of this kind was fitted to the same sixteen observations as equation (11.1), the corresponding coefficients b, and especially c, agreed quite well with (11.1). Hence this equation provided no reason to change the estimate of c. However, the equation gave estimates of ϱ which showed a substantially greater increase than those resulting from (10.3) from before to the periods after the First World War. Since the estimates of λ are generally less reliable than the other estimates, I prefer equation (10.3)'s estimates of ϱ, which are independent of λ.

Alternative 2(a) made λ the dependent variable, with ϱ prespecified. When an equation of this kind was fitted to the same sixteen observations as equation (11.1) the fit was poor ($\bar{R}^2$, weighted residuals, $= 0.328$). The coefficents all had the expected signs, and the estimates of b and c agreed reasonably well with estimates derived from (11.1). The most interesting feature of this result was a significant negative relationship between λ and s, given the other variables (i.e. l/ϱ and $g_L l/\varrho$), as required by my theory but not by orthodox theories. A test for simultaneous equations bias was made, since one could reasonably suppose that s depended negatively on λ. This still left the former negative relationship. Apart from this, the equation provided estimates of k_1 and k_2, the former being close to 0 and the latter close to 1. However, given the poor fit, little confidence could be placed in these.

Finally, alternative 2(b) resulted in an equation with ten explantory variables, of which only the constant had a t-statistic greater than 2, and only one other variable a t-statistic greater than 1. Most of the signs of the coefficients were incorrect.

(f) Summing up

Let me now attempt to sum up in three propositions this lengthy discussion of the factors that explain differences in labour's share between periods and countries. First, it is clear that, at best, the theory embodied in equation (11.1) explains only a modest fraction of the differences observed. I have had to call on several other explanations to account for some large divergences. Second, the other main explanations have related to the availability of agricultural land in relation to the demands placed upon it, changes in the monopsonistic power of employers and in unionization, differences in taxation and the availability of cheap fixed-interest finance, and possibly also differences in 'animal spirits'. Of these, the first was probably important in explaining the contrast between the UK and Japan on the one hand, and the USA (with a much higher labour share) on the other in the latter part of the nineteenth century. But as agricultural land dwindled in importance, the UK, Japan, and the USA all converged, although in the case of Japan this convergence probably did not take place until well into the post-Second World War period. Monopsony and unionization were probably more important in the UK and Japan than in the USA, and again help to explain the contrast between them in earlier years. Taxation and finance really need much more research than I have been able to devote to them (but see further in Chapters 14 and 15), and may, along with 'animal spirits', help to explain the apparently high values of λ for Japan after the Second World War. Third, and finally, even though all these (and possibly other) factors have been important parts of the explanation of what has happened in the past, the relationship expressed in equation (11.1), if true, is also very important. For it implies that the share of wages, and so the real wage at any given time, does make a big difference to the growth of employment that accompanies a given rate of investment. I return to this point in Chapters 15 and 16.

11.3 Explaining growth rates with a curved investment programme contour

The theoretical case for expecting the map of investment programme contours to be concave to the origin was given in Chapter 6. The evidence on the determinants of the share of wages, λ, just considered implies concavity, and I make use of it to derive a curved IPC below. This indirect approach is preferred to the more direct one, described below, of fitting a second-degree IPC to the data.

(a) The indirect approach

From the relation between the share of labour income, the rate of investment, and the labour intensity of investment established in the preceding section, one can derive a curved IPC to replace the straight line of Chapter 10. The equation to this is repeated for convenience:

$$\frac{q}{\varrho} = a + b \ \frac{l}{\varrho} - c \ \left(\frac{l}{\varrho}\right)^2. \tag{6.5}$$

In this equation, one can obtain the values of *a, b* and ϱ from the linear equation (10.3), and of *c* from equation (11.1), it being *half* of the coefficient of l/ϱ in that equation (see equations (6.2) and (6.6)). The resulting equation is as follows:

$$\frac{q}{\varrho} = 0.05228 + 0.9034 \frac{l}{\varrho} - 0.4193 \left(\frac{l}{\varrho}\right)^2 \quad (11.3)$$

with ϱ having the following values in the different periods:[21]

Pre-First World War	$\varrho = 1$
Interwar period	$\varrho = 1.6367$
Post-Second World War	$\varrho = 2.6220 - 1.0382 \ln cu.$

Since equation (11.3) was not obtained by any standard regression technique, one cannot provide the usual tests of significance for it. However, Figure 11.2 shows a scatter diagram in which the twenty-six observations are plotted, with q/ϱ on the vertical and l/ϱ on the horizontal axis. The regression line (10.3)[22] and equation (11.3) are both shown. Since the curvature in (11.3) is slight, the closeness of fit is much the same.

In order to measure this closeness of fit more precisely, one may compare the sum of the squared weighted residuals of equations (10.3) and an equation derived from (11.3). The latter is only slightly greater than the former.[23] We could argue that the introduction of an extra explanatory variable (i.e. the second-degree term, $(l/\varrho)^2$) should have enabled us to *reduce* the sum of the squared residuals. Had we chosen the coefficients in the curvilinear version of the equation so as to minimize the errors, we could indeed have done so—and in fact, an equation along these lines is presented in Section 11.3(b). The objection to that equation, however, is that, although it explains the rates of growth slightly more satisfactorily, it does not explain the data on shares of labour income so satisfactorily. The procedure I have followed has sought to provide as satisfactory an explanation for *both* sets of data as possible. It is recognized that some further improvements could be made by a process of iteration (or possibly by other more subtle ways which I hope others will devise). Whether very

[21] These values for ϱ are obtained from equation (10.3) as follows. We first arbitrarily define $\varrho = 1$ before the first World War. Note that the coefficient of *s* in equation (10.3) is $a\varrho$ (see equation (6.10)). Consequently, ϱ for other periods is the sum of the coefficients of *s* divided by the coefficient of *s* for the period before the First World War. Thus, for the interwar period, $\varrho = (0.05228 + 0.03329)/0.05228$, while for the post-Second World War period $\varrho = (0.05228 + 0.08480 - 0.05428 \ln cu)/0.05228$.

[22] After dividing through by $s\varrho$, with the values of ϱ just given above.

[23] By multiplying equation (11.3) through by $s\varrho$, we obtain an equation with *g* on the left-hand side, and this calculated value for *g* was subtracted from the actual value of *g* for each observation. If the residual is *u*, and the squares of the weights *w* (see Section 10.2), then one can calculate $\Sigma (wu^2)$. This sum of the weighted squared residuals was only 2.2% greater than the sum of the weighted squared residuals of equation (10.3).

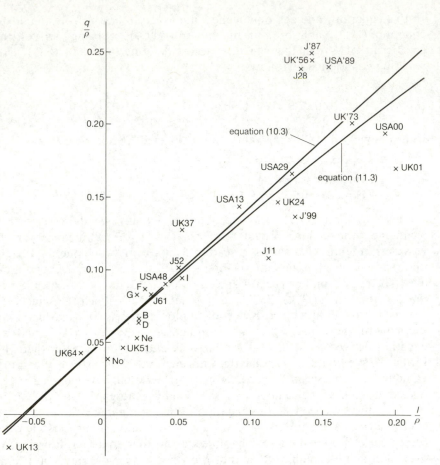

Fig. 11.2 Scatter diagram relating q/ϱ to l/ϱ
For key to periods see e.g. Table 10.1. Each period's first year is shown
above, and if this is in the nineteenth century it is shown with an
apostrophe; thus, USA '89 = USA 1889–1900

much improvement can be made with the available data is, however,
doubtful. For the present, I leave it there.

I used a similar test to that just described to choose between ϱ derived
from equation (10.3) and ϱ derived from equation (10.1). That is, I
obtained *a, b* and ϱ from equation (10.1), and I obtained *c* from an
equation similar to (11.1) but using ϱ derived from (10.1). (The resulting
value of *c* was 0.2580.) With these coefficients I obtained an equation
similar to (11.3) and then, following the procedure described in the fn. 23,
computed the sum of the weighted squared residuals. This sum was 3.5 per

cent greater than the sum of weighted squared residuals of equation (10.1), and 10.2 per cent greater than the sum of the weighted squared residuals found from equation (11.3). It therefore seemed preferable to derive ϱ from equation (10.3) rather than (10.1). It is also the case that equation (11.1), which explains $\lambda/(1 - s)$, fits much better when this is done. Thus, $\bar{R}^2$ (weighted residuals) is 0.679 when ϱ is derived from equation (10.3), but falls to 0.382 when ϱ is derived from equation (10.1).

(b)   The direct approach

If equation (6.5) is multiplied through by ϱs, the following equation results:

$$g = a\varrho s + bg_L - cg_L \frac{l}{\varrho} .$$

Two alternative ways of estimating this equation were attempted: (1) prespecifying ϱ by using equations (10.1) or (10.3), and (2) allowing the regression to determine ϱ.

   1. The first of these alternatives, in which ϱ was derived from equation (10.3),[24] gave results that were consistent with the preceding preferred method. Thus, the equation fitted to the twenty-six observations was:

$$g = 0.05092\varrho s + 0.9700g_L - 0.5285g_L \frac{l}{\varrho} . \tag{11.4}$$

$$(13.07) \qquad (7.20) \qquad (-0.57)$$

$\bar{R}^2$ (weighted residuals) $= 0.960$; R^2 (unweighted residuals) $= 0.881$
s.e. (weighted residuals) $= 0.00457$; s.e. (unweighted residuals) $= 0.00745$

If this equation is compared with the preferred one, (11.3), it will be found that the coefficients are similar and within less than one standard error of each other. The fit of this equation to the data is rather closer than that of either equation (10.1) or (10.3).[25] The last coefficient is of the correct sign, but is not significantly different from zero. Hence, on statistical grounds, this term should be dropped and the linear equation (10.1) or (10.3) preferred. Nevertheless, if one wants a curved IPC, the term must be retained. Although the fit of (11.4) is a little better than that of (11.3), I preferred the latter because, as already mentioned, the resulting value of c gives a better fit to the observed values of λ. However, it must be admitted that there is little to choose between them.

---

[24] The use of equation (10.1) rather than (10.3) to derive ϱ gave less satisfactory results. The fit was worse, the sum of the weighted squared residuals being 0.4607 compared with 0.2951 for equation (11.4). Also, the coefficients a and b agreed poorly with (10.1), and the value of c was much larger than in equation (11.1).

[25] The sum of the (weighted) squared residuals for equation (11.4) is 0.2951, which compares with 0.3255 for equation (10.1) and 0.2993 for equation (10.3).

2. The second alternative, in which ϱ is left to be determined by the regression, proved unsatisfactory. Perhaps the main reason for this is that it leads to an equation with nine variables to explain only twenty-six observations.[26] Not surprisingly, only two of the resulting coefficients appear to be statistically significant, and there are two other coefficients with incorrect signs. The results are not considered to be worth reporting.

(c) Explaining the residuals

Either the linear (equation (10.3)) or the curvilinear (equation (11.3)) version of the model 'explains' over 95 per cent of the (weighted) variance of growth rates in the twenty-six different periods and countries. Figure 11.2 enables one to comment on the remaining, unexplained, deviations from the regression lines. Many of these deviations are for earlier periods, when the statistical quality of the data is suspect: the UK 1856-73 and 1901-13, and the USA 1889-1900 and (for (10.3)) 1900-13, and Japan 1887-99 and 1899-1911. These periods accordingly receive less weight in the regressions.

It is also noteworthy that some consecutive pairs of periods are on opposite sides of the regression line, which might be due to an increase in the ratio of output to capacity (and so an observation lying above the regression line) being followed by fall in the ratio, or vice versa. This could apply to the Japanese observations for 1887-99, and 1899-1911, and for 1911-28 and 1928-36. Thus, the ratio of output to capacity could have been rising up to 1899 and then falling to 1911. It would have to have fallen further to 1928 and then risen sharply to 1936. Ohkawa (in Ohkawa and Shinohara 1979, 10-11, Table 1.2) specifies the following 'long-swing phases': up from 1887 to 1897, down from 1897 to 1904, up from 1904 to 1919, down from 1919 to 1930, and up from 1930 to 1938. This refers to smoothed series of real gross national expenditure, after taking a seven-year moving average (five years at the beginning and end). Ohkawa and Rosovsky (1973, 28, Table 2.2) give somewhat different phases. In estimating the trend rate of growth for the periods mentioned, observations for war years were excluded. I also excluded years of recession, defined as years lying below previous peaks. I tried, in this way, to eliminate cyclical changes in the output–capacity ratio, but may not have fully succeeded for these years. For the UK it does seem likely that the high rate of growth in 1937-51, and also the low rate of growth 1913-24, owe something to changes in the output–capacity ratio.

---

[26] In Section 10.3 it was explained how ϱ could be expressed as a linear function of a constant plus variables. Subsequently, three of the variables appeared to be significant (an interwar dummy, a post-Second World War dummy, and catch-up). Referring to the equation for g given on p. 331, it can then be seen that there are four terms in $a\varrho s$ and four in cg_L (l/ϱ), as well as the term in g_L, making nine in all. A rather unsatisfactory linear approximation was used for the term in l/ϱ.

It is interesting that the UK, the USA, and Japan all show abnormally low rates of growth in the first decade of this century. Regarding the UK, this has been much discussed by many authors.[27] Several explanations have been put forward. One is lack of effective demand owing to 'the long-swing fall in domestic construction and perhaps an adverse real-balance effect created by the rise in world prices' (Matthews *et al*. 1982, 543). This takes us back to the falling output–capacity ratio explanation. In coal-mining, an important sector, productivity declined as the better seams were worked out (Phelps Brown and Browne 1968, 177). More generally, there was a worsening of industrial relations which hindered the adoption of new methods, and there may also have been a reduction of effort and speed of work. This is discussed by Phelps Brown and Browne (1968, 185–90), who argue that, 'not only does it seem probable that labour was more militant or obstructive in the UK: it also seems to have met with less effective opposition from the employers there' (p. 188). Nevertheless, these authors conclude that,

though the changed attitude of labour took effect to offset or preclude some part of the normal course of productivity-raising change, we have to look beyond it to a shortfall of major innovations if we are to reach a sufficient explanation of a halt in the rise of productivity so complete and so long. . . . By 1900, the application of steam to power and transport, and of steel to equipment, had been largely worked through. New techniques . . . were being developed, but mostly as yet were only at the stage of the pilot plant: their impact would not be massive until after the First World War. (Phelps Brown and Browne 1968, 190–1; and see also Phelps Brown and Handfield-Jones 1952)

Britain seems to have lagged behind other countries, notably Germany and the USA, in the application of new techniques, and this has been attributed by some to a falling-off in entrepreneurial vitality—a conclusion disputed by others.[28] Sir Arthur Lewis concludes that

There is no evidence that British businessmen were any less enterprising after 1880 than their forefathers. . . . Yet something was lacking. Britian's competitive weakness was not in the old industries but in the new. These new industries were characterised by a higher scientific level than the old. . . . Between academic science and industry lay a big gulf which had to be bridged. The Germans bridged it in the first quarter of the nineteenth century, but the British failed to do so. (Lewis 1978, 129).

Whereas there is no lack of explanations for the UK's poor showing in the early years of this century, explanations for the USA and Japan seem to be in short supply. So far as the USA is concerned, my figures differ from those used by other authors. Thus, for example, Phelps Brown and Browne

---

[27] See Matthews *et al*. (1982, 113–17, 541–3, 606–7, and references therein). See also Thomas (1988) and the works cited below.
[28] Matthews *et al*. (1982, 115–17) survey the argument and give references.

contrast the UK with the USA, France, Germany, and Sweden as being the only country in which real income per occupied person in the whole economy stagnated from 1900 to 1913. There was not even any sign of slow-down in the growth rate for the USA, Germany, or Sweden (for France the figures before 1900 were lacking) (Phelps Brown and Browne 1968, 115–18). Consequently, what needed explaining was only the stagnation in the UK. Sir Arthur Lewis (1978) devotes a chapter to the slow-down in the UK, but, in a book that analyses the course of industrial production in the USA, France, and Germany as well, has no similar discussion for the USA. However, Thomas (1988) estimates that the rate of growth of multi-factor productivity in both Germany and the USA slowed down in the early years of the century, although not as much as in the UK.

So far as Japan is concerned, the slow-down in growth is noted by Ohkawa, but is left as 'an important problem to study in the initial phase of Japan's modern economic growth' (Ohkawa and Shinohara 1979, 16). And there I must leave it as well.

Olson (1982) has put forward the hypothesis that differences in growth rates between countries can be partially explained by the existence of 'distributional coalitions' (such as trade unions or other monopolistic groups), which are more numerous and powerful in some countries than others. Such coalitions are difficult to form, or to hold together, mainly because of the 'free-rider' problem. That is, one can often reap the benefits from the existence of such a coalition without having to join it. Consequently, it may take a long period for such coalitions to come into being to any substantial extent, and this has to be, of course, a period in which there is freedom to organize such coalitions. A war or a revolution may destroy existing coalitions. Olson then argues that the high growth rates experienced by France, Germany, Italy, Belgium, the Netherlands, and Japan since the Second World War, and the low growth experienced by the UK, can be at least partially explained by the disruption to the coalitions in the first group of countries as they were defeated and occupied, while in Britain there was no such disruption. The sclerotic British economy thus grew much more slowly than that of the other countries. The USA also grew more slowly, and, like Britain, avoided the trauma of defeat; but Olson is not prepared to claim this as further evidence in favour of his proposition, for various reasons.[29]

[29] See Olson (1982, 92–4). Other countries benefited from 'catch-up', and the US growth rate needs adjustment for that in any comparison with them. While distributional coalitions have been assisted by a long period of peace in the USA, the South was defeated and devastated in the Civil War, and 'for a century had no definitive outcome to the struggle over racial policy'. The USA has 'no direct legacy from the Middle Ages', and an unusually egalitarian beginning. For these reasons, Olson prefers to test his hypothesis by examining the relative growth performance of different regions of the USA, rather than by considering it in aggregate.

Olson's hypothesis could be interpreted in two ways. First, it could explain why *investment* (and so growth) was higher or lower in some countries than others. Investment is the cost of changing economic arrangements, and a high rate of investment implies that arrangements are being changed fast. A sclerotic economy would not permit a high rate of investment, and so would grow slowly for that reason. I referred to this version of the hypothesis in Chapter 8. It is, in my opinion, more closely in accordance with Olson's own arguments about the way in which distributional coalitions slow down growth (see p. 238). Second, it could explain why in some countries investment opportunities, as measured by ϱ in my theory, were greater than in others.

This second version of the hypothesis is not well supported by Figure 11.2. It is true that France and Germany lie above the regression line, and the UK lies below for 1951–64. But Japan is very close to the line, as also is Italy, while Belgium, Denmark, and the Netherlands are below it and the UK in the 1964–73 a little above it. I have confined attention to the post-Second World War periods since Olson largely does so as well, but I do not see that any clear support for this version of his thesis emerges from the earlier periods, either.

However, it should be recalled that, in Section 10.3, in the discussion of equation (10.2), I concluded that there *was* evidence that investment opportunities were more restricted in the UK than in the other countries, and that they were better in Japan. Equation (10.2) is fitted to all the periods, but most weight is given to those following the Second World War. Hence there is some evidence in favour of Olson's thesis, although, since equation (10.2) is not satisfactory, the evidence is not strong.

12

VERDOORN'S AND KALDOR'S LAWS

12.1 Introduction

In this chapter and the next I use the framework of analysis developed in previous chapters to attempt to explain some very interesting empirical regularities which have been discovered or alleged by others. These relate in the main to subdivisions of the GDP, and in particular to manufacturing industries, and so we revert in this chapter and in the next to the microeconomics rather than the macroeconomics of growth. The discoverers of the regularities, and their numerous followers, have put forward explanations of what they have found, and we shall consider some of these explanations in greater or lesser detail. Sometimes they will be neglected, as when they derive from orthodox growth theory which I have given reasons for rejecting. More usually, there are interesting ideas that need to be taken into account if we are to deepen our understanding of economic growth.

This chapter is concerned with comparisons of growth rates of output, employment, and productivity in similar industries between different countries, and with the ideas of Verdoorn and Kaldor, whose 'laws' (henceforth referred to without quotation marks) have aroused much interest. The next chapter considers comparisons of growth rates in dissimilar industries within one country, and the ideas of writers such as Fabricant, Salter, Kendrick, and Kennedy.

12.2 Verdoorn's Law

In equation (10.3), my preferred equation, differences in rates of growth of output in different countries and in different periods are explained in terms of two fundamental factors: the rate of growth in the quality-adjusted labour force, and the rate of investment. In addition to explaining such differences, the same equation also implicitly explains differences in the rates of growth of labour productivity. Thus, if

$$g = a\varrho s + bg_L, \tag{12.1}$$

then

$$g - g_L = a\varrho s + (b - 1)g_L. \tag{12.2}$$

Since my estimated value of b in (10.3) is 0.9034 with a standard error of 0.114, one can simplify further, to a fair approximation, by dropping the term in g_L on the right-hand side. The rate of growth of labour productivity then depends only on the rate of investment:

$$g - g_L = a\varrho s. \tag{12.3}$$

In an article published in 1949 in Italian, P. J. Verdoorn put forward a different explanation of differences in the rate of growth of labour productivity in industry between countries and periods, namely, that they depended on the rate of growth of output:[1]

$$g - g_L = a_4 + b_4 g. \tag{12.4}$$

Verdoorn (1949) gave a large number of estimates of the elasticity b_4. These were derived, in the main, simply by estimating the average rate of growth of labour productivity and of production in 'industry' for a particular country over a particular period, and then dividing the former by the latter. They therefore implicitly set $a_4 = 0$. The countries included Canada, the USA, Japan, and twelve in Europe, and the periods were mostly 1924–38, but also some pre-1914. Verdoorn's actual elasticities, found in this way, ranged from 0.25 to 1.67, but he himself chose a mean value of 0.45 with a range of 0.41–0.57 to represent the data. Verdoorn also gave estimates of the elasticity for particular subdivisions of manufacturing, mostly based on data for the USA for 1899–1937. Here, again, there was a wide range from 0.29 to 1.52.

Since Verdoorn's own explanation of a stable value for the elasticity (which his data scarcely supported) was in terms of a Cobb–Douglas production function, I shall not pursue it further here.

Perhaps because it was in Italian, Verdoorn's article did not attract a great deal of attention until Lord Kaldor's Inaugural Lecture in November 1966,[2] in which it formed an important part of his thesis that the UK's slow rate of growth in comparison with that of other countries was due to her greater economic maturity. This thesis, subsequently modified by Kaldor, is considered later in the chapter. Only three points will be made at this stage. First, Kaldor coupled the Verdoorn equation (12.4) with another equation which can be derived from it:

$$g_L = -a_4 + (1 - b_4) g. \tag{12.5}$$

---

[1] Verdoorn subsequently wrote 'Verdoorn's Law in Retrospect: A Comment' (Verdoorn 1980), which concluded 'The "law" that has been given my name appears therefore to be much less generally valid than I was led to believe in 1949.' However, this conclusion was derived from *a priori* reasoning based on a neoclassical production function allowing for disembodied technical progress and increasing returns to scale.

[2] Kaldor (1966), reprinted in Kaldor (1978); further references to the Inaugural Lecture are to this reprinted version.

In this equation, unlike (12.4), g does not appear on both sides. Hence errors of measurement in g will not result (as in (12.4)) in a correlation between the two sides which could be regarded as spurious.[3] Kaldor asserted in a later article that 'a *sufficient* condition for the presence of static or dynamic economies of scale is the existence of a statistically significant relationship between $[g_L]$ and $[g,]$ with a regression coefficient which is significantly less than 1' (Kaldor 1975b, 893).[4] Kaldor attached importance to such economies of scale, and I shall discuss them at length.

Second, Kaldor pointed out that part of the explanation for different rates of productivity growth in industry lay in different rates of investment. In fact, in a set of three lectures at Cornell University, delivered in October 1966, before his Inaugural Lecture at Cambridge, and which are an expansion of the latter, he provides a regression that is similar to (12.1); that is, the rate of growth of industrial output is explained in terms of the ratio of gross industrial investment to output and the rate of growth of industrial employment. Kaldor also introduces a constant (but without stating its significance, either statistical or in terms of his theory). Although the investment term is statistically significant, and its introduction into the equation reduces the coefficient of the employment term, it still leaves the coefficient significantly greater than 1, although not by a large margin.[5] Because it *is* still greater than 1, however (which corresponds to its reciprocal, $(1 - b_4)$ in (12.5), being less than 1), Kaldor claims that it 'implies that the rate of growth of productivity is positively correlated with the rate of growth of output and also with the rate of growth of employment' (1967, 83), and hence, presumably, that in his view there still is evidence here of static and dynamic economies of scale. This is further discussed below.

Finally, all of Kaldor's regression equations relate to comparisons of similar industries across countries. In that respect they are similar to the data I have used in Chapters 10 and 11, but there are some differences. First, I have confined attention thus far to the whole of non-residential business, whereas Kaldor considers some components of it separately: manufacturing, public utilities, construction, agriculture, mining, transport and communications, and commerce. In his view, static and dynamic economies of scale apply only, or mainly, in the first three of these sectors (called 'industry', collectively). Verdoorn's original article also confined attention to industry. Second, neither Kaldor's nor Verdoorn's measure of labour input is quality-adjusted. Third, all of Kaldor's data refer to broadly one

---

[3] See Kaldor (1975b, 891–2). Others who have discussed the question of spurious correlation at greater length are Fabricant, Salter, and Kennedy in the works cited in Chapter 13.

[4] I have altered Kaldor's original symbols e and q, to g_L and g to accord with my own.

[5] Kaldor gives two equations, the first including and the second excluding Canada, which he regards as something of a special case. The coefficients of g_L with their standard errors are, respectively, 1.367 (0.168) and 1.320 (0.085). See Kaldor (1967, 83; see also 1978 130).

time period (1953–4 to 1963–4). The countries covered include Austria and Canada, but are otherwise the same as my own.

Kaldor's lectures stimulated a great deal of subsequent work and criticism,[6] to some of which I refer below.

In Kaldor's view, economies of scale explained why a faster growth of output led to faster growth of productivity. However, the existence of a positive correlation between the growth of output and the growth of productivity is not enough to prove that. The causation could be, and was argued by some to be, in the reverse direction: productivity grew at different rates, and this caused demand and output to grow at different rates through its effects on relative costs and prices. It is worth while quoting Kaldor's attempt to rebut this view.

This alternative hypothesis is not, however, fully specified—if it were, its logical shortcomings would at once be apparent. If the rate of growth of productivity in each industry and in each country was a fully autonomous factor, we need some hypothesis to explain it. The usual hypothesis is that the growth of productivity is mainly to be explained by the progress of knowledge in science and technology. But in that case how is one to explain the large differences in the *same* period in different countries? How can the progress of knowledge account for the fact, for example, that in the period 1954–60, productivity in the German motor-car industry increased at 7 per cent a year and in Britain only 2.7 per cent a year? Since large segments of the car industry in both countries were controlled by the same American firms, they must have had the same access to the improvements in knowledge and know-how. This alternative hypothesis is tantamount to a denial of the existence of increasing returns which are known to be an important feature of manufacturing industry, quite independently of the Verdoorn Law, and one which is frequently emphasised in other contexts—as for example, in analysing the effects of economic integration. (Inaugural Lecture, Kaldor 1978, 108–9).

One might remark that, although the same American motor car manufacturers operate in Britain and on the Continent, comparisons of their factories equipped with very similar machinery have revealed much higher levels of productivity on the Continent. Their access to knowledge may have been the same, but it seems to have resulted in neither the same levels nor the same rates of growth of productivity. Nor is it at all clear that the explanation lies mainly in economies of scale reaped by the continental plants. The British government's Central Policy Review Staff, which reported on a comparison of this kind in 1975, attributed the lower levels of British productivity to overmanning, the failure of output to reach the levels that men and equipment should be able to achieve, and under-investment in capital equipment. Similar explanations have been put forward by others.[7]

[6] See in particular Cripps and Tarling (1973); Rowthorn (1975a, 1975b); Thirlwall (1980); and the Symposium on Kaldor's Growth Laws (1983), with contributions by A. P. Thirlwall, C. P. Blitch, J. S. L. McCombie, J. R. de Ridder, S. Gomulka, M. Chatterji, and M. R. Wickens.
[7] See Cairncross, Kay, and Silbertson (1977); Pratten (1976, 1977).

It may have been because of the argument quoted above that Kaldor chose to confine his attention to cross-country comparisons for the *same* industry in a given period. I call the relation between growth in productivity and growth in output which emerges from this type of comparison *Verdoorn's Law*, since that title has by now become firmly attached to it. There is a quite different type of comparison which has been frequently made, namely, that of rates of growth of productivity and output over a given period in *different* industries within one country. The earliest of these that I know of is by S. Fabricant in 1942 (i.e. earlier than Verdoorn's article). It therefore seems appropriate to refer to the whole set of relationships that Fabricant analysed and, so far as I can tell, indeed discovered, as *Fabricant's Laws*. Discussion of these is reserved for Chapter 13, but we may note here that static and dynamic economies of scale are considered at some length, as is also the question of the direction of causation in the relation between productivity growth and output growth.

12.3   Explaining Verdoorn's Law

Verdoorn's Law applies to my observations of growth rates of labour productivity and output of non-residential business. This can be seen from the regressions in Table 12.1. I fitted these to only the twelve post-Second World War observations in the data set because of the earlier finding that there was a marked shift in the relationship between output and input growth comparing this period with earlier ones. Furthermore, confining attention to a particular period is closer to the procedure followed by Kaldor. Had I taken all twenty-six observations, however, the broad conclusions would not have been different.[8]

The first equation in Table 12.1 is the Verdoorn equation, and shows that there is a strong positive relationship between productivity growth and output growth. The second equation is Kaldor's preferred reformulation, which gives a much weaker relationship. However, the coefficient of employment growth on output growth is quite significant and is also less than 1, which Kaldor would presumably regard as confirming the existence of economies of scale for non-residential business taken as a whole.

In the third and fourth equations I have substituted my preferred measure of labour input, which is quality-adjusted, for the more usual employment

---

[8] This can perhaps be readily seen if one considers the four coefficients in col. (4) of Table 12.1, but taking all 26 observations. The argument below in the text is supported by these figures in the same way as by those in Table 12.1.

coefficient	t-statistic
0.8585	14.0
0.1415	2.3
0.6051	7.0
0.3949	4.6

Table 12.1   Verdoorn regressions

	Dependent variable	Independent variable	Coefficients of		r^2
			Constant term	Independent variable, g	
	(1)	(2)	(3)	(4)	(5)
(i)	$g - g_N$	g	0.0052 (1.2)	0.7671 (9.8)	0.9060
(ii)	g_N	g	-0.0052 (1.2)	0.2329 (3.0)	0.4706
(iii)	$g - g_L$	g	0.0130 (2.3)	0.3898 (3.8)	0.5868
(iv)	g_L	g	-0.0130 (-2.3)	0.6102 (5.9)	0.7769

Notes

The equations were fitted to the 12 postwar observations for non-residential business (see the list in table SA I). *t*-statistics are shown in brackets beneath the relevant coefficients.

g = exponential rate of growth of output.

g_N = exponential rate of growth of numbers of full-time equivalent workers employed.

g_L = exponential rate of growth of quality-adjusted employment.

measure (adopted by both Verdoorn and Kaldor) of numbers employed. The result is interesting. The statistical fit of the employment equation, no. (iv), is now much improved as compared with equation (ii). At the same time, the fit of the Verdoorn equation (iii) is less good than that of equation (i). I think this demonstrates the wisdom of Kaldor's formulation, since I would maintain that it is the incorrect specification of labour input in equations (i) and (ii) that results in the poor fit in equation (ii), and, simultaneously, the good fit in equation (i), in which g appears on both sides.[9]

It should also be noted that the *coefficient* of g_L on g in equation (iv), although still below 1, is much closer to 1 than the coefficient of g_N on g in equation (ii). Hence, if the distance of this coefficient below 1 is taken as an index of the extent of economies of scale, as Kaldor's argument would seem to imply, then using g_L rather than the more usual g_N lessens that extent.

But why should the analysis be confined to two-variable regressions? In earlier sections it was shown that the relationship between output and inputs is best explained by equation (10.1) or (10.3), with the growth rate of output a function of not just the growth rate of employment, but also the rate of

[9] Thus, if g_N were a random variable quite unrelated to g, equation (ii) would have a zero correlation whereas equation (i) could still have a strong positive correlation so long as the variance of g_N was small enough.

investment. It was also shown that there have been significant shifts in this relationship from prewar to postwar. In both of my preferred equations, the terms for investment are significant, and so the explanatory power of the equation is weakened if these terms are dropped, as they are dropped in both Verdoorn's and Kaldor's formulations.

It will be recalled that Kaldor regarded a significant positive coefficient of employment on output, which was less than 1, as sufficient evidence of economies of scale. This coefficient, in a two-variable regression, can be regarded either as (a) an unbiased estimate of the corresponding coefficient in a multiple regression containing all the other significant explanatory variables, or as (b) some sort of reduced-form coefficient. Let us consider these two possibilities in turn.

If it is (a) that Kaldor had in mind, then the evidence from equations (10.1) and (10.3) is that the introduction of other significant explanatory variables makes an important difference, so that one cannot regard the two variable regressions as providing an unbiased estimate. In both (10.1) and (10.3) the coefficient of output on employment is *less* than 1, implying that if one takes the reciprocal of this coefficient, as in Kaldor's formulation, the coefficient of employment in output is *greater* than 1. Kaldor's argument for economies of scale, at least as far as non-residential business as a whole is concerned, cannot then be sustained. Of course, as we saw above, Kaldor applied his argument not to the whole of non-residential business, but only to manufacturing, public utilities, and construction. However, his *evidence* is very similar to that provided in Table 12.1 for non-residential business. If that evidence is unreliable for non-residential business, might it not also be unreliable for manufacturing, etc.? It is true that Kaldor did, as pointed out above, introduce investment into some of his equations, and that this still left the coefficient of employment on output less than 1 (although nearer to 1 than when investment was left out). However, Kaldor's employment variable was never quality-adjusted, and it is possible that, had it been so, the coefficient of employment on output would have been still further increased (as we found in Table 12.1). I conclude, therefore, that Kaldor's argument for economies of scale does not apply to non-residential business as a whole, and that it is also doubtful whether it applies to manufacturing, etc. All the same, there are other reasons for believing that such economies do exist, as we shall see in Chapter 13.

Let us now consider interpretation (b). One sort of relationship that could be in mind would be something like the following. Faster growth of output requires faster growth of inputs, but because a large part of those extra inputs are investment, the extra growth in employment is typically less than proportionate. Thus, 1 per cent extra output growth is typically accompanied by *less* than 1 per cent extra employment growth. This could indeed be the case, and, so far as the data in Table 12.1 are concerned, it does seem to have been the case. There is a positive correlation between the share of investment and the rate of growth of employment for that data, although not a strong one ($r^2 = 0.11$). We also saw, in equations (10.1) and 10.3), that investment and other variables (catch-up and shifts in ϱ) significantly explain differences in rates of growth of output and so, also, in rates of growth of productivity. Since the coefficient of output on employment in those equations was less than 1, Kaldor's argument for economies of scale does not apply.

Let me try to put the point quite generally. A given industry in country A grows faster than in country B for a number of different reasons: faster growth in employment as conventionally measured, faster quality improvement in the labour force, a higher rate of investment, because it is benefiting from 'catch-up', or because it has superior investment opportunities (higher ϱ) for other reasons such as better management, more co-operative labour, government assistance, etc. One might generally expect faster growth in employment to be *one* of the reasons, partly because labour input is so important and partly because growth feeds back on employment, especially if one is considering a *part* rather than the whole of an economy so that labour is free to move in from elsewhere. One might also generally expect there to be other reasons for faster output growth as well as faster employment growth. All of the other reasons must tend to increase productivity growth. Consequently, it is not very surprising if faster growth of *output* in A is associated with faster growth of *productivity* in A, and with less-than-proportionately faster growth in *employment* in A. There does not seem to be any reason to deduce from this combination of circumstances that this industry is subject to static or dynamic economies of scale, although there could be *other* evidence for that.

Finally, while the above combination of circumstances is hardly surprising, it is far from being an invariable feature of the economic scene. Verdoorn's Law does not always hold, whether in Verdoorn's or Kaldor's version.[10]

12.4 Kaldor's Growth Laws

In May 1983, the *Journal of Post Keynesian Economics* published a Symposium on Kaldor's Growth Laws. In what follows, I take that

---

[10] See, for example, Cripps and Tarling (1973, 23), whose data showed that, whereas Verdoorn's Law for manufacturing in 12 developed countries held for the 1950s and up to 1965, it appeared no longer to hold for the second half of the 1960s. It may also be recalled that Verdoorn's own data did not support a particularly stable relationship between productivity growth and output growth (see p. 337 above).

symposium and Kaldor's own writings as a guide. Paraphrasing Thirlwall, the laws are as follows:

1. Faster growth in manufacturing generates more extra growth in GDP than can be accounted for by the share of manufacturing in the GDP. 'The manufacturing sector of the economy is the "engine of growth" ' (Symposium 1983, 345).
2. Faster growth in manufacturing generates faster growth in productivity within manufacturing owing to static and dynamic economies of scale. This accounts for Verdoorn's Law, and has already been discussed.
3. Faster growth in manufacturing also generates faster growth in productivity outside manufacturing. This is because it draws labour and other resources from non-manufacturing sectors without reducing output there, or without reducing it very much. The scope for this varies from economy to economy, and in a 'mature' economy there may be little or no scope, which will tend to lower its rate of growth.
4. Faster growth in manufacturing depends on the growth of demand from outside manufacturing. Sometimes this outside demand may be exports to other countries, and this is the aspect stressed by Thirlwall (1983, 346; see also Kennedy and Thirlwall 1979). Kaldor certainly attached importance to it (see Kaldor 1971; also 1975b, 895-6), but it is open to the objection that, for the world as a whole (or for a closed, or nearly closed, economy), there are no exports. The alternative version of this law is to make the demand for manufactures depend on demand by 'agriculture'.[11] What this may mean is discussed below.

A fifth law could be added, namely, that success breeds success and failure failure, but that seems implicit in the above four laws.

These four laws, according to Kaldor, were not based on any particular deductive growth model (and he had produced more than one himself): rather, they were based on observed regularities in real economies.[12]

The empirical regularity underlying the first law is a regression of the annual percentage rate of growth of GDP on that of manufacturing output in twelve developed countries over the decade 1953/4–1963/4. Labelling the former rate of growth Y and the latter X, the regression given by Kaldor (1978, 103) is

$$Y = 1.153 + 0.614X, \qquad r^2 = 0.959$$
$$(0.040)$$

where the standard error of the coefficient of X is given beneath it. The fit is

---

[11] See Kaldor (1975a); see also the Introduction to Kaldor (1978).
[12] See the Introduction to Kaldor (1978, xvii): 'I tried to find what kind of regularities can be detected in empirically observed phenomena and then tried to discover what particular testable hypotheses would be capable of explaining the association.'

good and shows that 'rates of growth [of GDP] above 3 per cent a year are found only in cases where the rate of growth in manufacturing output is in excess of the overall rate of growth of the economy' (Inaugural Lecture, in Kaldor 1978, 103). Kaldor also provides a regression, based on the same data, which shows that the rate of growth of non-manufacturing output is positively associated with that of manufacturing output, the coefficients being very similar to those given above. This avoids the criticism which might be made that, in the first regression, manufacturing appears on both sides and is an important component of GDP. Kaldor further states that there is no correlation between the rate of growth of GDP and that of either agricultural production or mining. There is a significant positive relation between the rate of growth of GDP and that of services, but 'the fact that the coefficient is so near to unity and the constant is negligible suggests that the causal relationship here is the other way round—i.e. that it is the rate of GDP that determines the rate of growth of the 'output' of services' (Kaldor 1978, 123). Kaldor's explanation of these regressions takes us on to his other laws.

In his Inaugural Lecture, he emphasized the second law (the Verdoorn Law). Manufacturing, and also other 'secondary' industries such as public utilities and construction, benefited from increasing returns not, for the most part, because of static economies of scale, but because of dynamic economies of scale. Kaldor quoted Allyn Young (1928) with approval, and especially his idea that increasing returns were a macro phenomenon, i.e. that, 'because so much of the economies of scale emerge as a result of increased differentiation, the emergence of new processes and new subsidary industries, they cannot be "discerned adequately by observing the effects of variations in the size of an individual firm or of a particular industry" '(Kaldor 1978, 106). Agriculture and mining, however, are diminishing returns industries. In services, 'learning by experience must clearly play a role but economies of scale are not nearly so prominent and are exhausted more quickly' (p.111). In some parts (like education) productivity improvements are not properly measured. In others (like retailing) they are the passive result of increased throughput arising from the growth of industry.

Subsequently, Kaldor placed less emphasis on the Verdoorn Law. Thus, in 1975, in a reply to criticisms of his Inaugural Lecture by Rowthorn (1975a)[13] he referred to 'two remarkable correlations' found by Cripps and Tarling, which were:

[13] Rowthorn interpreted Kaldor's law as a positive relation between productivity growth ($g - g_N$ in our notation) and employment growth (g_N). Using Cripps and Tarling's data, as well as Kaldor's, Rowthorn showed that this positive relation was not very strong, and became statistically insignificant (and even negative in 1965–70) if observations for Japan were excluded. However, it is to be noted that g_N appears with opposite signs on the two sides of this regression, so that errors in measuring it would tend to reduce the magnitude of any

$$1950\text{--}65: \quad p_{\text{GDP}} = 1.172 + 0.534q_{\text{IND}} - 0.812e_{\text{NI}}, \quad R^2 = 0.805$$
$$(0.058) \qquad (0.202)$$

$$1965\text{--}70: \quad p_{\text{GDP}} = 1.153 + 0.642q_{\text{IND}} - 0.872e_{\text{NI}}, \quad R^2 = 0.958$$
$$(0.058) \qquad (0.125)$$

Here, the data are annual percentage growth rates of productivity in the whole GDP (p_{GDP}), output in (secondary) industry (q_{IND}), and employment outside of industry (e_{NI}). These equations show a positive association between the rate of productivity growth in the whole economy and the rate of growth of output in industry, together with a negative association with the growth of employment in non-industry. Kaldor then goes on:

> The important thing to note is—and herein lies Rowthorn's misunderstanding—that the existence of increasing returns to scale in industry (the Verdoorn Law) is not a necessary or indispensable element in the interpretation of these equations. Even if industrial output obeyed the law of constant returns, it could still be true that the growth of industrial output was the governing factor in the overall rate of economic growth (both in terms of total output and output per head) so long as the growth of industrial output represented a net addition to the effective use of resources and not just a transfer of resources from one use to another. This would be the case if (a) the capital required for industrial production was (largely or wholly) self-generated—the accumulation of capital was an aspect, or a by-product, of the growth of output; and (b) the labour engaged in industry had no true opportunity-cost outside industry, on account of the prevalence of disguised unemployment both in agriculture and services. There is plenty of direct evidence to substantiate both of these assumptions. (Kaldor 1975b, 894)[14]

These correlations, and the passage quoted, summarize Kaldor's reasons for his third law.

In his Inaugural Lecture, Kaldor had explained Britain's relatively low rate of growth by her 'maturity', meaning by this that 'real income per head has reached broadly the same level in the different sectors of the economy' (1978, 102), so that Britain could not expand industry rapidly by withdrawing workers from other sectors where their marginal productivity was low. In his reply to Rowthorn, however, Kaldor stated:

> I now believe that I was wrong in thinking in 1966 that the United Kingdom *had* attained the stage of 'economic maturity' (in the sense I defined that term) and that her comparatively poor performance was to be explained by inability to recruit sufficient labour to manufacturing industry rather than by poor market performance due to lack of international competitiveness. . . . I would now place more, rather than less, emphasis on the exogenous components of demand, and in

---

positive correlation. Kaldor, in his reply, had no difficulty in showing that the positive relation between g_N and g survived the removal of Japan.

[14] It would be interesting to see the 'direct evidence', but, unfortunately, Kaldor gave no reference.

particular on the role of exports, in determining the trend rate of productivity growth in the United Kingdom in relation to other industrially advanced countries. (Kaldor 1975b, 895–6)[15]

This takes us to the fourth law. Kaldor recognized that demand for industrial products was influenced by growth in industrial productivity through its effects on competitiveness. However, he also thought that this 'reverse causation' was 'far less regular and systematic' (1975b, 895) than the causation from demand to productivity growth, and that 'economic growth is demand-induced, and not resource-constrained' (p. 895). Indeed, as a previous quotation shows, he seemed to think that the supply of both capital and labour to industry had no opportunity cost.

While, for a particular country, exports (or exports net of imports of industrial products) may provide an important exogenous source of demand, for the world as a whole this cannot be true, nor was it true to an important extent for the United States for much of its recent history. While Kaldor did not make this point explicitly, he did refer in some of his most recent writings to a two-sector model of 'industry' and 'agriculture' on which he had been working, but which had not yet reached sufficient maturity to be published. The main discussions of this model that I have found are in the Introduction to Kaldor (1978) and in one of the essays there reprinted, 'What is Wrong with Economic Theory', dated 1974. The model may also, to some extent, have underlain his 'Capitalism and Industrial Development: Some Lessons from Britain's Experience', dated 1972 and reprinted in Kaldor (1978). The distinction between 'industry' and 'agriculture' seems to turn on the existence of increasing returns in the former and diminishing returns, together with the importance of land as a factor input, in the latter. The growth of 'industry' is demand-constrained but not resource-constrained, and Kaldor sometimes calls it the 'Keynesian sector'.

In such a model the ultimate constraint which governs the growth rate is not population growth or the rate of labour-saving innovations, but the progress of land-saving inventions which determine the growth of the 'agricultural surplus' at any given terms of trade between the products of Industry and Agriculture. . . . the growth rate of the 'Keynesian sector' is determined by the growth of the exogenous components of demand originating outside the sector and this yields a closed model which does *not* require the assumption of full employment. (Kaldor 1978, xxii)

Somewhat paradoxically, then, the 'engine of growth' in this Kaldorian growth model is not industry but 'agriculture', and the reference to land

---

[15] Kaldor referred to 'statistical studies that. . . make it doubtful whether I was correct in thinking that earnings in the service trades of the United Kingdom had come to be fully competitive with earnings in manufacturing or that the growth of manufacturing industry in the United Kingdom was constrained by labour shortages other than in a purely short-term sense'. The statistical study mentioned was Sleeper (1970).

suggests that he was not treating 'agriculture' as equivalent to 'non-industry', but that he really did mean agriculture and mining.

12.5 Some points of agreement

In reviewing and criticizing these Kaldorian laws of growth, let me begin by emphasizing points of agreement.

First, in regard to static and dynamic economies of scale, while I do not consider that Kaldor's or Verdoorn's evidence is persuasive (for the reasons given in preceding sections), I do not dispute the importance of the phenomenon. In my own terms, I would regard the factors referred to by both Kaldor and Allyn Young (and many others) as helping to explain why the IPC *persists* (i.e. why investment opportunities are always there, new ones replacing those that are taken up) and also why 'physical' returns to the rate of investment do not appear to diminish appreciably.

Second, the transfer of labour from agriculture (especially) and other low wage sectors to higher wage sectors does indeed seem to have been an important factor whose contribution to growth has been much greater in some countries than in others. The UK, in particular, has benefited less for many years from transferring workers from agriculture since the proportion of the work-force in that sector has been much smaller than in most other countries. In the analysis presented here, as in Denison's work, I have tried to quantify the contribution of this factor to growth through its effect on the difference between the quality-adjusted and unadjusted rate of growth of the labour force, $g_L - g_N$ (see Chapter 2).

Third, demand expectations are undoubtedly an important determinant of the rate of investment, and so of the growth of capacity to produce. This is discussed in Chapter 10 and Chapter 15 especially, as also is the related point that investment by A confers a benefit on B by helping to shift the demand curve for B's products faster to the right.

Fourth, I agree wholeheartedly with some of Kaldor's side-swipes at orthodox growth theory, for example the failure to take cognizance of imperfect markets, the futility of separating productivity growth which is due to capital accumulation from that which is due to improvements in technical knowledge, the robust statement that 'there is no such thing as a "set of blueprints" that reflect a "given state of knowledge",' and the scepticism regarding the production function.[16]

Finally, the attempt to explain empirical regularities, and to make one's theory empirically testable, must be applauded.

---

[16] These points are all made in the Introduction to Kaldor (1978).

12.6 Explaining Kaldor's Laws

The empirical regularity which Kaldor himself said had led him to put forward the views summarized above is the 'extraordinarily close correlation between the rate of growth of manufacturing output and the rate of growth of the GDP' (Kaldor 1978, xviii). This is undoubtedly a very interesting correlation, and I shall devote the following pages to an attempt to explain it. In my view, it is this correlation, together with Verdoorn's Law (already discussed), that poses the main challenge for anyone wanting to put forward an alternative view to that of Kaldor.

Before proceeding further, we may clear out of the way the supplementary correlation reproduced on p. 346, to which Kaldor also attached considerable importance. This may be written

$$p_{GDP} = a + bq_{IND} - ce_{NI}$$

where p, q, and e refer to rates of growth of productivity, output, and employment, respectively, and the suffixes refer to GDP, industry, and non-industry. My contention is that this correlation is little more than a rewriting of Kaldor's other correlation, the centrepiece of our discussion, between the rate of growth of GDP and that of manufacturing output. If we regard 'manufacturing' and 'industry' as being approximately the same, then we can rewrite the above as

$$q_{GDP} - (1 - W_{NM})e_M - W_{NM}e_{NM} = a + bq_M - ce_{NM}$$

where the suffix M is now manufacturing and NM is non-manufacturing, and where W_{NM} is the weight of non-manufacturing in total employment. Now if $W_{NM} \approx c$, which in fact it does, and if we accordingly cancel out the last term on each side, then the only remaining difference between this equation and Kaldor's first 'empirical regularity' is that this contains the term $(1 - W_{NM})e_M$ on the left-hand side. Now this term is likely to be small in relation to the other terms,[17] and so its inclusion may not matter very much. It is noteworthy that the values for a and b given by Kaldor for the period 1950–65 are 1.172 and 0.534, which are close to the values 1.153 and 0.614 in his original correlation of GDP growth on manufacturing growth

[17] Taking the wider concept of 'industry' equal to manufacturing, construction, and public utilities, the unweighted mean growth rate of employment in industry for Kaldor's 12 countries from 1954 to 1964 is 2.2% p.a., and the share of 'industry' in total employment in 1962/3 is 38.7% so the weighted employment growth rate is 0.9% p.a. This may be compared with the mean rate of growth of GDP of 4.8% p.a., and of manufacturing of 5.9% p.a., from 1953/4 to 1963/4. It seems very likely that the difference in means is also accompanied by a big difference in variances. Had we taken 'manufacturing' rather than 'industry', the disproportion would have been even greater. All figures derived from Kaldor's .Inaugural Lecture, (Kaldor 1978).

(see p. 344 above). Hence it seems fair to conclude that these 'two remarkable correlations' add virtually nothing to that original correlation,[18] and I accordingly now turn to it.

The more persuasive[19] form of this correlation is between growth in manufacturing output and growth in the rest of the economy, excluding manufacturing, which Kaldor also noted. Kaldor's Laws imply that 'demand'[20] is the main cause of the growth of manufacturing, and that faster growth of manufacturing in turn causes faster growth of the rest of the economy. However, if one asks what causes the initial 'demand', the answer seems to be, for any small country, demand for exports of manufactures; and we have already seen that this cannot be a complete answer for the world as a whole or for the USA. For them, the answer seems to be 'land-saving innovations' in 'agriculture'. Presumably this must also apply to some extent within any economy. Hence it is far from clear that Thirlwall is correct in interpreting Kaldor as regarding manufacturing as 'the engine of growth'. Nor is it at all clear why only *land-saving* innovations are thought to matter. Presumably any innovation that increases the productivity of labour or capital in any part of 'non-manufacturing' could equally well increase demand for manufactures.[21] Furthermore, since *some* increasing returns are allowed to exist in services (and, I would argue, they may even be found in 'agriculture'), the effect of innovations in manufacturing on demand for and productivity in non-manufacturing should not be neglected. Hence we seem to be left with a theory in which growth is fundamentally due to innovations, and in which the complementarity of the different parts of the economy is emphasized. This is hardly novel. It is also unsatisfactory, for the same reasons as those that are given elsewhere in criticism of the importance given to exogenous technical progress in orthodox growth theory.

[18] See also McCombie (1983, 423–4) for a criticism of these correlations which takes the view that they are merely the estimations of an identity in which the growth of productivity in the whole economy, p_{GDP}, is equal to the sum of the differences between the growth of output and employment in two parts of it, industry and non-industry, with two terms omitted (e_{IND} and q_{NI}).

[19] More persuasive because manuacturing growth does not then appear on both sides of the regression.

[20] Kaldor's main emphasis is on 'demand' without qualification, as quotations already given clearly show. However, he sometimes refers to competitiveness, and in one place he restates dependence on demand as 'putting it more finely, on the demand it is able to attract for its products' (Kaldor (1978) p.xxi). This seems to open the floodgates to what most would regard as *supply* factors. While I think they *should* be opened, this would obliterate many of the special features of Kaldor's growth laws.

[21] Kaldor might reply that, whereas land is scarce, labour and capital in non-manufacturing are not scarce; hence labour and capital-saving innovations in services do not increase demand for manufactures. I am not, myself, convinced that labour and capital are not scarce in services, and Kaldor's assertions are neither backed by empirical evidence nor *a priori* plausible.

Let us now consider what alternative explanation could be given for the correlation between manufacturing and non-manufacturing growth rates. We can learn something by seeing how far the correlation has persisted in recent years. Kaldor's data were for twelve countries for 1953/4–1963/4. Data for the same countries, both for that period and for a more recent period (1970–83), are used in Figure 12.1, which shows the relationship between the two growth rates. Some relevant regressions are given in Table 12.2, which also describes the sources used. The following points may be noted.

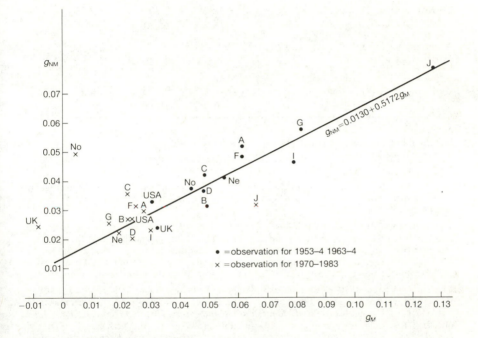

Fig. 12.1 Scatter diagram relating growth of non-manufacturing output to that of manufacturing

1. The regression line shown in Figure 12.1 is that fitted to 1953/4–1963/4, i.e. Kaldor's period. Although the data he used have been since revised somewhat, the regression and fit are little affected.

2. It is clear from Figure 12.1 and regressions (3) and (5) in Table 12.2 that, apart from 1970–83 for Norway, and to a lesser extent Canada, the UK and Japan, all the 1970–83 observations lie quite closely along the line fitted to the 1953/4–1963/4 data. Norway, and to a lesser extent Canada and the UK lie appreciably above it. For Norway and the UK this can be

Table 12.2   Regressions of the rate of growth of non-manufacturing output, g_{NM}, on that of manufacturing output, g_M, 12 countries, 1953/4–1963/4 and 1970–83

		r^2
All countries		
(1) 1953/4–1963/4	$g_{NM} = 0.0130 + 0.5172g_M$	0.897
	(3.61) (9.34)	
(2) 1970–83	$g_{NM} = 0.0293 - 0.0195g_M$	0.002
	(7.33) (−0.14)	
(3) Rows (1) & (2) pooled	$g_{NM} = 0.0208 + 0.3767g_M$	0.633
	(6.71) (6.16)	
All countries except Norway and the UK, 1970–83		
(4) 1970–83	$g_{NM} = 0.0240 + 0.1195g_M$	0.130
	(7.06) (1.09)	
(5) Rows (1) & (4) pooled	$g_{NM} = 0.0152 + 0.4689g_M$	0.835
	(6.08) (10.04)	

Notes

Figures in brackets below coefficients are their *t*-statistics

The 12 countries were Austria, Belgium, Canada, Denmark, France, Germany, Italy, Japan, Netherlands, Norway, UK, USA.

The rates of growth for 1953/4–1963/4 were average exponential rates between the averages of the years specified. Those for 1970–83 were exponential trends fitted by least squares to all the years mentioned.

The main source for 1953/4–1963/4 was *National Accounts of OECD Countries 1950–1968*, OECD Paris, 1970, using GDP at constant prices in manufacturing and the rest of the economy. However, for Belgium and Japan the growth rates for manufacturing were taken from Kaldor (1978, 103, Table 1), and non-manufacturing was derived as a residual from the GDP as given in the main source above. The coverage of 'manufacturing' is not the same in all countries.

The main source for 1970–83 was *National Accounts 1970–82 Detailed Tables, Vol. II*, OECD, Paris, 1984, with estimates for 1983 obtained from *OECD Economic Outlook*, December 1984, Table 12.1, for the whole GDP and *Main Economic Indicators. Historical Statistics 1964–1983*, OECD, Paris, 1984, for manufacturing production. However, for the Netherlands, GDP was entirely from *OECD Economic Outlook* and manufacturing from *Main Economic Indicators*, while for the UK both series were from the CSO *United Kingdom National Accounts*, 1984 edn., 1984, supplemented by the 1983 edn. for earlier years for manufacturing. The average estimate of GDP at factor cost was used and manufacturing subtracted to give non-manufacturing.

explained by the rapid growth of mineral fuel output, which raised the growth of non-manufacturing in that period; it may also have *depressed* the growth of manufacturing by raising the real exchange rate. Canada may also have experienced this phenomenon, as that country is a net mineral fuel exporter and real fuel prices rose sharply. Japan, well below the regression line in 1970–83, may have had the opposite experience, since it is especially dependent on imported oil. However, as is pointed out below, other factors enter into the situation, and it is noteworthy that the Netherlands is very close to the regression line despite the exploitation of natural gas fields there, which took place after the middle of the 1960s, and which left the country with close to zero net exports of mineral fuels.

3. One can characterize the changes from the earlier to the later period as being a shrinkage of growth rates back from whatever position a particular country held in the earlier period to approximately the same common position in the later one. This does not cover the four outliers mentioned in the preceding paragraph, but for the other eight countries the shrinkage was greater the faster was the rate of growth in the earler period, *and* was greater for manufacturing than for non-manufacturing (as predicted by the regression line). Japan's shrinkage for non-manufacturing was the greatest for any country, and did approximately bring its non-manufacturing growth rate back to the same level as the others. However, its manufacturing growth rate remained well above that of others, even though it shrank by more than the non-manufacturing growth rate, and by more than for any other country except Germany.

4. Since most countries clustered around common growth rates for manufacturing and non-manufacturing in 1970–83, and since there were the outliers already noted, the correlation between the two growth rates in that period disappeared (see regressions (2) and (4) in Table 12.2).

A good explanation of the above phenomena would require more research than I have been able to devote to the subject. What follows is very tentative.

In the first place, there were some factors common to all countries which reduced rates of growth in 1970–83 compared with 1953/4–1963/4. These are discussed in Chapter 16, but the main one, in my view, was the upsurge of inflation at the end of the 1960s and early 1970s, exacerbated by the commodity price boom and oil price increases of 1972-3-4, followed by the further oil price increase of 1979–80, which was not fully accommodated by government macroeconomic policies and, indeed, provoked counter-inflationary measures of varying degree.

Second, there were some changes in the composition of final demand which promoted manufacturing growth relatively to non-manufacturing in the earlier period, and which went into reverse in the later period.

Fast growth in the earlier period, coupled with income elasticities of demand in excess of 1, and further reinforced by the need to rebuild stocks depleted during the war and in the immediate postwar austerity years, resulted in consumer demand for clothing and durables expanding faster than GDP. In the later period, stocks had been replenished and the growth of incomes slowed down, and so consumer demand for these goods grew more slowly in relation to GDP. The rapid growth of output and high output–capacity ratios experienced in the years following the Second World

War steadily increased business confidence, and so fixed investment grew faster than GDP in nearly all countries. This went into reverse in the second period, when fixed investment grew more slowly than GDP. The behaviour of government final expenditure on goods and services was more or less the opposite of this. Following the Korean War, defence expenditures were cut back, and government expenditure generally grew more slowly than GDP in the earlier period (and this probably helped to contain inflationary pressures). In the later period, however, the relative rate of fall slowed down or became a relative rate of increase as health and education expenditures in particular were increased, and so government expenditures on goods and services often grew faster than before in relation to GDP (which probably tended to increase inflationary pressures).[22] These trends are illustrated in Table 12.3.[23] Now it seems probable that the direct and indirect manufacturing components of consumers' expenditure on clothing and durables and of fixed investment are relatively high, while those of government expenditures on goods and services are relatively low. Some estimates for the UK in 1954 are shown in Table 12.4. Hence the relatively rapid growth of manufacturing in the earlier period, and its failure to grow relatively quickly in the second, may have been due largely to the changes in the pattern of final demand, and they, in turn, were linked to overall rates of growth and inflation.

Third, we must consider trade in manufactures, whose importance is emphasized by Kaldor and others. One could measure the impact of trade by the change in the ratio of exports of goods and services to GDP at constant prices, i.e. in the same way as the other final expenditure components in Table 12.3. As Table 12.4 shows, at least for the UK in 1954, the manufacturing content of exports of goods and services was high. In fact, for nine out of the twelve countries,[24] the ratio of exports of goods and services to GDP at constant prices grew by more in 1971–1981 than in 1953–63. The figures are not reproduced here because a different measure is preferred. This is the change in the ratio of net exports (i.e. exports minus imports) of manufactures to GDP at current prices, which is given in Table 12.5.[25] This measure takes account of changes in *imports* of manufactures and also ignores trade in non-manufactures, and on both counts is preferable. On the other hand, the ratios are measured at current rather than constant prices, and some trade in manufactures is neglected (see note

[22] See Bacon and Eltis (1978), and Halberstadt, Goudswaard, and Le Blanc (1984) as well as other contributions to Emerson (1984).

[23] The table refers to data for single years near the beginning and end of each period for ease of computation. It would have been preferable to have fitted trends to all years.

[24] The three exceptions were Italy, the Netherlands, and Norway.

[25] As in Table 12.3, for ease of computation the figures given refer to single years near the beginning and end of each period, but it would have been better to have fitted trends to all the years.

Table 12.3   Changes in the ratios of consumers' expenditure on manufactures, fixed investment and government expenditure on goods and services to GNP or GDP at constant market prices
(Percentage of GNP or GDP)

Country	Consumers' expenditures on manufactures[a]		Gross fixed investment		Govt. expenditure on goods and services	
	1953–63	1971–81	1953–63	1971–81	1953–63	1971–81
Austria	1.1[b]	− 0.1	7.5	− 3.0	− 3.3	0.7
Belgium	2.6	1.9	2.2	− 4.0	0.6	1.5
Canada	0.3	1.5	− 2.2	1.6	− 4.1	− 2.7
Denmark	2.5	− 1.8	4.6	− 9.2	− 0.1	5.0
France	3.1	− 0.2	7.2	− 2.5	− 5.9	− 0.3
Germany	n.a.	− 1.3	5.3	− 4.2	− 0.4	1.2
Italy	0.8	− 0.1	6.5	− 2.7	− 2.5	− 0.3
Japan	n.a.	n.a.	12.3	− 2.6	− 6.0	− 0.3
Netherlands	5.5	n.a.	3.3	− 7.1	− 2.5	0.1
Norway	1.3	− 1.7	1.3	− 2.0	0.1	1.7
UK	2.9	0.8	3.2	− 4.5	− 4.7	1.5
USA	0.5	0.4	− 0.1	− 1.7	− 4.2	− 1.5

Notes

[a] 1953-63, expenditures on 'clothing' and 'durables'; 1971-81, expenditures on 'clothing and footwear', 'furniture, furnishings, and household equipment', and 'personal transport equipment'. Expenditure on 'household operation' is excluded, except for Germany. Food, drink, and tobacco are excluded throughout.

[b] 1956-63.

An example clarifies the meaning of the figures. In Austria in 1963, gross fixed investment was 24.5% of GNP at 1963 market prices. In 1953 it was 17.0% of GNP at 1963 market prices. So there was an increase of 7.5 percentage points from 1953 to 1963, as shown at the top of the third column of figures. For 1953 and 1963 the ratios were to GNP, while for 1971 and 1981 they were to GDP.

The price base was stated as being 1963 in the source for all of the 1953-63 changes; 8 out of 12 of the changes for 1971-81 were based on 1975 or 1976 prices. Canada was 1971, France and Italy were 1970, and Norway was 1980.

The sources used for all countries were the same OECD National Accounts publications referred to in the notes to Table 12.2, except that the data for the Netherlands for 1971 and 1981 were from *National Accounts, Main Aggregates*, Vol. I, 1953-82, OECD, Paris, 1984, p. 61.

(b) to the table). So far as they go, the figures show that net exports rose relatively faster (or net imports fell relatively faster) in the later period than the earlier one for all countries except Canada, Norway, and the UK (the three fuel-exporting countries, which we earlier remarked as lying above the regression line in Figure 12.1). Hence, with these three exceptions, trade in manufactures seems to have been a factor tending to work in the opposite direction to the changes in fixed investment and government expenditures; that is, in an accounting sense, it tended to make manufacturing production

Table 12.4 Direct and indirect manufacturing content of components of final expenditure in the UK, 1954

	Percentages of	
	Total inputs	Total inputs excluding indirect taxes and imports
Consumers' expenditure	19	29
Govt. expenditure on goods and services	20	23
Gross fixed investment	38	46
Exports of goods and services	44	56
Total final expenditure	25	34

Notes

The figures are derived from an input–output table for the UK for 1954 and show, on the assumption of fixed coefficients, the value added contribution made directly and indirectly by manufacturing industry to the various final expenditures components. The first column shows the contribution as a percentage of inputs from all industries, imports of goods and services, and net indirect taxes. The second column shows the contribution as a percentage of inputs from all industries only.

Source: Board of Trade and CSO, *Input–Output Tables for the United Kingdom 1954*, HMSO, 1961, Table 7.

grow faster than GDP, and so faster than non-manufacturing, in the later period as compared with the earlier one.

From a global point of view, there seem to have been two main explanations for these developments: the rise in the price of oil, and the high volume of lending to non-oil countries. Both of these had, as their counterpart, big increases in net exports of manufactures from industrialized to developing countries (including oil producers) between 1971 and 1981. Between 1953 and 1963, our twelve industrialized countries increased their net exports of manufactures in total from $15.5 billion to $21.6 billion. Between 1971 and 1981, however, their net exports of manufactures grew from $41.3 billion to $213.5 billion, a very much sharper increase. This second increase was roughly the same as that of all industrialized countries to the rest of the world, and it seems that about half of it went to OPEC and most of the rest to other developing countries.[26]

While one can account for the main differences in this way, it would require much further analysis to explain the individual behaviour of different countries in Table 12.5. The changes from 1971 to 1981 do not correlate at all closely with corresponding changes in net fuel exports,[27] and

[26] Based on data given in General Agreement on Tariffs and Trade, *International Trade 1974/75*, Geneva 1975, and *International Trade 1983/84*, Geneva 1984.

[27] Calculating net exports of mineral fuels (SITC, Section 3) as a percentage of GDP at market prices for 1971 and 1981, there was, as expected, a negative correlation between these

Table 12.5   Changes in the ratio of net exports of manufactures to GDP at market prices, at current prices
(Changes in percentages of GDP at market prices)

Country	1953–63 (%)	1971–81 (%)
Austria	− 6.0	1.8
Belgium–Luxemburg	− 2.4	− 0.8
Canada	1.0	− 1.5
Denmark	1.6	5.3
France	− 1.3	0.4
Germany	− 0.1	2.1
Italy	0.0	2.5
Japan	1.2	2.7
Netherlands	− 4.8	3.7
Norway	2.3	2.0
UK	− 2.7	− 3.7
USA	− 0.9	0.3

Notes

An example clarifies the meaning of the figures. Austria's net exports (exports − imports) of manufactures in 1953 were 4.9% of GDP at market prices; in 1963 they were − 1.1% (i.e. imports of manufactures exceeded exports). The change was accordingly − 6.0%, as shown at the top of the first column of figures.

'Manufactures' are defined as SITC sections 5–8 inclusive. Food, drink, and tobacco, and also fuels, are excluded. Hence value added in food, drink, and tobacco manufacturing and in petroleum refining are not covered.

Exports are f.o.b. and imports c.i.f., except for Canada and the USA, where they are f.o.b. For some countries the figures refer to general trade and for some to special trade.

Sources: trade figures from *United Nations Yearbooks of International Trade Statistics*. Where necessary, figures in US dollars have been converted to national currencies using conversion factors given there or in OECD trade statistics publications. GDP from the OECD sources cited in the notes to Table 12.2 and 12.3.

it is clear that there were other factors at work. Likewise, the changes from 1953 to 1963 need to be explained. For some countries (the UK and the USA, notably), the fall in net exports over this period was associated with a big fall in their shares of world exports of manufactures, and, in the case of the UK at least, many explanantions have been offered, including a tendency for export prices and wage costs per unit of output in manufacturing to rise relatively to that of competitors.[28] Germany, Italy, and Japan all increased their shares of world exports very markedly over this period, but, whereas Japan's export price and wage costs fell very

changes and those of net exports of manufactures in the second column of Table 12.5, but with a negligible $r^2 = 0.013$.

[28] See, for example, NEDC (1963, Tables 11 and 12). While US export prices rose even faster than the UK's, US wage costs per unit of output in manufacturing rose much more slowly.

markedly (as also did Italy's export prices), Germany's rose moderately (but less than those of the UK) (see NEDC 1963, Tables 11 and 12). Changes in export shares were not, in any case, always accompanied by changes in *net* exports as a share of GDP in the same direction. Table 12.5 shows that Japan did well in that respect, but Germany and Italy performed indifferently. For them, imports grew in absolute terms as fast as exports. In the case of the Netherlands and Austria, imports grew a great deal faster, perhaps in the former case partly because of rapidly increasing wage costs (see NEDC 1963, Table 12) and in the latter case partly because of rapidly growing earnings from tourism.[29]

Let me now summarize my tentative explanation of the 'empirical regularity' which Kaldor observed, and which is updated and illustrated in Figure 12.1. Various factors, discussed elsewhere, led to high rates of growth in the 1950s and 1960s, and also to a build-up of inflationary pressure then. In the 1970s the inflationary dam burst, and there was a commodity boom followed quickly by the first oil shock, with a second in 1979–80. Counter-inflationary measures resulted in a slow-down in growth. Growth rates in the earlier period differed widely between countries, for reasons discussed in Chapter 10 and 11, but with the slow-down the variation in growth rates was also reduced. In the earlier period high growth encouraged even higher growth in manufacturing because of high income elasticities of demand for consumer durables, the need to rebuild depleted stocks of them following war and postwar austerity, and growing business confidence which stimulated investment in plant and equipment. The relative decline in government expenditures, with their high service content, also favoured manufacturing in the earlier period. In the later period all this went into reverse, so that changes in the pattern of final demand worked against manufacturing or, at least, much less in its favour. Perhaps somewhat surprisingly, net exports of manufactures behaved in the opposite way to the factors so far mentioned. It was in the later period that a large net export surplus to OPEC and other developing countries was achieved. In the earlier period, some countries increased and others decreased their net exports, but this contributed little to an explanation of why manufacturing production generally grew faster than GNP.

In the light of this explanation, it does seem hopelessly oversimplified to attribute faster growth in non-manufacturing to faster growth in manufacturing, and the latter, in turn, to external demand. Kaldor made these attributions, but offered little more than assertion to back them up. His emphasis on export demand in particular seems misplaced. All the countries he studied were competing in much the same world markets for

---

[29] Austria's net receipts from travel in her balance of payments rose from 1.6% of GDP at market prices in 1953 to 4.9% of GDP at market price in 1963 (derived from IMF *Balance of Payments Yearbooks* and OECD *National Accounts Statistics*).

manufactures, and it is prima facie implausible to regard Japan's or Germany's success in relation to that of the UK or the USA as being due to differences in *demand*. In fact, Kaldor produced no statistics of foreign trade in manufactures at all in the writings I have referred to which contain, so far as I can judge, the evidence on which his laws of growth were based. He referred to 'the strong correlation between the growth of exports and the growth of manufacturing output' (1978, xviii), without actually presenting such a correlation or giving explicit references to where it could be found. There certainly *is* such a correlation (see, e.g., NEDC 1963, Table 9), but it raises the usual problems of the direction of causation. It seems more plausible to me that there are other factors that lead to faster or slower growth (which are discussed in other chapters), and which *also* lead to faster or slower growth in both exports and imports. Since both exports and imports are affected, there is no clear tendency for changes in *net* exports of manufactures to be correlated with rapid growth of manufacturing production, as is clear from our discussion of Table 12.5. Yet it is *net* exports of manufactures that are relevant if one is discussing the role of external demand, according to Kaldor himself:

Strictly speaking, it is the growth of *net* exports of manufactures which correlates with the growth of manufacturing output. But this qualification is only important in those cases (such as the UK or Japan) where the one measure is significantly different from the other, i.e. where the growth rate of exports of manufactures diverges to an important degree from the growth rate of imports of manufactures. (Kaldor 1978, xviii)[30]

Unfortunately, Table 12.5 suggests that this qualification *is* generally important. Making the growth of exports of manufactures the prime cause of the growth of GDP is not so much a case of putting the cart before the horse, but rather of forgetting, as both cart and horse career down hill, that there is such a thing as gravity.

[30] This quotation is a footnote to the previous quotation.

13

FABRICANT'S LAWS

13.1 Introduction

We turn now to a quite different sort of comparison from that made in previous chapters. Hitherto we have been concerned with growth rates of similar industries in different countries or time periods. We now consider growth rates of different industries within one country and one time period. A phenomenon similar to Verdoorn's Law seems better established for this type of comparison than for the earlier one, and, in seeking to explain it, we must take account of some other very interesting empirical regularities that have been found. Not only is there a tendency for faster productivity growth to accompany faster output growth, but both are correlated with savings in wage costs and materials costs per unit of output and with slower rates of growth of prices. The discoverer of these regularities, so far as I have been able to determine, was Solomon Fabricant, who described them (for the US economy) in a book published in 1942. This was followed by a great deal of further empirical and theoretical analysis[1] which confirmed the existence of similar phenomena in other countries and periods besides those originally studied by Fabricant. In what follows, I review some of the main studies in chronological order, and then use my own framework of analysis which leads to one particularly surprising conclusion, namely, that there is a tendency in a given economy over a given (long) period for labour productivity to grow at the same rate in all industries.

13.2 Fabricant's Laws and explanation of them

Fabricant's data relate to changes in index numbers of output, output per worker, employment, and various measures of costs and prices for some fifty manufacturing industries in the USA between various years in the period 1899–1939. The main laws are the correlations[2] between the following changes, these changes (for any particular correlation) being in the logarithms of index numbers[3] over a given period (as long as the data would permit):

---

[1] The three principle studies are Salter (1960); Kendrick (1961); and Kennedy (1971), which gives extensive references. Three more recent studies are, for the UK, Matthews *et al.* (1982) and Wragg and Robertson (1978); and for the USA, Kendrick (1982).

[2] Most of the correlation coefficients given by Fabricant are of ranks.

[3] For rank correlations it makes no difference whether absolute increases in index numbers

1. a positive correlation between increases in output per worker and in output, as in Verdoorn's Law. Fabricant in fact correlates output with employment, so as to avoid the danger of spurious correlation mentioned already (Fabricant 1942, 88);
2. a positive correlation between increases in the book value of the net capital stock and in both employment and output;
3. a positive correlation between increases in the book value of net capital stock per worker and output;
4. a negative correlation between increases in output per worker and wage costs per unit of output, implying that differential rates of increase in wage rates had not offset differential rates of increase of output per worker;
5. a positive correlation between increases in wage costs per unit of output and in value added per unit of output, with the non-wage element in value added at least not offsetting the differential rates of increase of wage costs;
6. a positive correlation between increases in value added per unit and in selling price, so that changes in materials costs per unit at least did not offset the changes in value added per unit;
7. a negative correlation between increases in selling prices and in output.

Fabricant explained this chain of relationships by causal factors working both from the supply and demand sides. Thus he sums up as follows:

The foregoing analysis has proceeded from change in unit labour requirements to change in output, in an attempt to trace the connection between them. We have observed that rate of decline in labor per unit has been associated with rate of decline in unit cost of fabrication; that costs of fabrication, in turn, have fallen or risen with selling price; and, finally, that selling price has dropped most precipitately in industries in which output has climbed most rapidly. The causal sequence may run in the other direction as well. Growth in output, whatever the initial stimulus, will tend to eventuate in economies of large-scale production, one of which frequently is a reduction in unit labor requirements. Capital equipment is more readily acquired when output is rising. As we have noted above, there is a fairly strong correlation between trends in output and in capital assets. Organizational changes are more easily introduced in growing industries. Even the rate of improvement and innovation in equipment, methods and organization may be stimulated more in growing than in declining industries. In this concatenation of relationships, also, we find reason to anticipate some degree of correlation (though not a high one) between decline in employment per unit of output and growth in output. (Fabricant 1942, 109–10)

Fabricant also pointed out that there was a *positive* correlation between growth of output per worker and employment. Rapidly growing product-

or changes in logarithms are taken, provided the index numbers are all equal in the initial period. Where Fabricant uses ordinary least squares regressions, he takes logarithms of the variables.

ivity was not (as many have feared) associated with declines in employment. Rather, the reverse was true, and employment grew fastest in those industries in which productivity grew fastest.

Fabricant's Laws have been broadly confirmed by many other studies, both for the USA and for other countries. Table 13.1 summarizes results based on data from six such studies. Four basic relationships are shown, these being the four regression equations given below the table. The first is the Verdoorn relationship of labour productivity growth on output growth, which is significant at the 1 per cent level in all six cases on a one-tailed test. The second is essentially the same relationship, but expressed in the form of labour input growth related to output growth so as to avoid the possibility of spurious correlation that some might think affected the first equation. The correlations are, in fact, stronger when the equation is written in this way, and, since the coefficient of employment growth on output growth is less than 1, the implication is that faster output growth is accompanied by faster productivity growth, just as in equation (1). The third and fourth equations require data on prices, which are available in only four out of the six cases. In the third equation, the growth of prices is shown to be negatively related to the growth of labour productivity, and in the fourth equation the growth of output is shown to be negatively related to the growth of prices. In only one of these cases is the significance of the relationship in doubt.

These four relationships are the laws on which I shall concentrate attention in what follows.[4] The main problem is to explain the first two, that is, to explain why productivity grows fastest where output grows fastest. We cannot make use of the same explanation as was used earlier for Verdoorn's Law. This is because we are no longer explaining differences in rates of growth of output in the same industry (or a similar mix of industries) in different countries, or at different times. Since we are comparing different industries, with very different capital intensities, it is no longer possible to explain different rates of growth of productivity by different investment ratios. A more capital-intensive industry may have a higher investment ratio, and yet a slower rate of growth of labour productivity, than a less capital-intensive one. Hence a different explanation is required and, whatever it is, it should be consistent with the relations shown in the third and fourth equations. In what follows, I first review the explanations provided by some other writers, and then make use of the earlier growth model, suitably adapted, to provide my own.

---

[4] All of Fabricant's seven correlations given above are relevant except 2 and 4, which make use of book values of capital stock. I have ignored these, as my framework of analysis does not require capital stocks. Such figures are in any case difficult to interpret, since they depend heavily on the accounting conventions used, and these may have little economic rationale.

13.3   Salter's analysis

After Fabricant's, the next substantial study which advanced matters further was that by Salter, published in 1960 (although the basic work was undertaken from 1953 to 1955). There were two parts to Salter's study, a theoretical part and an applied part. The former was an originator of putty–clay vintage models of growth, which are discussed in Chapter 3. Here I focus attention only on the applied part.

Salter applied Fabricant's analysis to UK data for a sample of twenty-eight industries (all from manufacturing except for electricity generation and coal mining) and with respect to changes in output, employment, costs, and prices between the years 1924 and 1950. He also considered similar US data, including Fabricant's. As well as confirming Fabricant's correlations, he extended them by measuring changes in the non-wage element of value added per unit of output (called 'gross margin cost') and in materials costs per unit of output separately. He found that both of these were positively correlated with wage costs per unit of output, showing that industries that were progressive tended to save on all factor inputs, and not just on one (see Fabricant's correlations 5 and 6 above). Salter did not, however, have any data on capital stock or investment.

More explicitly than Fabricant, Salter set out for discussion four possible explanations for the different rates of productivity growth in different industries. He considered each in turn to see how far it was consistent with the pattern of correlations he had found.

(a)   Increased personal efficiency of workers

Faster productivity growth in a particular industry is caused by the extra personal efficiency of the workers in it. Salter dismisses this explanation on the grounds that it is implausible that it could account for the very big differences in productivity growth he found, that it does not explain why changes in other costs are positively correlated with changes in labour costs per unit of output, and that one would expect that extra personal efficiency would be associated with extra labour earnings when in fact there is no correlation between labour productivity growth and growth in average earnings (see also Fabricant's correlation 4).

This last point is an important one, since it suggests that the inability of both Fabricant and Salter to measure quality-adjusted labour input did not matter very much. In so far as there were quality improvements or worsenings in labour, they were uncorrelated with the other variables, and also their variance was relatively small. This conclusion derives some further support from Table 13.1. One of the sets of data in that table, that

Table 13.1 Examples of Fabricant's Laws

Dependent variable	Values of:	USA 78 ind. 1899–1954 (1)	USA 32 ind. 1899–1953 (2)	USA 44 ind. 1947–73 (3)	USA 30 ind. 1948–76 (4)	UK 28 ind. 1924–50 (5)	UK 82 ind. 1954–73 (6)
(1) $g - g_L$	a_1, constant	0.0150 (11.5)	0.0130 (4.4)	0.0088 (2.3)	0.0181 (4.2)	0.0083 (4.7)	0.0261 (16.3)
	b_1, coeff. of g	0.2533 (8.0)	0.3297 (5.2)	0.4230 (5.0)	0.2984 (2.5)	0.4159 (8.4)	0.3660 (9.0)
	r^2	0.4554	0.4715	0.3747	0.1801	0.7318	0.5008
(2) g_L	a_2, constant	−0.0150 (−11.5)	−0.0130 (−4.4)	−0.0088 (−2.3)	−0.0180 (−4.1)	−0.0082 (−4.7)	−0.0263 (−16.4)
	b_2, coeff. of g	0.7467 (23.5)	0.6708 (10.5)	0.5770 (6.8)	0.7004 (5.8)	0.5823 (11.8)	0.6350 (15.5)
	r^2	0.8790	0.7871	0.5272	0.5457	0.8428	0.7504
(3) g_p	a_3, constant		0.0387 (13.4)		0.0451 (10.7)	0.0364 (11.4)	0.0689 (31.4)
	b_3, coeff. of $g - g_L$		−0.7565 (−7.5)		−0.6102 (−4.4)	−0.8488 (−5.9)	−0.8113 (−14.1)
	r^2		0.6531		0.4044	0.5730	0.7135
(4) g	a_4, constant		0.0643 (8.9)		0.0402 (4.8)	0.0517 (8.2)	0.0718 (9.0)
	b_4, coeff. of g_p		−1.2872 (−3.9)		−0.3033 (−1.1)	−1.3243 (−5.3)	−1.1967 (−6.6)
	r^2		0.3347		0.0419	0.5213	0.3533

Notes

The equations were all fitted by ordinary least squares to data consisting of exponential rates of change per annum between the years shown across industries. *t*-values are shown in brackets beneath the coefficients. The four equations fitted were:

(1) $(g - g_L) = a_1 + b_1 g$
(2) $g_L = a_2 + b_2 g$
(3) $g_p = a_3 + b_3(g - g_L)$
(4) $g = a_4 + b_4 g_p$.

It should be the case that $a_1 = -a_2$ and $b_1 + b_2 = 1$; however in some cases, owing to rounding errors in the basic data, these results are only approximately achieved.

g = exponential growth rate of output: this was generally measured either by base-weighted index numbers of gross output combined with value added weights, or by deflating gross output or alternatively value added by price index numbers. The separate estimation of gross output and material inputs at constant prices, with value added at constant prices obtained as their difference, although ideal, was generally not used. It was, however, used for farming in col. (2), for all industries in col. (3), and for a large proportion of industries in col. (4).

g_L = exponential growth rate of labour input: this is measured by man-hours in cols. (1), (2), and (4), by numbers of workers in cols. (5) and (6), and by quality-adjusted index numbers in col. (3).

g_p = exponential growth rate of price of output: this is generally intended to be the price of value added, excluding indirect taxes levied on output. It can only be a true price index of value added, however, where the volume of output has been estimated by subtracting the volume of material inputs from the volume of gross outputs (see note to g above): otherwise, it is a price index of gross outputs.

In general, the index numbers of quantity used price or value added weights referring to some fixed base year, and the index numbers of price were obtained by dividing index numbers of value by these index numbers of quantity, thus giving price index numbers with changing weights. However, col. (3) used a system approximating to a Divisia index of both prices and quantities.

Most of the industries included are manufacturing: entirely so in col. (1), 19 out of 32 in col. (2), 21 out of 44 in col. (3), 20 out of 30 in col. (4), 26 out of 28 in col. (5), and 80 out of 82 in col. (6). The other industries in cols. (2), (3), and (4) cover the non-manufacturing sector of the private domestic economy, except for finance and services (incl. residential housing) in col. (2), and real estate in col. (4). The only two non-manufacturing industries included in cols. (5) and (6) are coal mining and electricity generation. Whereas the other columns include the whole, or much the greater part, of manufacturing production, in col. (5) the industries are restricted to those for which adequate data existed, and cover only around a third of manufacturing. In cols. (1) and (2), beverages were excluded because of the prohibition era which fell within the period.

Sources: Cols. (1) and (2), Kendrick (1961); col. (3), Gollop and Jorgenson (1980); col. (4), Kendrick and Grossman (1980); col. (5), Salter (1960); col. (6), Wragg and Robertson (1978).

in column (3), is based on indexes of labour input that *are* quality-adjusted (see the source cited in the note to the table). It still remains true that productivity growth is quite strongly correlated with output growth, as also is employment growth with output growth. The coefficient of employment on output is, indeed, rather further below 1 than in the other sets of data, and the correlation coefficients are smaller than nearly all the others. Nevertheless, they are still very significant.

(b) Factor substitution

Labour productivity grows faster than average because capital or materials per unit of labour is growing faster than average, so enabling a greater than average saving in labour per unit of output to be made. Salter also dismisses this as a *major* part of the explanation: if it were, he argues, one would expect to find that increases in gross margin costs or materials costs would be positively correlated with increases in labour productivity, whereas the correlation is in the reverse direction.

This argument implicitly assumes that prices of capital or material inputs increased in broadly the same proportions in all industries, or at least that relative increases in prices were not negatively correlated with relative increases in quantities. Unless one assumes this, it is possible, for example, that faster-than-average labour productivity growth was due to a faster-than-average increase in the quantity of capital accompanied by a lower-than-average increase in the price of capital inputs into that industry. Salter does not appear to have recognized this possibility, and has no data on prices of capital inputs or materials to test it. However, so far as materials are concerned, a test was provided later by Kendrick (1961, 199–200), and there is also a careful discussion on this point by Kennedy (1971, 166–70), both of which confirm Salter's view. So far as capital inputs are concerned, there have been several studies which have measured changes in the quantities of capital inputs into different industries, and these have generally shown that little or none of the differences in rates of growth of labour productivity between industries can be explained by differences in the rates of change of capital-labour ratios.

These studies are well summarized and discussed by Kennedy (1971, 170–4), who points out, however, that conventional measures of the quantity of capital input do not properly allow for differential changes in the efficiency of these inputs. Consequently,

quality improvement in capital goods for use in an industry is counted not as an increase in volume of capital input, but as an increase in productivity. Changes in the quality of capital are generally caused by advances in technical knowledge, and these may bear with a substantial differential impact on the capital goods used in different industries. Hence the role of capital as a carrier of technological progress is not adequately taken into account in the above analysis of factor substitution. (Kennedy 1971, 173)

Needless to say, I think this criticism of conventional measures of capital inputs is very much to the point, but return to my own explanation below.

(c) Different rates of technical change

This is the explanation to which Salter attaches most importance. The data show that *all* factor inputs—labour, capital, and materials—per unit of output tend to move together. There are two plausible explanations for this, says Salter: technical change (which, he argues, generally makes absolute savings in all factors, even if it may also make the savings unevenly), and economies of scale (of which the same is true). However, economies of scale are linked to technical change, and major innovations can occur at different dates in different industries and lead to uneven rates of technical change and to the occurrence of economies of scale. The following passage from Salter is especially illuminating, and is one I shall revert to later:

Related to the character of scientific advance is the question of the age of an industry. An industry may be born around some new scientific principle—steam-power in the eighteenth century and electricity at the end of the nineteenth century, for example. Even though methods and techniques may be very crude, it is often economic to begin production almost immediately, because a high price can be charged. Subsequently, there is a great potential for improvements around the same basic principle. A new specialised technology arises and, for a period at least, brings forth a continuous flow of significant improvements and modifications. Something of this sort is going on with respect to nuclear-power generation at this very moment. At any one time, some industries are in this stage of rapid improvement, while others, more mature, find significant advances less frequent and less rewarding. For example, between 1850 and 1950 fuel consumption per draw-bar-horsepower of steam locomotives remained constant (although there have been other improvements); while in the more youthful field of electricity generation, coal consumption per kilowatt-hour has been reduced from 3.47 lb in 1908 to 0.09 lb in 1950.[5] New knowledge of economies of plant scale are important in this context. Young industries have only just begun to explore the possibilities of scale; for a period each new plant is bigger than its predecessors, very often with important economies. In the electricity industry this probing for the limits of scale-economies has extended over half a century and is still not completed: the first turbo-generators had a capacity of a thousand kilowatts; scale progressively increased until units of two hundred thousand kilowatts are in use.[6] Taking all these factors together, it is not unreasonable to expect substantial differences in the impact of improving technology on different industries. (Salter 1960, 133–4)

Salter thus argues that uneven rates of technical change lead to uneven

---

[5] Dunsheath (1951, 243, 125).   [6] Dunsheath (1951, 123).

rates of productivity increase and also uneven rates of savings in all factor costs. Furthermore, he argues that economies of scale are associated with technical change, and that there is a *general* tendency to substitute capital for labour. While substitution alone cannot account for the observed differences in productivity growth, the data are quite consistent with there having been some substitution as well as different rates of technical change. In my opinion, Salter's discussion of this point well illustrates the profitless complexity of describing the process in terms of movements along production functions ('substitution') and shifts of the function ('technical change').

(d) Economies of scale

Salter distinguishes three types of economies of scale. First, there are economies of firms and plants, such as those arising from mass production, standardization, spreading of overheads, distribution outlets, etc. Although all these economies should be realized in long-term competitive equilibrium, in practice they take time to achieve, and they are achieved more rapidly and easily when output grows rapidly than when it grows slowly. Salter cites the motor industry as a leading example.

Second, there are economies relating to the size of the industry arising, for example, from

the growth of specialist industries and services (such as materials and component suppliers), specialised education and training facilities, and the special cases where optimum plant scale is equal to or greater than industry output. A striking example of the importance of such economies is provided by the development of the grid system in electricity supply. . . . Similarly, the emergence of specialist suppliers has certainly been a critical factor in the growth of the motor industry. (Salter 1960, 141)

Third, there are what Salter calls 'dynamic scale and growth economies':

An expanding industry has a high morale; there is a willingness on the part of labour and management to adopt new methods; finance is readily available; and the very success of the industry tends to attract progressive management. Finally, since an expanding industry provides a good market for capital equipment, machine-manufacturers (and engineers within the industry) find it worth while to develop special-purpose machinery and, in addition, to employ mass-production methods in its manufacture. (Salter 1960, 142)

Another economy of growth, according to Salter, arises from the fact that faster growing industries will tend to have more recently installed plants embodying the latest, and most productive, techniques. However, as Salter himself points out (p. 81), this effect would be likely to be small. Also, an acceleration in the growth rate leads to a faster rate of growth of productivity only once-and-for-all, as the higher rate of investment shortens the average age of the capital stock. Once a steady rate of investment and growth is achieved, the average age would not change, and the rate of growth of productivity would relapse to its former steady-state level (see also Kennedy 1971, 187).

Salter pointed out that economies of scale could, in principle, account for all the observed pattern of correlations. They could be due to different rates of demand increase impinging on industries with similar potential economies of scale, which would then be realized to a greater extent where demand grew faster. Alternatively, industries' potential economies of scale might differ, and similar shifts in demand for them all could result in a more rapid fall in costs in some than in others, which in turn would feed back into faster growth in demand and ouput.

In conclusion, Salter argues that *all* factors mentioned are probably important, and that there is a complex set of interrelationships. Technical change and economies of scale in the first place affect best-practice techniques (i.e. the latest vintages), expand output, and drive down prices. Obsolete techniques are abandoned and so costs and prices fall throughout the industry. There is also substitution of capital for labour generally, and gross investment is necessary for the realization of the new techniques and economies of scale. *Increased* personal efficiency of workers may not explain differential productivity growth, but the *level* of personal efficiency may determine the rate at which new techniques can be absorbed.

13.4 Kennedy's analysis

While both Fabricant and Salter were eclectic in their explanation of Fabricant's Laws, Kennedy came down much more firmly on the side of demand and economies of scale as being the most important factors. Kendrick was also inclined to that view,[7] but since Kennedy presents the argument in a more compelling way, I shall concentrate on his exposition.

Salter had sought to explain different rates of labour productivity growth. Kennedy's main objective is to explain why faster labour productivity growth is associated with faster growth of output (see Kennedy 1971, ch. 6). After an illuminating discussion of the data, Kennedy makes the preliminary point that there are reasons why the association should be the opposite of that found. Rapid growth of output might lead to the

---

[7] See Kendrick (1961, esp. 209). Kendrick refers to an econometric analysis by N. E. Terleckyj, which attempted to discover the causes of differences between industries in their rates of growth of total factor productivity. The three causes that emerged as most important were: rates of change of output, amplitudes of cyclical fluctuations, and ratios of R&D outlays to sales, or of R&D personnel to total man-hours worked. This analysis was Terleckyj's unpublished doctoral dissertation for Columbia University entitled 'Sources of Productivity Change. A Pilot Study Based on the Experience of American Manufacturing Industries, 1899-1953' (1959). I have been unable to find subsequent references to this work, which is briefly described in Kendrick (1961, 181-7).

recruitment of less efficient labour, might reduce competitive pressures, and might increase the proportion of the increase of output accounted for by new entrants, which, according to Kennedy, 'would tend to lower productivity growth relative to output growth in the industry unless the new firms had a much higher level of productivity than the old' (p. 163). One might add that the faster productivity growth achieved in UK manufacturing in the early 1980s was attributed by some to the *contraction* of output, which, it is said, eliminated high-cost plants or firms and so achieved a once-for-all gain. It is thus all the more remarkable that there is a positive association between rates of growth of productivity and output, and all the more need to find convincing explanations.

Kennedy first discusses, and rejects, three explanations relating to the quantities of labour, materials, and capital inputs. Labour productivity for a particular industry is measured by an index of the quantity of gross output (rather than the quantity of value added) divided by an index of the numbers of workers or man-hours. Labour productivity might therefore increase because of unmeasured increases in the quality of labour input, or because of substitution of either materials or capital for labour. Kennedy's reasons for rejecting these possible explanations are similar to those already discussed.

Kennedy next discusses the explanation in terms of different rates of exogenous technical progress. Ignoring, for the moment, the possibility that faster output growth might itself make for greater or faster application of technological advances, this explanation is as follows. An industry in which technical progress happens to be more rapid will find its costs (all costs, and not just labour costs) falling faster. The consequent relatively faster fall in its prices will then cause demand for its products to grow faster, and thereby lead to the observed positive association of faster productivity growth with faster output growth. Kennedy argues that, while it is true that prices tend to fall fastest where productivity rises fastest, and it is also true that output tends to rise fastest where prices fall fastest, both the regression coefficients and correlation coefficients in these associations are too small to account for the rather strong positive association found between productivity and output growth. Much depends on how big the relevant price elasticities of demand are. Unfortunately, available empirical measurements of price elasticities of demand are not directly relevant since they refer mostly to final consumer goods. Such as they are, they do not suggest high price elasticities.[8] Furthermore, there is no observed tendency for the

---

[8] Kennedy argues (1971, 182) that, where prices are measured by unit values, the omission of quality changes results in errors in prices which are associated with equiproportionate errors in quantities in the opposite direction, and that this would normally tend to bias the elasticities upwards (arithmetically upwards, I assume). However, the resulting bias, in my opinion, would be towards unity; i.e., the true elasticities would be biased upwards only if they were smaller than 1. If they were greater than 1, omission of quality changes would bias them downwards.

productivity–output association to be stronger where the productivity–price and price–output associations are strongest. Kennedy also points out that rates of growth of demand do not depend only on relative price changes: income elasticities differ, and population growth, changes in the age distribution of the population, urbanization, and the distribution of income all impinge with different effects on different industries. In the case of open economies such as the UK and Ireland (for which Kennedy himself provided the data), shifts in foreign demand and supply can be important, and, while price elasticities may be high, the relevant price changes are not between domestically manufactured products, but between domestic and foreign substitutes, which may be quite different. However, if output happens to grow fast in some industry for reasons unconnected with reductions in its costs and prices relative to those of other domestic industries, why should this faster growth in output be associated with faster productivity growth when the latter is due only or mainly to exogenous technical progress? Surely there must be some way in which faster output growth itself *causes* faster productivity growth. To rely on causation running only in the reverse direction cannot explain the strong association between output and productivity growth which does exist.

Does faster output growth itself make for greater or faster application of (exogenous) technological advances? We have already seen that, while it may be true that faster growth shortens the average age of the capital stock and the lag in the application of new techniques, this effect is due to *acceleration* in growth, and hence is once-and-for-all. Even there, it is likely to be small. There may be some beneficial effects, but Kennedy is not inclined to give them a great deal of weight (1971, 189). He therefore turns to the hypothesis that the rate of technical progress in an industry is *not* exogenous but is, in fact, strongly influenced by the rate of growth of that industry's output. Endogenous technological progress of this kind is, he believes, an important part of the explanation that we are seeking.

The two principal authors cited by Kennedy in support of this hypothesis are Arrow (1962b) and Schmookler (1966). Arrow argued that the rate at which technological knowledge is acquired (i.e. the rate of 'learning') depends on experience in attempting to solve problems. If the same problems keep recurring, better and better solutions to them will be found, but the rate of improvement in the solutions will taper off. The rate of improvement will therefore be highest if new problems keep appearing. Gross investment leads to changes in economic arrangements and so brings new problems. A high rate of gross investment will thus result in a fast rate of learning and productivity growth. Arrow took as his index of learning cumulative gross investment, and he applied this to a vintage-type model. Kennedy argued that faster growth of output would be correlated with faster growth of the index and that this would explain the positive association of output and productivity growth. Arrow's model is discussed in Chapter 4 and is not considered further here. No substantial empirical evidence in support of it was provided.

By contrast, Schmookler did provide empirical evidence in support of his hypotheses. These were described in Chapter 5, but are summarized here for convenience. They were principally concerned with technical improvements in capital goods supplied to different industries. Such improvements in the *product* technology of the capital goods industries result in improvements in the *production* technology of the industries buying the capital goods. Conventional measurements of output omit many of the quality improvements resulting from better product technology, but include perhaps most of the productivity gains resulting from better production technology. Schmookler argues that most industries buy their capital goods from much the same range of capital-goods-producing industries. The scope for improvement (or 'inventive potential') of these industries may differ one from another and from time to time. However, wherever it exists it will be *directed* in whatever seems to be the most profitable use. The larger the volume of sales of capital goods to industry X, the more profitable, *ceteris paribus*, will it be to devote inventive effort to improving industry X's capital goods. So, if industry X is a big customer for all or most capital-goods-producing industries, they will all tend to devote more of their inventive effort to industry X's capital goods than to those of industry Y, which is a smaller customer. Since both X and Y buy from broadly the same set of capital goods industries, the *average scope* for improvement is much the same for X's or Y's purchases, but the *actual* improvements will be greater for X's since more effort will be devoted to them.

Schmookler's empirical evidence in support of his hypotheses is briefly surveyed in Chapter 5. Kennedy argues:

> If we accept his evidence and argument about the relation between gross investment in an industry and capital goods inventions for use in the industry, then, in so far as such inventions are responsible for raising productivity in the industry, the rise in productivity in a given period will depend on the amount of gross investment in that period, the level of productivity will, therefore, be related to the volume of cumulative gross investment from the beginning, and the rate of growth of productivity will be related to the rate of growth of cumulative gross investment. (Kennedy 1971, 197)

In a footnote, he states that this is 'exactly the same as Arrow's formulation of the learning hypothesis', although the argument leading to it is somewhat different.

I do not myself find this argument wholly convincing, since it does not clearly distinguish absolute and proportionate rates of growth. Gross investment could be bigger absolutely in industry X than in industry Y, and yet the proportionate rate of growth of output in Y could be bigger than in

X simply because the value of output was smaller in Y. Inventive effort, however, would presumably be directed towards capital goods for X. Hence productivity could be rising proportionately faster there although output was rising proportionately more slowly.

Kennedy provides an interesting argument as to why Schmookler's hypothesis also explains the association between relatively rapid output growth in an industry and relatively rapid falls in both the price and quantity (per unit of output) of its materials inputs. The rapid growth of the industry would induce a rapid growth of the industries supplying it with materials and so, by the mechanism just described, would induce relatively rapid improvements in both the product and production technologies of the materials-supplying industries. Improvements in product technology would show up as reductions in the measured quantity of materials per unit of output of the purchasing industry, since quality improvements are not properly allowed for. Improvements in production technology would show up as reductions in the price of the materials (Kennedy 1971, 199–201).

Economies of scale are divided by Kennedy into four types: those internal to a firm or plant, those external to it, static, and dynamic. After a very useful listing of the different kinds of static internal economies of scale, Kennedy argues that it is highly unlikely that their realization could, by itself, form an important explanation of the association between productivity and output growth. Thus, suppose that the scope for such economies is the same in all industries and that their realization is the only factor leading to productivity growth; then, since it is generally agreed that the scope for economies declines as output grows, one would expect to find that

the ratio of the rate of increase in productivity to the rate of increase in output would tend to be low in industries with very rapid rates of increase in output—something which is not supported by the data. More important, it is unrealistic to assume that the scope for static internal economies of scale would be the same in all industries and there is, therefore, no assurance that the industries with relatively rapid output growth would have as much scope for such economies as the industries with relatively slow output growth. (Kennedy 1971, 207)

However, one might counter this by reference to Salter's young and mature industries. The young industries are small and have more scope for static internal economies than the larger mature industries, and high rates of growth may be found more in the young than in the mature industries.

Static external economies of scale are dismissed by Kennedy as of little consequence for his argument (1971, 212), so we pass to dynamic economies of scale. These are reductions in costs (downward *shifts* in cost curves, as opposed to movements along downward-*sloping* cost curves) that are generally or partly irreversible (unlike static economies, which are reversible). I shall consider internal and external economies together, for brevity. Kennedy devotes most attention to the latter. The main sources of such economies are the development of skills resulting from greater specialization, as pointed out by Adam Smith (1776, I, i, ch. 1), and the development of machinery to undertake work formerly done by labour, which may become worth while only when there is a certain minimum amount of that work to be done, as pointed out by Allyn Young (1928). These economies occur within firms or industries that are growing rapidly and spread to the industries supplying them, since they in turn are induced to grow rapidly. Greater specialization made possible by the growth of output could be specialization of workers (including workers at all levels) or specialization of firms, the latter benefiting in turn from economies of scale as they grow in size. Young emphasized the way in which successive processes which had been combined within a single firm could be separated, mechanized, and performed by separate firms, the history of printing providing an example. Stigler (1951) extended Young's account by pointing out that some functions performed within a firm could be subject to economies of scale, and that specialist firms could come into existence to perform these functions once the industry reached a certain size. As Kennedy points out, the creation of new specialist firms and specialist industries causes difficulties in the definition and measurement of an 'industry's' rate of growth.

In conclusion, Kennedy accepts that exogenous technical progress could account for some of the association between output and productivity growth through its effects on costs and so on prices and so on demand. However, this effect, by itself, would result in only a weak association in view of the other strong influences on demand. Kennedy places most emphasis on endogenous technical progress and dynamic economies of scale. Because of these, faster output growth leads to faster productivity growth, there then, admittedly, being some feedback on output through price reductions, and so still further reinforcement of the association as output induces still further dynamic economies.

13.5 An explanation in terms of my own growth model

The growth model sketched out in earlier pages can be used to explain Fabricant's Laws, and this is of some value inasmuch as it enables one to do without concepts which should be abandoned for reasons given in Chapter 3. These include conventional definitions of the production function and its associated capital stock, the distinction drawn between movements along and shifts of the function ('factor substitution' versus 'technical change'), an exogenous rate of technical progress, and the measurement of total factor productivity. These concepts and measures were used to some extent by Fabricant, Salter, Kendrick, and Kennedy, and this mars their otherwise illuminating analyses. Furthermore, once we have jettisoned this unwanted ballast we can steer the ship into new ports which have not yet been properly visited or explored. The voyage, it must be stressed, needs to be followed by others. There is a great deal more to be done.

Chapter 9 explained how the equilibrium growth position of a firm or industry would be determined under various sets of assumptions. In this chapter I make use of that analysis, taking the simplest model which suffices for the purpose at hand. I assume, then, that the firms in a particular industry have access to a perfect capital market, so that in equilibrium the marginal rate of return is given by the market. They may or may not be subject to physical diminishing returns to the rate of investment, a point further discussed below. To ensure stability of equilibrium, as well as for greater realism, I assume that the firms are selling in imperfect markets. Whereas individual firms may diversify, I am concerned with *industries* producing essentially a given set of products, and so consider the typical firms in the industry in equilibrium to be constrained to grow at the rate given by the rate of shift of the demand curve for the industry's products. This assumption is unsatisfactory for a particular firm (which can diversify) as well as for a whole economy (where supply and demand factors are not easily separated), but it suffices for present purposes. For the moment I ignore the possibility that the *level* of prices affects the *rate of growth* of demand, but return to that later.

The upshot of these assumptions is that there is a dynamic supply curve for an industry which relates the equilibrium growth rate of supply to the level of the prices of its products, as in Figure 9.2, except that the supply curve could be either upward-sloping (as there), or downward-sloping. The curve would be upward-sloping only if there were sufficiently rapidly physical diminishing returns to the rate of investment. In the absence of these, access to a perfect capital market would ensure a downward-sloping supply curve. If we choose to assume an elastic, but less than infinitely elastic, supply of capital to the industry (as is plausible; see pp. 265 and 276), then the supply curve could be either upward- or downward-sloping, even with no physical diminishing returns. In any case, the dynamic demand curve confronting the typical firm is vertical, as in Figure 9.2, with its position determined by the rate of growth in the rest of the economy and by the income elasticity of demand for the industry's products.

The slope of the dynamic supply curve thus depends on the balance struck between tendencies making for physical diminishing returns to the rate of investment (e.g. Penrose effects), tendencies for the required rate of return on investment to rise as the rate of investment and growth is increased, both of which make for a rising supply curve, and opposing tendencies. The latter include economies of scale for all the reasons discussed earlier.

The distinction between economies that are internal to the plant or firm and those that are external to it but internal to the industry, and between those economies external to the industry but internal to the whole economy, become important here. If there are important economies of scale external to the firm but internal to the industry, then the investment programme contours perceived by the firm may be more subject to diminishing returns, and also less steeply sloping, than the real contours applicable to the whole industry. The economy-wide contours may be still less subject to diminishing returns, and still more steep. Indeed, our econometric results for the business sector as a whole, although not conclusive, rather support the conclusion that diminishing returns are not important, and so provide evidence for the importance of economies of scale.

The analysis is concerned with equilibrium growth rates. In equilibrium, an industry must grow at a constant exponential rate, with stable prices (in relation to the general price level), and a constant share of both investment and wages in value added. The rate of growth of labour productivity must then equal the rate of growth of real wage rates, which is determined in the rest of the economy. If this analysis is to be useful, I need to show that most industries are at least close to equilibrium for much of the time.

Of course, it is strictly impossible for all industries to be in equilibrium all of the time unless all have the same growth rate. There is nothing in the above that ensures that this will be so; indeed, I would regard it as something of a weakness in the model if it did, since growth rates of different industries differ quite widely over long periods. My use of the concept of steady equilibrium growth must therefore be regarded as no more than a useful first approximation. That is, over some given long period we can measure the actual average growth rates of different industries, and we can ask whether their behaviour over that period can be described as if it were equilibrium growth in terms of the above model to a first approximation. This inexactitude may not satisfy, but it is at least a step forward from a static or comparative-static analysis, and I do not know a better way to proceed.

To demonstrate the stability of growth equilibrium, it would be necessary to have a model of the behaviour of a typical firm away from equilibrium. The provision of such a model is highly desirable, but I must leave it to others. All I shall attempt here is to show that, in fact, most industries can be quite well approximated by the equilibrium just described. However, this is not true of all industries, some being better described as moving from one equilibrium to another, having been subject to some change in the exogenous determinants of equilibrium. I will start by considering this latter case, since it does give some insight into the question of stability, and also shows the role and importance of price changes. Only two kinds of shock will be considered. The first, from the supply side, is an improvement in the investment opportunities confronting an industry, such as might flow from a major invention. The second, from the demand side, is an increase in the rate of growth of demand for an industry's products arising from, say, an increase in the income elasticity of demand for those products. There are other types of shock which a fuller analysis should consider.

Although the first type of shock could alter the shape as well as the position of the IPC, I assume it only changes ϱ, and so leads to a uniform outward shift of the contour through F in Figure 9.1. This case was considered on pp. 248–9, where it was shown that such a shift will initially shift out the 'blown-up' IPC in the same proportion, since the prices of the industries' products will not initially change. Consequently, there will be a rise in the rate of return to investment, and growth will speed up, as also will the rate of growth of labour productivity. Since the dynamic demand curve has not shifted, faster growth of output must drive down prices. Equilibrium growth will then be restored with the same rate of return and shares of investment and wages as before the shock occurred. The fall in price will, in fact, neutralize the increase in ϱ, so that $P\varrho$ will be unchanged. In terms of dynamic supply and demand (Figure 9.2), there will be a fall in the supply curve leading to a fall in the prices of the industry's products and a restoration of the original rate of growth of output.

An industry subject to a shock on the supply side will then trace out exactly the sequence of events described by Fabricant and others. There will be faster growth in output associated with faster growth in productivity and slower growth in prices. The share of wages will be little affected. It will tend to fall, because of the faster growth of productivity, but it will tend to rise because of the slower growth of prices. In the final equilibrium the original share of wages will be regained, and so, on average during the transition to the new equilibrium, the share will not change. The same is true of the share of investment.

This sequence of events recalls the S-shaped logistic curve which has been used to typify the output histories of new products. The rate of growth of output may accelerate for a time, reach a maximum, and then decelerate to some new steady level. Meanwhile, prices of the new products tend to fall relatively to those of products-in-general. Some examples of this type of behaviour are to be found in Kuznets (1930), Dean (1951), and Mills (1955). See also the earlier quotation from Salter (p. 367).

The supply-side shock just considered is a fall in the dynamic supply curve, and the analysis can easily be adapted to refer to a rise. Our second type of shock is a shift in the (vertical) dynamic demand curve. Let us assume that this is a rightward shift, there being equally no difficulty in adapting the results for a leftward shift. It is clear from Figure 9.2 that a rightward shift in the dynamic demand curve must increase the rate of growth of output. Whether, in the new equilibrium, prices are higher or lower depends on the slope of the supply curve which, as we have seen, might be either upward or downward. If, then, demand-side shocks are to trace out the sequence of events described by Fabricant *et al.*, it is necessary that they should mostly slope downwards. For in that case the transition from one equilibrium to another would involve the same sequence of faster growth in both output and productivity, as the rate of investment is increased, accompanied by a fall in (relative) prices. If the dynamic supply curve sloped upwards, however, there would have to be a *rise* in (relative) prices, and that is not what is generally observed. What this suggests is that either economies of scale and elastic supplies of savings are important (so that supply curves slope downwards), or most shocks are on the supply side, not the demand side. We return to this question below.

Even if dynamic supply curves slope downwards, there is another possible difference between the two types of shock. In the supply-side shock, neither λ nor s changes, or changes very much. In the demand-side shock, however, both could change appreciably. It seems likely that a rightward shift in the dynamic demand curve would result in a fall in λ and a rise in s (see p. 247).

Let us now consider what would be the salient features of an economy in which most of the industries were close to equilibrium for most of the time, but in which a minority were subject to the kinds of shocks just described.

The industries that were close to equilibrium would exhibit the following features. Their rates of growth of output would, in general, differ, but not their rates of growth of productivity (see p. 376 above). Consequently, differences in rates of growth of output would be matched by equal differences in rates of growth of employment. A regression of employment growth on output growth should have a coefficient of 1, and there should be a zero correlation between output growth and productivity growth, i.e. for these industries, Verdoorn's Law would *not* apply. These industries should also have stable prices or, once changes in the general price level are allowed for, should have approximately zero variance in their relative rates of price growth. Likewise, they should have approximately zero variance and zero mean in their rates of growth of λ. It is possible to test for the above using data from the sources already cited.

Turning now to the industries out of equilibrium, one might expect some rather different features. In so far as supply-side shocks of the kind described above prevailed, one would expect to find the phenomena described by Fabricant's Laws: rates of growth of output positively correlated with rates of growth of productivity, and both negatively correlated with rates of growth of prices. There would still, however, be little change in λ. In so far as demand-side shocks as described above prevailed, and assuming elastic supplies of capital and little in the way of physical diminishing returns to the rate of investment, the same would be true, except that changes in λ would occur.

If the model of equilibrium growth is to be useful, most industries should conform to it. Fabricant's Laws should, then, be due to a minority of industries being out of equilibrium, while for most industries the laws would not apply. How far do the available data bear this out? In what follows I use the same data as in Table 13.1, but seek to divide the industries into two groups: those approximately in equilibrium, and those out of it.

As a preliminary, we may note from Table 13.2 that four out of the six sets of data have frequency distributions of productivity growth rates that are more humped or peaked than normal; that is, they are *leptokurtic*. This could be due to a majority of industries having productivity growth rates close to the mean so that they are in, or near, equilibrium in the sense described above. There is also some evidence of leptokurtosis in growth rates of output, although it is marked in only two out of the six sets of data. All of the four available distributions of growth rates of λ, the share of wages, are leptokurtic.

In order to see whether one could describe most industries as being approximately in equilibrium, each of the six sets of data in Table 13.1 was divided into two parts: those two-thirds with rates of labour productivity growth that differed least from the mean, and the remaining one-third whose rates of labour productivity growth differed (positively or negatively) most from the mean. The two-thirds fraction was arbitrary. The results of fitting the same equations to each of these sets of data are given in Tables 13.3 and 13.4, and Table 13.5 contains relevant data on the extent of variation in growth rates comparing all industries with the $\frac{2}{3}$ 'equilibrium' industries.

The available data for columns (1), (2), (3), and (6) in the tables supports my hypotheses well; the data in columns (4) and (5) provide much less satisfactory support for it. It must be remembered that the hypotheses are concerned with *trends* in capacity and other magnitudes, and that one would not expect them to hold over short periods where the end-years being compared have different ratios of output to capacity. This may partly explain why column (4), in which 1948 is compared with 1976, a year of appreciably lower output in relation to capacity in the USA, does not support the hypotheses well. Column (5) refers to a much more restricted sample of manufacturing industries (only about a third of the total) than do the other columns, and that may help to explain its poor showing.

Let us first consider equation (1) in Tables 13.3 and 13.4. If I am right, this equation should have a negligible or small coefficient of productivity growth on output growth in the $\frac{2}{3}$ 'equilibrium' industries, with a negligible or small r^2. By contrast, the coefficient should be sizeable and the r^2 large for the $\frac{1}{3}$ 'disequilibrium' industries. All the columns in Tables 13.3 and 13.4 bear this out, except for column (5) in Table 13.3 (although even there the coefficient b_1 is fairly small, 0.23) and column (4) in Table 13.4, where the r^2 and the coefficient are not very significant.

Table 13.2 Kurtosis of the distributions of rates of growth of productivity, output, and the share of wages across industries

Kurtosis of exponential growth rates of:	USA 78 ind. 1899–1954 (1)	USA 32 ind. 1899–1953 (2)	USA 44 ind. 1947–73 (3)	USA 30 ind. 1948–76 (4)	UK 28 ind. 1924–50 (5)	UK 82 ind. 1954–73 (6)
Labour productivity	5.0	3.9	4.7	2.6	2.7	5.2
Output	5.9	3.0	4.8	3.1	2.9	3.3
Share of wages		5.2		3.6	3.5	4.0

Note
Kurtosis is measured by $\mu_4/\mu_2{}^2$, where μ_4 is the fourth moment about the mean, and μ_2 the second moment (i.e. the variance). For the normal distribution this measure is 3, and values in excess of 3 denote leptokurtosis or peakedness above normal. For sources and other details of the data used, see the notes to Table 13.1

Table 13.3 Tests of Fabricant's Laws for $\frac{2}{3}$ of industries with least variance of productivity growth rates

Dependent variable	Values of:	USA 52 ind. 1899–1954 (1)	USA 21 ind. 1899–1953 (2)	USA 29 ind. 1947–73 (3)	USA 20 ind. 1948–76 (4)	UK 19 ind. 1924–50 (5)	UK 54 ind. 1954–73 (6)
(1) $g - g_L$	a_1, constant	0.0181	0.0193	0.0221	0.0264	0.0119	0.0318
		(21.9)	(7.6)	(8.8)	(6.3)	(7.3)	(30.3)
	b_1, coeff. of g	0.0880	0.1179	−0.0091	−0.0238	0.2282	0.0964
		(3.7)	(2.0)	(−0.1)	(−0.2)	(3.9)	(2.9)
	r^2	0.2139	0.1792	0.0008	0.0019	0.4676	0.1429
(2) g_L	a_2, constant	−0.0181	−0.0193	−0.0221	−0.0263	−0.0119	−0.0319
		(−21.9)	(−7.6)	(−8.8)	(−6.2)	(−7.3)	(−30.1)
	b_2, coeff. of g	0.9120	0.8821	1.0091	1.0217	0.7698	0.9036
		(38.2)	(15.2)	(16.2)	(7.8)	(13.0)	(27.4)
	r^2	0.9669	0.9244	0.9064	0.7733	0.9089	0.9351
(3) g_p	a_3, constant		0.0275		0.0594	0.0437	0.0649
			(4.7)		(9.5)	(8.1)	(11.0)
	b_3, coeff. of $g - g_L$		−0.2853		−1.2388	−1.2787	−0.6925
			(−1.2)		(−5.3)	(−4.2)	(−4.1)
	r^2		0.0715		0.6068	0.5108	0.2418
(4) g	a_4, constant		0.0429		0.0268	0.0363	0.0493
			(2.6)		(3.4)	(3.9)	(3.1)
	b_4, coeff. of g_p		−0.1240		0.1274	−0.7175	−0.6920
			(−0.2)		(0.5)	(−2.0)	(−1.9)
	r^2		0.0014		0.0124	0.1834	0.0618

Note

The same equations were fitted as in Table 13.1 to those $\frac{2}{3}$ of the industries whose productivity growth rates differed least from the mean productivity growth rate for each set of data. t-values are shown in brackets beneath the coefficients. For further details of data and sources, see the notes to Table 13.1.

Table 13.4 Tests of Fabricant's Laws for $\frac{1}{3}$ of industries with most variance of productivity growth rates

Dependent variable	Values of:	USA 26 ind. 1899–1954 (1)	USA 11 ind. 1899–1953 (2)	USA 15 ind. 1947–73 (3)	USA 10 ind. 1948–76 (4)	UK 9 ind. 1924–50 (5)	UK 28 ind. 1954–73 (6)
(1) $g - g_L$	a_1, constant	0.0147	0.0123	0.0048	0.0161	0.0049	0.0208
		(5.1)	(2.4)	(0.7)	(1.8)	(1.4)	(6.5)
	b_1, coeff. of g	0.3441	0.4548	0.6290	0.4387	0.5261	0.5489
		(6.1)	(4.6)	(4.6)	(2.0)	(7.2)	(8.6)
	r^2	0.6107	0.7022	0.6209	0.3409	0.8803	0.7406
(2) g_L	a_2, constant	−0.0147	−0.0124	−0.0048	−0.0161	−0.0047	−0.0211
		(−5.1)	(−2.4)	(−0.7)	(−1.8)	(−1.3)	(−6.6)
	b_2, coeff. of g	0.6559	0.5459	0.3710	0.5606	0.4718	0.4533
		(11.7)	(5.5)	(2.7)	(2.6)	(6.5)	(7.1)
	r^2	0.8508	0.7725	0.3630	0.4567	0.8563	0.6582
(3) g_p	a_3, constant		0.0405		0.0456	0.0337	0.0692
			(8.3)		(6.7)	(5.5)	(22.0)
	b_3, coeff. of $g - g_L$		−0.8233		−0.5060	−0.7513	−0.8239
			(−5.9)		(−2.7)	(−3.7)	(−11.7)
	r^2		0.7935		0.4718	0.6558	0.8392
(4) g	a_4, constant		0.0646		0.0600	0.0625	0.0798
			(7.3)		(3.3)	(8.1)	(7.7)
	b_4, coeff. of g_p		−1.6134		−0.8677	−1.7468	−1.3214
			(−4.1)		(−1.5)	(−5.8)	(−5.9)
	r^2		0.6550		0.2307	0.8258	0.5746

Note

The same equations were fitted as in Table 13.1 to those $\frac{1}{3}$ of the industries whose productivity growth rates differed most from the mean productivity growth rate for each set of data. t-values are shown in brackets beneath the coefficients. For further details of data and sources, see the notes to Table 13.1

Table 13.5 Extent of variation in growth rates of output, productivity, price of value added, and share of wages across industries

		USA 78 ind. 1899–1954 (1)	USA 32 ind. 1899–1953 (2)	USA 44 ind. 1947–73 (3)	USA 30 ind. 1948–76 (4)	UK 28 ind. 1924–50 (5)	UK 82 ind. 1954–73 (6)
Standard deviation of:							
(1) g	All	0.0296	0.0243	0.0260	0.0175	0.0267	0.0321
(2)	$\frac{2}{3}$	0.0221	0.0183	0.0186	0.0123	0.0195	0.0250
(3) $g - g_L$	All	0.0111	0.0117	0.0180	0.0123	0.0130	0.0166
(4)	$\frac{2}{3}$	0.0042	0.0051	0.0060	0.0068	0.0065	0.0064
(5) g_p	All		0.0109		0.0118	0.0146	0.0159
(6)	$\frac{2}{3}$		0.0054		0.0108	0.0117	0.0090
(7) g_λ	All		0.0076		0.0053	0.0085	0.0078
(8)	$\frac{2}{3}$		0.0062		0.0036	0.0073	0.0077
(9)	$\frac{1}{3}$		0.0100		0.0070	0.0110	0.0083
Ratio of standard deviations of:							
(10) g and $g - g_L$	All	2.7	2.1	1.4	1.4	2.1	1.9
(11)	$\frac{2}{3}$	5.3	3.6	3.1	1.8	3.0	3.9
(12) g and g_p	All		2.2		1.5	1.8	2.0
(13)	$\frac{2}{3}$		3.4		1.1	1.7	2.8
(14) g and g_λ	All		3.2		3.3	3.2	4.1
(15)	$\frac{2}{3}$		2.9		3.5	2.7	3.3
(16)	$\frac{1}{3}$		3.4		3.6	3.5	5.2

Note

The first nine lines of the table give standard deviations of exponential growth rates of output (g), productivity ($g - g_L$), the price of value added (g_p), and the share of wages in value added (g_λ). The remaining seven lines show the ratios of the standard deviations of the growth rate of output to the other standard deviations. All standard deviations are calculated using the formula $\sigma = \sqrt{[\{\Sigma(x - \bar{x})^2\}/(n - 1)]}$ where x is the variate, $\bar{x}$ is its arithmetic mean, and n is the number of observations. For further details of the data and sources used, see the notes to Table 13.1

Next, consider equation (2) in these tables. If I am right, this equation in the $\frac{2}{3}$ industries should have a coefficient of 1 of employment growth on output growth, which should be highly significant. For the $\frac{1}{3}$ industries the coefficient should be positive, but less than 1. All columns bear both predictions out, except that column (5) in Table 13.3 has a coefficient of 0.77, which is not as close to 1 as might be hoped.

Next, consider the extent to which the degree of variation in productivity growth rates is lower for the $\frac{2}{3}$ industries than for all the industries. According to my hypothesis, it should be much lower. In making this comparison, it is useful to relate the variation in productivity growth rates to that in output growth rates. One might expect (e.g. from Verdoorn's Law, or because of Kennedy's arguments considered above) that, if the growth rate of output varied less, so would the growth rate of productivity, but the perhaps surprising feature of my hypothesis is that, in equilibrium, there remains considerable variation in growth rates of output without any variation in growth rates of productivity. From Table 13.5 it can be seen that, first, there is an appreciably smaller standard deviation of productivity growth rates in the $\frac{2}{3}$ industries than in all—not surprisingly, since that is how they were selected. Second, the standard deviation is itself quite small, and especially so for columns (1) and (2), which cover the longest periods. In their cases the standard deviations of productivity growth rates are around 0.5 per cent per year or less for the $\frac{2}{3}$ industries, whereas they are more than twice as great for all industries (and three to four times as great for the $\frac{1}{3}$ industries). Third, the standard deviation of the growth rate of output is much greater in relation to that of productivity for the $\frac{2}{3}$ industries than for all industries. This is true for all columns, although the increase is least marked for columns (4) and (5).

Next, we consider the extent to which the degree of variation in growth rates of the price of value added is lower for the $\frac{2}{3}$ industries than for all the industries. According to my hypothesis, it should be much lower. Again, one can relate the standard deviation to that of output growth as a sort of numeraire. Unfortunately, there are no data available for two of the 'good' columns, (1) and (3). The other two 'good' columns, (2) and (6), do support the hypothesis, as can be seen from Table 13.5. However, the 'bad' columns, (4) and (5), do not: although they show some reduction in price variation, it is proportionately less than the reduction in the standard deviation of the growth rate of output.

Finally, consider the variation in the growth rate of the share of wages as measured by its standard deviation in rows (7), (8), and (9) of Table 13.5. My hypothesis states that this should be small for the $\frac{2}{3}$ industries, but it could also be small for all industries, for the reasons given above if supply shocks rather than demand shocks predominate. Since the standard deviation is small both for all industries and for the $\frac{2}{3}$ industries, this suggests that supply shocks are dominant. In other words, where industries are out of equilibrium, it is mainly because of factors such as some invention or group of inventions which has shifted the investment programme curve out, or else because of some falling off in the supply of inventions which has shifted the curve in. It is these, rather than changes in income elasticities of demand, that have pushed industries out of equilibrium. Had changes in income elasticities been more important, one would have expected bigger changes in λ in the $\frac{1}{3}$ industries for the reasons given earlier. In fact, although the standard deviation of the growth rate of the share of wages *is* bigger in the $\frac{1}{3}$ industries than in the $\frac{2}{3}$, in relation to σ_g it is *smaller* (see Table 13.5). However, the conclusions that supply shocks have been dominant must be regarded as tentative. Only two kinds of shock were distinguished in the earlier analysis, and there may have been other kinds whose effects should be considered.

13.6   Does labour productivity tend to grow at the same rate in all industries?

For myself, and perhaps for others too, the most surprising conclusion to emerge from the preceding analysis is that labour productivity tends to grow at the same rate in all industries in a given economy in a given time period. This conclusion does not hold for different time periods; as we have seen, productivity grew much faster in the quarter-century following the Second World War than ever before. Nor does it apply to different economies, in some of which productivity grows much faster than in others. However, within one economy, and across different industries in that economy over a given period, which could be as long as you please and must be long enough to average out the effects of cyclical fluctuations, the tendency does seem to hold.

It is only a *tendency*. About two-thirds of the industries covered in the various sets of data we have reviewed conform to it quite closely so far as their average behaviour over the periods surveyed is concerned. This behaviour approximated to equilibrium growth, and, given that the working of the labour market ensured that the rate of growth of wage rates was approximately the same in all industries within the economy, this *required* uniformity in rates of growth of labour productivity in order that the shares of labour, λ, in each industry should not change, or not by very much. For the remaining one-third of industries this was not so, but it is still possible that their behaviour could be described as subject to the same tendency. That is, although their rates of growth of productivity differed widely, it is possible that this was because of random shocks (such as major inventions), following which productivity grew either faster or more slowly than the mean for the whole economy, but nevertheless regressed towards that mean. Regression towards the mean is implicit in my explanation of Fabricant's Laws for these $\frac{1}{3}$ industries, and so there is evidence that it did occur.

What is the explanation for this tendency towards a uniform rate of labour productivity growth? There are two essential elements: first, the point already made that the labour market appears to work in such a way that wage rates rise at about the same rate in all industries; second, the role of price changes as a substitute for changes in investment opportunities: the substitutability of P and ϱ. It is this second point which is the novel element in the theory put forward here, and which is therefore perhaps worth recapitulating.

Let us imagine two industries, one of which is 'backward' in the sense that labour productivity is growing much more slowly than the average for the rest of the economy, and the other of which is 'forward', with labour productivity growing much faster than average. In the backward industry, prices (of value added) will be tending to rise relatively to prices-in-general, while in the forward industry they will be tending to fall. The rise in prices in the backward industry has the effect of reducing the burden of a given real rate of investment there. In terms of our usual symbols, a given $\sigma = S/Q$ will imply a smaller and smaller $s = S/PQ$ as P rises. Since it is s, rather than σ, that measures the economic burden for investors in the industry, the chances are that σ will rise as P rises. But a higher σ, which is a faster rate of real investment, will tend to increase the rate of growth of labour productivity. The backward industry will then appear less backward. The rise in P has had the same economic effect, so far as the industry is concerned, as if there had been a favourable outward shift in investment opportunities, ϱ. The story is just the same, *mutatis mutandis*, for the forward industry, which will cease to appear so forward as its prices fall and the burden of a given real rate of investment there increases.

I suspect that this tendency to regress to the mean is widespread. It may, of course, be interrupted from time to time by shocks, and the more narrowly we define the industry, the more important will such disturbances appear. Nevertheless, the tendency can probably be detected at work even in such 'industries' as domestic service, where, prima facie, the scope for labour productivity growth might seem to be severely limited. If one could measure the output of domestic service as the amounts of meals prepared, clothes made presentable, rooms kept clean, flowers grown, and lawns kept green and smooth, etc., and if the labour inputs included not just paid servants but also master, mistress, and children, then I suggest that the rise in labour productivity over the past century has been marked in Western countries, where the prices paid for cooking, working, cleaning, and gardening have risen faster than prices-in-general, but has probably been much less marked in Eastern countries, where their relative prices have risen by much less. This, however, is mere speculation!

Errors of measurement of quality improvement could, if persistent, conceal the tendency to regress to the mean. The measured rate of growth of labour productivity in some service industries has lagged behind that in manufacturing over long periods, and prices of services, as measured, have risen faster. This could be due to a failure to measure the output of services properly. Indeed, in some cases output is measured by labour input, which reduces apparent labour productivity growth to zero.

13.7   Economies of scale reconsidered

It will be recalled that both Kennedy and Kendrick believed that the strong positive correlation between productivity growth and output growth was to a great extent due to various static and dynamic economies of scale, and that, because of these, faster output growth *caused* faster productivity growth. What light do my model and the above data shed on this? One possible way in which economies of scale could feature in my model is through reducing the extent to which there are 'physical' diminishing returns to the rate of investment. We have noted at several points that the evidence for such diminishing returns is weak, and so this does support the contention that economies of scale are important.

One could, however, give another interpretation to the economies-of-scale argument. It could be taken to mean that ϱ, the parameter defining the distance out of the 'physical' investment programme contour, increases as output increases. For an economy with output generally increasing, the aggregate investment programme contour would then shift gradually outwards, and the contours for those industries whose output was growing most rapidly would shift outwards most rapidly. We saw in Section 10.3 that there has indeed been an outward shift of the aggregate contour, and I gave as possible explanations the improvement in communications, in the expertise of management, and in the education of the work-force, all of which may have increased the awareness and improved the selection of investment opportunities. Might not static and dynamic economies of scale also be part of the explanation?

Turning to individual industries, and assuming that the *scope* for economies of scale is the same for all industries, the implication of the argument in terms of Figure 9.1 would be that the faster growing industries would experience a faster-than-average outward shift in their 'physical' investment programme contours, i.e. in point F, over any given period. It would be possible then for industries to reach growth equilibria in which differential rates of shift of point F were exactly offset by differential rates of change in prices. As we saw earlier, price changes can substitute for shifts in investment opportunities, and so they could offset them. Both the equilibrium point E and point C in Figure 9.1 would remain stationary. Rates of growth of output and employment would be constant, as would the rate of growth of prices. Hence the rate of growth of the *value* of output for each industry would be constant, and this would have to equal the rate of growth of the value of the wage bill so as to keep the share of wages constant. The share of investment in value terms would also remain constant, and so would the average rate of return. In this growth equilibrium, let us focus attention on two equations which need to be modified to allow for prices changing at the rate g_p in equilibrium:

$$g = v\bar{g} - \epsilon g_p \qquad (13.1)$$

$$g_w = g - g_L + g_p. \qquad (13.2)$$

The first of these equations explains the rate of growth of demand for the industry's products in terms of the general growth of the economy, $\bar{g}$, multiplied by the income elasticity of demand for those products, v, and the rate of price increase of those products, g_p, multiplied by their price elasticity of demand, ϵ (defined so as to be positive). It must be remembered that we assume zero inflation, so that g_p is the *relative* rate of price increase. The second equation is the requirement for constancy of the share of wages. By eliminating g_p from these equations, we obtain

$$g - g_L = g_w - \frac{v}{\epsilon}\bar{g} + \frac{1}{\epsilon}g. \qquad (13.3)$$

This is a Verdoorn-type equation, with the rate of growth of productivity positively related to the rate of growth of output.

It thus seems possible to explain this relationship in terms of a causal relationship between growth of output and growth of investment opportunities, arising from static and dynamic economies of scale. Unlike my earlier explanation, this is an *equilibrium* relationship. Does it plausibly explain the data?

So far as the $\frac{1}{3}$ industries in Table 13.4 are concerned, it does provide a plausible explanation. There we do observe a strong positive correlation between productivity and output, and also a strong negative correlation between output and prices. The coefficient on prices in this second relationship (i.e. equation (4) in Table 13.4) ranges from -0.9 to -1.7, and if we interpret this as an unbiased estimate of the price elasticity of demand, $-\epsilon$, the resulting coefficient for g in equation (13.3) seems too big, since $1/\epsilon$ would range from 1.1 to 0.6, whereas the coefficient of g in equation (1) of Table 13.4 ranges from 0.6 to 0.3. However, it is quite possible that the estimates of the price elasticities are biased downwards in absolute terms in equation (4) of Table 13.4, owing to failure to allow adequately for quality changes, for example. Hence the evidence in Table 13.4 could be consistent with the economies-of-scale explanation.

It is when we turn to Table 13.3, for the $\frac{2}{3}$ industries, however, that this explanation runs into difficulties. Very little remains of the positive correlation between the growth of productivity and the growth of output for these industries, and very little of the negative correlation between growth of output and growth of prices. It is not as if we have, by our selection of industries, removed all these whose growth of *output* varies appreciably. There is, admittedly, less variation in output in the $\frac{2}{3}$ industries than in the $\frac{1}{3}$ industries, but it is still quite considerable. For example, the standard deviation of output growth for the $\frac{2}{3}$ of 82 (i.e. 54) industries remaining in column (6) is 0.0250 (see Table 13.5, second row), which is greater than the standard deviation of output growth of 0.0243 for all 32 industries in column (2) (see Table 13.5, first row). Yet for the former group of industries the coefficient of productivity growth on output growth is only 0.0964, and r^2 is 0.1429, whereas for the latter the coefficient is 0.3297 and r^2 is 0.4715. If the causation runs strongly from output growth to productivity growth, it is hard to explain this difference, or, indeed, most of the other results for the $\frac{2}{3}$ industries.

It seems, therefore, that if the economies-of-scale explanation is interpreted as requiring a strong causal relation from faster output growth to faster productivity growth, it cannot easily be reconciled with data that show that, for about $\frac{2}{3}$ of all industries, there is little or no positive correlation between the two. I am therefore inclined to put little weight on this explanation, although it *does* seem to me that there is a case for believing that economies of scale of various sorts prevent 'physical' returns to investment from diminishing appreciably.

13.8   The effect of the price level on the rate of growth of demand

Hitherto I have assumed, as is customary, that the level of demand for a particular industry's products depends upon the level of its prices, other prices being given. There are reasons for believing, however, that a lower *level* of prices could induce a faster *rate of growth* of demand, which we may now consider. We also consider what difference this possibility makes to the preceding analysis.

We have already seen that price changes are a substitute for shifts in real investment opportunities. A rise in price shifts the investment programme curve outwards, and, if rates of return and shares of investment in value added remain unchanged, this will result in a faster rate of growth of output so long as price remains at its new, higher, level. The opposite would occur if price fell. These are all effects on *supply*. However, there is a close relation between the supply of industry A and the demand for substitutes or complements of A produced by industries B and C, respectively. If A's price level is lower, this will in all probability lower prices for substitute industry B and raise them for complement industry C. As a result, the rate of growth of B's output will tend to be reduced and that of C's increased. Both of these effects will react back on A, tending to make the *rate of growth* of demand for A increase. It is therefore quite possible that not just the level but also the rate of growth of demand for A will depend on the level of its prices in relation to the general level of prices in the economy as a whole. These effects might, perhaps, be especially important where A, B, and C are traded products, or intermediate goods, but they might also occur for final consumer goods.

In the growth equilibrium described in earlier sections (other than the immediately preceding one), prices do not change. We maintain that assumption (or definition?) here, but we still need to modify equation (9.1), which explains the rate of growth of demand. We must add a term for the price level of output, which could be as follows:

$$g = v\bar{g} - \alpha P^\beta \tag{13.4}$$

where both α and β are greater than 0. This modification greatly complicates the equilibrium solution, since g is no longer determined simply by the exogenous rate of growth of the economy's output multiplied by the income elasticity of demand. However, there is still an equilibrium solution, and the characteristics of a group of industries that are approximately in equilibrium are still the same as described earlier. My analysis of the $\frac{2}{3}$ industries is therefore not affected.

My analyses of the shifts in equilibrium resulting from major inventions and from changes in the rate of growth of demand arising from changes in v are, however, affected. An outward shift in the investment programme contour, increasing ϱ, increases the rate of growth and drives prices down. Because of this fall in prices, the new equilibrium growth rate will be higher than before, instead of remaining unchanged, as in my earlier analysis. Hence, instead of C in Figure 9.1 shifting out and then back to its previous position, it will have to end up further to the right. It will still be the case that, in the transition, the rates of growth of both output and productivity will be faster, and that prices will fall (i.e. that Fabricant's Laws will be obeyed); but now, in addition, λ, the share of wages, will generally change.

My previous analysis still applies for the second kind of shock, an increase in v. However, the final increase in the rate of growth of output will be greater because the fall in price will add to it. This supposes no physical diminishing returns to the rate of investment. If they were to occur, and to require a rise rather than a fall in the equilibrium price level, then this would tend to reduce the rate of growth of output in the new equilibrium.

The upshot of all this is to leave the previous analysis not much affected. Nevertheless, from other points of view it could be of considerable interest to know whether the *rate of growth* of demand is a function of the *level* of an industry's prices in relation to the general level of prices, and further work on this question would be desirable.

14

TAXATION AND GROWTH

14.1 Introduction

With taxation taking 35–40 per cent of GDP at market prices in OECD countries,[1] there should be no need to justify a chapter on taxation and growth. Yet few books on economic growth mention the subject.[2] Perhaps this is because the authors believe that most taxes have little effect on growth in the long run, and this is understandable if the dominant factors are thought to be the growth of the labour force and 'technical progress'. Since I have discarded the latter, and since I believe that material investment is a very important factor, I cannot escape so easily. Prima facie, taxes at current rates might affect investment adversely, and a badly designed tax system might bring down the rate of growth by a substantial amount.

I start by considering three taxes, each assumed to be at a uniform rate: a tax on wages, a tax on take-out from enterprises, and a tax on savings/investment. Actual taxes are often amalgams of all three of these, and, in addition, are levied at different rates on particular kinds of wages, capitalists' consumption, or savings. However, my main interest is in the effects of taxation on rates of growth and factor shares, and these three taxes provide a reasonable starting point.

Taxation is used mainly to finance government expenditure on goods and services and to redistribute income. Government expenditure on goods and services may be on the products of general government employees (e.g. civil servants, armed forces, teachers, doctors) or on the products of the business

---

[1] See, for example, *OECD Economic Outlook*, December 1983, Table 11, p. 36. Social security contributions are included as taxes.

[2] An exception is Giersch (1981), which contains a paper by H. G. Peterson. This reports various regression equations relating both the level and rates of growth of GDP to ratios of total, direct, and indirect taxes to GDP. The equations provide no support for the view that OECD countries have already reached the downward branch of the 'Laffer curve' where higher tax rates diminish tax revenue. There are some rather weak negative relationships between tax ratios (especially direct) and growth. However, as was pointed out by F. Neumark in the same volume, the regressions could be criticized because they omit other important variables influencing growth besides tax ratios, and because it is marginal tax rates rather than average tax ratios that are relevant (see Section 14.6 below). Another commentator, J. Meister, argued that government borrowing could discourage investment and growth, and might, in the short to medium run, accompany lower tax ratios, thus influencing the simple relation between growth and tax ratios. Peterson also discusses the growth-promoting effects of a switch from income to expenditure taxation, which is discussed in Section 15.7 below. A theoretical study of taxation policy in relation to growth is Phelps (1965). This is considered further in Chapter 15.

sector (weapons, buildings, pink string, and sealing wax). General government employees are outside the business sector to which all my analysis, empirical and theoretical, refers. However, they are a source of demand for business sector output, and so the taxes paid by that sector are recycled back to it in that way. In so far as the government directly buys the output of the business sector, that also recycles its taxes back to it.

There are certain effects of taxation and government expenditure on the distribution of incomes and output in the economy which it is convenient to deal with first. In general, since taxes reduce the real incomes of taxpayers, they tend also to reduce their savings. Whether this reduces the rate of growth of the business sector of the economy depends on how the government spends the proceeds and on how this expenditure is regarded by those benefiting from it. If the taxes are simply paid back by way of transfers (e.g. social security payments), the initial reduction in savings will be partly or wholly offset, and the outcome will depend on the marginal propensities to save of taxpayers compared with those of the recipients of transfers.

If the taxes are spent on current goods and services, then the incomes of taxpayers are reduced, but they and others benefit from government expenditure. They may benefit by more than if the taxes had not been levied or the expenditure not incurred, in which case their real incomes will have been raised by the whole operation, and so their savings may also be higher on balance. If the savings are all invested in the business sector, the latter should grow faster than before.

In fact, the business sector could grow faster even if total savings were unchanged. This is because the *size* of the sector could be reduced in so far as government expenditure was on wages and salaries of public employees, rather than on purchases of goods and services from the business sector. If the size of the business sector is reduced, and the amount invested in it is unchanged, then the rate of investment, s, will have increased, and so also the sector's rate of growth. However, the mere fact that the rate of growth is higher is not sufficient to prove that an increase in government expenditure on public employeees drawn from the business sector, and financed by taxation, is beneficial. In fact, a marginal change of this kind is neutral if the workers transferred earn the same wage in both sectors, if the business sector is competitive, if we ignore any other costs or distortions involved in levying the taxes required, if the social value of the output of the workers in government employment is measured by their wages, and if the marginal rate of return in the business sector equals the social rate of discount.[3]

---

[3] Suppose, first, that the ratio of investment to output in the business sector is kept unchanged at s. Let one more worker, earning w in both sectors, be transferred from business

If government current expenditure financed by taxation creates less benefit than it destroys, however, then it seems likely to reduce savings and growth in the business sector. One should include in this calculation the actual costs of collecting the taxes, and of any distortions they may cause. Since taxes inevitably have costs of these kinds, £1 of tax collected should normally be required to provide more than £1 of social benefit by way of extra government expenditure in terms of its equivalent private consumption. More than £1 of private consumption will have been destroyed to provide £1 of tax.

Governments may, of course, raise taxes in order to finance their own capital expenditure, or to make loans to the business sector. Here again, the net effect of this on the business sector or on the whole economy depends very much on the productivity of the investment so financed, and on how taxpayers and beneficiaries react. The terms of any government loans are also relevant. Some capital expenditures could be highly beneficial (e.g. on roads, sewers, prisons, defence), with the result that the rate of growth of the business sector is enhanced. Equally, of course, such expenditure could have low or negative returns (e.g. Concorde, or parts of the UK nuclear power programme) (see Henderson 1977). No simple generalization seems possible.

In the rest of this chapter I consider mainly the distorting effects of different kinds of taxes and their effects on growth and factor shares, ignoring the use to which the revenues are put. I also continue to ignore the effects of fiscal (or monetary) policy on the ratio of output to capacity. For the most part, I consider only the simplest model of the economy, with perfect markets, no diminishing returns to investment, and no borrowing. This suffices to make the main points. In the following chapter I consider the effects of tax changes on growth and factor shares after relaxing these assumptions.

---

to government. The loss of *output* in business (taking my simplest competitive model) is $w\mu/\lambda$, the marginal product being greater than the wage in the ratio μ/λ. However, because of the fall in value added, investment must be reduced so as to keep s unchanged. Hence the fall in consumption is $(1 - s)(w\mu/\lambda) = w$, since $\mu(1 - s) = \lambda$. Assume that the worker and his progeny grow at g_L in either sector. The loss of consumption from the business sector is then w growing at $g_L + g_w = g$, and the present value of that loss is $w/(r - g)$. In the government sector, the wage is assumed to grow at the same rate as in the business sector, g_w, and so the growth in the value of the worker's wage, and his progeny's, is $g_w + g_L = g$. If the wage in government always measures its social value (with consumption as numeraire), then the present value of the worker's output in government is again $w/(r - g)$, and so the transfer has led to neither loss nor gain. If we now assume that the total absolute amount of saving is restored to its previous level, before the transfer, this involves a marginal cut in consumption compared with the above scenario. Its investment in the business sector will earn the marginal rate of return, thus resulting in a zero change in social present value.

14.2 A tax on wages[4]

The effects of tax on the *level* of the supply of labour, L, and real wage rates, w, must be distinguished from the effects on the *rate of growth* of the supply of labour, g_L. Another important distinction is between the effects of a given rate, or structure of rates, of tax and the effects of changes in the rate, or structure of rates.

Let us first consider the effects of a given uniform tax on *levels* of wages, assuming that g_L is unaffected. That assumption implies that the equilibrium values of s, g, and λ are also unaffected. On simple and plausible assumptions, it then appears that increasing the tax rate will reduce real wage rates after tax but will have little effect on either output or real wages before tax.[5] But these are once-for-all effects which leave rates of growth and pre-tax factor shares, i.e. our main concerns, unaffected.

A uniform tax on wages could affect g_L by influencing demographic factors, by affecting the rate of investment in education and training, or by affecting labour mobility. I have nothing useful to say about the first of these, and so will continue to assume that there is no effect. Unless tax rates are very high or real wages are very low, that seems plausible.

In many developed countries, much education and quite a lot of training are compulsory and are provided free by the state. Hence I take their amounts as being exogenously determined, and unrelated to the level of tax rates on wages. However, there still remains in many countries considerable scope for education and training which is either wholly or partly privately financed. Even where the state pays all the more obvious costs, such as teachers and buildings, it may not pay the cost of the forgone earnings incurred by the pupils (assuming they have some choice in the matter). Hence, to some extent, taxes on wages could impinge on individual decisions to invest in human capital, and so could affect the rate of growth

---

[4] In this and succeeding sections, tax rates are always tax-inclusive; that is, the tax levied is included in both the numerator and the denominator of the relevant fraction.

[5] Using a static analysis, and assuming that the output elasticity of employment is a and the elasticity of supply of labour is b, then, given that the share of wages (pre-tax) in total output is the fixed equilibrium share λ, it can be shown that

$$\frac{\partial w}{\partial T_w} = \frac{wb}{\{1/(1-a)\} + b}, \text{ and } \frac{\partial w(1 - T_w)}{\partial T_w} = (1 - T_w)\frac{\partial w}{\partial T_w} - w$$

where w is the real wage rate, and T_w is the tax rate on wages. The elasticity of supply of labour with respect to the real wages rate, b, could be positive or negative, and it seems likely to be small. If $b = 0$, neither output, nor employment nor the pre-tax wage are affected by an increase in T_w, and the post-tax wage is reduced by the full amount. See p. 64 above for some discussion of the sign and magnitude if b.

of the quality-adjusted labour force. One could go further and argue that the *effects* of a given provision of education or training, even when it is both free and compulsory, depend upon the pupil's efforts to learn, and that is to some extent affected by taxes on wages.

Whether a tax on wages reduces the return to investment in human capital depends on the nature of the costs incurred. I consider only four kinds. First, there may be expenditure on goods of various kinds (e.g. books, equipment, buildings, etc.) whose prices are assumed to be fixed in relation to consumption goods independently of the tax on wages, and which I call 'goods' for short. 'Goods' are the numeraire. Second, there may be expenditure on labour (e.g. teachers). Third, there may be a loss of earnings by the pupil, so-called forgone earnings. Finally, there is the effort expended by the pupil, which may consist of a loss of leisure time or simply paying attention. If we can regard effort as being equivalent to leisure at the margin, then it can also be regarded as equivalent to earnings forgone at the margin. Hence the last two categories can be merged as 'forgone earnings'.

Now suppose that, without any tax, at a present cost of C in terms of goods one can achieve a benefit in extra wages worth B in terms of consumption goods when discounted to the present. If a tax at the rate of T_w per unit on wages is imposed, and assuming that neither the cost nor the discount rate nor wages *before tax* are changed, the benefit falls to $B/(1 + T_w)$.

The tax might, however, change labour supply, and so alter the wage before tax, to k times its previous level, and so alter the benefit also to k times $B/(1 + T_w)$. It seems improbable that this could reverse the fall in the benefit, and it might well make the fall (slightly) greater if labour supply increased because of the tax.

In so far as the cost consists of labour (e.g. teachers), with the same other assumptions the cost becomes kC and the benefit $k\{B/(1 + T_w)\}$. The ratio of benefit to cost thus still falls when the tax is imposed.

In so far as the cost consists of forgone earnings, there is no effect on the rate of return, since both cost and benefit are multiplied by $k/(1 + T_w)$. This last case is undoubtedly important, since forgone earnings are a large part of the total costs of education and training, and may represent virtually the whole of it for the private individual where the state bears the other costs. Nevertheless, it seems somewhat extreme to suggest that one can conclude that a uniform tax on wages leaves investment in human capital unaffected.[6] Because of the other categories of cost, which are substantial and which quite often do fall on the private individual, the net effect of such a tax must be to reduce such investment. The conclusion is reinforced if one considers the likely effect of the tax on pupil's efforts to learn. Despite the

[6] See Boskin (1975), as quoted in Eaton and Rosen (1980, 705-6). See also Heckman (1976, S12, S14).

marginal equivalence of effort with post-tax wages, it is surely plausible that higher tax rates would reduce pupils' efforts, and so reduce the rate of real investment in human capital.

The above leaves out of account some other effects. In so far as a tax on wages increases or reduces the future hours of work of the individual contemplating making the investment, it increases or reduces its attractiveness. The 'utilization' of the extra human capital is thereby increased or reduced (see Eaton and Rosen 1980). If investment in human capital is reduced, and g_L falls, this will probably reduce r (see below), and this, in turn, will tend to increase the attractiveness of investment in human capital, thus damping the whole effect but not, of course, reversing it. Finally, allowing for the uncertainty of investment in human capital has ambiguous effects on the tax (see Eaton and Rosen 1980). I do not myself believe that any of these effects is likely to be substantial, and conclude that the net effect of a tax on wages is to reduce investment in human capital.

The effects of a tax on wages on the return to changing jobs, and so on labour mobility, can be analysed in a similar way. There is a cost incurred by the worker, which could consist partly of goods, partly of labour, and partly of forgone earnings. There is a benefit in terms of a future increase in wages, which is taxed. The imposition of the tax reduces the return to the investment.

It seems likely for the above reasons that taxes on labour reduce the rate of investment in human capital, and so reduce g_L. The importance of this effect requires more investigation.[7] There can be little doubt about the importance of taxes on wages, and some estimates are given later in the chapter.

Let us now consider the effects of a fall in g_L in my model of the whole system. Figure 8.1 represents the simplest version of this model, which can be used to answer the question. In Appendix C to Chapter 15 a more complicated version is described, and Table 15A.1 shows the effect of changing g_L on various endogenous variables for a country resembling the USA in 1948–73. In that case a fall in g_L reduces g and all three measures of the rate of return there given. It increases the (before-tax) share of wages, λ, and the rate of investment, s. However, the direction of these last two effects could alter if g_L were initially negative or if the IPC were more sharply curved than I have supposed.

There is one other way in which a given tax on wages could affect the rate of growth that should be mentioned. It is not possible for such a tax to cover *all* employment. Many kinds of self-employment or family

---

[7] The only (very tentative) estimate I know is by Rosen (1980, 174–5), who gives calculations suggesting that the US federal income tax reduces the probability of enrolling in college by 3.5 percentage points, which he apparently regards as an understatement of the likely effect; also it is derived from a non-representative sample.

employment, including the grey area between leisure and work, cannot be taxed efficiently or at all. Raising tax rates on wages must tend to drive people out of the labour market and into these pursuits, some of which form the 'black' economy in which tax is illegally evaded, but in which risks may be high and there may be a loss of economies of scale. This disruption of the market system and increase in insecurity will tend to reduce both the amount and the efficiency of investment, and so the rate of growth.

A tax on wages can be regarded as a tax on consumption out of wages and a tax at the same rate on savings out of wages. As I argue in Section 14.4 that taxes on savings do affect growth and factor shares, it might be thought that a tax on wages must also affect them in so far as it is a tax on savings out of wages. However, this is not the case. The rate of return received by the worker on his savings is not affected by the wage tax (apart from any effect *via* changing g_L, which we are not concerned with here). If he chooses to give up an extra £1 of consumption now, the amount of extra consumption he will get in the future as a result is not subject to the wage tax since the return is not a wage. It is true that workers' real incomes are reduced by a wage tax, and that the tax will tend to reduce their savings, but that effect was discussed in Section 14.1.

To conclude this section, let us briefly consider the effects of changing, say increasing, the rates of tax on wages. Such increases may be resisted by wage-earners, who may attempt to pass on the higher taxes by pressing for bigger wage increases—the phenomenon of real wage resistance, which has attracted much attention in recent years. This can have serious consequences for growth, since it may result in a profits squeeze as governments sooner or later refuse to accommodate faster inflation. There may then be a rather extended period of rising unemployment, excess capacity, and slow growth, until aspirations and expectations are adjusted to the new reality. The developments in many countries since the late 1960s exemplify this, and are further discussed in Chapter 16.

14.3 A tax on take-out from enterprises

It will not surprise those familiar with the subject that a tax on enterprises' take-out has no effects on the magnitudes that concern us. The forumulae for r and μ in (8.2) and (8.3) are unchanged, and so are all the equilibrium equations.[8]

One way of expressing the above conclusion, which may have intuitive appeal, is to say that a tax at the rate T_c on take-out makes the government a sleeping partner in the firm. Of any distributions (whether of dividends or

---

[8] The result that pre-tax and post-tax rates of return are equal with an expenditure tax is demonstrated in, for example, Institute for Fiscal Studies (1978). For a brief history and illuminating discussion of the expenditure tax, see Kaldor (1955).

capital) by the firm, the government receives a share equal to T_c and the legal owners and creditors receive $1 - T_c$. Of any receipts by the firm from these three entities (government, owners, creditors), the government subscribes T_c and the others $1 - T_c$.[9] Because the government and the others participate in the same proportions, whether one is paying out or paying in, their rates of return are equalized, and this common rate of return is the pre-tax rate of return.

This argument prompts the question, If a tax on take-out has no ill effects, why not raise it to 100 per cent? One answer is that very high rates of tax would divert take-out into various forms of business expenses. Owners and creditors would be recompensed by business entertainment, tied houses, business cars, a share in the physical output of the firm (e.g. cross-channel ferries), and so on, rather than by monetary payments attracting tax. Another is that firms that were efficient at evading tax would flourish at the expense of socially more efficient firms. As with high taxes on wages, high taxes on take-out would tend to disrupt the market system and increase insecurity, and so reduce the efficiency and amount of investment and decrease growth.

VAT and other consumption taxes, in so far as they fall on consumption financed by dividends, interest, rent, or other profit, are taxes on take-out in the above sense. So too is income tax on these types of income, although that is, in addition, a tax on savings. Probably, most tax revenues that do not come from employees' earnings come from take-out.

14.4 A tax on savings and investment

A uniform tax on savings, which is equivalent in my simplified model to a tax on investment, affects the rate of return equation in my model (i.e. equation (8.2)) so that it becomes

$$r = (1 - T_s) P (q - \lambda l). \qquad (14.1)$$

Here, T_s is the tax-inclusive rate of tax on savings. A proof of this result is given in the appendix to this chapter. As is also shown in that appendix, equation (8.3), which is repeated here for convenience, is unaffected if expressed in terms of the tax-inclusive savings rate, s^*.

$$\mu = \frac{\lambda}{1 - s^*}. \qquad (14.2)$$

However, here appearances are misleading. s^* is defined as the ratio of tax-inclusive savings, S^*, to the value of output, PQ. My numeraire is, as always, consumption, and S^* is the consumption sacrificed by the saver or investor. However, the actual value of investment in terms of consumption

[9] A subscription of £1 $- T_c$ by shareholders or creditors to the firm reduces take-out *after tax* by £1 $- T_c$, and so must reduce take-out before tax by £1 and tax payments by £T_c.

is $S = S^*(1 - T_s)$, with $T_s S^*$ accruing to the government. It is convenient to distinguish between S^* and $S = S^*(1 - T_s)$, and we may call the former 'savings' and the latter 'investment', so that s^* is the savings ratio and $s = s^*(1 - T_s)$ is the investment ratio. Clearly, the introduction of the tax *has* altered the relation between μ and λ and the investment ratio.

We must also note that equations (8.5) are altered so that they refer to investment ratios:

$$P s^*(1 - T_s)l = \bar{g}_L; \ P s^*(1 - T_s)q = g. \tag{14.3}$$

Apart from these changes, the model, which consists of equations (8.1)–(8.5), is unaffected. The model assumes that the rate of growth of quality-adjusted employment, g_L, is exogenously fixed,[10] and so is most suitable for considering the effect of taxation in a whole economy. It is not difficult to provide a geometrical analysis on the lines of Figure 8.1. Increasing the tax rate on savings, T_s, then has exactly the same effect as a reduction in the price level, P; that is, the 'blown-up' IPC though C shrinks inwards towards the origin in the proportion T_s, so that, for example, a tax rate of 50 per cent would bring C back halfway to O along the ray OC. That this is the effect is clear from equations (14.1) and (14.3). These are the only equations in the model in which P appears, and it is always multiplied by $(1 - T_s)$. This geometrical analysis is not further pursued here. Instead, in Chapter 15 I use a more complex version of the model to estimate the effects of the taxation of savings on growth, rates of return, investment, savings, and the share of wages.

What kinds of taxation bear on savings? As already noted, income tax and profit tax are taxes on both savings and take-out. Their incidence on savings is, however, lessened or even offset completely by the tax exemption of pension fund contributions and of the income of pension funds, by the tax deductibility of interest payments, by depreciation allowances of varying degrees of generosity, and by investment grants, all of which often discriminate markedly between different types of asset, different geographical regions, and different industries.

Indirect taxes, such as VAT, commonly exempt investment, but not always. It is difficult, for example, to distinguish between building maintenance and improvements, or between motor cars for personal consumption or for business use, and so both are often taxed at the same rate.

It is important to note that indirect taxes on consumption which do not

---

[10] In fact, a reduction in the rate of return on material investment could be expected to stimulate investment in human capital, and so increase g_L. Thus Heckman (1976, S27–8) argues that an income tax, which is a tax on wages *and* on interest (and so savings), will lower rates of discount and thereby increase investment in human capital. While this seems correct so far as the discount rate effect is concerned, it ignores the fact that some of the costs of education and training are *not* forgone earnings.

fall on *material* investment are neutral if we exclude the effects on human investment and so on g_L. Thus, for example, a uniform VAT of 10 per cent, confined to consumption, is equivalent to a 10 per cent wages tax,[11] a similar tax on take-out, and zero tax or subsidy on investment. Although such a tax would lower the ratio of a given real amount of investment (measured in real consumption forgone) to a given real amount of output (measured in consumption goods), when both are expressed at market (i.e. purchaser's) prices, it would not change the ratio at factor cost (i.e. producer's prices) or in terms of consumption as a numeraire.

14.5   Uneven rates of tax

Thus far we have considered taxes at uniform rates on wages, take-out, and savings/investment. In practice, and for a wide variety of reasons, including administrative cost, equity, history, and acceptability by the taxpayer (whose co-operation is much needed), taxes are levied at different rates. There is usually a progressive tax on wages. Corporations may be taxed more heavily than unincorporated enterprises, especially small ones, which may evade tax. Different types of consumer goods and services bear different tax rates (justified, for example, by different elasticities of demand, or by differences in their importance to rich and poor consumers), as do different types of investment expenditure. Without considering the arguments in favour of such differentiation, let us ask whether there is any *general* argument concerned with growth against it. In the end, decisions must be based on both types of argument, but here I can consider only the second.

There is a well-known general argument against uneven tax rates which is that they reduce the *level* of output, or of the welfare resulting from that output, below what could be achieved with uniform tax rates. They do this by preventing sundry marginal rates of transformation and substitution from being equalized. In turn, there are other arguments in favour of uneven tax rates of the kind already mentioned and which suggest, on the contrary, that output and welfare are higher. None of these arguments concerns us here, since all relate to *levels*, whereas our concern is *growth*.

Let us consider, to begin with, uneven rates of tax on consumption, and let us assume, in order to point up the argument, that they have no justification on other grounds. Let us further assume that only consumption is taxed, that private returns to investment are the same for all

---

[11] This is still true even if part of wages is saved. The whole of a given pre-tax real wage is effectively reduced by 10%. It is obvious that that part of wages that is spent immediately on consumption buys 10% less in real terms, but it is also true that the present value of any real savings is reduced by 10%, since rates of discount are unaffected (as we have seen, and assuming g_L is unaffected) and future expenditure buys 10% less in real terms.

goods, and that markets are perfect. We further assume that social returns to investment to expand the output of goods bearing the average rate of tax are the same as private returns. Then social returns to expand the output of highly taxed goods will exceed private returns, while for lightly taxed goods the reverse will apply. In this situation, we could achieve a once-for-all gain in output by making the taxes uniform. This would increase investment in highly taxed goods and force down their prices, and reduce investment in lightly taxed goods, forcing up their prices. By undertaking more investment with higher-than-average social returns and less with lower-than-average social returns, we would increase the social rate of return on all investment on average and so the rate of growth from a given total investment. This gain, however, must eventually disappear, since eventually all investment will earn the same social (and private) return, which, so far as I can see, will be the same average return as before. A higher return will have been earned for a time, but only for a limited time.

It therefore appears that the existence of uneven tax rates on consumption does not, on the above assumptions, affect the rate of growth in the long run. It is true that it results in uneven social rates of return being earned on investment, but there seems to be no reason to think that it either increases or reduces the *average* social return. There is scope for a once-for-all gain to be made, but it is once-and-for-all.

Let us next consider uneven rates of tax on investment. Here it does seem likely that unevenness reduces the rate of growth. It does so because, unlike the previous case, it continually reduces the average social rate of return on a given amount of investment. An extreme example may make this clear. Suppose a law were passed that prohibitive tax rates should be levied on the one hundred most socially profitable investment projects coming up each year. The effect must surely be to reduce the average social return to a given amount of investment, and so to reduce the rate of growth. Of course, such a law would not be passed, but there are some laws, or administrative practices, which are a step in that direction. High marginal rates of tax on income, capital gains, or wealth mean that the businessmen who get richest quickest are taxed at the highest rates. Taxes on investment in buildings coupled with subsidies on investment in machinery mean that investment in the former is discouraged while investment in the latter is encouraged. But, just because of these taxes and subsidies, the social return to investment in buildings is likely to exceed that on investment in machinery.

Finally, let us consider uneven rates of tax on wages. Suppose a wage tax is levied at higher marginal rates, the higher are wages. This is likely to reduce the return to investment in human capital even when the costs consist entirely of forgone earnings. The pupil's forgone earnings will in general be lower than his earnings after he has been educated and trained, and so the tax will reduce the benefit from the investment in greater proportion than the cost. Progressivity is likely to reduce the return for other types of investment cost (goods and teachers) as well, since the education and training are likely to put the pupils into a higher-than-average tax bracket. Tax discrimination between those in different occupations earning the same rates of pay does not seem likely to affect the rate of growth. This case is similar to tax discrimination between consumer goods, and it results in the same scope for once-for-all gains, but not for continuing gains.

14.6 Estimates of marginal effective tax rates

Despite the many volumes that have been written on public finance, usable estimates of marginal effective tax rates on labour, capitalists' consumption, and savings are thin on the ground. Tax systems are extraordinarily complex, but precisely because of this it is disappointing that more and better empirical studies have not been undertaken in this field.

It must be emphasized that what is needed are estimates of *marginal effective* tax rates, and not simple ratios of taxes received to incomes paid out, which is what is sometimes provided by existing studies. While these average ratios are of interest, they do not measure the incentives provided by taxation and subsidies. The tax rates must be *marginal* so that they relate to decisions to invest or save or work more or less. They must be *effective* in taking into account all changes in taxes and subsidies that are affected by the relevant decisions. Studies frequently omit relevant taxes or subsidies. The structure of the tax and subsidy system is also important. It is quite possible, for example, for taxes on profits to equal 50 per cent of profits earned, while the marginal rate of profits taxation on investment is zero.[12] Or the reverse could apply, with no taxes being actually paid on profits, while investors had to reckon with a 50 per cent tax rate on profits at the margin.[13] Likewise, the *effective* tax rate on certain employees can be 100 per cent at the margin without any taxes being paid.[14]

There is therefore no escape, if one wants to provide economically relevant estimates, from the necessity of assembling information on the actual tax rates in force, as opposed to the much easier task of showing the amounts of revenue received. Furthermore, because of the myriad different tax rates relevant to different possible transactions, a way has to be found to represent the system in terms of suitable average marginal rates and

[12] This would be the case with a profits tax somewhat in excess of 50% (depending on the rate of investment), against which one could write off investment expenditure in full as soon as it occurs.

[13] This would be the case for companies that had accumulated sufficient tax allowances from past losses or investments to offset all their current tax liabilities, but which expected to revert to paying taxes on profits in the (near) future.

[14] This could result from loss of social security or other benefits when taking employment.

spreads of rates. None of this is easy, and the difficulties no doubt explain the lack of good studies.

A few very recent studies are much the best available. King and Fullerton (1984) is the leading one so far as the taxation of investment or savings is concerned.[15] A recent OECD study is the only one which, so far as I am aware, seriously attempts to estimate marginal effective tax rates on wages in a number of different countries and taking account of all the main relevant taxes (McKee, Visser, and Saunders 1986, 45–101).

Table 14.1, which is reproduced from the OECD study, shows estimates of marginal effective tax rates on wages in OECD countries in 1983, and subdivides the taxes into five kinds: payroll taxes, employer's and employee's social security contributions, personal income tax, and indirect taxes. All tax rates are calculated for a single average production worker in manufacturing industry. Estimates are also given in the source for a similar worker who is married with two children, but for ten of the countries they are the same, and for another eight they are around or less than 6 per cent of total compensation lower, leaving only two countries where they are substantially lower (France and Luxembourg).

It could be argued that at least *part* of employers' and employees' social security contributions are regarded by those concerned not as a tax, but rather as payment of pension contributions or insurance. Private payments of that nature are not treated as a tax, and although the state contributions that are shown in the table are compulsory, it is still possible that they are regarded to some extent in the same light as are private contributions. This means that there is uncertainty about the size of effective marginal tax rates on wages. Nevertheless, unless one is prepared to believe that employees would freely contribute most of the amounts shown *at the margin* for pension or insurance, many of the figures in the first column of the table do seem very high. Even if the total supply of labour measured in terms of man-hours is not much affected by taxes at these rates, the allocation of labour between more or less skilled occupations, and the effort devoted to acquiring skills, could be much affected. The incentive to avoid tax by unpaid self-employment, or by illegal means, is correspondingly strong in some countries.[16]

Estimates of tax rates on savings or investment in the UK and the USA in three postwar years are given in Table 14.2. In making these estimates, I

---

[15] See also King (1977) and Hills (1984). The OECD study (McKee *et al.* 1986) also applies King and Fullerton's methodology to a number of other countries.

[16] Unpaid self-employment (e.g. painting and repairing your own house) enables the worker to avoid virtually all taxes. Illegal avoidance may, however, provide escape only from some. Thus, indirect taxes may still have to be paid even if social security and income tax are not. The avoidance or evasion of taxes by jobbing builders could be defended on the grounds that they have to compete with untaxed do-it-yourselfers!

Table 14.1 Marginal effective tax rates on wages in 1983, single worker at APW
level
(Percentage of total compensation including all taxes)

Country	Total	Payroll tax	Social security contributions Employers'	Social security contributions Employees'	Personal income tax	Indirect tax
Australia	42.3	4.8	0.0	0.0	28.6	9.0
Austria	64.0	1.6	17.9	12.4	22.5	9.6
Belgium	66.9	0.0	19.4	8.7	31.6	7.1
Canada	42.7	0.0	0.0	0.0	29.4	13.3
Denmark	71.2	0.0	0.0	4.5	55.9	10.8
Finland	62.5	0.0	5.2	2.6	43.8	10.9
France	68.8	4.6	30.2	9.7	16.8	7.4
Germany	60.9	0.0	15.6	14.6	23.2	7.5
Ireland	70.2	0.0	10.4	7.6	40.3	11.9
Italy	62.7	0.0	31.3	5.9	18.2	7.2
Japan	43.7	0.0	10.2	9.1	20.2	4.3
Luxembourg	67.2	0.6	16.3	10.1	33.7	6.5
Netherlands	73.5	0.0	19.7	31.2	17.0	5.6
New Zealand	40.3	0.0	0.0	0.0	31.3	9.1
Norway	69.5	0.0	13.9	8.7	32.7	14.1
Portugal	46.9	0.0	17.7	9.5	7.6	12.2
Spain	46.7	0.0	23.6	4.2	14.4	4.5
Sweden	73.0	4.2	22.4	0.0	39.0	7.4
Switzerland	42.2	0.0	9.3	9.2	17.8	5.9
UK	54.5	1.3	9.3	8.1	26.8	9.1
USA	48.6	0.0	7.8	6.2	30.7	3.9

Note
The worker is assumed to have a total income equal to the average earnings of a production
worker in manufacturing. Payroll taxes, unlike social security contributions, are not linked to
the receipt of benefits. Personal income tax rates allow only for standard reliefs available to all
taxpayers irrespective of marital or family status. Indirect taxes exclude property taxes on, e.g.,
homes.

Source: McKee, Visser, and Saunders (1986, 71, Table 7).

have used King and Fullerton's data, and have also followed their
methodology in many respects. However, there are some important
differences, and my estimates result in lower tax rates and also less
variability of tax rates between the different categories of investments.[17]
Full details are given in Appendix C to this chapter.

[17] Thus, King and Fullerton's average tax rate for the UK in 1980 on their 'fixed-*r* basis'
(which is closest conceptually to the estimates given here) is 30.0%, as compared with my
estimate of 4.9%. For the USA in 1980, King and Fullerton gave 49.9% compared with 19.9%

Table 14.2 Effective rates of taxation on saving
(Percentages)

Destination of saving, or ownership	UK			USA		
	1960	1970	1980	1960	1970	1980
'Machinery'	3.6	− 23.3	− 15.9	22.4	15.6	4.5
Buildings	40.4	29.6	26.9	33.4	34.5	37.9
Inventories	70.4	63.0	50.0	51.4	48.4	47.2
Manufacturing	23.6	1.9	− 9.5			
Other industry	18.2	− 1.8	1.9			
Commerce	36.7	25.2	27.1			
Households	26.4	11.8	8.7	29.5	25.7	21.6
Tax-exempt	20.8	− 2.2	2.8	26.8	22.3	17.0
Insurance	22.0	1.7	4.5	27.0	22.6	17.4
All	24.9	6.6	4.9	29.0	24.8	19.9

Notes
If the pre-tax real rate of return is p, and the post-tax real rate of return is r, then the effective tax rate is $(p - r)/r$. The estimates refer to hypothetical marginal investments undertaken by companies and financed largely by retained profits but also by some debt and new share issues. All investments are assumed to earn a real return which would be just over 5% p.a. (i.e. 0.05 exponential return) for a tax-exempt owner. 'Machinery' includes plant equipment and vehicles and, in the case of the USA, public utility structures. 'Other industry' consists of construction and public utilities (including transport and communications). 'Commerce' excludes financial services. For further details, explanations and sources, see Appendices B and C to this chapter.

Even if the variability in tax rates is less than the King–Fullerton estimate, it is still considerable, especially the contrast between subsidies or low tax on investment in 'machinery' and high taxes on investment in inventories, with buildings in between. This discrimination partly results from the shorter lives for machinery than for buildings assumed in tax codes. If the conclusions of Chapter 7 are accepted, this is a doubtful basis for more favourable tax treatment, although one can admit that in *some* cases of abnormally short lives it would be justified. Whether it is for the class of 'machinery' as a whole is more questionable. However, discrimination has gone further than just allowing the taxpayer to write off the asset over a

here. The spread in some of King and Fullerton's estimates of percentage tax rates for 1980 is as follows:

	UK	USA
Machinery	−57.5	26.4
Buildings	56.4	54.1
Inventories	45.9	54.5
Households	104.6	73.4
Tax-exempt	−34.5	−21.3
Insurance	14.5	22.4
All	30.0	49.9

shorter life. In the USA in 1980 investment grants of the order of 10 per cent of the purchase price were made for machinery and equipment and for public utility structures. In the UK, free depreciation (i.e. 100 per cent immediate write-off) as well as investment grants for investment in depressed areas were in force in 1980, and in some earlier years there were investment grants applicable to all areas.[18] Investments in 'machinery' and also in manufacturing industry were regarded with especial favour, and one may ask, why?

Further research is needed to answer this question. One reason may have been the view that technical progress is the mainspring of productivity growth, and that such progress has to be embodied in 'machines', so more machines means faster productivity growth. This seems to me to imply too limited a view of the way in which investment leads to productivity growth. More buildings and inventories, not to mention education, R&D, management, or marketing expenditures, also means greater productivity growth, so long as these investments are well chosen. The favour shown to investment in manufacturing (in the UK at least) may have owed something to Lord Kaldor's advocacy. His views on the importance of manufacturing as the engine of growth are discussed in Chapter 12. I do not find them persuasive. A further reason for favouring investment in 'machines' over some other kinds of investment relates to the scope for learning. It seems plausible to believe that *any* investment, by changing the world, may suggest new investment opportunities to other businessmen which they would not otherwise have thought of. Furthermore, the extent to which this occurs probably differs from one investment to another. More investment opportunities, and scope for learning, probably resulted from building the first factory to make motor cars in the UK than from building a typical housing estate. This may be so, but what is much less certain is that the creation of opportunities and scope for learning attaches to a particular category of investment like 'machinery'. It is notoriously difficult for politicians or civil servants or even businessmen to spot the winners in advance and, that being so, the case for discriminatory tax treatment on these grounds is weak.

It may also be questioned whether tax discrimination achieves its ostensible objectives. The discrimination in favour of manufacturing in the UK, for example, may simply have depressed the prices of manufactured goods relative to other (especially non-traded) goods and services. It would, presumably, have done this as a result of encouraging investment and so output in manufacturing, with the temporarily higher growth of output forcing down its price. Then, in equation (14.1), the effect on r of a lower rate of tax, T_s, could be offset by a lower (relative) price, P, and growth

---

[18] For a detailed description of the system, and of how it has changed since 1945, see King and Fullerton (1984, ch. 3) and also Melliss and Richardson (1976).

would resume at its previous rate. There is still, however, a *general* effect on growth. So long as the lower tax on investment in manufacturing is not offset by higher taxes on investment elsewhere, the *average* tax rate on all investment is reduced. It is precisely the fall in manufactured goods prices which generalizes the tax cut, so that all investment gets some benefit. In non-manufacturing, P rises (relatively) and so r increases, and investment is encouraged. Hence, what starts out as an attempt to encourage investment in manufacturing over investment elsewhere ends up as a general encouragement to all investment.

There is evidence that tax discrimination has affected the pattern of saving. Thus, Hills (1984) divides twelve different categories of household saving in the UK into two groups, five privileged and seven penalized. 'Privileged' here means that the relevant tax rate is below the taxpayer's marginal income tax rate,[19] while 'penalized' means that it is above that rate. He considers changes in the personal sector's net wealth between 1957 and 1981, and concludes that:

At the start of the period both groups accounted for the same proportion, 45%, of personal sector net worth. By the end of the period, however, the privileged group represented 64% of personal sector net worth while the penalised group represented only 26% of personal sector net worth: 84% of the real savings flow over the period had gone into the first group, but only 2% into the second. (Hills 1984, 70–1)

Hill's privileged groups include investment in dwellings (net of mortgages) and consumer durables, which together absorbed 84 per cent of the real saving within the privileged group. The other types of saving were financial. Savings in the form of pension rights, insurance contracts, and building society accounts grew rapidly,[20] while direct share ownership and holdings of gilt-edged securities and other marketable debt declined in real terms.

The tax-exempt status of pension funds must partly explain their rapid growth in the postwar period in the USA as well as the UK. Thus, King and Fullerton's estimates, reproduced in Appendix Table 14A.1, show that the share of pension funds in the total equity owned by them, households (directly), and insurance companies rose from 8 per cent in 1960 to 41 per cent in 1980 in the UK, and from 11 to 22 per cent over the same period in the USA. The Wilson Committee to Review the Functioning of Financial Institutions drew attention to these developments in the UK both in its interim report (March 1979), and in its final report (June 1980) and was in

---

[19] This is not explicitly defined by Hills, but appears to be the marginal tax rate that would apply to income from ordinary interest or dividends, including the investment income surcharge then in force. The calculations were done for three types of taxpayer whose marginal tax rates were zero, the 'standard rate', and the top rate.

[20] Building society accounts grew despite being penalized by the tax system, perhaps because the owners of the accounts wished to improve their standing with the societies in order to borrow on mortgage from them, or for other reasons discussed by Hills (1984, 72).

no doubt that the tax privileges to saving through these institutions had considerably influenced its volume (Committee 1980, para. 701).

In some of the evidence given to the Committee, concern had been expressed about some possible or alleged effects of this. Thus, it was said that the stock market had become more volatile because insurance and pension fund managers tended to react similarly to similar information. A study undertaken for the Committee, however, did not support this view.[21] It was also said that the investing institutions tended to be unduly risk-averse and to prefer shares in larger companies, and to neglect small ones; but here again the evidence was unclear.[22] All those giving evidence thought it desirable that institutions should take an active interest in the performance of the companies whose shares they held. The Committee remarked: 'We share this view, though it is possible to exaggerate the advantages and overlook some of the potential difficulties. It is clearly in the public interest that weak or inadequate management should be changed and that efficient management should be kept on its toes' (Committee 1980, para. 920). Some further discussion of the extent to which managements are 'disciplined' by shareholders appears in Chapter 9 above.

Let us now consider the general level of taxation on saving. The estimates in Table 14.2 suggest that savings in the UK, in so far as they are invested in companies, were taxed at about 25 per cent in 1960, but that the rate fell sharply in the 1960s, and was only about 5 per cent in 1980. In the USA the average level also fell, but not so much—from about 30 to about 20 per cent. Estimates for earlier years are lacking, but before 1914 tax rates on saving were probably very low. They would have been higher between the wars, although whether as high as in 1960 is uncertain. Melliss and Richardson's estimates for manufacturing industry in the UK suggest that effective tax rates were higher in the late 1940s and in the 1950s than subsequently.[23]

Estimates for other countries that are comparable to those in Table 14.2 are not available.[24]

---

[21] See the final report (Committee to Review the Functioning of Financial Institutions (henceforth 'Committee')) (1980 paras. 662, 663).

[22] See Committe (1980, paras. 664–6). The proportion of the total market value of share issues held by investing institutions in three size categories over £4 million at end 1975 was remarkably uniform. For the smallest size category of £4 million and under it was much lower, but, as the Committee pointed out, one reason for this may have been 'the prevalence among companies of this size of strongly entrenched family-controlled shareholdings which rarely come onto the market'. See also Hills (1984, ch. 5), who provides a comparative analysis of the equity portfolios of a sample of persons, insurance companies, pension funds, and investment trusts in the UK in 1983. He concludes that pension funds and insurance companies display a surprisingly strong aversion to shares of high specific risk, given their ability to diversify their holdings (p. 97).

[23] In Whiting (1976: see esp. Table 8, p. 37 and Chart 4, p. 41).

[24] King and Fullerton (1984) provide estimates for Germany and Sweden, as well as the USA, and King (1985, 235) also provides some estimates for Japan in 1985. McKee, Visser, and

This chapter has discussed the ways in which taxation affects investment and growth, and has presented some estimates of effective marginal tax rates. In Chapter 15 I use these estimates in a simple model to calculate how growth would change it taxes were changed.

Appendix A: A uniform tax on savings and investment

This appendix presents proofs of equations (14.1) and (14.2) for the rate of return and slope of the EPC. The simplifying assumptions listed on p. 394 are maintained. In brief, we consider a steadily growing self-financed firm selling and buying in perfect markets.

We start with the first proof of the rate-of-return formula without taxation given in Chapter 7, and then consider the proof of the formula for the slope of the EPC given in Section 6.4, equation (6.2).

When investment is taxed, we must distinguish between the cost of the investment to the investor, which includes the tax, and which we denote by S^*, and the actual opportunity cost of the investment in terms of consumption goods and services, which we continue to denote by S. If the tax rate is T_S (on a tax-inclusive basis), then the latter quantity is $S = S^*(1 - T_S)$, and the value of the resources accruing to the government is S^*T_S measured in terms of consumption forgone. The disposal by the government of those resources is discussed in Section 14.1, and is not further considered here.

With taxation of investment, the fundamental identities defining q and l become

$$g \equiv Ps^*(1 - T_S)q; \qquad g_L \equiv Ps^*(1 - T_S)l \qquad (14A.1)$$

where $s^* \equiv S^*/PQ$.

As in Chapter 7, we may now consider a firm which increases its rate of investment by δs^* for a short interval of time δt, so that the total amount of take-out sacrificed by the owners is $PQ\, \delta s^* \delta t$. As a result of this higher rate of investment, at the end of the interval δt, and neglecting second-order terms, output and employment are δQ and δL higher than they would otherwise have been, and

$$\delta Q = PQ\, \delta s^*(1 - T_S)\delta t\, q; \qquad \delta L = PL\, \delta s^*(1 - T_S)\delta t\, l. \qquad (14A.2)$$

In order to revert to the previous rate of investment, s^*, a fraction s^* of this extra output must be invested. Consequently, at the end of δt the rate of take-out is increased by δC, where

$$\delta C = P\, \delta Q(1 - s^*) - w\, \delta L$$
$$= PQ\, \delta s^*(1 - T_S)\delta t\, P\{q(1 - s^*) - \lambda l\}. \qquad (14A.3)$$

This increase in take-out grows at g as before, and its present value is therefore $\delta C/(r - g)$. Setting this equal to the initial take-out sacrificed, and dividing through by $PQ\, \delta s^* \delta t$, gives

$$1 = \frac{(1 - T_S)\, P\, \{q(1 - s^*) - \lambda l\}}{r - g}, \qquad (14A.4)$$

Saunders (1986) provide estimates for 19 OECD countries in 1983. However, none of these estimates can safely be compared with those in Table 14.2. (See Appendix C to this chapter for further discussion of the differences.)

from which, after multiplying through by $r - g$, we get

$$r = (1 - T_S)P(q - \lambda l), \tag{14A.5}$$

which is equation (14.1). Here $P(q - \lambda l)$ is the pre-tax rate of return, which we shall call p.

The proof of equation (14.2) follows easily from the proof that $\mu = \Delta q/\Delta l = \lambda/(1 - s)$ which appears in Section 6.4. In the equation on p. 155, setting the change in take-out to zero, viz.

$$P \delta Q - \delta S - w \delta L = 0,$$

all the terms are the same on the left-hand side except that we must now replace δS by $\delta S^* = s^* P \delta Q$. Consequently, the remainder of the proof holds if we replace s by s^*, which gives equation (14.2).

Appendix B: Existing systems of taxing savings and investment

The preceding appendix considered the simplest case of a uniform tax. Here, we move nearer to reality by considering a corporation tax, a personal income tax, tax allowances for depreciation, investment grants, and the different tax treatment of finance by way of debt, new share issues, and retentions. The taxation of inventory profits arising from inflation and, more generally, interactions between inflation and the tax system are also considered. In all this analysis I follow the path-breaking studies of King and Fullerton (1984) and King (1977), whose data and estimates I use. I do not, however, use their actual formulae for pre-tax real rates of return on investment (p) required to earn given real post-tax rates of return (r). Since the effective tax rate, T_S, is defined as $(p - r)/p$, my tax rates differ from theirs. A comparison of the two is made in Scott (1987), which also explains why King and Fullerton's formulae are rejected in favour of those given here. So far as possible I have used their symbols, but some changes were necessary to conform with the rest of this volume. The approach adopted is the same as in the preceding section, but essentially the same formulae can be found in other ways (see, for example, Scott 1987).

As before, we consider a steadily growing firm which undertakes a marginal increase in its rate of investment for a short interval of time and then relapses to a condition of steady growth. Now, however, the firm is subject to a more complex tax regime whose parameters must be defined, and this interacts both with a more complicated financing system and with inflation.

The firm is subject to a tax on profits at rate τ. Nominal interest received is included in taxable profits, and nominal interest paid is deducted before arriving at taxable profits. There is one nominal rate of interest ruling in the market, which is i. The rate of inflation is π, so that the real rate of interest is $i - \pi$.

The firm benefits from a system of tax allowances on its assets. These can take a wide variety of forms, ranging from the ability to write off the whole expenditure on the asset against tax when the expenditure is incurred (i.e. so-called free depreciation), to writing off a certain amount of the original expenditure each year, to writing off nothing at all. In addition, there may be government grants to encourage particular forms of investment, or investment in particular regions. I adopt King and Fullerton's simplification of this intricate system by writing A for the present value to the firm of all these allowances or grants per unit expenditure on the assets that concern us. Consequently, the net cost to the firm of an investment costing 1 unit (e.g. £1) in the market is $1 - A$. The value of A will depend on the particular assets bought by the firm, and it is expressed in terms of value, equivalent to the firm's own retained profits. If, for example, the asset concerned qualified for free depreciation, then $A = \tau$, since the expenditure of 1 on the asset would reduce the firm's taxable profits by 1 and so its tax bill by τ. This assumes, as I assume throughout, that the firm has sufficient profits to be able to claim all its allowances—it does not suffer from 'tax exhaustion'. A is further discussed in the notes to Tables 14A.1 and 14A.2.

The treatment of dividends differs under different forms of corporation profit tax. Under the classical system (as in the USA), the firm simply pays tax at τ on all its profits, and then its dividends are subject to personal income tax in the hands of its shareholders at rates depending on their individual incomes. Their marginal rate of income tax is assumed to be m. This system results in dividend distributions being generally more heavily taxed than retentions. Under the imputation system (as in the UK) the firm still pays tax at τ on all its profits, but cash dividends are accompanied by a tax credit equal to $c/(1 - c)$ times the dividends, where c is the so-called rate of imputation. For income tax purposes, the dividend receiver is deemed to have received an income, per unit cash dividend, of $1 + \{c/(1 - c)\} = 1/(1 - c)$ gross of income tax, and to have paid $c/(1 - c)$ of tax. If his marginal rate of tax is m, he ends up receiving $(1 - m)/(1 - c)$ net of all income tax. Clearly, if $m = c$ he ends up with exactly the unit cash dividend, and there is no further tax adjustment. To save administrative cost, c is chosen in the UK to equal the so-called standard rate of tax, which is the marginal tax rate of many taxpayers. If, however, the recipient's marginal tax rate is above c, he has to pay more tax, and if it is less (as with pension funds or charities, which are tax-exempt) he can claim a refund. For the standard rate taxpayer, the system results in the rate of *all* tax (i.e. profits and income tax) on dividends being the same as on retentions, i.e. it is simply τ; but for other taxpayers that is not the case. In order to cover both the classical system and the imputation system and other systems as well, King (1977) used the symbol θ. In King and Fullerton (1984), θ is the value of the dividend *before personal income tax*, which can be paid at the sacrifice of 1 unit of retentions. Consequently, with the classical system, $\theta = 1$, but with the imputation system $\theta = 1/(1 - c)$. It follows that the sacrifice of 1 unit of retentions enables the shareholder to receive $\theta(1 - m)$ units after paying all taxes.

In deciding how to finance its investments, the firm faces complex problems. The tax deductibility of interest may make debt attractive, as also may low rates of real interest. However, if the firm increases the proportion of debt to equity, it will tend to increase the fluctuations in the profit attributable to the equity, since that is the residual claim. There is also an increased risk of bankruptcy. There is therefore a hidden marginal cost of extra debt, over and above the interest cost, and this may rise sharply when the proportion of debt exceeds some 'safe' value. The firm may therefore reject further debt finance at some point, even though the apparent return on a project financed by debt is above the rate of return required by shareholders.

The choice between new share issues and retentions, the two forms of equity finance considered here, is also difficult. Suppose, for example, that there is a classical corporation tax, as in the USA, and that all shareholders are subject to some additional personal income tax, so that $m > 0$. It would then seem to be a mistake to pay dividends at a time when new shares are being issued. If, instead, the firm simply cuts back its dividends by $X, it would enable $X of extra investment to be financed at a cost to shareholders of only $X(1 - m)$, whereas new share issues would cost them $X. Yet firms do pay dividends simultaneously with issuing new shares, and the explanation may be that shareholders regard dividends as an indicator of the directors' opinion of the profitability of the firm. They like a rather stable, or (especially) a rapidly growing, dividend, and regard a cut in dividends as signalling danger. The result of cutting the dividend may therefore be that the share price falls, and if shares are issued they have to be issued unduly cheaply.

To handle these points satisfactorily would require a more complex analysis than is possible here. One cannot, it seems, expect firms to equalize the *apparent* costs to shareholders of different forms of finance at the margin, since these apparent costs omit hidden costs which can be important. The expedient adopted here is to assume that a steadily growing firm will find some optimum balance between the three forms of finance mentioned. Marginal profits will, in general, be financed in proportions that could differ from the average proportions, but, as will appear in the sequel, I shall confine attention mainly to the simplest case in which the marginal and average proportions are the same.

I therefore assume that, when the rate of investment is stepped up for a short while, a fraction of it f_b^* is financed by borrowing and a fraction f_s^* by the issue of new shares, the rest being financed by retentions. When investment relapses to its previous steady rate, I assume that the corresponding fractions are f_b and f_s. Subsequently, I make the simplifying assumptions that $f_b^* = f_b$ and $f_s^* = f_s$.

I consider the pre-tax and post-tax returns to investment financed only by this *combination* of methods. It is not difficult to rewrite the formulae so that they refer to financing by only one or the other method, but that does not seem realistic for the reasons given.

The tax system just described clearly does *not* consist of a simple tax on investment. Nevertheless, it is possible to translate it into the equivalent of such a tax at the margin. In the preceding section, I referred to and defined investment, S^*, as its *tax-inclusive* value, since that accords with my general treatment of taxes, and created no difficulties in that simple case. However, when we come to this more complicated and realistic case, it is easier to refer to the various magnitudes as they would normally be measured. To avoid confusion, I therefore write the various equations in terms of S, the tax-exclusive value of investment, as it would normally be measured at market prices (expenditure taxes on investment expenditures usually being small). This is assumed to be its opportunity cost in terms of consumption, which is our numeraire. Throughout most of the analysis I use S, not S^*, which I define at the conclusion as the tax-inclusive value, where 'tax' refers to the *equivalent marginal tax rate*, which I now proceed to calculate.

Defining $s \equiv S/PQ$, we can rewrite (A 14.2) as

$$\delta Q = PQ \, \delta s \, \delta t \, q; \qquad \delta L = PL \, \delta s \, \delta t \, l. \qquad (14A.6)$$

Before calculating the increase in the rate of take-out which results at the end of δt, we must first consider how to deal with interest payments. Most payments and receipts that concern us are not fixed in nominal terms, but grow in real terms at the same rate as the firm (i.e. at g) and so at $g + \pi$ in nominal terms. Interest, however, on any given amount borrowed is assumed to be fixed in nominal terms. I therefore handle it in the same way as tax allowances for depreciation, which are also fixed in nominal terms; that is, I work out present values. There are two different streams of interest payments. First, there is interest on the borrowing which partly finances the marginal investment made during δt. The amount of this investment is $PQ \, \delta s \, \delta t$, of which a fraction $(1 - A)$ has to be financed. The amount borrowed for this is $f_b^* \, PQ \, \delta s \, \delta t$, and the interest on that is i times as much, fixed in nominal terms. This interest has to be met, ultimately, from shareholder's take-out, since to meet it from retentions would reduce the firm's other investment which we must leave undisturbed. On each unit of interest paid, since corporation tax is saved at rate τ, and since each unit of after-tax profits translates into θ units of dividends before personal tax, the ultimate cost in shareholder's net-of-tax receipts is $(1 - \tau)\theta(1 - m)$. This perpetual nominal flow must be discounted at the shareholder's nominal discount rate, which is $r + \pi$. Consequently, the lump-sum equivalent of the future interest payments on the borrowing which finances part of the extra investment during δt is

$$I_1 = \frac{(1 - \tau)\theta(1 - m) \, i \, f_b^* \, PQ \, \delta s \, \delta t}{r + \pi}.$$

The second stream of interest payments to consider is that associated with the financing of the extra (and growing) stream of investment which accompanies the higher output from the end of δt onwards. Because output is higher by δQ, the rate of investment is raised by $P \, s \, \delta Q$ in order that the previous share of investment in output, s, shall be maintained. Of this extra investment, a fraction f_b is financed by borrowing, and, by similar argument to that just given, the present value of the interest payments on that borrowing is

$$I_2 = \frac{(1 - \tau)\theta(1 - m) \, i \, f_b \, P \, s \, \delta Q}{r + \pi}.$$

One further preliminary to be dealt with concerns the taxation of spurious inventory profits. These profits can arise if stocks are valued on a first-in–first-out (FIFO) basis and if there is inflation. They will not, in general, arise if stocks are valued on a last-in–first-out (LIFO) basis. There may also be special provisions which exempt such profits from taxation (as in the UK from 1975 to 1984). I assume that a fraction v of investment gives rise to inventory profits at rate $v\pi$ and results in extra corporate tax payments of $v\pi\tau$, and so to reduced take-out, after personal taxation, of $\theta(1 - m)v\pi\tau$. I do not treat the 'profits' so taxed as being part of true profits or output. This being so, there are then two streams of extra taxation to be considered, just as with borrowing. There is, first, that associated with the extra investment undertaking during δt, which gives rise to extra taxation, which grows at π (since the value of the extra inventories, a fixed quantity, grows with the general price level) and which therefore must be discounted at r to give its present value, viz.

$$V_1 = \frac{\theta(1 - m)v\pi\tau \, PQ \, \delta s \, \delta t}{r}.$$

Second, there are the extra inventory profits arising from investment which accompanies the higher rate of output at the end of δt. A fraction v of this investment is also assumed to give rise to inventory profits and extra taxation as above. The present value of that extra taxation, discounting at r, is

$$V_2 = \frac{\theta(1 - m)v\pi\tau \, P s \, \delta Q}{r} .$$

Let us now consider the components of the increased rate of take-out at the end of δt, resulting from the marginal investment during δt.

There is, first, the extra trading profit, after paying corporation tax but ignoring interest, which is $(P\delta Q - w\delta L)(1 - \tau)$.

Second, one must deduct from this the extra investment needed to keep the share of investment at s, its previous level. This is $Ps \, \delta Q$, but only $(1 - A)$ of it needs financing, and f_b of the investment is financed by borrowing and f_s by new share issues, leaving the rest to come out of take-out. Hence on this account we must deduct

$$(1 - A - f_b - f_s)Ps \, \delta Q.$$

The above two items, taken together, must be multiplied by $\theta(1 - m)$ to give their value to the shareholder, and we must then also deduct I_2 and V_2, which are already expressed in terms of their value to the shareholder. Finally, we must also deduct the new share issues subscribed to by the shareholder to get his *net* take-out, which come to $f_s Ps \, \delta Q$. Hence the increased rate of net take-out at the end of δt is, after some regrouping of terms,

$$\delta C = \theta(1 - m) \, [\![P \, \delta Q \langle 1 - \tau - s[1 - A - f_b\{1 - \frac{(1 - \tau)i}{r + \pi}\} - f_s\{1 - \frac{1}{\theta(1 - m)}\}]$$

$$- \frac{v\pi\tau s}{r} \rangle - w \, \delta L(1 - \tau)]\!].$$

$$(14A.7)$$

This increased take-out grows at $g = Psq$, and so its present value is given by dividing by $r - g$. This present value equals the value of the sacrifice of take-out made by shareholders to finance the extra investment during δt. That is the investment itself, $PQ \, \delta s \, \delta t$, adjusted for the present value of depreciation, etc., for borrowing, and its associated interest I_1, for new share issues, and for the present value of taxation on extra inventory profits, V_1. The amounts expended by the firm have to be multiplied by $\theta(1 - m)$ to give the corresponding take-out sacrificed by shareholders. Hence their total sacrifice is

$$\theta(1 - m)PQ \, \delta s \, \delta t(1 - A - f_b^* - f_s^*) + I_1 + V_1 + f_s^* PQ \, \delta s^* \, \delta t.$$

If we now substitute from (14A.6) into (14A.7), and if we set $\delta C/(r - g)$ equal to the sacrifice, then we can divide through by $\theta(1 - m)PQ \, \delta s \, \delta t$. We then need to solve for r, but this is simply done only if $f_b^* = f_b$ and $f_s^* = f_s$. I therefore make that simplifying assumption, and the equation for r is then

$$r = \frac{(1 - \tau)P(q - \lambda l) - v\pi t}{1 - A - f_b\{1 - \frac{(1 - \tau)i}{(r + \pi)}\} - f_s\{1 - \frac{1}{\theta(1 - m)}\}} .$$

$$(14A.8)$$

r still appears on both sides of this equation, which is a quadratic in r, and the solution is not given here. In fact, I use the equation to find $P(q - \lambda l)$ for given r in the way described below.

The above equation can be rewritten as earlier (see 14A.5):

$$r = (1 - T_S)P(q - \lambda l),$$

with

$$1 - T_S = \frac{(1 - \tau) - v\pi\tau/P(q - \lambda l)}{1 - A - f_b\left\{1 - \dfrac{(1 - \tau)i}{r + \pi}\right\} - f_s\left\{1 - \dfrac{1}{\theta(1 - m)}\right\}}. \qquad (14A.9)$$

It can be easily shown that the usual equation $\mu = \lambda/(1 - s^*)$ holds so long as we interpret s^* as the tax-inclusive investment rate. Hence, if s is the investment rate as ordinarily measured, then $s^* = s/(1 - T_S)$.

It must be pointed out that the above definition of marginal tax rate on investment incorporates an effect that is due to the particular financing methods employed. T_S does measure the gap between the pre-tax return on investment, which is $P(q - \lambda l)$, and the post-tax return return received by the *shareholder*, which is r. This gap, however, depends not only on the various tax parameters A, τ, v, θ, and m, but also on the fractions of investment financed by fixed-interest borrowing, f_b and new issues of shares, f_s, *and* on the interest cost of borrowing, i, and the rate of inflation, π. Consequently, there could be a gap (positive or negative) even if all tax rates were zero. Thus, we have combined in this formula for the 'tax rate' the effects of both tax rates and methods of financing. While this is unsatisfactory in some respects, it does simplify what is in any case very complicated, and it serves my purpose well in Chapter 15, where I seek to explain the gap between the rate of return received by the shareholder and the pre-tax rate of return on investment.

Equation (14A.8) can be used to estimate the average rate of tax on marginal investments in the following way. Assume that the capital market works in such a way that different suppliers of capital receive the same real rate of return on their savings at the margin and *before* deduction of personal income tax. The common real rate of return of r^* is assumed to be obtainable by investing in ordinary shares whose (pre-tax) dividend yield is constant at d, and whose real dividends grow at rate g. The tax-exempt funds will earn $r^* = d + g$ after tax, while other taxpayers, whose personal income tax rates are m, will earn

$$r = d(1 - m) + g = r^* - md.$$

Note that this implies that some savers may not purchase particular securities. For example, if there is a market rate of interest i in nominal terms, a taxpayer will earn a real rate of return after tax of $i(1 - m) - \pi$, and this will vary with m. I have assumed that in the inflationary economies of postwar years i is in practice set at a level that enables tax-exempt funds to earn a real rate of return of r^*. Hence $i - \pi = r^*$. This implies that, for all other savers for whom $m > 0$, the real return received by lending at i is

$$i(1 - m) - \pi = r^* - mi$$
$$= (r^* - md) - m(i - d).$$

Now if such savers can earn a real return of $r^* - md$ elsewhere, they will lend at i only if $i \leq d$,[25] or if they receive some other benefit from lending, such as extra

---

[25] Which it could hardly be, given our assumptions about tax-exempt funds and the capital market.

liquidity. While it is quite realistic to assume that there is a benefit from extra liquidity, the implication is that savers' *marginal* real return after taking this extra benefit into account is *more* than $i(1 - m) - \pi$. For much of the postwar period in the UK, for example, $i(1 - m) - \pi$ was negative for very many taxpayers. That does not, however, imply that their marginal real rates of return on savings, and so their real rates of discount, were negative. On the contrary, such savers could earn positive real rates of return after tax by investing in ordinary shares, and so it seems more realistic to assume that their real rates of discount were also positive.

The effective rate of tax on savings varies with r^*. However, in order to preserve as much simplicity as possible, only one value of $r^* = 0.05$ has been taken in the estimates given here. It is thought that this is, in fact, a realistic estimate of the real rate of return obtainable by a tax-exempt fund during much of the postwar era. It is also the rate chosen by King and Fullerton in their 'fixed-r' case.

Given r^*, and hence r for a given m, and given the other tax parameters, τ, v, and θ, and given also estimates of π, A, f_b, and f_s obtained in the manner set out in Tables 14A.1 and 14A.2 described below, equation (14A.8) enables one to calculate the pre-tax real rate of return $p = P(q - \lambda l)$ required to yield a post-tax real rate of return of r for the saver. This value of p applies to a *particular* saver who has invested in a *particular* project, since m varies from one saver to another, while A varies according to both the industry and the asset in which his savings are invested. Thus, for the ith project, the *tax wedge* may be defined as $p_i - r_i$, and the *effective tax rate* as

$$T_{Si} = \frac{p_i - r_i}{p_i}.$$

The possible permutations of saver, industry, and asset are numerous, and for my purposes it is useful to calculate a weighted average. Since the rates of return are on gross investment, it is appropriate to use gross investment weights. Thus, if S_i is gross investment in the ith project, the weighted average pre-tax real rate of return is

$$p = \frac{\Sigma_i (S_i p_i)}{\Sigma_i S_i}$$

Similarly, the weighted average post-tax real rate of return is

$$r = \frac{\Sigma_i (S_i r_i)}{\Sigma_i S_i}.$$

Finally, the weighted average effective rate of tax is

$$T_S = \frac{p - r}{p} = \frac{\Sigma_i (S_i p_i T_{Si})}{\Sigma_i (S_i p_i)}.$$

Hence the individual tax rates must be weighted by $S_i p_i$, not by S_i alone, to obtain an average tax rate which is consistent with the average p and r.

Appendix C: Application of the formulae to the UK and the USA

The formula in (14A.8) was used to estimate effective rates of taxation of savings for the UK and the USA in three postwar years: 1960, 1970, and 1980. Tables 14A.1 and 14A.2 plus section (*c*) and (*d*) set out the data used, much of it derived from King and Fullerton (1984). While in many respects their methodology was also adopted,

(a) *Data used to estimate effective tax rates on savings, I*

Table 14A.1 Miscellaneous data

	UK			USA		
	1960	1970	1980	1960	1970	1980
(1) Rate of inflation p.a., π	0.0350	0.0392	0.1239	0.0234	0.0252	0.0661
(2) Nominal interest rate p.a., $i = \pi + 0.05$	0.0850	0.0892	0.1739	0.0734	0.0752	0.1161
(3) Marginal rate of personal tax, m						
(a) Households	0.5610	0.5800	0.4500	0.4310	0.4130	0.4750
(b) Tax-exempt	0	0	0	0	0	0
(c) Insurance	0.2604	0.2560	0.1765	0.0780	0.0720	0.0690
(4) Real rate of discount p.a., $r = 0.05(1 - m)$						
(a) Households	0.0220	0.0210	0.0275	0.0285	0.0294	0.0263
(b) Tax-exempt	0.0500	0.0500	0.0500	0.0500	0.0500	0.0500
(c) Insurance	0.0370	0.0372	0.0412	0.0461	0.0464	0.0466
(5) Rate of corporation tax, τ	0.5063	0.4063	0.5200	0.5320	0.5040	0.4950
(6) Opportunity cost of retentions in terms of gross dividends, θ	1.633	1.0000	1.4290	1.	1.	1.
(7) Fractions of inventory investment on which taxable stock appreciation	1.	1.	0.	0.	0.	0.
(8) Fraction of investment financed by debt, f_b	0.07	0.07	0.07	0.16	0.16	0.16
(9) Fraction of investment financed by new share issues, f_s	0.05	0.05	0.05	0.04	0.04	0.04
(10) Ownership fractions of:						
(a) Households	0.8037	0.7130	0.4360	0.868	0.815	0.743
(b) Tax-exempt institutions	0.0833	0.1367	0.4070	0.105	0.155	0.216
(c) Insurance	0.1130	0.1503	0.1570	0.027	0.030	0.041

Note
Rates of inflation, interest, and discount are all exponential.

Sources: Lines 3, 5, 6, 7 and 10 are from King and Fullerton, 1984. Line 1 is the average rate of increase in the implicit deflator for consumers' expenditure in the national accounts for the ten years ending in the year shown. Lines 2 and 4 are further explained in the text. Lines 8 and 9 are based on flow-of-funds accounts for industrial and commercial companies (U.K.) or non-financial corporate business (USA) over the years 1965–71 and are further explained in the text. The sources used were *National Income and Expenditure 1972*, H.M.S.O., Tables 13, 28 and 73; and *The Federal Reserve Bulletin*, November 1969, p. A 71.4, and October 1974, p. A 59.5.

(b) Data used to estimate effective tax rates on savings, II

Table 14A.2 Depreciation allowances and investment grants in the UK, 1960–1980

	1960		1970		1980	
	Mfg. & other	Commerce	Mfg. & other	Commerce	Mfg. & other	Commerce
'Machinery'						
(11) Fractions of investment entitled to:						
(a) Standard depreciation, f_1	0.9	0.9	0.8	0.8	0	0
(b) Immediate depreciation, f_2	0.3	0.3	0.2	0.2	1	1
(c) Grants, f_3	0	0	0.93[a]	0.69	0.323[b]	0
(12) Declining balance exponential rate of depreciation a	0.153	0.153	0.2	0.2	0	0
(13) Rate of grant g	0	0	0.261	0.261	0.1946	0
Buildings						
(14) Fractions of investment entitled to:						
(a) Standard depreciation, f_1	0.95	0	0.7	0	0.5	0.04
(b) Immediate depreciation, f_2	0.15	0	0.3	0	0.5	0.01
(c) Grants, f_3	0	0	0	0	0.821[c]	0
(15) Life of asset, L	50	n.a.	25	n.a.	12	n.a.
(16) Rate of grant, g	0	0	0	0	0.1476	0

Notes
For definition of industries, see Section (*d*) below.
[a] This figure is for manufacturing; for other industry it is 0.84
[b] This figure is for manufacturing; for other industry it is 0.004
[c] This figure is for manufacturing; for other industry it is 0.007.

The above data were used to estimate the present value of tax allowances per unit of gross investment. The formulae follow King and Fullerton (1984 ch. 2), viz.:

$$A = f_1 A_d + f_2 \tau + f_3 g.$$

For 'machinery' (i.e. plant, equipment, and vehicles), standard depreciation is on the declining balance method, and the present value of tax saved is:

$$A_d = \frac{\tau a}{a + r + \pi}.$$

(continued at foot of page 420)

there were some important differences noted below, and, as already noted, (14A.8) is not the same as their formulae. The net result of all the differences is that my tax rates are substantially lower than theirs (p. 406 above).

Since retained profits are easily the largest source of finance for gross investment, the most important difference between King and Fullerton's formulae and (14A.8) relates to the treatment of such retentions. King and Fullerton reduce the post-tax return in relation to the pre-tax return by an amount that increases with the rate of tax on capital gains. In (14A.8) there is no such reduction, and my reasons for questioning King and Fullerton's formula are given in Scott (1987). This is one reason why the average tax rates estimated here are below theirs.

A second difference is that I have omitted economic depreciation, whereas King and Fullerton include it. My pre-tax rate of return is $P(q - \lambda l)$, which is the same as their gross rate of return, MRR. Their pre-tax rate of return $p = MRR - \delta$, where δ is the exponential rate of economic depreciation. My reasons for omitting δ are given in Chapter 7 above. They are relevant to normal or average investment, which is what my estimates refer to. It is not denied that some allowance for supernormal depreciation would be required for *particular* investments, but, equally, so would some allowance for subnormal depreciation or appreciation. In most cases, the effect of setting $\delta = 0$ is to reduce the effective rate of tax.

A third difference is that I have used gross investment weights rather than capital stock weights to average pre-tax rates of return. Since this gives more weight to plant and equipment on which tax rates tend to be lowest, this also tends to lower the average tax rate.

A fourth difference is that I assume that the saver's real rate of return after tax is $r^*(1 - m)$, with $r^* = 0.05$. King and Fullerton present two sets of calculations. The set that is closest conceptually to mine is their so-called 'fixed-r case'. In this, the real rate of *interest* is set at 0.05, and savers are assumed to get a real rate of return of $i(1 - m) - \pi$ after tax. Since $i - \pi = 0.05$, the real rate of return received by savers is $0.05 - mi$. For tax-exempt funds, this coincides with the assumption made here, but for households, especially where inflation is high, it is lower. For example, for the UK in 1980, the rate of inflation is 0.1239 and for households $m = 0.45$ (see Table 14A.1). Consequently, King and Fullerton's real rate of return post-tax for households would be $(0.05 + 0.1239)(1 - 0.45) - 0.1239 = -0.0238$. By contrast, my real rate of return for households is $0.05 (1 - 0.45) = 0.0275$. This is, admittedly, an extreme example, but in my opinion it shows that King and Fullerton's assumptions lead to results that look less realistic than those flowing from the assumptions taken here. While a higher rate of return for savers increases

---

For buildings, standard depreciation is on the straight-line method, and the present value of tax saved is:

$$A_d = \frac{\tau[1 - \exp\{-(r + \pi)L\}]}{(r + \pi)L} .$$

For inventories, all the parameters are zero in all the years.

Sources: King and Fullerton (1984, ch. 3). However, f_1 and f_2 for buildings for commerce in 1970 are mistakenly given by them as 0.7 and 0.3. The correct figure of 0 in each case is taken here.

the estimated tax wedge, it makes little difference to the effective tax rate.[26] It does, however, reduce the variability in post-tax returns received by different classes of saver.

As well as their 'fixed-r case', King and Fullerton present results based on the assumption that the pre-tax real rate of return, p, is the same for all projects, which is called the 'fixed-p case'. The resulting weighted averages are generally below, and often substantially below, those resulting from the 'fixed-r case'.[27] Since the 'fixed-r case' is closer to my own, and since it seems to simulate the working of the capital market better than the 'fixed-p case', I have confined attention to the former as far as possible.

A fifth difference is that local property taxes ('rates' in the UK) have been omitted here, but are included by King and Fullerton; this lowers my effective tax rates compared to theirs somewhat.

A final difference concerns the estimated weight of different sources of finance. King and Fullerton derived their estimates from a combination of balance sheet and flow-of-funds data, and they are concerned with changes in the net capital stock, whereas my concern is the financing of real gross investment. Because of this, I confined attention to flow-of-funds data. A difficult issue is the best way to handle the large investment made by companies in financial assets, an issue not fully discussed by King and Fullerton. If one takes the *gross* inflow of funds, a large fraction of this comes from the issue of debt of various kinds. However, companies also acquire a lot of financial assets. It does not seem appropriate to regard the relevant fraction of debt finance, f_b in (14A.8), as being that relating to the *gross* inflow. This would mean that, for a company that turned over its portfolio of securities very rapidly, or had large flows in and out of its bank account, the financial flows would dominate everything else. The course adopted here therefore has been to net out financial transactions, so that it is only the excess of borrowing over lending that contributes towards the financing of real gross investment. The effect of this is to reduce the proportion of finance coming from debt as compared

---

[26] This can be seen as follows. Assume that $v = 0$ (as is the case for the USA for all years, and for the UK in 1980). Then (14A.8) may be rewritten, ignoring the terms multiplying f_b and f_s, both of which are small, as

$$p = \frac{(1 - A)}{(1 - \tau)}\, r.$$

Hence

$$p - r = r\left(\frac{1 - A}{1 - \tau} - 1\right),$$

and

$$T_S = \frac{p - r}{p} = 1 - \frac{(1 - \tau)}{(1 - A)}.$$

Since A is not very sensitive to r, the magnitude of T_s is not sensitive to r either, but $p - r$ varies directly with r.

[27] King and Fullerton explain the difference by the positive correlations between p_i and t_i in the 'fixed-r case' in the formula for the weighted average T_S (see King and Fullerton 1984, 16, also p. 417 above). In the 'fixed-p case' there is no correlation, since by assumption all p_i are the same.

with King and Fullerton's estimates. Since they estimate that rates of tax are lower on debt finance than on equity finance, this tends to raise my tax rates compared with theirs.

It must be admitted that the shares of debt finance that I have used are somewhat arbitrary. I took average proportions for the years 1965–71. In earlier years, the share of debt finance on my net basis was often negative for the UK, and occasionally for the USA as well. However, so long as the proportions are small, the estimated rates of taxation are little affected.

Both King and Fullerton's and my estimates omit some indirect taxes on investment, which are generally rather small. As an offset, subsidies to research and development (e.g. to research in universities), which ought to be included as part of investment, are also omitted.

(c) Data to estimate effective tax rates on savings, III: Depreciation allowances and investment grants in the USA

Investment is divided into three types of asset: (1) 'equipment', which includes vehicles, machinery, and plant as well as public utility structures; (2) 'structures', which includes industrial and commercial buildings, hotels, etc.; and (3) inventories. Using the same symbols as in Table 14A.2, for 'equipment' and 'structures', $f_1 = 1$ and $f_2 = 0$ in all years, while $f_3 = 0$ in 1960 and 1970. For inventories, all the parameters are 0 in all years. We therefore need A_d for 'equipment' and 'structures' for all years, and $f_3 g$ for them in 1980. Thirty-four types of 'equipment' and 'structures' are distinguished in King and Fullerton (1984, Tables 6.5 and 6.29), but ten of these were excluded as being in excluded industries (see Section (d) below). That leaves twenty-one types of 'equipment' and three types of 'structures'. For each of these, King and Fullerton provide lifetimes permitted under the tax laws current and, for 1980, $f_3 g$. For 'equipment', businesses were permitted in all years to use the double-declining balance (DDB) system under which, if L is the permitted life, a fraction $2/L$ of the written-down value of the asset could be allowed against tax each year. DDB was also permitted for 'structures' in 1960, but in 1970 and 1980 only a fraction $1.5/L$ could be written off each year. Business was permitted to switch to the sum-of-the-years' digits (SYD) system when it appeared advantageous for 'equipment' in all years, and for 'structures' in 1960. For the last, however, they could switch to straight line only in 1970 and 1980. According to King and Fullerton, it was advantageous to make these switches at various points in the assets' lives, although it is uncertain how far firms took advantage of this. To preserve simplicity, I have ignored the switching possibility, and assumed that either $2/L$ or $1.5/L$ was written off throughout the assets' lives. Accordingly, the present values of tax saved were

$$A_d = \frac{\tau(x/L)}{x/L + r + \pi}$$

with $x = 2$ or 1.5 as appropriate. Thus, compared with King and Fullerton's calculations, those given here exaggerate the tax rate on investment on this account. The values of A_d were computed for each type of asset (and added to $f_3 g$ in 1980), and then weighted by the gross investment weights described in the next section.

(d) Data used to estimate effective tax rates on savings, IV:
    Gross investment weights

It is appropriate for the methodology followed here to use gross investment weights for fixed investment rather than the capital stock weights used by King and Fullerton. In order to eliminate cyclical fluctuations, ten-year averages were used. In the case of the USA, investment in constant dollars analysed by the required twenty-four types of asset (see Section (c) above) was available in the *National Income and Product Accounts 1929–1976*, and the average of the years 1962–71 was used for all the calculations for simplicity. In the case of the UK, only data in current values in the necessary detail was available, which meant that the later years received more weight because prices were higher. Again, the years 1962–71 were averaged, the data coming from *National Income and Expenditure 1972*. The same sources also gave investment in inventories (excluding stock appreciation).

The definitions of industries for the UK were:

Manufacturing	as defined in the source
Other industry	construction, gas, electricity, water, railways, road passenger transport, shipping, harbours, docks and canals, air transport, postal telephone and radio communications
Commerce	wholesale and retail distribution, and 'other transport and services'

Excluded industries were agriculture, forestry, fishing, coal mining, other mining and quarrying, insurance, banking, finance and business services, dwellings, universities, colleges, etc., other education, health, personal social services, roads, etc., sewerage and land drainage, and miscellaneous public services.

The weights for the UK were rounded for simplicity and were as follows:

	Mfg.	Other industry	Commerce	Total
Machinery	0.29	0.29	0.12	0.70
Buildings	0.07	0.10	0.07	0.24
Inventories	0.03	0.01	0.02	0.06
TOTAL	0.39	0.40	0.21	1.00

15

THE OPTIMUM RATE OF INVESTMENT AND GROWTH

15.1 Introduction

Should investment be taxed or subsidized? Is the rate of growth too high or too low? In this chapter I look for answers to these questions, in so far as any emerge from the conclusions of previous chapters. I am very conscious that these are large issues to which many other considerations are relevant. The analysis given is only a beginning, and the answers are very tentative.[1]

My approach is to consider and compare various rates of return. Chapter 7 gave estimates of average social rates of return in my standard periods and countries, and contrasted these, for the postwar years in the UK and the USA, with rates of return accruing to savers, that is, to ordinary shareholders and to bondholders. Roughly speaking (and there is considerable uncertainty about the estimates), average social returns were about double savers' returns, even if income tax is not deducted from the latter. Prima facie, this suggests that savers would be prepared to finance a higher rate of investment if they were allowed to receive more of its fruits. The existing rates of investment, and of growth, would then be judged to be too low.[2] There are, however, other considerations which need to be taken into account, of which only one will be mentioned in this introduction. The *marginal* social rate of return may be much less than the *average*. Since a marginal increase in the rate of investment would earn only the marginal social rate of return, it is that which must be compared with the marginal returns received by savers. Hence we need to know how the marginal social return compares with the average. Such evidence as I have suggests that it does not lie far below it, and, if that is so, rates of investment and growth are less than optimal.

How can we explain the gap between marginal social and private rates of return? The first, and obvious, explanation is taxation. However, it seems

---

[1] Two discussions of government policy towards economic growth, written when it was in the forefront of economists' concerns, are Phelps (1965) and Tobin (1964). The latter also includes interesting comments by Johnson and Stein, but is somewhat marred, in my view, by over-preoccupation with the so-called Golden Rule of Accumulation. That (mistaken) rule is further discussed in Appendix D to this chapter.

[2] Both Solow (1963, 96) and Tobin (1964, 13–15) note the large gap in the USA between private and social real rates of return to investment and those typically received by savers, together with the implication that investment is sub-optimal.

quite likely that this does not explain the whole of the gap, and two further possibilities are considered. First, there may be a 'learning' externality to investment. The typical business may learn from investments undertaken by others. Given *their* rate of investment, an individual business's investment opportunities are then limited by the lessons they provide. If all businesses were to increase their rates of investment together, this source of diminishing returns would be removed and the externality for the individual firm would be internalized for the whole economy. Second, the existence of market imperfections means that the rate of growth of demand limits an individual firm's investment opportunities. If it invests at a faster rate, it must either accept lower prices, or incur higher selling costs of various kinds, or diversify faster into new products or markets where returns are lower. Again, there is an externality, so that if all firms invested more together this particular source of diminishing returns would disappear and the externality for the individual firm would be internalized for the whole economy.

It is possible to give some tentative estimates of rates of taxation on investment, and of the gap between average and marginal private returns which is due to the learning externality and to market imperfections. Each of these could explain a large part of that gap. Indeed, when consideration is given to the relation between market imperfections and the share of wages in value added, it is difficult to resist the conclusion that there must be some other factor impelling firms to invest and increase output beyond what would maximize their present values. The motivations of managerially controlled firms were discussed in Chapter 9. The evidence at hand suggests that growth is an important motive, which offsets, at least partly, the otherwise anti-growth bias in the system caused by market imperfections. Putting it simply, 'animal spirits' oppose monopoly.

The two externalities just mentioned, from learning and growth of demand, provide a case for subsidizing investment, but the existence of 'animal spirits' lessens the need for such subsidies. One must also remember the general need to raise tax revenues. Most taxation is harmful at the margin, but is still worth imposing to secure the benefits of various public expenditures. Before one can decide whether investment is taxed too heavily, then, one must weigh up the harm this does against the harm done by further increases in other forms of taxation or by cuts in public expenditure.

The argument just sketched relies in several places on quantitative estimates. To see how these fit in, one must first understand the formulae for private and social, marginal and average, rates of return, and for the relation between the share of wages, λ, and the proportionate marginal product of labour, μ, which are given in the next section. This involves a tedious number of symbols, which have featured in previous chapters and which, regrettably, cannot be avoided. Readers of the chapter are, however, spared proofs which they can find elsewhere.

After this necessary chore, we can launch into the argument itself. We consider the magnitude of 'physical' diminishing returns to all investment taken together in Section 15.3. We then examine how far the gap between marginal social and private returns can be explained by taxation in Section 15.4. In Section 15.5 we discuss the learning externality, and in Section 15.6 the demand externality arising from the existence of imperfect markets. The final section draws together the strands of the argument. Four factors are identified which account for the gap between marginal social and private returns. Setting each of these factors at optimum levels, I estimate the optimum rates of growth for the UK and the USA using a more realistic (and complicated) version of the growth model sketched out in Chapter 8. This more realistic version is set out in Appendix C below. The model is also used to estimate the effect on growth of removing taxes on savings and investment, on the assumption that they can be shifted to labour and capitalists' consumption with negligible harmful effects. The existence of externalities to investment indeed suggests that one should go beyond that, and subsidize investment. The model indicates that a subsidy of around 50 per cent of investment would be needed to achieve optimum growth, but there are several objections that can be raised to paying such a large subsidy as that.

My definition of optimum growth is very different from that underlying the so-called Golden Rule of Accumulation. That rule was framed on the assumptions of orthodox growth theory, which I reject. In Appendix D to the chapter it is shown that, if the Golden Rule were followed, it would lead, according to my theory, to wildly excessive growth and investment. In fact, the whole of output would have to be devoted to investment, leaving nothing for consumption. Perhaps it should be re-christened the Miser's Rule?

In this chapter we consider the main reasons that have been suggested as to why investment is sub-optimal. Two further arguments are examined in Appendix E. One is that private individuals discount the future too heavily, and that this should be corrected by the government. In Chapter 8 this component of pure time preference, or impatience, was allowed for in the coefficient α, but, despite recognizing its existence, I do not believe that it requires offsetting action by the government. The other argument is that individuals might be willing to save more if they knew that others would do so as well—the so-called 'Isolation Paradox'. Again, I do not find this a persuasive argument for governmental action.

15.2 Comprehensive formulae for the private and social rates of return and proportionate marginal product of labour

In previous chapters, various formulae have been given for the private rate of return, r, and the proportionate marginal product of labour, μ. It has been shown how the simplest formulae need to be modified to allow for 'physical' diminishing returns to the rate of investment (Chapter 7 appendix), for imperfect markets (Appendix A to Chapter 9), for borrowing (Appendix B to Chapter 9, and Chapter 14 appendix), and for taxation (Chapter 14 appendix). As we need, in this chapter, formulae that are the best approximations we can find to reality, all four of these relaxations of my original assumptions must be made simultaneously. The last two—borrowing and taxation—are in effect combined in the formulae for the tax rate T_s, as was noted in Appendix B to Chapter 14 (p. 416). The 'tax rate' includes both the effects of the taxation of investment and the method of financing on the gap between the pre-tax rate of return and the rate of return received by the shareholder, r_{sha}. I adopt this simplification here as it is easier to apply empirically than the various alternatives discussed in Chapter 9. The resulting formulae for r and μ are stated without proof:[3]

$$r = (1 - T_s)\left\{ P\,(\eta q - \lambda l)\,\frac{\varrho_m}{\varrho} + g\left(1 - \frac{\varrho_m}{\varrho}\right)\right\} \qquad (15.1)$$

where

$$\frac{\varrho_m}{\varrho} = \frac{\gamma\sigma}{e^{\gamma\sigma} - 1}$$

$$\mu = \frac{\lambda}{\eta + an - \dfrac{s}{1 - T_s}} \qquad (15.2)$$

The symbols have their standard meanings, which are given in the List of Main Abbreviations and Symbols at the front of the book.

The *average* private pre-tax rate of return on investment is still given by my simplest formula, so

$$r_a = P(q - \lambda l). \qquad (15.3)$$

In Appendix A to this chapter I prove the following formula for the marginal *social* rate of return on investment:

$$r_s = P\{q - \mu\,(1 - s)l\}\,\frac{\varrho_{ms}}{\varrho} + g\left(1 - \frac{\varrho_{ms}}{\varrho}\right) \qquad (15.4)$$

where

$$\frac{\varrho_{ms}}{\varrho} = \frac{\gamma_s\sigma}{e^{\gamma_s\sigma} - 1}$$

ϱ_{ms} is the 'radius' of the marginal IPC considering the marginal *social* benefits of investment, and γ_s is similar to γ but, again, takes account of the marginal *social* benefits.

This result is achieved by assuming that all firms together increase their rate of investment by a marginal amount in such a way that the (given) growth of labour input is unaffected. This brings about an increased rate of

---

[3] A proof could, for example, follow the first rate-of-return proof in Chapter 7, and is not difficult for r or for μ.

consumption, growing at g, whose present value, discounted at r_s, is equal to the real sacrifice of consumption incurred to obtain it. It may be noted that the marginal social rate of return equals the marginal private rate of return in (15.1) if $T_s = 0$ (no taxation of savings or investment), $\eta = 1$ (no market imperfections), $\lambda = \mu (1 - s)$ (which would be the case in the absence of taxation of savings and of market imperfections if firms maximized their present values so that $an = 0$), and $\gamma = \gamma_s$. As explained in Appendix A to this chapter, γ_s will generally be less than γ because of the existence of an externality to learning from other firms' investments, which is discussed further below. Equality of social and private returns thus also requires the absence of such an externality.

The formula for the *average* social rate of return is

$$r_{as} = P\{q - \mu (1 - s)\, l\}. \tag{15.5}$$

This is simply (15.4) with $\gamma_s = 0$. The conditions under which it could equal the average private pre-tax rate of return in (15.3) are those that make $\lambda = \mu (1 - s)$ (see above).

Finally, I denote the rate of return received by shareholders, after paying profits tax (i.e. corporation tax) but before paying personal income tax, as r_{sh}. The corresponding rate of return after paying personal income tax as well is r_{sha}. These rates of return are not necessarily the same as r, the rate of return after tax to the owners of the firm on marginal investments by the firm, because the firm may be controlled by a management that does not seek to maximize the present value of the firm to its owners. Thus shareholders may show, by the price they are willing to pay for shares, that they discount future dividends at a higher or lower rate than the post-tax rate of return being earned for them on marginal investments by their companies. To maximize share values, the two rates of return should be equalized; but positive 'animal spirits' will make r less than r_{sha}.

15.3 'Physical' diminishing returns to collective investment

How much of the gap between average social returns to investment, r_{as}, and the rate of return received by shareholders, r_{sh}, is due to 'physical' diminishing returns to collective investment? This is simply the gap between r_{as} and r_s, and to estimate it using (15.4) and (15.5) we need to estimate the coefficient γ_s. Before doing so, some general considerations may be given.

First, it must be remembered that we are not here discussing short-term variations in the rate of investment, such as are relevant to the analysis of trade cycles, and to which most econometric investment equations refer. An upsurge in investment demand will, sooner or later, result in shortages developing in capital goods industries, and this will lower marginal returns to investment, whether because capital goods prices rise, or order books lengthen, or inferior substitutes have to be purchased. None of this is relevant here, since we are essentially comparing different steady-state rates of growth and investment. Where investment is higher, and the output of the investment goods industries forms a larger share of total output, that is a situation to which all have adjusted since it has ruled and is expected to continue to rule for a considerable time.

Second, there is a general argument for believing that there are diminishing returns, namely, that investment opportunities can be expected to differ and the best will be done first.

Third, however, while that seems very convincing, there are many other arguments which have been adduced in favour of increasing returns and dynamic economies of scale. As these were discussed in Chapters 12 and 13, they are not repeated here, although one is considered in the following section.

The *a priori* arguments are not, then, compelling either way; nor have I been able to locate empirical studies of this question. My own empirical studies on the whole suggest that the assumption of constant returns to investment (from a collective point of view—*not* the investment of an individual firm) is a reasonable one (i.e. $\gamma_s = 0$). Thus, for example, if one takes equation (10.1), which is statistically the preferred one for the explanation of growth rates based on our standard periods and countries, the addition of a term in s^2 to it, which would allow for the possibility of diminishing returns to s, resulted in a coefficient that was positive (i.e. implying increasing, not diminishing, returns) but small, with a t-statistic of only 0.31, implying that it was not significantly different from zero.

However, as was pointed out in Chapter 10, there is one equation which does provide rather weak support for the existence of diminishing returns, and that is (10.2). The apparent absence of diminishing returns in (10.1) could be due to country differences in the scope for investment, as measured by ϱ. Thus, for other reasons, ϱ may be high in Japan and low in the UK. That would certainly accord with popular belief. Rates of investment are also high in Japan and low in the UK. Hence the existence of diminishing returns to investment may be being concealed by these other factors which offset the fall in ϱ arising from high s in Japan, and the rise in ϱ arising from low s in the UK. Equation (10.2) attempts to allow for this possibility by using country dummies, and the result is a negative coefficient for s^2, which indicates diminishing returns. This coefficient is not statistically very significant ($t = -1.07$), and the whole equation is less satisfactory than equation (10.1) or (10.3). Nevertheless, it does seem worth while using the estimate, at least as an indicator of the extent to which diminishing returns may explain the gap between r_{as} and r_s.

Equation (10.2) is of the general form

$$g = As - Bs^2 + \mu g_L.$$

If we divide this through by s, we get

$$q = A - Bs + \mu l,$$

which may be compared with the linearized equation for the IPC, which, after multiplying by ϱ, is

$$q = a\varrho + \mu l.$$

Hence $a\varrho = A - Bs$, and

$$\frac{1}{\varrho} \frac{\partial \varrho}{\partial s} = \frac{-B}{A - Bs}.$$

Now in Appendix A to this chapter, I have assumed that the way in which increases in s result in diminishing returns is to lower ϱ as in equations (15A.1) and (15A.2).[4] From these we can derive equation (15A.3), which relates $(1/\varrho)(\partial\varrho/\partial s)$ to γ_s, which can then be solved for γ_s making use of the above estimate for $(1/\varrho)(\partial\varrho/\partial s)$. We can, then, use this estimate of γ_s, together with the other known magnitudes in (15.4) and (15.5), to estimate both r_{as} and r_s, and so the gap between them. Estimates for the UK, the USA, and Japan for postwar years are given in Table 15.1, columns (1) and (2); the estimated values of γ_s are in column (5).[5] It can be seen that the existence of diminishing returns as estimated from equation (10.2) lowers the marginal social rate of return by amounts ranging from 0.02 to 0.04, but leaves the marginal return still well in excess of the return of around 0.063 received by shareholders (before income tax) in the UK and USA in the postwar years (Table 7.3, column (3)).

Columns (3) and (4) in Table 15.1 perform a similar exercise, but start from a lower estimated average social rate of return. This lower estimate simply splits the difference between the estimates based on our standard period data (i.e. as in column (1) here) and those based on conventional ratios of net profits to net capital stock at current prices for the non-financial corporate sector (i.e. as in column (2) of Table 7.3). The resulting estimates of marginal social rates of return are lower now, but still well above returns to shareholders.

It must be emphasized that these estimates of the differences between average and marginal social rates of return are very uncertain, and that it would be quite reasonable to assume that, in fact, there were no differences at all.

---

[4] These equations are written in terms of $\sigma = S/Q$ rather than $s = S/PQ$ for the reason given in Appendix A to this chapter. However, here, where we are considering only the whole economy, and so the representative firm in it, we can set $P = 1$ without loss of generality, so that $\sigma = s$.

[5] Since (10.2) is not consistent with equation (15A.1), but only gives a linear approximation, the estimates of γ_s vary between country and period.

Table 15.1   Average and marginal social rates of return to investment

Country	Period	Period data		Modified data		Estimated γ_s
		Average r_{as} (1)	Marginal r_s (2)	Average r_{as} (3)	Marginal r_s (4)	(5)
UK	1951–64	0.127	0.105	0.112	0.093	2.85
	1964–73	0.186	0.143	0.132	0.103	3.16
	1951–73	0.153	0.123	0.121	0.098	2.97
USA	1948–73	0.154	0.130	0.134	0.114	2.98
Japan	1952–61	0.258	0.221	n.a.	n.a.	1.99
	1961–73	0.214	0.171	n.a.	n.a.	2.51
	1952–73	0.231	0.190	n.a.	n.a.	2.28

Notes
Col. (1) is the same as in col. (1) of Table 7.1. Equation (15.5) is used with our standard period data. Col. (2) is derived from the same data as col. (1), using equation (15.4) and the estimates of γ_s in col. (5). Col. (3) is the arithmetic mean of the estimates for each period and country in cols. (1) and (2) of Table 7.3. Col. (4) starts from the estimates in col. (3) instead of those in col. (1), but otherwise is similar to col. (2). Col. (5) estimates are derived from econometric equation (10.2) in the way described in the text. γ_s is the coefficient in equation (15A.1) which determines the rapidity with which returns to investment diminish. $\gamma_s < 0$ implies increasing returns. For the UK and Japan, the estimates for 1951–73 and for 1952–73 respectively are based on the weighted averages of growth rates for the sub-periods shown, the weights being the lengths of the sub-periods.

15.4   The extent of the gap arising from taxation of investment and from borrowing

The estimates of marginal tax rates in the UK and the USA given in Table 14.2 provide an indication of the pre-tax marginal rates of return that companies must earn in order to yield shareholders a given post-tax rate of return. It is only an indication, since the assumptions underlying the estimates can be queried (see further below), and since I have estimates for only three years—1960, 1970, and 1980. Of these, 1960 seems the most relevant, as it lies roughly in the middle of the postwar period we are considering. The rate of tax, T_s, on a tax-exempt shareholder is then 20.8 per cent for the UK and 26.8 per cent for the USA. I take a tax-exempt shareholder, since I apply these rates to the rates of return in Table 7.3 which are those received by shareholders before deduction of income tax. These are 0.064 for the UK in 1951–73 and 0.063 for the USA in 1948–73. The resulting required pre-tax rates of return work out at 0.081 for the UK and 0.086 for the USA. These rates of return allow for the existence of fixed-interest borrowing and inflation.

All the estimated social rates of return (which are pre-tax) in Table 15.1 are in excess of these required rates. The extent of the excess depends on which estimates one chooses. At one extreme—r_{as} in column (1)—we have rates of 0.151 for the UK and 0.154 for the USA. At the other extreme—r_s in column (4)—we have rates of 0.097 for the UK and 0.114 for the USA. These estimates suggest, then, that, while taxation (together with fixed interest borrowing and inflation) explains much of the gap between returns to investment and returns to shareholders, it by no means explains it all.

However, it may be that taxation explains rather more than the tax rates in Table 14.2 allow. In constructing the estimates for 1960 for the USA, I assumed zero marginal taxation of spurious inventory profits, because firms had the option of adopting the LIFO method of inventory valuation which would have eliminated such profits. In this I followed King and Fullerton. However, in fact, most inventories in the USA were valued on the FIFO method, so that there were spurious inventory profits and taxes levied on them. For this reason one might reasonably argue that marginal tax rates in the USA were higher than assumed in Table 14.2. Another factor tending to increase the required pre-tax return on material investment was investment by companies in non-interest-bearing financial assets (notably, trade credit and cash), for which no special allowance is made in Table 14.2. To allow for these and some other, less important, factors, I recomputed the US effective tax rate for 1960, which produced a revised tax rate of 30.8 per cent (instead of 26.8 per cent).[6] The required pre-tax rate of return is then 0.091 (instead of 0.086). A similar revision was not attempted for the UK, partly because taxation of inventory profits is already allowed for in the estimates for 1960 in Table 14.2. While the gap is somewhat reduced by the revision to the US figure, it still remains.

In view of the uncertainties about tax rates, it is worth while considering other estimates which shed light on the question being discussed. These are estimates of the valuation ratio, v. It was shown in Chapter 7 that, in the absence of taxation, and if the average rate of return equals the rate of discount used by shareholders and other creditors of the firm, and if rates of return are constant and expectations are fulfilled, and if depreciation is measured in such a way as to make investment net of depreciation equal to the rate of change of the present value of the firm, V, then $v = V/K = 1$, where K is the net capital stock. This is a catalogue of assumptions, but for the moment let us maintain all but two of them. Let us allow for the existence of taxation and for its effects on the rate of discount used by shareholders and creditors. For a firm with given output, wages, invest-

---

[6] It was assumed that 80% of investment in inventories was subject to taxation of inventory profits, and that investment in non-interest-bearing financial assets effectively doubled the interest rate paid by a firm on its *net* borrowing. Both these estimates are based on Furstenberg (1977, Table 1 and p. 361).

ment, and growth, it is clear that taxation will not alter K, nor will it alter the average pre-tax rate of return r_a. However, taxation will reduce the amounts (after tax) taken out by shareholders and creditors. The question is, then, how far taxation can be expected also to reduce r_{sha} (post-tax) below r_a, and whether the effect of this in increasing V is offset by the fall in take-out.

The simplest case would be if we were dealing with a static firm with no depreciation and no investment and with a rate of tax on profits of τ. We would then have[7]

$$K = \frac{PQ\,(1 - \lambda)}{r_a}$$

If, for the moment, we ignore borrowing and personal income taxation, and assume that all profits after tax accrue to shareholders, and if their rate of discount were lower than r_a *only* because of tax, so that $r_{sh} = r_a\,(1 - \tau)$, then we would have

$$V = \frac{PQ\,(1 - \lambda)\,(1 - \tau)}{r_a\,(1 - \tau)} = K.$$

Hence, with these assumptions, we should have $v = 1$. If, in fact, we find $v > 1$, this would point to shareholders' rate of discount being even lower than could be explained by taxation, i.e. $r_{sh} < r_a\,(1 - \tau)$.

It can be shown (see Appendix B to this chapter) that, in the more complicated case of a steadily growing firm in which there is both investment and depreciation, the effect of taxation is to reduce V below K. The fall in the rate of discount is not then sufficient to outweigh the fall in take-out. This then strengthens the conclusion that, if $v > 1$, shareholders' rate of discount, r_{sh}, must be lower than r_a by more than can be explained by taxation.

Still for the moment maintaining our other assumptions, let us now consider the first eight estimates of v for US companies in various postwar periods up to 1973 in Table 15.2. In these estimates, V is the estimated current market value of the companies' shares plus that of their net financial debt. K is the estimated current value of the firm's net capital stock, using the perpetual inventory method.[8] As there are various ways in which both of these magnitudes can be estimated,[9] it is not altogether

[7] On p. 198 it is shown that, for a firm growing at g, K equals take-out divided by $(r_a - g)$. The formula in the text applies to a static firm with $g = 0$ and no investment, so that take-out is $PQ(1 - \lambda)$.

[8] See pp. 90–1 for a brief description of the method.

[9] For example, Furstenberg (row (6) in Table 15.2) adds net non-interest-bearing financial assets to the capital stock, whereas others net them out against debt in V. Furstenberg also includes land in K, while Summers, for example, omits it. Market values are usually estimated by capitalizing flows of dividends, or interest, and different rates of capitalization can be used depending on which yields one thinks are representative.

Table 15.2 Estimates of the valuation ratio for companies

Author	Country	Period	Ave. valuation ratio, v
(1) Brainard, Shoven, Weiss	USA	1958–73	1.45
(2) Economic Report of the President	USA	1958–73	1.12
(3) Tobin, Brainard	USA	1960–73	2.16
(4) Lindenberg, Ross	USA	1960–73	1.69
(5) Ciccolo	USA	1958–73	1.48
(6) Furstenberg	USA	1958–73	0.89
(7) Summers	USA	1958–73	1.14
(8) Summers	USA	1948–73	0.99
(9) Summers	USA	1948–73	1.003
(10) Bank of England	UK	1964–73	1.256

Notes

Estimates (1)–(8) are, so far as I can judge, not adjusted for taxation, while estimates (9) and (10) are adjusted.

Estimate (9) is stated by the author to be equivalent, 'in a taxless world', to unadjusted v *less* 1, so presumably one should add 1 to it to obtain comparability with estimate (10).

Estimates (1)–(6) inclusive are from Brainard, Shoven, Weiss (1980, Table 2), which lists the sources. The precise coverage of the estimates is not always stated.

Estimates (7)–(9) inclusive are from Summers (1981, Table 3), and refer to all non-financial corporate business. ·

Estimate (10) is from figures kindly supplied by the Bank of England and refers to all industrial and commercial companies. The original method of calculation was set out in two articles by Flemming *et al.* (1976), which gave end-of-year estimates back to 1960, the average for 1960–3 being 1.188. Subsequently, the methodology was revised. The latest series available when this was prepared (June 1986) went back to only 1967, so an older series back to 1964 is used in the table. The latest series is appreciably higher for 1967–73 (i.e. 1.308 compared with 1.214 for the series in the table).

surprising that different investigators have come up with different values of v for what appear to be similar groups of companies. The size of the differences is, all the same, rather worrying.[10]

Of the first eight estimates of v, six are above 1, one is only just below it, and one is not far below it. If our other assumptions were fulfilled, we could take this as rather strong evidence that the gap between r_a and r cannot all be explained by taxation. We must now reconsider those assumptions.

One assumption that was questioned in Chapter 7 relates to the way in which depreciation and the capital stock are estimated. I concluded there that conventional estimates of the capital stock at current replacement costs almost certainly overstate its true value, while (for the USA) conventional

[10] The first six estimates in Table 15.2 are all presented by Brainard, Shoven, and Weiss (1980), who remark: 'The various estimates show significantly different levels—which are difficult to reconcile—but nevertheless show similar patterns through time' (p. 466).

estimates of depreciation are probably only slightly below true values ('true values' in both cases being those that give effect to the assumptions made here). This, then almost certainly strengthens the above conclusion, since it implies that true v is even greater than the estimates in Table 15.2 suggest.

A second point we must reconsider is the neglect of borrowing by the firm. Since in practice there is borrowing, and the market value of debt is included in V, the relevant rate of discount, r_{sh}, is no longer that of shareholders alone. Instead, it is a weighted average of shareholders' and other creditors' rates of discount. Since other creditors certainly earned lower real rates of return than did shareholders in the period under discussion (see Table 7.3), the weighted average is below shareholders' rate of return. Let us call this weighted average r_c (for 'cost of capital'). What the argument shows is that the gap between r_a and r_c is not wholly due to taxation. The excess of r_{sh} (i.e. shareholders' rate of discount) over r_c is wholly due to the existence of borrowing. It follows that the argument still shows that the gap between r_a and r_{sh} is not wholly explained by taxation and borrowing taken together.

Two further assumptions made above are that rates of discount and return are constant and that expectations are fulfilled. Unfortunately, there seems to be no simple way of knowing how far, or even in what direction, failure of these assumptions affects the data and conclusion. All one can say is that they add to its uncertainty.

In addition to the first eight estimates of r in Table 15.2, which, so far as I know, are not adjusted in any special way for taxation, there are two estimates, (9) and (10), that are so adjusted. In both cases these adjustments are complex, and only those for estimate (10) will be briefly outlined here.[11] So far as estimate (9) is concerned, it should be noted that the figure shown is *not* the ratio V/K but one that is more akin to (although not the same as) $V/K - 1$. Hence it is a *positive* value here, which carries the same implications as a value greater than 1 for estimate (10).

Turning to estimate (10), the amount available for distribution, both as dividends and as interest after tax, is computed for a static firm whose gross investment equals depreciation at current replacement cost. Call this C. As before, the estimated current market value of the firm (including its net debt) is V. As before, again, the net capital stock at current replacement cost estimated by the perpetual inventory method is K. However, a *tax-adjusted* value of K, which is $(1 - A)K$, is used instead of K, where A is the present value of taxes saved per unit of investment by way of depreciation allowances and also of investment grants. Then we have

$$r_a \text{ (after tax)} = \frac{C}{(1 - A)K}$$

$$r_c \text{ (after tax)} = \frac{C}{V} .$$

$$v \text{ (tax-adjusted)} = \frac{V}{(1 - A)K} = \frac{r_a}{r_c}$$

In a nutshell, therefore, the objective of making the adjustments in estimate (10) is to ensure that, when $v = 1$, the average rate of return on investment equals the 'cost of capital', r_c, *both* being measured after tax. Consequently the fact that v averaged more than 1 over the period shown implies that r_c lay below r_a, the post-tax average rate of return. The tax-adjusted estimates in both rows (9) and (10) of Table 15.2 therefore point to the same conclusion as earlier: that taxation and borrowing are insufficient to explain the gap between the average pre-tax rate of return and the shareholders' rate of return.

To conclude, these estimates of valuation ratios have shown that taxation and borrowing together do not explain by any means the whole of the gap between r_a and r_{sh}. Since r_{as} is approximately the same as r_a (because $\lambda \approx \mu$ $(1 - s)$—see equations (15.3) and (15.5), and columns (1) and (2) of Table 7.1), the conclusion therefore also relates to the gap between r_{as} and r_{sh}. By stretching it a bit, we can finally relate it to the gap between r_s and r_{sh}–that is, so long as r_s is not much below r_{as} (see Section 15.3), and as long as v is well above 1.

15.5   Externality to investment arising from learning

In Chapter 6 we discussed the way in which the typical firm's investment opportunities are affected by its ability to learn from investments undertaken elsewhere. This has some similarities to Arrow's idea of learning-by-doing, and, like Arrow, I find it implies an externality to investment.[12] Because of increased investment opportunities created for other firms, the individual investor will usually not capture all the benefits resulting from his investment. If all firms were to increase their rates of investment together,[13] they would find that the set of investment opportunities confronting them had improved, since there was more to learn. ϱ would accordingly increase, and so would the average rates of return to investment. Most people would probably regard this effect as obvious so far as a great deal of investment in R&D is concerned, but, as is pointed out in Chapter 6, almost any investment can have the same effect, although to a greater or lesser extent. Any investment changes the world, and may suggest investment opportunities to others that they would not otherwise have thought of.

[11] The sources cited in the note to Table 15.2 should be consulted for further details.
[12] Arrow (1962b). See also Solow (1963, 63–8) for a discussion of the gap between private and social rates of return which occurs in Arrow's model.
[13] Investment by 'all firms' here must be taken to include research and development undertaken by, for example, universities, research institutes and government departments.

The existence of some sort of learning effect must underlie the catch-up effect, for which evidence is given in Chapter 10. Some might also want to say that the learning effect at least partly explains the outward shift of the IPC, which seems to have occurred in a great many countries after the Second World War. Rates of investment were probably much higher then than in any previous period, and so probably were rates of return and ϱ (see Chapters 7 and 10). However, to conclude that this was so would be to imply increasing rather than diminishing returns to a collective increase in the rate of investment, and my econometric results do not support that. As was noted in Section 15.3, there is some weak evidence in favour of diminishing returns, but it is only weak. It is quite plausible to assume constant returns, given the evidence at hand. All we can say, then, is that the learning effect counteracts other factors which make for diminishing returns, leaving, quite probably, little net effect either way.

The learning effect explains why there may be diminishing returns to the rate of investment for an individual firm but not (or to a lower extent) for all firms taken together. The flow of new ideas to the individual firm is limited by the rate of investment of all other firms, so that, if the individual firm raises its rate of investment, it may have to make do with worse, or less relevant, ideas. But if all firms invest more together, they thereby increase the flow of ideas for all. The learning effect is therefore one reason why the marginal return to the firm is lower than its average return, and why the marginal private return is below the marginal social return.

15.6 Externality to investment arising from its effect on demand: 'market' diminishing returns

It is important to guard against a possible misunderstanding at the outset. We are *not* here concerned with the short-term, Keynesian, effects of an increase in investment on aggregate demand. Our concern is with a comparison of steady-growth states, in one of which the rate of investment, s, is higher than the other. Where s is higher, the rate of growth of capacity is faster, and so it is possible for the rates of growth of demand and output to be faster without increasing the ratio of output to capacity. This is quite different from the Keynesian effect of an increase in investment on aggregate demand, which does increase the ratio of output to capacity. By doing so, it tends to increase inflationary pressure, which may or may not be thought desirable, depending in particular on the starting position. None of that is our concern here. The ratio of output to capacity may be assumed to be maintained at whatever is thought to be the optimum ratio, but, in any case, it does not vary either over time or as between the two growth states being compared.

The rate of growth of demand *does* vary as between the states, and this is brought about by a higher s in one of them. What I seek to show is that, in helping to bring this about, investment in a typical individual firm confers a substantial benefit on other firms which the firm itself does not capture, so that there is an externality. At the same time, this results in the marginal private rate of return being well below the average private return, and also being well below the marginal social return. The only requirements to be fulfilled are that there must be imperfect markets and the investment in question must be output-increasing.

In principle, the externality could apply to supply as well as demand.[14] I have, throughout this book, neglected material inputs to the firm, and have assumed a very elastic supply of labour. I continue with this in what follows, merely noting the need for further research to determine whether a more accurate treatment would make much difference.

In order to isolate the effect I wish to consider, I simplify by assuming that there are no physical diminishing returns, no taxation, and no learning externality. The average private return, r_a, the marginal private return, r, and the marginal social return, r_s, are then given by the following equations, from which I have eliminated λ by using equation (15.2):

$$r_a = P\{q - \mu(\eta + an - s)l\}$$
$$r = P\{\eta q - \mu(\eta + an - s)l\}$$
$$r_s = P\{q - \mu(1 - s)l\}.$$

The externality exists only if, and to the extent that, markets are imperfect, that is if $\eta < 1$, i.e. to the extent that marginal net revenue is less than price. If markets were perfect, with $\eta = 1$, the effects of demand would be mediated entirely though prices and, at market prices, the individual firm could sell as much as it pleased. With $\eta < 1$, however, that is no longer the case. It is clear that the firm's marginal rate of return is below its average rate of return, and also below the marginal social rate of return on its investment. Thus

$$r_a - r = (1 - \eta) Pq$$
$$r_s - r = (1 - \eta) P\left\{ q - \mu\left(1 - \frac{an}{1 - \eta}\right) l\right\}.$$

Both of these differences are positive with $\eta < 1$ so long as $q > 0$ (i.e. so long as investment is expanding, rather than contracting, output, as we can normally expect), and given that we must always have $q > \mu l$, and given also that $an \geq 0$.

The fact that the marginal social return exceeds the marginal private return to investment is sufficient to prove the existence of the externality. It may be helpful, however, to explain more fully how it comes about.

[14] Two writers who have drawn attention to the externality arising from market imperfections of both supply and demand are Scitovsky (1954) and Tobin (1964). The former coined the phrase 'pecuniary external economies' to distinguish these from the 'technological external economies' of the bees-and-apples variety referred to in Meade (1952).

By raising the aggregate rate of investment, the individual firm *permits* aggregate output to grow faster. Other firms can then invest more and expand their output faster without having to cut prices or incur a higher ratio of selling costs to output. On this investment, these firms can therefore earn average returns which, as we have seen, are above their marginal returns. It is this excess of average over marginal returns for other firms that constitutes the benefit for them, and it is a benefit that the original firm does not capture. Furthermore, all this takes place without any change in the ratio of output to capacity, and so without any increase in inflationary pressure on that account. Naturally, the higher rate of investment must be matched by a higher rate of saving, and so, if one is considering the initiation of such a process, there has to be a cut-back in consumption (as compared with what would otherwise have occurred) to make room for the increase in investment. Subsequently, both consumption and investment grow faster than before.

Here, as elsewhere in this book, I do not attempt to trace through the route by which an increase in the rate of investment leads to a faster rate of growth of demand. The rate of growth of demand in the rest of the economy is an important determinant of the rate of investment in each part of it, given market imperfections. In that sense, I believe the accelerator theory of investment is profoundly true. However, when one considers the behaviour of the whole of a closed economy, the rate of growth of demand that can be sustained over the longish periods that are the main concern of this book depends on the rate of investment, which in turn must depend on the rate at which people are prepared to save. In the final version of my growth model, which is used later in the chapter (and set out in Appendix C below), the rate of growth of demand is endogenous, as also is the rate of saving and investment. I have not attempted to explain how macroeconomic equilibrium is maintained, important though that question is. That Pandora's box has been kept firmly closed. Consequently, the word 'permit' in the last paragraph was used advisedly. It could be the case that no government intervention of any kind is required, the economy naturally maintaining a constant ratio of output to capacity, or cycling around a trend ratio that is constant. Alternatively, the government may be intervening through monetary and fiscal policies to maintain what it considers to be an optimum ratio. The choice between these alternatives is left to readers.

There is a close analogy between the externality we are considering and the 'locomotive effect'. Governments have, from time to time, exhorted other governments to expand their economies so as to increase world aggregate demand and to pull other economies along behind them. The view that the major countries should all expand demand together has also been expressed on many occasions. It is feared that if one country tries to go it alone it will run into balance of payments difficulties, which can be overcome only at the cost of devaluation and a serious worsening of the expanding country's terms of trade. If all expand together, this worsening in terms of trade can be largely avoided. Such a worsening is conceptually the same as the price cuts (or increased selling expenses) which a firm must make if it wants to grow faster unilaterally. The 'locomotive' idea, and that of concerted expansion, have usually been viewed as short-term macroeconomic policy measures. They encounter the objection that they would raise output–capacity ratios and increase inflationary tendencies. The same objection does not apply if the faster growth results from a faster rate of investment matched by increased (*ex ante*) savings.

Since the magnitude of the externality we are considering depends on market imperfections, it is important to gain some idea of the size of η for a typical firm. The formula for η, which is explained in p. 256 and Appendix A to Chapter 9, shows that it depends on two magnitudes, thus:

$$\eta = 1 - \frac{1}{\epsilon' (1 - ma)}. \tag{15.6}$$

Here ϵ' is the price elasticity of demand for *gross* output (i.e. gross of materials costs), and ma is the ratio of material costs to gross output (excluding selling costs, in principle: see Appendix A to Chapter 9). We therefore consider, now, estimates of ϵ' and ma respectively.

The relevant price elasticity of demand is that confronting the typical firm, and it is a *long-term* elasticity, since I have used it in that sense in the equations.[15] The elasticity is not the *consumers'* price elasticity of demand, but is mainly dependent on the behaviour of *producers*. Even if consumers' elasticity for a particular good were zero, the relevant elasticity could be close to infinity because the typical firm's sales might be very sensitive to the price it charged if other competitors produced very close substitutes. Many econometric studies of demand relate to consumers' price elasticities, and are therefore, unfortunately, irrelevant.

One set of econometric studies that is relevant is that relating to price elasticities of demand in foreign trade. For example, estimates of the price elasticity of demand for UK exports of manufactures should give some idea of the relevant elasticity for a typical manufacturer. Unfortunately, one must reject for this purpose the elasticities found in recent econometric models of the UK economy. For example, Brooks and Henry's re-estimation of the National Institute's model found price elasticities of demand for UK exports of manufactures of about 0.5 and for imports of manufactures rather smaller than this. For exports of services the elasticity was about 1 (Brooks and Henry 1983, 63–4). Likewise, the elasticities given by Enoch (1978, 189) (which appear to be consistent with the Bank of

---

[15] The equations simplify reality by assuming an instantaneous effect on demand which lasts for ever.

England's model of the UK economy in 1979: Bank of England 1979, 22) for exports of manufactures were around 1, and for imports, between 1 and 2. If a typical manufacturer were indeed confronted by a demand curve having an elasticity as low as any of these estimates, it is difficult to believe that he would not raise his price, perhaps very considerably, and at any rate until the elasticity had become much higher. With an elasticity of 1, his sales receipts would be unchanged, while his costs must be lower. With an elasticity less than 1, his sales receipts would be increased. In fact, the conventional static theory of monopoly requires the producer to equate marginal cost (MC) and marginal revenue (MR) where

$$MR = P\left(1 - \frac{1}{\epsilon}\right).$$

This formula suggests that the mark-up of price over marginal cost would be infinite if $\epsilon = 1$, and would be 100 per cent of cost (50 per cent of price) even if $\epsilon = 2$. In practice, mark-ups are far smaller than this.

How can one reconcile this with the apparently low values of the price elasticity found in econometric studies?[16] One important part of the explanation lies in the inappropriate measures of relative prices which have to be used. These refer to aggregates of goods whose composition is different for different countries. Changes in composition may then lead to relative 'price' changes that bear no simple relation to changes in quantities demanded. Where the basic price index numbers are unit values obtained by dividing values by some imperfect indicator of quantity (e.g. number or tonnage), as they often are, the resulting errors of measurement could bias the estimated elasticities towards 1.[17] Another explanation lies in the confusion of demand and supply effects. It is difficult to separate these out in a study dealing with aggregates, but the result may be that a low apparent elasticity of demand may partly reflect a low elasticity of supply. A further explanation could be that the short-run effects are indeed rather small, and that, despite their use of lagged variables, the studies have failed to capture all the long-run effects, which could be spread over several years.

There are some econometric studies of demand in international trade which have arrived at higher estimates of price elasticities of demand than those so far mentioned, sometimes using methods other than the usual analysis of economic time-series. A typical value for the price elasticity of demand for exports of manufactures in other studies is 3.[18] My own study of UK imports concluded that:

[16] See Orcutt (1950) for a discussion of the reasons for expecting a downward bias in ordinary least squares estimates of these elasticities.

[17] Enoch (1978) provides a good discussion of different price indices which have been used to measure 'competitiveness'.

[18] See (a) MacDougall (1951, 1952): this was a cross-section study of more than 100 different manufactured exports of the USA and the UK (and some other countries as well) in

the size of the price elasticity of substitution depends on the nature of the product. For standard semi-manufactures like textile yarns and steel it is large, perhaps 15 or even larger. For more complicated manufactures, or for goods sold more directly to private persons where branding and advertising may be more important, the elasticity may be around 5. . . . (Scott 1963, 184)

For UK imports of manufactures as a whole, I estimated the price elasticity of demand at about 6, with a range of possible values extending from 4 to 13. This estimate was based mainly on the sharp and very large (44 per cent) fall in the quantity of UK imports of manufactures following the imposition of tariffs and the devaluation of the pound in 1931–2, (Scott 1963, 158–72).

A recent study which avoids the pitfall mentioned earlier of confusing demand with supply effects is that of Riedel (1988) for the exports of Hong Kong. He shows that, if the traditional procedure of fitting a reduced-form equation which implicitly assumes an infinite elasticity of supply is followed, a low price elasticity of demand (0.7) is indeed estimated. If, however, one models supply separately from demand, which is feasible given Hong Kong's special situation with virtually all manufacturing devoted to export, then the estimated price elasticity of demand is infinite. A large fraction of Hong Kong's exports consist of clothing and similar consumer goods sold to wholesalers or buyers from multiple stores. In my view the price elasticities of demand may well be very high for such goods, but lower for other manufactures where product differentiation and the producer's reputation are more important—machinery, instruments, vehicles, etc. A representative elasticity may then be much less than infinite, although much more than the low elasticities found by most econometric studies thus far.

The preceding estimates all relate to manufactures. We may therefore take them in conjunction with an estimate of *ma* which also relates to manufactures. For the UK in 1963, *ma* can be put at 0.63.[19] The resulting

the interwar years, which concluded that the elasticity of substitution between them was probably of the order of 3 (*Economic Journal*, September 1952, 495). (b) Vries (1951): this study used a novel method. The US Tariff Commission was asked in 1945 what would be the long-run effects of a 50% reduction or a 50% increase in the US tariff on a large number of products. Their estimates, made by 'experts' familiar with the industries concerned, formed the basis for de Vries's conclusion that the typical price elasticity of demand for 176 commodities was about 2.5. (c) A more conventional time-series study which estimated elasticities of 3 to 5 was Junz and Rhomberg (1965). Other time-series studies yielding estimates around 3 were Kreinen (1967); Gregory (1971); and Zelder (1958).

[19] This estimate is based on CSO, *Input–Output Tables for the United Kingdom 1963*, HMSO, 1970, Table B, and equals, for all manufacturing industries, (total inputs *less* net indirect taxes and *less* value added, i.e. the sum of gross trading profits and income from employment) ÷ (total inputs *less* net indirect taxes). 1963 was chosen as a year near the mid-point of the period considered. As is pointed out in Appendix A to Chapter 9, ideally, selling costs should be excluded from both materials costs and gross output (i.e. total inputs *less* net indirect taxes), but the data for making this exclusion were not available. This would not bias the resulting estimate of η for given ϵ' if selling costs form the same proportion of value added (e.g. some employees are salesmen) as of 'material' inputs (e.g. if some inputs are payments for advertising).

estimates of η for different values of ϵ' are shown in column (2) of Table 15.3.[20]

If we can take these estimates of η as sufficient to represent its value in non-residential business as a whole in both the UK and the USA, we can derive estimates of the coefficient *an* ('animal spirits'). These are shown in columns (3) and (4) of Table 15.3, and make use of equation (15.2), using

Table 15.3 Estimates of η, *an*, and *r* for various values of ϵ' for the UK 1951–73, and the USA, 1948–73

ϵ'	η	*an*		*r*	
UK & USA	UK & USA	UK	USA	UK	USA
(1)	(2)	(3)	(4)	(5)	(6)
2	−0.35	1.39	1.39	−0.001	−0.017
3	0.10	0.94	0.94	0.017	0.005
4	0.32	0.71	0.71	0.026	0.016
5	0.46	0.58	0.58	0.032	0.023
6	0.55	0.49	0.49	0.035	0.027
7	0.61	0.42	0.42	0.038	0.030
10	0.73	0.31	0.31	0.043	0.036
13	0.79	0.24	0.25	0.045	0.039
15	0.82	0.22	0.22	0.046	0.040
20	0.86	0.17	0.17	0.048	0.043
∞	1.00	0.04	0.04	0.054	0.049

Note
The table shows estimates of η (the marginal net revenue (value added) per unit of extra output as a fraction of the price of value added), *an* (the premium attached to an extra unit of output as a fraction of the price of value added — 'animal spirits'), and *r* (the marginal post-all-taxes real rate of return for a typical shareholder household), given the values of ϵ' (the observed, or empirical, price elasticity of demand for gross output, allowing selling costs to vary) in col. (1). The formulae used are (15.6), (15.2), and (15.1), respectively. The values of g, g_L, g_N, λ, and s (and so q and l) are from Table SA I, the two postwar periods for the UK being combined using weights proportionate to their lengths. μ is derived from equation (11.3) and is 0.9046 for the UK and 0.8685 for the USA. $1 - T_s$ is from Table 14.2 for households in 1960 and is 0.736 for the UK and 0.705 for the USA. *ma* is 0.63 for both countries, based on manufacturing for the UK in 1963 (see fns. 19 and 20 in the text), and so the estimates of η are the same for both. γ is derived from (15.7) and (15.8), assuming $\alpha = 0.013$ and $\beta = 1.5$ (see p. 231). Since we are dealing with the typical firm in the whole of non-residential business, we can set $P = 1$ and $\sigma = s$.

[20] The value of *ma* chosen relates to manufacturing because the estimates of ϵ' cited also do. It is assumed that η is the fundamental quantity, so that a different *ma* would imply a different ϵ' rather than a different η. If, despite this, one were to take the same ϵ' and a value of *ma* that is lower and relates to the whole of non-residential business, η would be bigger, *an* smaller, and *r* bigger. Using the same source as in the preceding footnote, *ma* for non-residential business in the UK in 1963 may be put at 0.51, compared with 0.63 for manufacturing alone. If, for example, one takes the row in Table 15.3 for $\epsilon' = 6$, and puts *ma* = 0.51, this gives the following estimates for cols. (2)–(6) respectively compared with *ma* = 0.63:

	col. (2)	col. (3)	col. (4)	col. (5)	col. (6)
ma = 0.63	0.55	0.49	0.49	0.035	0.027
ma = 0.51	0.66	0.38	0.38	0.040	0.033

values for the other magnitudes for the postwar years in the UK and the USA derived as explained in the note to the table.

In view of the considerable uncertainty about the size of the typical elasticity of demand, ϵ', I have presented a wide range of estimates in Table 15.3. Is there any way of narrowing this range?

If the elasticity were as low as 2, it would imply, as the table shows, that the marginal net revenue per unit of extra output, η, was actually negative. A very remarkable degree of 'animal spirits' is required to offset that! It also implies, given the assumption discussed below, that the marginal real rate of return earned on investment is negative. The picture of growth-obsessed managements completely out of shareholders' control which this portrays must surely be rejected.

The very large elasticities are also implausible. An infinite value for ϵ' would imply that the typical producer could sell as much as he liked so long as he increased selling expenditures in the same proportion as sales, and without the need for any price cuts. If this were true, it is not clear why many producers should attach so much importance to demand, whether as explanations of their output or their investment.

Unfortunately, these considerations still leave a very wide range of elasticities possible. Somewhat arbitrarily, and relying mainly on the slender evidence on elasticities already cited, I shall confine attention in what follows mainly to a value for ϵ' of 6, chosen as my best guess for the average good. This does imply a very sizeable average premium given to output of around 50 per cent, which some may reject as too large to be plausible. I must admit that it does seem large. This may reflect the high level of business confidence in the postwar years; or perhaps the elasticity should be higher and so the premium lower; or there may be some other explanation which I have not found.

The estimates in Table 15.3 have the interesting implication that, whatever is the magnitude of 'market' diminishing returns, 'animal spirits' more or less exactly offset it. This is because, for both countries, it so happens that $\eta + an \approx 1$, as observant readers may already have noticed by adding column (2) in the table to either column (3) or column (4). There is no *necessity* about this, and rough estimates for other periods and countries suggest that it is not always so. I have no good estimates of tax rates for these, and hence do not consider it worth while reproducing my guesses. However, so far as they go, they suggest that, for postwar Japan and continental Europe, the situation was similar to that in the UK and USA. The premium was probably much lower in the UK and Japan before 1939, although not in the USA, where it may even have been higher before 1914. However, all the other determinants of the share of wages in output that were discussed in Chapter 11, such as the availability of cheap food, are relevant, and no firm conclusions can be drawn.

'Animal spirits', *an*, as was pointed out in Chapter 9, not only influence the share of wages in output through their effect on the choice of the labour intensity of investment (equation (15.2)), but also drive companies to accept marginal rates of return on investment below those that would maximize share values. In other words, the marginal return (post all taxes) earned on investment, *r*, is below the shareholders' (post all taxes) rate of discount, r_{sha}. As a result, companies invest more, and grow faster, than their shareholders want them to. Or, at least, this seems to have been the case in the postwar years up to 1973, as we shall see.

If the managements were consistent, they ought to have attached a uniform premium to output, both in selecting the labour intensity of investment (as in equation (15.2)) and in selecting the *amount* of investment. It seems to me that this should require that the marginal rate of return earned on investment (post all taxes) for the shareholder should have been equated to his rate of discount *after* taking account of the premium, *an*. Then, if we make the appropriate modification to *r* in equation (15.1) to allow for the premium on output, this should make it equal to r_{sha}. Hence we should have

$$r_{sha} = (1 - T_s) \left\{ P((\eta + an) q - \lambda l) \left(\frac{\gamma \sigma}{e^{\gamma \sigma} - 1} \right) + g \left(1 - \frac{\gamma \sigma}{e^{\gamma \sigma} - 1} \right) \right\}.$$

(15.7)

Now, following the Ramsey approach, we have (see equation (8.1))

$$r_{sha} = \alpha + \beta (g - g_N).$$

(15.8)

Combining these equations, we already have estimates for the UK and USA in the postwar years for all the magnitudes concerned except for γ, the coefficient of diminishing returns to the rate of investment. Some of these estimates are admittedly shaky, and in particular those of α and β (see Chapter 8) and of T_s. Nevertheless, it seems worth while deriving an estimate of γ in this way, as no other estimates of it are available. The estimates, it should be noted, are *independent* of ϵ' or η. All we require is ($\eta + an$), and this is given in terms of μ, λ, s, and T_s by equation (15.2). So, as long as we can make the consistency assumption just described (i.e. that the same premium, *an*, features in equation (15.7) as in (15.2)), the uncertainty attaching to our estimates of ϵ', and η, and *an* can be ignored. The resulting estimates of γ are 9.87 for the UK and 14.59 for the USA.[21] These estimates are sensitive to the particular values of α, β, and T_s chosen, and, in view of their uncertainty, the footnote shows how small changes in these magnitudes would affect γ for the USA.[22] One cannot attach much

---

[21] See the sources given in the note to Table 15.3
[22] A small (1%) increase in each of α, β, and $(1 - T_s)$ was made and the resulting change in γ calculated keeping all the other relevant magnitudes constant. The resultant estimates of

significance to the difference between the UK and US figures.[23] Of more significance is the fact that both estimates of γ are appreciably greater than our earlier estimate of γ_s, which is consistent with there being an appreciable externality to learning. We return to this later.

The above estimates of γ provide us with all we need to estimate r from equation (15.1) for each value of η, and these estimates are given in columns (5) and (6) of Table 15.3. Because of 'animal spirits', an, all of these rates of return lie below r_{sha}, the shareholders' rate of discount. That has a unique value for each country given by either (15.7) or (15.8), which is 0.055 for the UK and 0.051 for the USA.[24] Naturally, the *extent* of the gap between the two is bigger, the bigger is an (and hence the smaller are η and ϵ'). If ϵ' were infinite, and $\eta = 1$, there would be virtually no gap at all. The firm would not be faced by market diminishing returns, and it would (according to my estimates) then be approximately maximizing share values. This result occurs because of the point already noted, that $\eta + an \approx 1$. So, if $\eta = 1$, $an \approx 0$ and the discrepency between r_{sha} and r is virtually eliminated. Hence the Marris view that managements of firms push investment and growth beyond the point that would best please their shareholders is borne out by my estimates, so long as one takes the view (as I do) that price elasticities of demand confronting firms are appreciably less than infinite.

15.7   Explanation of the excess of the marginal social return over the marginal private return to investment: the optimum rate of growth

We can now draw the different strands of the argument together. Four reasons have been given for the difference between the marginal social

partial derivatives and elasticities were as follows:

$$\frac{\partial \gamma}{\partial \alpha} = -384; \qquad \frac{\alpha}{\gamma}\frac{\partial \gamma}{\partial \alpha} = -0.342$$

$$\frac{\partial \gamma}{\partial \beta} = -9.74; \qquad \frac{\beta}{\gamma}\frac{\partial \gamma}{\partial \beta} = -1.00$$

$$\frac{\partial \gamma}{\partial (1 - T_s)} = 22.5; \qquad \frac{(1 - T_s)}{\gamma}\frac{\partial \gamma}{\partial (1 - T_s)} = 1.09.$$

[23] Perhaps returns diminish more sharply in the USA because that country operates more closely to the frontiers of knowledge than does the UK, where there is still scope for considerable catching-up. My rough guesses suggest that, for Japan, γ was still lower than in the UK in the postwar years.

[24] In reality, different shareholders face different rates of marginal tax, and that alone is enough to lead to different post-tax real rates of discount. Presumably, these are accompanied by different rates of growth of real consumption per head, or by different values of α and β. Here, as elsewhere, I neglect all this and focus on the average. I have taken the marginal tax rates applicable to households (i.e. ignoring pension funds and life insurance) in 1960 in Table 14.2. Since households were not, in general, free to invest as much as they wished in pension funds and life insurance (as legislation limited their ability to exploit the tax advantages), their marginal savings were subject to higher rates of taxation.

return to investment and the marginal private return. Taxation, the learning externality, and the demand externality each tend to reduce the private return in relation to the social return. 'Animal spirits', however, leads to firms behaving as if private returns were higher than they really are. The first three result in the return to the shareholder falling short of the return to society as a whole and so in sub-optimal investment. The fourth, considered by itself, drives investment above what would (if the other three did not exist) be optimal. Since the other three do exist, 'animal spirits' to some extent redress the balance.

My estimates enable me to quantify each of these four factors for the UK and the USA for the postwar years up to 1973. Readers are once again reminded of the tentative nature of these estimates. They are given here at all only because no others are available and in the hope that others will be stimulated to improve upon them. I believe they are interesting, and better than nothing—but unreliable.

From Table 15.1, the marginal social return, r_s, in the postwar years up to 1973 in the UK could be put as high as 0.151 or as low as 0.097. The first of these estimates rests solely on the standard period data and assumes there are no collective physical diminishing returns to the rate of investment. The second is a compromise between the standard period data and estimates based on the conventional ratio of net profits to net capital stock, as well as allowing for some diminishing returns. To simplify matters I shall, in what follows, use an intermediate estimate which is based on the standard period data but allows for diminishing returns, as in column (2) of Table 15.1. This is 0.123 for the UK and 0.130 for the USA.

Taking $\alpha = 0.013$ and $\beta = 1.5$, on the basis of the estimates described in Chapter 8, and using equation (15.8), the marginal after-tax return to a typical shareholder household in the period, r_{sha}, averages 0.055 for the UK and 0.051 for the USA.[25] Hence the gap to be explained is 0.068 for the UK and 0.079 for the USA. Both gaps are large, and Table 15.4 presents an analysis of them.

The allocation of responsibility for the gap between the four factors is inevitably somewhat arbitrary, and the method used is explained in the note to the table. It is essentially the same as that used in Table 15.5, which is described below (that being a more important table). It is obvious that the magnitude of the demand externality, and of the approximately offsetting 'animal spirits' effect, depends crucially on one's view of the size of the

---

[25] These values of r_{sha} differ from those in Table 8.1, which are rather lower. The values in the text here are consistent with the model in Appendix C to this chapter, and assume steady growth, with take-out growing at the same rate as output, whereas in Chapter 8 the (lower) actual average real rate of growth of dividends (without deducting g_N) is used. There are also differences in tax rates. In the text here, T_s is the estimate for households from Chapter 14. This includes an allowance for company taxes based on 1960 tax rates. In Chapter 8, since the estimates are based on actual dividends, no estimate of company tax rates is required.

Table 15.4 Analysis of the excess of r_s over r_{sha}

	UK 1951–73	USA 1948–73
(1) Marginal social return, r_s	0.123	0.130
(2) *less* marginal taxation (net of borrowing gain)	−0.026	−0.028
(3) *less* learning, etc., externality	−0.044	−0.054
(4) *less* demand externality	−0.036	−0.032
(5) *plus* 'animal spirits'	+0.039	+0.035
(6) equals marginal after-tax return to typical shareholder, r_{sha}	0.055	0.051

Note
There is no uniquely correct way to allocate responsibility for the gap between r_s and r_{sha} between the four factors, since the order in which they are taken determines their effects. It may be noted that the formula for r_{sha}, (15.7), is equivalent to that for r_s (15.4), provided that (i) $T_s = 0$; (ii) $\gamma = \gamma_s$; (iii) $\eta = 1$; and (iv) $an = 0$. Accordingly, the difference made when each of these four assumptions was held, instead of keeping T_s, γ, η, and an at their actual estimated values, was calculated. In each case only one variable was changed, the others being kept at their actual estimated values. Thus, four effects were calculated. Another four effects were calculated by starting at the other end, and finding the difference made to r_s when, for example, T_s was given its actual value instead of 0, and likewise for the other three. The arithmetic average of each pair of differences was then found, and these (after slight adjustment) are shown above. Their sum was close to the actual total difference between r_s and r_{sha}. Throughout, it was assumed that $\epsilon' = 6$.

typical price elasticity of demand, ϵ'. In the table, this is assumed to be 6. Higher values would reduce the importance of both of these factors—to vanishing point if $\epsilon' \longrightarrow \infty$. While I have selected what I believe is a reasonable estimate of ϵ', other values are also reasonable. However, the effects shown in rows (2) and (3) would not be altered if different values of ϵ' were chosen. All that would happen is that rows (4) and (5) would alter, but not their sum.

Before commenting on Table 15.4, it is useful to consider another way of measuring the effects of the four factors, as this leads us directly to an estimate of the optimum growth rate. I define this as the growth rate that would occur if the four variables I have isolated all took optimum values.[26] If we can assume that taxation of saving could be eliminated, and replaced by additional taxation of labour and of capitalists' consumption with negligible effects on growth or on the level of output,[27] then the optimum level of T_s would be 0, provided that, in addition, the other three variables

[26] This may not be practically possible, for reasons discussed later in the chapter. The 'optimum' growth rate is then merely a convenient point of reference, and a system is not condemned just because it fails to achieve that growth rate. The relevant question is whether or not it does better than some other achievable system. See the pertinent comparison of the 'nirvana' and 'comparative institution' approaches by Demsetz (1969).

[27] See the discussion in Chapter 14.

could somehow be optimized. If the learning externality could somehow be internalized, then the only remaining causes of physical diminishing returns to investment would be those that apply to investment as a whole. Then we would have $\gamma = \gamma_s$. If product markets could be perfected so that no price cuts were needed to increase sales by an individual firm, then $\eta = 1$.[28] Finally, 'animal spirits' would have to disappear, so that managements faithfully reflected the preferences of their shareholders and maximized share values; so $an = 0$.

In order to estimate what the rate of growth would become if all these conditions were simultaneously fulfilled, I have used the model developed in Chapter 8. The details are set out in Appendix C to this chapter. As well as estimating the optimum rate of growth, I have used the model to allocate responsibility for the gap between the optimum rate of growth and the actual rate of growth to each of the four factors. This allocation is inevitably somewhat arbitrary, since the factors interact. Thus, one can work out the increase in the actual growth rate that would occur if, for example, all taxes on savings were abolished, so that $T_s = 0$. One can also work out the increase in the actual growth rate if $\gamma = \gamma_s$, or if $\eta = 1$, or if $an = 0$ (a reduction rather than an increase in this case). But the sum of these separate four effects falls a good deal short of their combined effect on growth. Alternatively, one can work out the *reduction* from optimum growth that would occur if T_s took its actual value instead of 0. One can also work out the reduction from optimum growth if $\gamma_s = \gamma$, or if η or an took their actual estimated values (with the increase in an increasing growth). In this case the sum of the four separate effects adds up to much more than the total effect when all four are changed simultaneously. In Table 15.5 I have simply taken the arithmetic average of each pair of effects, which, with a slight adjustment, adds up to the total effect. This method of allocation is essentially the same as that followed in Table 15.4.

As in Table 15.4, I have assumed that $\epsilon' = 6$, and this assumption is crucial in determining the effects of the demand factor and the 'animal spirits' factor; but their combined effect, and so the optimum rate of growth and the effects of taxation and learning, would be unchanged if we were to assume that ϵ' took some other value. So long as we keep the sum of η and an unchanged, the results are unchanged.[29]

All the estimates are, as has been repeatedly stressed, very tentative. Taking them as they stand, they point to the following conclusions (the results for both countries being remarkably similar).[30]

---

[28] I do not assume that selling costs can be eliminated, but the result that $\eta = 1$ follows if there are constant returns in selling expenditures.

[29] This is because, in the model set out in Appendix C, it is the *sum* of η and an that appears in equations (15.2) and (15.7). η appears by itself in equation (15.1) which determines r, but that affects nothing else.

[30] This is partly, of course, simply the consequence of the assumptions. Thus I have assumed the same values of η, α, and β for each country. Other similarities, however, reflect reality rather than just assumptions.

Table 15.5   Estimated effects of four factors on growth

	UK 1951–73	USA 1948–73
(1) Optimum growth rate	0.045	0.054
(2) *less* effect of taxing saving	−0.006	−0.006
(3) *less* effect of learning etc. externality	−0.012	−0.014
(4) *less* effect of demand externality	−0.008	−0.006
(5) *plus* effect of animal spirits	0.007	0.005
(6) equals actual growth rate	0.027	0.033

Note

The optimum growth rate and the effects of the four factors were all calculated using the model set out in Appendix C to this chapter. The optimum growth rate is found by setting $T_s = 0$, $\gamma = \gamma_s$, $\eta = 1$, and $an = 0$. The effects of each of the four factors were found by a similar method to that used in Table 15.4. Again, there is no uniquely correct way of allocating responsibility for the gap between optimum and actual growth. The difference made to actual growth when each of the above four variables was given the 'optimum' value specified was calculated, in each case the other three variables being held at their actual estimated values. Another four effects were calculated by starting at the other end, and finding the difference made to the optimum growth rate when, for example, T_s was given its actual value instead of 0, and likewise for the other three. The arithmetic average of each pair of differences was then found, and these (after slight adjustment) are shown above. Their sum was close to the total difference between optimum and actual growth. Throughout, it was assumed that $\epsilon' = 6$.

First, and most importantly, the saver's return in Table 15.4 is a long way below the social return from investment at the margin. In optimum growth this gap is closed, and, since the coefficient of collective physical diminishing returns to the rate of investment is not particularly high ($\gamma_s = 2.97$ for the UK and 2.98 for the USA: see Table 15.1), and since the estimate of the elasticity of marginal utility of consumption with respect to increases in consumption is also not particularly high ($\beta = 1.5$: see Chapter 8), the closing of the gap is accompanied by a large increase in the rate of investment and in the rate of growth, with only a moderate fall in the marginal rate of return.[31] From Table 15.5 it can be seen that the rate of growth increases from 0.027 to 0.045 in the UK, and from 0.033 to 0.054 in the USA. These are big increases. It is interesting that the optimum rate of growth of ouput per worker (i.e. $g - g_N$) is about the same for each country, since the rate of growth of workers is about 0.009 faster in the USA than in the UK. The increase in the rate of investment required to procure this is from 0.18 to 0.39 as a share of output in the UK, and from 0.14 to 0.42 in the USA. Investment thus has to increase to rates well above the highest covered by our data (which is 0.32 for Japan in 1961–73).

---

[31] In optimum growth, the marginal social and private return is 0.083 for the UK and 0.082 for the USA. The rates are similar in the two countries because, as noted in the text, the rates of growth of output per worker are similar, and because α and β are assumed to be the same.

Furthermore, this rise in the share of investment requires a very big rise in the share of profits and fall in that of wages: down from 0.72 to 0.55 for the UK, and from 0.73 to 0.51 for the USA. Although these shares of profits and wages would have looked normal in the UK, and probably in Japan as well, in the nineteenth century, it is hard to imagine that they could come about today. Nevertheless, they would, of course, be accompanied by very rapidly growing real wage rates. The rate of growth of real wages per worker would go up from 0.028 to 0.046 in the UK, and from 0.025 to 0.046 in the USA. The sacrifice made by wage-earners of about a quarter or more (after allowing for tax: see below) of their present wages would enable them to receive much higher wages subsequently, and there would be very substantial increases in their wealth, measured as the discounted present value of their future wages. The wealth of capitalists would also increase so long as the bulk of the tax on savings was shifted on to labour and not on to capitalists' consumption.[32] The tax revenues share in the general increase in growth, and hence so do government expenditures. The benefits from this should be taken into account. It is assumed that any extra taxation of labour does not affect its supply.[33]

Whether this large increase in the growth rate is either desirable or feasible raises issues that go well beyond the scope of this chapter, or the book as a whole. Some further remarks on feasibility are given below, as we now turn to consider the four factors that have been isolated in Tables 15.4 and 15.5.

[32] Using the rate of discount ruling with optimum growth to calculate wealth both before and after the change, the wealth of workers and capitalists can be estimated as follows, expressed as ratios to current GDP in NRB:

	UK		USA	
	'Now'	'Optimum growth'	'Now'	'Optimum growth'
Workers	12.8	14.7	14.8	18.4
Capitalists (excl. tax on savings)	0.7	1.6	1.5	2.4
Tax (assuming revenues share in general growth)	1.1	1.7	1.2	2.1

These are the discounted values of future streams of wages (before deducting any taxes) and capitalists' take-out and tax (on savings initially), assuming steady growth. Wage-earners are assumed to consume all their wages, and capitalists are assumed all to be shareholders. No allowance is made for other taxes on wages or capitalists' consumption, and all the revenues, and so government expenditures, are implicitly assumed to maintain constant shares of income. Borrowing is neglected, the whole of T_s being regarded as a tax.

[33] See the discussion in Section 14.2, where it is concluded that high taxes on wages are likely to reduce human investment and so to reduce g_L. The effect may be rather small, especially in view of the much larger tax base of wages than of savings. Thus income from employment in non-residential business was five times as big as investment in the USA in 1948–73. A given reduction in tax rates on savings would then result in a much smaller increase in tax rates on wages, with total tax revenue unchanged. Nevertheless, the estimates do exaggerate the increase in growth somewhat on this account.

This brings us to the second conclusion to be drawn from the estimates, which is that taxation and borrowing together account for little more than a third of the difference between social and private marginal rates of return. Likewise, they explain little more than a third of the gap between optimum and actual growth rates. However, the elimination of taxation of savings is probably the single most feasible way of stimulating growth in the long term which is open to governments, since it is not easy to see how the other obstacles to achieving optimal growth could be overcome. As was noted in Chapter 14, the substitution of expenditure taxes for income taxes has been advocated by various writers and committees, and this would exempt savings from tax, while still leaving labour and capitalists' consumption taxed. The increase in growth obtained by eliminating the tax on savings (assuming 1960 tax rates as in Table 15.5) would not be quite as much as the 0.6 per cent per annum shown in Table 15.5 if this were the *only* change made. As already pointed out, the changes of all four factors reinforce each other. If the tax on savings alone were eliminated, the increase in the growth rate would be around $\frac{1}{2}$ per cent per annum in both the UK and the USA according to my model. This requires an increase in the share of investment of 5 percentage points, which would be accompanied by a rise in the (pre-tax) share of wages of about 3 percentage points and, of course, by an increase in the rate of growth of real wages per worker of about $\frac{1}{2}$ per cent per annum. Even if all the tax on savings were transferred to labour, and even if one ignores the benefit resulting from the faster growing government expenditure made possible if tax revenues share in the general growth, labour's wealth would be substantially increased, as would that of capitalists.[34]

These estimates of the benefits flowing from the replacement of taxes on savings by taxes on labour (and capitalists' consumption) are considerably larger than those made by some earlier writers.[35] Reviewing this work in the

[34] A similar calculation to that in fn. 32, but using the rate of discount ruling after taxes on saving are eliminated with the other three factors unchanged from their estimated actual levels, gives the following results for wealth, expressed as ratios to current GDP in NRB:

	UK		USA	
	'Now'	'No tax on savings'	'Now'	'No tax on savings'
Workers	19.8	23.7	28.9	36.9
Capitalists (excl. tax on savings)	1.1	1.4	2.9	3.4
Tax (assuming revenues share in general growth)	1.8	2.1	2.4	3.0

[35] See Boskin (1978) and Feldstein (1978). Both of these writers estimated the annual welfare gains resulting from removing the tax on saving in the USA at about $50–$60 billion. This is equivalent to about 4% of my definition of income in US non-residential business in 1977. Assuming that the benefit were to remain a constant proportion of that income, and that it grew at the average rate applicable to 1948–73 of 0.03352 p.a., and discounting it at the rate of

context of a life-cycle savings model, King concluded that the optimality of an expenditure tax (i.e. a system that did *not* tax saving) depended sensitively on the parameters of the model, about which little firm information was available. It was difficult to argue strongly for either an income tax or an expenditure tax on efficiency grounds, and the main argument in favour of the latter was that given in the Meade Report (Institute for Fiscal Studies 1978) that

it represents the only practicable alternative to the present mess, which has arisen, at least partly, from an unworkable distinction between capital and income. To bolster this argument the Meade Committee has drawn attention to the enormous range of effective tax rates on capital income according to the type of asset and financial medium through which savings are channelled'. (King 1980, 32)

The existence of this 'enormous range' was further documented in King and Fullerton (1984) and is referred to in Chapter 14. While agreeing that its removal, and the resultant simplification of the tax system, and its inflation-proofing, constitute powerful arguments for expenditure taxation, I would also maintain that there are likely to be substantial benefits to growth as well. King's life-cycle model makes it uncertain whether the rate of saving will rise or fall when taxes on savings are reduced, but reasons for rejecting such a model were given in Chapter 8. King's growth model makes the rate of growth in the long run independent of the rate of investment, and that also must be rejected. King's scepticism is thus not well founded, although I must admit that my own estimates are very uncertain.

My third conclusion is that the remaining factors explaining the gap between marginal social and private returns, and that between the optimum and actual growth rate, account for most of these gaps. Both Tables 15.4 and 15.5 show the learning externality as the most important factor, and the demand externality and 'animal spirits' approximately cancelling each other out. It must be admitted that these are all very shaky estimates. However, what is less shaky is that there is a large gap between the marginal social and private returns still to be explained *after* we have allowed for taxation and borrowing. It also seems likely that, if whatever is responsible for this gap could be eliminated, the rate of growth would rise appreciably. Whether I have attributed the right proportions to the three remaining factors is more doubtful, and it is possible that there is some other factor I have neglected which provides an important part of the explanation. However, as I have been unable to identify any other such factor, I will proceed as if it did not exist.

discount used in fn. 34, 0.058, it amounts to about twice annual income in US non-residential business. In contrast, my estimate of the present value of the benefits is about nine times such income (see fn. 34). Both of the writers cited assumed that the benefits would accrue as a result of a better allocation of consumption over individuals' lifetimes. Neither allowed for any increase in the long-term rate of growth.

There are some well-known ways in which the loss of growth arising from the learning externality can be reduced. These include the subsidization of basic research, and also of some applied research and development, the use of patents, providing extension services and common research facilities, and the encouragement of exchanges of information through conferences, productivity missions, and other visits. Governments have also from time to time attempted to subsidize or otherwise encourage the use of new technologies, or so-called 'high technology' industries. In developing countries, laws that favour investment in 'new and necessary industries' are often to be found. While these and similar measures can be important and helpful, one may still question whether they do more than scratch the surface of a problem to which no simple or easy solution may exist.[36] Increasing the average size of firms may help to internalize more of what would otherwise be an externality, but this encounters at least two serious disadvantages. It may reduce competition, thus (in terms of our four factors) reducing γ only at the cost of also reducing η. It may also lead to bureaucracy, over-centralization, and so inefficiency.[37] Some big firms have, in fact, preferred to avoid the latter disadvantage by creating independent profit centres and encouraging them to compete. They may also, however, maintain central research and advisory facilities, and the central management is in a position to apply lessons learned in one part of the business to other parts. They may then be able to get some of the best of both worlds. But there clearly is an inherent conflict between the advantages to be gained by decentralization of decision-making with competition, and those flowing from the freer exchange of information and so better scope for learning which single ownership and control can provide. While there are ways of lessening this conflict, perhaps it can never be altogether avoided and some compromise solution is the best available.[38]

[36] The existence of the learning externality, and of an excess of social over private benefit from private expenditure on R&D expenditure, has been long known, although the literature has mainly referred to such expenditure, whereas the point is made here that all investment expenditure creates externalities of this kind to a greater or lesser extent. For an early discussion, see Pigou (1932, 185). A more recent and extended analysis is by Arrow (1962a). This was criticized by Demsetz (1969). For an economic analysis of the patent system, see Taylor and Silberston (1973). An extensive discussion of governmental policies towards R&D and science generally is in the various OECD *Reviews of National Science Policy*. See, in particular, that for the United States, 1968. An extract from it, together with the articles by Arrow and Demsetz and other interesting articles and bibliography, are in Lamberton (1971).

[37] Kamien and Schwartz (1982) conclude: 'Empirical studies over the last fifteen years have consistently shown that, although there may sometimes be certain advantages of size in exploiting the fruits of R&D, it is more efficiently done in small or medium-size firms than in large ones' (p. 66).

[38] For a recent survey of the relationship between competition, monopoly, and innovation, see Kamien and Schwartz (1982), which takes as its main starting point J. A. Schumpeter's three books (1934, 1939, and 1950). The issues were discussed in Richardson (1960), and they are also treated more briefly in the articles by Arrow and Demsetz mentioned in the preceding footnote.

My method of estimation has resulted in the last two of my four factors—that is, the demand externality resulting from imperfect markets (η < 1) and 'animal spirits' (an > 0)—approximately offsetting each other. This is because, in equation (15.2), the values of the known variables (μ, λ, s, and T_s) are such for both the UK and the USA that $\eta + an \approx 1$. So, if both took their optimum values, with $\eta = 1$ and $an = 0$, little would change. That does *not* imply that we can simply forget both of them. Their offsetting may be due to chance, and it is also possible that my estimates are at fault. It could be that $\eta < 1$, which explains most of the gap between marginal social and private returns not arising from taxation. The learning externality might in reality be quite minor (i.e. $\gamma \approx \gamma_s$) and an might also be quite small, and so might fail to offset the demand externality effect.

While this possibility must be admitted, one would then have to find some other explanation for the observed relation beween μ, λ, s, and T_s in equation (15.2), or would have to change the estimates of one or more of these magnitudes. Further research on all this is desirable, but for the present I proceed on the assumption that the estimates of γ, η, and an are broadly correct.

There may, indeed, be a real causal link between η and an which results in a tendency for the one to offset the other. This would be a happy result if it were true. The link could occur in the following ways. Consider a firm that strengthens its monopolistic position by gaining a larger share of its market, or in some other way: η then will fall, and the firm's marginal rate of return will fall in relation to its average, and the firm will also be inclined to choose less labour-intensive (and so output-increasing) investments (if it wants to maximize its share value). Two important effects will follow. First, since the share of profits devoted to investment will fall, the firm's pay-out ratio (i.e. the ratio of dividends to net profit after tax) will increase. Second, the share of wages in value added by the firm will fall. The first effect relaxes the constraint that shareholders place upon the firm's conduct. Instead of paying out what management could regard as unnecessarily generous dividends, the profits could be retained and invested by the firm, thus driving the marginal return further below the rate of return received by shareholders. The second effect could meet with resistance by the firm's work-force. Furthermore, with shareholders kept happy by sufficiently generous dividends, the management may be just as anxious to keep the work-force happy by avoiding redundancies. It may also derive a sense of power and achievement from expanding output and employment. All of this, in terms of our model, amounts to an increase in 'animal spirits' an, which at least partially offsets the fall in η.

There is another way of looking at the question which points to a similar answer. The logic of maxization means that it is *marginal* costs and benefits, *marginal* rates of return in relation to *marginal* rates of discount, which ought to count in decision-making. However, all published accounts, and most of the figures available to decision-makers, refer to *average* costs and benefits. It is not at all easy to find out what a firm's marginal return on investment is, but an average return can be calculated. Likewise, the average cost of capital and the average cost of labour are calculable, while marginal costs may not be, or not easily so. Decision-makers may therefore have to operate with hard information on average magnitudes, but only rough judgements on marginal ones. Shareholders, and others who monitor firms' performance, have even less information at their disposal than managements. Judged by its performance in terms of average rates of return and average shares of wages, a firm with a low η offset by a high *an* will be indistinguishable from another with a high η and a low *an*. The two firms will, in reality, be confronted by very different investment opportunities and marginal value products of labour, but that will be, at best, known only to their managements. To their shareholders and work-force, they will appear to be performing similarly, and so it is possible that that is how, in the end, they will indeed perform. That may be how market forces really operate.

If lower η is offset by higher *an*, can the same be said of higher γ? In Table 15A.1 of Appendix C to this chapter I have worked out the effects of small changes in η, *an*, and γ (as well as other exogenous variables and parameters) on the endogenous variables of the system, using the model there described, which is also that used to construct Table 15.5. It can be seen that the effects of changes in η and *an* exactly match each other (apart from their effects on r). It can also be seen that, for some variables, higher *an* would also tend to offset higher γ, but there is not the same matching as with η.

A rise in γ (just like a fall in η) tends to reduce growth g, the share of investment, s, and the shareholders' return, r_{sha}. All these changes, whether arising from a rise in γ or a fall in η, could be offset by a rise in *an*. However, the required rise in *an* would increase the share of wages, λ, and cut the payout ratio, *po*, both by substantial amounts, in the case of a rise in γ. In the case of a fall in η, on the contrary, λ and *po* would end up unchanged. Hence shareholders' and workers' positions would be affected in the one case and not in the other. In so far as managements respond to, and are monitored by, average magnitudes such as the payout ratio and the share of wages, there is thus more reason to believe that 'animal spirits' will tend to offset monopoly than that they will tend to offset physical diminishing returns to the rate of investment.

The upshot of the above discussion is that there are some reasons for believing that 'animal spirits' naturally tend to offset market, but not physical, diminishing returns, with the policy implication that the two main obstacles in the way of achieving optimal growth are taxation and the learning externality. Nevertheless, I would not want to press the argument so far as to conclude that market diminishing returns and the demand externality can be safely neglected. Monopolists may pursue other objectives besides the growth of output (see Williamson 1967, 169), and an increase in the degree of monopoly might lead to that best of all monopolistic rents—a quiet life—and thus to low investment and growth. Policies that increase competition, or at least maintain it at a reasonably high level, are safer.

Given the externalities described above, it is natural to ask whether investment should not be subsidized. Using the model in Appendix C to this chapter, it can be calculated that a subsidy of about 60 per cent to investment in the UK, and of about 50 per cent in the USA, would suffice to procure the optimum rate of growth.[39] However, there are some objections to paying such a high rate of subsidy.

In the first place, in these estimates I have treated investments as if they were homogeneous with respect to their learning externalities. It seems unlikely that they are even approximately so. It seems probable, for example, that more could be learned, and was learned, from Henry Ford's first use of assembly methods to make motor cars, and the factory he constructed, to do this, than from the houses in a typical suburban housing estate. The learning externality to R&D expenditures, and to basic research in particular, is probably especially large. It is, no doubt, the realization of the heterogeneity of investments in this respect that has led governments to discriminate in their tax and subsidy treatment of different types of investment. Their attempts to spot the winners were probably not very successful, since it is so difficult to predict the consequences of innovations. Indeed, if my theory of growth is true, it is to some degree impossible. We can only choose current investments in the light of what we already know, and by changing the world we alter what is known and reveal hitherto unknown opportunities. A uniform subsidy on all investment would thus over-subsidize some while leaving others under-subsidized. Investment choices, and so growth, could still be further improved in principle, and would not have been optimized.[40] Governments granting the subsidy would be aware of all this, and would inevitably seek to avoid uncalled-for subsidies here, while giving generous subsidies there. Special pleading and political favouritism could hardly be avoided, and inefficiency on a large scale might be the result. A zero tax and subsidy avoids many of these

[39] If the model is run with $1 - T_s = 1.6$ for the UK, or 1.5 for the USA, the variables g, s, μ, r_{sha}, r_s, and ϱ all take their optimum values; λ and po are both appreciably higher, and r somewhat lower.

[40] But what does optimization mean? An infeasible solution can hardly be an optimum one, and it is very difficult to say what degree of discrimination in subsidization would *in practice* improve matters. See fn. 26 above.

dangers, as well as eliminating administrative costs, and, given our ignorance, has much to recommend it.

Second, while I have neglected the adverse effects of raising taxes elsewhere to compensate for the loss of taxes on savings, there would be some losses, and these would increase, per pound of extra cost, as the subsidy grew larger.

Finally, even with a uniform subsidy to investment, it would not be easy to establish what the best subsidy rate would be, or precisely what expenditures should qualify. The line between maintenance and investment expenditures is not always easy to draw (see Chapter 1). The practical problems of administering a sizeable subsidy might be severe.

My conclusion is, therefore, that there is a good case for eliminating existing taxes on savings and investment,[41] but less to be said for subsidies. The learning externality is perhaps best tackled by the types of measures discussed earlier (p. 454) and the demand externality by measures to promote competition, although it is possible that some of the benefits flowing from that will be offset by a decline in 'animal spirits'.

There is one further means to increase savings and investment which must be considered. If private savings are sub-optimal for one reason or another, can they not be supplemented by public savings?[42] The proposition that public savings contribute to total national savings has, however, been disputed. It has been argued that the actions of the public sector will be offset by reactions in the private. Suppose, for example, that a given increase in expenditure on defence is financed by (a) raising extra taxation or (b) borrowing. Consider a closed economy, and assume that, after the process of adjustment is completed, the ratio of output to capacity is the same under both options. Government saving will be higher under (a) than (b), but will national saving? Some would argue that it would be higher, although admittedly not as much as the difference in government saving. Somehow, resources have to be freed for defence expenditure. Under (a), most of the work is done by the extra taxation, and this will impinge mainly on private consumption. There may be some rise in the price level and in

---

[41] This is quite consistent with leaving the proceeds of *past* investment taxed. A uniform expenditure tax would subject expenditure financed by income from past investment to taxation, while exempting current and future saving from tax.

[42] I avoid discussion here of the best way to measure the budget surplus or deficit in order to gauge its effect on total investment in the non-residential business sector, which is the main concern of this book. There are several difficult questions involved. For example, should one measure the current surplus or the surplus available after financing public sector investment? If the former, how far are expenditures for health and education, for example, to count as capital rather than current? If the latter, should investment by public enterprises in the non-residential business sector be excluded from public sector investment? What allowance should be made for future liabilities for social security? How should the published accounts be adjusted for inflation? For a useful discussion of these and other issues, some touched on briefly later in the text, see papers in the Symposium on Government Borrowing and Economic Policy (1985).

interest rates (the money supply being held constant under both options), and so some fall in private investment and savings, but there will be less than under (b). Under that option, most of the work of freeing resources has to be done by higher prices and interest rates, and so private investment will fall more and so too must national savings. This, I think could be regarded as the orthodox view, and the view implicit in most econometric forecasting models. Government borrowing is less deflationary than taxation.

However, it has been pointed out that taxpayers could well anticipate that borrowing would lead to higher taxes in the future to pay interest on the loans and perhaps to repay the loans themselves. The discounted value of these future tax payments could be as big as the extra taxation raised under (a). Rational taxpayers might then react to borrowing in just the same way as to extra taxation, and the effects of (a) and (b) on national saving and investment would then be the same.[43]

There are reasons for thinking that this is an extreme conclusion, however. Perhaps the main reason in most peoples' minds is a simple disbelief that taxpayers behave in the way supposed, however, rational it might be to do so. Some convincing empirical support for the 'Ricardian[44] equivalence theorem' is needed, but, so far as I am aware, is lacking. Political leaders in a democracy commonly believe that it is difficult to raise taxes in order to reduce a budget deficit, which suggests that *they* at least do not think that taxpayers regard taxation and borrowing as equivalent. Many taxpayers have no or very little marketable wealth throughout their lives. They spend all their net receipts more or less as they get them. Extra taxation reduces their spending, but a vision of extra taxation to come does not. Furthermore, borrowing need not result in higher taxation in the future, but could result instead, at least to some extent, in lower

[43] See Barro (1974) for an ingenious exposition of this point of view which also deals with some counter-arguments.

[44] See Ricardo (1951, I, 244-9, IV, 185-200). While Ricardo pointed out that the payment of taxes to finance a war was equivalent (in present-value terms) to the subsequent payment of taxes to pay interest on debt incurred for the same object, he did *not*, so it seems to me, believe that the two systems of finance would have the same effects, or that they were equally beneficial. On the contrary, he firmly asserted that taxation was to be preferred to borrowing, and that the latter would reduce saving and 'blind us to our real situation':

From what I have said, it must not be inferred that I consider the system of borrowing as the best calculated to defray the extraordinary expenses of the State. It is a system which tends to make us less thrifty—to blind us to our real situation. If the expenses of war be 40 millions per annum, and the share which a man would have to contribute towards that annual expense were 100 l. from his income. By the system of loans, he is called upon to pay only the interest of this 100 l., or 5 l. per annum, and considers that he does enough by saving his 5 l. from his expenditure, and then deludes himself with the belief, that he is as rich as before. (Ricardo 1951, I, 247)

It is clear that the authority of Ricardo cannot be cited in favour of the practical truth of the equivalence theorem.

government expenditure. It is hard to see why the private sector should curb its expenditure now because it expects cuts in defence expenditure, let us say, in the future. Other counter-arguments have been put forward to which readers may refer.[45]

My own belief is that government saving does indeed contribute to national saving, and that, since investment is sub-optimal for the reasons already given, there is a case for increasing it. If the proceeds of budget surpluses are used to retire public debt, the destination of the extra savings will be left to private savers to determine, so that there is no necessary implication that the choice of investments will then be made by the government, to which some would object. Some other means would be needed when the debt was eliminated, but I expect that that bridge will not be crossed for quite some time.

Appendix A: The social rate of return

In this appendix, I prove the formula for the social rate of return to investment. The externalities that may pertain to an individual firm's investment can be internalized if we consider a closed economy in which all firms increase their rate of investment together. As in the appendix to Chapter 7, I assume that there are 'physical' diminishing returns to this collective increase in the rate of investment, so that the radius of the marginal *social* investment contour, ϱ_{ms}, shrinks by an amount given by

$$\varrho_{ms} = \bar{\varrho}_0 e^{-\gamma_s \sigma}. \tag{15A.1}$$

In this formula, and in what follows, I define $\sigma \equiv S/Q$ as the real, tax-exclusive, rate of investment. The coefficient γ_s, which determines the amount by which ϱ_{ms} shrinks for a given increase in σ, is not necessarily equal to γ, the corresponding coefficient for the individual firm in (7A.2). This is because the learning externality discussed in Chapter 15 has now been internalized. Consequently, one would expect that γ_s would be smaller than γ.[46]

I first explain how γ_s has been estimated. In the appendix to Chapter 7, equation (7A.3) gives the relation between the radius of the average IPC, ϱ, and that of the IPC with zero investment, ϱ_0, for an individual firm. Since I assume that a similar functional relationship applies for collective investment as for individual investment

---

[45] See Buchanan (1976) and the works there cited. It is noteworthy that Tobin (1964, 10) explicitly considered the possibility that increased public saving would be offset by reduced private saving, only to reject it when discussing governmental measures to promote growth.

[46] It might be, though, that a collective increase in the rate of investment would result in bottlenecks appearing in the investment goods industries, which would be more severe than if an individual firm were to increase investment. However, the analysis seeks to determine the marginal *long-term* yield to investment, and it therefore seems right to assume that the investment goods industries have time to adapt (and, in effect, foresee) the increased demand placed upon them. Here, as elsewhere, we are not concerned with short-term investment behaviour.

(i.e. since (15A.1) has the same functional form as (7A.2)), a similar equation to (7A.3) can be derived, namely:

$$\varrho = \frac{\bar{\varrho}_0}{\sigma} \left(\frac{1 - e^{-\gamma_s \sigma}}{\gamma_s} \right). \tag{15A.2}$$

Here, all the variables refer to all firms taken together, and it is assumed that the investments of all change together. If we then differentiate this with respect to the rate of collective investment, σ, we obtain, after suitable rearrangement,

$$\frac{1}{\varrho} \frac{\partial \varrho}{\partial \sigma} = \frac{\gamma_s}{e^{\gamma_s \sigma} - 1} - \frac{1}{\sigma}. \tag{15A.3}$$

Now we can obtain an estimate of the left-hand side of this equation in the way explained in the text (p. 430). Since we know the average rate of investment, σ, we can then solve the equation for γ_s, and the resulting estimates are given in Table 15.1.

The relation between the radius of the marginal social investment contour, ϱ_{ms}, and the marginal investment contour for the typical firm, ϱ_m, may be briefly considered. Since the firm is *typical*, it must have the same *average* radius as that of all firms taken together, which is ϱ. Now it was shown in the appendix to Chapter 7 that

$$\frac{\varrho_m}{\varrho} = \frac{\gamma \sigma}{e^{\gamma \sigma} - 1}$$

and by similar reasoning it can be shown that

$$\frac{\varrho_{ms}}{\varrho} = \frac{\gamma_s \sigma}{e^{\gamma_s \sigma} - 1}.$$

Now the expression $\gamma \sigma / (e^{\gamma \sigma} - 1)$ is a decreasing function of γ for positive finite values of γ and σ, which are those that concern us. It follows that if $\gamma_s < \gamma$, because of the learning externality, for finite positive values of σ, γ_s, and γ, we must have

$$\varrho_m < \varrho_{ms}.$$

Society as a whole, therefore, invests at the margin on a higher contour than does the individual typical firm, because of the externality. Now if the individual typical firm were to cut back investment to zero by itself, its marginal investment contour would be ϱ_0 (see the appendix to Chapter 7), while from (15A.1) we can see that if all firms together cut back investment to zero their marginal investment contour would be $\bar{\varrho}_0$. The relation between ϱ_0 and $\bar{\varrho}_0$ depends on the rate of investment of all firms taken together. Let us now call that rate $\bar{\sigma}$ and distinguish it from the rate of investment of the individual (and otherwise typical) firm, which is σ. It can easily be proved that

$$\frac{\varrho_0}{\bar{\varrho}_0} = \left(\frac{1 - e^{-\gamma_s \bar{\sigma}}}{\gamma_s} \right) \div \left(\frac{1 - e^{-\gamma \bar{\sigma}}}{\gamma} \right) \tag{15A.4}$$

The expression $(1 - e^{-\gamma \sigma})/\gamma$ is a decreasing function of γ for positive finite values of σ and γ. It follows that, if $\gamma_s < \gamma$, $\varrho_0 > \bar{\varrho}_0$. Hence, if the individual firm cuts back investment, it eventually confines itself to investment opportunities that are better than those that would rule if all firms cut back investment together. This is because, in the latter event, all lose the benefit of learning from each others' investments. If all cut back together, so that $\bar{\sigma} \to 0$, then it can be seen from (15A.4) that $\varrho_0 \to \bar{\varrho}_0$. Each firm thus faces a deterioration of its investment opportunities when all cut back, and an improvement when all increase investment together.[47]

This digression should have clarified the way in which the assumed functional relations relate to the learning externality. We now return to the derivation of the formula for the marginal social rate of return. We follow the same type of argument as proof no. 1 in Chapter 7, and so consider what happens when all firms together increase their rate of investment by a small amount, $\delta\sigma$, for a short interval, δt, and then relapse back to steady growth. The extra investment takes place at the marginal investment contour, ϱ_{ms}, and if it took place on the same ray from the origin as average investment, whose characteristics are (q, l), then the characteristics of this marginal investment would be simply ϱ_{ms}/ϱ times those of average investment. There is, however, an important difference between the collective increase in investment we are now considering and an increase by an individual firm. Since I assume that the rate of growth of total labour input in the whole economy is given,[48] it is not possible for the additional investment to have the marginal characteristics just described. In fact, there has to be a small increase in the wage rate sufficient to reduce the labour intensity of all investment occurring in the interval δt so that the growth of labour input is unaffected, despite the higher rate of investment. Let us suppose that the *average* characteristics of investment are thereby changed to $(q - \delta q, l - \delta l)$, while the *marginal* characteristics are the average ones multiplied by ϱ_{ms}/ϱ.

We can now work out the effect of the additional investment in the rates of output and employment at the end of the short interval. The proportionate increment in output is given by

$$\frac{\delta Q}{Q} = \left\{ (q - \delta q)\,\sigma + (q - \delta q) \left(\frac{\varrho_{ms}}{\varrho} \right) \delta\sigma - \sigma q \right\} \delta t.$$

In effect, there are three parts: the increment arising from average investment taking place with the new average characteristics, the increment arising from marginal investment, and from the sum of these we must subtract the increment that would have occurred at the old rate of investment with the old average characteristics.

By similar reasoning, we have

$$\frac{\delta L}{L} = \left\{ (l - \delta l)\sigma + (l - \delta l) \left(\frac{\varrho_{ms}}{\varrho} \right) \delta\sigma - \dot{\sigma l} \right\} \delta t.$$

This equals 0, since total labour input growth cannot be affected.

Remembering that $\mu = \delta q/\delta l$ and that $\sigma = Ps$, we can readily obtain

$$\delta Q = PQ\,\delta s\,\delta t(q - \mu l) \, \frac{\varrho_{ms}}{\varrho}.$$

[47] From (15A.4) it can easily be shown that $\partial\varrho_0/\partial\sigma > 0$ as long as $\gamma_s < \gamma$.

[48] Since we are discussing long-term growth, I ignore possible changes in the rate of unemployment.

A proportion s of the increased value of output must be invested to maintain the old rate of growth. Hence the increased rate of consumption at the end of the short interval is

$$\delta C = P \, \delta Q \, (1 - s).$$

The extra consumption sacrificed to obtain δC is measured by the tax-exclusive value of the additional investment, $PQ \, \delta s \, \delta t$, and this must equal the present value of the increased consumption, which is growing at g, discounted at the marginal social rate of return, r_s. If we then divide through by $PQ \, \delta s \, \delta t$, we get

$$1 = \frac{P \, (q - \mu l) \, (\varrho_{ms}/\varrho) \, (1 - s)}{r_s - g}.$$

Remembering that $Psq = g$, we obtain, after rearrangement,

$$r_s = P\{q - \mu \, (1 - s) \, l\} \, \frac{\varrho_{ms}}{\varrho} + g \left(1 - \frac{\varrho_{ms}}{\varrho}\right). \tag{15A.5}$$

Appendix B: The valuation ratio for a growing firm with taxation

In this appendix I examine the effect of taxation on the valuation ratio of a steadily growing firm. I neglect borrowing throughout. Let the pre-tax average rate of return for the firm be r_a, and let the effective rate of tax on investment be T_s; then the average post-tax rate of return received by shareholders is $(1 - T_s)r_a$.[49] If their take-out, after tax, is C, which is growing at g, and if they were to use the average post-tax of return as their rate of discount, then the value of the firm to them would be

$$V = \frac{C}{(1 - T_s) \, r_a - g}. \tag{15A.6}$$

If the net capital stock of the firm is K, I shall show that, on these assumptions, and as long as labour productivity grows,

$$v = \frac{V}{K} < 1. \tag{15A.7}$$

Since the data in Table 15.2 on the whole suggest that $v > 1$, and at any rate that v is not far below 1, it follows that shareholders' discount rate is probably *less* than $(1 - T_s) \, r_a$.

To simplify matters, I assume that there are only two relevant parameters of the tax system: a rate of profits tax of τ, and the present value of tax saved per unit of investment of A through depreciation allowances, etc. Hence the effective tax rate on investment is given by[50]

$$1 - T_s = \frac{1 - \tau}{1 - A}.$$

---

[49] See fn. 50.

[50] See equation (14A.9), when v, f_b, and f_s are all set equal to 0. Note that v in this footnote, and in equation (14A.9), does *not* refer to the valuation ratio.

Take-out after tax is then[51]

$$C = PQ\{(1 - \lambda)(1 - \tau) - s(1 - A)\}.$$

It is shown in Chapter 7 that the net capital stock equals what take-out would be if there were no tax, divided by $(r_a - g)$. Hence

$$K = \frac{PQ(1 - \lambda - s)}{r_a - g}.$$

Substituting in (15A.6) and (15A.7), we then have

$$v = \frac{\{(1 - \lambda)(1 - \tau) - s(1 - A)\}(r_a - g)}{(1 - \lambda - s)\{(1 - T_s)r_a - g\}}$$

$$= (1 - A)\frac{\{(1 - \lambda)(1 - T_s) - s\}(r_a - g)}{(1 - \lambda - s)\{(1 - T_s)r_a - g\}}.$$

If, now, ignoring the factor $(1 - A)$, which lies between 1 and 0, we subtract the denominator from the numerator, we get

$$T_s\{g(1 - \lambda) - r_a s\} = T_s\{g(1 - \lambda) - P(q - \lambda l)s\}$$

$$= T_s\lambda(-g + g_L).$$

Hence, as long as $g > g_L$, that is as long as labour productivity grows, this is a negative quantity, and so the denominator exceeds the numerator even before we have multiplied the numerator by $(1 - A)$. Hence, for a growing firm with growing labour productivity, $v < 1$ on the above assumptions.

Appendix C: Model for the analysis of optimum growth

In this appendix I give the model referred to in the text which underlies the analysis of the factors explaining the gap between actual and optimum growth rates in Table 15.5. It is basically the same one as in Chapter 8, but some of the equations are modified (for example, to allow for physical and market diminishing returns to the rate of investment), and some additional equations are required for additional variables. It is the most realistic (and so also the most complicated) of the models in this book, and I have used it to provide a set of estimates of the effects on growth and other endogenous variables of making small changes in the exogenous variables. This is Table 15A.1, which is useful for purposes of reference. All the estimates in the table refer to the USA 1948–73. It must be emphasized that these estimates are all very uncertain. Furthermore, for the reasons discussed in the text, the exogenous variables cannot really be regarded as being independent of one another. For example, both g_L and g_N are exogenous, but a higher value of g_N would almost certainly result in a higher value of g_L (although the reverse is less likely). In a better model, more equations relating these variables would be given; but that awaits further research.

Throughout the equations that follow, since we are dealing with the whole of non-residential business and with the typical firm in it, we can set $P = 1$ and $\sigma = s$. Nearly all the symbols have been explained in the text and an additional one is

---

[51] I ignore personal income tax, which is an additional tax on take-out, as this does not affect the conclusions.

explained below. (See also the List of Main Abbreviations and Symbols at the front of the book.) The first seven equations of the model are those already given in the text which define r (15.1), r_a (15.3), r_s (15.4), r_{as} (15.5), r_{sha} (15.7), the Ramsey Approach equation (15.8), and the equation for μ (15.2). There is also (15A.2) for ϱ.

There are two equations, similar to (8.3) and (8.4) which relate to the IPC:

$$\frac{q}{\varrho} = a + b \; \frac{l}{\varrho} - c \; \frac{l^2}{\varrho^2}. \tag{15A.8}$$

$$\mu = b - 2c \; \frac{l}{\varrho}. \tag{15A.9}$$

There are two equations which derive from the definitions of q and l:

$$g = sq. \tag{15A.10}$$

$$g_L = sl. \tag{15A.11}$$

Finally, I define an additional variable, po, which is the net payout ratio. This is the ratio of take-out to profits net of both tax and depreciation. The measure of depreciation used is that explained in Chapter 7, but modified to allow for taxation of saving and investment.[52] So:

$$po = \frac{1 - \lambda - s/(1 - T_s)}{1 - \lambda - \dfrac{\lambda \, (g - g_L)}{r_a \, (1 - T_s) - g}}. \tag{15A.12}$$

This formula does not allow for the taxation of capitalists' consumption, but, provided that is a constant proportion of take-out, it does not affect po. The numerator of po is evidently reduced by the taxed proportion, but so is the denominator, since the latter is a measure of the maximum sustainable consumption level if the whole of the firm's income is taken out.

The above 13 equations suffice to determine the 13 endogenous variables:

$$r, r_a, r_s, r_{as}, r_{sha}, \mu, \lambda, \varrho, q, l, g, s, po.$$

The exogenous variables and parameters of the system are:

$$\bar{\varrho}_0, g_L, g_N, T_s, \eta, an, \gamma, \gamma_s, \alpha, \beta, a, b, c.$$

Appendix D: The Golden Rule of Accumulation

The so-called Golden Rule of Accumulation, which has been propounded by several writers,[53] is that the ratio of saving and investment to output should equal the share of profits in output. A related proposition is that the marginal rate of return to capital should equal the rate of growth.

The growth models used to derive the above rules are orthodox in that technical progress is exogenously given, and so the rate of growth is independent of the rate of investment in the long run. The problem of choice is therefore not that selecting the

[52] The modification can be derived from a similar analysis to that given in Chapter 7. One way of expressing it is to say that it is the after-tax average rate of return, $r_a (1 - T_s)$, which is used instead of the average rate of return, r_a.

[53] See Phelps (1961); also Phelps (1966, 3), which lists five other writers who independently derived the 'Rule', and on p. 4 Phelps mentions still others who derived particular cases of it.

Table 15A.1 Estimated effects of exogenous variables in the model

Effect of variable x given below	Base value	Effect on variable given in col. heading									
		g 0.03326		s 0.1421		λ 0.7264		μ 0.8684		r_{sha} 0.0508	
		$\dfrac{\partial g}{\partial x}$ (1)	$\dfrac{x}{g}\dfrac{\partial g}{\partial x}$ (2)	$\dfrac{\partial s}{\partial x}$ (3)	$\dfrac{x}{s}\dfrac{\partial s}{\partial x}$ (4)	$\dfrac{\partial \lambda}{\partial x}$ (5)	$\dfrac{x}{\lambda}\dfrac{\partial \lambda}{\partial x}$ (6)	$\dfrac{\partial \mu}{\partial x}$ (7)	$\dfrac{x}{\mu}\dfrac{\partial \mu}{\partial x}$ (8)	$\dfrac{\partial r_{sha}}{\partial x}$ (9)	$\dfrac{x}{r_{sha}}\dfrac{\partial r_{sha}}{\partial x}$ (10)
(1) $\bar{Q}_0$	3.2182	0.0069	0.6722	0.0072	0.1622	0.0013	0.0059	0.0122	0.0450	0.0104	0.6598
(2) g_L	0.0155	0.7177	0.3354	−1.3481	−0.1474	−0.4471	−0.0096	−2.5190	−0.0451	1.0765	0.3292
(3) g_N	0.0080	0.3969	0.0959	3.5561	0.2012	−3.7944	−0.0420	0.7010	0.0065	−0.9047	−0.1431
(4) $1 - T_s$	0.7050	0.0175	0.3714	0.1572	0.7798	0.0799	0.0776	0.0308	0.0250	0.0263	0.3645
(5) η	0.5495	0.0077	0.1273	0.0690	0.2670	0.7948	0.6013	0.0136	0.0086	0.0116	0.1250
(6) an	0.4885	0.0077	0.1132	0.0691	0.2374	0.7948	0.5348	0.0136	0.0077	0.0116	0.1111
(7) γ	14.5911	−0.0007	−0.2969	−0.0061	−0.6215	0.0064	0.1295	−0.0012	−0.0202	−0.0010	−0.2914
(8) γ_s	2.9831	−0.0015	−0.1322	−0.0015	−0.0322	−0.0003	−0.0012	−0.0026	−0.0090	−0.0022	−0.1298
(9) α	0.0130	−0.2641	−0.1032	−2.3641	−0.2163	2.5204	0.0451	−0.4680	−0.0070	0.6039	0.1544
(10) β	1.5000	−0.0066	−0.2986	−0.0592	−0.6250	0.0631	0.1303	−0.0118	−0.0203	0.0152	0.4482

Effect of variable x given below	Base value	Effect on variable given in col. heading							
		r 0.0268		r_s 0.1290		ϱ 2.6231		po 0.6948	
		$\dfrac{\partial r}{\partial x}$ (11)	$\dfrac{x}{r}\dfrac{\partial r}{\partial x}$ (12)	$\dfrac{\partial r_s}{\partial x}$ (13)	$\dfrac{x}{r_s}\dfrac{\partial r_s}{\partial x}$ (14)	$\dfrac{\partial \varrho}{\partial x}$ (15)	$\dfrac{x}{\varrho}\dfrac{\partial \varrho}{\partial x}$ (16)	$\dfrac{\partial po}{\partial x}$ (17)	$\dfrac{x}{po}\dfrac{\partial po}{\partial x}$ (18)
(1) $\bar{\varrho}_0$	3.2182	0.0083	0.9953	0.0329	0.8210	0.7888	0.9677	0.0168	0.0779
(2) g_L	0.0155	0.0142	0.0083	1.4446	0.1740	4.9039	0.0291	−3.7049	−0.0829
(3) g_N	0.0080	0.2324	0.0697	−1.0682	−0.0666	−12.9292	−0.0396	−4.9447	−0.0572
(4) $1 - T_s$	0.7050	0.0427	1.1225	−0.0471	−0.2574	−0.5710	−0.1535	0.1593	0.1616
(5) η	0.5495	0.0336	0.6896	−0.0207	−0.0883	−0.2510	−0.0526	−0.2840	−0.2246
(6) an	0.4885	−0.0153	−0.2798	−0.0207	−0.0785	−0.2511	−0.0468	−0.2840	−0.1997
(7) γ	14.5911	−0.0007	−0.3872	0.0018	0.2062	0.0220	0.1226	0.0084	0.1768
(8) γ_s	2.9831	−0.0018	−0.1960	−0.0142	−0.3294	−0.1674	−0.1904	−0.0036	−0.0155
(9) α	0.0130	−0.1553	−0.0753	0.7112	0.0717	8.6000	0.0426	3.2878	0.0615
(10) β	1.5000	−0.0039	−0.2188	0.0178	0.2074	0.2155	0.1232	0.0824	0.1778

Note

The base values of all the variables are shown below or beside them. They are equal to, or close approximations to, those for the USA 1948–73. The effects were found by increasing each variable shown in column x by 1% of itself, while holding the others at their base values, and noting the difference made to the solution of the model.

best steady-state rate of growth, since it is exogenously given. Instead, the problem is to choose the best capital–output ratio and best ratio of investment to output, s, which will determine the *level* of consumption per head at each moment of time along the growth path. A higher s implies a higher capital–output ratio, and so a higher output per head. However, it does not necessarily imply higher *consumption* per head. The higher is the capital–output ratio, the more investment is required merely to maintain that ratio constant (as it must be maintained along a steady-growth path). Assuming diminishing returns to the capital stock in the production function, raising the capital–output ratio and so the capital–labour ratio eventually increases output per head by less than it increases required investment per head, so resulting in a cut in consumption per head. The Golden Rule pushes s to the point at which consumption per head is maximized.[54]

Reasons for rejecting orthodox growth theory are given in Chapter 3. In the growth theory developed in this book, higher s increases the steady-state rate of growth. Consequently, the problem of optimizing s is not the same as in orthodox theory. Following the Golden Rule of Accumulation would, in my model, lead to far too high a rate of investment and growth, as well as some other unacceptable results. In what follows, I assume perfect markets, no taxation, no externalities, and no 'animal spirits', as those assumptions conform to the ones adopted in most discussions of the Golden Rule.

We may recall the following four essential equations of my model for the whole economy with g_L given:

$$r = (q - \lambda l) \; \frac{\varrho_m}{\varrho} + g \left(1 - \frac{\varrho_m}{\varrho} \right). \qquad (15A.13)$$

$$\mu = \frac{\lambda}{1 - s}. \qquad (15A.14)$$

$$r_{sh} = \alpha + \beta (g - g_N). \qquad (15A.15)$$

$$g = sq. \qquad (15A.16)$$

If we set $s = 1$ and $\lambda = 0$, it can be seen from (15A.13) and (15A.16) that $r = g$, in accordance with the Golden Rule. Furthermore, s will then also equal the share of profit, which is 1. In terms of my usual diagram (with no diminishing returns to the rate of investment: Figure 8.1), points E and C will coincide (since $OE/OC = s = 1$) and OL must equal the given g_L. μ will be the slope of the IPC at C, and will be a finite positive number. Hence, as $s \to 1$, we must have $\lambda \to 0$ for (15A.14) to be satisfied. Since $\tan CRS = \lambda$, the angle $CRS \to O$, and R shifts up to Q. Hence $r = OR \to g = OQ$.

Hence obedience to the Golden Rule does not, in my model, maximize consumption per head, but rather the rate of growth. In fact, consumption is minimized, since it has to fall to zero, the whole of output being required for

---

[54] Readers may recall the analogy in Chapter 3 in which, according to orthodox theory, an escalator (i.e. exogenous technical progress) is taking you up the mountain. Climbing up the escalator adds to enjoyment of the view (i.e. increases the level of consumption at a given point in time) until the time and energy spent in pressing the successively harder treadmills round (i.e. the need to invest to maintain the higher capital–output ratio) becomes so great as to prevent further gains to enjoyment.

investment. This clearly is excessive by any standards! With g far in excess of any plausible value of g_N, when $s = 1$, and with the value of β of 1.5 which I consider plausible, equation (15A.15) will give a value for r_{sh} which is well above r and g, again indicating that investment is excessive.

Appendix E: Impatience and the isolation paradox

This appendix examines two arguments which have been put forward to show that saving and investment are sub-optimal, implying the need for corrective action by the government. Neither, in my view, is persuasive. We consider them in turn.

(a) Impatience

It is a widely held opinion that individuals discount future benefits and costs simply because they are in the future; this pure time preference, or impatience, is recognized in Chapter 8, where it is represented by the coefficient α. Some writers have taken the view that its existence implies that the government should act to promote saving. Thus, Pigou argues:

Generally speaking, everybody prefers present pleasures or satisfactions of given magnitude to future pleasures or satisfactions of equal magnitude, even when the latter are perfectly certain to occur. But this preference for present pleasures does not—the idea is self-contradictory—imply that a present pleasure of given magnitude is any *greater* than a future pleasure of the same magnitude. It implies only that our telescopic faculty is defective, and that we, therefore, see future pleasures, as it were, on a diminished scale. . . . This reveals a far-reaching economic disharmony. For it implies that people distribute their resources between the present, the near future, and the remote future on the basis of a wholly irrational preference. . . . The inevitable result is that efforts directed towards the remote future are starved relatively to efforts directed towards the present. . . . This, however, is not all. Since human life is limited, such fruits of work or saving as accrue after a considerable interval are not enjoyed by the person to whose efforts they are due. . . . No doubt, this obstacle to investment for distant returns is partly overcome by stock-exchange devices. If £100 invested now is expected to reappear after 50 years expanded at, say, 5 per cent compound interest, the man who originally provides the £100 may be able, after a year, to sell his title in the eventual fruit for £105; the man who buys from him may be able similarly to get his capital of £105 back with 5 per cent interest after one year; and so on. . . . But, of course, in actual fact this device is of very narrow application. As regards investments, such as planting a forest or undertaking drainage development on one's own estate, which can only be accomplished privately, it is not applicable at all. (Pigou, 1932, 24 *et seq.*)

There are some criticisms to be made of this argument. It is far from clear that the 'device' is of 'very narrow application'. Improvements to a private estate will affect its marketable value, as well as its mortgageable value. The illustrations that Pigou subsequently uses to show that men habitually neglect the future relate to wasteful exploitation of minerals, over-fishing, and exhaustion of soil fertility. In many cases the harm is done because of an absence of enforceable property rights, not because of a defective telescopic faculty. In other cases, such as the 'wasteful' use of minerals, whether there is indeed waste depends on the future development of substitutes, a point ignored by Pigou.

It is also the case, as is pointed out in Chapter 8, that it is rational to discount future satisfactions in a world in which destruction of oneself and one's heirs has always to be reckoned with. Pigou admits this argument when he says:

Nobody, of course, holds that the state should force its citizens to act as though so much objective wealth now and in the future were of exactly equal importance. In view of the uncertainty of productive developments, to say nothing of the mortality of nations and eventually of the human race itself, this would not, even in the extremest theory, be sound policy. (Pigou 1932, 29)

Let us, however, admit that α is greater than a reasonable allowance on these grounds, and does reflect some genuine impatience; the question must then be asked as to whether a democratic government should, for *this* reason, seek to promote investment. I do not see how one can expect it to, if it reflects the wishes of its citizens. There are some who believe that governments can be expected to take a longer view than individual citizens, but the opposite seems to me more plausible in many cases. I argued in Chapter 8, against the life-cycle view of savings, that the urge to perpetuate oneself is perhaps the most fundamental one governing our existence. By contrast, 'a week is a long time in politics'. If we are seeking arguments to convince a democratic government that it should promote investment, they need to be grounded firmly on the preferences of its citizens, but that is not the case with this argument.

(b) The Isolation Paradox

In contrast to Section (a), the argument here is that citizens acting collectively *will* want there to be more investment than, acting as individuals, they are willing to save for. This is due to what Sen (1961) has termed the 'Isolation Paradox'. Baumol (1952), briefly, and Marglin (1963) also propounded this argument, but I will concentrate on Sen's version of it. He imagines an individual with a constant and consistent set of preferences who knows exactly what others will save:

Now, this individual faces a choice, let us say, between one unit of consumption now and three units of consumption in twenty years time. He knows, for some reason, that in twenty years he will be dead. He cares for the future generations, but it is not enough, let us assume, to make him sacrifice a unit of his present consumption for three units for the generation living in twenty years' time. He decides, therefore, to consume the unit; but another man comes and tells him that if he saves one unit of consumption the other man will also save one unit. It would not be, by any means, irrational for the first man to change his mind now and to agree to save a unit. The gain to the future generation is much greater, and he can bring it about by sacrificing himself only one unit of consumption. (Sen 1961, 487–8)

Of course, while the gain to future generations is much greater, there is also a greater sacrifice on the part of the current generation, and presumably the man takes account of that. Sen notes this point, and says that it may look as if the conflict between the individual and the collective decision

arises because the person concerned values the gains of the future generations but does not care at all about the sacrifices of the others in the present generation. This is not so. The possibility of the conflict is present whenever the person values the sacrifice (of one unit, in the above example) of present consumption of others less than the corresponding gain (three units) of the future generation, so that he would like them to save more. (Sen 1961, 488)

As a preliminary point, one can criticize the lumping together of the whole future generation. Individuals generally save for their heirs. Hence they may have little concern at all for the amounts other individuals save for *their* heirs. The first individual may be quite indifferent when the second one tells him that he will save more for the latter's heirs, and so be unmoved to save more himself.

Let us admit, however, that individuals do have some concern for the welfare of others, and not just their own family or heirs. Why should one individual believe that others are saving too little? We must put aside, at this point, all the *other* arguments for believing that saving and investment are sub-optimal. We are seeking here an *additional* argument. Naturally, if there are other arguments and externalities, that will indeed result in a conflict between individual and collective decisions. However, in their absence, I can see no reason why I should want others to save more than they freely decide to save themselves. To return to Sen's example, the first individual does not believe an extra benefit of three units to the future generation is worth the sacrifice of an extra unit himself, yet he is supposed to believe that the situation is different for others. So far as they are concerned, a sacrifice of one unit is worth *less* than the benefit of three units to the future generation. Yet they confront, presumably, the same market rates of interest and the same opportunities. (Or, at least, any differences in this respect are not mentioned in the argument—nor would there be anything special about it if they existed.) I therefore conclude that this argument for governmental intervention is not persuasive.

16

THE SLOW-DOWN IN PRODUCTIVITY GROWTH AFTER 1973

16.1 Introduction

When I started this book, although only a few years had passed since 1973, it was enough to show that a sharp break had occurred. It seemed best for the empirical analysis to end with that year *provisionally*. I expected to need several years to complete the book, and so postponed writing about the post-1973 years until the rest was complete. This provided more years' data for that period, although it left me uneasy as to whether I should be able to continue to keep theory and fact wedded together as comfortably as up to 1973.

Writing this chapter has, in fact, resulted in some revisions to the earlier chapters. This has encouraged me, rather than the reverse. It has driven home the lesson of the earlier chapters, that theory should benefit from, and be strengthened by, confrontation with experience. From the experience of the slow-down I have learned the importance of factors such as inflation, deflation, boom, and slump for productivity growth, and have understood better how and why they affect it.

The chapter begins with a very compressed survey of events of the period up to 1985, followed by an equally compressed account of some of the main explanations that have been offered of the slow-down. I then make use of the book's growth model, and show that an unmodified application of it leaves much unexplained. One needs to look more closely at the growth of the quality-adjusted labour force, at capacity utilization, and at evidence on abnormal scrapping and mistaken investments. When this is done, it is possible to provide an explanation without having to assume that there has been any fundamental worsening of investment opportunities. The implication is that, if other aspects of macroeconomic behaviour could be restored to their pre-1973 norms, so, for the greater part, could the trend growth of (quality-adjusted) labour productivity. Likewise, a sufficiently rapid growth of employment could be secured to bring down unemployment substantially in Europe, where it has risen much more than in the USA or Japan. There is no need to hypothesize some new technical revolution, which either would make productivity growth much more difficult or, its opposite, would make millions of workers inevitably redundant. This is the conclusion to which I am drawn, and which, I hope, we may all see fulfilled.

16.2   A brief sketch of events up to 1985 [1]

The year 1973 was a turning point in the world economy. The long postwar boom came to an end, and most countries entered on a period of greater instability and slower growth of output, employment, and productivity. I shall focus attention on three countries—the USA, Japan, and the UK—for which I have data comparable with that for earlier years referring to the non-residential business sector (and excluding North Sea oil and gas for the UK). However, in this preliminary sketch I include data for OECD Europe as a whole[2], and generally refer to the whole of the gross domestic product as conventionally measured. The slow-down in growth in these countries is clear from Table 16.1. It was most marked in Japan. Employment growth in the USA, exceptionally, was maintained, and this was accompanied by a near-disappearance of productivity growth.

Table 16.1   The slow-down in growth

Exponential rates of growth of:	Period	OECD Europe	USA	Japan	UK
GDP	1960–73	0.046	0.040	0.092	0.031
	1973–85	0.019	0.023	0.038	0.013
Employment	1960–73	0.004	0.019	0.013	0.003
	1973–85	0.001	0.019	0.008	− 0.002
GDP per person	1960–73	0.042	0.021	0.079	0.028
employed	1973–85	0.018	0.005	0.029	0.015

Sources: OECD National Accounts Main Aggregates, Vol. I, Paris, 1986; *OECD Economic Outlook December 1986*; *OECD Labour Force Statistics 1962-1982*, and *1964-1984*; *OECD Employment Outlook*, September 1986.

The timing of the slow-down more or less coincided in very many countries. Bruno and Sachs fitted two trend lines to annual data of real GDP, GDP per employee, and manufacturing output per employee in nineteen separate OECD countries for 1960–82. In each case they found the year t such that, with one trend for 1960 to t and the second for t to 1982, the fit was best. 'In most cases the estimated turning point falls within the period 1972–75 (in 55 out of 72 cells . . .). In some cases it falls somewhere at the end of the 1960s (1968–70). Only the US aggregate GDP and GDP per employee series (but not manufacturing) dates the turning point around

[1] In what follows, I have drawn heavily on various OECD studies, periodicals, and statistics, including in particular McCracken *et al.* (1977), and *OECD Economic Outlook* (OECD 1986).

[2] Austria, Belgium, Denmark, Finland, France, Germany, Greece, Iceland, Ireland, Italy, Luxembourg, Netherlands, Norway, Portugal, Spain, Sweden, Switzerland, Turkey, UK.

1966–67' (Bruno and Sachs 1985, 248–9). As they point out, this coincidence of turning points suggests that there were common causes at work.

Inflation accelerated after 1967, generally became still worse after 1972, and did not begin to subside until the early 1980s in many countries (see Table 16.2). To add to the catalogue of miseries, unemployment grew to levels untouched since the 1930s, the highest ones being reached in Europe (see Table 16.3).

Table 16.2   The speed-up of inflation

Exponential rates of growth of:	Period	OECD Europe	USA	Japan	UK
GDP price deflator	1960–67	0.037	0.020	0.051	0.036
	1967–73	0.060	0.050	0.067	0.067
	1973–82	0.098	0.076	0.061	0.140
	1982–85	0.073	0.038	0.010	0.049

Sources: See Table 16.1.

Table 16.3   Increasing unemployment
(Standardized[a] unemployment as a percentage of the total labour force)

	Some[b] EEC countries	USA	Japan	UK
1965	2.1	4.4	1.2	2.3
1973	2.9	4.8	1.3	3.0
1985	11.9[c]	7.1	2.6	13.0[c]

[a] i.e., adjusted by the OECD Secretariat so far as possible to preserve comparability over time and to conform with the definitions drawn up by the International Labour Organization; see *Standardised Unemployment Rates, Sources and Methods*, OECD, Paris, 1985.
[b] Belgium, France, Germany, Italy, Netherlands, Spain (for 1973 and 1985 only), and the UK.
[c] New estimates based on labour force surveys and given in *OECD Economic Outlook*, December 1987, are 11.1 for EEC and 11.2 for UK. These are described in *OECD Economic Outlook*, June 1987, pp. 30–1.

Sources: OECD Economic Outlook, July 1981 and December 1986. There are minor differences (0.1 in the rate shown) between the 1973 estimates in these sources for the EEC countries and the USA.

How can these untoward developments be explained? The most obvious place to start from is the first oil shock of 1973, which was both closely preceded and followed by sharp increases in the prices of other primary commodities. The coincidence of turning points at or near 1973 strongly suggests that these price increases and the slow-down in growth were closely connected. However, all was not well even before 1973. As we have seen, the US turning point may have been around 1967, and inflation started to accelerate then or soon afterwards. Table 16.3 shows that unemployment also was rising in this period. The oil shock greatly reinforced an already existing inflationary tendency, and it was because the forces behind that tendency were so strong that the ensuing developments were both severe and long drawn-out. The commodity price increases that followed the outbreak of the Korean War in 1950 were similar to those in 1972-3, but they were not followed by the same prolonged slow-down—quite the contrary. I believe that the main difference lay in peoples' expectations and attitudes, conditioned by their experience in the preceding years.

The First World War was a traumatic experience for Europeans especially, and was succeeded by years of difficulty and distress. There was the immediate postwar boom and slump. There was high or hyper-inflation in several countries. There was the deep recession of the 1930s with very heavy unemployment. This led up to the trauma of the Second World War, which devastated Europe even more, but also Japan, and involved the USA to a much greater extent than the First. At the end of it one was thankful to be alive, and one's expectations were modest.

In the event, Europe, North America, and Japan were launched upon a period of prosperity and growth without precedent. The Korean War was a minor interruption, enforcing temporary hardships in some of these countries (but heavy losses in Korea itself) which were quickly reversed. Gradually, peoples' expectations changed. They became more and more convinced that Beveridge's fifth giant of Idleness enforced by mass unemployment had really been slain (Beveridge 1944): 'experience showed that rises in pay that had been resisted as too big to be viable were in fact compatible with the maintenance of employment and a progressive rise in the standard of living. There seemed no reason why the next rise should not be bigger still' (Phelps Brown 1975).[3]

Meanwhile, attention turned to the other four giants of Want, Disease, Ignorance, and Squalor. Governments were expected to upgrade public benefits and services to levels previously found only in writings described as utopian. Political parties competed with one another to satisfy these demands. As a result, as Table 16.4 shows, in the years up to 1973 taxation in various forms and disguises took a larger and larger share of people's incomes, especially in Europe.

This larger tax take could fall on either profits or wages. It had to be one or the other—or both. In so far as it fell on profits, it could either fall on savings and investment at the margin or could cut capitalists' consumption. Such data as I have for the USA and the UK suggest a fall rather than a rise in the marginal tax rate on savings between 1960 and 1970.[4] However, these

---

[3] I owe much to this perceptive article.
[4] See Table 14.2. King and Fullerton (1984) gives estimates showing a fall in Germany and a rise in Sweden from 1960 to 1970.

Table 16.4   The growing tax burden
(*Current receipts of government as a percentage of GDP*)

Period	OECD Europe	USA	Japan	UK
1960	31.3	26.3	20.7	30.1
1967	34.9	27.1	19.3	36.2
1972	37.0	29.3	21.5	37.5
1974	38.8	30.3	24.5	40.6
1985	45.8	31.1	31.2	43.7

Source: 1967–85 from *OECD Economic Outlook December 1987;* 1960 from *OECD Economic Outlook Historical Statistics 1960–1983*, Paris, 1985, except for USA, from *NIPA 1929–82.*

data refer to the explicit taxes on and subsidies to saving and investment. The tax burden could have been shifted on to savers simply by a rise in the share of wages and a fall in that of profits. The data on the share of wages in the non-residential business sector in the USA, Japan, and the UK in Table SA II show different patterns in each. In the USA there was no clear trend in the share from 1948 to 1973. In Japan the share of wages fell in the 1950s but then flattened out to 1972. In the UK the share of wages showed no clear trend until the latter half of the 1960s, when it rose moderately. Apart from the UK this does not suggest that labour was able to pass on the growing tax burden to capitalists in these countries, but then the burden increased most in Europe, and only the UK is European. Profits were probably squeezed more in, for example, Germany, Italy, and the Netherlands (see Hill 1979, 124, Table 6.3 and 130, Diagram 6.3). They appear to have fallen as a share of value added in the business sector in OECD countries on average.[5]

However, the share of taxes and other deductions from wages also increased.[6] In the UK, for example, the share for a 'typical' wage-earner is estimated to have gone up from about 20 to 28 per cent from 1963 to 1973.[7] Indeed, from 1964 to 1968, real post-tax earnings in the UK scarcely grew at

[5] See Lindbeck (1983, 20, Fig. 2), which shows a decline in the ratio of gross operating surplus, adjusted by OECD to account for the labour income share of the self-employed, to value added in the business-sector, unweighted average of 11 countries (Canada, Finland, France, Germany, Italy, Japan, Netherlands, Norway, Sweden, UK and USA) over the years 1961–73 (and beyond to 1978).

[6] See Lindbeck (1983, 21, Fig. 3), which shows that from 1964 to 1973 the rate of growth of the real product wage was consistently above or equal to that of real earnings obtained by employees, the former being deflated by value added prices and the latter by consumer goods prices. The series refer to unweighted averages for manufacturing in ten countries (Belgium, Canada, Denmark, France, Germany, Italy, Japan, Sweden, UK, and USA).

[7] The deductions consist of income tax, compulsory social security contributions, and local rates for an average male married worker with no children and no property income other than his own house. See Bacon and Eltis (1978, 212–13).

all. The Labour government which came in at the start of this period made a succession of agreements with the trade unions to prevent wages increasing, hoping to avoid a devaluation of the pound. In 1967 devaluation was accepted, and it seemed all the more necessary to prevent the competitive gains from being lost by domestic wage and price increases, and so the efforts to hold these back continued. Eventually, with an election in 1970, restraint was abandoned and there was a wage explosion.

Greater wage explosions had already occurred on the Continent: in France, following *les événements de mai 1968*; in Germany, following an over-expansionary budget in 1967, drawn up to escape from the first significant postwar recession; and in Italy following the 'hot summer' of 1969. In all three countries there was an upsurge of strikes, as there was, to a lesser extent, in the UK and also in the USA. It seems likely that labour leaders were encouraged by militancy in other countries, and the timing may well have been influenced by the student unrest which started in 1967 in the USA and then spread round the world. That the time was ripe was due to the factors already mentioned: the fading of memories of earlier hard times, the growing confidence that wage increases did not result in job losses, and, in some cases, exasperation with attempts to hold back wage increases when taxation was biting into them more and more.

The end of the 1960s thus witnessed a serious weakening in people's confidence in the stability of wage and price levels, but not in the ability and determination of governments to maintain full employment. The 1970s opened with a mild recession in nearly all the major countries, as governments reacted to the inflation of the previous years. Unemployment thereupon grew, albeit from generally low levels. The rather extraordinary boom that followed in 1972–3 was partly a response to that—perhaps the last occasion for many years when the governments of so many large countries would react in that way. Some governments were probably influenced by the serious labour unrest and by fears of 'ungovernability' if unemployment were allowed to grow (McCracken *et al.* 1977, 52). The years 1972–3 also saw elections in Canada, France, Germany, Italy, Japan, and the USA. Balance of payments constraints on expansion were removed by the abandonment of fixed exchange rates, the US deficit, and the resulting enormous increase in international liquidity;[8] and this same increase, since governments either would not or could not neutralize its effects on their money supplies, resulted in rapidly rising domestic liquidity and negative real interest rates.

Superimposed on this inflationary situation came the commodity price shocks. Crop failures in many countries in 1972 found grain stocks seriously

---

[8] International liquidity grew at 2.5% p.a. from 1964 to 1969. From the end of 1969 to the end of 1973 it grew at 23.7% p.a. reaching an astonishing 43.5% in 1971 (see McCracken *et al.* (1977, 269).

Table 16.5   Gains and losses from changes in the terms of trade
(Percentage of GDP)

	OECD Europe	USA	Japan	UK
1960	1.4	1.8	4.8	−0.2
1972	3.2	3.1	7.9	1.2
1974	0.9	1.3	5.7	−4.8
1980	0.0	0.0	0.0	0.0
1984	−0.5	3.8	−0.4	−0.3

Note
The figures are the percentage of GDP gained (if positive) or lost (if negative) owing to the difference in each country's term of trade on goods and services between the year in question and 1980. The gain is measured as the net balance on goods and services at current prices in year t, B_t, expressed at 1980 prices by deflating by the implicit price index of public and private consumption, P_t/P_{80}, *less* the net balance at 1980 prices when exports and imports are separately deflated by their own price index numbers, B_{t80}, all expressed as a percentage of GDP at 1980 prices, Y_{t80}. Hence the gain is

$$100 \left(B_t \frac{P_{80}}{P_t} - B_{t80} \right) \Big/ Y_{t80}.$$

For a justification of this measurement of gain, see text and Scott (1979). The source from which all the data were obtained was *OECD National Accounts, Main Aggregates*, Vol. I, *1960–1984*, Paris, 1986.

depleted, so that food prices shot up first. Then industrial materials prices responded to the boom in demand. Finally, the *coup de grâce* was given by the quadrupling of the oil price following the outbreak of war in the Middle East in October 1973 and the cuts in oil production that ensued.

These commodity price increases sharply reversed a long period of improvement in industrial countries' terms of trade, as can be seen from Table 16.5. The table shows the gain in a particular year from the terms of trade then ruling as compared with the position in 1980, the arbitrarily selected base year. The *change* in the gain from one year to another then measures the gain or loss over that period from changes in the terms of trade between them.[9] The gain is measured by the difference made to the cost of achieving a given balance on goods and services (i.e. of acquiring the foreign assets, positive or negative, which that balance provides) by differences in the terms of trade. By a 'given balance' is meant a balance with a given purchasing power over consumption, since this is our preferred measure of any investment, foreign or domestic, at constant prices. The formula used is given in the note to the table, and a fuller justification may be found in the reference cited therein.

Between 1960 and 1972, the countries shown in the table gained between 1

[9] It would have been preferable to have measured gains or losses from one year to the next by a Divisia-type index, instead of using the arbitrary year 1980 as base, but time was lacking for this calculation.

and 3 per cent of GDP (i.e. 0.1–0.25 per cent per annum) from improvements in their terms of trade. While not large, this was a significant counterweight to the increasing tax burdens shown in Table 16.4. In the next two years OECD Europe, the USA, and Japan each lost about 2 per cent, while the UK lost 6 per cent, and this at a time when tax burdens increased by 1–3 per cent. Profits and wages had, therefore, somehow or other to share between them a cut in income of 4, 3, 5, and a staggering 9 per cent of GDP in these areas respectively. This would have been difficult enough in a period of rapidly rising output, but, in fact, output either grew more slowly or fell in 1974, which is indeed one reason why the tax burden rose so much.

In several of the large countries, policy turned to restriction of demand in 1973, before the oil shock. Memory of the inflationary period at the end of the 1960s was still fresh, and wages were reacting to price increases more rapidly. The need for counter-inflationary policy was thus evident. In the USA and the UK attempts had been made to moderate both wage and price increases by guidelines or controls of various kinds: but, while the initial impact of these seemed helpful, their existence may well have aggravated inflation after the oil price shock.[10] In the main, countries relied on monetary and fiscal measures of the traditional kind to reduce demand, and the inevitable result, given the impetus behind price and wage increases, as well as the unforeseen oil price increase, was to cut output, although the timing and extent of this varied. Unemployment also rose, although in some countries employment losses were borne by immigrant workers to a substantial degree.

Although countries pulled out of the severe recession of 1974–5, the recovery was fragile. Governments were understandably nervous of any measures that might strengthen inflation. However, fiscal policy was generally expansionary for the rest of the 1970s in most OECD countries (except, after 1975, the USA), while real short-term interest rates remained negative or very low.[11] By 1979, OECD countries had experienced four years of steady, if unspectacular, growth averaging nearly 4 per cent per annum out of the trough of the recession. Unemployment and inflation both remained stubbornly high by postwar standards.[12]

[10] In the USA, the period of decontrol coincided with the commodity boom and oil crisis. In the UK, provisions for automatic pay increases ('threshold agreements') meant that the oil price rise unexpectedly triggered these, thus speeding up the wage–price spiral. Subsequently in the UK the 'Social Contract' between the Labour government and the trade unions, which had begun laxly, was tightened up sufficiently in the foreign exchange crisis of 1976 to result in real wage cuts in 1976 and 1977; this reduced the rate of inflation to single figures in 1978. However, as had happened before, restraint was followed by labour unrest in the 'Winter of Discontent' in 1978–9 and by a wage explosion.

[11] See Chart D (p. 12) on fiscal policy influences and Chart C (pp. 7–8) on real short-term interest rates in OECD (1986).

[12] For all OECD countries, consumer prices rose by 11.3% in 1975 over the previous year, and still by 9.8% in 1979 over 1978. The standardized unemployment rate averaged 5.1% in 1975 and 5.0% in 1979 (sixteen countries only). See OECD (1986, Tables R10 and R12).

Then came the second oil price shock. The already very high spot price approximately trebled in 1978–9, with the import price lagging behind to reach a similar peak in early 1981 (see OECD 1986, 57, Chart R). Once again, the terms of trade of many OECD countries worsened sharply, and especially those of Italy and Japan. By this time, however, the UK was a substantial oil producer, and only a small net importer of fuels, and so was little affected. Hence, as Table 16.5 shows, while Japan lost 5.7 per cent of GDP through the worsening of her terms of trade from 1974 to 1980, the UK gained nearly as much. In OECD Europe and the USA, the losses were both around 1 per cent.

Getting inflation down was by now the top priority for many governments, and the reaction to the oil price rise was accordingly more severe than in 1973–4. Although many budgets were in deficit, and continued to be so until the end of the period under review, the OECD's measure of 'fiscal impact' shows a generally less expansionary stance than in the earlier period. On the monetary side, nominal interest rates were raised until real short-term rates became substantially positive, and were held there. Inflation did indeed at last fall, with consumer prices rising at less than 5 per cent per annum on average by 1985 and slowing down further after that (OECD 1986, Charts D, C, and K).

However, this prolonged deflationary squeeze meant that output grew on average by only 2 per cent per annum from 1979 to 1985 in the OECD area as a whole, and that unemployment rose still further, from 5 to 8 per cent (and to 12 per cent in the EEC). Weak demand exerted its most powerful effects on commodity prices, with many falling in dollar terms. With the significant exception of the USA, however, the available data suggests that wages held on to part of the higher share of business output that they had secured since 1972. As usually happens in a recession, the wage share rose in Japan and the UK from 1972 to 1975. In both countries the share in 1984 (Japan) and 1985 (UK) had fallen back, but it still remained above its 1972 level, and very markedly so in Japan. In the USA, however, the wage share was actually lower in 1985 than in 1972 (see Table SA II). OECD estimates suggest that the wage share in business output rose from 1972 to 1985 in France, Italy, Finland, Belgium, and Sweden, and was about the same in Germany.[13] We return later to the relation between the wage share and employment growth, but remark here that employment grew much faster in the USA than in Europe. This could be part of the explanation (or result?) of different behaviours in wage shares. However, tax burdens continued to grow in both Europe and Japan, but not to any appreciable extent in the USA (Table 16.4), and that could be another part.

[13] See OECD (1986, 49–50, Chart P), which shows profit shares in the business sector, assumed here to move inversely to the wage share.

Let me now summarize what is already a very compressed summary of events. Rather serious inflationary pressures began to make themselves felt in many countries at the end of the 1960s, and were in places accompanied by growing industrial unrest and riots. Governments reacted by deflationary measures, but then, alarmed by increasing unemployment and still committed to using expansionary fiscal or monetary measures to preserve full employment, set 'all-systems go'[14] in an unusually synchronized and rapid boom in 1972–3. Superimposed on this came those commodity price increases: in food, owing to harvest failures and low stocks; in materials, owing to the boom; and, 'o'er topping all', in oil, triggered by war in the Middle East. Despite deflationary measures leading to the worst postwar recession, and a sharp and persistent rise in unemployment, inflation remained stubbornly high. Fiscal and monetary policies switched to expansion, and real growth out of the recession lasted for four years until the second oil shock in 1979–80. With inflation once again soaring, governments became even more determined to counter it, and this time they were successful in bringing it down substantially. But real interest rates had to be pushed up significantly, unemployment rose still further, and output grew much more slowly.

16.3   The productivity puzzle: some possible explanations

Why was the slow-down in the rate of growth of output from 1973 to 1985 accompanied by a slow-down in productivity growth as well? Some would not regard that as a puzzle at all, and would claim that it is quite usual for slower growth in output to have this effect, whether in the long run or the short run. In both cases, they would argue, there is abundant evidence of increasing returns. So far as the long run is concerned (and that is our main concern), we have seen in Chapters 12 and 13 that the association between output and productivity growth is by no means universally found, and so is not to be explained by any simple reference to increasing returns. Such as it is, the model in this book can explain it. However, to explain the association in recent years requires some special factors, as we shall presently see.

The short-run association of output and productivity growth is essentially due to a fuller utilization of spare capacity (for capital or overhead labour) and to the failure of *measured* direct labour inputs to correspond to *actual* inputs. Firms commonly pay direct labour for more hours than are actually worked, and, as output expands in a boom, actual hours worked increase

---

[14] McCracken *et al* (1977); 'With the benefit of hindsight we would judge that the shift of policies, particularly monetary policies, in 1971 to settings which were effectively "all-systems go" in many countries simultaneously was the most important mishap in recent economic policy history' (p. 51).

faster than hours paid for, with the reverse happening in a slump.[15] This phenomenon means that it is important to compare years in which the ratio of output to capacity is approximately the same if one wants to measure productivity trends, a point to which we return below.

There is already an enormous literature on the slow-down in output and productivity growth, and I do not intend to review it here.[16] I will refer, however, to some of the studies in order to list the main explanations that have been suggested and to see whether they appear sufficient.

The leading study is that of E. F. Denison for the slow-down in the USA.[17] Denison finds that real national income per person employed in non-residential business grew at 2.45 per cent per annum from 1948 to 1973, falling to −0.26 per cent per annum from 1973 to 1982. Of this decline of 2.71 percentage points, rather more than half—1.47 percentage points—is left unexplained after taking account of fourteen separate factors which he has quantified (Denison 1985, 37).[18] Denison considers possible explanations for this 1.47 point decline under five separate headings.[19]

The first of these relates to technological knowledge. Denison estimates that in 1948–73 organized R&D in the USA contributed about 0.2 percentage points to the growth rate arising from the residual, viz. 1.38 percentage points, in non-residential business (Denison 1985, 28, 42, 100). Since the relevant R&D expenditure at constant prices grew rapidly up to 1979 and more slowly thereafter, one would have to posit a big drop in its contribution per unit of expenditure at constant prices in order for its total contribution to fall after 1973. Expert opinion differs on whether there has been any drop in yield. Denison accepts Mansfield's view 'that it is un-

[15] There are numerous studies which show that measured labour productivity rises in a boom and falls in a slump. See for a good example Brechling and O'Brien (1967, 277–87). This study covers 12 OECD countries. So far as I know, it was Fair (1969), who first drew attention in this context to the difference between hours actually worked and hours paid for. A sophisticated attempt to measure the difference between hours worked and paid for in UK manufacturing is in Muellbauer (1984). Smith-Gavine and Bennett have conducted surveys to measure the percentage utilization of labour (PUL): see the reference in Muellbauer et al (1986, xiii).

[16] For international comparisons and analysis, see Matthews (1982); articles by A. Lindbeck, H. Giersch and F. Wolter, E. F. Denison (with comments by D. J. Morris and S. J. Prais) in Economic Journal, March 1983; Kendrick (1984) Bruno and Sachs (1985); Muellbauer et al. (1986); Maddison (1987). A survey of studies relating to the USA is Wolff (1985).

[17] Denison (1979, 1985). Most references are to the second of these.

[18] The factors are: hours, age–sex composition, education, reallocation from farming, reallocation from non-farm self-employment (i.e. all the factors included in g_L besides changes in numbers), inventories, non-residential structures and equipment, land, weather in farming, pollution abatement, worker safety and health, dishonesty and crime, economies of scale, and intensity of demand. The last allows in principle for the difference in capacity utilization between 1973 and 1982 (and 1948 and 1973).

[19] Denison quickly dismisses a sixth possibility: 'It is occasionally suggested that the productivity slow-down never happened and is merely the product of bad statistics. This cheerful illusion has no basis in reality' Denison (1985, 56).

certain whether a slackening of technological advance contributed at all to the productivity slow-down but that it probably did although there is no strong evidence that its contribution was very large' (Denison 1985, 40–1). He gives reasons for rejecting Kendrick's view that the effect was as large as a drop of 0.2 percentage points (p. 42). He also gives reasons for rejecting the view that the ageing of the capital stock since 1973 has (as in vintage theory) made much difference through lengthening the lag between average and best-practice techniques (Denison 1985, 43–4).[20]

Denison's second heading relates to managerial knowledge and performance. He believes that advances here accounted for a large part of the 1.38 percentage points of his residual for 1948–73, so that deteriorations *could* be important. Furthermore, he cites many reasons and expert opinions suggesting that managerial knowledge and performance in the USA *have* deteriorated. This could be because an increasing amount of management time and effort has had to be devoted to relations with government, new regulations and legislation, and purely financial matters as inflation has speeded up, exchange rates have become more volatile, and interest rates have varied more. Alternatively (or in addition), it could be because management style and philosophy have become too preoccupied with decentralization and short-term profits and not enough with technological improvements or with real complexities which require more 'hands-on' experience. There is, it is alleged, insufficient attention to some points which Japanese managements handle better: quality control, consensus-building, promotion of company loyalty, etc. On the other hand, as Denison points out, it is difficult to explain why this deterioration in managerial performance occurred as suddenly as it must have done if it is to explain what happened; nor is it clear why it should have occurred in so many countries. After all, the fall in productivity growth was much greater in Japan than in the USA (Table 16.1). Hence, although Denison includes a deterioration in managerial performance as 'among the more probable main causes of the slow-down in the growth of residual productivity' (1985, 46–7), it does not seem altogether convincing.

Declining work effort is the third heading. Although many have alleged that this is *the* explanation, similar allegations have appeared in the past, and no convincing evidence is available. Again, the suddenness of the change and its international character make it somewhat implausible. There is, however, a more plausible version of the argument which has been suggested by Muellbauer:

This is that with reduced real income generating capacity in the industrial countries there was a sharpened conflict between reality and the aspirations for real wage

---

[20] Even on extreme vintage assumptions, Denison argues that only 0.16 percentage points of the slow-down could be accounted for in this way.

growth of workers and their representatives. This conflict may have resulted in increased use of restrictive practices, strikes and other modes of non-cooperation that showed itself in reduced productivity growth. (Muellbauer *et al.* (1986, iv)

Judged by time lost in industrial disputes, conflict increased in the larger OECD countries in the late 1960s and during the 1970s. However, with growing unemployment and inflation subsiding, time lost in disputes generally fell in the first half of the 1980s, and so, if this can be taken as a reliable indicator, productivity should have recovered to a great extent by the end of our period so far as this factor is concerned.

The fourth heading relates to the misallocation of resources, and is in turn subdivided. There is the misallocation of workers between occupations and jobs resulting from the implementation by employers of successive guidelines issued by the US federal government under the Civil Rights Act of 1964. These guidelines caused employers to abandon selecting employees by means of tests which, there is evidence to show, did allocate workers successfully. Since workers differ very greatly in their aptitudes and abilities, the result could have been a lowering in the productivity of newly hired workers. But it might have spread beyond this to older workers as general standards of work adapted to those of the newer workers, once the latter formed a critical mass. Denison cites the work of F. L. Schmidt and J. E. Hunter, and accepts that they have demonstrated that these effects *could* have been important, although he reserves judgement until more evidence is assembled. I do not know of evidence of a similar development in other countries.

There is misallocation of capital arising from tax distortions. Denison refers to the varying rates on tax on capital which started, he thinks, with the introduction of accelerated depreciation in 1954, with subsequent chops and changes culminating in the Accelerated Cost Recovery System of 1981. Chapter 14 gave estimates, based on King and Fullerton (1984), showing the wide variation of tax rates, in the UK as well as the USA, and it was argued that such variation could reduce the rate of growth of output for a given rate of investment. I have not been able to quantify this effect. Denison's rough estimates suggest that it would be small, but his underlying model is not one that I accept. Again, however, the change in productivity trend seems too sharp and to coincide in too many countries for this to be a plausible major common cause.

A second cause of misallocation of capital is that arising from unusually rapid obsolescence or scrapping as a result of unusually rapid shifts in demand or techniques. Denison cities M. N. Baily, and E. R. Berndt and D. O. Wood, who have argued that this was an important factor in the slow-down. As Denison says, it could be described either as more misallocation of capital, or as a reduction in the quantity of capital. He does not believe that it accounted for much of the slow-down, partly because 'most of the stock could not have been affected by oil prices' (the factor stressed by Berndt and Wood), partly because much of the stock in his final year, 1982, was acquired after 1973, and partly because he sees no reason to assume that there was accelerated obsolescence. I return to this point below, as I believe, on the contrary, that it is a most important cause of the slow-down.

The last cause of misallocation of resources Denison considers is that arising from increasing trade barriers. While accepting that these have increased, he points out that so has trade, suggesting that the barriers have not increased substantially. Furthermore, past estimates suggest that the losses in efficiency arising from such barriers in the USA in the recent past have not been great, so that *changes* in them, of the sort that seem to have occurred, probably had rather minor effects on total output.

Denison's fifth, and last, heading of possible explanations for the decline of the residual concerns energy prices and use. Some economists have regarded the sharp rises in energy prices that occurred in 1973 and also in 1978–80 as an important *direct* cause of slower productivity growth (see, e.g., Rasche and Tatom 1977a, b). By 'direct' I mean to abstract from indirect, macroeconomic effects which aggravated inflation and so increased the deflationary squeeze that followed. The rise in energy prices could have had a direct effect, it is alleged by some, by requiring the use of labour and capital to substitute for energy when the price of the latter rose. If, for example, the same output level was produced with less energy but more capital and labour, then this would have reduced output per unit of capital and labour taken together. It would thus, so it is argued, have reduced the residual. By assuming that the quantity of extra capital and labour costs the same as the quantity of energy saved, one can estimate by how much the residual was reduced. Denison provides estimates, based on work he cites by Alterman, which suggest that only about 0.1 percentage point of the 1.4 percentage point decline in the growth rate of the residual from 1948–73 to 1973–82 can be explained in this way (Denison 1985, 54–6).

It must be pointed out that, if one were to confine attention to value added by labour and capital (as opposed to gross output of labour, capital, and energy), and to measure changes in output and input by Divisia-type index numbers, so that at every change, in effect, current relative prices were used, and if one were to make the above assumption that each £1 of energy saved required £1 of capital and/or labour, then substitution would have absolutely *no* effect on the residual. This is simply because each extra £1 of capital or labour used would result in £1 of extra value added, by assumption. Consequently, if one gets the result that the residual is *reduced* by such substitution, it must be due to either of two things. One may measure output gross of energy inputs, but exclude energy from the inputs considered. There would then be an unexplained fall in the productivity of the other inputs (capital and labour) when energy inputs were reduced and they were increased. One could regard this as simply a mistaken way of measuring productivity, since growth accounting seeks to be as comprehensive as possible. The mistake should not be important. For some countries (like Japan and Italy) nearly all primary energy is imported, and is therefore included as neither an input nor an output. For others (like the USA and the UK) a large part of primary energy is domestically produced. The capital and labour required to produce it are therefore included as inputs, and their output is part of GDP. It is then not clear why substitution of the kind supposed affects the residual.

The second way in which the residual might be affected is that output and input are not measured by a close approximation to a Divisia index. It then depends very much on whether the base year used for weighting outputs and inputs is before or after the big rise in energy prices. If it is before, then the saving in energy inputs will be given a smaller value than the increase in capital and labour substituting for them. There will then appear to be a decline in the residual. The opposite, of course, is true if energy prices are relatively higher in the base year than in the year when substitution occurs. For the USA and the UK, 1982 price weights are stated to be those used for the period 1973–85, while for Japan 1980 price weights are stated to be those used for the period 1973–84. Relative oil prices reached their peak in the years 1980–2 (see OECD 1986). It therefore seems unlikely that this weighting factor is an important explanation of the decline in the residual.[21]

Denison gives two others reasons why the rise in energy prices was probably not an important *direct* cause of the decline in residual productivity growth. First, according to his estimates, the latter decline started in the second quarter of 1973, months before the major oil price rise occurred. Second, as he points out, 'if reduced energy was the major cause of the productivity slow-down, managements should be aware of it'. He then cites two surveys of managers, one in the USA and one in the UK, neither of which supports the view that it was a major cause (Denison 1985, 52–3).

One can sum up Denison's study of the slow-down in the USA as follows. Fourteen measured factors together account for rather less than half the fall in total factor productivity growth. Of the five groups of factors considered by Denison as possible explanations of the remainder, he himself regards only two as being possibly important: a deterioration in management performance, and a misallocation of labour arising from the imple-

---

[21] See Lindbeck (1983, 23–4 and Appendix TA. 3) for a good discussion of the points made above. Lindbeck estimates that, for OECD countries, the 'loss' of annual productivity growth owing to substitution away from both energy and raw materials in the years 1973–9, measured at *initial* relative prices, was 0.1 percentage points for the whole economy and 0.2 percentage points for manufacturing. Using 1980 or 1982 relative prices as weights, the effects would presumably have been much smaller still, or could even have been in the opposite direction. See also Jackman's comment on Bruno in Matthews (1982, 105–10).

mentation of the Civil Rights Act of 1964. I find the first of these implausible myself, but believe the second must be kept in mind, along with a third factor which Denison does not believe important, namely, what he calls misallocation of capital and I will call abnormal required maintenance and also mistaken and wasted investments. These are discussed later on.

Another economist who has attempted to quantify the factors explaining the slow-down in productivity growth is Lindbeck (1983), not just for the USA, but for the OECD countries as a whole. Many of the factors he considers have already been mentioned or (like 'catch-up') are taken into account in the next section. However, Lindbeck makes the interesting point that, whereas the *timing* of the slow-down, and its *abruptness*, are best explained by the macroeconomic disturbances of 1972–4, there were other gradual factors at work as well: the rising inflation trend; the fall in profitability; a deterioration in the functioning of markets and the efficiency of economic incentives as higher tax rates and inflation interacted to produce various distortions, and as legislation made it more difficult to dismiss labour; and an increasing tendency of both employers and employees to count on governments to accomodate wage and price increases and to bail individual firms out of difficulties.

When all these various system changes, in the form of market distortions, disincentives, inflexibilities and uncertainties, are considered, it is tempting to speak of an emerging 'arteriosclerosis' of the western economic systems accentuated by the resistance to change and the fights about income shares, by organised interest groups. (Lindbeck 1983, 17)

16.4   The productivity puzzle: using this book's model

Having considered the different ways in which orthodox growth accounting explains, or fails to explain, the decline in productivity growth, let us now see what light can be cast on this problem if we use the model developed in this book. The first point to be made is that there is, indeed, something to be explained. In what follows I use equation (11.3) as the explanatory hypothesis. It is convenient to express the equation in terms of g (the exponential growth rate of output), g_L (that of quality-adjusted employment), s (the gross investment ratio), and ϱ (the measure of the efficiency of investment or radius of the IPC), as follows:[22]

$$\frac{g}{\varrho} = 0.05228s + 0.9034 \, \frac{g_L}{\varrho} - 0.4193 \left(\frac{g_L}{\varrho} \right)^2 \frac{1}{s} . \qquad (16.1)$$

For the period 1973–85[23] one can calculate g, g_L, and s using the same procedures as were used for the standard, earlier, periods. I thus ignore

[22] Equation (11.3) is multiplied through by s, and I put $g = sq$, $g_L = sl$.
[23] In what follows I refer to the period being considered as 1973–85 for convenience, but the data for Japan are for 1973–84.

output and employment in slump years (i.e. those years in which output was less than in a previous year) and fit exponential trends to the remaining years to obtain g and g_L. s is the mean ratio of gross investment to output at current prices for all years except the final one. All magnitudes refer to non-residential business. This being done, one can solve the quadratic in ϱ,[24] and the resulting values are in the column for ϱ in Table 16.6.

Table 16.6 Explaining growth in USA, Japan, and the UK, 1973–1985

	Growth rate of capacity	Growth rate of quality-adjusted employment	Investment ratio	Radius of IPC	Ditto relative to radius before 1973
	g	g_L	s	ϱ	
USA	0.0240	0.0225	0.1633	0.6588	0.2484
Japan[a]	0.0315	0.0174	0.2576	1.1983	0.3441
UK	0.0056	−0.0107	0.1820	1.6198	0.5498

Notes
[a] 1973–84.

Growth rates are exponential. The value of ϱ is calculated from equation (11.3), given g, g_L, and s, as described in the text. In the last column, this value of ϱ is divided by the corresponding value for the period before 1973, calculated in a similar way. These values are given in col. (8) of Table 16.13 for the following periods: USA, 1948–73; Japan, 1961–73; UK, 1951–73.

As is clear from equation (16.1), and so long as g_L is small, doubling ϱ, for example, doubles the marginal contribution of s to growth of output. We discussed in Chapter 10 various explanations for the remarkable improvement in investment opportunities which occurred from before to after the Second World War. A glance at the estimates of ϱ in Table 16.6 shows that what now needs to be explained is why they deteriorated so markedly after 1973. The IPC apparently shrank back to a point that was inferior to the interwar position and even, in the case of the USA, inferior to pre-1914.

A fall in ϱ, and hence in the yield of investment, is only one possibility. There could be other explanations for the results in Table 16.6, of which the following are the main ones we consider.

1. The rate of growth of quality-adjusted employment may have been less than I have estimated for a variety of reasons.
2. Capacity utilization may have fallen, with three results. First, the rate of growth of capacity may have been higher than my estimate of the rate of

[24] Writing the three constants in (16.1) as a, b, and c (a positive number) respectively, the solution is

$$\varrho = \frac{g - bg_L \pm \sqrt{\{(g - bg_L)^2 + 4acg_L^2\}}}{2as},$$

taking the positive root.

growth of output, g. It is really the rate of growth of capacity that equation (16.1) explains. Second, the ratio of investment to output in 1973–85 may be exaggerated by comparison with earlier years. It is really the ratio of investment to capacity output (or, at least, to output which is some normal fraction of capacity output) to which equation (16.1) refers. Third, a drop in capacity utilization would tend to reduce employment, although not to the same proportionate extent.

3. The investment ratio, s, may be exaggerated by comparison with earlier years for another reason. During 1973–85 there may have been much greater scrapping of assets that could still contribute significantly to output at current prices than in earlier years. If an asset that could contribute to output is scrapped, required maintenance is thereby increased. Hence another way of expressing the point is that required maintenance may have been abnormally high in 1973–85. That being so, investment net of required maintenance would have been a lower fraction of measured s than in earlier years.

The above three possibilities, which are further explained below, all imply that, for one reason or another, my measures of g_L, g, and s are faulty. Naturally, if we change their values we shall change the resulting estimates of ϱ which are derived from equation (16.1). As we shall see, it is quite possible that, in a fundamental sense, there has been no fall at all in ϱ since 1973. Before a judgement on this can be formed, however, we must first consider the three possibilities at length.

16.5   Has employment grown more slowly than estimated?

There are two kinds of evidence that can be examined to see whether quality-adjusted employment, L, has grown more slowly than my estimates suggest. The first relates to changes in the industrial allocation of employment (apart from its allocation between agriculture and the rest, which is already allowed for in the estimates for g_L for the USA and Japan, and which was of negligible effect for the UK), and the second to changes in the proportion of employment in smaller versus larger enterprises. As regards the first, it has been pointed out that the share of employment in manufacturing has declined while the share of employment in services has risen since 1973, and that these changes have been more marked than in the preceding twenty-five years.[25] Since some of the service industries (e.g. retailing, hotels, and catering) pay relatively low wages, this shift would

[25] See, e.g. Maddison (1987). He estimates that the changes in the structure of employment growth between industries (including agriculture) made substantial differences to the growth rates of GDP in the USA, Japan, and the UK comparing 1950–73 with 1973–84. However, his calculations implicitly assume that relative *marginal* products of labour equal relative *average* products, whereas the assumption I prefer is that relative wages are a better guide to the former.

have tended to lower the quality of employment, measuring quality by weights proportionate to relative wage rates. As regards the second, some have asserted that a large proportion of the growth in employment in recent years has been in small firms.[26] Since small firms tend to pay below-average wage rates, this could also have reduced the quality of employment.

A problem that is encountered in measuring each of these effects is that it is uncertain how far they are additional to effects already allowed for. For example, my estimate of g_L already allows for the effect on quality of a shift in the sex composition of employment. Many service industries employ a higher proportion of women than do manufacturing industries on average. Hence a shift of employment away from manufacturing and in favour of service industries is likely to be accompanied by an increase in the proportion of women in total employment, and this has in fact occurred. One can calculate each effect separately, but to add them together would seem to involve some double-counting. Unfortunately, there is insufficient data to determine how much, and it could be large or small. Lower wages in service industries could be due partly to the greater proportion of women employed, but could also be due to lower wages for any particular category of man or woman. To estimate g_L satisfactorily, one needs a fully articulated set of estimates of employment in which each group of workers is as nearly homogeneous as possible. Such estimates are lacking, and one has to make do with indirect and partial estimates. In what follows I look in each case at changes in rates of change between the years before and after 1973 (or a neighbouring year). For example, I measure the rate of growth of quality arising from industrial reallocation before and after that date, and I then assume that the change in this rate of growth resulted in an equal change in g_L. It is possible, because of double-counting, that this exaggerates the change in g_L, but both the extent of the exaggeration and even its existence are uncertain. With access to a finer industrial analysis, for example, my estimated effect might have been greater, and this could have offset, or even more than offset, the double-counting element.[27]

(a) Industrial reallocation of employment

Table 16.7 gives estimates of the rates of growth of the quality of employment arising from changes in the industrial pattern of employment for our three countries. All the effects are small, and so are the changes from before to after 1973. g_L may have increased about 0.2 per cent per annum more slowly after 1973 than before in the USA and the UK, while

[26] See, for example, Birch (1981, 3–14); and the Survey on Small Businesses in the *Financial Times*, 12 June 1984.

[27] For example, the construction industry in the USA is treated as a homogeneous unit in the industrial analysis of employment in the next section. However, there has been a shift *within* that industry. 'This industry once employed largely highly-skilled union workers; now it is predominantly non-union, and its members are relatively unskilled labourers' (Baily 1981, 45).

Table 16.7   Estimated effects of changes in the industrial allocation of employment on the rate of growth of its quality

	No. of separate industries	Period	Estimated effect on rate of growth of quality of employment		
			Laspeyres-weighted	Paasche-weighted	Fisher-weighted
USA	56	1948–73	0.0001	− 0.0007	− 0.0003
		1973–85	− 0.0016	− 0.0021	− 0.0018
		Change	− 0.0018	− 0.0014	− 0.0016
UK	10	1951–73	n.a.	0.0003	n.a.
		1973–85	− 0.0003	− 0.0018	− 0.0011
		Change	n.a.	− 0.0021	n.a.
Japan	7	1953–73	− 0.0013	− 0.0011	− 0.0012
		1973–84	− 0.0013	− 0.0012	− 0.0012
		Change	0.0000	− 0.0001	0.0000

Sources: Official national income accounts publications of the countries concerned, supplemented for the UK by publications of the Department of Employment.

Notes

The quality index for year 1, with year 0 as base, is

$$Q_L \text{ (Laspeyres-weighted)} = \frac{\Sigma(w_0 n_1)}{\Sigma(w_0 n_0)} \div \frac{\Sigma(n_1)}{\Sigma(n_0)}$$

$$Q_P \text{ (Paasche-weighted)} = \frac{\Sigma(w_1 n_1)}{\Sigma(w_1 n_0)} \div \frac{\Sigma(n_1)}{\Sigma(n_0)}$$

$$Q_F \text{ (Fisher-weighted)} = (Q_L \, Q_P)^{\frac{1}{2}}$$

where w = average income from employment per employee in each industry, and n = numbers of employees in each industry (full-time equivalents in the case of the USA) and the summation is across all industries.

Agriculture is included for the UK but not for the USA and Japan, since the estimates for g_L for the last two countries already allow for reallocation between it and other industries.

Owing to changes in industrial classification, the UK estimates for 1951–73 link separate estimates for 1951–9 and 1959–73, while those for Japan link 1953–61 with 1961–73 and 1973–80 with 1980–4.

the difference for Japan was negligible. It is of some interest that most of the effects were negative, especially after 1973, indicating a slight shift of employment towards lower-paid industries. For both the USA and the UK, the Paasche-weighted index numbers grew more slowly than the Laspeyres-weighted ones. This implies that employment tended to grow most rapidly in those industries in which average earnings grew most slowly. In Japan the weighting made scarcely any difference.

(b) Employment growth in smaller versus larger enterprises or establishments

Employment may be classified by the size of the *enterprise* in which it occurs, or by the size of the *establishment*, size in each case being measured by numbers of persons employed. 'In broad terms, establishments are physically separate centres of productive activity, most readily identified with plants. Enterprises, on the other hand, are separate legal and financial entities, which may consist of a number of establishments, and are generally recognised as firms.'[28] For both types of entity, there is evidence that average earnings as well as other fringe benefits tend to be lower the smaller the entity.[29] This is due to a variety of reasons, such as more part-time employment,[30] more very young or very old workers, more women, or workers with fewer years of formal education,[31] or workers with lower rates of unionization.[32]

In a period in which profits are being squeezed by cost pressures, small firms may grow faster than big ones. In smaller firms, real wages and profit margins may be more flexible downwards, the threat to survival is greater, and new small firms may spring up to fulfil new needs which large firms are less aware of or are less capable of adapting to meet. By contrast, in a boom period the advantages may lie more with bigger firms, which can obtain finance more easily and undertake large investments for rapid growth. At all events, there is evidence that small firms[33] suffer smaller net employment losses in a recession[34] and make a greater contribution to net job growth in slow-growing or declining industries than large firms,[35] and that small firms provide a larger share of employment in some service industries (such as wholesale and retail distribution, hotels and catering, and some miscellaneous services) than in manufacturing. Because the years since 1973 have been characterized by weak demand, slow growth, and a relative decline in manufacturing production in most OECD countries, one might therefore expect that employment would have shifted more towards small firms since 1973 than in the boom years before. Furthermore, because of the lower wages in small firms, this should have depressed the rate of growth of labour quality by comparison with the earlier period. Again, the problem of double-counting rears its ugly head. Changes in part-time work,

[28] Quoted from OECD (1985, 64). This invaluable survey of recent work in this area is the basis for much of what follows.

[29] See OECD (1985, 78 and 79, Tables 31 and 32). The data refer to the USA and Japan and (for average earnings) to some West European countries.

[30] See OECD (1985, 78 and 79, Table 32). The data refer to the USA and Japan and show a doubling of the share of part-timers in the smallest size category.

[31] See US Small Business Administration (1984, 240, Table 4.2, 242, Table 4.3, and 246, Table 4.6) for data for the USA in 1979.

[32] See Millward and Stevens (1986, 58–9, Table 3.4).

[33] The OECD (1985) study defines enterprises employing less than 20 people as *very small*, those employing less than 100 people as *small*, those employing 100–499 workers as *medium-sized*, and those employing 500 or more as *large*. In what follows, I retain those definitions.

[34] The OECD study (1985, 76) cites the Canadian Federation of Independent Business, *A Study of Job Creation: 1975 to 1982 and Forecasts to 1990*, on this point.

[35] The OECD study (1985, 73) cites Birch and MacCracken (1982) and Armington and Odle (1982) on this point.

age and sex composition, and educational attainment are in principle already allowed for in our measure of g_L, so that their contribution to explaining lower wages in small firms should be excluded. However, wage rates are probably lower for similar workers in smaller firms, partly because of lower unionization, partly because the conditions of work are more attractive to some workers, and partly because such firms operate under more competitive conditions which compel them to pay less if they can. One might expect that their ability to do so would be increased by the recessionary atmosphere and growth in unemployment since 1973. Self-employed and family workers are also more important in very small firms, and their earnings are often well below average.

The evidence for a shift of employment towards small firms since 1973 is mixed and subject to some controversy. There are two ways in which it has been measured. Most straightforwardly, one can compare 'snapshots' of the distribution of employment by firm size (or, failing that, by establishment size) at different dates. Some evidence of this kind is presented below. It points to a sizeable shift in Japan, and also in UK manufacturing, *if one compares the years since 1973 with the years before*. It is that comparison which is the relevant one if one wants to find out whether g_L has fallen by more than my first estimates suggest. For the USA, unfortunately, the latest data that I have been able to obtain refer to 1977. There is, then, only a rather small shift comparing 1972–7 with 1958–72. However, there is some reason to believe that the shift may have become more pronounced in the early 1980s (see below).

The second way in which the contribution of small firms to employment growth has been measured is by means of what are called 'longitudinal' studies. It has been pointed out that the straightforward 'snapshot' comparison of the distribution of employment by firm size may not give a good measure of the extent to which employment growth in small firms accounts for the total growth of employment. The following quotation makes the point with admirable clarity:

Take, for example, employment growth in firms of less than 20, and 20 or more, employees. If, at the time of the initial survey, a particular firm had 15 employees, and at the time of the next survey had grown by ten to 25 employees, with all else unchanged, the snapshot data would show employment by very small firms falling by 15, and employment by larger firms growing by 25. However, the true situation is that very small firms have in fact contributed ten jobs to net employment growth. The difficulty here arises from firms crossing the boundaries of the size groupings as they expand or contract, affecting the picture on contributions to net employment growth. (OECD 1985, 72)

This problem can be overcome by using data that refer to the employment histories of the firms concerned. Unfortunately, such data are not widely available, and some of the available studies suffer from various limitations.[36] The OECD (1985) study surveys a number of these, of which the most important are those for the USA already referred to: Birch and MacCracken (1982) and Armington and Odle (1982). The former found that some 70 per cent of private sector net employment growth from 1978 to 1980 came from small enterprises, whereas the latter claimed that only about 40 per cent (i.e. about the same as small firms' share of employment) had done so (although about 78 per cent of net job growth occurred in small *establishments*). In a subsequent study for the US Small Business Administration (1985), Armington and Odle found that in the years 1976–82 small firms accounted for 53 per cent of net employment growth, while the US Small Business Administration itself (1984b) found that in the recession period 1980–2 much more than all net employment growth was due to small firms. Unfortunately, these studies, and in fact nearly all of those mentioned in the OECD (1985) study, refer only to periods ending well after 1973, and so do not permit a comparison to be made of the change between the years before and those after that year. It is significant that the one longitudinal study quoted as providing data for the earlier years (for manufacturing in Scotland: *Scottish Economic Planning Department 1980*) found that, for existing establishments over the 1954–74 period, employment fell in all size categories, but more so in establishments with less than twenty-five employees. The conclusion of the OECD study is that, while there are serious data problems for the longitudinal studies, 'it seems reasonable to conclude that small firms have been particularly important in net job growth over the past ten or fifteen years. The same finding also holds, perhaps with a little more certainty, for establishments' (OECD 1985, 80). It seems quite likely that an even stronger conclusion holds for the contrast between pre- and post-1973.

Can any estimate be made of the implications for the growth of g_L? In order to provide some very rough estimates, I have used the available 'snapshot' data, for the USA, the UK, and Japan. As we have seen, there are reasons why this may exaggerate the adjustments required to g_L as first measured, and there are also reasons why it may understate the adjustments. Not much weight can then be placed on the estimates, but they are the best I can obtain. They are given in Table 16.8.

So far as they go, the estimates show, first, that in all three countries there was a shift towards smaller enterprises (for the USA) or establishments (for the UK and Japan), which would have tended to reduce g_L in the years after 1973. However, the data for the USA, which extend just to 1977, show only a very small shift to have occurred. For the UK the shift was appreciable, reducing the rate of growth of labour quality by 0.3 per cent per annum, but the data refer only to manufacturing industry. The

---

[36] For example, if a sample of existing firms are asked to provide past histories of their employment growth, the sample will be biased by the exclusion of firms that have disappeared.

Table 16.8   Estimated effects of the allocation of employment between different sizes of enterprises or establishments on the rate of growth of its quality

	Nature & no. of size classes	Sector covered	Weighting system	Period	Estimated effect on g_L
USA	Enterprises, 5 classes	See below[a]	Earnings per employee, 1977	1958–72	0.0013
				1972–77	0.0006
				Change	−0.0007
UK	Establishments, 6 classes	Mfg.	Fisher-wtd earnings per employee, 1951, '73, '83	1951–73	0.0012
				1973–83	−0.0021
				Change	−0.0033
Japan	Establishments, 3 classes	Private non-agriculture	Earnings per month, 1981	1957–72	0.0036
				1972–81	−0.0025
				Change	−0.0061

[a] Minerals, manufacturing, wholesale trade, retail trade, selected services, and (from 1967) construction.

Sources: USA: from (1) US Small Business Administration, *The State of Small Business*, March 1982, Tables A1.28 and 29 and (2) *The State of Small Business*, March 1984, Table A2.24. *UK:* from (1) Board of Trade, *Census of Production for 1951, Summary Tables Part I*, HMSO, 1956, Table 4; (2) Dep. of Industry, Business Statistics Office, *PA 1002 Business Monitor 1973 Report on the Census of Production Summary Tables*, HMSO, 1976, Table 6; and (3) Dept. of Trade and Industry, Business Statistics Office, *PA 1002 Business Monitor Report on the Census of Production 1983 Summary Volume*, HMSO, 1986, Table 6. *Japan:* from *Statistical Yearbook 1983*, Tables 3–27 and 4–3.

shift was apparently greatest for Japan, amounting there to a reduction in the rate of growth of labour quality of some 0.6 per cent per annum.

Japan has an unusually large proportion of employment in very small firms, in which average earnings per employee are usually low by comparison with those in larger enterprises. As they are of particular interest, the Japanese data used to estimate the quality change are shown in Table 16.9. It may be seen that the share of employment in establishments with fewer than five persons fell from 1957 to 1972, but then rose slightly to 1981. In contrast, the share in establishments with thirty or more persons engaged rose in the earlier period, and then fell from 1972 to 1981. Average earnings in the first group in 1981 were only a half of those in the second, so that this shift had a pronounced effect on the quality index, that index being simply average earnings assuming that, in each size class, earnings per person remained as in 1981.[37]

[37] If wages for size class i in 1981 were w_i, and if the proportion employed was k_{it} in year t, then the quality index for year t is $\Sigma_i(w_i \, k_{it})$. More detailed data of persons engaged in 9 different size classes of establishment, ranging from 1–4 persons to over 1,000 persons, were available in the source, but not matching earnings data. However, an attempt was made to

Table 16.9   Proportions of persons engaged in private non-agricultural establishments in Japan, average monthly cash earnings and quality index.

	Proportions of persons engaged in establishments of size				Quality index[b]
	1–4 persons	5–29 persons	30+ persons	All	
1957	0.2752	0.3304	0.3944	1.0000	213.9
1972	0.1953	0.3237	0.4810	1.0000	225.8
1981	0.2054	0.3694	0.4253	1.0000	220.8
Earnings[a]	136	201	279		

[a] Average monthly cash earnings of regular workers in 1981 (thousands of yen).
[b] $\Sigma_i(w_i k_{it})$ = avg. monthly earnings assuming earnings for each size class are as shown in 1981.
Source: Statistical Yearbook 1983, Tables 3–27 and 4–3.

To summarize the above: for all three countries the evidence does suggest that shifts in the composition of the labour force occurred after 1973 at a faster rate than before that date, which had the effect of reducing the growth of labour quality. If we take the calculations at their face value, they point to an extra decline in g_L of some 0.0022 in exponential growth terms for the USA, 0.0061 for Japan, and 0.0034 for the UK.[38] We have seen reasons why these differences might exaggerate, and also reasons why they might understate, the true effects. In the case of the USA, however, there seem to be particularly good reasons for thinking that true g_L is exaggerated, even after adjustment. This is because later data than I have been able to use suggest that the shift to small firms continued; and, probably still more important, the studies by Schmidt and Hunter referred to in Denison (1985) suggest that there was substantial misallocation of labour in recent years as a result of the implementation of the Civil Rights Act of 1964. Another possibility is the extent and pattern of immigration into the USA in recent years. According to Borjas (1987), the flow of legal immigrants has both increased and worsened in quality, in the sense that immigrants' earnings have fallen relative to those of native-born Americans. In addition, the flow of illegal immigrants may also have increased, and their earnings would again tend to be below those of

piece together the latter from various sources and so to construct a quality index using all 9 size classes. The resulting change in the rate of growth of quality from 1957–72 to 1972–81 was virtually the same as that calculated for the three size classes.
[38] For the USA and Japan, the changes shown in the last columns of Tables 16.7 and 16.8 have been added to obtain the figures given. For the UK, the Paasche-weighted change in Table 16.7 was added to 0.4 times the change shown in the last column of Table 16.8, 0.4 being the average weight of manufacturing in business sector employment.

comparable native-born workers. One could justify a further reduction in g_L in the USA of, say, 0.005 or even more for these reasons.[39]

16.6   Capacity utilization

The importance of variations in capacity utilization in any empirical study of growth is stressed in Chapter 2, and readers are reminded of it in several later chapters. A glance at almost any chart of output shows fluctuations which must result in variations in the rate of capacity utilization. Growth theory seeks to abstract from these, and to explain changes in capacity rather than in actual output. However, it is the latter and not the former to which published data refer. The rate of growth of capacity is similar to the rate of growth of output only if changes in capacity utilization (the ratio of output to capacity) are small. If we knew the changes in utilization we could infer the changes in capacity from those of output. How, then, can changes in utilization be estimated?

Before considering possible answers to this question, let us first examine the notion of capacity more closely. In much theoretical discussion, a firm's capacity is defined as the output it would produce if it were to minimize its average costs.[40] A distinction has been drawn between the short run and the long run: in the former the firm's capital stock is taken as fixed, whereas in the latter all factors except, presumably, entrepreneurship, are variable. While this concept may be useful for a discussion of the static theory of imperfect competition, attempts to dynamize it rapidly become complex. It does not provide us with an operational criterion by which we can estimate the changes in capacity utilization that have actually occurred.

Let us consider briefly why such changes do occur in the first place.[41] The demand for a typical firm's output varies for numerous reasons: according to the time of day, the day of the week, the season of the year, and the state of the trade cycle. Firms do not vary their inputs to match all these fluctuations in demand, nor do they attempt to eliminate them altogether by varying their prices. Presumably, they consider that it would be unprofitable to do so. Many items of fixed capital have to be ordered, built, and installed over long periods, and must then be planned years in advance of their utilization. Inventories can be increased or decreased quickly, but in fact are used as a buffer between sales and output, or consumption and purchases. The first effect of unexpectedly high demand is to deplete them,

---

[39] See p. 484 above for further discussion. An offsetting consideration is that Denison's quality adjustments for US employment growth, which I have used, allow for shifts from non-farm self-employment to the rest of the economy, and this overlaps the shift from or towards employment in small firms.

[40] Kaldor (1935), Cassels (1937), Klein (1960), Berndt and Morrison (1981), and Morrison (1985).

[41] See Denison (1974, 294–5) for a good brief discussion.

and they pile up when demand is unexpectedly low. Much labour is similar to fixed capital: it has to be trained over long periods, and cannot be hired quickly. In principle, it could be fired quickly, but it might then be difficult and costly to re-hire, and contracts, explicit or implicit, often require long notice. Furthermore, workers' morale, and so their work efficiency, would suffer if they were laid off whenever output was temporarily reduced. As we saw earlier,[42] measured hours worked are usually more than actual hours worked for those paid by the hour, so that 'utilization' even of hourly paid workers varies considerably.

It is clear that many firms must expect to operate with excess capacity for most of the time, if they are to be able to cope with temporary peaks in demand. This is manifestly true of many shops, transport systems, power and water supplies, and a variety of other services, Factories will also often have excess capacity inasmuch as working hours can be increased, or extra shifts worked. There will also often be stand-by equipment which can be called into use if required, but which is less efficient than the equipment normally used. What 'capacity' means will thus vary depending on the nature of the good or service provided, and on whether one is referring to hourly, daily, weekly, or annual output levels. An electric power system, for example, might be able to deliver a maximum of X units of electricity in any given hour, but its annual maximum capacity would be much less than X multiplied by the number of hours in the year. This is because annual demand is inevitably uneven, and so the system could cope with temporary peaks only if the average hourly demand were much lower than X. The system's annual capacity would not be related in any simple way to its actual use during particular hours.

Because of this variety and complexity of meaning, there is no simple way of defining what is meant by 'capacity'. It is not surprising to discover that measuring changes in capacity, or in its utilization, is fraught with difficulty. With our expectations suitably lowered, let us now consider the different ways in which this has been, or could be, done. I confine attention to four.

Output moves cyclically, and the first method assumes that successive peaks in the cycle represent points of equal utilization of capacity. Variations in utilization are then equivalent to deviations in output from its trend, the trend being given by the rate of growth from one cyclical peak to the next. Unfortunately, while this method may be useful for an analysis of cyclical behaviour, it is useless for our purpose. We cannot beg the question of what the trend is since that is what we are trying to discover.

The second method is a variant of the first. Trend output is now given by some production function, the inputs to which can be measured. Deviations in output from trend again correspond to changes in capacity utilization. This method is equally useless for our purpose. The production function makes assumptions about the yield of investment (or, in orthodox terms, the rate of technical progress), which beg the question we are seeking to answer.

The third method is one devised by Denison,[43] and is in principle a useful one for the purpose in hand. Denison regarded it as impossible to measure utilization directly. Instead, he used another series, which moved like utilization and from which the latter could be inferred. He discarded the percentage of labour force unemployed and also variations in hours worked. Both refer only to labour inputs. Unemployment is affected by extraneous changes in the size of the labour force. Hoarding labour in a recession would tend to increase estimated utilization, whereas the reality would be the reverse of this. One might add the point, already made, that measured hours diverge from actual hours worked. The series chosen by Denison was the share of profits (strictly, non-labour income) in corporate national income. This share tends to rise in a boom and fall in a slump, and so to move in the same way as utilization. This behaviour can be explained by the constancy of profit margins in relation to normal (i.e. cyclically adjusted) costs, while actual costs per unit of output vary cyclically, with overheads per unit of output falling in a boom and rising in a slump. Denison accordingly regressed deviations of non-residential business output per unit of input from its trend value on annual deviations of the share of profits from its trend value over the years 1948–69. An additional explanatory variable—the deviation from trend of the ratio of average compensation per hour to the implicit deflator of national income in the sector—was brought in to allow for erratic changes in profit margins arising from price controls, for example, but this did not much affect the estimates of utilization.

The correlations were reasonably good,[44] and enabled Denison to estimate the 'normal'[45] deviation of output per unit of input from its trend value for any given deviation of the share of profits from *its* trend value. The former deviation gave Denison an index of utilization, which is all that is needed to adjust output to a constant degree of utilization. Furthermore, while the regression equation was based on a period (1948–69) when the trend of productivity appeared uniform, so that he could be reasonably confident that deviations from trend were being properly measured, the method enabled him to estimate capacity utilization in the years after 1973, when the trend was unclear. All that was needed was the profit share (and the wage/price term).

[43] The fullest description is in Denison (1974, 294–311, Appendix 0). Some later revisions are made in Denison (1979, Appendix I; and 1985, 70–4).

[44] In the equation Denison used, $R^2 = 0.898$ (see Denison 1985, 72).

[45] That is, as given by the regression equation.

Table 16.10 Capacity utilization in the USA around 1973 (%)

	Non-labour share of nat. income in non-financial corporations with inventory 'profits'		Utilization ratio for		
	excluded	included	NRB (Denison)	GDP (OECD)	Mfg. (Fed. Reserve Board)
(1)	(2)	(3)	(4)	(5)	(6)
1971	16.61	17.40	97.5	98.3	94.0
1972	17.02	18.03	97.9	100.9	100.2
1973	16.73	19.38	97.9	103.6	105.0
1974	14.35	19.31	94.2	100.5	100.5
1975	16.74	18.10	95.9	96.7	87.4

Sources: Col. (2): Denison (1985, Table I–1, col. (1)), but without adjustment for oil and gas; see his note (a). If oil and gas were excluded, the adjusted percentages for 1974 and 1975 would be 13.62 and 16.03. Denison used these adjusted figures in calculating col. (4), but the unadjusted figures are given for comparison with col. (3). Inventory 'profits' means the inventory valuation adjustment, this adjustment being made (and so the spurious 'profits' subtracted) in col. (2) but not in col. (3).

Col. (3): *NIPA 1929–76*, Table 1.13. This is the same source as Denison used for col. (2), but here inventory 'profits' (see above) are added both to national income and to non-labour income.

Col. (4): Denison (1985, Table 5–1, col. (9)), but rebased so as to make the average for 1948–72 = 100. The figures would have been negligibly different had the average for 1964–72 been set equal to 100 as in col. (5).

Col. (5): *OECD Economic Survey 1986/7 Japan*, Nov. 1986, read off Diagram 22, p. 88, and the percentages rebased to make the average for 1964 (the earliest figure shown) to 1972 equal to 100. Utilization is measured by the deviation of actual output (GDP) from phase-average trend output.

Col. (6): Federeal Reserve Board index of capacity utilization in manufacturing rebased so that the average for 1948–72 = 100. Figures from 1964, from *OECD Main Economic Indicators Historical Statistics 1964–1983*, Paris, 1984; earlier years from *Federeal Reserve Bulletin*, Nov. 1976, p. 903.

Denison's method is both ingenious and plausible. However, it does yield an estimate of utilization for 1973 that seems implausible, and this is rather important in the present context. Table 16.10 shows his index of capacity utilization for USA non-residential business when the average of the index over the years 1948–72 is set equal to 100. Somewhat surprisingly, the level of the index in 1973 is 2 per cent below average. This contrasts sharply with other possible measures of capacity utilization. Thus, for example, Denison's own estimate of the deviation of output per unit of input from its trend in 1947–73 is *plus* 0.8 per cent.[46] The OECD gives a measure of 'economy-wide capacity utilization . . . as measured by the deviation of

[46] Denison (1985, Table I-2, col. (6)). However, if the trend of output per unit of input is fitted to the years 1947–69 instead of 1947–73, the deviation in 1973 is *minus* 0.3 per cent.

actual output (GDP) from phase-average trend output' for the USA, which has 1973 as the year with the highest degree of utilization of any shown. The years run from 1964 to 1985, and the index of utilization in 1973 is about $3\frac{1}{2}$ per cent above the average of the preceding nine years (see column (5) of Table 16.10). Finally, the Federal Reserve Board's index of capacity utilization in manufacturing industry gives 1973 as about 5 per cent above the average of 1948–72 (see column (6) of the table).

A possible explanation of the discrepency between Denison's and the other estimates for 1973 is the behaviour of inventory 'profits' in that year. Firms using the FIFO method of inventory valuation make what are generally regarded as spurious profits on their inventories during periods when prices are rising, as they were very sharply in 1973. National income statisticians deduct these spurious profits (called 'stock appreciation', or 'inventory valuation adjustment') in calculating national income, and Denison's share of non-labour income is calculated making that deduction. However, if firms adopt a price mark-up which is based on material costs as they are recorded in their accounts, then it is the ratio of profits *gross* of inventory profits to total output which is the relevant measure for Denison's purpose.[47] Columns (2) and (3) of Table 16.10 compare the two different ways of measuring profits (non-labour income) as a share of output. It can be seen that the share in 1973 is not particularly high in column (2), when inventory profits are deducted, but *is* high in column (3), when they are left in. It is also significant that in 1974, when inventory profits were much greater even than in 1973 (so that the share of profits was very low in column (2)), Denison's estimated utilization ratio in column (4) is also very low, and this is shown as recovering in 1975 (when inventory profits were much reduced). Yet the course of output and other measures of utilization point to a *decline* in utilization from 1974 to 1975 (see columns (5) and (6)). This all suggests that it might be possible to improve Denison's method by making some allowance for changes in inventory profits. That, however, requires further research. Until it is done, it seems unsafe to use the method for years in which violent movements in prices occurred, as they did in the period under examination.

This brings us to the fourth method of measuring capacity utilization, which is by business surveys. These vary greatly in the questions asked and in the extent to which all the relevant information that could be obtained is in fact obtained. In the UK,[48] for example, the Confederation of British

---

[47] The relation between the mark-up and historic versus replacement cost pricing of materials was discussed long ago by Parkinson (1955, 177–196). It is interesting that his article was provoked by another massive increase in materials prices—that accompanying the Korean War.

[48] The following information for both the UK and Japan is based on OECD Department of Economics and Statistics, *Main Economic Indicators Sources and Methods: Business Surveys*, No. 37, April 1983.

Industry conducts monthly and quarterly surveys addressed to a stratified sample of about 2,000 enterprises accounting (in 1982) for about a half of employment in manufacturing. The question asked is, 'Is your present level of output below capacity (i.e. are you working below a satisfactory full rate of operation)?', to which the answers can be 'Yes', 'No', or 'Not applicable'. The proportion of 'No' answers is interpreted as the proportion of respondents operating at full capacity, but, since no information is sought or obtained on the *degree* of utilization, this seems an imperfect measure compared with what might be obtained. The Japanese quarterly survey by the Bank of Japan seems little better. Firms are asked to express a judgement generally based on machinery utilization, and the available answers are 'Excessive', 'Adequate', or 'Insufficient'. The OECD publishes the difference between those replying 'Excessive' and those replying 'Insufficient', expressed as a proportion of total replies.[49]

By contrast, the Federal Reserve Bulletin's index of capacity utilization for US manufacturing seems to be based on much better information. Since the procedures used are eclectic, they are not easily summarized.[50] Broadly speaking, business surveys of utilization rates are used, in conjunction with production index numbers, to provide benchmark estimates of capacity. For some materials, such as steel, and for utilities, estimates of physical capacity are made by trade associations, and these are also used, as are some other surveys of capacity. The Bureau of Economic Analysis's capital stock data are used as well, but less reliance has been placed on them because the other series show that capacity in recent years has grown more slowly in relation to the estimated capital stock than formerly[51]—a point to which we return below. Interpolations between the capacity estimates are made by fitting various trend lines and by using the available relevant series on materials capacity. Since the estimates are prepared for subdivisions of manufacturing, as well or for mining and utilities, various consistency checks are possible. In some cases, peak-to-peak trends in output are used. The final utilization ratios are the ratios of output index numbers to capacity index numbers.

The survey method has the great advantage that it provides estimates of utilization which are independent of estimates of trend output, thus permitting one to identify changes in trends of capacity. Furthermore, the concept of utilization is mainly left to businessmen themselves to decide, so that it refers to their norms. I do not see any other way at present of

[49] An alternative index of the ratio of output to capacity in manufacturing, based on a survey by MITI, is referred to in the note to Table 16.11.

[50] What follows in based on 'New Estimates of Capacity Utilization: Manufacturing and Materials', *Federal Reserve Bulletin*, November 1976, pp. 892–905; and 'New Federal Reserve Measures of Capacity and Capacity Utilisation', *Federal Reserve Bulletin*, July 1983, pp. 515–21.

[51] See *Federal Reserve Bulletin*, July 1983, p. 520, and also Bosworth (1982, 286–90).

obtaining an operational definition. However, there is a danger that norms may shift. If utilization remains low on average for some years, that may come to be regarded as normal, leading to an upward drift in apparent utilization rates. There could equally be a downward drift if, subsequently, utilization reverted to its previously higher average level. There is thus a good deal of uncertainty about the available data on capacity utilization.

A further problem is that the data relate, in the main, to *manufacturing*, whereas what we need are estimates for the whole non-residential business sector. Since manufacturing output is generally more volatile than service output (as measured), some way of allowing for this has to be found. I have simply regressed the utilization ratios for manufacturing on the ratios of non-residential business output to its trend value over the longest period available ending in 1973. This procedure also deals with the difficulty that both the UK and Japanese data do not directly measure utilization ratios as such, but are merely indicators of them. It is vulnerable to the criticism that the relation between utilization in manufacturing and in the rest of business may have changed after 1973. Even before 1973, the correlation coefficients were not particularly high. The resulting estimates are in Table 16.11, the note to which also gives the correlation coefficients.

The estimates imply that capacity utilization was lower in the years following 1973 than in earlier years. The rate of growth of capacity was also somewhat greater than that of trend output measured according to my standard procedure (i.e. g in Table 16.6). On both counts, one needs to make adjustments before estimating ϱ from equation (16.1).

The drop in average capacity utilization means that s, the ratio of investment to output, needs adjustment. s should be measured at a constant ratio of output to capacity. The fall in average utilization after 1973 means that unadjusted s is exaggerated by comparison with s for earlier years. Column (5) for each country in Table 16.13 then gives a suitable adjustment for s.[52]

As we would like to measure the trend rate of growth of *capacity*, rather than *output*, for the variable g, the most straightforward procedure would seem to be to fit a trend line to the index numbers of capacity in Table 16.11. While this seems satisfactory for the USA and Japan, where estimated capacity rose in every year, it is not so for the UK. Inspection of

---

[52] s is measured as the average ratio of investment to output for all the years in each period except the last (see p. 47 above). The adjustments to s in col. (5) for each country in Table 16.13 were made in proportion to the changes in average utilization for the following periods:

Country	Earlier period	Utilization	Later period	Utilization
USA	1948–72	0.993	1973–84	0.971
Japan	1966–72	1.002	1973–83	0.945
UK	1964–72	0.999	1973–84	0.979

Thus, for example, the Japanese adjusted s of $0.243 = 0.258 \times (0.945/1.002)$

Table 16.11 Utilization ratios and index numbers of capacity in non-residential business in the USA, Japan, and the UK, 1973–1985

	Utilization ratios			Capacity		
	USA (1)	Japan (2)	UK (3)	USA (4)	Japan (5)	UK (6)
1973	1.021	1.029	1.011	1.000	1.000	1.000
1974	0.996	0.993	0.988	1.006	1.023	1.010
1975	0.920	0.903	0.972	1.077	1.103	0.997
1976	0.967	0.905	0.967	1.087	1.136	1.018
1977	0.985	0.915	0.979	1.132	1.168	1.016
1978	1.002	0.916	0.982	1.186	1.221	1.040
1979	1.011	0.950	0.993	1.201	1.252	1.046
1980	0.967	0.964	0.968	1.238	1.296	1.038
1981	0.965	0.950	0.957	1.270	1.347	1.018
1982	0.908	0.937	0.963	1.303	1.390	1.009
1983	0.936	0.931	0.973	1.304	1.429	1.030
1984	0.980	0.958	0.991	1.342	1.453	1.039
1985	0.977	0.965	1.004	1.383	n.a.	1.076

Note

For sources and method of estimation, see text. The utilization ratios are all close to 1.000 for the period ending in 1973 for which trends in NRB output were judged uniform and utilization estimates were available (USA 1948–73, mean ratio 0.994; Japan 1966–73, mean ratio 1.005; UK 1964–73, mean ratio 1.000). The regressions of ratios of NRB output to its trend value on the various indicators of utilization in manufacturing mentioned in text were made for the periods just mentioned with the following r^2: USA, 0.74; Japan, 0.57; UK, 0.52. An alternative index of utilization for manufacturing in Japan, based on MITI surveys for 146 products, gives a similar result to the above (although with a rather larger drop in utilization after 1973) if the index is regressed on ratios of NRB output to its trend value for the same years, 1966–73, as above, with a rather higher $r^2 = 0.66$. If, however, the years 1961–73 are used (this utilization index being available then), the correlation is much worse, $r^2 = 0.33$, and the drop in utilization after 1973 is much smaller.

column (6) in that table shows that capacity is estimated to have moved cyclically, with a particularly marked fall from 1979 to 1982. There is the further problem that output, and probably estimated capacity as well, was affected by the miners' strike which lasted for a year from March 1984. The slope of the regression for the UK, which is in any case small, is an unreliable measure of the trend rate of growth of capacity in this period. It seems better to take the estimated rate of growth between capacity in 1973 and in 1985. For the sake of uniformity, the same was also done for the USA and Japan (1973 and 1984), although there it made little difference.[53]

[53] The average rates of growth of capacity between 1973 and 1985 (1984 for Japan) were: USA, 0.0272; Japan, 0.0340; UK, 0.0061. The fitted trend rates of growth of capacity were: USA, 0.0273; Japan, 0.0347; UK, 0.0038. This trend for the UK is below the unadjusted figure of 0.0056 and has a lower $r^2 = 0.48$.

Finally, allowance must be made for the effect of changes in capacity utilization on employment. If output falls in relation to capacity, so too will employment, although probably not so much proportionately. This is because there is some overhead labour, and because hours actually worked fall in relation to measured hours (see p. 482). In what follows, I assume that for every 1 per cent decline in the ratio of output to capacity, employment, as measured by L (and therefore including the effect on hours worked), falls by two-thirds of 1 per cent. This is similar to the relationship found by Okun for the USA (Okun 1973) for an earlier period, and it may have changed since, and may also be different in Japan and the UK. Further investigation is needed.[54]

16.7 Abnormally high required maintenance after 1973

An important reason why s as measured may exceed true s is that required maintenance may have increased, and this increase may not have been allowed for in the ordinary way as a current cost of production.

The argument that follows has some similarities to the arguments of those who believe that there has been abnormally rapid obsolescence leading to abnormal scrapping of capital since 1973.[55] It is generally held that depreciation tends to reduce the capital stock and the value of the services rendered by it. Abnormal obsolescence (arising, for example, from the rise in oil prices) would then tend to reduce the rate of growth of the capital stock and capital services below the rate calculated in the ordinary way by the perpetual inventory method. That method *assumes* fixed lengths of lives of assets. If, then, lives were shortened by the events since 1973, actual K may have grown more slowly than K as estimated on the assumption of unchanged lives. This could explain the slow-down in the growth of both output and labour productivity.

I believe that the main idea underlying this argument is sound, and that events after 1973 did lead to both mistaken new investments and abnormal scrapping of past investments. The question is how precisely this affected the growth of output and productivity. Careful readers of Chapter 1, if they have retentive memories, will realize that I consider the argument as just stated to be unacceptable. I argued there that the scrapping of worthless assets does not reduce output, and that their physical deterioration can be ignored, just as national income statisticians ignore the effects of wind and weather on ruined castles and deserted villages. If a rise in the price of oil

[54] The two-thirds figure does not allow for cyclical quality shifts in employment which Okun found for the USA, which would tend to increase it. If they were included, the already very small estimated effects of changes in utilization on labour productivity given in Table 16.14, col. (3), would virtually disappear.

[55] See Baily (1981; 1982, 423-53). See also the articles by Muellbauer *et al.* (1986).

prematurely eliminates the quasi-rent earned by, say, a gas-guzzling taxi, and the owner then drives it for the last time to the junk-yard, no output is lost thereby. The fuel used by the taxi, the driver's labour, and any other inputs associated with it are worth as much or more than their joint output with the taxi, *ex hypothesi*. So long as they can earn as much elsewhere, output should not fall when the taxi is scrapped. And if the driver, perhaps, becomes unemployed, that still leaves the conclusion intact, because the value of his labour will be subtracted from the total of inputs and so the consequential fall in output will be fully explained. There is nothing so far that helps to explain the *un*explained fall in output and productivity.

If we are to explain *that*, and if we are to remain consistent with Chapter 1 and the rest of this book, the abnormal-scrapping argument (as we may call it) needs to be carefully interpreted. I believe that this improves it and adds to its plausibility. The essential requirement, if scrapping is to help in the explanation, is that *the assets scrapped should not be worthless from a social point of view*. Thus, to continue with our example of the taxi, it must be the case that some quasi-rent is still being earned on the taxi when it is scrapped. One naturally asks, then, why the owner should scrap the taxi in such circumstances. This is where care is required. Essentially, one must have imperfect markets and price inflexibility, both of which exist despite the efforts of some economists to ignore them.

To make the point clearly, let us contrast the behaviour of a competitive economy with flexible prices with one in which competition is imperfect and *real* prices (including factor prices) are more inflexible. Imagine that they have similar production structures, and that both are subjected to a supply shock, which for concreteness I shall assume consists of a rise in the price of oil. In the competitive flexible-price economy, there is no reason to suppose that assets will be either under-utilized or scrapped as long as it is both privately and socially profitable to use them. Changes in relative prices will make some assets obsolete earlier than would have been the case had oil not risen in price. They will therefore be scrapped sooner. However, for the reasons already given in Chapters 1 and 3 and in the taxi example above, this scrapping will not reduce total output at constant prices.[56] Total gross investment will still give a reasonable approximation to net investment from society's point of view—as good, at any rate, as it does in any other period. There is then no mileage to be gained in explaining the slow-down in the growth of output or productivity by reference to abnormal scrapping. Indeed, it is unclear whether *in aggregate* there will be abnormal scrapping, since, while some assets will be scrapped sooner (steelworks, say), others should be given a new lease of life (coal mines, say).

---

[56] Output at constant prices is to be measured by a Divisia index, so that any change in output is, in effect, measured at current prices, or at prices differing to a negligible extent from current prices.

Matters are different in the less competitive and more inflexible-price economy. Both capitalists and workers then have good reasons for preferring to cut output rather than prices or wage rates. A monopolist may believe that closing down one factory out of three producing a similar product will be more profitable than keeping all three going at a much lower price. Oligopolists will fear the consequences of a price war. Trade unions will want to preserve real wages for 90 per cent of their members, accompanied by employment cuts of 10 per cent, rather than start down the road of accepting wage cuts which could lead to *all* their members (they fear) being substantially worse off.

Given such behaviour, it will be the case that assets earning positive, and sometimes large, quasi-rents at current prices will either be allowed to stand idle or be scrapped. The associated labour may find alternative work, or may become unemployed, but that should not, in principle, upset my growth accounting. If the new work is lower-paid (e.g. if more employment is in lower-paid services, or in smaller firms), I attempt to allow for that in the measure of labour inputs; and if employment falls, labour input is reduced. Where error arises is in the measurement of capacity output and of net investment. Normally, it is assumed that actual output is an approximately constant proportion of capacity output and that gross investment as conventionally defined is a close approximation to net investment (see Chapter 1). However, in a period in which the events just described are occurring on a large scale, this will no longer be true. The ratio of output to capacity will fall, and required maintenance will increase, so that an abnormally large part of gross investment will be required to offset the fall in output arising from the scrapping of assets earning positive quasi-rents at current prices.

It should be emphasized that I am not assuming that businessmen or workers are acting irrationally. The decisions taken may appear to be the best that could be taken, given all the circumstances. The fact that an asset *could*, if the demand were there, earn a positive quasi-rent at current prices does not mean that it is foolish to scrap it, or to leave it idle. Admittedly, from a social point of view it would be better to operate the asset and lower prices all round, but the owners of such assets might then lose far more. The gainers would be those who buy its output, but the owners may understandably ignore their gains. Likewise, workers who remain employed may reasonably, from their point of view, prefer to maintain wages at the cost of unemployment of their fellow-workers, while the social interest would be better served by lower wages and more employment for all. Both the unemployed and consumers could gain thereby.

One might ask why the discarded assets are not bought for a song by competitors and operated at cut prices, which would yet be profitable; or why the unemployed workers do not offer themselves at lower wages in competition with their employed fellow-workers who have, apparently, let them go to the wall. Some such competition may indeed appear, but existing asset-owners and employed workers have means at their disposal to suppress it. There may be agreements to scrap capacity which can be enforced to a greater or lesser extent. Economies of scale, or lack of know-how, may make it difficult or impossible to compete with established firms. Collective agreements, the threat of strikes, and the risk of alienating their work-forces may make employers unwilling to attempt to lower wages or to take on workers at lower wages than those already employed. This is not the place to analyse such behaviour in any detail or depth. Suffice it to say that there is abundant evidence that it occurs, although elements of competitive behaviour and price and wage flexibility are also to be found. The real situation is never simple.

Let us now review some of the available evidence which shows that there was abnormal scrapping leading to abnormally high required maintenance in 1973–85. Unfortunately, there is no very *direct* evidence, since no one attempts to collect statistics of the quasi-rents earned at current prices on assets that are taken out of use, and that is what is required. We have therefore to fall back on a variety of indirect pieces of evidence.

First, the rate of business failures increased very markedly after 1973,[57] as may be seen from Table 16.12. While the liabilities of those failing were very small in relation to total business output, they approximately doubled their ratio to output in the USA and the UK, and this serves as an indicator of a higher rate of scrapping. Big firms do not often go bankrupt, so that *their* scrapping would not show up in these figures, but they were subject to the same pressures as small firms. Of course, an increase in business failures would not necessarily imply that useful assets were being taken out of production. The assets might be of little real value, or they might be bought up by other firms and put to use. One cannot be sure of the general importance of these possibilities.

An interesting detailed study of closures and adjustment in 1974–84 in the British cutlery industry sheds light on its experience, which may have at least some similarities with those of others. Although machinery was sometimes sold to competitors, the author estimates that there was a big fall in capacity but that, despite this, a lot of excess capacity remained. The study shows that, while firms that survived tended on average to be more profitable than those that were closed down, 'the failing firms did not comprise the most unprofitable firms in the industry. Of the 10 firms which earned the lowest return on capital during 1978–82, four were survivors at the end of 1984, while three of the failures were not among this "bottom ten" ' (Grant 1985, 18). One of the largest and fastest-growing firms failed,

[57] For the USA and the UK, the increase was especially marked after 1980, the highest year being 1985 for the USA and 1984 for the UK. For Japan, however, the highest year was 1977.

Table 16.12 Liabilities of bankrupt enterprises as a percentage of output in non-residential business

	Ave. of years up to 1973		Ave. after 1973	
	Period	%	Period	%
USA	1960–73	0.25	1974–85	0.49
Japan	1970–73	0.58	1974–84	0.84
UK	1960–73	0.066	1974–85	0.133

Sources: For each country, the data on liabilities for each year were divided by the current value of GDP in non-residential business, obtained as in the Statistical Appendix, and the arithmetic mean of the percentages for the years shown was calculated. The liabilities data were obtained as follows:

USA: US Dept. of Commerce, *Business Statistics* and *Survey of Current Business.* The series refer to current liabilities, i.e. 'all accounts and notes payable and all obligations, whether in secured form or not, known to be held by banks, officers, affiliated companies, supplying companies, or the Government'. They do not include long-term publicly held obligations, and offsetting assets are not taken into account.

Japan: Japan Statistical Yearbooks, 'suspension of business transactions with banks', 'amount of liabilities'. A continuous series is available only from 1970, but an estimate is given for the depressed year 1965 when the corresponding percentage was 1.57.

UK: CSO, *Annual Abstract of Statistics,* 'liabilities of debtors adjudicated bankrupt' in England and Wales with corresponding items for Scotland and Northern Ireland.

and one reason for failure was that firms persisted in high investment despite falling profits. They then became saddled with heavy bank debts, and profits turned to losses when interest rates shot up in the early 1980s. Smaller, conservative, family firms with low investment rates were better able to survive as they had very little debt. Grant is not convinced that it was always the firms with the worst long-term prospects that failed.[58] Hence, while the process of Darwinian selection worked after a fashion, this experience suggests that it may work differently in times of prosperity as compared with recession. In prosperous times, an increasing share of output may be secured by bold, growth-oriented, larger firms. In recessions such firms can come to grief, while slower-growing, more cautious, firms survive.[59]

The steel industry provides a striking, perhaps extreme, example of the effects of the changed business climate after 1973.[60] Throughout the postwar period, output and capacity had expanded strongly, although there

[58] 'Those firms which had invested most heavily in long-term adjustment were among the most vulnerable to the upheaval of 1980–82, and conversely, the firms which had the capacity to survive this period were very often firms which appear to have limited longer-term potential' (Grant 1985, 22).

[59] As usual, however, generalization is risky. Some well-managed larger firms continued both to invest and prosper in the cutlery trade in the early 1980s.

[60] The following draws on Hogan (1983), and Mény and Wright (1987).

had been cycles with shortages in some years and excess capacity in others. In many countries there were ambitious investment plans in the early 1970s, and the drop in demand which had affected all the main producers by 1975 was at first regarded by many as just another (if rather severe) cyclical downturn. Capacity continued to grow, as there are long lags involved, and as decisions to expand further were not quickly revised.

There seems little doubt that many of the investments made in this period earned very low, if not negative, returns. Steel production has tended to be dominated by cartels for a variety of reasons, but these had been of less importance in the years of expansion; furthermore, some governments and international organizations had frowned upon them. The situation changed when both steel prices and capacity utilization fell drastically in 1975 and afterwards. Cartels were then encouraged, to restrict production and investment and to raise prices.

In the EEC, various plans were introduced which began on a voluntary basis, but shifted towards controls enforced by firms, and were coupled with import restrictions and 'voluntary' export restraints. These measures were often taken in response to short-term swings in demand, but it was eventually realized that the crisis was a prolonged one. 'Restructuring' then became the aim of medium-term policy; that is, 'steel producers were strongly encouraged to close down gradually their old and inefficient plants. The reduction of productive capacity in the steel sector would have to be accompanied by new investment which would raise productivity, and hence competitiveness' (Tsoukalis and Strauss, in Mény and Wright 1987, 207). Indeed, the European Commission intended to give aid or approval 'only if the capacity increases resulting from any proposed investment were offset by capacity reduction elsewhere' (p. 201). Meanwhile, national governments subsidized their steel producers in order to enable them to keep going and to slow down the contraction in employment. After 1979, total capacity fell in the nine EEC steel-producing countries taken as a whole,[61] in the USA,[62] and in Japan.[63]

It seems probable that much of the capacity that was eliminated was profitable at current prices. 'Profits' in this context must include subsidies (since output is measured at factor cost), interest, and depreciation. There need be no profits for shareholders. If capacity had been unprofitable, why were controls needed to eliminate it? Presumably they were needed because prices had not been allowed to sink far enough to perform the elimination. It is interesting that one study of steel investment and closures in the UK

[61] Tsoukalis and Strauss, in Mény and Wright (1987, 192, Table 1). The countries are Belgium, Denmark, France, Germany, Ireland, Italy, Luxembourg, Netherlands and UK.
[62] See *Federal Reserve Bulletin*, July 1983, p. 517.
[63] See *Japan Statistical Yearbook*, 1986. The fall did not occur until 1983 as Japanese steel producers continued investing heavily until the late 1970s (see Hogan 1983, ch. 4).

argues that the British Steel Corporation 'wasted huge sums of money on unnecessary capital plant (harbours, unloading facilities, blast furnaces etc.)—we estimate about £1.5 billion worth; [and] closed many perfectly viable steel plants, for example, those at Corby, Shotton, Consett, Bilston and Shelton' (Bryer, Brignall, and Maunders 1982, 3). One important reason for the closures was that the output from these plants could be replaced by output from large new plants which, the authors argue, were 'unnecessary'. If these authors are correct in their view that the closed plants would have been 'viable', this implies again that prices were not low enough to make them unprofitable, or, in other words, that some of the capacity that was scrapped was capable of earning positive quasi-rents at current prices.

The record of the steel industry thus exemplifies several phenomena which were to be found to a greater or lesser extent in other industries: strengthening business confidence in the years up to 1973, which led to high levels of investment and the rapid growth of capacity;[64] a long time-lag between the ending of the boom and corresponding adjustments in investment, so that much investment was wasted and earned low returns; and efforts to mitigate the downward pressure on prices and profitability by a variety of measures to restrict output and investment and scrap capacity. There were many other industries in which absolute declines in total capacity occurred.[65] Such declines were quite unusual in the postwar period, during most of which capacity grew strongly. Slow growth of capacity, and a fortiori absolute declines, point to abnormal scrapping.[66]

We saw earlier that, in the USA, manufacturing capacity as measured by the Federal Reserve Board has grown more slowly than formerly in relation to official estimates of the capital stock based on the usual perpetual inventory method (see p. 502 and fn. 51). This suggests that asset lives shortened, which is consistent with abnormal scrapping and/or mistaken or wasted investments.

Wadhwani and Wall (1986) have made an interesting attempt to measure abnormal scrapping in UK manufacturing industry using company accounts. Their general conclusion is that their evidence does suggest that,

---

[64] See Hogan (1983, 15); and for Japan in particular, which was an extreme example of unbounded confidence, see Hogan (1983, 64–5).

[65] In the USA, capacity as measured by the Federal Reserve Index declined from 1979 to 1982 in petroleum refining and motor vehicle and parts, as well as in iron and steel (*Federal Reserve Bulletin*, July 1983, p. 517). In Japan there were declines in fabricated metal products (1982–5), ceramics (1980–5), chemicals (1983–5), petroleum and coal products (1982–5), pulp and paper (1981–5), and textiles (1975–85) (*Japan Statistical Yearbook*, 1986). There were also world-wide excesses of shipping capacity as oil cargoes shrank, which resulted in excess ship-building capacity.

[66] Two cross-section studies of the slow-down in productivity growth in individual industries in the USA and the UK, mainly within manufacturing, provide evidence consistent with the abnormal scrapping hypothesis: Baily (1982) and Kilpatrick and Naisbitt (undated).

because of abnormal scrapping, the official estimates of real gross capital stock overstate the rate of growth of the stock in the period 1974–82, but that the overstatement accounts for only a small part of the productivity slow-down that occurred. However, this second part of their conclusion is based on growth-accounting assumptions which are criticized in Chapter 3. In fact, if one takes their estimates at face value, they imply a very big offset to gross investment resulting from abnormal scrapping, averaging close to two-thirds of gross investment in the years 1975–82.[67] This, however, greatly overstates the case, because it makes the assumption that each £1 of assets disposed of (assumed scrapped) contributes as much to output as each £1 of gross investment. That, of course, is the standard assumption made in calculating the gross capital stock, since the change in that stock is equal to gross investment minus scrapping. As I argued in Chapter 1, this is inappropriate, since in competitive conditions each £1 of assets scrapped should contribute nothing to output, so that nothing should be deducted for scrapping. However, in the circumstances of the later 1970s and early 1980s, it seems quite likely that on average assets *were* scrapped which could have contributed to output at current prices. The reasons for this have been discussed, and the reasons for thinking that the situation differed from the earlier postwar years are discussed below. If this is accepted, one can take Wadhwani and Wall's figures as providing an upper bound to the likely importance of abnormal scrapping in manufacturing. Thus, if, for example, each £1 of assets scrapped contributed one-third as much to output on average as each £1 of gross investment, then abnormal scrapping could have offset about a fifth ($0.64 \div 3$) of gross investment in the period considered. This is still a substantial amount, but it has to be recognized that the estimates are very uncertain.[68]

The last piece of indirect evidence for abnormal scrapping to be considered relates to business confidence, or 'animal spirits', *an*. The

[67] This figure was arrived at as follows. Wadhwani and Wall's estimates refer to 333 manufacturing companies accounting for 26% of manufacturing employment in 1979. They provide estimated annual percentage changes in the gross capital stock in manufacturing at 1980 prices for the years 1972–82 both as officially estimated and as estimated from the accounts of their sample. There are four versions of the latter. Taking what appears to be their preferred version (Measure (iv) in Table 2), one finds that from 1972–74 the gross stock grew 0.84% p.a. faster than the official estimates, while from 1974 to 1982 it grew 1.45% p.a. more slowly. One could then assume that abnormal scrapping, not allowed for in the official estimates, reduced the rate of growth of the gross stock by about 2.3% p.a. in the years 1975–82 inclusive. Using the official estimates of the gross stock at 1980 prices and of gross fixed investment in manufacturing in the 1986 Blue Book, one can then easily calculate that, on average, abnormal scrapping equalled 64% of gross fixed investment in the years 1975–82.

[68] See Wadhwani and Wall (1986) for their own warnings about the assumptions they had to make to derive their estimates. Clearly, the small and non-random nature of their sample is one important cause of uncertainty. Another is their assumption about the average age of assets disposed of. They had to make some assumption in order to convert historic cost figures to replacement costs.

influence of this was first mentioned in Chapter 9, and its importance in post-Second World War years was gauged in Chapter 15. *an* measures the shadow premium that growth-orientated managements give to output, which results in their choosing more labour-intensive investments, with higher q and l, than if they were seeking to maximize the present value of the firm to the shareholders (see p. 277). The estimates in Chapter 15 suggested that in the period 1948–73 firms on average in the USA and the UK were attaching a substantial premium to output, so much so that they were behaving as if they were operating in perfect markets, and therefore as if the price of output equalled its marginal revenue (see p. 444–6). *an* was then high enough to compensate for, and offset, the actual imperfection of markets (i.e., $\eta + an \approx 1$: p. 444). The implication of this finding is that scrapping, where it occurred, should have had a negligible effect on output, just as if markets really had been perfect. Assets would not be scrapped so long as their quasi-rents were positive at current prices.

After 1973, business confidence was badly shaken. The recessions experienced in many countries were the worst since the 1930s, profits were squeezed, and bankruptcies increased. One would expect, then, that *an* would fall, with the following consequences. In the first place, this should result in either a less labour-intensive form of investment being chosen (lower q and l), or a lower rate of investment (s), or in a lower share of wages in value added (λ), or some combination of these. The evidence that this did indeed occur is considered later (p. 521). Second, with managers attaching relatively more importance to profits and less to growth, they would adopt a harder line on scrapping. Marginal revenue would now be treated as being less than price, and it would be quasi-rents in marginal revenue terms which would now be relevant. An asset whose quasi-rent was still positive at current prices could have a zero or negative quasi-rent if one substituted marginal revenue for price. Scrapped assets would then no longer be valueless from a growth accounting point of view. This change in business priorities would explain both an increase in the rate of scrapping and an increase in the importance, per pound of assets scrapped, of their effects on output.

It seems likely that business confidence was also weak in the 1930s—and, in the UK at least, in the 1920s as well. In Chapter 10 we showed that ϱ was much lower then than in 1948–73. The above argument suggests that part of the explanation for the lower ϱ was this weaker business confidence, leading to lower *an* and more scrapping with a bigger impact on output than in the postwar boom years.

In conclusion, there does seem to be plenty of indirect evidence that the years since 1973 have witnessed much more abnormal scrapping of assets with potentially positive quasi-rents at current prices than in earlier postwar years. Unfortunately, no firm estimates can be made as to how much extra required maintenance resulted from this, but in what follows I shall, for illustrative purposes, assume that it was equivalent to one-fifth of gross investment. Besides this additional required maintenance, the evidence points to a large amount of mistaken and wasted investment, whose effect must have been to reduce ϱ.

16.8 Conclusions on the causes of the slow-down

Many possible explanations of the slow-down in productivity growth have now been considered. In what follows, these are fitted into the framework used throughout this book. This enables us to assess their relative importance, and also to answer the obvious question about their permanence. Should we expect the lower rate of productivity growth to persist? Or can we hope for a return to the golden postwar years of rapid growth?

Table 16.13 summarizes the relevant data for our three countries, each for two periods, before and after 1973. This is used in Table 16.14 for an analysis of the slow-down. The notes to the tables explain how the figures were obtained. g_L for 1973–85 differs from its value in Table 16.6 because of the adjustments suggested in Section 16.5 above. Likewise, s in column (7) of Table 16.13 is adjusted for the reasons set out in Sections 16.6 and 16.7, and also shown in columns (5) and (6). Finally, ϱ for 1973–85 in column (8) of Table 16.13 is substantially greater than in Table 16.6 because of these adjustments to g_L and s. There is still a fall in ϱ comparing pre- and post-1973 values, but it is much reduced by these adjustments.

Turning to Table 16.14, the first five columns analyse the change in $g - g_L$, post-1973 *less* pre-1973, into five components using equation (16.1). The total change is shown in column (6). Let us consider each of these in turn.

From Table 16.13, we can see that for each country there was a fall in the rate of growth of quality-adjusted employment, g_L, and this tended to *increase* the rate of growth of productivity, since the coefficient b is less than 1, and also because of diminishing returns to labour. (The IPC is concave viewed from the origin.) However, the effects here were small in the USA and the UK.

The effects of changes in the rate of investment, s, as measured were also in the direction of increasing productivity growth in the USA, where s actually rose. There was, however, a substantial fall in s in Japan which reduced productivity growth by about 1 per cent a year. In the UK the difference on this account was negligible.

The effects of the fall in capacity utilization in all three countries were very small.

Given my illustrative assumption that abnormal required maintenance

Table 16.13 Annual exponential growth rates and other variables before and after 1973

Country	Period	g (1)	g_N (2)	g_L (3)	s as measured (4)	Capacity utilization effect on s (5)	Abnormal maintenance effect on s (6)	s adjusted (cols. (4), (5), & (6)) (7)	ϱ (8)
USA	1948–73	0.034	0.008	0.016	0.142	0.000	0.000	0.142	2.65
	1973–85	0.024	0.019	0.015	0.163	−0.003	−0.033	0.127	1.81
	Change	−0.010	0.011	0.000	0.021	−0.003	−0.033	−0.015	−0.85
Japan	1961–73	0.089	0.013	0.035	0.318	0.000	0.000	0.318	3.48
	1973–84	0.031	0.007	0.011	0.258	−0.015	−0.052	0.191	2.24
	Change	−0.057	−0.006	−0.023	−0.060	−0.015	−0.052	−0.126	−1.24
UK	1951–73	0.027	−0.001	−0.001	0.179	0.000	0.000	0.179	2.95
	1973–85	0.006	−0.008	−0.014	0.182	−0.004	−0.036	0.142	2.53
	Change	−0.021	−0.007	−0.013	0.003	−0.004	−0.036	−0.037	−0.42

Notes

g, g_N, and s in col. (4) were calculated as in the standard way for other periods (see Ch. 2), as also was g_L for the earlier period. g_L for years post-1973 was adjusted as in Section 16.5.

The capacity utilization effect on s was obtained by multiplying s as measured by average estimated capacity utilization in the later period (with utilization in the earlier period set equal to 1). See Table 16.11 and fn. 52 in the text. The abnormal maintenance effect on s was assumed to be one-fifth of s as measured in the later period (see p. 514) Col. (7) is the sum of cols. (4), (5), and (6). The value of ϱ in col. (8) was calculated from g, g_L, and s in cols. (1), (3), and (7) as in fn. 24, except that g for the later period was the estimated growth rate of capacity rather than output (see p. 504) and that g_L was assumed to grow faster than in col. (3) by two-thirds of the capacity utilization effect on g (see p. 505).

Table 16.14 Analysis of the slow-down in productivity growth

Differences (later period minus earlier) in annual exponential growth rates of productivity, $g - g_L$, arising from changes in cols. (1) – (8)

	g_L	s	Capacity utilization	Abnormal required maintenance	ϱ	Total difference in $g - g_L$ cols. (1) –(5)	Difference in $g_L - g_N$	Difference in $g - g_N$ cols. (6) & (7)
	(1)	(2)	(3)	(4)	(5)	(6)	(7)	(8)
USA	0.000	0.002	−0.001	−0.004	−0.006	−0.009	−0.011	−0.020
Japan	0.003	−0.011	−0.001	−0.008	−0.017	−0.034	−0.017	−0.051
UK	0.001	0.000	0.000	−0.005	−0.004	−0.008	−0.006	−0.014

Note

The periods being compared are as in Table 16.13. The differences in cols. (1) – (5) were calculated from equation (16.1) which gives g as a function of g_L, s, and ϱ. The increment in g arising from changes in g_L, for example, was calculated in two ways. In one, the values of s and ϱ were set at earlier period levels and the increase in g for the observed change in g_L was calculated. In the other, the values of s and ϱ were set at later period levels, and again the increase in g for the observed change in g_L was calculated. The arithmetic mean of these was then taken, and (in the case of g_L only) the increase in g_L was then subtracted to give the figures in col. (1). Cols. (2) and (4) were calculated in a similar way. Col. (3) was the sum of two effects: (i) the excess of the rate of growth of capacity over the rate of growth of output in the later period, and (ii) minus two-thirds of (i) owing to the assumed faster growth of g_L needed if output had grown as fast as capacity. Col. (4) was based on an assumed offsetting of one-fifth of actual s in the later period owing to abnormal required maintenance. The values of g, g_L, s, and ϱ used in the calculations are given in Table 16.13, but the value of s in the later period was the sum of cols. (4) and (5) there, and the capacity utilization effect on g is given by comparing col. (1) in Table 16.13 with the estimated growth rates of capacity given in fn. 53 between the first and last years of the period. Cols. (6) and (7) can also be derived from that table.

offset one-fifth of s, the resulting falls in productivity growth were quite substantial (column (4)): about 0.5 per cent each for the USA and the UK, and over 0.75 per cent for Japan.

Finally, the effect of the residual fall in ϱ on productivity growth shown in column (5) was large for Japan (1.7 per cent per annum) and important still for the USA and the UK. There were several different factors behind this. Both Japan and the UK had caught up further with the USA and hence presumably profited less from imitation. Using the estimated catch-up factor from equation (11.3), one can estimate that about one-sixth of the fall in ϱ for Japan, and half of that for the UK, was due to that. A second explanation for the fall in ϱ was the deterioration in the terms of trade. The country's IPC shrinks inwards because the 'price' of its output has fallen in relation to consumption goods in general. If one assumes that this shrinkage is adequately measured by the terms-of-trade effects estimated in Table 16.5, then the resulting fall in ϱ explains about 3 per cent of the total fall in ϱ for the USA, about 8 per cent for Japan, and about 13 per cent for the UK.[69]

A third explanation for the fall in ϱ in the USA, and possibly in the other countries as well, was the group of factors referred to by Denison as the 'legal and human environment', including legislation on pollution abatement and worker safety and health, and the cost of increased dishonesty and crime. Denison estimates that these factors reduced the measured growth rate in 1973–82 by 0.16 per cent per annum as compared with 1948–73 (Denison 1985, 107, Table 7-1). That would be equivalent to about a quarter of the fall in ϱ for the USA. A fourth explanation for the fall in ϱ in Japan was labour-hoarding. According to Maddison, there was probably significant labour-dishoarding in the postwar years up to 1973, but this was reversed after 1973. Hoarding resulted both from the employment of family workers (which is, however, to some extent already allowed for in our adjustment to g_L for the shift in the composition of employment between larger and smaller establishments), and from the 'lifetime' commitment to male workers in large firms (see Madison 1987).

Fifth, ϱ would have fallen in all three countries because of the slow-down in other countries: each would have benefited less from the externalities of investment arising from learning and demand growth which were discussed in Chapter 15.[70] A final explanation of the fall in ϱ in all countries was the

---

[69] There is considerable doubt about these estimates, since, apart from anything else, they refer to *national* changes in terms of trade whereas all estimates in Table 16.14 are for the non-residential business sector. One has to assume that the sector shared propoportionately in any losses. In the UK, in particular, with North Sea oil and gas excluded from our definition of the non-residential business sector, this assumption is questionable.

[70] See Sections 15.5 and 15.6. The loss of externality arising from learning is doubtful, however. Does the externality depend on measured gross investment, which actually rose in the USA and the UK, or on gross investment less abnormal required maintenance, which fell in all three countries given our illustrative assumption?

increase in mistaken and wasted investment. This probably accounted for the remaining fall in ϱ.

To what extent were these factors temporary or reversible and to what extent permanent? By 'reversible' I mean that, if macroeconomic performance, apart from productivity growth, returned to the norms of 1948–73 (so that large cycles in output and generally depressed conditions of demand with under-utilization of capacity were avoided, as well as very large fluctuations in relative prices), then productivity growth would also revert to its norm. I assume that s would revert to its pre-1973 levels, but that the post 1973 levels of g_L would be maintained. This is consistent with the treatment of s as endogenous and g_L as exogenous.

Most of the major factors mentioned in the discussion of Table 16.4 are in this sense reversible or temporary. That applies to all the changes in s (columns (2), (3), and (4)) and to both the 'mistaken investment' and the 'externalities' components of the change in ϱ. It probably also applies to the component arising from changes in the terms of trade, since such changes tend to reverse themselves. In fact, the permanent factors are confined to the changes in g_L and those owing to catch-up and the legal and human environment. It seems likely that three-quarters or more of the fall in $g - g_L$ is temporary or reversible. In particular, there is no need to suppose that there has been any fundamental deterioration of the quality of investment opportunities. That conclusion is important, but scarcely surprising. The timing of the slow-down, and its coincidence in so many countries, strongly suggest that common factors associated with macroeconomic behaviour were at work. It follows that a reversion of that behaviour to pre-1973 norms would also reverse most of the slow-down. However, that does not mean that such reversal will be either easy or rapid.

Before discussing that further, let us consider the last two columns of Table 16.14, which account for the difference between $g - g_L$ and $g - g_N$. It is the latter measure of productivity growth that enters more into popular discussion, and it is also of more importance for living standards. The difference between the two is, of course, $g_L - g_N$, which is shown in column (7) of the table. In each of the three countries there was a substantial fall in this growth rate—that of the quality of the employed labour force. What explains this fall? Once again, I attempt to distinguish temporary and reversible factors from more permanent ones.

The shift of employment towards small firms was probably largely reversible—a phenomenon of depression, not boom (see p. 492). That accounted for 0.006 out of the total 0.017 fall in $g_L - g_N$ in Japan, and 0.003 out of the total of 0.006 fall for the UK. For the USA, however, the available data showed only a small fall. A fall in hours worked, faster than before 1973, was observed in all three countries, and some of that was probably due to depression. But these effects were moderate—around 0.002 for each country. All the other causes of the fall in $g_L - g_N$ must be classified as 'permanent'. These include the reduction in the gains from the reallocation of labour between agriculture (and, for the USA, non-farm self-employment[71]) and the rest of the economy; the effects of legislation in the USA on the allocation of labour; changes in the extent and pattern of immigration into the USA; changes in the age and sex composition of employment; and changes in education.[72] The upshot is that, whereas for the USA and Japan the bulk of the fall in $g_L - g_N$ (say, 1 per cent per annum in each country) was probably 'permanent', in the UK most of the fall was not.

In conclusion, therefore, the answer to the question of whether productivity can be expected to recover or not depends on the following main consideration: can we return to the relatively smooth macroeconomic behaviour of the years before 1973? If we can, then most of the reduction in $g - g_L$ can be expected to be reversed. On the other hand, while a similar conclusion applies just as strongly to the UK for the reduction in $g - g_N$, it must be weakened for the USA and Japan, where $g_L - g_N$ can be expected to remain around 1 per cent per annum lower than before 1973. These conclusions perhaps over-confidently ignore Lindbeck's remarks about emerging 'arteriosclerosis' which were quoted earlier (see p. 487). They result from a rather mechanical extrapolation of the past, and could be upset by fresh changes yet to come. The failures of prophecy are well enough known.[73]

16.9   'Animal spirits', the shares of wages and profits, and the growth of employment

The following discussion starts from the formula for μ, the proportional marginal product of labour, which is also the slope of the IPC at the equilibrium growth point:

$$\mu = \frac{dq}{dl} = \frac{\lambda}{\eta + an - \dfrac{s}{1 - T_s}} \tag{16.2}$$

[71] Denison's estimates, which form the basis of those used here, allow for this particular form of reallocation of labour. To some extent this offsets the failure to allow properly for shifts to small firms in the USA: see fn. 39.

[72] For both Japan and the UK, I extrapolated other economists' estimates of the improvements in labour quality owing to education. Consequently, the changes here were either zero or very small by assumption. For the USA, Denison's estimates covered the years up to 1982.

[73] 'The human race, to which so many of my readers belong, has been playing at children's games from the beginning. . . . And one of the games to which it is most attached is called . . . "Cheat the Prophet". The players listen very carefully and respectfully to all that the clever men have to say about what is to happen in the next generation. The players then wait until all the clever men are dead, and bury them nicely. They then go and do something else. That is all. For a race of simple tastes, however, it is great fun.' Chesterton (1904, bk. 1, ch. 1).

where $g = sq$; $g_L = sl$; λ is the share of 'wages' in value added; η is marginal revenue divided by price; *an* is 'animal spirits', i.e. the premium added by management to η which reflects their preference for growth and output over profits; and T_s is the marginal tax rate on savings, including an allowance for fixed-interest borrowing. All these terms, and the equation itself, are explained in earlier chapters.

Since the IPC is concave to the origin because of diminishing returns to labour, μ diminishes as l, the labour intensity of investment, is increased. From Table 16.15 it can be seen that in both Japan and the UK l fell after 1973, while in the USA it rose. The implication is that μ rose in Japan and the UK and fell in the USA. *Ceteris paribus*, that would have resulted in a rise in the share of wages, λ, in Japan and the UK, and a fall in the USA, as can be seen from equation (16.2); and that indeed is what happened, although the fall in the USA was negligible (see Table 16.15).

Table 16.15   The labour intensity of investment (l), the share of wages (λ), and 'animal spirits' (*an*)

	Period	l	λ	*an*
USA	1948–73	0.109	0.726	0.488
	1973–85	0.138	0.725	0.655
	(adj.)	0.120		0.463
Japan	1961–73	0.109	0.613	0.502
	1973–84	0.068	0.685	0.537
	(adj.)	0.059		0.426
UK	1951–73	−0.005	0.716	0.486
	1973–85	−0.059	0.744	0.446
	(adj.)	−0.099		0.400

Note

$l = g_L/s$. The adjusted values of l use the adjusted values of g_L *and s* shown in Table 16.13, while the unadjusted values for 1973–85 (or '84) are as in Table 16.6. λ is the share of wages calculated in the standard way; i.e., it is the unweighted average of the shares for all years in the period except the last, and excluding 'slump' years when output was below its previous peak.

an is calculated from the formula for μ as described in the text. The adjusted values for *an* use the adjusted values of g_L and s. For the post-1973 period two values of *an* were calculated from these adjusted values, one allowing for and the other not allowing for the drop in average capacity utilization from 1948–73 to 1973–85 for those years for which λ was calculated, and the mean of these is shown in the table. (See text for further explanation.)

However, equation (16.2) shows that there are other variables that could have changed, either offsetting or reinforcing the effect of a change in μ on λ. By inserting estimates or guesses for all the variables in (16.2) save one, it is possible to calculate the implied value of the remaining variable. I have assumed no change in η, and have estimates for all the other variables[74] except *an*, thus permitting it to be calculated. The results are shown in the last column of Table 16.15.[75] The main point that emerges is that, *if one uses the adjusted estimates of g_L and s* for the years after 1973, then *an* falls. If, however, one uses the unadjusted estimates, *an* rises for the USA and Japan, and falls only moderately for the UK. Since a fall in 'animal spirits' almost certainly occurred, the adjustments are to some extent vindicated. In other words (and given, of course, the theory underlying the whole argument), it is plausible to suppose that g_L and s in these countries were appreciably lower than my initial measurements suggest, since this results in a fall in the estimated value of *an*.[76]

What would be the implications of a return to the smoother macroeconomic behaviour of the years before 1973 for the share of wages, λ? Let us assume that this would restore all the variables in the denominator on the right-hand side of (16.2) to their pre-1973 levels.[77] Then whether λ was likewise restored would depend on whether μ, and so l, would have to be higher than before if we wanted g_L to be higher. In the UK (and probably in several continental European countries as well), a faster growth of employment is much to be desired as a means of reducing existing high levels of unemployment. The implication is, then, that λ should be lower in order to encourage more labour-using forms of investment, and perhaps considerably lower than the levels to which it had climbed by 1985.[78] In

[74] $\mu = b - 2c\,(l/\varrho)$, and so can be calculated from equation (16.1) which gives $b = 0.9034$ and $c = 0.4193$, and with l and ϱ as in Tables 16.15 and 16.13. Table 16.15 also gives λ. I have set $\eta = 0.55$ as in Table 15.3 with $\epsilon' = 6$, s is as in Table 16.13, and $1 - T_s$ is from Table 14.2 for the USA and the UK, using the 1960 estimate for households (as the marginal supplier of finance) for the years before 1973 and the 1980 estimate for the years after 1973. For Japan a guess of $1 - T_s = 0.9$ was used for both periods.

[75] For the post-1973 period, two estimates of *an* were made for each country, and the average of these is shown. In one, it was assumed that business regarded the lower average rates of capacity utilization which occurred in the later period (for the years for which λ was calculated) as normal. On that assumption, the actual values of λ and s were used in applying equation (16.2). In the other, it was assumed that business still regarded the pre-1973 average rates of capacity utilization as normal. On that assumption, s in the later period was multiplied by the utilization rate in the later period and divided by that in the earlier period. The adjustment to λ was similar, but allowed for an increase in employment accompanying a rise in capacity utilization in line with the assumption described on p. 505. In practice, business may have started with this second view and moved towards the first view, and this justified the taking of an average.

[76] This assumes that η was constant from before to after 1973. One might plausibly argue that η rose, and could provide an alternative explanation for a fall in *an*. However, in my view it would be still more plausible to retain the adjustments to g_L and s and to accept that, if η did rise, then *an* fell even further than Table 16.15 suggests.

[77] There has already been a move in the UK towards raising T_s from its low 1980 level back towards higher, earlier, levels, and the same applies to the USA.

[78] i.e. 0.773, which was well above the average of 0.716 for 1951-73, or even 0.744, for the years used in our standard averaging procedure for 1973-85.

Japan, g_L will very likely remain substantially below its very high pre-1973 level, and so a higher λ may be sustainable. In the USA, the adjusted g_L in 1973–85 was little different from 1948–73, and if that remained the case no change in λ would be required. In all countries it would be possible to sustain higher shares of labour without adverse effects on the labour intensity of investment if competitiveness could be sharpened (higher η), business confidence raised (higher an), or taxation of saving reduced (lower T_s). On the other hand, λ may have to be lower if higher growth is to be achieved via a faster rate of investment.

16.10 Final conclusions

This book is about long-term economic growth, yet in this chapter we have had to consider matters that would usually be regarded as the province of short-term macroeconomics: inflation, deflation, and cyclical fluctuations in output and capacity. The obvious lesson is that these are of great importance for long-term growth. I conclude that the slow-down and its cure both depend on such factors. The slow-down in productivity growth is not to be explained by a fundamental worsening of investment opportunities; nor is rising unemployment in many European countries to be explained by the very opposite (as some would have us believe)—a sudden acceleration in productivity growth which makes more and more workers redundant. On the contrary, both are quite explicable in other terms.

That, unfortunately, makes neither of them easy to deal with. My analysis of the slow-down attributed part of the blame to the rise in oil prices, OPEC I and OPEC II. But the greater part of the inflationary upsurge of the 1970s was due, in my view, to rising aspirations and strengthening confidence in full employment and growth in the 1950s and 1960s. Expectations of rising real wages were coupled with expectations of a rising 'social wage'—of better and better collectively provided services and more generous pensions and other transfers from the state. These rising expectations collided with a lower ceiling imposed by worsening terms of trade in the early 1970s. Where moderation was quickly accepted, the damage was limited; but where moderation was replaced by militancy, the eventual reconciliation of aspirations to reality took longer and was much more costly.

Although some errors were made, I do not, myself, believe that the subsequent deflation and rising unemployment were due mainly to errors in macroeconomic policy which could easily have been avoided by recourse to some superior alternative policy. The proponents of that view have not shown that such an alternative was available, and it seems implausible that so many governments would have ignored it had it been so. If this is accepted, the principal problem that has to be overcome in returning to the rapid growth experienced after the war is that of readjusting expectations and aspirations. On the one hand, wage-earners' expectations, and the expectations of those benefiting from public services and transfers, have to become sufficiently modest. On the other hand, businessmen's 'animal spirits' have to recover. A good deal of progress has been made in both directions, and there is no reason why it should not continue. The contention of this chapter, that most of the slow-down in quality-adjusted labour productivity growth can be reversed, should then be tested. That contention is still conjectural, but let us hope it will eventually be demonstrable.

STATISTICAL APPENDIX

1 Introduction

This appendix gives some further details of the sources and methods used to derive the basic statistics analysed, mainly, in Chapters 10 and 11. The statistics themselves are also given: those for periods in Table SA I, and those for individual years for the USA, Japan, and the UK in Table SA II.

While it is hoped that enough explanation has been provided for most readers, it seemed impractical to describe all the estimates in full. The next three sections deal with particular topics—the derivation of the variable used to measure the scope for catch-up, *cu*, the derivation of the weights used in the regressions, and an explanation of how the effects of changes in hours of work on labour productivity were estimated. These three sections are followed by four more describing the sources and methods used for the USA, Japan, the UK, and the continental European countries.

2 The scope for catch-up, *cu*

As noted in Chapter 10, a variable measuring the scope for catch-up, *cu*, was introduced to help explain differences in growth rates between different countries in the years since the Second World War. This section describes how the variable was estimated.

The aim was to measure output per man in non-residential businesses (but excluding agriculture) in each country in each year relative to the corresponding output per man in the USA, taken as being the leading country. For any particular period, *cu* was then the arithmetic mean of those relatives for the years in the period. Agriculture was excluded because it was thought that relative output per man there was not a good indicator of the scope for catch-up, since productivity was much influenced by special factors such as the availability of good-quality land and heavy protection.

In principle, output in each country needed to be valued, for this comparison, at the same prices as for the USA. This could be done using either the country's own prices or US prices, the former showing, in general, an appreciably lower level of output relative to that of the USA than the latter. Countries tend to produce relatively more output of goods that are relatively cheaper. It seemed best to take the geometric mean of these two price comparisons, i.e. an intermediate set of price weights. If one were to imagine the lower-productivity country growing over a period so as to catch up the USA, while that country stood still, then growth in the catching-up country would on average be measured using an intermediate set of price weights, assuming some approximation to a Divisia index. If one were instead to use either the country's own initial price weights or US price weights to measure growth, it would either exceed or fall short of this and so would not correspond to the gap that actual growth performance would reveal.

In principle, the input of labour in the productivity comparison needed to be quality-adjusted, since some of the differences between countries were due to differences in labour quality, and, in so far as this was the case, there were no corresponding differences in the scope for catch-up. There might be corresponding differences in the scope for improving labour quality, but that would show up in g_L, not in ϱ.

The main sources used for labour inputs were Denison with Poullier (1967), and Denison and Chung (1976). Each country was compared with the USA in 1960, except for Japan, for which the comparison was made in 1970. Denison provides estimates of the differences in labour input arising from: annual hours of work (allowing for differences in the efficiency of work, owing to differences in hours of work); the age and sex composition of employment; education; and the proportion of self-employment and unpaid family workers (excluding agricultural workers). Outputs were compared using the work of Gilbert and Kravis (1954), Gilbert and associates (1958), and Kravis *et al.* (1975). The first two of these are cited in Denison with Poullier (1967) and were used for all countries except Japan, for which the last was used.

Both outputs and labour inputs were adjusted so far as possible to correspond to NRB, excluding agriculture, for the year of comparison (1960 or 1970). However, extrapolating the ratios to earlier or later years, index numbers of Q/L for the country concerned relative to those for the USA were used as the best indicators readily available. These index numbers refer to the whole of NRB.

Output per (quality-adjusted) man employed in NRB (excluding agriculture) in each country relative to the USA in the base year was estimated. These figures are given in Table SA.1.

Table SA.1 Output per (quality-adjusted) man employed in non-residential business[a] in each country

Country	Relative output per quality-adjusted man employed (USA = 1)	Base year
Japan	0.563	1970
UK	0.443	1960
Belgium	0.572	1960
Denmark	0.544	1960
France	0.588	1960
Germany	0.567	1960
Italy	0.471	1960
Netherlands	0.492	1960
Norway	0.621	1960

[a] Excluding agriculture.

3 Weights used for the regressions

As noted in Section 10.2, in fitting equations by least squares to the twenty-six observations for different countries and periods, each observation was multiplied by a weight. These weights consisted of the square roots of the products of three variables: namely, for each period, the number of years in the period, the mean population of the relevant country in that period, and an index of statistical reliability of the data for that period. Mean populations were taken simply as the geometric means of populations in the first and last years of each period, the sources used being as follows.

USA: 1929-73; *Survey of Current Business,* Special Supplement, July 1981, Table 8.2; 1889-1929, linked at 1929 using *Historical Statistics of the United States 1789-1945*, series B31.
Japan: 1889-1970, Ohkawa and Shinohara (1979), Table A53, interpolating to get mid-years; 1970-3, *United Nations Monthly Bulletin of Statistics*, October 1982.
UK: 1856-1962, Feinstein (1972), Table 55, column (1); 1962-1973, CSO *Monthly Digest of Statistics*, November 1982.
Continental European countries: OECD *Manpower Statistics 1954-1964,* 1965, Table 1.

The three components of the weights are shown in Table SA.2, together with their rounded products. The observations were multiplied by the square roots of this last column of figures.

4 The effects of changes in hours of work on labour productivity

This section provides a fuller explanation and discussion of that in Section 2.2. When hours of work are long, a reduction can generally be expected to result in some offsetting increase in output per man-hour. The offset is greater the longer are hours per week or per year; indeed, hours can be so long that a reduction in hours per year actually increases output per year. As Sidney Webb and Harold Cox (1891, 4) concluded, 'in the arithmetic of labour, as in that of the Customs, two from ten is likely to produce, not eight, but even eleven' (quoted in Denison with Poullier 1967, 59). As Denison points out,

Shorter hours result in less fatigue, greater intensity of work, fewer mistakes, better quality of output, less wastage, and less absenteeism. This personal effect is greatly reinforced by an institutional factor. Many jobs require an individual's presence so long as an establishment is open, but do not fully occupy him throughout this time so that he can readily compress the same amount of work into fewer hours. (Denison with Poullier 1967, 59)

Denison mentions several other studies which have concluded that the offset exists, some of which have estimated its magnitude, and these include studies by the International Labour Organization, an expert report to the European Economic Community, the French Planning Commission, the Dutch Planning Bureau, the Norwegian government, the National Institute of Economic and Social Research, a

Table SA.2   Weights used for the regressions

Country	Period	No. of years	Mean population (m)	Statistical reliability	Weighting factor
UK	1856–73	17	30.0	0.5	255
	1873–1901	28	36.6	0.5	512
	1901–13	12	43.5	0.5	261
	1913–24	11	45.3	0.333	166
	1924–37	13	46.1	1	599
	1937–51	14	48.8	0.5	341
	1951–64	13	52.1	1	677
	1964–73	9	54.9	1	494
USA	1889–1900	11	68.6	0.5	377
	1900–13	13	86.1	0.5	560
	1913–29	16	108.9	0.5	871
	1929–48	19	133.7	1	2540
	1948–73	25	175.7	1	4392
Japan	1887–99	12	40.8	0.333	163
	1899–1911	12	46.5	0.333	186
	1911–28	17	55.7	0.333	316
	1928–36	8	66.0	0.333	176
	1952–61	9	89.7	1	807
	1961–73	12	101.1	1	1214
Belgium	1955–62	7	9.0	1	63
Denmark	1955–62	7	4.5	1	32
France	1955–62	7	45.2	1	316
Germany	1955–62	7	54.6	1	382
Netherlands	1955–62	7	11.3	1	79
Norway	1955–62	7	3.5	1	25
Italy	1955–62	7	49.2	0.5	172

German research institute for the German government, and P. J. Verdoorn and L. Reynolds. (See Denison with Poullier 1967, 59-62, for details.) Matthews *et al.* (1982) also allowed for a productivity offset in their study.

While the weight of expert opinion is therefore very much on the side of making some allowance for increased productivity as hours fall, authors disagree as to how much should be allowed. I have adopted Denison's estimates so far as he provided data for the USA, Japan, and continental Europe, and I have attempted to follow his assumptions in constructing estimates for the UK and for years not covered by him for other countries. The method used is described below. Apart from the evidence in favour of *some* adjustment, some econometric evidence in favour of the particular adjustments made here is discussed in Section 10.5. While this is not compelling, I think that labour input is better measured with the adjustment made than without. However, both measures are provided (L is with and H without the adjustment).

Denison applies his adjustment only to full-time non-farm workers. In 1960, male workers in this category in the USA worked an average of 42.3 hours per week, after reductions to allow for vacations, other holidays, sickness, and absences for other reasons. Denison assumes that a small reduction in hours of work (whether as a result of a shortening of the normal working week, or increased vacations, etc.) would have led then to a 30 per cent offset in output per man-hour. He further assumes that, had average hours worked per week been ten hours longer, at 52.3 hours per week, the offset would have been complete, so that output per year would have been unaffected by a small reduction in hours of work. 'Intermediate points are set by proportional interpolation'.[1]

While Denison does not set out his assumptions in terms of a formula, it is convenient to do so here. Let y be output per man-hour, h be average hours worked per week by full-time male workers, and k be the proportionate productivity offset. Then, by definition,

$$k = \frac{-h}{y} \quad \frac{dy}{dh}. \tag{SA.1}$$

Assumes that k increases linearly with hours worked, so

$$k = a + bh \tag{SA.2}$$

where a and b are constants. Integrating (SA.1), and using (SA.2) to eliminate k, we get

$$-\ln y = a \ln h + bh + c \tag{SA.3}$$

where c is a constant which depends on choice of units. The values of a, b, and c, can be obtained as follows. First, when $h = 42.3$, we have $k = 0.3$, and when $h = 52.3$, $k = 1$. From (SA.2) it follows that

$$1 - 0.3 = 10b.$$

$$b \qquad = 0.07$$

and

$$a \qquad = -2.661.$$

If we now, for example, choose to set $y = 1$ when $k = 42.3$, then from (SA.3) we can find

$$c = 7.00388.$$

Equation (SA.3) then enables y to be determined for given values of h. The adjusted index of man-hours can then be obtained by multiplying unadjusted man-hours by y. The results so obtained agree with Denison's.

In using this method to obtain adjusted man-hours for the UK, some modifications of Denison's procedure were necessary. First, only data on average

---

[1] See Denison with Poullier (1967, 63) and Denison (1979, 37–8), where revised estimates of hours worked in the USA in 1960 are given.

hours worked by male and female full-time workers taken together were available whereas Denison used separate series for males and females. An adjustment to 'male-equivalent' hours was made to allow for this. Second, the y-index was used to multiply *all* man-hours worked, including those by part-time workers, the self-employed, and farmworkers. Denison treated these groups differently, assuming that for part-time workers $k = 0$, and for farmworkers and the self-employed $k = 1$. Since these groups are small in the UK for much of the period covered, and since they offset each other to some extent, it is not thought that the difference is important. Finally, the above formula implies that when (male-equivalent) hours per week fall below 38.0, k becomes negative. In other words, further reductions in hours worked below 38.0 *reduce* rather than *increase* productivity. It seemed preferable to assume that there was simply no further change.[2]

5 USA: sources and methods

General

For the period 1889-1929, the main source was Kendrick (1961). For the period 1929-73, the main sources were the *National Income and Product Accounts of the United States 1929-76* (abbreviated to *NIPA 1929-76*), together with Denison (1979) and Kendrick with Pech (1973) for labour input. For the period 1973-85 the main sources were *NIPA 1929-82*, the *Survey of Current Business*, July 1986 (henceforth *SCB* July 86), and Denison (1985). Alaska and Hawaii are partly omitted before 1960 in the *NIPA* statistics, but, so far as possible, adjustments are made to remove this discontinuity.

Output at constant prices, Q

The main steps in the calculation were as follows.

1. Conventional estimates of GDP at constant prices were obtained. Up to 1929 the estimates are at market prices, and thereafter at factor cost.

2. These were adjusted by subtracting gross domestic investment expenditure as conventionally estimated at constant prices and adding back gross domestic investment expenditure at current prices deflated by the implicit price index of private plus public consumption.

3. Further adjustments consisted in subtracting output at constant prices as conventionally estimated of government (but not government enterprises), households and non-profit institutions (but see below for 1889-1928), and dwellings.

The base years used for weighting are mentioned below. For 1889-1928, Kendrick (1961) gives all the series required except the output of households and non-profit institutions and dwellings. The output of households and non-profit institutions was, accordingly, not subtracted in step 3. (I am not clear, in any case, how far it is included in the original estimates.) However, the output of government (excluding government enterprises) is given by Kendrick, and subtracted, and an estimate was made of the output of dwellings to be subtracted in each year using estimates of

---

[2] In fact, no change was assumed in y for the UK for 1973-85. Owing to an oversight, some very minor reductions in y were left in for 1970-3.

consumers' outlay on rent in Kuznets (1946, 144). These estimates are for overlapping decades at current and 1929 prices, from which annual estimates were constructed by trial and error. Kendrick's estimates are given in 1929 prices, but are based on a chain index with price weights varying every few years (Kendrick 1961, 54–5). For 1929–73, *NIPA 1929–76* gives all the series required. My understanding of the explanation given in the source of the weighting system adopted is that all quantities were weighted by 1972 prices *(NIPA 1929–76*, xiii). In general, one would expect this to result in a downward bias in the quantity index, as compared with a chain-linked index in which the prices are changed every few years. However, at least over the period 1929–53, Kendrick found very little difference between a chain-linked index and one using *1929* weights (see Kendrick 1961, 55). It is also noteworthy that the rate of growth of real GNP over the period 1948–74 was scarcely affected by the revisions made when the base year for price weights was shifted from 1958 to 1972 (see *SCB*, p. 1, January 1976, 25–6). For 1973–85, *NIPA 1929–82* gives all the series required up to 1982, and this was updated to 1985 using *SCB*, July 1986. The price weights are 1982.

Output at current prices, Y

The main steps in the calculation were as follows.
1. The gross domestic product at factor cost as conventionally defined was estimated. The average of estimates from the expenditure and income approaches was taken where both were available (i.e. from 1929 onwards).
2. From this, the output of government (but not government enterprises), households and institutions, and dwellings was subtracted.

For the period 1889–1929 the main source was Kendrick (1961). However, no estimate of GDP at current factor cost is given by him. Accordingly, the starting point was GNP at current market prices in Kendrick's Table A-IIb. From this was subtracted his estimate of net factor income from abroad at 1929 prices (Table A-III), converted to current prices using the implicit price index for GNP (see Kendrick 1961, 248). The correction from market prices to factor cost was combined with a general proportionate adjustment of the resulting estimate for 1929 to make it equal that derived from *NIPA 1929–76* and referred to below. It was assumed that this proportionate adjustment was constant throughout the period. Output of government was obtained by converting Kendrick's estimates at 1929 prices to current prices using three linked deflators. The first, for 1909–29, was the implicit deflator for government output in *NIPA 1929–76*. The second, for 1890–1909, was an index of average earnings of clerical workers in manufacturing and steam railroads from *Historical Statistics of the US, 1789–1945*, series D142. This gave similar results to the third index, Kendrick's implicit deflator for government purchases of goods and services, which was used to link 1889–1890. Output of households and institutions was not subtracted, but some allowance is made for it by the proportionate adjustment in the 1929 figure, assumed constant in other years, already referred to.

Finally, output of dwellings was obtained by multiplying the output at 1929 prices (see 'Output at constant prices *Q*' above) by an index of rents. For the years 1913–29 the Bureau of Labour Statistics (BLS) index given in *Historical Statistics* series L44, was used, which seems consistent with Kuznets (1946), Table III-10, p. 144, and also p. 105 so far as can be judged. Kuznets (1946, 138 and 105) implies that he used Carl Snyder's index for rents for years prior to 1913, and that that index 'practically does not change from 1875 to 1895, then rises gradually from 1895 to 1913'. This statement, plus Kuznets's overlapping-decades estimates, guided the annual estimates made here. For the period 1929–73, all the series required were obtained from *NIPA 1929–76*. For the period 1973–85 they were obtained from *NIPA 1929–82* and *SCB* July 1986.

Domestic gross investment at current prices, S

This is domestic gross investment as conventionally defined, including the value of the physical change in inventories, but excluding gross investment in dwellings and gross investment by government and institutions. For 1889–1929 the main source was Kendrick (1961), starting from gross private domestic investment (Table AIIb, the sum of columns (7) and (8)) and subtracting gross investment in dwellings and institutions using other sources. For non-farm residential investment Grebler, Blank and Winnick (1956, 338, Table B-6), was used. For farm residential investment 1897–1929, Goldsmith (1955, 761) was used, his estimates being extrapolated back to 1889 by guesswork. For institutions, Goldsmith (1955, 619–20) was used. For 1929–73, all the statistics are from *NIPA 1929–76*, and for 1973–85 they are from *NIPA 1929–82* and *SCB* July 1986.

Labour income at current prices, W

This is the sum of compensation of employees (including taxes and contributions for social insurance and employers' contributions for private pension and welfare funds) and the estimated labour component of income from self-employment, excluding compensation of employees in government (but not government enterprises), households, and institutions. For the period 1889–1928, no annual estimates were made. However, averages for the standard periods (1889–1900, 1900–13, 1913–29) were constructed as follows. The first two periods were based on Budd (1960, 387 and Appendix C), which provides estimates for overlapping decades from 1869 to 1913. However, his estimates of the deemed labour earnings of self-employed workers were reduced by a small amount in the light of Dension's comments on them (Budd 1960, 402) and my use of Denison's estimates for 1929 and later (see below).

It should be noted that the resulting averages of labour income *share* ($\lambda = W/Y$) are not strictly comparable with those for later periods or other countries, since recession years are not excluded. As λ tends to be high in recession years, it is somewhat overstated in 1889–1900 and 1900–13 by comparison with those other estimates. The estimate for 1913–29 was based on Kuznets with Epstein and Jenks 1941, 216–17, Table 22), which gives annual estimates for compensation of employees and 'entrepreneurial income' for 1919–38. These were each linked to corresponding items for the series from 1929 onwards and are described below. Adjustments were made to exclude labour income of government, households, and institutions. It was assumed that 0.74 of linked entrepreneurial income was labour income, since this was the ratio for 1929 which corresponded to the estimate (based on Denison) for that year described below. In making the estimate of λ for 1913–29, as for later periods and other countries, recession years, war years, and the final year of the period were excluded. In this case, however, 1913 was also excluded since no estimate for that single year was available. For the period 1929–73 the source for total compensation of employees, and for the amounts subtracted for employees in government and households and non-profit institutions, was *NIPA 1929–76*. Labour income of unincorporated business was as estimated in Denison (1979), and derived from his Tables G-1 and G-3 (pp. 170, 172). For the period 1973–85 similar estimates were made using *NIPA 1929–82*, *SBC* July 1986, and Denison (1985). The latter's estimates of labour income of unincorporated business were, however, adjusted upwards. This was because they were based on estimates of unincorporated business earnings as in *NIPA 1929–76*, and these were appreciably increased in the revised estimates in *NIPA 1929–82* (see *SCB* December 1985, p. 10). Following this adjustment, the estimates of λ for 1973 based on *NIPA 1929–82* agreed closely with that based on *NIPA 1929–76*.

Numbers employed, full-time equivalents, N

The sources used give employment in terms of full-time equivalents. For the period 1889–1929, Kendrick (1961, 305–6, Table A-VI) was used, taking his estimate for the total private economy (which includes government enterprises). Employment in households and institutions was *not* subtracted as no separate estimates were available. For the period 1929–48, Kendrick with Pech (1973, 243–4, Table A-19) gives an index of persons engaged in the private domestic economy which was linked to the preceding series at 1929. Again, no subtraction for households and institutions was made. For the period 1948–73, a series consisting of the following items from *NIPA 1929–76* Table 6.11B was used, linked to the preceding series at 1948: persons engaged in production in private domestic industries *plus* government enterprises *less* full-time equivalent employees (Table 6.8B) in educational services, social services, and membership organizations, private households, and half of those in health services. These figures exclude unpaid family workers, and so the estimates of these in Denison (1979, 154 Table B-1) were added. For the period 1973–85, similar estimates were made using *NIPA 1929–82*, *SCB* July 1986, Denison (1985), and the US Bureau of Labour Statistics *Employment and Earnings*, issues for January 1983–6.

Man-hours worked per annum, H

The only difference between H and L is the allowance made for the changing efficiency of hours worked. This section is therefore best read after that describing L, which follows immediately. For the years covered by Denison (i.e. 1929, 1940–1, 1947–82), the adjustment to L consisted simply in removing the index of 'efficiency of an hour's work as affected by changes in hours due to intra-group changes', as in Denison (1979, Table 3-1, column (5)) for the years up to 1973 and in Denison (1985, Table 3-1, column (5)) for the years 1973–82. Changes in efficiency arising from 'specified intergroup shifts' were not removed (see Denison 1979, 40–1, and

Denison 1974, 42–3). The removal was effected in a similar way to that in which the addition of the reallocation effect was made, which is described in the note to L below. For the interpolated years 1930–9 and 1942–6, two changes were involved in the procedure described in the note to L. First, the input of labour to farm business was measured in man-hours rather than in persons engaged, and, second, the adjustment made for changes in the efficiency of hours worked in non-farm business was omitted. For the years 1889–1929 the same two changes were made to the procedure described in the note to L. For the years 1982–5 Denison's index of changes in efficiency arising from intra-group changes was projected (and used to adjust L as described above) by regressing the index, for the years 1972–82, on average annual hours worked per full-time equivalent employee in private business plus government entrerprises ($r^2 = 0.988$). The latter were obtained from *NIPA 1929–82* Table 6.7B and 6.11, and was also available for 1983–5 in *SCB* July 1986.

Labour input, L

The quality-adjusted index of labour input after 1928 is based on Denison's estimates as in Denison (1979) for the years 1929, 1940–1, and 1947–73, and in Denison (1985) for the years 1973–82. It is convenient to describe this first, and then to describe the sources used to interpolate the other years, 1930–9, 1942–6, and, finally, the sources used for the years 1889–1929 and 1983–5.

Denison provides an index of labour input into the non-residential business sector which adjusts for changes in age and sex composition, for education, and for changes in hours worked. The allowance made for the last of these includes an allowance for changes in the effciency of hours worked which is discussed in Section 4 above. In addition, Denison estimates the contribution made to the growth of output resulting from the transfer of labour from farming, and from non-farm self-employment, to the rest of the sector. I have combined these effects with the other quality and quantity changes in labour input to produce an index of labour input including them all. For the years covered by Denison, it is this adding on of the reallocation of labour effects that is the only modification made here to Denison's labour input series. The adding on is most simply described for the years for which Denison gives a continuous series, i.e. for 1947–82. He estimates the contribution of the change in labour input from, for example, 1947 to 1948 to the proportionate growth of national income in non-residential business between those years as

$$\lambda_{D47} \; \frac{L_{D48} - L_{D47}}{L_{D47}},$$

that is, as the product of the labour share of national income in non-residential business in 1947, λ_{D47}, and the proportionate increase in his index of labour input (L_D). He also provides an estimate of the proportionate growth of national income in non-residential business arising from the reallocation of labour. Let us call this $R_{47/48}$. I add these together to obtain my proportionate increase in the quality-adjusted labour input as

$$\frac{L_{48} - L_{47}}{L_{47}} = \left\{ \lambda_{D47} \; \frac{L_{D48} - L_{D47}}{L_{D47}} + R_{47/48} \right\} \Big/ \lambda_{D47}.$$

It follows that, if the proportionate increase in my index is multiplied by λ_{D47}, I will get the same contribution to proportionate growth of national income as does Denison from his index of labour input plus his reallocation effect. My index of labour input is then obtained by accumulating the year-to-year proportionate changes obtained as just described. For the years up to 1973 the source used was Denison (1979). For the years 1973–82, linked at 1973, the source used was Denison (1985).

For years where a continuous series is not provided by Denison (i.e. 1929, 1940, 1941, 1947), one can follow a similar method, making the assumption that the proportionate rates of growth of output and labour input are uniform over each period. While this was not the case, it is thought that any resulting error is small.

For the years 1930–9 and 1942–6, not covered by Denison, the following sources were used to estimate an index of labour input (which included 1929, 1940–1, and 1947) which was then used to interpolate between the years he covered. Index numbers of persons engaged in farm business and man-hours worked in non-farm business were obtained from Kendrick with Pech (1973, Table A-22 and A-21). Index numbers of the age–sex compositional effect and of the education effect were obtained by interpolation of Denison's figures. An index of average hours worked in non-farm business was obtained from Kendrick with Pech (1973), and this was used to calculate an index of the changing efficiency of hours worked as described in Section 4 above. The index of persons employed in farm business was not adjusted for changes in hours worked following Denison (1979, 40), who points out that full-time farmworkers work very long hours, so that any changes in hours worked are likely to be fully offset by changes in efficiency. However, in so far as shifts in average hours worked in non-farm business were due to what Denison calls 'inter-group effects', e.g. a shift from full-time to part-time work, my attempt to allow for changes in the efficiency of hours worked departs from his more careful calculations. My index of labour input for interpolation was calculated from the above series by combining the index of persons employed in farm business with the index of man-hours worked in non-farm business (after first multiplying by the age–sex and the hours-efficiency effects) using the labour earnings weights for 1948 given in Kendrick with Pech (1973, 231). The resulting combined index was then multiplied by the education effect index. Its increase over the period 1929–47 was 35 per cent as compared with the increase of 40 per cent of the index based directly on Denison.

For the years 1889–1929, the method used was similar to that just described for the interpolating series. Index numbers of persons engaged in farm business and man-hours worked in non-farm business were obtained from Kendrick (1961, Tables A-VI and A-X), as also was an index of average hours worked in non-farm business. The last was used to calculate an index of the efficiency of hours worked in non-farm business as described in Section 4 above. It was assumed that there was no change in age–sex composition. An index of education effect is given in Denison (1962, 72 and 85). This extends from 1909 to 1958. A comparison with Denison's later estimates (Denison 1979) suggests that the earlier ones are upward-biased as compared with the later ones. Since I have used the later ones above, I adjusted the earlier ones downwards by one-third. I also assumed that the index 1889–1909 grew at the same rate as from 1909 to 1920. The weights used to combine farm and non-farm labour inputs were obtained from Kendrick (1961, 267) and refer to the years 1919–29.

For the years 1983–5 a series was built up from the components described below and this was linked on at 1981 (not 1982, because, while Denison's estimate was retained for that year, it was thought to be likely to be subject to more revision than his estimate for 1981. Also, in reconstructing the series back to 1972, there was closer agreement with Denison's series for 1981 than for 1982.) The components used were the index of N, described above; an index of annual hours per full-time equivalent employee in private business plus government enterprises (described in the note to H); an index of the efficiency of an hour's work as affected by changes in hours arising from intra-group changes (also described in the note to H); an index of age and sex composition effects using data from *Earnings and Hours* and following Denison's method so far as possible; an index of the effect of education, which was simply a projection of Denison's index for 1972–82; and an index of gains from reallocation of labour based on employment data from *NIPA 1929–82* and *SCB* July 1986. The resulting index of L agreed reasonably well with the index already described for 1972–82.

6 Japan: sources and methods

General

For the period 1952–65 (and for some series 1952–71), the data are based mainly on Denison and Chung (1979); for subsequent years they are based on various official sources mentioned below, but mainly the *Annual Reports on National Accounts* of the Economic Planning Agency of the Government of Japan (referred to as 'EPA (1981)' etc.). For the period 1941–51 no data are given. For the period 1885–1940 the main source was Ohkawa and Shinohara (1979). Annual estimates of the share of wages could not be made for this last period, although some very rough averages were estimated for the standard sub-periods (see below). While the post-Second World War series were linked to the earlier ones, so that Q, N, H, and L are all expressed as index numbers on the base 1913 = 100, this link is especially weak.

Output at constant prices, Q

The main steps in the calculation were as follows.

1. Conventional estimates of GNP or GDP at constant prices were obtained.

2. These were adjusted by subtracting estimates of gross domestic investment expenditure at constant prices, as conventionally measured, and adding back gross domestic investment expenditure at current prices deflated by the implicit price index of private plus public consumption.

3. Further adjustments consisted in subtracting output at constant prices as conventionally measured of public administration and defence, professional services (to cover health and education), domestic servants and dwellings, and also net factor income from abroad at constant prices where appropriate.

The price weights used are noted below for each period. For 1885–1940, steps 1 and 2 were based on Ohkawa and Shinohara (1979, Tables A1, A2, A3, A38 and

A39), using the series at current and constant 1934–6 prices. Their Table 3.2 was also used to provide estimates of inventory investment for years for which such estimates are not given in the other tables. For step 3, net domestic product at 1934–6 prices in 'public adminstration' (which includes defence), 'professional' and 'domestic servants, etc' as in Table A25 was subtracted, as also was personal consumption expenditure at 1934–6 prices on housing from Table A36. For 1952–65, steps 1 and 2 were based on Denison and Chung (1976), supplemented by EPA 1969 and 1973 for gross domestic investment at current and constant prices. For the constant price series, 1965 price weights were used. Outputs of general government, households, and institutions, and dwellings at constant prices were subtracted for step 3 using Denison and Chung (1976). The link from 1938 to 1952 was based mainly on data from Ohkawa and Shinohara (1979) at 1934–6 prices, supplemented by Denison and Chung (1976) and Ohkawa and Rosovsky (1973). The output of public administration and defence, and professional services and domestic servants, was based on employment data which may not be comparable, since it came from different sources for 1938 and 1952. For 1965–73, the constant price series use 1975 price weights and are mainly from EPA 1981 for all three steps but are supplemented by Denison and Chung (1976) to adjust EPA series for dwellings and the output of households and non-profit institutions to a basis comparable with that of Denison and Chung. For 1973–84, EPA 1986 was mainly used, with similar adjustments, using 1980 price weights.

Output at current prices, Y

The main steps in the calculation were as follows.

1. Conventional estimates of GNP (up to 1940) or GDP (from 1952 on) at market prices were obtained using the mean of estimates from the income–output approach and from the expenditure approach. For the earlier period it was necessary to correct for bias in the estimates before calculating the mean (see Ohkawa and Shinohara (1979, 66–8).

2. Net indirect taxes, the output of public administration and defence, professional services, domestic servants, dwellings, and (for the GNP series) net factor income from abroad were subtracted. Up to 1940, the main source was Ohkawa and Shinohara (1979); for 1952–65 the main source was Denison and Chung (1976); for 1965–73 the main source was EPA 1981; for 1973–84 the main source was EPA 1986. For the period 1952–65, the categories subtracted for public administration and defence, professional services, and domestic servants are those labelled by Denison and Chung as 'general government', 'private households', 'private non-profit institutions' (which includes private medical, health, and education institutions, as well as religious and other non-profit institutions), and 'foreign governments' (i.e. income of Japanese employees of foreign governments in Japan). For later years similar categories are given in the EPA figures, but, whereas the 'general government' figures agree closely with Denison and Chung's, the EPA figures for households and non-profit institutions are much smaller. According to Denison and Chung (1976, 140), this is because private education and health are excluded. The EPA figures were therefore increased proportionately to make them comparable with those of Denison and Chung.

Domestic gross investment at current prices, S

This equals gross domestic capital formation (including the value of the physical change in stocks) as conventionally defined but excluding investment in dwellings and government structures (or 'general government' post-Second World War). Military investment is excluded. Loss of stocks in 1923 arising from the Kanto earthquake is allowed for, but not damage to 'buildings', since it is assumed that most was to dwellings. However, damage to 'factories' and 'ships' is allowed for. The sources were the same as for Y, except that for 1952–65 EPA 1969 and 1973 were used.

Labour income at current prices, W

Annual estimates are given only for 1952 onwards. For earlier years the data are unreliable, but some rough estimates for our standard periods are given. These are based on annual data for non-agriculture and five-year averages for agriculture given in Ohkawa and Shinohara (1979, Tables A47 and 4.5). The non-agricultural data are for net domestic product, so capital consumption from Table A7 was added. The agricultural data are for *shares* of total costs of production, and these were converted to current yen using the data in Table A16. Wages of self-employed workers were imputed as described in the source. Income from dwellings is excluded, and wages of public administration and defence, professions, and domestic servants were subtracted as for Y. The period averages exclude recession and war years. That for 1899–1911 is based on data for 1906–11, 1906 being the earliest year for which data for non-agriculture are given in the source. The estimate for 1887–99 is simply the same as for 1899–1911. For 1952–65 the estimates are derived from Denison and Chung (1976), these being linked at 1965 to the estimates for 1965–73. The latter were based on EPA 1981, being the sum of compensation of employees in the whole economy, plus 0.6834 times income from unincorporated enterprises in agriculture, forestry, and fishing, plus 0.8917 times other income of unincorporated enterprises, less income of general government, households, and non-profit institutions as in Y. The multiplying factors of 0.6834 and 0.8917 are the estimated labour components of the income of unincorporated enterprises, and are those estimated by Denison and Chung for 1970, and used by them for other years in their study (Denison and Chung 1976, 174). For 1973–84 the same method was followed using data from EPA 1986.

Numbers employed, N

For the period 1885–1940, the numbers of 'gainful workers' in the whole economy are given in Ohkawa and Sinohara (1979, Table A53). These appear to include the armed forces, but not those overseas. For the years 1920, 1930, and 1940, Lockwood (1954, 465, Table 40) gives the numbers in the civilian labour force and the armed forces. His estimates agree closely with those in Ohkawa and Shinohara. Lockwood also specifies the number in 'government and the professions' and 'domestic'. For 1920, 1930, and 1940, these categories, together with the armed forces, were subtracted from the Ohkawa–Shinohara series to give numbers in non-residential business. For other years, the Lockwood figures for the subtraction were projected backward, or interpolated, using the output at constant prices of public administration and defence, professional services, and domestic servants as in Q. No corrections for part-time workers could be made. For the period 1952–71, the estimates of employment in non-residential business in Denison and Chung (1976, Table 3-4) were taken. The link from 1938 to 1952 used the 'gainful workers' series in Ohkawa and Shinohara (1979, Table A53), subtracting, for 1938, the numbers in the armed forces, the government, the professions, and domestic servants as obtained above and, for 1952, numbers employed in general government and households and non-profit institutions and foreign governments (i.e. their Japanese employees in Japan) as in Denison and Chung (1976, Tables A-1 and A-2). In view of the different series used for prewar and postwar years, the change over the war period is of doubtful reliability. For the period 1971–3, the following series was linked to the Denison–Chung figures at 1971. Total numbers employed were obtained from *Monthly Statistics of Japan*, Statistics Bureau, Prime Minister's Office, and from these were subtracted numbers employed in government, households, and non-profit institutions as in EPA 1981. For the period 1973–84 numbers employed in the whole economy and in government, households, and non-profit institutions were all obtained from EPA 1983 (for 1973–80) and EPA 1986 for 1980–4, linking at 1980. For the years 1952–72, no adjustment was made for part-time workers. From statistics given by Denison and Chung (1976, Table F-1–F-3), it seems likely that N would have grown slightly faster, perhaps by 0.2 per cent per annum, owing to a decline in the proportion of part-time workers, had an adjustment been made. For the years 1973–84, an adjustment was made, counting those working thirty-four hours or less a week as one-half of a full-time worker, using data from *Monthly Statistics of Japan*. Over this period, part-time working increased as a proportion of the whole, and the adjustment reduces the rate of growth of N by about 0.2 per cent per annum.

Man-hours worked per annum, H

For 1885–1940, and for the link 1938–52, this is the same as L (q.v.), since no adequate data on hours of work were available for these years,[3] and hence no hours efficiency offset was calculated. According to Minami and Ono, from 1888 to 1969 'there was no substantial changes in hours and days worked per worker' (see Ohkawa and Shinohara 1979, 210). For 1952–71 the figures are derived from the series for L (see below) by the same method as that adopted for the USA, that is, the effect of changes in the efficiency of an hour's work as affected by changes in hours arising from 'intra-group' changes was removed, this being the only difference. This effect is as calculated by Denison and Chung (1976, Table 4-3, column (5)). The effect arises from the improvement in productivity resulting from a fall in hours worked by full-time workers. (See Section 4 above for further discussion.) In the

[3] Ohkawa and Rosovsky (1973, 49) remark that 'pre-World War II working-hour statistics are extremely limited, and therefore not usable for present purposes'. They quote some estimates for particular years 1923–39 which do not suggest any clear or marked trend, up or down, but say that 'In the opinion of most experts, these figures are not reliable enough to indicate changes in *actual* working hours. They pertain rather to [regular or standard working hours].'

case of Japan, hours of work were so long in this period that virtually the whole of any fall in full-time hours was assumed to be offset. For 1971-3, there is a negligible difference between the H and L series, since available figures suggested little change in average hours of work. For 1973-84 average annual hours worked in the whole economy (from estimates kindly supplied by A. Maddison, and which include the effects of part-time working) were used in place of the allowance made for changes in hours and efficiency in calculating L (see below). Apart from that, the series is the same as L.

Labour input, L

Five components of the index of labour input may be distinguished: (i) the growth in numbers, (ii) the increase in productivity arising from shifting workers out of agriculture and into the rest of the economy and, in the years 1952-71 only, out of non-farm self-employment into the rest of the economy, (iii) changes in hours of work, including the resulting effects on the productivty of an hour's work, (iv) changes in the age and sex composition of the work-force, and (v) changes in the amount of education received by members of the work-force. For the years 1952-71, Denison and Chung's (1976) estimates of all five components were taken, but for earlier and later years only some of the components could be estimated.

For these other years, the method used to estimate (ii), while similar to Denison and Chung's (see their Appendix J), is not exactly the same, although it is thought that the results of the two methods are close to each other. It seemed both simpler and more straightforward to combine (i) and (ii) together in the following way. As with their method, the calculation proceeds one year at a time. It is assumed that the marginal product of labour is directly proportionate to its wage in each sector. Suppose that employment in sector i from year t to year $t + 1$ increased in proportion n_{it}. Suppose that the share of wages in GDP in sector i, at current factor cost in year t, is λ_{it}. Suppose that we are measuring output at constant prices of base-year T, and that the share of sector i in GDP at factor cost at base-year prices in year t is y_{it}. Then the proportionate growth of labour input from t to $t + 1$ arising from (i) and (ii) together is given by

$$\frac{\Sigma_i \, (n_{it} \, \lambda_{it} \, y_{it})}{\Sigma_i \, (\lambda_{it} y_{it})}.$$

In words, the proportionate growth of L from one year to the next is given by the weighted sum of the proportionate growth of employment in each sector, the weights being proportionate to output elasticities of employment in each sector[4] and to the shares of total output of each sector. Denison and Chung assume that the output elasticity in non-agriculture is proportionate to the share of labour, but for

---

[4] If the marginal product of labour equals its wage, then $\lambda_i = w_i \, L_i / Y_i = (L_i / Y_i) \, (\partial Y_i / \partial L_i)$, which is the output elasticity of employment in sector i. This is the conventional justification for using λ_i. According to the theory in this book, the output elasticity (with perfect markets) is not λ_i but $\lambda_i / (1 - s_i)$ in steady growth. Hence it has to be assumed that s_i is the same in all sectors for the formula in the text to apply. With imperfect markets there is a further assumption of uniformity required, and it is clear that the formula is, at best, only a rough approximation.

agriculture they assume an output elasticity of 0.25, which is much lower than the share of labour income (0.65–0.75, according to them), 'because labour could be withdrawn from many farms with little loss of output (and it was, of course, from such farms that it predominantly was drawn)' (Denison and Chung 1976, 226–7).[5] Denison and Chung remark that, when Ohkawa and Watanabe saw their estimates of the gains from the reallocation of labour, they thought they were too small. However, a careful examination by Denison and Chung of possible explanations for this leads them to the conclusion that they do not need to revise their estimates. Indeed, as they point out, it would not greatly increase the gain from reallocation if they were to assume that labour lost from agriculture (or unincorporated business) caused *no* drop in output there (pp. 229–34).

The opposite view, i.e. that there were *no* gains from reallocation, at least before the First World War, has been expressed by Kelley and Williamson (1974, 44–50). They argue that *some* wage differential between agriculture and industry is to be expected because of cost-of-living differences and quality differences, but that these are consistent with a close-to-perfect labour market. In the period 1887–1915 there is no evidence, they say, that industrial wages rose faster than rural ones (although average labour productivity did), and this is also consistent with a close-to-perfect labour market. However, I do not myself find their arguments persuasive. Although the data they give (Table A.2) do not suggest a large gap between *daily wage rates* in agriculture and manufacturing before the First World War (and see also Ohkawa and Shinohara 1979, Figure 13.1), there does seem to have been a large gap between average *annual labour earnings* in agriculture and the rest of the economy. Kelly and Williamson appear to dismiss annual earnings data as being 'less useful' (1974, 223). As only a small fraction of employment in agriculture consisted of wage labourers (Ohkawa and Shinohara 1979, 238), it seems quite possible that the marginal annual product of workers leaving agriculture was much below that of labour hired by the day. It is also quite posssible for the gap to persist for many years, while migration proceeds, and yet for daily wage rates in agriculture to keep in step with those in industry. One needs to know more about the locality and seasonality of employment of daily workers, and about the unpleasantness of the tasks they were asked to perform, before one can judge whether there is much validity in Kelley and Williamson's arguments. In the absence of such information, I prefer to accept the more orthodox view that the reallocation of workers from agriculture to the rest of the economy contributed substantially to economic growth as conventionally measured.

For the years 1885–1940, components (i) and (ii) were estimated as above using the numbers of gainful workers in agriculture and forestry, and in non-agriculture, as in Table A.53 of Ohkawa and Shinohara (1979). GDP or GNP in each sector was estimated from the same source (see Q and Y above), as also was the share of wages in non-agriculture at current prices (see their Table A. 47: this commences at 1906, and for earlier years the average for 1906–14 of 0.7 was assumed). For agriculture, Denison and Chung's output elasticity of 0.25 was assumed. Employment in public administration and defence, professional services, and domestic services was

---

[5] For labour moving out of non-farm unincorporated business, Denison and Chung assume that the marginal product of each worker there was only one-fourth as much as that of labour in the rest of the economy (excluding agriculture).

removed using the series calculated for Q and Y above. Component (v), changes in labour quality owing to education, was estimated using data and weights given in Ohkawa and Rosovsky (1973, Table 3.6 and pp. 56–8). Their data start at 1900, and it was assumed that the rate of growth of eductional quality from 1885 to 1900 was the same as from 1900 to 1910. No direct information on the remaining components (iii) and (iv), hours and age–sex composition, was available. Ohkawa and Rosovsky (1973, 55) take the view that the effect of changes in age and sex composition were probably slight, and, as already quoted, Minami and Ono state that changes in hours of work were probably small. However, it was decided to make a small upward adjustment in the index of L of 0.00264 per year, mainly to allow for a possible understatement of quality improvements arising from education and for reallocation out of self-employment in non-agriculture. This figure was the difference between the rate of growth of labour input over the years 1953–63, after quality adjustment, and after allowing for reallocation between sectors, in Denison and Chung (1976) over the rate of growth for the same period calculated using the same sources and methods as for 1885–1940. There were several sources of difference between those two estimtes, and it is uncertain that their magnitudes would have been the same in 1885–1940. The estimate of the growth of L in that period is correspondingly uncertain.

For the link between 1938 and 1952, essentially the same sources and methods were used as for 1885–1940. However, it was assumed that there were no net changes in quality arising from hours, age and sex composition, and education. Since employment in agriculture grew rather faster than in the rest of the economy (excluding government, etc.) over this period, the index of L grew rather more slowly than that of N.

For 1971–3, the method used for components (i) and (ii) was similar to that for 1885–1940, the data coming from EPA 1981 and from *Monthly Statistics of Japan* (as for N). However, the output elasticities in agriculture and non-agriculture were assumed constant, and were based on Denison and Chung's figures for 1963 (Denison and Chung 1976, 227). There was a negligible change for (iii), hours of work. The effects of changes in age and sex composition, item (iv), were calculated using data in *Monthly Statistics of Japan* using weights based on Denison and Chung (1976, Table G-1 and G-3) for 1971. Quality improvements owing to education were simply projected at the same rate as for 1961–71 as in Denison and Chung (1976, Table 4.3). The addition of 0.00264 mentioned above for 1885–1940 was not made.

For 1973–84, components (i) and (ii) were calculated in the same way as for 1971–3, except that the employment and GDP data were from EPA 1983 and 1986. Component (iii), changes in hours of work and in the efficiency of an hour's work, was assumed to be given by the index of N divided by the index of numbers employed with no adjustment for part-time working. Consequently, this component reflected only that part of the reduction in average hours worked which was due to the increase in part-time working (and, by counting part-time workers as equal to 0.5 of a full-time worker, when their hours of work were probably a smaller proportion than this, closer to 0.4 (see Denison and Chung 1976, Tables F-1–F-3), made an allowance for greater efficiency of part-time workers' hours). It was assumed that the remaining reduction in hours (which was small) was wholly offset by increased efficiency of work. Components (iv) and (v) were calculated as for 1971–3.

7 UK: sources and methods

General

Up to 1920, Southern Ireland is included in the UK; thereafter it is excluded.

Output at constant prices, Q

The main steps in the calculation were as follows.

1. A 'compromise' index of conventional GDP at constant factor cost was obtained by taking the equally weighted arithmetic mean of index numbers based on output, expenditure, and income data.

2. This was adjusted by subtracting gross domestic investment expenditure at constant prices, as conventionally measured, and adding back gross domestic investment expenditure at current prices deflated by the implicit price index of private plus public consumption.

3. Further adjustments consisted in subtracting output at constant factor cost as conventionally measured of dwellings, professional and scientific services (to cover health and education), public administration and defence, and domestic servants. From 1970 to 1985, the output of the industries extracting mineral oil and natural gas was excluded (their output was negligible before then).

The price weights used varied between periods. In the main, 1900 prices were used for 1856–1913, 1938 prices were used for 1913–38, and a Fisher 'Ideal' index of 1938 and 1948 prices was used for 1938–48. However, in some cases weighting was done using other years' price weights, depending on availability of data. For the years after 1948 the system of price weighting is described in the Blue Books. Broadly speaking, the price weights are updated every five years or so, and the base year is used to calculate output at constant prices for the years adjacent to the base year both before it and after it. Series over longer periods are the result of linking together the five-year series. This method gives an approximation to a Divisia index, and seems preferable to either a Laspeyres or a Paasche index in which the base year remains fixed for long periods. Up to 1948 the principle source was Feinstein (1976, 1972), and thereafter various issues of *Economic Trends Annual Supplements* and the Blue Books of *National Income and Expenditure*.

Output at current prices, Y

The main stages in the calculation were as follows.

1. Conventional GDP at factor cost was obtained as the equally weighted arithmetic mean of estimates based on income and expenditure data.

2. This was adjusted by subtracting output at current factor cost of dwellings, professional and scientific services (to cover health and education), public administration and defence, domestic servants, and the imputed rent of public capital. From 1970 the output of industries extracting mineral oil and natural gas

was also excluded. (Their output was negligible before then.) The main sources used were the same as for Q.

Domestic gross investment at current prices, S

This is gross domestic capital formation (including the value of the physical change in stocks) as conventionally defined but excluding investment in dwellings, social and other public services investment (including highways and bridges), and, from 1970 onwards, gross fixed investment in the petroleum and natural gas industries. The main sources used were as for Q, but prior to 1920 the gross fixed investment series in Feinstein (1976, 1972) was replaced by a revised series kindly provided by Feinstein which was consistent with the series used in Matthews *et al.* (1982), although still subject to further revision.

Labour income at current prices, W

This is the sum of income from employment (including taxes and social security contributions) and the estimated labour component of income from self-employment, excluding income from employment in professional and scientific services, public administration and defence, domestic servants, and, from 1970 onwards, income from employment in petroleum and natural gas extraction industries. The main sources used were the same as for Q. For the years up to 1973, the share of income from self-employment which was deemed to be labour income is that underlying Figure 6.1, p. 165 in Matthews *et al.* (1982), the figures being kindly supplied by Feinstein. The method used to estimate this was to subdivide the economy into twelve sectors, and to assume that, within each sector, labour earnings per self-employed worker were the same as per employee. For years prior to 1920, however, rougher methods were used. After 1973 my own estimates were rough, the 1973 estimate being extrapolated using numbers of self-employed (as in *Economic Trends Annual Supplement*) and average income from employment per employee in the whole economy.

Numbers employed, full-time equivalents, N

The following magnitudes were estimated:

1. total numbers employed in the whole economy (including self-employed), N_T;
2. the proportion of these consisting of part-time workers, p;
3. the ratio of hours worked by part-time workers to full-time workers, r;
4. the ratio of man-hours worked in non-residential business to those worked in the economy, h.

Then $N = hN_T(1 - p + pr)$.

As regards magnitude 1, up to 1959 the main sources were Feinstein (1976, Table 57) and Matthews *et al.* (1982, Table D.1), which gives benchmark years. For subsequent years, the *Department of Employment Gazette* for October 1975, December 1976, and later issues, and *Economic Trends Annual Supplements* were the main sources. For magnitude 2, Matthews *et al.* (1982, Table D.1) gives benchmark years 1856-1973, and intervening years were interpolated. For subsequent years annual estimates were made using various issues of the *New Earnings Survey* of the Department of Employment. For magnitude 3, estimates were made of average full-time hours per week and average part-time hours per week. For the former, the estimates were mainly based on Matthews *et al.* (1982), supplemented by Department of Employment and Productivity (1971) and also the *British Labour Statistics Yearbooks* and various *New Earnings Surveys*. The same sources were used to estimate average part-time hours. For magnitude 4, see the note for *H* below, item (2).

Man-hours worked per annum, H

(1) An estimate of man-hours worked in the whole economy was first prepared, and then multiplied by (2) the estimated ratio of man-hours worked in the non-residential business sector to those in the whole economy. This was then multiplied by a further factor (3), which adjusted for changes in age and sex composition and also for education. Item (1) used the series $N_T(1 - p + pr)$ described above in the note for *N*, multiplied by average full-time hours per week, and adjusted further so as to allow for annual and public holidays, absences for sickness, and days lost through strikes, estimates for these being derived from the same sources. For the years 1973-85 estimates of annual hours per worker were kindly supplied by A. Maddison. The ratio (2) for years 1856-1913 was that for 1913 (see below) multiplied by the ratio of (total employment in the whole economy *less* employment in the armed forces and employment in the rest of public and professional services) to total employment in the whole economy. The latter was obtained as in item 1 of the note for *N* above. Employment in the armed forces is from Feinstein (1976, Table 57), and employment in the rest of public and professional services was obtained by interpolation and extrapolation of the figures for census years, 1861-1911, in his Table 60. For years 1913-73, Matthews *et al.*'s estimates of man-hours worked by industry for benchmark years 1924-73 was the main source, and they provide a rough estimate for 1913 in Table 8.1. Interpolation was done on the basis of annual figures of employment by industry. The preceding estimates did not remove domestic servants from total man-hours, and for this (and for man-hours in oil and natural extraction gas from 1970) a different method of adjustment was used, based on the ratio of earnings by domestic servants (and oil and natural gas extraction workers) to total earnings (obtained as for *W* above). In effect, man-hours were then weighted by earnings per hour. The adjustments for item (3) followed those estimated by Matthews *et al.* (1982, Table 4.7), which gave rates of growth arising from these factors between benchmark years 1856 and 1973. The rates of growth were assumed to be constant between benchmark years, and also to be the same in the non-residential business sector as in the whole economy. For 1973-85 estimates were made based on *New Earnings Survey Data*, and (for education) on a projection of the rate of growth for 1964-73 from Matthews *et al.* (1982, Table 4.7).

Labour input, L

Labour input equals man-hours worked adjusted for age and sex composition and for education (i.e. *H*) multiplied by a further factor, *y*, which allows for the changing efficiency of an average hour's work. (See Section 4 above for further discussion.) This factor is a function of the average hours worked in a year by a full-time worker estimated from the sources mentioned in the note to N, item 3. For 1973-85, y was assumed constant, being close to its maximum value according to the formula used.

8 Continental European countries: (Belgium, Denmark, France, Germany (Federal Republic), Italy, Netherlands, Norway): sources and methods

General

The statistics throughout refer to the years 1955-62 since it was only for these years that a quality-adjusted index of employment was available from Denison (Denison with Poullier 1967). The various national income statistics needed were, in the main, derived from the same sources as those used by Denison, namely, the OECD's *National Accounts Statistics 1955-1964*, (Paris, 1966) (henceforth referred to as OECD 1966) and, for France and Germany, the OECD's *General Statistics, January 1965*. The latter was needed so as to enable a link to be formed between earlier and later series on slightly different bases. In what follows, only OECD 1966 is referred to, although this should be taken to include the January 1965 publication as well. In addition to these sources, some reference to national sources was necessary, as detailed below.

Output at constant prices, Q

The main steps in the calculation were as follows.

1. Conventional estimates of GDP at constant 1958 factor cost were obtained for 1955 and 1962.

2. These were adjusted by subtracting gross domestic investment expenditure as conventionally estimated at constant 1958 prices and adding back gross domestic investment expenditure at current prices deflated by the implicit price index of private plus public consumption.

3. Further adjustments consisted in subtracting output at constant 1958 prices as conventionally estimated of dwellings and of public administration, defence, education, and health.

All the figures were from OECD 1966. For France and Germany, GDP at market prices was used. For Denmark, France, Italy, Netherlands, and Norway, the growth rate of GDP was adjusted by the same amount as the growth rate of national income was by Denison for irregularities in the pressure of demand and in agricultural output (see Denison with Poullier 1967, 302-16). Because of these adjustments, the growth rate was measured as simply the average exponential growth rate between the end-years of the period, 1955 and 1962. Denison made no adjustment to the German growth rate for the above reasons, and his adjustment to the Belgian growth rate for the government deflation procedure was irrelevant, since the output of government is excluded here. His adjustment for construction deflation procedures in France was also irrelevant here, since investment expenditures are deflated by the price index of consumption. For the Netherlands, since the output of dwellings at constant 1958 prices was not shown separately in the source, output at current prices was deflated by the implicit price index of consumers' expenditure on rent.

Output at current prices, Y

This is GDP at factor cost *less* the output of dwellings and of public administration, defence, health, and education, the figures coming from OECD 1966. For France and Germany, output of dwellings is at market prices, but no correction to factor cost was made, so the result is to understate Y for them slightly, and overstate s and λ. Estimates for each year 1955–62 were made. Only one estimate of GDP at factor cost was available for each year in the source, so there was no averaging of estimates made from the income and expenditure approaches, as in the USA, Japan, and the UK.

Domestic gross investment at current prices, S

This is gross domestic fixed asset formation plus change in stocks less gross domestic fixed asset formation in dwellings and less gross fixed asset formation by general government. Estimates for each year 1955–62 were made. The source used was OECD 1966.

Labour income at current prices, W

This is compensation of employees plus the estimated labour component of the income of independent traders less compensation of employees in public administration, defence, health and education. Denison with Poullier (1967, 38) gives the share of the first two components of W (i.e. without the deductions for public administration, etc.) in national income as conventionally defined for the average of 1955–9 and also of 1960–2. From OECD 1966 annual estimates of national income were obtained, and the average ratio of it to Y for 1955–62 was calculated. This, combined with Denison's estimates, then gives an estimate of the average ratio of W to Y for 1955–62 before deductions for public administration, etc. Annual estimates of compensation of employees in public administration (etc.) were made using OECD 1966 by subtracting depreciation and other operating provisions in general government from GDP in this sector. Again, the average ratio to Y for 1955–62 was estimated, and this ratio was then subtracted from the preceding ratio of W (without deductions) to Y to give the final estimated average ratio of W to Y for 1955–62. This average ratio was all that was needed, and annual estimates of W were therefore not made.

Numbers employed, full-time equivalents, N

According to Denison (Denison with Poullier 1967, 65), only in Italy, of the countries considered here, was there an important change in the ratio of full-time to part-time workers. Hence, with that exception, N was simply taken as total numbers employed excluding those in the armed forces, as in Denison with Poullier (1967, 47, 49), and also excluding those in public administration, health, and education. These last were estimated using mainly national statistical yearbooks. Estimates were made only for

1955 and 1962. For Italy an adjustment was made to allow for the sharp fall in the proportion of part-time workers based on information given in Denison with Poullier (1967, 65, 369).

Man-hours worked per annum, H

The only difference between L and H is the allowance made for the changing efficiency of hours worked. This section is therefore best read after that describing L, which follows immediately. From Denison with Poullier (1967, 66 Table 6.6), one can, for each country, compute three index numbers for 1962, with 1955 = 1, which are for non-agricultural wage and salary workers only, viz.: (1) average annual hours per person employed (columns (1) and (3) of the table), (2) the (improved) quality of an hour's work arising from the fall in annual hours (columns (4) and (6)), and (3) the quality of a year's work (columns (7) and (9)). The third of these is simply the product of the first two, and is the one that was used in estimating L. For H, the only difference is that the first index number was used in place of the third.

Labour input, L

For each country, for 1955 and 1962, numbers employed in three different groups were estimated: (1) agriculture, forestry, hunting, and fishing, (2) non-agricultural employers and own-account workers and unpaid family workers, and (3) wage and salary workers in the rest of NRB. All the necessary figures are given in Denison with Poullier (1967, 47, 49), except that it was necessary to exclude wage and salary workers in public administration, health, and education from group (3). This was done using the estimates mentioned in the section above on N. Quality-adjusted index numbers of employment for each of these groups for 1962, with 1955 = 1, were then constructed and combined using estimated relative marginal products of labour in each as weights, and this weighted index of employment was L. The quality adjustments were as follows. For each of the three groups it was assumed that the adjustments for changes in age and sex composition, and for improved education, were the same, and were as given in Denison with Poullier (1967, Tables 7.7, p. 77 and Table 8.6 (A), p. 89). For group (3) only, the index of quality of a year's work given in Denison with Poullier (1967, 66, Table 6.6, columns (7) and (9)) was used to adjust employment in that group. This allowed both for changes in hours worked in the group and for the assumed effect on efficiency of falling hours of work. For groups (1) and (2), no allowance was made for changes in hours of work (either here or by Denison). It is quite likely that any changes that did occur were wholly offset by changes in the efficiency of each hour worked. The weights used to combine the index numbers of employment for each group were as follows: for group (1), one-quarter of national income per worker in the sector, except for Denmark, where the proportion was 0.33, and for Italy, where it was 0; for group (2), one-quarter of estimated average earnings of non-agriculture employees; for group (3), estimated average earnings of non-agricultural employees. All the weights were derived from estimates for 1955, and are based on the assumptions made in Denison with Poullier (1967, 214, 216).

Table SA I Data for Periods

Country	Period	g	g_L	g_N	g_H	s	λ	cu	π
UK	1856–73	0.02413	0.01418	0.00834	0.01066	0.0993	0.5419	0.5909	0.06
	1873–1901	0.02116	0.01798	0.00999	0.01715	0.1059	0.5995	0.5752	0.29
	1901–13	0.01613	0.01930	0.01143	0.01760	0.0961	0.6190	0.4806	0.58
	1913–24	−0.00125	−0.00354	−0.00400	−0.01283	0.0532	0.6540	0.4417	0.91
	1924–37	0.01939	0.01570	0.00893	0.01672	0.0812	0.6717	0.4360	0.46
	1937–51	0.01876	0.00768	0.00335	0.00548	0.0903	0.6900	0.4316	0.36
	1951–64	0.02650	0.00680	0.00448	0.00592	0.1690	0.7072	0.4347	0.15
	1964–73	0.02721	−0.01200	−0.00933	−0.01247	0.1938	0.7298	0.4794	0.00
	1973–85	0.00563	−0.01065	−0.00842	−0.01062	0.1820	0.7435	0.5553	0.75
USA	1889–1900	0.04018	0.02597	0.01840[a]	0.02285	0.1684	0.7436	1	0.27
	1900–13	0.03335	0.03340	0.02387	0.02833	0.1731	0.6771	1	0.31
	1913–29	0.03164	0.02012	0.01305	0.01504	0.1353	0.7266	1	0.31
	1929–48	0.02366	0.01855	0.00987	0.01508	0.0879	0.7257	1	0.68
	1948–73	0.03352	0.01554	0.00804	0.01511	0.1424	0.7261	1	0.16
	1973–85	0.02400	0.02253	0.01877	0.02171	0.1633	0.7247	1	0.42

Japan	1887–99	0.03280	0.01892	0.00539	0.01892	0.1323	0.5420	0.4655	0.33
	1899–1911	0.01541	0.01466	0.00344	0.01466	0.1127	0.5420	0.4182	0.50
	1911–28	0.02438	0.02530	0.00258	0.02530	0.1387	0.5636	0.4070	0.41
	1928–36	0.05275	0.03034	0.01137	0.03034	0.1360	0.5179	0.3801	0.00
	1952–61	0.09605	0.04848	0.01961	0.04991	0.2510	0.6761	0.3203	0.00
	1961–73	0.08869	0.03470	0.01312	0.03438	0.3175	0.6126	0.4537	0.00
	1973–84	0.03148	0.01744	0.00712	0.01715	0.2576	0.6849	0.5529	0.18
Belgium	1955–62	0.03469	0.01257	0.00449	0.00949	0.1647	0.6807	0.5689	0.14
Denmark	1955–62	0.04027	0.01496	0.01008	0.01091	0.1914	0.6959	0.5389	0.00
France	1955–62	0.05003	0.01607	−0.00226	0.01516	0.1829	0.6875	0.5743	0.00
Germany	1955–62	0.05867	0.01491	0.01157	0.00586	0.2228	0.6546	0.5462	0.00
Netherlands	1955–62	0.03956	0.01625	0.01048	0.01340	0.2278	0.6578	0.4885	0.14
Norway	1955–62	0.03443	0.00236	−0.00162	−0.00169	0.2839	0.6363	0.6086	0.14
Italy	1955–62	0.06133	0.03441	0.00607	0.02913	0.1931	0.6386	0.4655	0.00

Note

For the meaning of the symbols, see List of Main Abbreviations and Symbols at the front of the book. All growth rates are exponential, and the way in which the various averages were calculated is explained in Chapter 2.

[a] Owing to an error, g_N for this period was taken as 0.01527 in all the regressions in which it appears.

Table SA II   Annual data for USA, Japan, and the UK
(Years marked by an asterisk are those judged to be substantially affected by excess capacity or war, and so were excluded in fitting trends of output and employment or in calculating averages of wage shares.)

USA, non-residential business

| Year | Index numbers (1913 = 100) | | | | Ratios | |
	Q	L	N	H	s	λ
1889	38.61	46.43	57.59	50.65	0.1243	
1890	41.50	48.43	59.50	52.97	0.1918	
1891	43.34	50.13	61.01	54.77	0.1794	
1892	47.72	52.13	62.83	57.12	0.2097	
1893*	44.92	52.03	62.57	56.34	0.1687	
1894*	43.79	50.83	61.22	53.82	0.1643	
1895	49.78	54.32	64.41	58.14	0.1811	
1896*	48.71	54.81	64.72	58.16	0.1497	
1897	53.93	57.00	66.62	60.52	0.1642	
1898	55.02	57.70	67.17	61.02	0.1503	
1899	61.69	62.28	71.29	66.70	0.1686	
1900	62.28	63.73	72.40	67.77	0.1887	
1901	69.26	67.37	75.43	71.58	0.1889	
1902*	68.68	71.55	78.75	75.64	0.1988	
1903	71.78	74.40	81.11	78.41	0.1879	
1904*	70.40	74.37	80.72	77.11	0.1593	
1905	76.40	78.91	84.46	81.94	0.1585	
1906	87.06	83.07	87.80	86.03	0.1865	
1907	87.81	85.66	89.80	88.50	0.1824	
1908*	78.29	83.49	87.51	84.04	0.1278	
1909	89.55	89.06	92.02	89.81	0.1775	
1910*	89.39	92.13	94.41	92.86	0.1758	
1911	92.38	94.22	95.82	94.90	0.1495	
1912	96.15	97.91	98.60	98.57	0.1686	
1913	100.00	100.00	100.00	100.00	0.1808	
1914*	90.16	98.81	98.63	97.50	0.1073	
1915*	93.07	99.61	98.98	97.15	0.0997	
1916*	108.6	108.1	105.6	106.1	0.1445	
1917*	103.7	110.9	107.5	108.5	0.1201	
1918*	109.8	111.4	107.3	107.6	0.1043	
1919*	116.1	111.8	107.5	104.2	0.1658	
1920	118.7	112.6	108.0	105.8	0.2192	
1921*	111.6	105.2	102.1	95.28	0.0969	
1922*	117.4	113.1	107.8	103.7	0.1155	

	Index numbers (1913 = 100)				Ratios	
Year	Q	L	N	H	s	λ
1923	135.8	123.0	114.8	113.8	0.1648	
1924	140.1	120.9	112.8	111.0	0.1025	
1925	142.3	125.4	115.8	115.8	0.1477	
1926	152.6	130.5	119.2	121.0	0.1475	
1927	153.5	131.6	119.2	121.5	0.1295	
1928	154.8	133.6	120.4	123.0	0.1182	
1929	166.0	138.0	123.6	126.5	0.1502	0.7123
1930*	148.4	130.6	117.4	117.7	0.1118	0.7432
1931*	132.7	119.8	109.1	106.9	0.0672	0.7837
1932*	109.9	107.5	100.2	94.07	0.0024	0.8376
1933*	106.4	108.1	99.54	94.30	0.0216	0.8437
1934*	115.1	112.9	105.9	95.01	0.0537	0.7802
1935*	128.9	119.3	109.3	101.2	0.0994	0.7691
1936*	144.4	130.2	114.1	111.9	0.1150	0.7398
1937*	159.6	138.0	119.1	119.8	0.1456	0.7557
1938*	145.1	128.5	112.2	110.0	0.0723	0.7674
1939*	159.1	136.6	116.1	117.7	0.0951	0.7524
1940*	175.5	144.6	120.9	125.0	0.1304	0.7226
1941*	208.2	163.9	130.5	142.0	0.1455	0.6992
1942*	232.8	177.3	137.5	155.5	0.0631	0.6983
1943*	249.3	185.3	139.5	165.1	0.0305	0.7059
1944*	255.4	182.6	136.4	163.9	0.0386	0.7043
1945*	248.5	175.9	132.2	155.9	0.0609	0.7233
1946*	242.7	184.9	140.3	160.0	0.1450	0.7635
1947	246.3	193.1	146.8	165.8	0.1221	0.7391
1948	267.2	196.0	149.8	168.6	0.1484	0.7254
1949*	258.4	187.7	144.3	160.5	0.1038	0.7299
1950	286.9	194.9	147.4	167.0	0.1500	0.7102
1951	306.6	208.0	153.0	178.4	0.1600	0.7049
1952	314.0	213.6	154.5	182.2	0.1275	0.7274
1953	326.3	219.3	156.5	186.9	0.1229	0.7380
1954*	319.5	211.2	151.4	180.3	0.1146	0.7443
1955	348.0	219.3	154.4	186.9	0.1440	0.7172
1956	358.6	224.5	157.2	191.7	0.1492	0.7373
1957	360.8	224.0	157.1	190.5	0.1412	0.7412
1958*	351.3	215.8	150.2	183.5	0.1176	0.7458
1959	378.5	225.2	153.6	191.5	0.1388	0.7304
1960	381.4	226.5	154.2	192.7	0.1347	0.7432
1961	386.0	225.8	152.1	191.9	0.1279	0.7389
1962	407.0	231.6	154.1	197.5	0.1384	0.7276
1963	423.1	235.7	154.6	201.6	0.1371	0.7209

	Index numbers (1913 = 100)				Ratios	
Year	Q	L	N	H	s	λ
1964	447.9	241.2	157.0	206.1	0.1406	0.7190
1965	479.0	250.6	162.1	214.6	0.1604	0.7078
1966	506.7	260.8	167.8	222.6	0.1724	0.7068
1967	516.3	264.6	170.6	224.9	0.1599	0.7183
1968	541.9	271.5	174.1	230.7	0.1538	0.7213
1969	557.9	278.3	178.9	236.5	0.1612	0.7361
1970*	550.2	275.7	177.2	233.4	0.1498	0.7526
1971	566.4	275.6	176.2	233.4	0.1502	0.7398
1972	604.3	284.3	180.9	240.5	0.1546	0.7362
1973	644.6	298.0	189.6	251.6	0.1706	0.7370
1974*	632.4	300.3	192.3	252.7	0.1673	0.7520
1975*	625.8	291.6	185.7	245.2	0.1377	0.7282
1976	662.9	300.9	191.4	252.6	0.1533	0.7268
1977	703.2	312.6	199.3	262.2	0.1642	0.7204
1978	749.6	328.6	210.2	275.4	0.1763	0.7189
1979	766.1	340.9	218.0	285.5	0.1735	0.7287
1980*	755.3	339.6	217.3	283.7	0.1603	0.7388
1981	773.8	344.7	219.3	287.4	0.1807	0.7275
1982*	746.4	338.0	214.6	281.8	0.1525	0.7385
1983*	770.2	348.5	216.5	291.2	0.1443	0.7253
1984	830.5	372.2	228.7	311.2	0.1789	0.7135
1985	852.6	384.0	234.1	320.7	0.1648	0.7169

Japan, non-residential business

	Index numbers (1913 = 100)				Ratios		
Year	Q	L	N	H	s	λ	cu
1885	47.46	62.35	88.33	62.35	0.0915		0.3994
1886	51.07	62.45	88.40	62.45	0.0989		0.4258
1887	55.04	63.01	88.60	63.01	0.1056		0.4513
1888	58.35	64.58	89.18	64.58	0.1348		0.4633
1889	61.76	66.92	90.01	66.92	0.1256		0.4696
1890*	58.04	68.36	90.62	68.36	0.1200		0.4192
1891	65.28	69.85	91.14	69.85	0.1275		0.4574
1892*	63.86	71.66	91.72	71.66	0.1217		0.4119
1893	68.43	73.24	92.18	73.24	0.1294		0.4579
1894	70.25	71.15	91.81	71.15	0.1338		0.4849
1895	75.14	71.38	92.03	71.38	0.1432		0.4860
1896	77.31	75.80	93.31	75.80	0.1595		0.4856

Year	Index numbers (1913 = 100)				Ratios		
	Q	L	N	H	s	λ	cu
1897*	75.39	78.37	94.05	78.37	0.1588		0.4302
1898*	76.98	79.39	94.47	79.39	0.1274		0.4303
1899	81.90	80.96	95.00	80.96	0.1032		0.4321
1900*	79.13	82.13	95.37	82.13	0.1039		0.4172
1901*	81.86	82.64	95.51	82.64	0.1017		0.4077
1902*	78.38	83.58	95.86	83.58	0.0909		0.4134
1903*	75.71	83.20	95.83	83.20	0.0975		0.3991
1904*	82.38	81.13	95.50	81.13	0.0936		0.4539
1905*	80.94	81.20	95.45	81.20	0.1385		0.4356
1906*	82.86	83.05	96.44	83.05	0.1324		0.4028
1907	89.01	88.91	97.69	88.91	0.1249		0.4132
1908*	88.79	90.25	97.92	90.25	0.1198		0.4439
1909	90.60	93.13	98.23	93.13	0.1113		0.4094
1910	93.13	96.11	98.76	96.11	0.1343		0.4453
1911	99.99	95.99	98.98	95.99	0.1475		0.4495
1912*	96.80	97.85	99.45	97.85	0.1347		0.4262
1913*	100.0	100.0	100.0	100.0	0.1424		0.4231
1914*	101.2	101.7	100.4	101.7	0.1460		0.4614
1915*	110.9	111.2	101.0	111.2	0.1409		0.4516
1916*	121.3	114.4	101.4	114.4	0.1568		0.4466
1917*	133.0	112.8	101.5	112.8	0.2068		0.5335
1918*	136.4	118.0	100.6	118.0	0.2278		0.4962
1919*	128.2	109.3	98.30	109.3	0.1806		0.4779
1920	132.6	120.2	100.8	120.2	0.1876		0.4428
1921	135.7	123.2	101.4	123.2	0.1305		0.4393
1922	138.4	127.0	101.8	127.0	0.1369		0.4442
1923*	131.9	134.7	102.2	134.7	− 0.0907		0.3753
1924*	133.7	133.5	101.8	133.5	0.1443		0.3657
1925*	137.4	139.3	102.6	139.3	0.1224		0.3678
1926	140.0	142.4	102.9	142.4	0.0966		0.3557
1927	151.0	144.1	103.0	144.1	0.1473		0.3801
1928	157.1	145.7	103.3	145.7	0.1277		0.3937
1929	157.4	151.1	105.2	151.1	0.1349		0.3664
1930	162.3	159.9	107.7	159.9	0.1443		0.3780
1931	167.1	164.8	109.4	164.8	0.1420		0.3873
1932	168.2	167.0	110.6	167.0	0.0913		0.4169
1933	187.1	170.9	111.0	170.9	0.1078		0.4706
1934	209.6	176.0	111.7	176.0	0.1625		0.4943
1935	222.9	183.1	112.6	183.1	0.1777		0.4767
1936	228.4	187.8	113.9	187.8	0.1889		0.4640
1937*	250.8	187.6	112.3	187.6	0.2424		0.4891

| Year | Index numbers (1913 = 100) | | | | Ratios | | |
	Q	L	N	H	s	λ	cu
1938*	261.7	195.1	114.0	195.1	0.2194		0.5026
1939*	275.9	200.6	114.9	200.6	0.2375		0.4996
1940*	288.4	211.8	118.7	211.8	0.2507		0.4747
1941							
1942							
1943							
1944							
1945							
1946							
1947							
1948							
1949							
1950							
1951							
1952	236.0	232.4	137.5	232.4	0.2516	0.7100	0:2923
1953	255.2	247.2	146.1	247.8	0.2051	0.7075	0.2936
1954	272.7	254.9	147.9	257.2	0.1891	0.6852	0.2992
1955	300.6	261.6	152.3	264.2	0.2155	0.6935	0.3064
1956	334.2	278.2	155.1	283.2	0.2712	0.6869	0.3182
1957	383.0	299.5	159.5	305.3	0.3149	0.6547	0.3359
1958	388.6	312.4	160.7	317.6	0.2414	0.6642	0.3233
1959	427.3	326.2	161.6	331.0	0.2669	0.6584	0.3298
1960	500.7	343.9	165.7	349.3	0.3032	0.6243	0.3658
1961	572.6	356.4	166.5	360.2	0.3973	0.6131	0.3977
1962	610.9	371.7	168.9	368.0	0.3119	0.6220	0.3957
1963	656.2	382.9	170.2	376.1	0.3113	0.6313	0.4040
1964	723.9	398.7	172.3	390.2	0.3211	0.6253	0.4137
1965	750.2	415.9	175.7	419.0	0.2769	0.6314	0.3993
1966	835.1	434.2	179.7	437.4	0.2817	0.6179	0.4189
1967	942.7	448.7	183.4	454.1	0.3160	0.6075	0.4556
1968	1065	464.4	186.4	464.7	0.3279	0.6018	0.4861
1969	1201	476.7	187.7	476.0	0.3340	0.5903	0.5318
1970	1308	492.4	189.6	489.4	0.3446	0.5817	0.5632
1971	1326	506.5	189.8	501.5	0.3020	0.6109	0.5390
1972	1433	519.7	189.5	515.6	0.2853	0.6177	0.5489
1973	1584	544.9	194.1	539.7	0.2989	0.6468	0.5686
1974*	1565	550.4	192.5	528.0	0.3090	0.6744	0.5713
1975*	1534	550.7	189.9	524.3	0.2601	0.6990	0.5492
1976	1584	573.7	194.8	549.4	0.2471	0.7044	0.5303
1977	1646	586.5	197.3	562.8	0.2370	0.7016	0.5279
1978	1721	597.3	199.5	574.7	0.2309	0.6909	0.5344

Year	Index numbers (1913 = 100)				Ratios		
	Q	L	N	H	s	λ	cu
1979	1832	609.2	200.9	590.5	0.2517	0.6942	0.5662
1980	1925	622.4	202.2	604.5	0.2585	0.6770	0.5884
1981	1971	629.9	203.6	608.1	0.2558	0.6786	0.5898
1982	2006	637.1	204.8	615.5	0.2484	0.6827	0.6033
1983	2048	650.9	207.8	630.6	0.2366	0.6882	0.6024
1984	2143	658.2	208.2	644.8	0.2480	0.6816	0.6174

UK, non-residential business

Year	Index numbers (1913 = 100)				Ratios		
	Q	L	N	H	s	λ	cu
1856	31.06	39.22	60.07	46.02	0.0979	0.5763	0.5902
1857	31.25	39.32	59.93	46.15	0.0569	0.5577	0.5878
1858	31.74	38.29	58.07	44.94	0.1016	0.5403	0.6084
1859	32.35	41.11	62.03	48.24	0.0750	0.5755	0.5731
1860	33.18	41.90	62.91	49.17	0.0774	0.5739	0.5723
1861	34.26	41.65	62.17	48.76	0.0991	0.5438	0.5899
1862	34.24	41.04	60.93	47.95	0.0808	0.5299	0.5938
1863	34.66	42.23	62.34	49.22	0.1091	0.5247	0.5796
1864	35.98	43.99	64.57	51.15	0.1247	0.5229	0.5732
1865	37.26	44.63	65.13	51.77	0.1330	0.5363	0.5806
1866	37.73	44.72	64.94	51.88	0.1072	0.5368	0.5823
1867*	36.86	43.52	62.85	50.37	0.0783	0.5464	0.5800
1868	38.77	43.75	62.82	50.52	0.1228	0.5348	0.6022
1869	38.72	44.75	63.91	51.56	0.0745	0.5335	0.5835
1870	42.42	46.40	65.90	53.34	0.1091	0.5265	0.6118
1871	45.29	48.09	67.91	55.16	0.1362	0.5084	0.6255
1872	45.21	49.69	69.21	54.89	0.1047	0.5491	0.5996
1873	46.93	50.63	69.78	54.09	0.1269	0.5660	0.6062
1874	47.36	51.12	69.69	52.83	0.1082	0.5724	0.6012
1875	48.29	51.56	69.74	53.29	0.1292	0.5709	0.6032
1876	48.53	51.55	69.17	53.27	0.1302	0.5770	0.6016
1877	48.61	51.71	68.83	53.44	0.1208	0.5888	0.5962
1878	48.58	51.22	67.65	52.93	0.1093	0.5781	0.5969
1879	49.63	49.35	64.65	50.99	0.1100	0.5908	0.6281
1880	51.44	53.45	69.46	55.23	0.1125	0.5596	0.5964
1881	53.50	55.37	71.40	57.22	0.1019	0.5736	0.5942
1882	55.52	57.38	73.40	59.30	0.1398	0.5799	0.5905
1883*	55.20	58.23	73.89	60.17	0.0983	0.5960	0.5741

	Index numbers (1913 = 100)				Ratios		
Year	Q	L	N	H	s	λ	cu
1884*	54.90	55.54	69.92	57.39	0.0894	0.5890	0.5941
1885*	54.30	55.63	69.49	57.49	0.0792	0.5924	0.5821
1886*	55.10	55.95	69.32	57.82	0.0729	0.5846	0.5828
1887	58.12	58.90	72.41	60.87	0.0953	0.5860	0.5795
1888	61.23	62.00	75.61	64.07	0.0867	0.6006	0.5755
1889	66.11	65.43	79.16	67.61	0.1435	0.6127	0.5843
1890	66.34	66.63	79.98	68.86	0.1198	0.6306	0.5588
1891*	64.65	66.71	79.42	68.81	0.0760	0.6416	0.5391
1892*	61.48	65.95	77.90	68.02	0.0605	0.6600	0.4898
1893*	61.28	66.28	77.65	67.62	0.0559	0.6652	0.5150
1894	67.35	68.12	79.18	69.69	0.1032	0.6374	0.5519
1895	69.89	70.48	81.28	72.16	0.1005	0.6385	0.5204
1896	73.55	73.91	84.54	75.58	0.1101	0.6412	0.5385
1897	74.29	75.33	85.49	76.78	0.1039	0.6419	0.5013
1898	78.61	77.32	87.05	78.60	0.1275	0.6321	0.5128
1899	83.12	79.53	88.83	81.05	0.1359	0.6109	0.5074
1900*	82.22	79.91	88.55	81.27	0.1165	0.6135	0.5063
1901*	80.85	80.35	88.33	81.55	0.1332	0.6236	0.4707
1902*	82.30	81.14	88.50	82.37	0.0866	0.6102	0.5082
1903*	81.03	82.13	88.87	83.24	0.0836	0.6267	0.4918
1904*	81.99	82.09	88.13	83.07	0.0979	0.6151	0.5074
1905	84.92	84.41	89.90	85.40	0.1167	0.6067	0.4997
1906	88.44	87.47	92.43	88.33	0.1143	0.6077	0.4640
1907	90.48	89.15	93.46	89.88	0.0928	0.6250	0.4761
1908*	84.93	86.13	89.59	86.55	0.0524	0.6329	0.5057
1909*	87.68	87.63	90.42	88.18	0.0904	0.6243	0.4786
1910	90.80	92.30	94.51	92.61	0.0980	0.6250	0.4876
1911	93.97	95.80	97.31	95.94	0.0963	0.6229	0.4811
1912	95.55	97.07	97.87	96.76	0.0913	0.6264	0.4821
1913	100.00	100.00	100.00	100.00	0.1170	0.6204	0.4809
1914*	98.69	97.92	97.35	99.22	0.1181	0.6428	0.5312
1915*	98.16	92.70	91.70	95.34	−0.0341	0.6363	0.5450
1916*	93.63	89.35	87.93	91.81	−0.0756	0.6582	0.5016
1917*	91.48	86.49	84.70	88.75	0.0243	0.6189	0.5440
1918*	91.56	86.84	84.61	89.01	0.0835	0.6227	0.5144
1919*	89.89	95.93	93.99	91.66	0.1101	0.6587	0.4339
1920*	93.51	104.3	104.8	95.05	0.0651	0.6729	0.4090
1921*	84.61	88.77	91.78	79.00	0.0607	0.6708	0.4321
1922*	90.94	91.30	92.59	81.90	0.0584	0.6553	0.4615
1923*	93.85	93.95	94.27	84.60	0.0578	0.6675	0.4351
1924	98.63	96.18	95.70	86.84	0.0768	0.6703	0.4256

Year	Index numbers (1913 = 100)				Ratios		
	Q	L	N	H	s	λ	cu
1925	105.1	97.53	96.80	87.83	0.1182	0.6359	0.4567
1926*	98.97	95.87	96.54	85.30	0.0765	0.6606	0.4246
1927	108.3	103.3	99.97	94.11	0.0841	0.6710	0.4323
1928	109.6	103.9	100.3	94.21	0.0862	0.6654	0.4378
1929	113.4	106.0	101.8	96.07	0.0898	0.6593	0.4277
1930*	112.2	102.8	99.40	92.26	0.1045	0.6490	0.4619
1931*	104.3	99.89	96.47	89.44	0.0745	0.6900	0.4533
1932*	105.3	101.2	96.90	90.40	0.0650	0.7061	0.4890
1933*	109.3	103.9	98.36	93.44	0.0392	0.7154	0.5140
1934	116.9	107.7	102.2	97.67	0.0798	0.6954	0.5120
1935	122.3	113.2	104.1	103.3	0.0774	0.6855	0.4809
1936	129.0	117.8	107.6	107.8	0.0841	0.6909	0.4749
1937	134.8	122.8	111.2	112.6	0.1078	0.6769	0.4565
1938	135.5	120.3	110.8	108.0	0.1102	0.6559	0.4797
1939*	139.5	129.1	115.2	118.1	0.1149	0.6655	0.4462
1940*	143.3	125.5	110.7	115.4	0.1288	0.6419	0.4524
1941*	152.5	126.0	109.4	117.1	0.0879	0.6224	0.4582
1942*	152.0	127.4	109.8	118.3	0.0467	0.6221	0.4370
1943*	154.8	125.0	107.0	116.0	0.0634	0.6232	0.4427
1944*	145.2	120.6	103.5	110.2	0.0094	0.6403	0.4140
1945*	136.9	114.4	99.6	102.8	0.0092	0.6750	0.4074
1946*	140.0	120.1	104.9	107.2	0.0635	0.6823	0.4271
1947	150.4	126.5	111.9	111.8	0.1395	0.7058	0.4483
1948	159.5	129.7	114.0	114.6	0.1379	0.6972	0.4338
1949	166.1	131.6	115.1	116.1	0.1331	0.6939	0.4409
1950	170.0	134.6	116.2	119.0	0.1113	0.7100	0.4126
1951	181.6	137.3	117.1	121.5	0.1877	0.7083	0.4315
1952*	177.9	135.8	116.2	119.8	0.1344	0.6915	0.4286
1953	186.5	138.0	116.9	121.9	0.1407	0.6834	0.4368
1954	193.8	141.2	118.5	124.9	0.1416	0.6907	0.4363
1955	204.2	144.2	120.1	127.7	0.1675	0.7021	0.4292
1956	206.4	145.1	120.6	128.3	0.1701	0.7113	0.4283
1957	209.4	145.0	120.5	127.9	0.1778	0.7103	0.4312
1958*	207.3	142.9	119.0	125.8	0.1711	0.7119	0.4286
1959	215.2	145.3	119.6	128.1	0.1757	0.7062	0.4238
1960	229.0	147.7	121.9	129.9	0.1993	0.7050	0.4428
1961	234.2	148.6	123.3	130.4	0.1911	0.7195	0.4434
1962	235.2	147.9	123.2	129.5	0.1683	0.7275	0.4352
1963	246.3	148.3	122.7	129.8	0.1713	0.7151	0.4449
1964	261.2	151.7	124.2	133.0	0.2054	0.7144	0.4459
1965	267.1	151.1	124.7	132.2	0.1972	0.7199	0.4448

Year	Index numbers (1913 = 100)				Ratios		
	Q	L	N	H	s	λ	*cu*
1966	271.3	147.7	124.3	128.9	0.1907	0.7281	0.4547
1967	274.8	144.4	121.1	126.0	0.1934	0.7278	0.4690
1968	287.2	143.8	119.7	125.5	0.1979	0.7252	0.4812
1969	294.7	144.1	119.3	125.8	0.2006	0.7348	0.4906
1970	300.5	141.7	118.4	123.6	0.1990	0.7563	0.5110
1971	304.6	136.2	115.4	118.8	0.1858	0.7310	0.5233
1972	314.3	135.3	115.0	118.2	0.1742	0.7307	0.5256
1973	344.0	139.6	117.1	121.8	0.2098	0.7265	0.5479
1974*	339.5	137.1	116.5	119.6	0.2067	0.7656	0.5655
1975*	329.9	135.0	115.2	117.8	0.1509	0.7909	0.5476
1976*	334.9	132.5	112.6	115.6	0.1755	0.7645	0.5517
1977*	338.0	132.1	112.6	115.3	0.1888	0.7419	0.5470
1978	347.3	132.1	113.0	115.3	0.1934	0.7384	0.5542
1979	353.5	134.2	114.6	117.2	0.2073	0.7656	0.5637
1980*	341.7	131.5	114.0	114.8	0.1689	0.7982	0.5619
1981*	331.1	121.6	108.1	106.2	0.1583	0.8100	0.5833
1982*	330.5	120.8	105.5	105.4	0.1656	0.8013	0.5958
1983*	340.7	117.8	103.5	102.9	0.1758	0.7847	0.6293
1984*	350.3	121.0	105.4	105.6	0.1824	0.7890	0.6240
1985	367.3	122.7	105.8	107.1	0.1870	0.7730	0.6484

REFERENCES

Abramovitz M. (1956), 'Resource and Output Trends in the United States since 1870', *American Economic Review*, Papers and Proceedings, 46.

_____ and others (1959), *The Allocation of Economic Resources*, Stanford University Press.

Ahmad, S. (1966), 'On the Theory of Induced Invention', *Economic Journal*, 76.

Allen, R. G. D. (1967), *Macroeconomic Theory*, Macmillan, London.

Andrews, P. W. S., and Brunner, E. (1959), *The Life of Lord Nuffield*, Basil Blackwell, Oxford.

Armingtom, C., and Odle, M. (1982), 'Small Business—How Many Jobs? *The Brookings Review*, Winter.

Arrow, K. J. (1962a), 'Economic Welfare and the Allocation of Resources for Invention', in Nelson (1962).

_____ (1962b), 'The Economic Implications of Learning by Doing', *Review of Economic Studies*, 29.

Artis, M. J., and Nobay, A. R. (eds.) (1977), *Studies in Modern Economic Analysis*, Basil Blackwell, Oxford.

Atkinson, A. B., and Harrison, A. J. (1978), *Distribution of Personal Wealth in Britain*, Cambridge University Press.

Atkinson, A. B., and Stiglitz, J. E. (1969), 'A New View of Technological Change', *Economic Journal*, 79.

Bacon, R., and Eltis, W. (1978), *Britain's Economic Problem*: *Too Few Producers* (2nd edn.), Macmillian, London.

Baily, M. (1981), 'Productivity and the Services of Capital and Labour', *Brookings Papers on Economic Activity*.

_____ (1982), 'The Productivity Growth Slow-down by Industry', *Brookings Papers on Economic Activity*.

Bank of England (1979), *Bank of England Model of the UK Economy*, Discussion Paper no.5, London.

Barna, T. (1957), 'The Replacement Cost of Fixed Assets in British Manufacturing Industry in 1955', *Journal of the Royal Statistical Society*, ser. A 120.

_____(1962), *Investment and Growth Policies in British Industrial Firms*, Cambridge University Press.

Barro, R. J. (1974), 'Are Government Bonds Net Wealth?' *Journal of Political Economy*, 82.

_____ (1984), *Macroeconomics*, John Wiley, New York.

Baumol, W. J. (1952), *Welfare Economics and the Theory of the State*, Harvard University Press, Cambridge, Mass.

_____ (1959), *Business Behaviour, Value and Growth*, Macmillan, New York.

_____ and McLennan, K. (1985), *Productivity Growth and US Competitiveness*, Oxford University Press.

Beckerman, W. (1980), 'Comparative Growth Rates of "Measurable Economic Welfare": Some Experimental Calculations', in Matthews (1980).

Begg, D., Fischer, S., and Dornbusch, R. (1984), *Economics* (British edn.), McGraw-Hill, Maidenhead.

Berndt, E. R., and Morrison, C. J. (1981), 'Capacity Utilisation Measures: Underlying Economic Theory and an Alternative Approach', *American Economic Review*, 71.

Beveridge, Sir William (1944), *Full Employment in a Free Society*, Allen and Unwin, London.

Birch, D. L. (1981), 'Who Creates Jobs?', *The Public Interest*, no.65.

_____ and MacCracken, S. (1982), 'The Small Business Share of Job Creation: Lessons Learned for the Use of a Longtitudinal File', unpublished paper, Massachusetts Institute of Technology Program on Neighbourhood and Regional Change, Cambridge, Mass.

Black, J. (1962), 'The Technical Progress Function and the Production Function', *Economica*, 29.

Board of Inland Revenue (1950), *Income Tax Wear and Tear Allowances for Machinery or Plant*, HMSO, London.

Borjas, G. J. (1987), 'Immigration', *NBER Reporter*, Fall.

Boskin, M. J. (1975), 'Notes on the Tax Treatment of Human Capital', mimeo, National Bureau of Economic Research Working Paper no.116, Stanford, Cal.

_____ (1978), 'Taxation, Saving and the Rate of Interest', *Journal of Political Economy*, 86.

_____ (ed.) (1979), *Economics and Human Welfare*: *Essays in Honor of Tibor Scitovsky*, Academic Press, New York.

Bosworth, B. (1982), 'Capital Formation and Economic Policy', *Brookings Papers on Economic Activity*.

Bottomley, A. (1971), *Factor Pricing and Economic Growth in Underdeveloped Rural Areas*, Crosby Lockwood, London.

Bowley, A. L. (1937), *Wages and Income since 1860*, Cambridge University Press.

Brainard, W. C., Shoven, J. B., and Weiss, L. (1980), 'The Financial Valuation of the Return to Capital', *Brookings Papers on Economic Activity*.

Branson, W. H. (1979), *Macroeconomic Theory and Policy*, Harper and Row, New York.

Brechling, F. and O'Brien, P. (1967), 'Short-run Employment Functions in Manufacturing Industries: An International Comparison', *Review of Economics and Statistics*, 49.

Brittain, J. A. (1978), *Inheritance and the Inequality of Material Wealth*, Brookings Institution, Washington, DC.

Britto, R. (1973), 'Some Recent Developments in the Theory of Economic Growth: An Interpretation', *Journal of Economic Literature*, 11.

Bronfenbrenner, M. (1971), *Income Distribution Theory*, Macmillian, London.

Brooks, S., and Henry, B. (1983), 'Re-estimation of the National Institute Model', *National Institute Economic Review*, no.103.

Brunhild, G., Burton, R. H. (1974), *Macroeconomic Theory*, Prentice-Hall, Englewood Cliffs, NJ.

Bruno, M., and Sachs, J. (1985), *Economics of World-wide Stagflation*, Basil Blackwell, Oxford.

Bryer, R. A., Brignall, T. J., and Maunders, A. R. (1982), *Accounting for British Steel*, Gower, Aldershot.

Buchanan, J. M. (1976), Barro on the Ricardian Equivalence Theorem, *Journal of Political Economy*, 84.

Budd, E. C. (1960), 'Factor Shares, 1850-1910', in Conference on Research in Income and Wealth (1960).

Burgess, G. J., and Webb, A. J. (1974), 'The Profits of British Industry', *Lloyds Bank Review*, no.112.

Cairncross, Sir A., Kay, J. A., and Siberston, Z. A. (1977), 'The Regeneration of Manufacturing Industry', *Midland Bank Review*; reprinted in Matthews and Sargent (1983).

Carré, J.-J., Dubois, P., and Malinvaud, E. (1976), *French Economic Growth*, Stanford University Press.

Cassels, J. M. (1937), 'Excess Capacity and Monopolistic Competition', *Quarterly Journal of Economics*, 51.

Chesterton, G. K. (1904) *The Napoleon of Notting Hill*, Bodley Head, London.

Christensen, L. R., and Jorgenson, D. W. (1969), 'The Measurement of US Real Capital Input, 1929-1967', *Review of Income and Wealth*, series 15.

_____ (1970), 'US Real Product and Real Factor Input, 1929-1967', *Review of Income and Wealth*, series 16.

Collard, D.A., Helm, D. R., Scott, M. FG., and Sen, A. K. (eds.) (1984), *Economic Theory and Hicksian Themes*, Clarendon Press, Oxford.

Commission on Money and Credit (1963), *Impacts of Monetary Policy*, Prentice-Hall, Englewood Cliffs, NJ.

Committee to Review the Functioning of Financial Institutions (1979), *The Financing of Small Firms* (Chairman: The Rt. Hon. Sir Harold Wilson), *Interim Report*, Cmnd. 7503, HMSO, London.

_____ (1980), *Report* (Chairman: The Rt. Hon. Sir Harold Wilson), Cmnd. 7937, HMSO, London.

Conference on Research in Income and Wealth (1951), *Studies in Income and Wealth*, Vol. 14, National Bureau of Economic Research, New York.

_____ (1957), *Problems of Capital Formation*, Studies in Income and Wealth, Vol. 19, National Bureau of Economic Research, New York, and Princeton University Press.

_____ (1958), *A Critique of the United States Income and Product Accounts*, Studies in Income and Wealth, Vol. 22, National Bureau of Economic Research, New York, and Princeton University Press.

_____ (1960), *Trends in the American Economy in the Nineteenth Century*, Studies in Income and Wealth, Vol. 24, Princeton University Press.

_____ (1964), *The Behaviour of Income Shares*, Studies in Income and Wealth, Vol. 27, Princeton University Press.

Conlisk, J. (1969), 'A Neoclassical Growth Model with Endogenously Positioned Technical Change Frontier', *Economic Journal*, 79.

Cripps, T. F., and Tarling, R. J. (1973), *Growth in Advanced Capitalist Economies*, Cambridge University Press.

Crombie, A. C. (ed.) (1963), *Scientific Change* (Symposium on the History of Science at the University of Oxford, 9–15 July 1961), Heinemann, London.

CSO (various dates), *National Income and Expenditure*, HMSO, London.

Cyert, R., and March, J. (1963), *A Behavioural Theory of the Firm*, Prentice-Hall, Englewood Cliffs, NJ.

Dawkins, R. (1986), *The Blind Watchmaker*, Longman Harlow, Essex.

Dean, G. A. (1964), 'The Stock of Fixed Capital in the United Kingdom in 1961', *Journal of the Royal Statistical Society*, ser. A, 127.

Dean, J. (1951), *Managerial Economics*, Prentice-Hall, Englewood, Cliffs, NJ.

Demsetz, H. (1969), 'Information and Efficiency: Another Viewpoint', *Journal of Law and Economics*, 12.

Denison, E. F. (1954), 'Income Types and the Size Distribution', *American Economic Review*, 44.

_____ (1962), *The Sources of Economic Growth in the United States and the Alternatives before Us,* Supplementary Paper no. 13, Committee for Economic Development, New York.

_____ (1964), 'The Unimportance of the Embodied Question', *American Economic Review*, 54.

_____ (1974), *Accounting for United States Economic Growth 1929–1969*, Brookings Institution, Washington, DC.

_____ (1979), *Accounting for Slower Economic Growth*, Brookings Institution, Washington, DC.

_____ (1985), *Trends in American Economic Growth 1929–1982*, Brookings Institution, Washington, DC.

_____ and Chung, W. K. (1976), *How Japan's Economy Grew So Fast*, Brookings Institution, Washington, DC.

_____ , assisted by Poullier, J–P. (1967), *Why Growth Rates Differ*, Brookings Institution, Washington, DC.

Department of Employment and Productivity (1971), *British Labour Statistics Historical Abstract 1886–1968*, HMSO, London.

Derry, T. K., and Williams, T. I. (1960), *A Short History of Technology*, Clarendon Press, Oxford.

Diamond Commission (1975), *Royal Commission on the Distribution of Income and Wealth* (Chairman: Lord Diamond), Report no.1, *Initial Report on the Standing Reference*, Cmnd. 6171, HMSO, London.

_____ (1977), *Royal Commission on the Distribution of Income and Wealth* (Chairman: Lord Diamond), Report no.5, *Third Report on the Standing Reference*, Cmnd. 6999, HMSO, London.

Dixit, A. K. (1976), *The Theory of Equilibrium Growth*, Oxford University Press.

Dornbusch, R., and Fischer, S. (1978), *Macroeconomics*, McGraw-Hill Kogakusha, Tokyo.

Downie, J. (1958), *The Competitive Process*, Duckworth, London.

Drandakis, E. M., and Phelps, E. S. (1966), 'A Model of Induced Invention, Growth, and Distribution', *Economic Journal*, 76.

Dunsheath, P. (ed.) (1951), *A Century of Technology, 1851–1951*, Hutchinson, London.

Eaton, J., and Rosen, H. S. (1980), 'Taxation, Human Capital, and Uncertainty', *American Economic Review*, 70.

Eisner, R., and Strotz, R. H. (1963), 'Determinants of Business Investments', in Commission on Money and Credit (1963).

Eltis, W. A. (1973), *Growth and Distribution*, Macmillan, London.

―――― (1984), *The Classical Theory of Economic Growth*, Macmillan, London.

Emerson, M. (ed.) (1984), *Europe's Stagflation*, Claredon Press, Oxford.

Enoch, C. A. (1978), 'Measures of Competitiveness in International Trade', *Bank of England Quarterly Bulletin*, 18.

Fabricant, S. (1942), *Employment in Manufacturing 1899-1939* National Bureau of Economic Research, New York.

―――― (1954), 'Economic Progress and Economic Change', *34th Annual Report of the National Bureau of Economic Research*, NBER, New York.

Fair, R. C. (1969), *The Short-run Demand for Workers and Hours*, North-Holland, Amsterdam.

Feinstein, C. H. (1972), *National Income, Expenditure and Output of the United Kingdom, 1855-1965*, Cambridge University Press.

―――― (1976), *Statistical Tables of National Income, Expenditure and Output of the UK 1855-1965*, Cambridge University Press.

Feldstein, M. (1970), 'Inflation, Specification Bias, and the Impact of Interest Rates', *Journal of Political Economy*, 78.

―――― (1978), 'The Welfare Cost of Capital Income Taxation', *Journal of Political Economy*, 86.

―――― and Summers, L. (1977), 'Is the Rate of Profit Falling?' *Brookings Papers on Economic Activity*.

Fettber, R. (ed.) (1967), *Determinants of Investment Behaviour*, Universities-National Bureau Conference Series, no.18, Columbia University Press, New York.

Fisher, I. (1906), *The Nature of Capital and Income*, Macmillian, London.

―――― (1930), *The Theory of Interest*, Macmillan, New York; part reprinted in Parker and Harcourt (1969).

Flemming, J. S., Price, L. D. D., and Byers, S. A. (1976), 'The Cost of Capital, Finance and Investment', *Bank of England Quarterly Bulletin*, 16.

Flemming, J. S., with Price, L. D. D., and Ingram, D. H. A. (1976), 'Trends in Company Profitability', *Bank of England Quarterly Bulletin*, 16.

Freeman, C., Clark, J., and Soete, L. (1982), *Unemployment and Technical Innovation*, Frances Pinter, London.

Friedman, M. (1953), *Essays in Positive Economics*, University of Chicago Press.

―――― (1957), *A Theory of the Consumption Function*, Princeton University Press for the National Bureau of Economic Research.

Furstenburg, G. M. von (1977), 'Corporate Investment: Does Market Valuation Matter in the Aggregate?' *Brookings Papers on Economic Activity*.

Galbraith, J. K. (1952), *American Capitalism*, Hamish Hamilton, London.

―――― (1967), *The New Industrial State*, Hamish Hamilton, London.

George, K. D. (1968), 'Concentration, Barriers to Entry and Rate of Return', *Review of Economics and Statistics*, 50.

Giersch, H. (ed.) (1981), *Towards an Explanation of Economic Growth*, Institut für Weltwirtschaft an der Universität Kiel, J. C. B. Mohr (Paul Siebeck), Tübingen.

Gibert, M., and associates (Beckerman, W., Edelman, J., Marris, S., Stuvel, G., and Teichart, M.) (1958), *Comparative National Products and Price Levels: A Study of Western Europe and the United States*, OEEC, Paris.

Gilbert, M., and Kravis, I. (1954), *An International Comparison of National Products and the Purchasing Power of Currencies: A Study of the United States, the United Kingdom, France, Germany and Italy*, OEEC, Paris.

Gilfillan, S. C. (1970), *The Sociology of Invention*, MIT Press, Cambridge, Mass.

Glyn, A., and Sutcliffe, R. B. (1972), *British Capitalism, Workers and the Profits Squeeze*, Penguin Books, Harmondsworth, Middx.

Goldsmith, R. W. (1955), *A Study of Saving in the United States*, Vol. 1, Princeton University Press.

Gollop, F. M., and Jorgenson, D. W. (1980), 'US Productivity Growth by Industry, 1947–73', in Kendrick and Vaccara (1980).

Grant, R. M. (1985), 'Capacity Adjustment and Restructuring in the UK Cutlery Industry 1974–84', *Economic Working Papers* no.21, National Economic Development Office, London.

Grebler, L., Blank, D. M., and Winnick, L. (1956), *Capital Formation in Residential Real Estate*: *Trends and Prospects*, National Bureau of Economic Research, New York.

Green, H. A. J. (1960), 'Growth Models, Capital and Stability', *Economic Journal*, 70.

Gregory, R. G. (1971), 'United States Imports and Internal Pressure of Demand, 1948–68', *American Economic Review*, 61.

_____ and James, D. W. (1973), 'Do New Factories Embody Best Practice Technology?' *Economic Journal*, 83.

Griffin, T. (1976), 'The Stock of Fixed Assets in the United Kingdom: How to Make the Best Use of the Statistics', *Economic Trends*, CSO, London.

Griliches, Z. (1957), 'Hybrid Corn: An Exploration in the Economics of Technical Change', *Econometrica*, 25.

Haavelmo, T. (1960), *A Study in the Theory of Investment*, University of Chicago Press.

Hacche, G. (1979), *The Theory of Economic Growth: An Introduction*, Macmillan, London.

Hahn, F. H. (1971), *Readings in the Theory of Growth*, Macmillian, London.

_____ and Matthews, R. C. O. (1964), 'The Theory of Economic Growth: A Survey', *Economic Journal*, 74.

Halberstadt, V., Goudswaard, K., and Le Blanc, B. (1984), 'Current Control Problems with Public Expenditure in Five European Countries', in Emerson (1984).

Haley, B. F. (1968), 'Changes in the Distribution of Income in the United States', in Marchal and Ducros (1968).

Hamberg, D. (1971), *Models of Economic Growth*, Harper and Row, New York.

Harberger, A. C. and Bailey, M. J. (eds.) (1969), *The Taxation of Income from Capital*, Brookings Institution, Washington DC.

Harbury, C. D. (1962), 'Inheritance and the Distribution of Personal Wealth in Britain', *Economic Journal*, 72.

_____ and Hitchens, D. M. W. N. (1979), *Inheritance and Wealth Inequality in Britain*, Allen & Unwin, London.

_____ and McMahon, P. C. (1973), 'Inheritance and the Characteristics of Top Wealth Leavers in Britian', *Economic Journal*, 83.

Harrod, R. F. (1948), *Towards a Dynamic Economics*, Macmillan, London.

Hartwell, R. M. (1983), 'The Origins of Capitalism: A Methodological Essay', in Pejovich (1983).

Hay, D. A., and Morris, D. J. (1979), *Industrial Economics: Theory and Evidence*, Oxford University Press.

Hayek, F. A. (1941a), *The Pure Theory of Capital*, Routledge & Kegan Paul, London.

_____ (1941b), 'Maintaining Capital Intact: A Reply' *Economica*, 8; reprinted in Parker and Harcourt (1969).

Heckman, J. J. (1976), 'A Life-cycle Model of Earnings, Learning and Consumption', *Journal of Political Economy*, 84.

Heertje, A. (1977), *Economics and Technical Change*, Weidenfeld & Nicolson, London.

Helliwell J. F. (ed.) (1976), *Aggregate Investment: Selected Readings*, Penguin, Harmondsworth, Middx.

_____ Sturm, P., Jarrett, P., and Salon, G. (1986), 'The Supply Side in the OECD's Macroeconomic Model', *OECD Economic Studies*, no.6.

Henderson, P. D. (ed.) (1966), *Economic Growth in Britain*, Weidenfeld & Nicolson, London.

_____ (1977), 'Two British Errors: Their Probable Size and Some Possible Lessons', *Oxford Economic Papers*, 29.

Hicks, J. R. (1932), *The Theory of Wages*, Macmillian, London.

_____ (1942), 'Maintaining Capital Intact: A Further Suggestion', *Economica*, 9; reprinted in Parker and Harcourt (1969).

_____ (1946), *Value and Capital* (2nd edn.), Clarendon Press, Oxford.

_____ (1965), *Capital and Growth*, Clarendon Press, Oxford.

Hill, T. P. (1979), *Profits and Rates of Return*, OECD, Paris.

Hills, J. (1984), *Savings and Fiscal Privilege* (rev. edn.), Institute for Fiscal Studies, London.

Hirschman, A. O. (1958), *The Strategy of Economic Development*, Yale University Press, New Haven, Conn.

_____ (1977), 'A Generalized Linkage Approach to Development, with Special Reference to Staples', *Economic Development and Cultural Change*, 25, Supplement.

Hirshleifer, J. (1977), 'Economics from a Biological Viewpoint', *Journal of Law and Economics*, 20.

H. M. Treasury, Department of Trade and Industry and Bank of England (1984), 'Industrial and Commercial Companies' Real Rates of Return: Differences between Figures derived from National Accounts and Company Accounts', *Economic Trends*, CSO, London.

Hogan, W. T. (1983), *World Steel in the 1980s*: *A Case of Survival*, Lexington Books, Toronto.

Hotelling, H. (1925), 'A General Mathematical Theory of Depreciation', *Journal of the American Statistical Association*, 20; reprinted in Parker and Harcourt (1969).

Howrey, E.P., and Hymans, S. H. (1978), 'The Measurement and Determination of Loanable-funds Savings', *Brookings Papers on Economic Activity*.

Hughes, G. A., and Heal, G. M. (eds.) (1980), *Public Policy and the Tax System*, Allen & Unwin, London.

Institute for Fiscal Studies (1978), *The Structure and Reform of Direct Taxation*, Report of a Committee chaired by Professor J. E. Meade, Allen & Unwin, London.

Jewkes, J., Sawers, D., and Stillerman, R. (1969), *The Sources of Invention* (2nd edn.), Macmillan, London.

Johnson, D. G. (1954), 'The Functional Distribution of Income in the United States, 1850–1952', *Review of Economics and Statistics*, 36.

Johnson, H. G. (1973), *The Theory of Income Distribution*, Gray–Mills Publishing, London.

Johnson, P. S. (1975), *The Economics of Invention and Innovation*, Martin Robertson, London.

Jones, H. (1975), *An Introduction of Modern Theories of Economic Growth*, Nelson, Sunbury-on-Thames.

Jorgenson, D. W. (1971), 'Econometric Studies of Investment Behaviour: A Survey', *Journal of Economic Literature*, 9.

—— and Griliches, Z. (1967), 'The Explanation of Productivity Change', *Review of Economic Studies*, 34.

Junz, H. B., and Rhomberg, R. R. (1965), 'Prices and Export Performance of Industrial Countries', *International Monetary Fund Staff Papers*, 12.

Kaldor, N. (1935), 'Market Imperfections and Excess Capacity', *Economica*, 2.

—— (1955), *An Expenditure Tax*, Allen & Unwin, London.

—— (1957), 'A Model of Economic Growth', *Economic Journal*, 67.

—— (1966), *Causes of the Slow Rate of Economic Growth of the United Kingdom*, Cambridge University Press; reprinted in Kaldor (1978).

—— (1967), *Strategic Factors in Economic Development*, New York State School of Industrial and Labour Relations, Cornell University, Ithaca, NY.

—— (1971), 'Conflicts in National Economic Objectives', *Economic Journal*, 81; reprinted in Kaldor (1978).

—— (1975a), 'What is Wrong with Economic Theory', *Quarterly Journal of Economics,* 89; reprinted in Kaldor (1978).

—— (1975b), 'Economic Growth and the Verdoorn Law—A Comment on Mr Rowthorn's Article', *Economic Journal*, 85.

—— (1978), *Further Essays on Economic Theory*, Duckworth, London.

—— and Mirrlees, J. A. (1962), 'A New Model of Economic Growth', *Review of Economic Studies*, 29.

Kamerschen, D. R. (1968), 'The Influence of Ownership and Control on Profit Rates', *American Economic Review*, 48.

Kamien, M. I., and Schwartz, N. L. (1982), *Market Structure and Innovation*, Cambridge University Press.

Kay, J. A. (1976), 'Accountants, Too, Could Be Happy in a Golden Age: The Accountant's Rate of Profit and the Internal Rate of Return', *Oxford Economic Papers*, 28.

Kelley, A. C., and Williamson, J. G. (1974), *Lessons from Japanese Development: An Analytical Economic History*, University of Chicago Press.

Kendrick, J. W. (1961), *Productivity Trends in the United States*, Princeton University Press.

_____ (1982), *Interindustry Differences in Productivity Growth*, American Enterprise Institute, Washington, DC.

_____ (ed.) (1984), *International Comparisons of Productivity and Causes of the Slowdown*, American Enterprise Institute, Washington D.C.

_____ and Grossman, E. S. (1980), *Productivity in the United States: Trends and Cycles*, Johns Hopkins University Press, Baltimore.

_____ , assisted by Lethem, Y., and Rowley, J. (1976), *The Formation and Stocks of Total Capital*, Columbia University Press for the National Bureau of Economic Research, New York.

_____ assisted by Pech, M. R. (1973), *Postwar Productivity Trends in the United States, 1948-1969*, National Bureau of Economic Research, New York.

_____ and Sato, R. (1963), 'Factor Prices, Productivity and Economic Growth', *American Economic Review*, 53.

_____ and Vaccara, B. N. (1980), *New Developments in Productivity Measurement and Analysis*, National Bureau of Economic Research, Conference on Research in Income and Wealth, Chicago.

Kennedy, C. (1964), 'Induced Bias in Innovation and the Theory of Distribution', *Economic Journal*, 74.

_____ (1966), 'Samuelson on Induced Innovation', *Review of Economics and Statistics*, 48.

_____ (1973), 'A Generalisation of the Theory of Induced Bias in Technical Progress', *Economic Journal*, 83.

_____ and Thirlwall, A. P. (1972) 'Technical Progress: A Survey', *Economic Journal*, 82.

_____ (1979), 'Import Penetration, Export Performance, and Harrod's Trade Multiplier', *Oxford Economic Papers*, 31.

Kennedy, K. A. (1971), *Productivity and Industrial Growth*, Oxford University Press.

Kennedy, P. E. (1979), *Macroeconomics*, Allyn & Bacon, Boston.

Kerr, C. (1957), 'Labor's Income Share and the Labor Movement', in Taylor and Pierson (1957).

Keynes, J. M. (1936), *The General Theory of Employment Interest and Money*, Macmillan, London.

Killingsworth, M. R. (1983), *Labour Supply*, Cambridge University Press.

Kilpatrick, A., and Naisbitt, B. (undated), 'A Disaggregated Analysis of the Slowdown in Productivity Growth in UK Manufacturing Industry in the 1970s', *Economic Working Papers*, no.12.

King, M. A. (1977), *Public Policy and the Corporation*, Chapman & Hall, London.

_____ (1980), 'Savings and Taxation', in Hughes and Heal (1980).

_____ (1985), Tax Reform in the UK and US', *Economic Policy: A European Forum*, no.1.

_____ and Fullerton, D. (eds.) (1984), *The Taxation of Income from Capital: A Comparative Study of the United States, the United Kingdom, Sweden, and West Germany*, University of Chicago Press.

King, W. I. (1919), *The Wealth and Income of the People of the United States*, Macmillan, New York.

Klein, L. R. (1960), 'Some Theoretical Issues in the Measurement of Capacity', *Econometrica*, 28.

Koopmans, T. C. (1960), 'Stationary Ordinal Utility and Impatience', *Econometrica*, 28.

Kravis, I. (1959), 'Relative Income Shares in Fact and Theory', *American Economic Review*, 49.

_____ , Kenessey, Z., Heston, A., and Summers, R. (with the assistance of others) (1975), *A System of International Comparisons of Gross Product and Purchasing Power*, Johns Hopkins Press for the World Bank, Baltimore.

Kreinen, M. E. (1967), 'Price Elasticities in International Trade', *Review of Economics and Statistics*, 49.

Kuehn, D. A. (1975), *Takeovers and the Theory of the Firm*, Macmillan, London.

Kuznets, S. (1930), *Secular Movements in Production and Prices*, Houghton Mifflin, Boston.

_____ (1946), *National Income: A Summary of Findings*, National Bureau of Economic Research, New York.

_____ (1966), *Economic Growth and Structure*, Heinemann, London.

_____ (1974), *Population, Capital and Growth*, Heinemann, London.

_____ assisted by Epstein, L., and Jenks, E. (1941), *National Income and Its Composition, 1919–1938*, Vol.1, National Bureau of Economic Research, New York.

_____ , assisted by Jenks, E. (1961), *Capital in the American Economy*, Princeton University Press for the National Bureau of Economic Research.

Lamberton, D. M. (ed.) (1971), *Economics of Information and Knowledge*, Penguin, Harmondsworth, Middx.

Lamfalussy, A. (1963), *The United Kingdom and the Six: An Essay on Economic Growth in Western Europe*, Macmillan, London.

Langrish, J. *et al.* (1972), *Wealth from Knowledge*, Macmillan, London.

Lawriwsky, M. L. (1984), *Corporate Structure and Performance*, Croom Helm, London.

Lebergott, S. (1964), 'Factor Shares in the Long Term: Some Theoretical and Statistical Aspects', in Conference on Research in Income and Wealth (1964)

Levinson, H.M. (1954), 'Collective Bargaining and Income Distribution', *American Economic Review*, 44.

Lewis, Sir W. A. (1978), *Growth and Fluctuations 1870–1913*, Allen & Unwin, London.

Lindahl, E. (1933), 'The Concept of Income', in *Economic Essays in Honour of Gustav Cassel'*, Allen & Unwin, London; reprinted in Parker and Harcourt (1969).

Lindbeck, A. (1983) 'The Recent Slow-down of Productivity Growth', *Economic Journal*, 93.

Little, I. M. D. (1950), *A Critique of Welfare Economics*, Clarendon Press, Oxford.

_____ , (1981) Comment on S. Kuznets' "Driving Forces of Economic Growth: what can we learn from history?" in Giersch (1981).

Lockwood, W. W. (1954), *The Economic Development of Japan*, Princeton University Press.

Lutz, F. A. and Hague, D. C. (eds) (1961), *The Theory of Capital*, Macmillan, London.

MacDougall, G. D. A. (1951), 'British and American Exports: A Study Suggested by the Theory of Comparative Costs. Part I', *Economic Journal*, 61.

_____ , (1952), 'British and American Exports: A Study Suggested by the Theory of Comparative Costs. Part II', *Economic Journal*, 62.

Maddison, A. (1982), *Phases of Capital Development*, Oxford University Press.

_____ (1987), 'Growth and Slowdown in Advanced Capitalist Economies: Techniques of Quantitative Assessment', *Journal of Economic Literature*, 25.

Mansfield, E. (1968), *Industrial Research and Technological Innovation; an Econometric Analysis*, Longmans, London.

_____ (1969), *The Economics of Technical Change*, Longmans, London.

Marchal, J., and Ducros, B. (eds.) (1968), *The Distribution of National Income*, Macmillan, London.

Marglin, S. A. (1963), 'The Social Rate of Discount and the Optimal Rate of Investment', *Quarterly Journal of Economics*, 77.

Marris, R. (1964), *The Economic Theory of 'Managerial' Capitalism*, Macmillan, London.

_____ (1964–5), 'Income Policy and the Rate of Profit in Industry', *Transactions of the Manchester Statistical Society*.

_____ and Wood, A. (eds.) (1971), *The Corporate Economy*, Macmillian, London.

Marshall, A. (1920), *Principle of Economics*, (8th edn.), Macmillan, London.

Martin, R. F. (1939), *National Income in the United States, 1799–1938*, National Industrial Conference Board, New York.

Matthews, R. C. O. (ed.) (1980), *Economic Growth and Resources*, Vol.2. *Trends and Factors*, International Economic Association, Macmillan, London.

_____ (ed.) (1982), *Slower Growth in the Western World*, Heinemann, London.

_____ (1984), 'Darwinism and Economic Change', in Collard *et al.* (1984).

_____ , Feinstein, C. H., and Odling-Smee, J. C. (1982) *British Ecomomic Growth 1856–1973*, Clarendon Press, Oxford.

_____ and Sargent, J. R. (eds.) (1983), *Contemporary Problems of Economic Policy*, Methuen, London.

Maurice, R. (ed.) (1968), *National Accounts Statistics: Sources and Methods*, CSO, HMSO, London.

Mayer, C. *et al.* (1985), 'Recent Developments in Industrial Economics and their Implications for Policy', with contributions by J. Vickers, G. Hay, T. Sharpe, and G. Yarrow, *Oxford Review of Economic Policy*, 1.

McCain, R. A. (1972), 'Induced Technical Progress and the Price of Capital Goods', *Economic Journal*, 82.

McCloskey, D. N., and Nash, J. (1984), 'Corn at Interest: The Extent and Cost of Grain Storage in Medieval England', *American Economic Review*, 74.

McCombie, J. S. L. (1983), 'Kaldor's Laws in Retrospect', *Journal of Post Keynesian Economics*, 5.

McCracken, P., Carol, G., Giersch, H., Karaosmanoglu, A., Komiya, R. Lindbeck, A., Marjolin, R., and Matthews, R. (1977), *Towards Full Employment and Price Stability*, OECD, Paris.

McKee, M. H., Visser, J. J. C., and Saunders, P. G. (1986), 'Marginal Tax Rates on the Use of Labour and Capital in OECD Countries', *OECD Economic Studies*, no.7.

Meade, J. E. (1952), 'External Economies and Diseconomies in a Competitive Situation', *Economic Journal*, 62.

—— (1961), *A Neo-classical Theory of Economic Growth*, Allen & Unwin, London.

—— (1968), *The Growing Economy*, Allen & Unwin, London.

Melliss, C. L., and Richardson, P. W. (1976), 'Value of Investment Incentives for Manufacturing Industry 1946 to 1974', in Whiting (1976).

Mény, Y., and Wright, V. (eds.) (1987), *The Politics of Steel; Western Europe and the Steel Industry in the Crisis Years (1974-1984)*, de Gruyter, Berlin.

Merrett, A. J., and Sykes, A. (1973), *Capital Budgeting and Company Finance*, Longman, London.

Merton, R. K. (1961), 'Singletons and Multiples in Science', *Proceedings of the American Philosophical Society*, 105; reprinted in Merton (1973).

—— (1973), *The Sociology of Science*, University of Chicago Press.

Meyer J., and Kuh, E. (1957), *The Investment Decision*, Harvard University Press, Cambridge, Mass.

Mills, F. C. (1955), *Statistical Methods* (3rd edn.) Pitman, London.

Millward, N., and Stevens, M. (1986), *British Workplace Industrial Relations 1980-1984*, Gower Aldershot.

Minami, R., and Ono, A. (1979), 'Factor Incomes and Shares', ch. 11 in Ohkawa and Shinohara (1979).

Mitchell, B. R., and Deane, P. (1962), *Abstract of British Historical Statistics*, Cambridge University Press.

Modigliani, F. (1958), 'New Developments on the Oligopoly Front', *Journal of Political Economy*, 66.

—— and Miller, M. H. (1958), 'The Cost of Capital, Corporation Finance and the Theory of Investment', *American Economic Review*, 49.

—— (1961), 'Dividend Policy, Growth, and the Valuation of Shares', *Journal of Business*, 34.

Morrison, C. J. (1985), 'On the Economic Interpretation and Measurement of Optimal Capacity Utilisation with Anticipatory Expectations', *Review of Economic Studies*, 52.

Muellbauer, J. N. J. (1984) 'Aggregate Production Function and Productivity Measurement: A New Look', Centre for Economic Policy Research, Discussion Paper no.34.

—— , Berndt, E. R., Wood, D. O., Batstone, E., Wadhwani, S., Wall, M., Rossi, V., Walker, J., Todd, D., and Lennon, K. (1986), 'Productivity and Competitiveness in British Manufacturing' (and other related articles), *Oxford Review of Economic Policy*, 2.

Mueller, M. G. (1971), *Readings in Macroeconomics* (2nd edn.), Holt, Rinehart & Winston, London.

Musgrave, J. C. (1976), 'Fixed Non-residential Business and Residential Capital for the United States 1925–75', US Department of Commerce, *Survey of Current Business*, 56.

NEDC (National Economic Development Council) (1963), *Export Trends*, HMSO, London.

Needham, J. (1963), 'Poverties and Triumphs of the Chinese Scientific Tradition', in Crombie (1963).

Nelson, R. R. (1959), 'The Simple Economics of Basic Scientific Research', *Journal of Political Economy*, 67.

―――― (ed.) (1962), *The Rate and Direction of Inventive Activity*, Princeton University Press.

―――― and Winter, S. G. (1974), 'Neoclassical vs. Evolutionary Theories of Economic Growth: Critique and Prospectus', *Economic Journal*, 84.

―――― (1982), *An Evolutionary Theory of Economic Change*, Belknap Press, Cambridge, Mass.

Nickell, S. J. (1978), *The Investment Decisions of Firms*, Cambridge Economic Handbooks, James Nisbet, Welwyn Garden City, and Cambridge University Press.

Nordhaus, W. D. (1969), 'An Economic Theory of Technical Change', *American Economic Review*, Papers and Proceedings, 59.

―――― (1973), 'Some Skeptical Thoughts on the Theory of Induced Innovation', *Quarterly Journal of Economics*, 87.

―――― and Tobin J. (1972), 'Is Economic Growth Obsolete?' in National Bureau of Economic Research Fiftieth Anniversary Colloquium, *Economic Growth*, NBER, New York.

Nyman, S., and Silberston, A. (1978), 'The Ownership and Control of Industry', *Oxford Economic Papers*, 30.

OECD (1985), 'Employment in Small and Large Firms: Where Have The Jobs Come From?', *OECD Employment Outlook*, September.

―――― (1986), *OECD Economic Outlook*, December.

Ogburn, W. F., and Thomas, D. S. (1922), 'Are Inventions Inevitable?' *Political Science Quarterly*, 37.

Ohkawa, K. (1968), 'Changes in National Income Distribution by Factor Share in Japan', in Marchal and Ducros (1968).

―――― and Rosovsky, H. (1973), *Japanese Economic Growth*, Stanford University Press.

―――― and Shinohara, M. (eds.), with Meissner, L. (1979), *Patterns of Japanese Economic Development*: *A Quantitative Appraisal*, Yale University Press, New Haven, Conn.

Okun, A. (1973), 'Upward Mobility in a High-pressure Economy', *Brookings Papers on Economic Activity*.

Olson, M. (1982), *The Rise and Decline of Nations*: *Economic Growth, Stagflation, and Social Rigidities*, Yale University Press, New Haven, Conn.

Orcutt, G. H. (1950), 'Measurement of Price Elasticities in International Trade', *Review of Economics and Statistics*, 32.

Ott, D. J., Ott, A. F., and Yoo, J. H. (1975), *Macroeconomic Theory*, McGraw-Hill, New York.

Oulton, N. (1976), 'Inheritance and the Distribution of Wealth', *Oxford Economic Papers*, 31.

Parker, J. E. S. (1964), 'Profitability and Growth of British Industrial Firms', *Manchester School*, 32.

Parker, R. H. and Harcourt, G. C. (eds.) (1969), *Readings in the Concept and Measurement of Income*, Cambridge University Press.

Parker, R. H., Harcourt, G. C., and Whittington, G. (eds.) (1986), *Readings in the Concept and Measurement of Income* (2nd edn.), Philip Allan, Oxford.

Parkinson, J. R. (1955), 'The Terms of Trade and the National Income 1950–2', *Oxford Economic Papers*, 7.

Pejovich, S. (ed.) (1983), *Philosophical and Economic Foundations of Capitalism*, Lexington Books, Lexington, Mass.

Penrose, E. (1959), *The Theory of the Growth of the Firm*, Basil Blackwell, Oxford.

Petersen, H. G. (1981), 'Taxes, Tax Systems and Economic Growth', in Giersch (1981).

Phelps, E. S. (1961), 'The Golden Rule of Accumulation: A Fable for Growth Men', *American Economic Review*, 51.

―――― (1965), *Fiscal Neutrality toward Economic Growth*, McGraw-Hill, New York.

―――― (1966), *Golden Rules of Economic Growth*, W. W. Norton, New York.

Phelps Brown, Sir Henry (1975), 'A Non-monetarist View of the Pay Explosion', *Three Banks Review*, no.105.

―――― and Browne, H. M. (1968), *A Century of Pay*, Macmillan, London.

―――― and Handfield-Jones, S. J. (1952) 'The Climacteric of the 1890s: a Study in the Expanding Economy', *Oxford Economic Papers*, 4.

Phillips, J. D. (1960), 'Labor's Share and "Wage Parity" ', *Review of Economics and Statistics*, 42.

Pigou, A. C. (1932), *The Economics of Welfare* (4th edn.), Macmillan, London.

―――― (1941), 'Maintaining Capital Intact', *Economica*, 8; reprinted in Parker and Harcourt (1969).

Pratten, C. F. (1976), *Labour Productivity Differentials within International Companies*, Cambridge University Press.

―――― (1977), 'The Efficiency of British Industry', *Lloyds Bank Review*, no.123.

Radice, H. K. (1971), 'Control Type, Profitability and Growth in Large Firms', *Economic Journal*, 81.

Ramsey, F. P. (1928), 'A Mathematical Theory of Saving', *Economic Journal*, 38.

Rasche, R. H. and Tatom, J. A. (1977a), 'The Effects of the New Energy Regime on Economic Capacity, Production and Prices', *Federal Reserve Bank of St Louis Review*, 59.

―――― (1977b), 'Energy Resources and Potential GNP', *Federal Reserve Bank of St Louis Review*, 59.

Ray, G. F. (1984), *The Diffusion of Mature Technologies*, Cambridge University Press.

Reder, M. W. (1959), 'Alternative Theories of Labor's Share', in Abramovitz and others (1959).

Redfern, P. (1955), 'Net Investment in Fixed Assets in the United Kingdom, 1938–53', *Journal of the Royal Statistical Society*, ser. A, 118.

Ricardo, D. (1951), *The Works and Correspondence of David Ricardo*, edited by P. Sraffa with the collaboration of M. H. Dobb, Cambridge at the University Press for the Royal Economic Society: Vol. 1, *On the Principles of Political Economy and Taxation*; Vol. IV, *Pamphlets and Papers written for Publication 1815–1823*.

Richardson, G. B. (1956), 'Demand and Supply Reconsidered', *Oxford Economic Papers*, 8.

_____ (1960), *Information and Investment*, Oxford University Press.

Riedel, J. (1988), 'The Demand for LDC Exports of Manufactures: Estimates from Hong Kong', *Economic Journal*, 108.

Robertson, Sir Dennis (1963), *Lectures on Economic Principles*, Collins/Fontana Library, London.

Robinson, J. (1956), *The Accumulation of Capital*, Macmillan, London.

_____ (1959), 'Depreciation', *Rivista di Politica Economica*; reprinted in Robinson (1960).

_____ (1960), *Collected Economic Papers*, Vol.2, Basil Blackwell, Oxford.

_____ (1962), *Essays in the Theory of Economic Growth*, Macmillan, London.

Rosen, H. S. (1980), 'What is Labour Supply and do Taxes Affect It?' *American Economic Review*, 70.

Rosenberg, N. (1974), 'Science, Invention and Economic Growth, *Economic Journal*, 84.

Rosenstein-Rodan, P. N. (1957), 'Notes on the Theory of the Big Push', paper submitted to the Rio Roundtable of the International Economic Association, mimeo.

Rowthorn, R. E. (1975a), 'What Remains of Kaldor's Laws?' *Economic Journal*, 85.

_____ (1975b), 'A Reply to Lord Kaldor's Comment', *Economic Journal*, 85.

Ruggles, R., and Ruggles, N. D. (1956), *National Income Accounts and Income Analysis* (2nd edn.), McGraw-Hill, New York.

Salter, W. E. G. (1960), *Productivity and Technical Change*, Cambridge University Press.

Samuelson, P. A. (1965), 'A Theory of Induced Innovation Along Kennedy–Weizsäcker Lines', *Review of Economics and Statistics*, 47.

_____ (1966), 'Rejoinder, Agreements, Disagreements, Doubts and the Case of Induced Harrod-neutral Technical Change', *Review of Economics and Statistics*, 48.

_____ (1973), *Economics* (9th edn.), McGraw-Hill Kogakusha, Tokyo.

Schmookler, J. (1966), *Invention and Economic Growth*, Harvard University Press, Cambridge, Mass.

Schultz, T. W. (1951), 'The Declining Economic Importance of Agricultural Land', *Economic Journal*, 61.

Schumpeter, J. A. (1934), *The Theory of Economic Development*, Harvard Economic Studies Vol. 46, Harvard University Press, Cambridge, Mass.

_____ (1939), *Business Cycles: A Theoretical, Historical and Statistical Analysis of the Capitalist Process*, McGraw-Hill, New York.

Schumpeter, J. A. (1950), *Capitalism, Socialism and Democracy* (3rd edn.), Allen & Unwin, London.

Scitovsky, T. (1952), *Welfare and Competition*, Allen & Unwin, London.

—— (1954), 'Two Concepts of External Economies', *Journal of Political Economy*, 17.

—— (1964), 'A Survey of Some Theories of Income Distribution', in Conference on Research in Income and Wealth (1964).

Scott, M. FG. (1963), *A Study of United Kingdom Imports*, Cambridge University Press.

—— (1976), 'Investment and Growth', *Oxford Economic Papers*, 28.

—— (1977), 'The Test Rate of Discount and Changes in Base-level Income in the United Kingdom', *Economic Journal*, 87.

—— (1979), 'What Price the National Income?' in Boskin (1979).

—— (1980), 'Net Investment in Education in the United Kingdom, 1951–1971', *Oxford Review of Education*, 6.

—— (1981), 'The Contribution of Investment to Growth', *Scottish Journal of Political Economy*, 28.

—— (1984), 'Maintaining Capital Intact', in Collard *et al.* (1984).

—— (1986a), 'Some Economic Principles of Accounting: A Constructive Critique of the Sandilands Report', in Parker, Harcourt and Whittington (1986).

—— (1986b), 'Explaining Economic Growth', 1986 Keynes Lecture, *Proceedings of the British Academy*, 72.

—— (1987), 'A Note on King and Fullerton's Formulae to Estimate the Taxation of Income from Capital', *Journal of Public Economics*, 34.

Scottish Economic Planning Department (1980), 'Small Units in Scottish Manufacturing', *Scottish Economic Bulletin*, Spring.

Sen, A. K. (1961), 'On Optimising the Rate of Saving', *Economic Journal*, 71.

—— (ed.) (1970), *Growth Economics*, Penguin, Harmondsworth, Middx.

—— (1979), 'The Welfare Basis of Real Income Comparisons: A Survey', *Journal of Economic Literature*, 17.

—— (1980), 'The Welfare Basis of Real Income Comparisons: A Reply', *Journal of Economic Literature*, 18.

Sharpe, W. F. (1981), *Investments* (2nd edn.), Prentice-Hall, Englewood Cliffs, NJ.

Simler, N. J. (1961), 'Unionism and Labor's Share in Manufacturing Industries', *Review of Economics and Statistics*, 43.

Simons, H. C. (1938), *Personal Income Taxation*, University of Chicago Press; part reprinted in Parker and Harcourt (1969).

Singer, C. (1959), *A Short History of Scientific Ideas to 1900*, Clarendon Press, Oxford.

Singh, A. (1971), *Takeovers: Their Relevance to the Stockmarket and the Theory of the Firm*, Cambridge University Press.

—— and Whittington, G., with Burley, H. T. (1968), *Growth, Profitability and Valuation*, Cambridge University Press.

Sleeper, R. (1970), 'Manpower Redeployment and the Selective Employment Tax', *Bulletin of the Oxford University Institute of Economics and Statistics*, 32.

Smith, A. (1776), *An Inquiry into the Nature and Causes of the Wealth of Nations*, Macmillan edn., London 1936.

Smith, A. D. (1987), 'A Current Cost Accounting Measure of Britain's Stock of Equipment', *National Institute Economic Review*, no.120.

Solow, R. M. (1956), 'A Contribution to the Theory of Economic Growth', *Quarterly Journal of Economics*, 70.

_____ (1957), 'Technical Change and the Aggregate Production Function', *Review of Economics and Statistics*, 39.

_____ (1958), 'A Skeptical Note on the Constancy of Relative Shares', *American Economic Review*, 48.

_____ (1963), *Captial Theory and the Rate of Return*, North-Holland, Amsterdam.

_____ (1970), *Growth Theory: An Exposition*, Clarendon Press, Oxford.

_____ (1971), 'Some Implications of Alternative Criteria for the Firm', in Marris and Wood (1971).

Stern, N. (1977), 'The Marginal Valuation of Income', in Artis and Nobay (eds.) (1977).

Stigler, G. J. (1951), 'The Division of Labor is Limited by the Extent of the Market', *Journal of Political Economy*, 59.

Stiglitz, J. E., and Uzawa, H. (eds.) (1969), *Readings in the Modern Theory of Economic Growth*, MIT Press, Cambridge, Mass.

Streissler, E. (1980), 'Models of Investment-dependent Economic Growth Revisited', in Matthews (1980).

Stuvel, G. (1986), *National Accounts Analysis*, Macmillan, London.

Summers, L. H. (1981), 'Taxation and Corporate Investment: A *q*-Theory Approach', *Brookings, Papers on Economic Activity*.

Surrey, M. J. C. (1976), *Macroeconomic Themes*, Oxford University Press.

Swan, T. W. (1956), 'Economic Growth and Captial Accumulation', *Economic Record*, 32.

Sylos-Labini, P. (1962), *Oligopoly and Technical Progress*, Harvard University Press, Cambridge, Mass.

Symposium on Government Borrowing and Economic Policy (1985), *National Institute Economic Review*, no. 113.

Symposium on Kaldor's Growth Laws (1983), *Journal of Post Keynesian Economics*, 5.

Taylor, C. T., and Silberston, Z. A. (1973), *The Economic Impact of the Patent System*, Cambridge University Press.

Taylor, G. W., and Pierson, F. C, (eds.), (1957), *New Concepts in Wage Determination*, McGraw-Hill, New York.

Taylor, L. (1970), 'Saving out of Different Types of Income', *Brookings Papers on Economic Activity*.

Thirlwall, A. P. (1980), 'Rowthorn's Interpretation of Verdoorn's Law', *Economic Journal*, 90.

Thomas, M. (1988), 'Slow-down in the pre-World War I Economy', *Oxford Review of Economic Policy*, 4.

Tobin, J. (1964), 'Economic Growth as an Objective of Government Policy', *American Economic Review*, Papers and Proceedings, 54.

Todd, J. E., and Jones, L. M. (1972), *Matrimonial Property*, HMSO, London.

Townsend, J. C. (1976), 'The Personal Savings Ratio', *Bank of England Quarterly Bulletin*, 16.

United Nations (1968), *A System of National Accounts*, Department of Economic and Social Affairs, Statistical Office of the United Nations, Studies in Methods, Series F, No. 2, Rev. 3, New York.

US Department of Commerce (1972), 'The Measurement of Productivity', *Survey of Current Business*, Vol. 52, No. 5, Part II.

US Small Business Administration (1984a), *The State of Small Business*, US Government Printing Office, Washington DC.

—— (1984b), *Job General, Economic Policy in the Eighties: The Small Business Factor*, Office of the Chief Council for Advocacy, Washington DC.

—— (1985), *The State of Small Business*, US Government Printing Office, Washington DC.

Usher, D. (1976), 'The Measurement of Real Income', *Review of Income and Wealth*, 22.

—— (1980a), *The Measurement of Economic Growth*, Basil Blackwell, Oxford.

—— (1980b), 'The Welfare Basis of Real Income Comparisons: A Comment'. *Journal of Economic Literature*, 18.

—— (ed.) (1980c), *The Measurement of Capital*, Studies in Income and Wealth, Vol.45, National Bureau of Economic Research, Conference on Research in Income and Wealth, University of Chicago Press.

Verdoorn, P. J. (1949), 'Fattori che regolano lo sviluppo della produttivita del lavoro', *L'Industria*, 1.

—— (1980), 'Verdoorn's Law in Retrospect: A Comment', *Economic Journal*, 90.

Vries, B. A. de (1951), 'Price Elasticities of Demand for Individual Commodities Imported into the United States', *International Monetary Fund Staff Papers*, Vol.I.

Wadhwani, S., and Wall, M. (1986), 'The UK Capital Stock—New Estimates of Premature Scrapping', in Muellbauer *et al.*(1986).

Walker, J. L. (1974), 'Estimating Companies' Rate of Return on Capital Employed', *Economic Trends*, CSO, London.

Webb, S., and Cox, H. (1891), *The Eight Hours Day*, Walter Scott, London.

Weiss, L. W. (1963), 'Average Concentration Ratios and Industrial Performance', *Journal of Industrial Economics*, 11.

Whiting, A. (ed.) (1976), *The Economics of Industrial Subsidies*, HMSO, London.

Whittington, G. (1983), *Inflation Accounting: An Introduction to the Debate*, Cambridge University Press.

Williamson, O. E. (1967), *The Economics of Discretionary Behaviour*, Markham, Chicago.

—— (1970), *Corporate Control and Business Behaviour*, Prentice-Hall, Englewood Cliffs, NJ.

Wolf, J. (1912), *Die Volkswirtschaft der Gegenwart u. Zukunft*, Leipzig.

Wolff, E. N. (1985), 'The Magnitude and Causes of the Recent Productivity Slowdown in the United States: A Survey of Recent Studies', in Baumol and McLennan (1985).

Wonnacott, P. (1974), *Macroeconomics*, Richard D. Irwin, Homewood, Ill.

Wragg, R., and Robertson, J. (1978), *Post-war Trends in Employment, Productivity, Output, Labour Costs and Prices by Industry in the United Kingdom*, Department of Employment, Research Paper no.3.

Wright, C. (1969), 'Saving and the Rate of Interest', in Harberger and Bailey (1969).

Wright, F. K. (1964), 'Towards a General Theory of Depreciation', *Journal of Accounting Research*, 2; reprinted in Parker and Harcourt (1969).

Yamada, S., and Hayami, Y. (1979), 'Agriculture', ch.4 in Ohkawa and Shinohara (1979).

Young, A. A. (1928), 'Increasing Returns and Economic Progress', *Economic Journal*, 38.

Young, A. H. (1975), 'New Estimates of Capital Consumption Allowances Revision of GNP in the Benchmark', US Department of Commerce, *Survey of Current Business*, 55.

Zahn, F. (1975), *Macroeconomic Theory and Policy*, Prentice-Hall, Englewood Cliffs, NJ.

Zelder, R. E. (1958), 'Estimates of Elasticities of Demand for Exports of the US, 1921–38', *The Manchester School*, 26.

INDEX OF PERSONS

n = footnote   t = table (including notes)   f = figure

INDEX OF SUBJECTS

n = footnote   t = table (including notes)   f = figure